Karen LaMonte

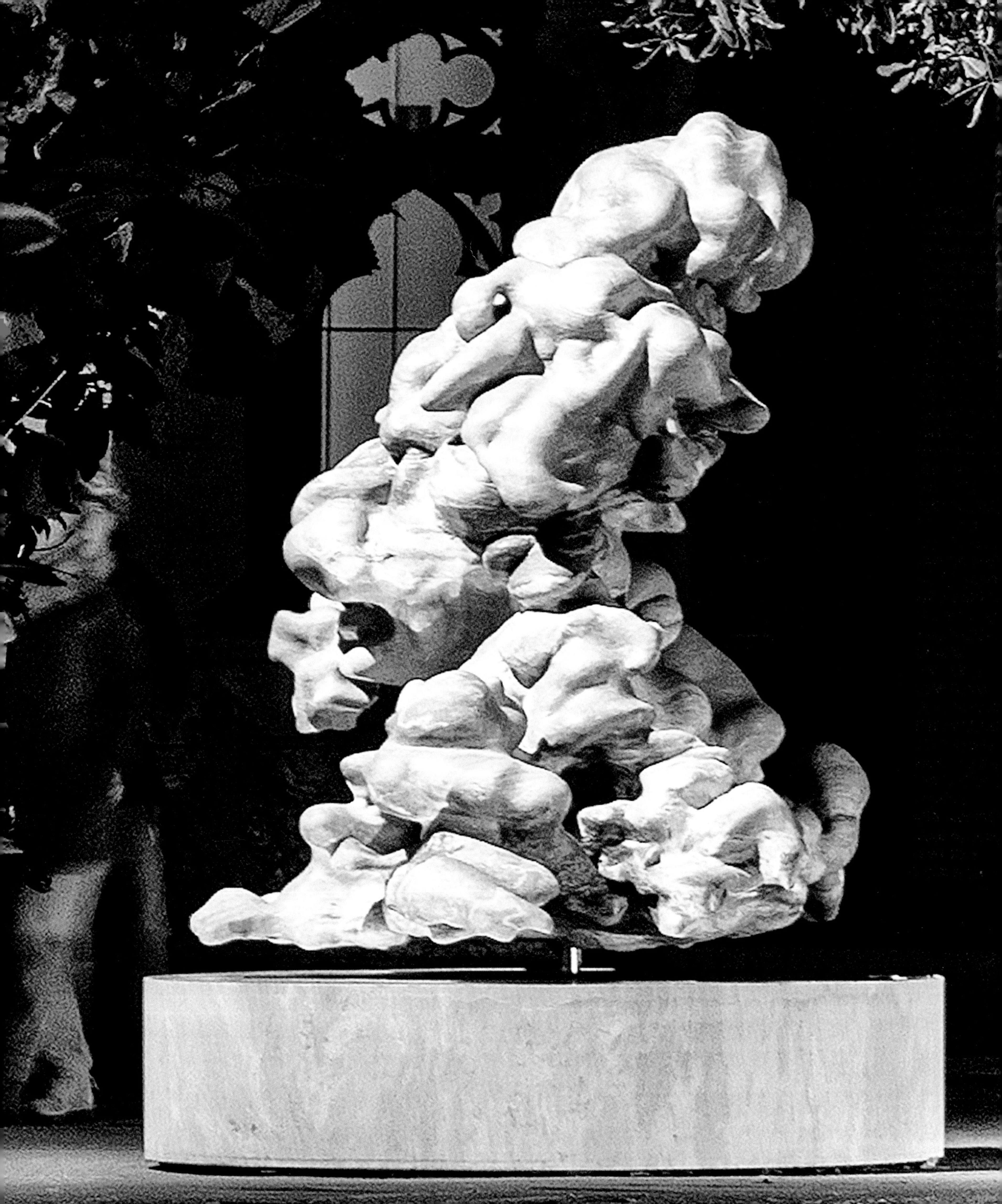

PREVIOUS
Cumulus 1:2, 2017
Exhibition *Glasstress*, 2017, Fondazione Berengo
57th Biennale Arte, Venice, Italy

OPPOSITE
Studio, Czech Republic, 2012.

FOLLOWING
Undine, 2007
Exhibition *Contemporary Among the Classics*, 2009
Chrysler Museum of Art, Norfolk, VA

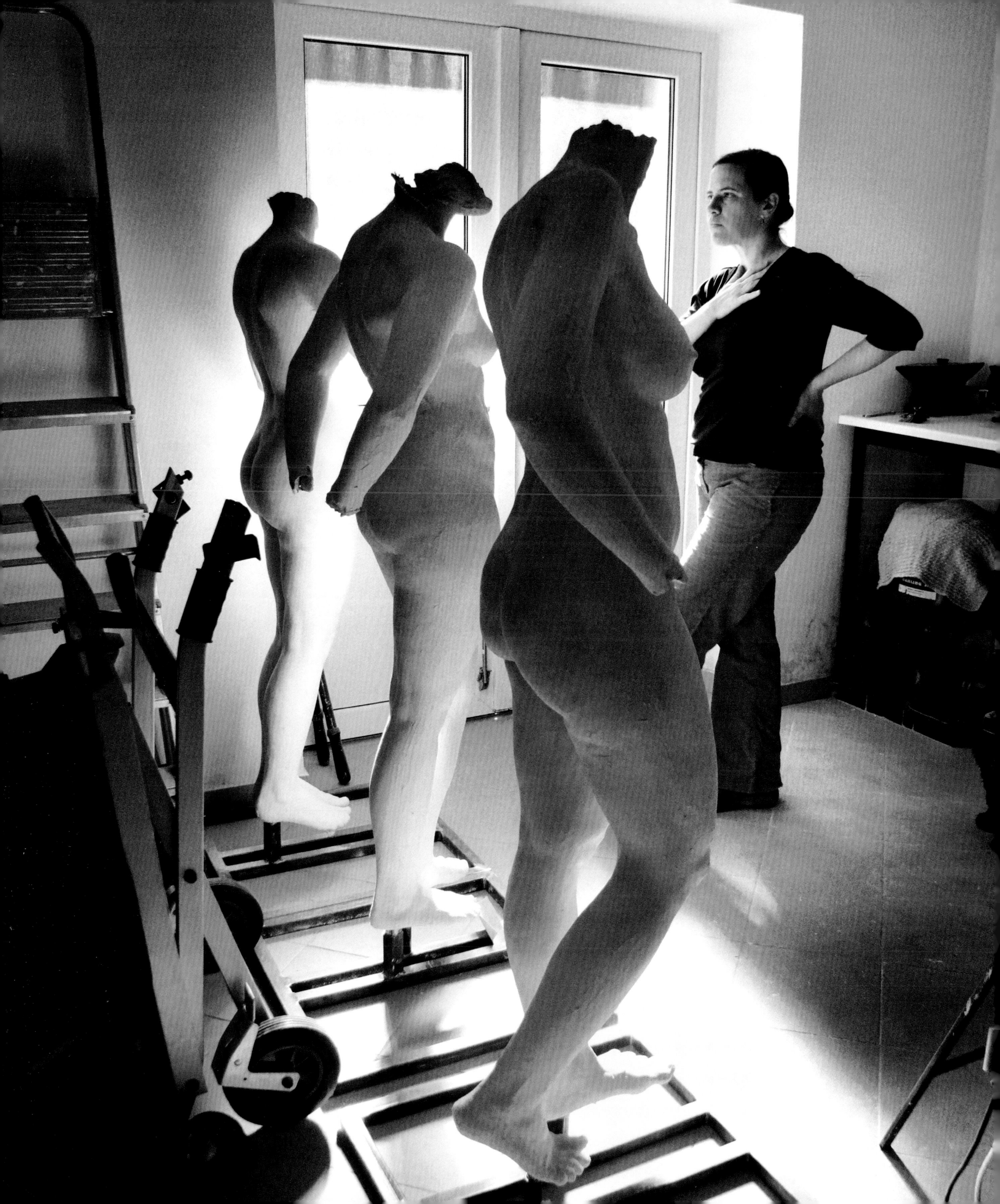

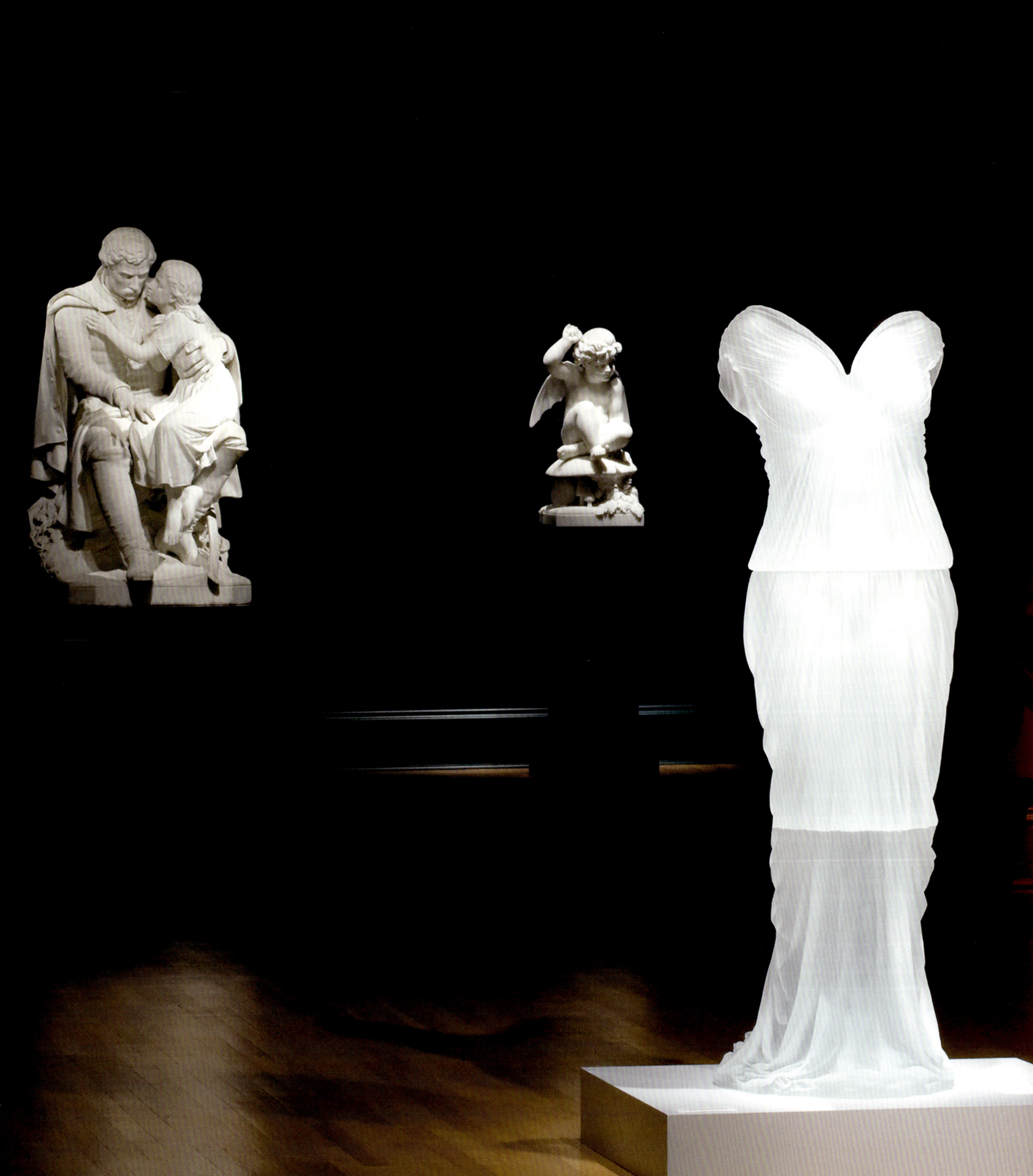

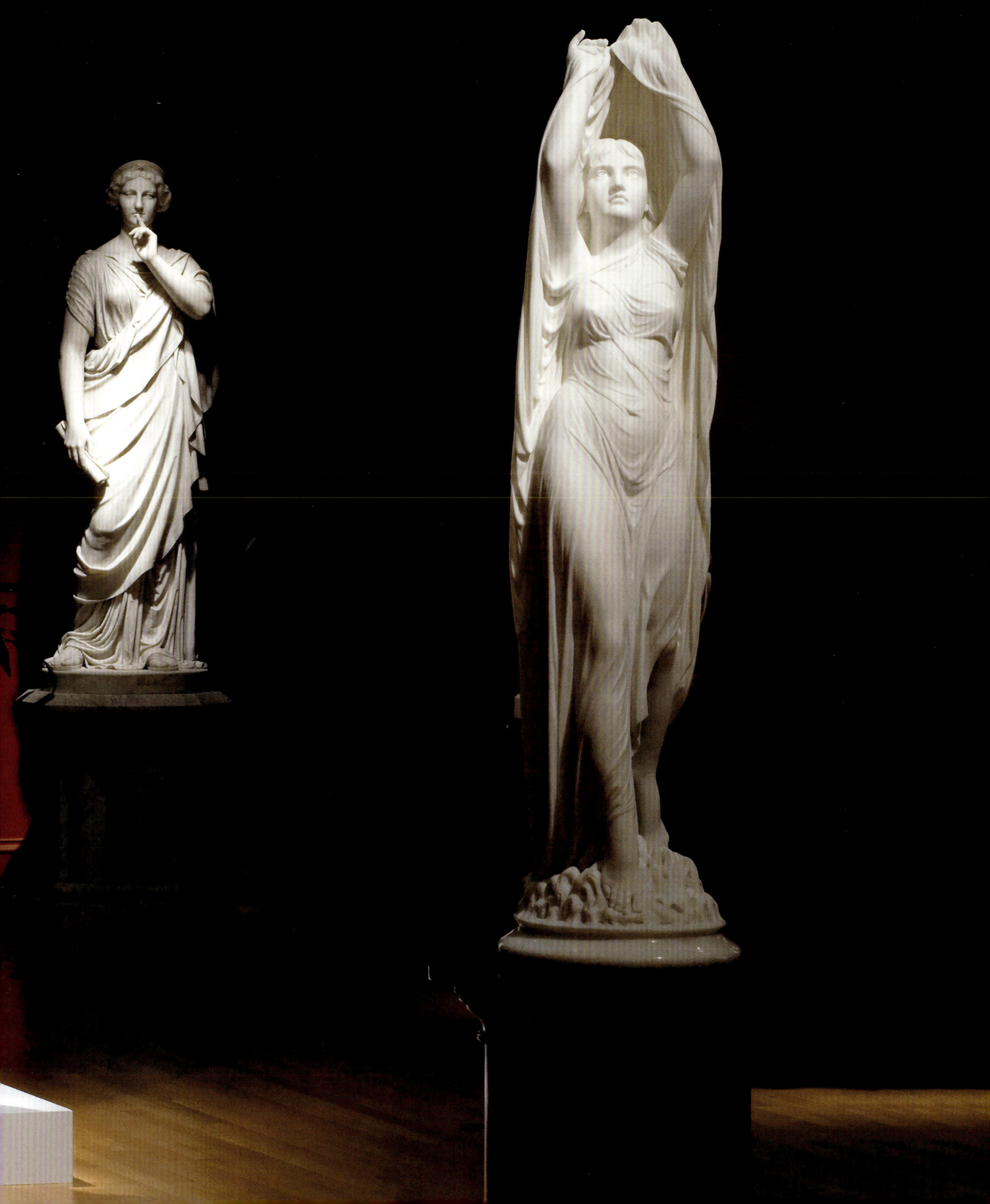

Karen LaMonte

FOREWORD STEVEN A. NASH
INTRODUCTION LUCY R. LIPPARD

WITH ESSAYS BY

BRETT LITTMAN

ARTHUR C. DANTO

LAURA ADDISON

TINA OLDKNOW

STEVEN A. NASH

KAREN LAMONTE

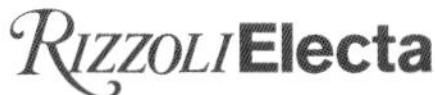

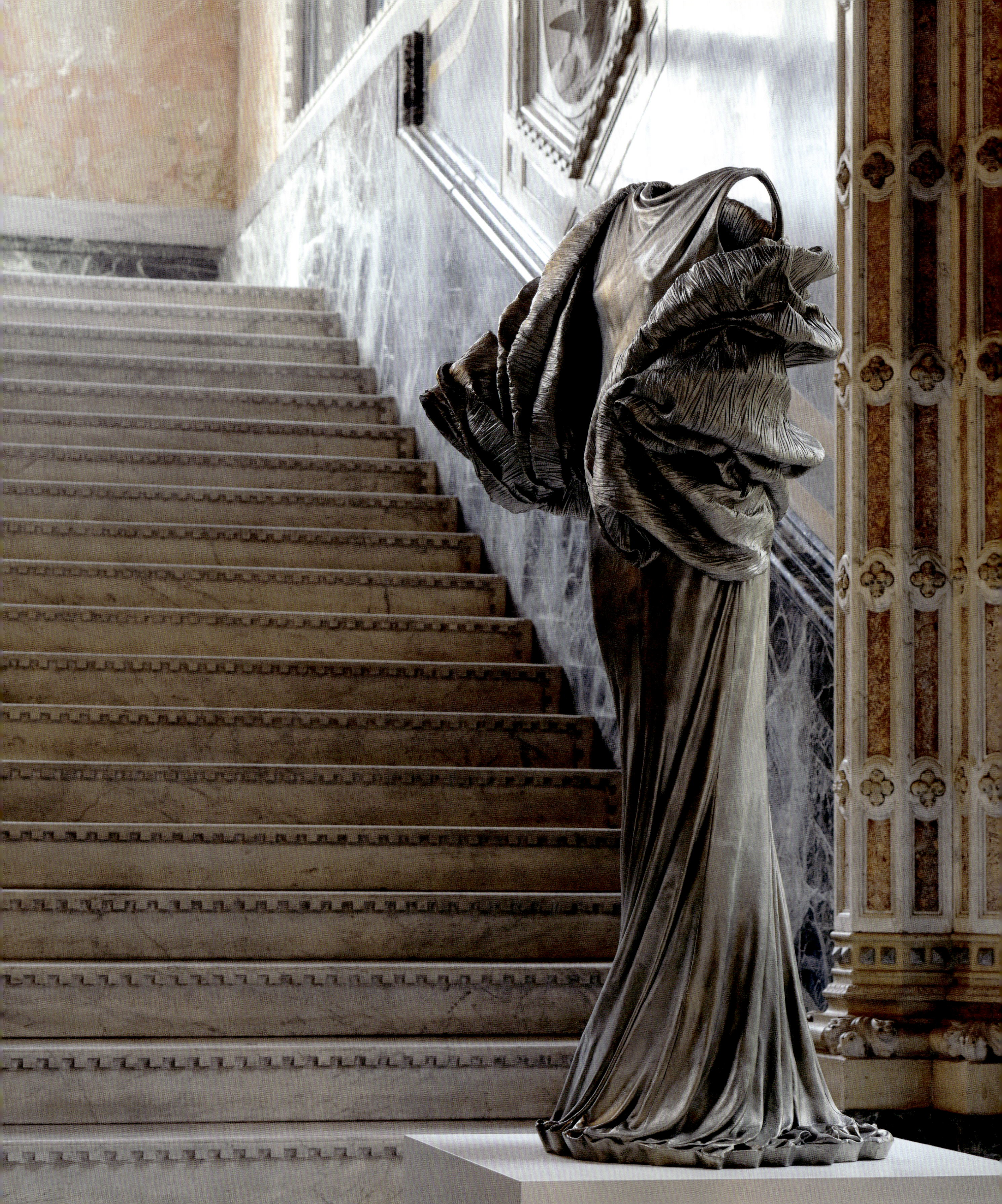

Nocturne 3, 2015
Exhibition *Glasstress,* 2017, Fondazione Berengo
57th Biennale Arte, Venice, Italy

FOLLOWING
Detail of *Bijin (Kintsugi)*, 2011
Ceramic, 49 × 20½ × 24 in. (124 × 51.5 × 61.5 cm)

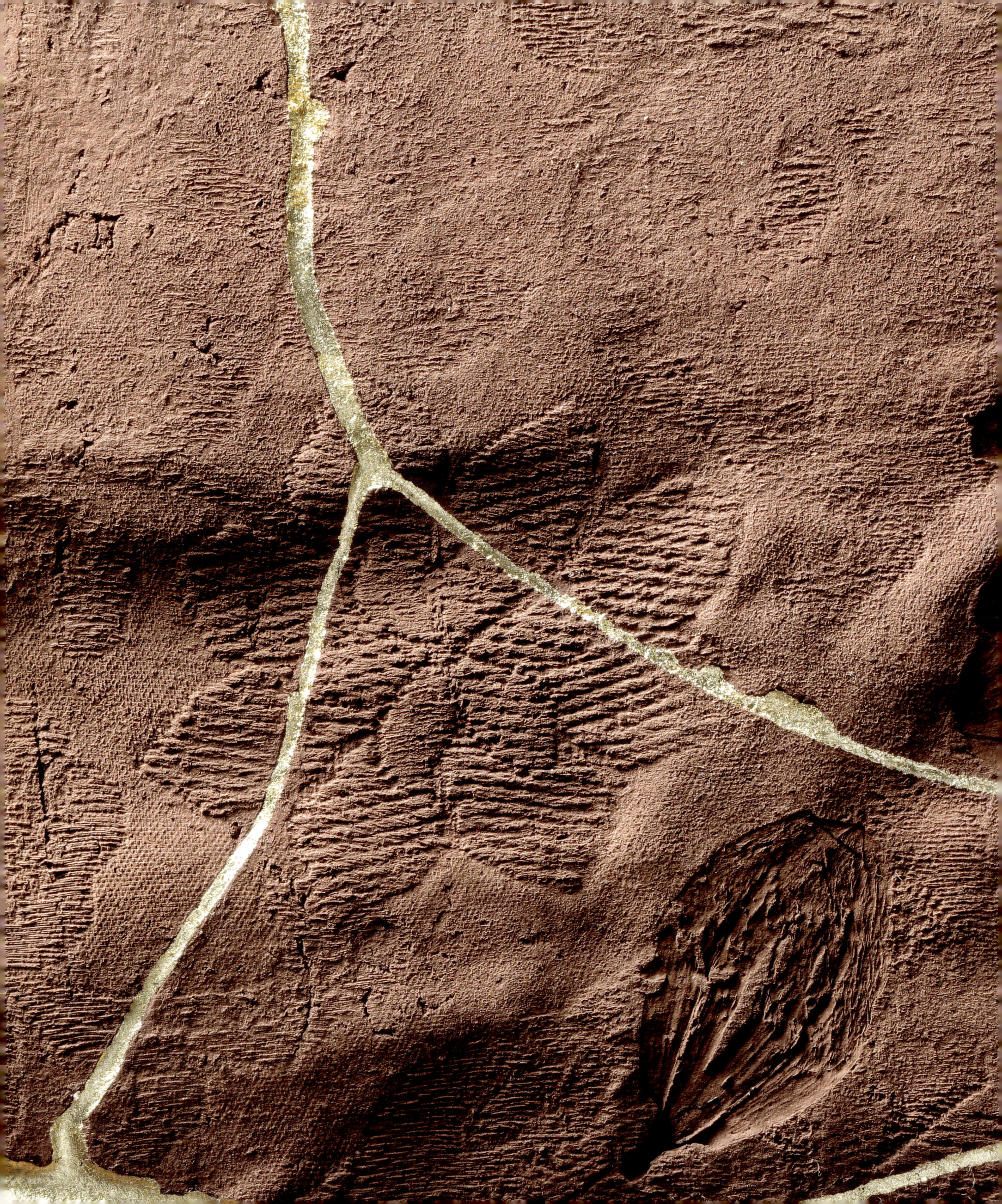

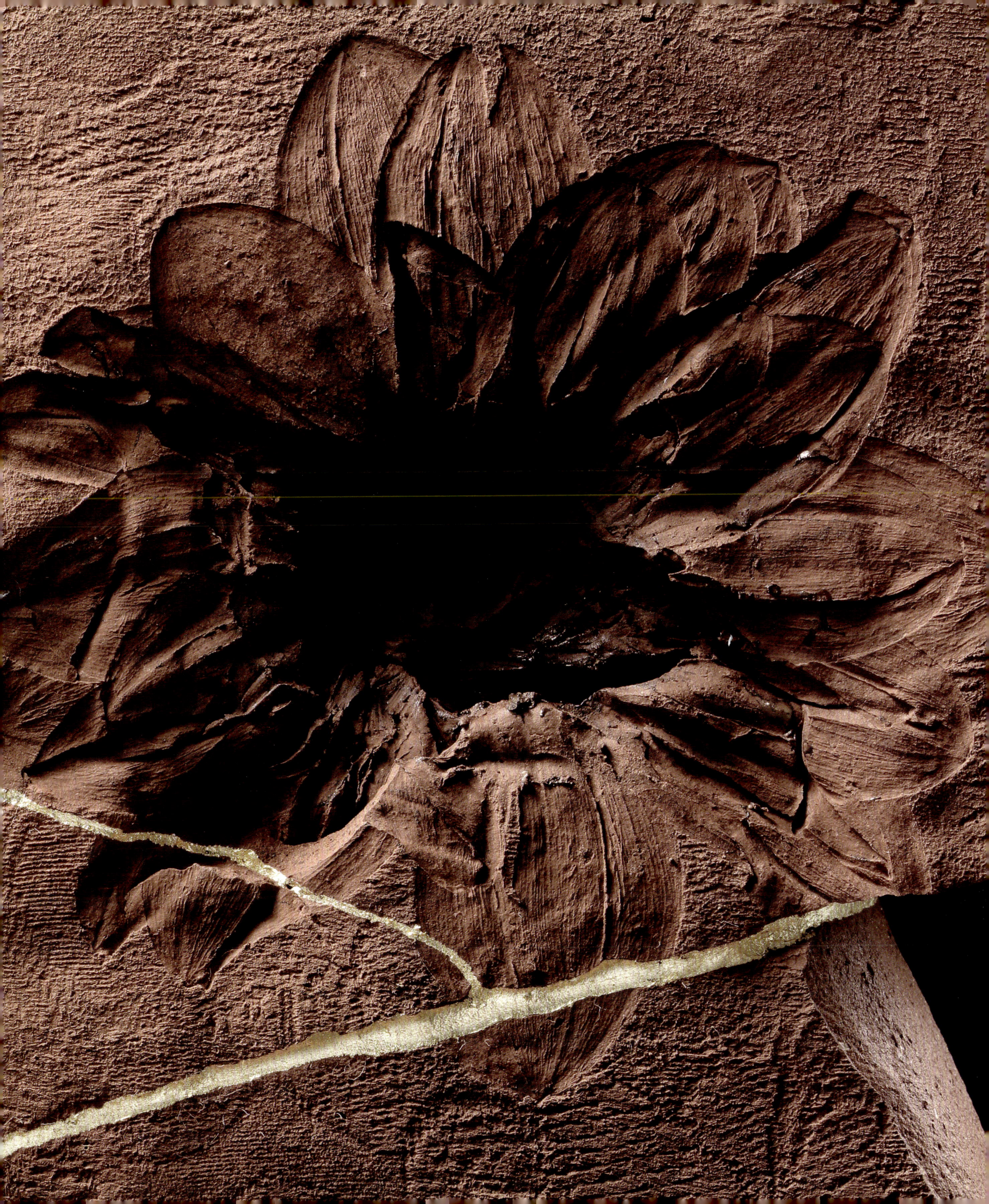

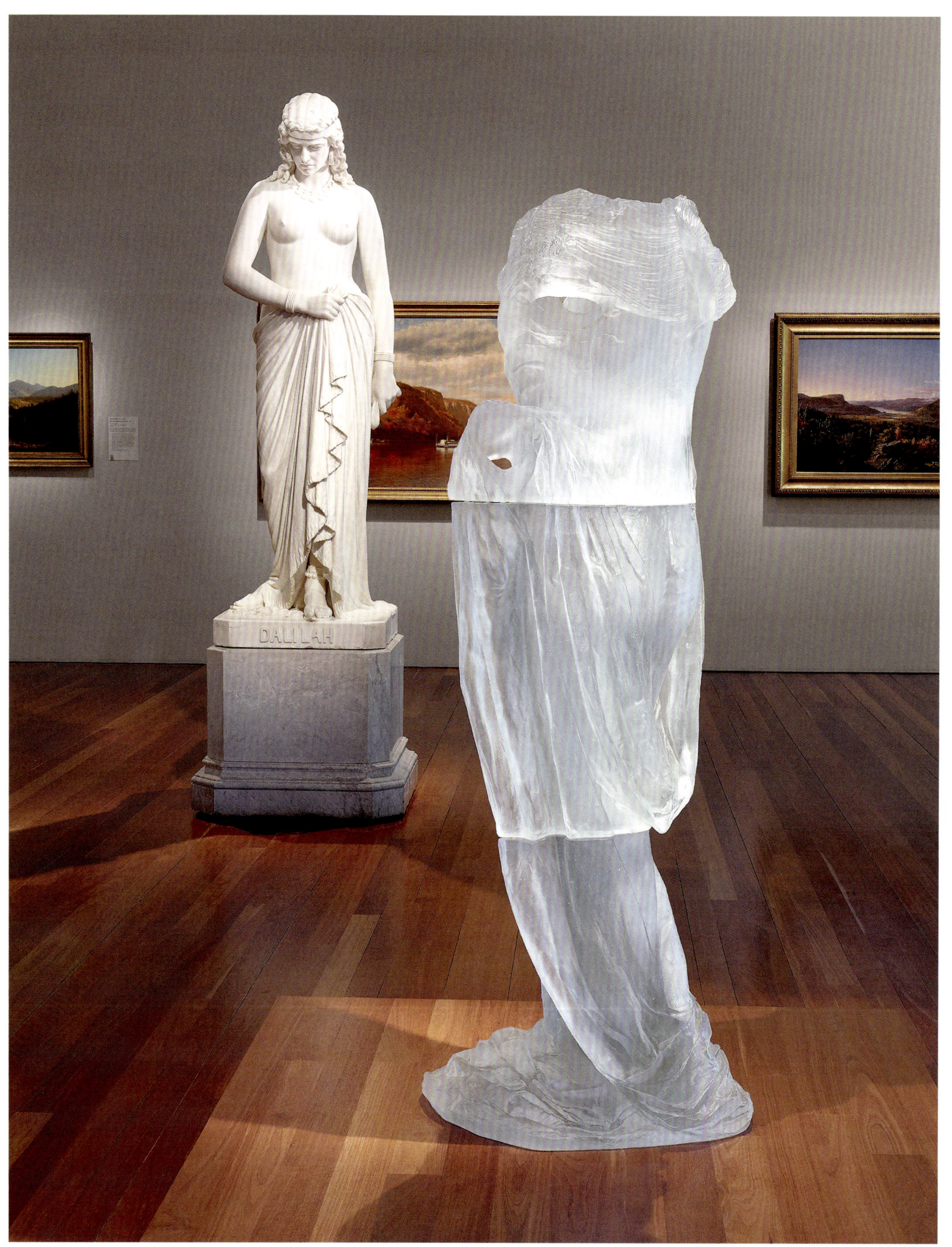
DALILAH

Foreword

Steven A. Nash

Dress 3, 2001
Collection of de Young Museum/
Fine Arts Museums of San
Francisco, San Francisco, CA

It is unusual for a mid-career artist to have investigated along her way a wide diversity of different ideas, materials, and modes of expression, and yet, this is precisely the course of Karen LaMonte's practice. Her career, stretching from her days at Rhode Island School of Design in the late 1980s to today, is marked by steady exploration and an underlying consistency of purpose and vision. Her thematics involve explorations of the integrity of solid form in space—the truthfulness, clarity, and articulateness of such a form—as well as the inherent qualities of her materials, the beauty of the female form, how draping of the body with textiles affects our perception of its visual and cultural meaning, and light as a sculptural property.

This monograph thoroughly documents an evolution of projects that all embody one or more of these principles. Having studied in the glass department at RISD, LaMonte turned to cast glass, making over the next seven years mainly small-scale figures, animals, dresses, and other objects. Coming under the influence of the great Czech masters of large-scale glass casting (she had moved to Prague by then), she ambitiously studied the elements of their control over this difficult medium and began to produce the large transparent dresses for which she soon became well known. Radiant in their refraction of light and evocative in their hollow castings that reveal the imprint of now-vanished women, these works set the stage for much of what came later, including the recurrent investigation of the strong cultural influence of fashion on identity, self-expression, and perceptions of feminine beauty.

LaMonte's next development involved an expansion of cultural focus and a deep dive into the history and societal meanings of the Japanese kimono tradition. With the ensuing kimono sculptures, she added bronze, iron, and ceramics to her practice. Her work in all these materials features a concerted effort to express the inherent character and textural beauty possessed by each. Soon she branched out further into a series of works involving large castings of sheets of drapery whose waves of folds inspire associations with landscape.

It was then back to European and American haute couture but with a new moodiness and a transformation of her use of light. Her *Nocturnes* have the same classical stateliness as the earlier glass dresses but with a much different aura, one of dreamlike shadowy settings, of longing and meditation. With her glass, she developed a new formula that produces a dusky coloration. She started to use white bronze for its effects of gray, and the slow rusting of iron, as in her kimono sculptures, for its powdery, ineffable surfaces. Then, in a complete change of pace, some of LaMonte's most recent sculptures are huge carvings in marble of cumulus clouds, taking her work to a new position, on the edge of abstraction.

This developmental track adds up to an impressive artistic record that is as diverse in formal expression and iconography as it is with materials. Its path has been chronicled by a number of publications as well as important museum exhibitions at, among others, Prague's Czech Museum of Fine Art (2004); the Museum of Glass, Tacoma, Washington (2005); the Chrysler Museum of Art, Norfolk, Virginia (2009); the Chazen Museum of Art, Madison, Wisconsin (2017); and the Hunter Museum of American Art, Chattanooga, Tennessee (2018), all contributing to LaMonte's expanding reputation.

This monograph is the first to study the full scope of Karen LaMonte's career and work. Her place in contemporary art is still being defined, but she already has made remarkable contributions. One can hardly wait to see where this adventurous artist leads us next.

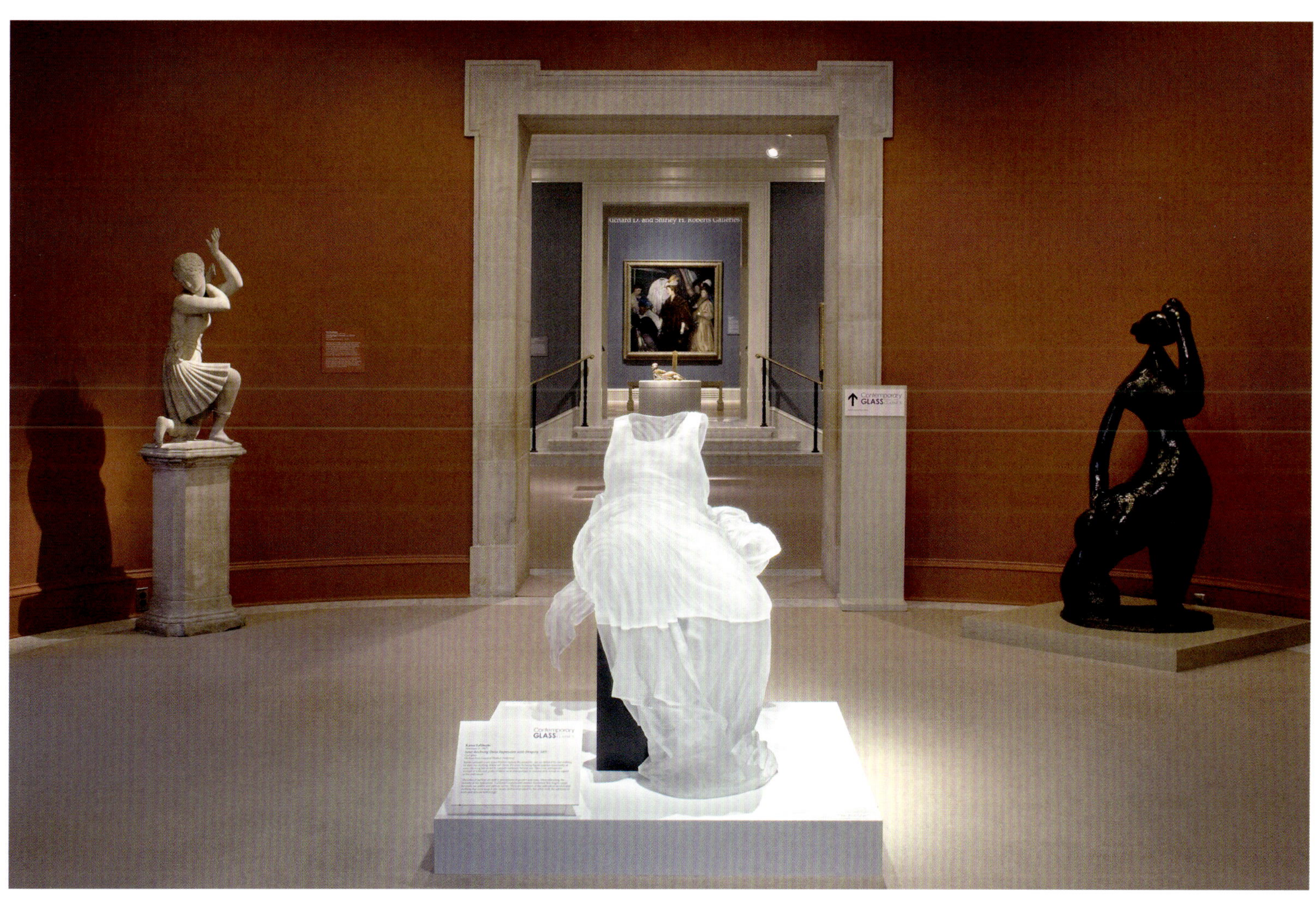

Semi-Reclining Dress Impression with Drapery, 2005
Exhibition *Contemporary Among the Classics*, 2009
Chrysler Museum of Art, Norfolk, VA

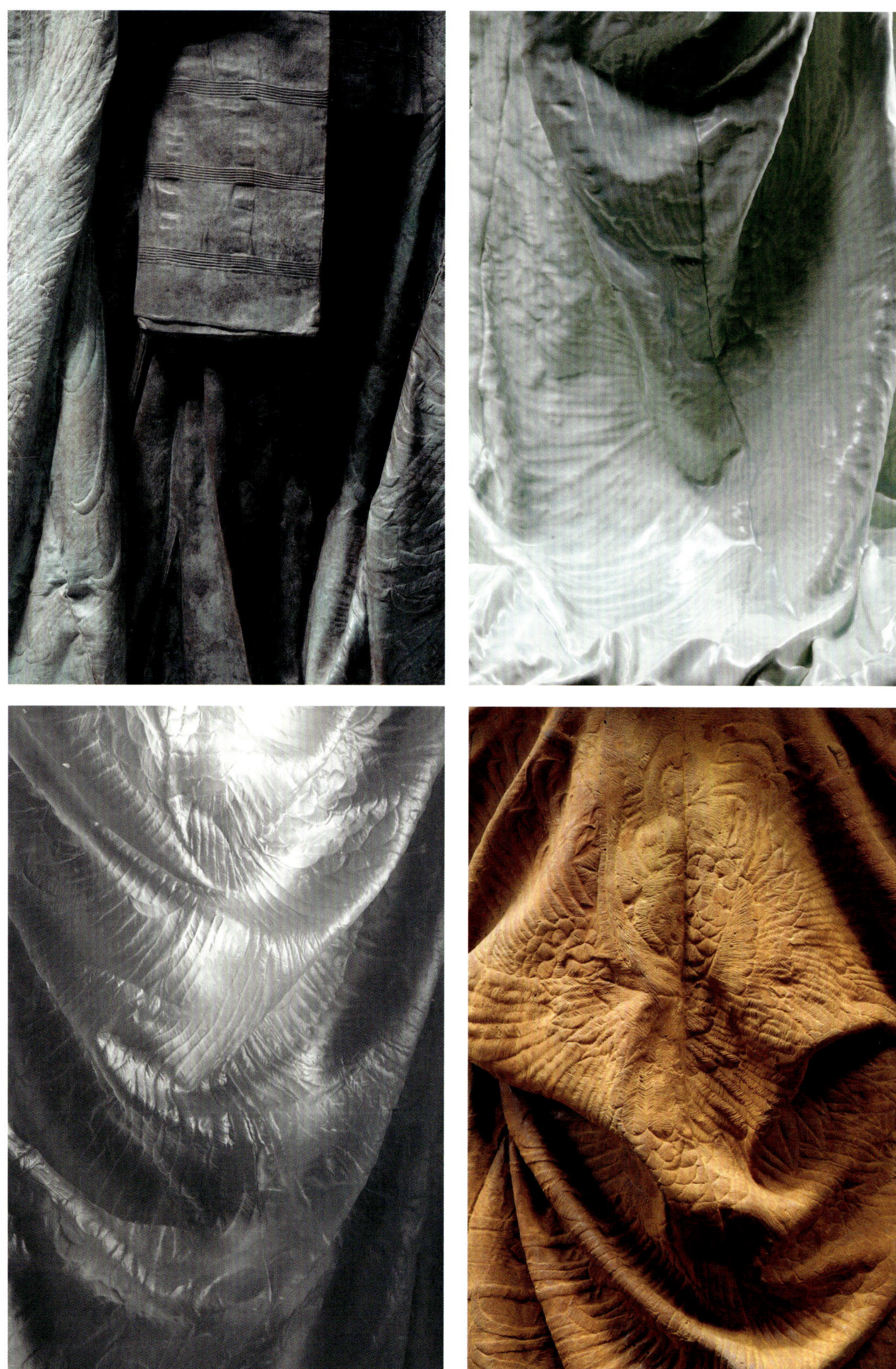

Clothes Make the Woman, Clouds Make the Sky

Lucy R. Lippard

As I was writing this, thinking about Karen LaMonte's art, I found myself mesmerized by the hills and valleys of draping fabric and the ever-shifting piles of bulbous clouds encountered in daily life. LaMonte's simultaneous devotion to the romantic, the realist, and the scientific combines to produce her unique body of work . . . body being the operative word. In the freestanding gown sculptures for which she is best known, the role of artifice and illusion vies with impressive physical presence. She writes that her Eureka moment was a dress she found in a Warsaw costume shop in 1999, the basis for *Vestige* (a nice play on words), her first large cast glass sculpture: "The instant I saw it in glass for the first time, I could see the hollow interior shape, and I knew in that moment that I wanted the hollow to be an articulated impression of a body, an absent woman."[1] The robust and ethereal gowns and the simultaneous absence of the invisible but imagined human body incorporate (another key word) history, nostalgia, fashion, and art. Asked why she chose dresses, LaMonte replied, "I'm a girl."

Clothes, of course, are our second skin. Some women prefer a neutral presence, conservative or casual. Others are fashionistas, following the trends. Others deploy all their creativity in their wardrobe from pantsuits to hippie robes. Some, like me, shop mainly at thrift shops, enjoying the unknown histories of found objects and other bodies. Most women, no matter how dismissive of fashion, have experienced the glow of "dressing up," the attraction of sensuous fabrics, of unaccustomed elegance. LaMonte, however, is less interested in superficial

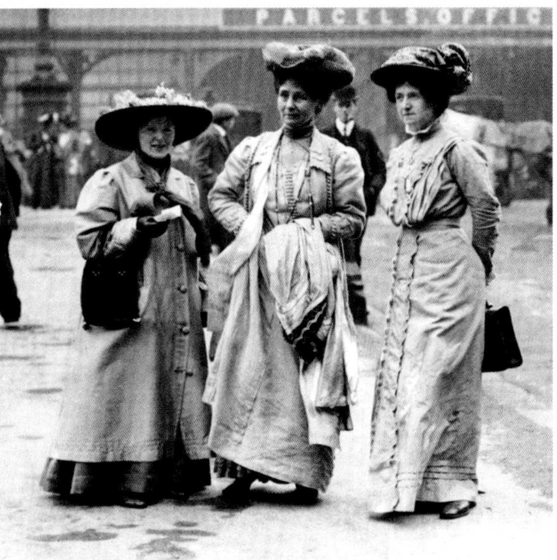

Suffragettes, circa 1913.

Details of *Kabuki* in bronze, ceramic, rusted iron, and cast glass. Collection of Imagine Museum, St. Petersburg, FL

glamour than in the *weight* of things, present and absent. She thinks and makes, calling on the metaphysical and the physical. The tumultuous Baroque garments and the more orderly and traditionally regulated draperies of Greek classical sculpture and Japanese kimonos have led her to unexpected places. Sometimes her work has been shown in museum halls along with the ancient figures she has studied—a dialogue the viewer can almost overhear.

In the mid-1990s, LaMonte was working at UrbanGlass in Brooklyn, having graduated from Rhode Island School of Design in 1990. She made some shiny little blown glass clothes hanging on a line and three-dimensional glass puppets, also hollow, indicative of her theatrical preoccupations with costume and setting. In 1995, she planted her *Atmospheres*—bronze and glass flowers under bell jars (some painted with clouds)—on the margins of Burning Man in Nevada's Black Rock Desert. In 1998, a Fulbright took her to Prague in a successful search for the expertise to make life-size cast glass sculptures. (She and her husband have since settled there.)

The dresses, which transcend the mannequins they initially resemble, evoke other eras—thousands of years ago for the classical Greek/Roman look, and perhaps the kimonos as well; a century or so for twentieth-century garb. The dresses are timeless rather than contemporary, although early reliefs include a more generic little girl's dress and a man's suit. No jeans or leggings or shirts or shorts. The sensuous appeal of softly falling fabrics, diaphanous skirts, loosely clinging tops accommodating full breasts beneath are not available to many of us, though we have found other ways to expose our bodies, revealing décolletage, wardrobe malfunctions, tight pants. In LaMonte's world, obesity does not exist, nor does anorexia. Her invisible women are full bodied, confident, relaxed, as in earlier pieces like the

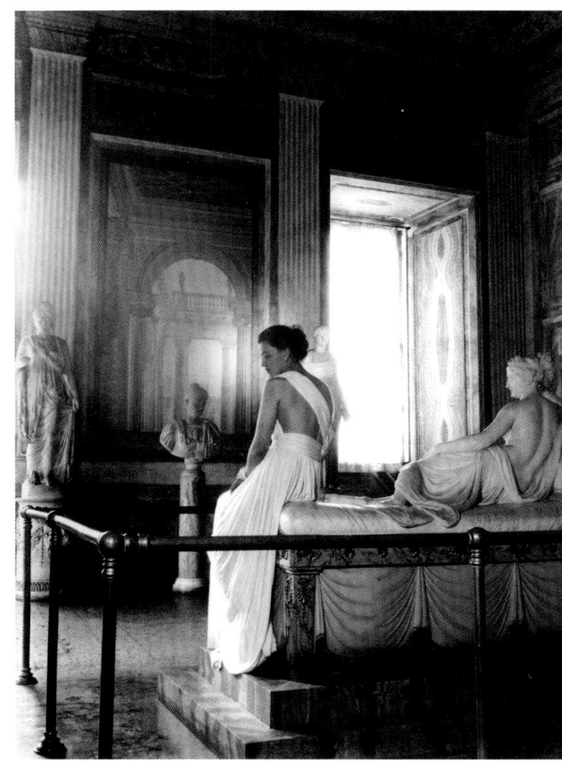

Pasquale De Antonis (1980–2001). Antonio Canovas's statue of Pauline Bonaparte Borghese with model wearing cape by Balzani Galleria Borghese, 1947

hollow cast glass *Semi-Reclining Dress Impression* (2005) and *Seated Dress* (2005). These are among my favorites because the positions are dynamic, and because of the strength implied by the absent bodies and their poses—legs sturdily apart, contrasted with a dress that literally floats and a medium that is so spectacularly fragile. Such a combination of strength and vulnerability is at the core of much feminist art and life. LaMonte notes that she "subverted the tradition of the odalisque . . . by taking away the body." Clothes make the woman? The woman makes the clothes? For anyone who has raided her dead mother's closet, as I have, LaMonte's embodiment of garments evokes the memories they hide in their very folds, both a ghostly touch and a firm embrace. The figures are glamorous but they also convey a certain melancholy, suggesting sensual expectation or the potential loss of glamour, youth, an insistence on mortality.

Forty years ago, some postmodern feminists might have been critical of this work, accusing it of the dreaded "essentialism." I always felt that argument was misguided, since feminism is about the essences of female experience and its potential to be smart, tough, courageous, caring, generous, and empathetic, abjuring conventional "femininity" in favor of something bolder, riskier, and politically astute. LaMonte has no dog in this fight. She is probably too young to remember these annoying divisions in the movement and she is her own woman, following an intensely demanding trajectory to her hard-won and technically groundbreaking embodied sculptures.

Given her focus on life-size freestanding sculptures, LaMonte's *Lark Mirror* series (2004–8) is something of an anomaly. It transforms a small object associated with vanity into apparent *memento mori*, identifying with the birds caught in lark mirror traps. Fleeting, not portrait, photographs are etched on the reflective surfaces. Some of the subjects are children, others are sleeping, some look frightened. One is titled *Hysteria*. The ornately framed, handheld glass mirrors seem to have captured psychological secrets visible only in the privacy of the "looking glass," phantoms passing through.

Beauty is a component often dismissed or neglected by contemporary art, but LaMonte is clearly in its thrall. "I have always been fascinated by how conceptions of beauty define desire," she has written, "and generate the building blocks of allure—the language of attraction." Beauty, as we know it, is in the eye of the beholder, changing drastically from one person to another, one situation to another, one culture to another—some of which focus on brilliant body painting rather than clothing per se, a different sort of second skin. LaMonte's prime subjects, body and weather, are universal, but beauty itself is culturally determined. LaMonte is curious about what constitutes the beautiful and the monstrous in different cultures, through different lenses; her favorite book is Mary Shelley's *Frankenstein*, with its insights into both science and humanity.

In 2006, seeking cross-cultural depth and a new starting point, LaMonte went to Kyoto, Japan, where she immersed herself in the highly codified culture of the kimono. It carries various subtle messages about the wearer's place in society and, in a broader sense, the ephemeral qualities of beauty, the body, and thus life itself. She discovered that contrary to Western fashion conventions, "putting on a kimono is literally about erasing the individual's identity and joining the group." Inspired by the *ukiyo-e* tradition (sorrowful or floating world), she adopted Japanese concepts of impermanence. (In 2012, a group of her terra-cotta kimonos exploded; some were painstakingly reassembled with the multiple cracks filled with gold, a tactic at the heart of the philosophy of *wabi-sabi* and its focus on transience and imperfection.) After researching the population, LaMonte settled on the body of an average forty-year-old Japanese woman, or everywoman. The viewer unaware of this underlying structure relates more intimately to the absent body.

Casting the same kimono in four different mediums—glass (fragile transparency), clay (earthy density), rusted iron ("an expression of transience"), and the sedate permanence of bronze—allowed similarities and differences to surface, plumbing the depths of each image, each medium, and even subtly suggesting the personalities of each invisible model. If the body is a shadow, the cast glass clothing is light, the bronzes are darkness, the clay perhaps distance. The choice of medium determines the ultimate identity of the figure. LaMonte is a poet of materials.

As she was looking into Greek myths about the chaos that preceded the planet we know, the goddess of infinite night caught her imagination: "I was inspired to make female figurations of night—somber, seductive, and inscrutable"—a useful description for much of her art. Studying the physiological effects, she realized that "night brings together body and universe, finite and infinite," as we stare up into the Milky Way, our home away from home. For two years, she worked with a German scientist "to formulate a color and light absorption appropriate for penumbral garments." She developed a dense glass that "gathered darkness." Installed together, women rising up from a darkened pool into night, as she put it, suggest a fragmented narrative thrown up into a starry night.

LaMonte studied couture across historical time, seeking fabrics that folded or draped in ways that evoked light and atmosphere at nightfall, making connections between the emptiness of the dresses and "the empty darkness of the night . . . a sculptural interpretation of Tenebrism. . . . As I worked, I felt I was gathering darkness around the body," like a garment for the cosmos. Having read about the *Théâtre de la Mode* in a war-torn Paris at the end of World War II, LaMonte got the idea of installing six of the life-size sculptures on empty stages faced by empty seats, reinforcing the inherent drama of light and lack thereof inherent in the project. The artwork in this case was the photograph of the *tableau vivant,* shot in the brief window of time between performances in the eighteenth-century Estates Theater in Prague, where Mozart had once performed, and later in a theater in a Baroque castle, also in the Czech Republic. Frédéric Chopin and John Field provided the dazzling soundtrack.

The *Nocturnes* led to the celestial. With hindsight, it seems inevitable that LaMonte would be attracted to the landscape references in the metaphorical hills and valleys of body and clothing. In 2009, while working on a joint Kohler/Corning grant at the famous Kohler factory (an eye-opening experience), LaMonte made a series of "abstract" bas-reliefs of drapery that suggested clouds, water, and other natural phenomena. She

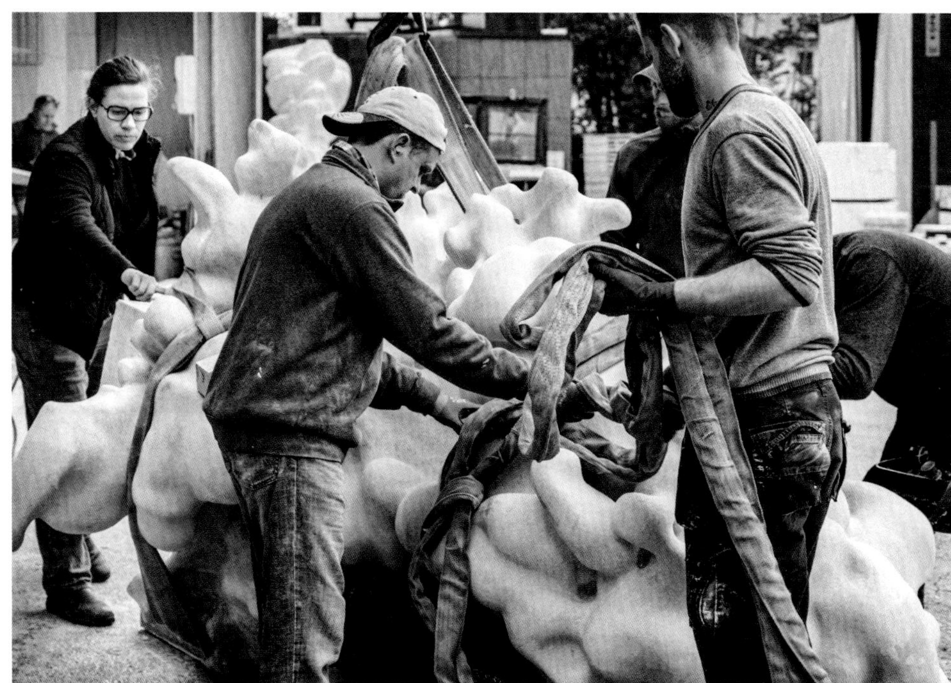

Rigging *Cumulus 1:2* for rotation, 2017.

was increasingly drawn to materials revealing the forces of nature and weather, a subject all too pertinent today as we face climate catastrophe. "My figurative work was a celebration of empowered femininity," she says. "In moving into landscape, I am looking at a grand feminine archetype, which is the earth."[2] Land and female body are an age-old construct. With her usual thoroughness, LaMonte studied three-dimensional models of weather, worked with climatologists, focusing on clouds, the process of their formation and interaction with light, from earth below or airplane windows above. Her interest in weight and weightlessness was provoked when she learned that something as "light and airy" as a cumulus cloud could weigh 220 tons. Having decided to make a heavy marble cloud sculpture, she worked not from photographs, which provide only incomplete information, but from the equations determining the structure of clouds. She spent five days on a supercomputer in Switzerland with scientist Tapio Schneider, who told her that "[c]louds are hugely important for the climate. How much warmer it will get depends on what happens to cumulus clouds." Transforming "everycloud" into marble called for more technology with the help of a software program and an actual robot to "make the diaphanous solid and the intangible permanent."[3] Just as humans have always gazed at clouds and associated fleeting (floating) images, the marble cloud offers similarly evocative territory.

Unlike many artists (though Agnes Denes comes to mind), LaMonte is an avocational scientist or valuable scientific collaborator, bringing together the artist's curiosity with the scientist's factual caution. The recent work takes a logical turn toward another orbit. Suggesting that we look to Nature as a "Model, Measure, and Mentor," and noting that we are in the age of "synthetic biology," LaMonte became interested in biomimetics—defined as "a new science that studies nature's models and then imitates or takes inspiration from these designs and processes to solve human problems,"[4] with sustainability as an objective. In her biomimetic work, she returns to the body that was invisible in the garment pieces. One figurine is a pregnant nude, lounging on a couch. The sculptures are smaller, referred to as figurines, but not as small as the generative object—the forty-thousand-year-old Venus of Hohle Fels, which is only two and one-half inches high. These ancient artifacts are usually interpreted as fertility symbols and one of LaMonte's figurines is a pregnant nude, lounging on a couch. Although these realistic figures do not convey the sensuous reality of the "empty" gowns, they offer fresh subject matter. The emphasis is on "new technologies and materials that mimic human biology." Experimenting once again with scientists, LaMonte found novel uses for bioglasses—both "tooth glass" (she calls it mimetic ivory) and an unstable bioactive glass. The third (non-bioactive) material is an opalized glass, which, with its prismatic flashes, interacts with light like the sky. Given their exotic materials, the resultant figures—unstable and impermanent—might be said to be proxies for life as much as they are art.

LaMonte writes that she is "terrified of writing and speaking about" her work: "My greatest hope is that every viewer will have their own personal relationship with the work, unmediated by me." (It must be doubly terrifying to have writers like me and my colleagues weigh in.) Yet artists, unless they choose to be anonymous, cannot escape mediation. And better it comes from the artist than from critics, whose role is to analyze, explain, and perhaps embellish after the fact. LaMonte's texts and her recorded lectures are articulate and illuminating about the complex intellectual and material processes that define her art, as well as her enthusiasm for (and contributions to) cutting-edge science. Knowing the history and intelligence and years of hard work behind her sculptures can only deepen their effect, guiding the grateful viewer. It would be a shame to ignore any component of these memorable sculptures. "To me," writes LaMonte, "exploring [an] expansive expression of inherent beauty is one of the most exciting aspects of reinventing an ancient icon. . . . I like to challenge the boundary between representation and reality."

NOTES

1 *Presences* was the title of Harmony Hammond's headless female figures made of colorful strips of rags (1972), and the title of Hammond's recent retrospective—*Material Witness*—offers parallels to LaMonte's very different work. The dresses of Nancy Youdelman, Judith Shea, and Beverly Semmes, among others, are also precedents in feminist art. Unless otherwise noted, all quotations by the artist are from her recorded interviews and statements, plus personal communications with he author.

2 Karen LaMonte, quoted in Tina Oldknow, "Karen LaMonte: Charting the Iconography of Desire," in *Karen LaMonte: Drapery Abstractions* (New York: Heller Gallery, 2010), 4.

3 Judy Hill, "Cloud Sourcing," Caltech, Fall 2017, accessed at magazine.caltech.edu/post/cloud-sourcing.

4 Janine M. Benyus, *Biomimicry: Innovation Inspired by Nature* (New York: Harper Perennial, 2002).

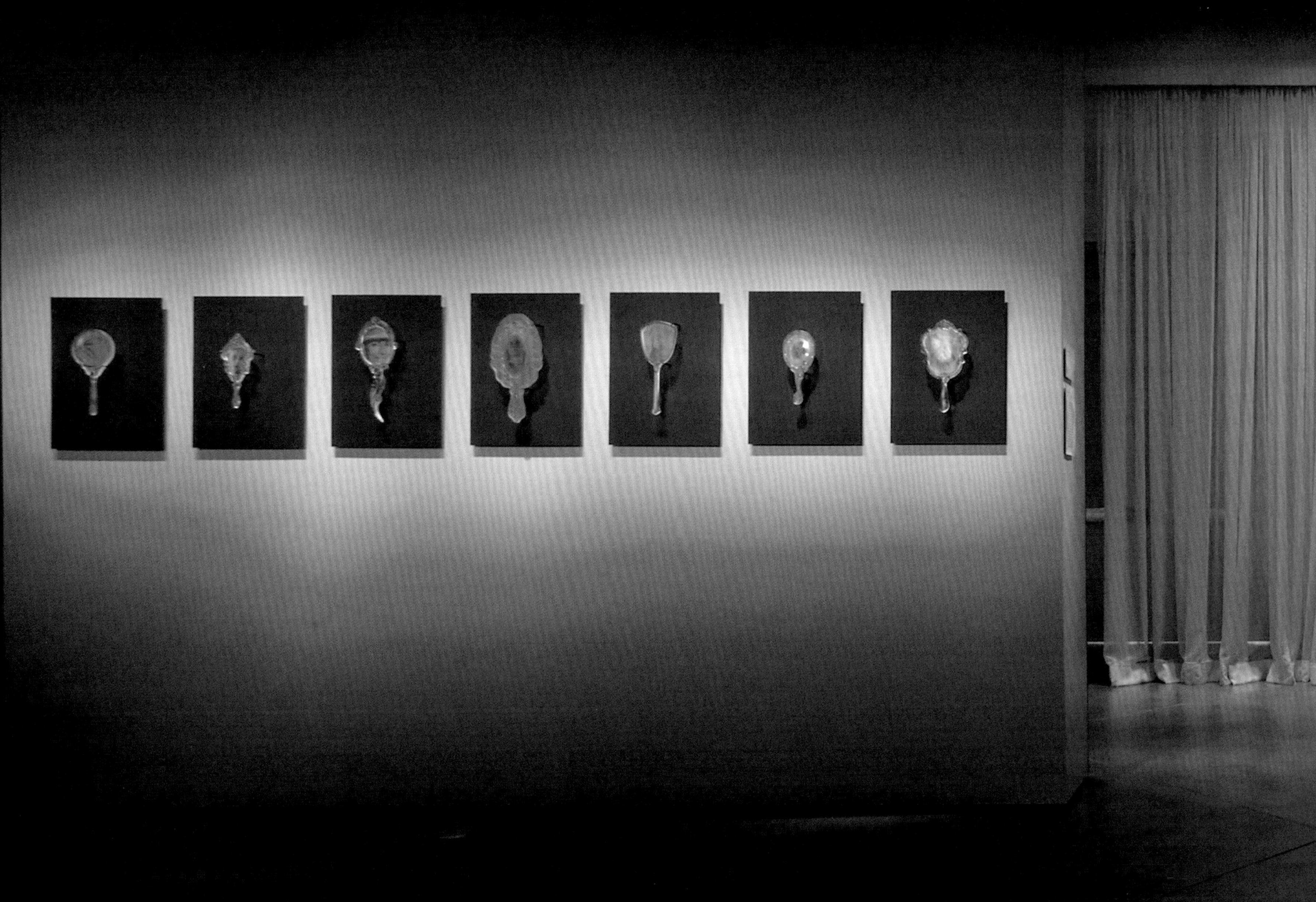

Exhibition *Absence Adorned*, 2005
Museum of Glass International Center
for Contemporary Art, Tacoma, WA

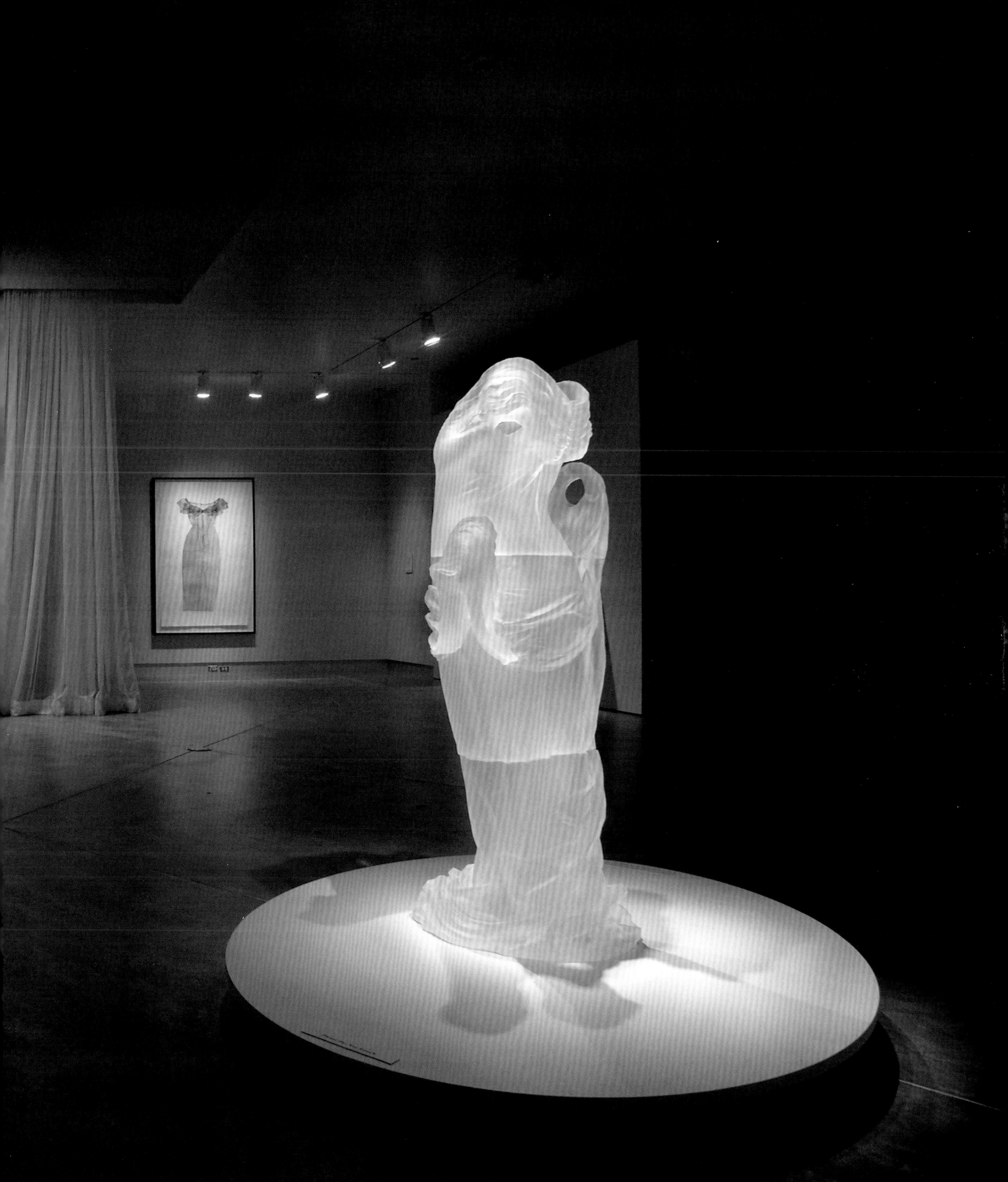

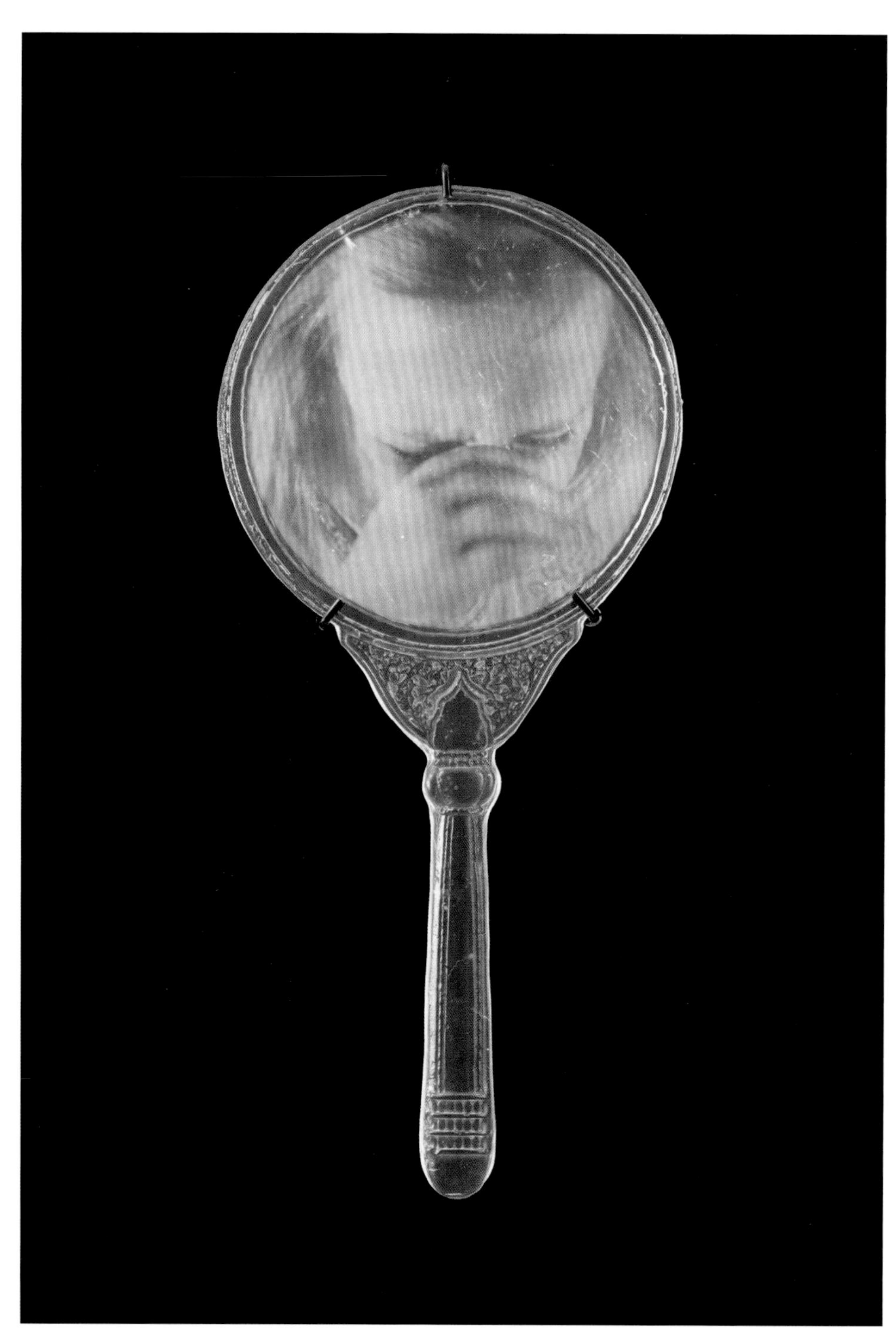

Down the Rabbit Hole

Brett Littman

I first met Karen LaMonte in 1995 at UrbanGlass, a nonprofit glassworking facility in Brooklyn, New York, where she was the organization's education director and I was its associate director. Both of us were relatively recent college grads trying to make our way in the art world—she as a practicing artist and I as an art professional in nonprofits. Karen and I not only worked together, but also talked about shows and exhibitions we saw, got into philosophical discussions about art, and socialized after work with many of the artists who were part of the UrbanGlass community at the time. It truly was a "golden era" at the institution, and one that was extremely formative for many of us who were there.

The mid-1990s at UrbanGlass under John Perreault's direction was also artistically a very interesting time. The intersection between the fine art world and the glass art world—maybe more than any other time that I can remember in the last twenty years—was quite intense, positive, and fluid. There were many artists in the UrbanGlass orbit including Kiki Smith, Rachel Feinstein, Matthew Barney, Charles Long, Tony Oursler, Robert Rauschenberg, Maya Lin, Louise Bourgeois, and Dennis Oppenheim, all making or having glass fabricated at the studio, all interested in using glass as a material and highlighting the handmade and process-oriented nature of glassworking in their art. Since I didn't study art or craft history (I had been a philosophy and poetry major at University of California San Diego), I didn't really see much difference between glass art and fine art sculpture. I wrote a lot about glass between 1996 and 2002 and generally took the position that materiality and process were important to understanding contemporary aesthetics; if the artist grasped what was at stake in making sculpture using glass (as opposed, let's say, to putting a bunch of exquisite vessels on a table and calling it an installation), then I was willing to address it critically as art with no qualifiers.

Because Karen studied both sculpture and glass at Rhode Island School of Design, she was one of a handful of people at the studio who really understood how to think through her ideas in sculptural ways, and she excelled at it. I saw her earliest three-dimensional works—a series of blown glass puppets and, later, small dresses made from recycled bottles and hung on a

Lark Mirror, 2004
Cast glass, 11½ × 5½ × ½ in.
(29 × 14.5 × 1.5 cm)
Collection of Alexander Tutsek-Stiftung Foundation, Munich, Germany

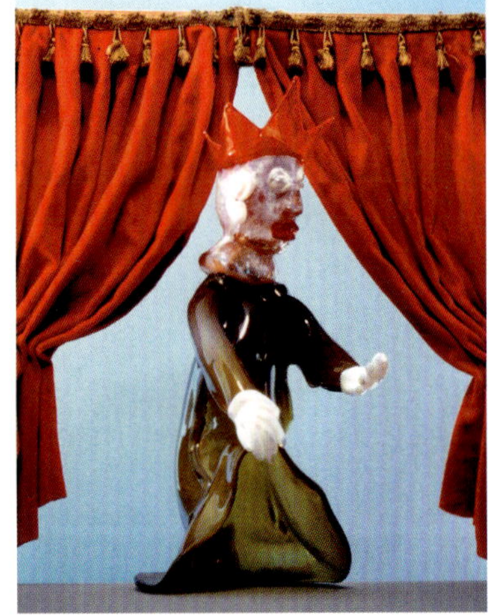
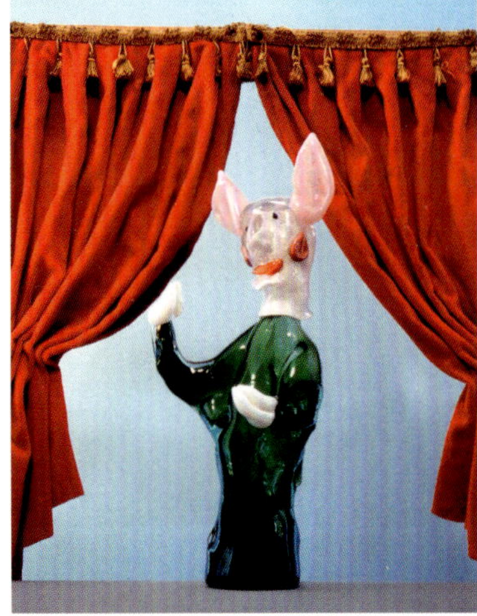
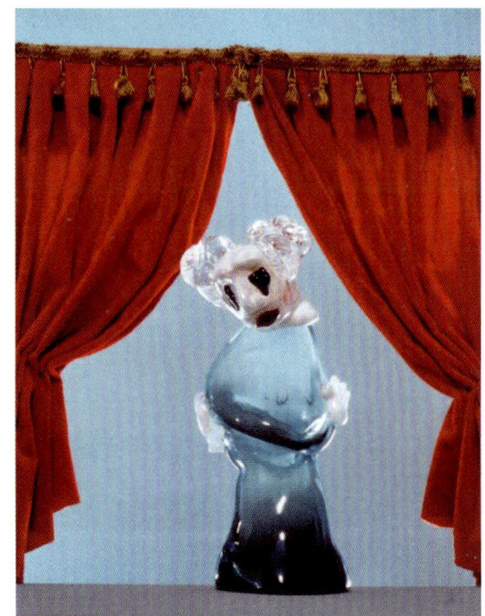
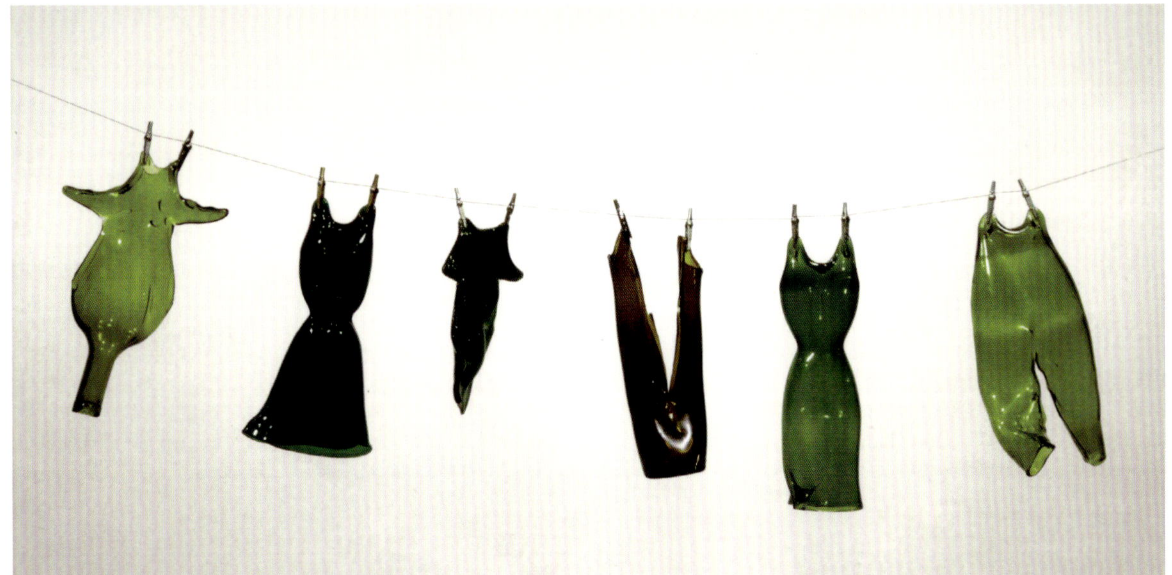

Three puppets, 1994
Blown glass, each approx.
16 × 8 × 8 in. (40 × 20 × 20 cm)

Bottle Clothesline, 1995
Blown glass, 15 × 40 × 4 in.
(38 × 102 × 10 cm)
Collection of Tucson Museum of Art, Tucson, AZ

clothesline—and remember being immediately impressed. Karen was thinking about how glass could represent the human form and emotions and embody presence and absence. Her early work showed a level of maturity and seriousness that made it stand out among her peers and other glass artists at UrbanGlass.

Karen has always had an absolute dedication to research and going "down the rabbit hole" to learn more about what she was interested in. She is a rare breed of artist willing to spend the time necessary to dive deep into a topic before actually trying to make something. Karen left UrbanGlass in 1998 after she got a Fulbright grant to go to the Czech Republic to study glass casting. By 2001, when I visited her and her husband, Steve Polaner, in Prague to write an article for *Glass* magazine, Karen had already made incredible strides in perfecting her series of epically scaled life-size glass dresses. While I was there, I watched Karen work with master mold makers on her hollow-walled molds, which allowed her to articulate the interior structure of a woman's body as well as the exterior folds and details of draped fabric. Karen's dedication to and research into the history, tradition, and limits of glass casting truly allowed her to push the technical and artistic limits of the medium. As well, these early glass dress sculptures allowed Karen to explore the social and material culture of fabric, draping, and what "dressing" signifies, adding another layer of meaning to the work that propelled them far beyond conversations about the decorative, beauty, and skill.

From her earliest sculptural experiments in glass with her blown glass puppets and dresses, which were almost elemental in form and execution compared to what she is doing today, she has shown singular focus in her pursuit of her own ideas. For example, Karen's research on dressing and the body took her to Japan on a fellowship in 2006 to study the kimono and *yuzen* dyeing techniques, which eventually led to her *Floating World* series. Simultaneously, a fortuitous encounter with fishing nets, together with the development of a series of reclining figures in which the drapery looked like topography of the natural environment, grew into a branch of research that inspired a new body of work based on the idea of landscape, *Drapery Abstractions*.

Continuing to push her work in new directions, Karen has incorporated printmaking and large-scale bronze, iron, and ceramic casting as well as photography, bioglass, and monumental carved marble into her repertoire as ways to express these ideas. Her work still focuses on the dress and the body as objects but she has made a conscious choice to be more abstract in her approach, echoing an earlier shift that Tina Oldknow referred to when describing *Drapery Abstractions*: "While this differentiation might seem subtle to some, it represented a fundamental conceptual shift for LaMonte: she had moved from object/figure/beauty to a territory of landscape/nature/sublime."[1]

I have known Karen for twenty-four years; she is probably the artist whose work and career I have followed the longest. As I trace the exciting interconnections and evolutions of her "rabbit holes," from those early discussions and small glass works to her current diverse explorations, I cannot wait to see where they take her next.

NOTES

1 Tina Oldknow, "Karen LaMonte: Charting the Iconography of Desire," in *Karen LaMonte: Drapery Abstractions* (New York: Heller Gallery, 2010), 3.

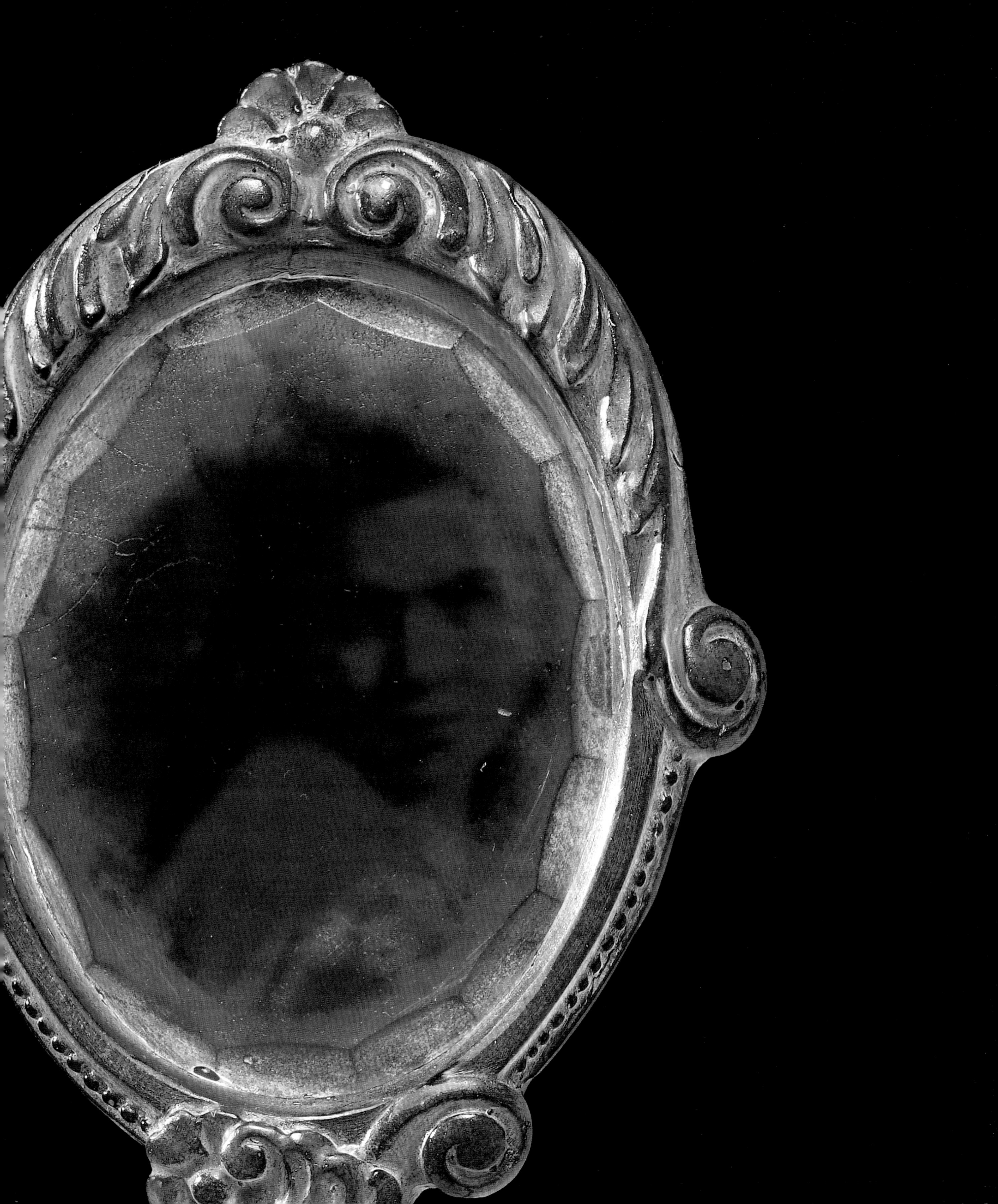

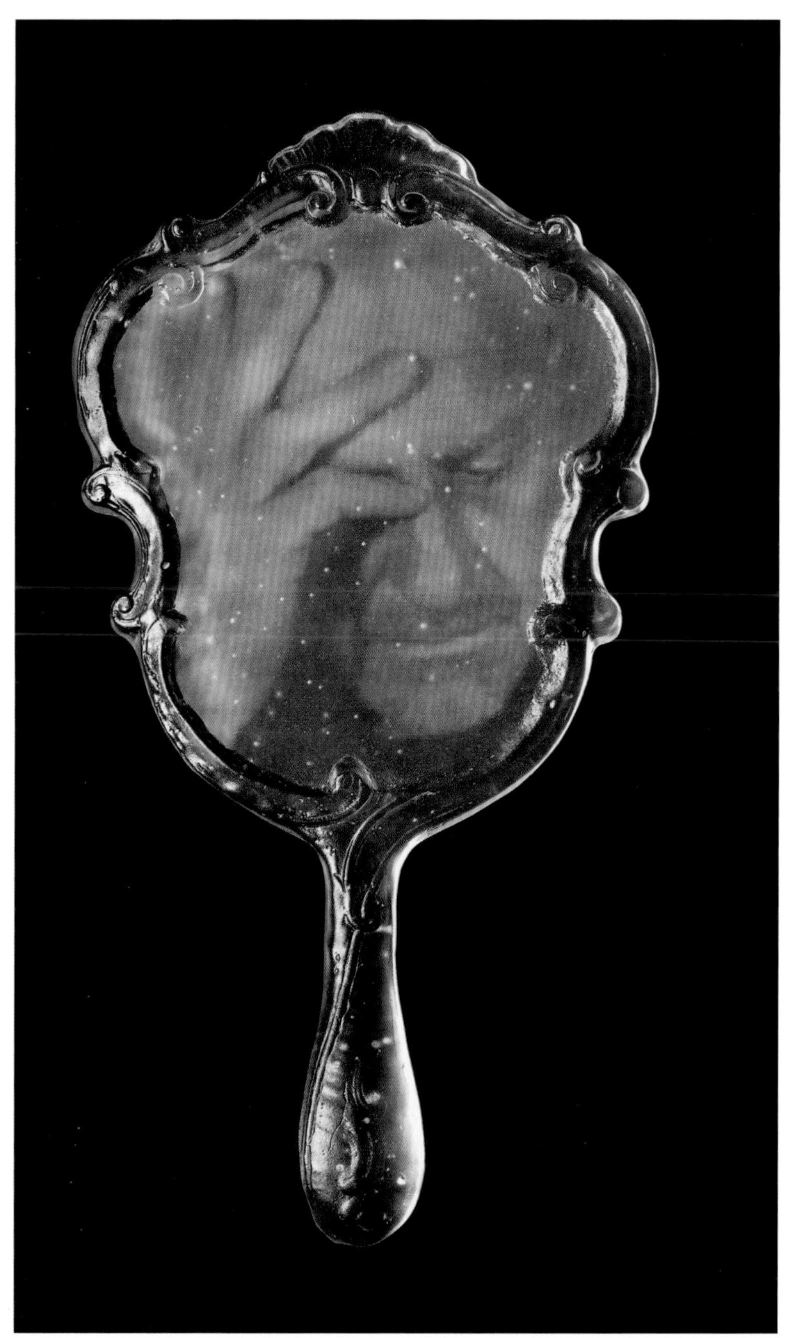

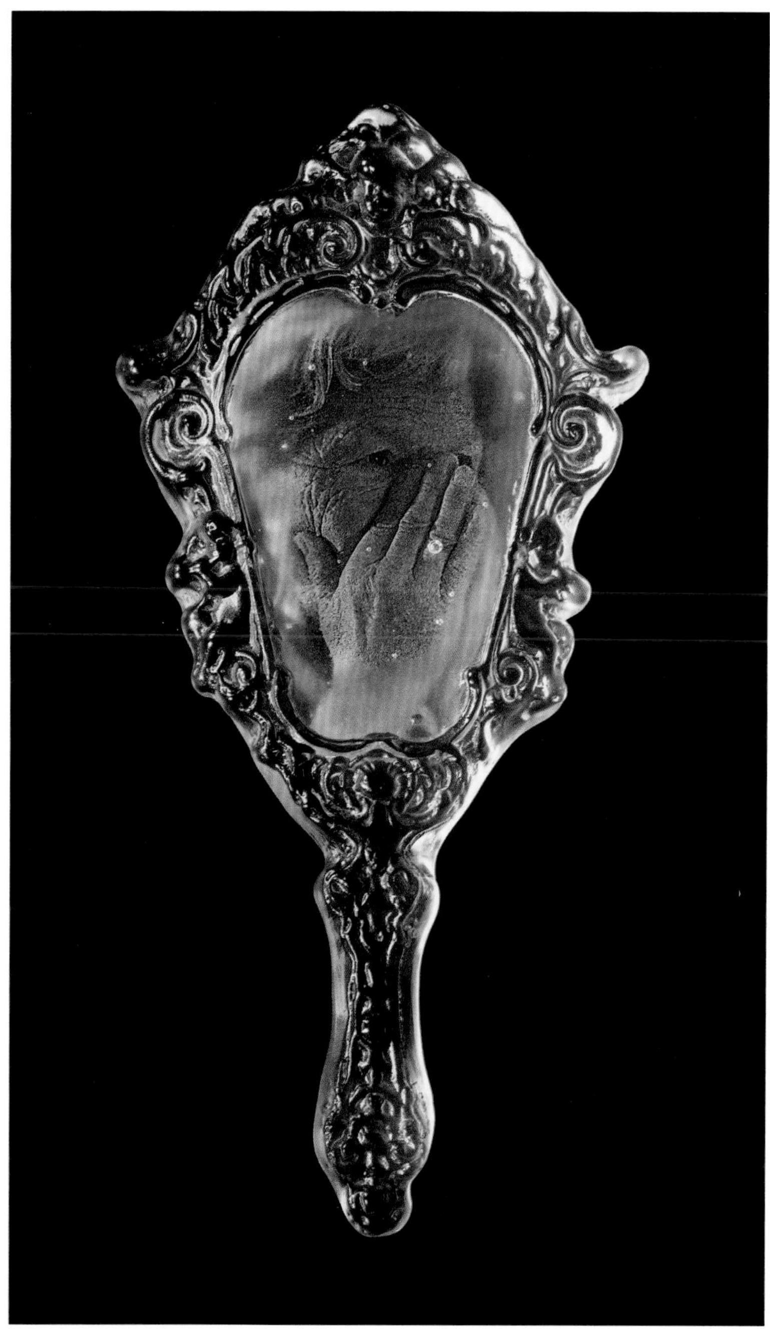

OPPOSITE
Lark Mirror (Hysteria), 2008
Cast glass, 14 × 5½ × ½ in. (35.5 × 14.5 × 1.5 cm)
Collection of Musée des Arts Décoratifs, Paris

ABOVE LEFT TO RIGHT
Lark Mirror, 2004
Cast glass, 12½ × 6½ × 1 in. (31.5 × 16 × 2 cm)

Lark Mirror, 2004
Cast glass, 10 × 4½ × 1 in. (25 × 12 × 2 cm)

Impression 4, 2001
Sartoriotype, 58½ × 42½ × 3 in.
(149 × 107.5 × 7 cm)

FOLLOWING
Impression 2, 2001
Sartoriotype, 79 × 57 × 3 in.
(200 × 145 × 7 cm)
Collection of Corning Museum of Glass,
Corning, NY

Impression 8, 2001
Sartoriotype, 62 × 42 × 3 in.
(157.5 × 107 × 7 cm)

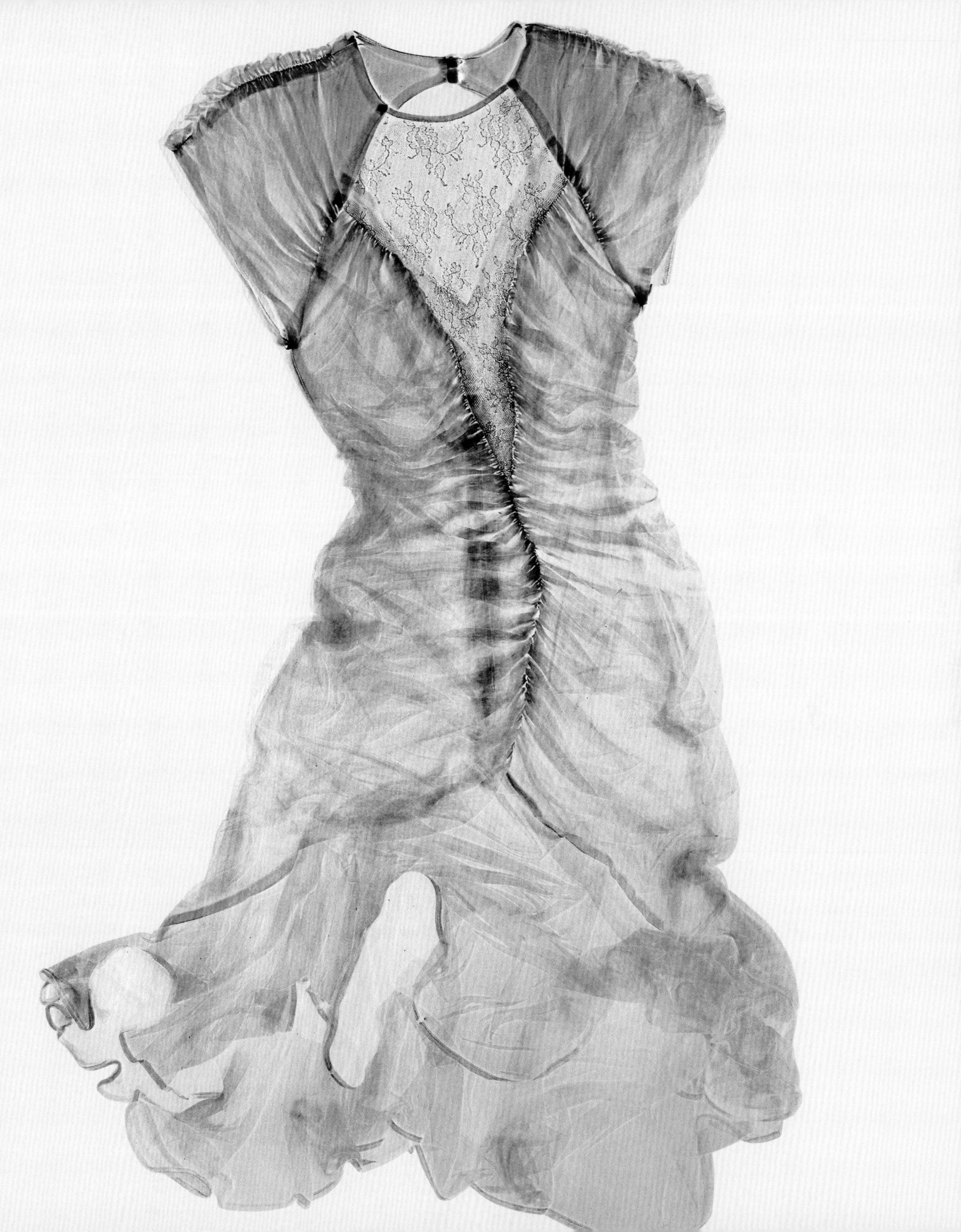

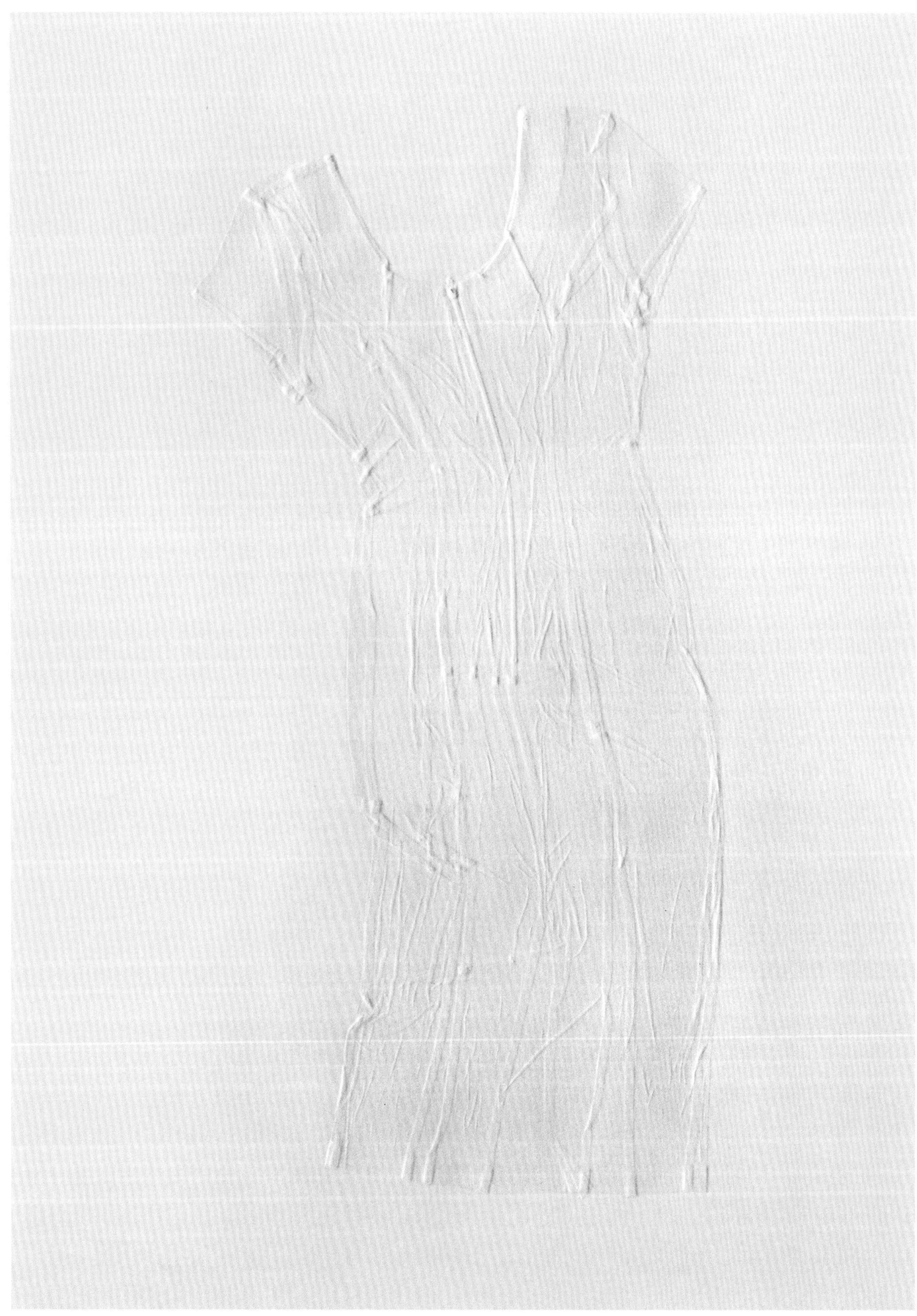

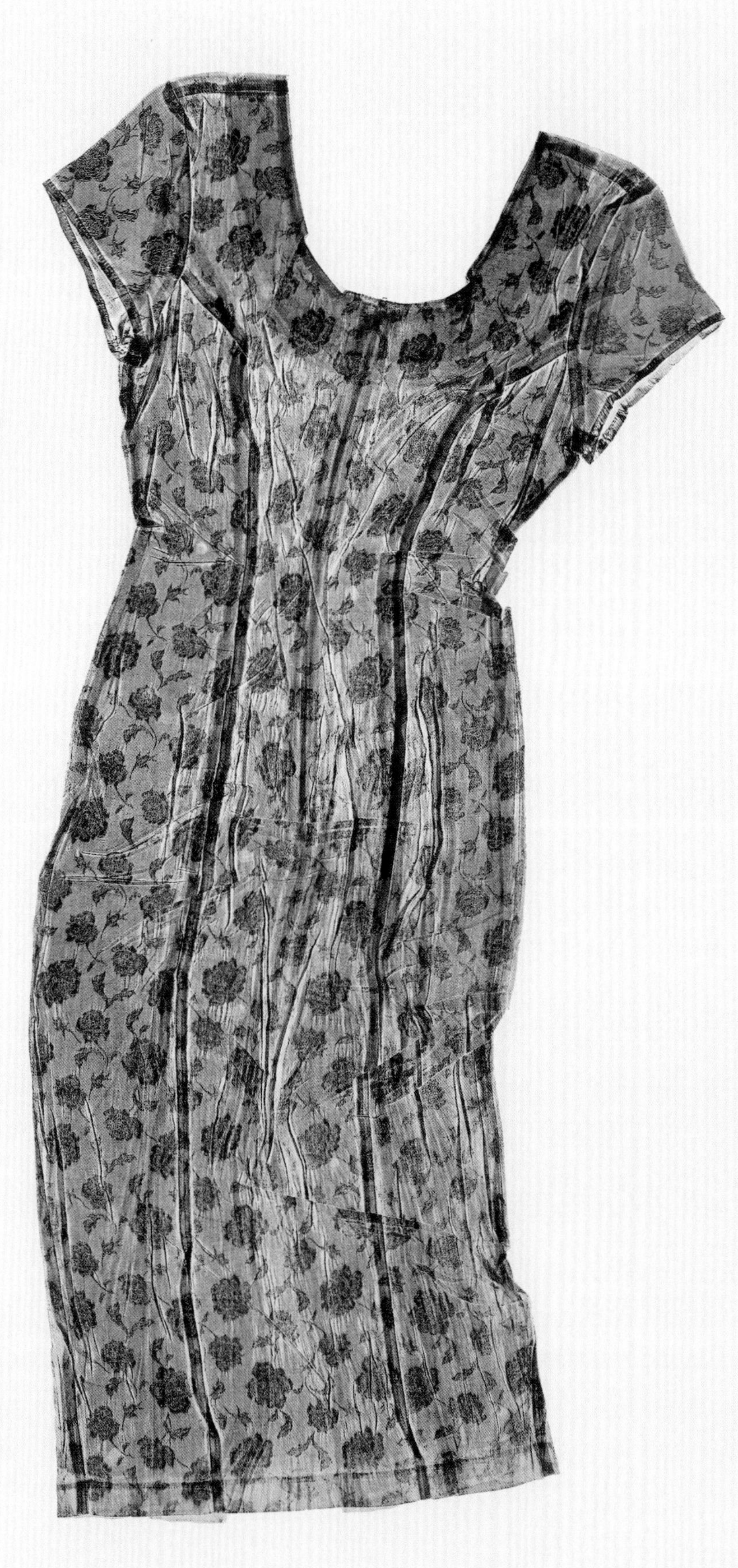

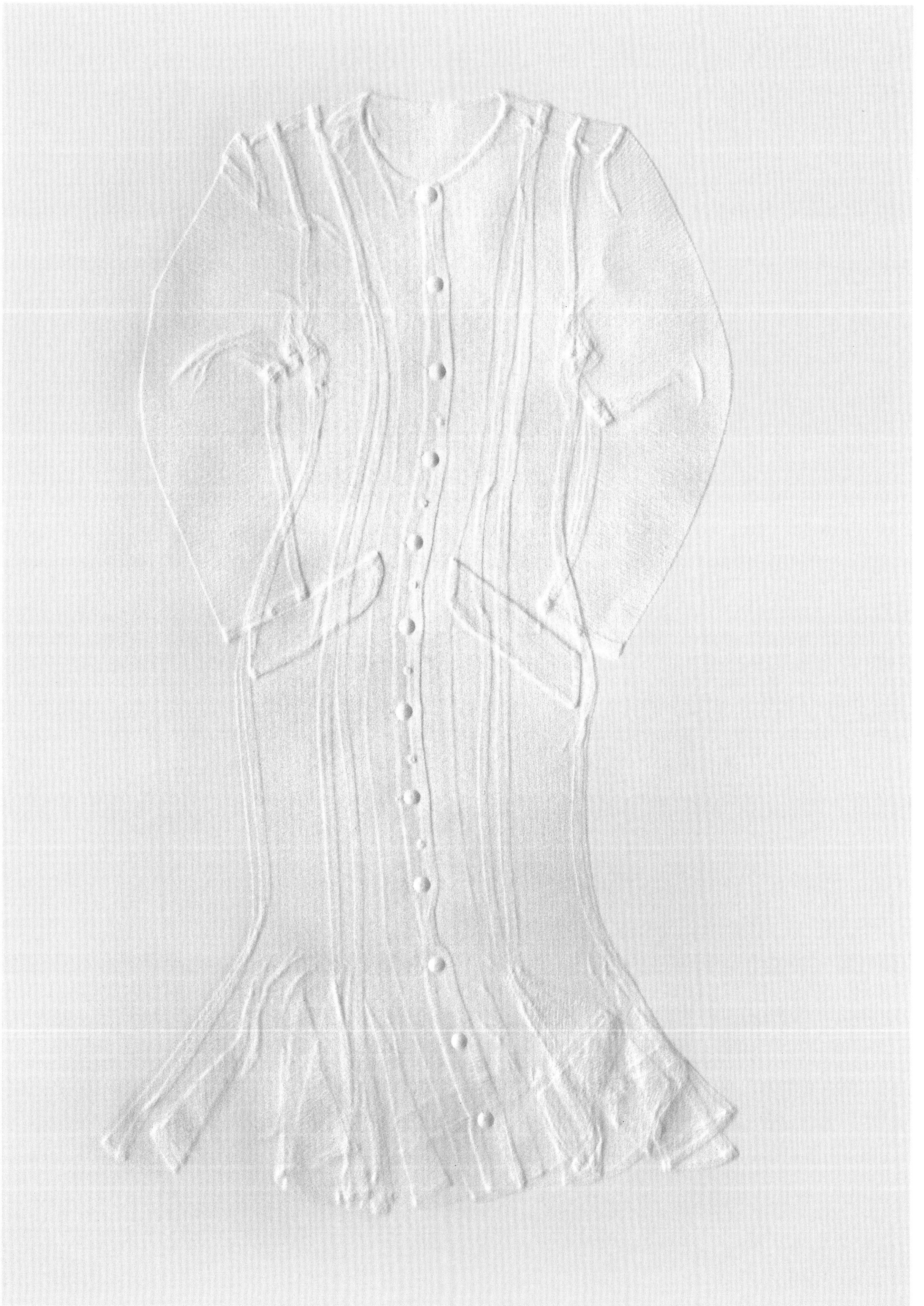

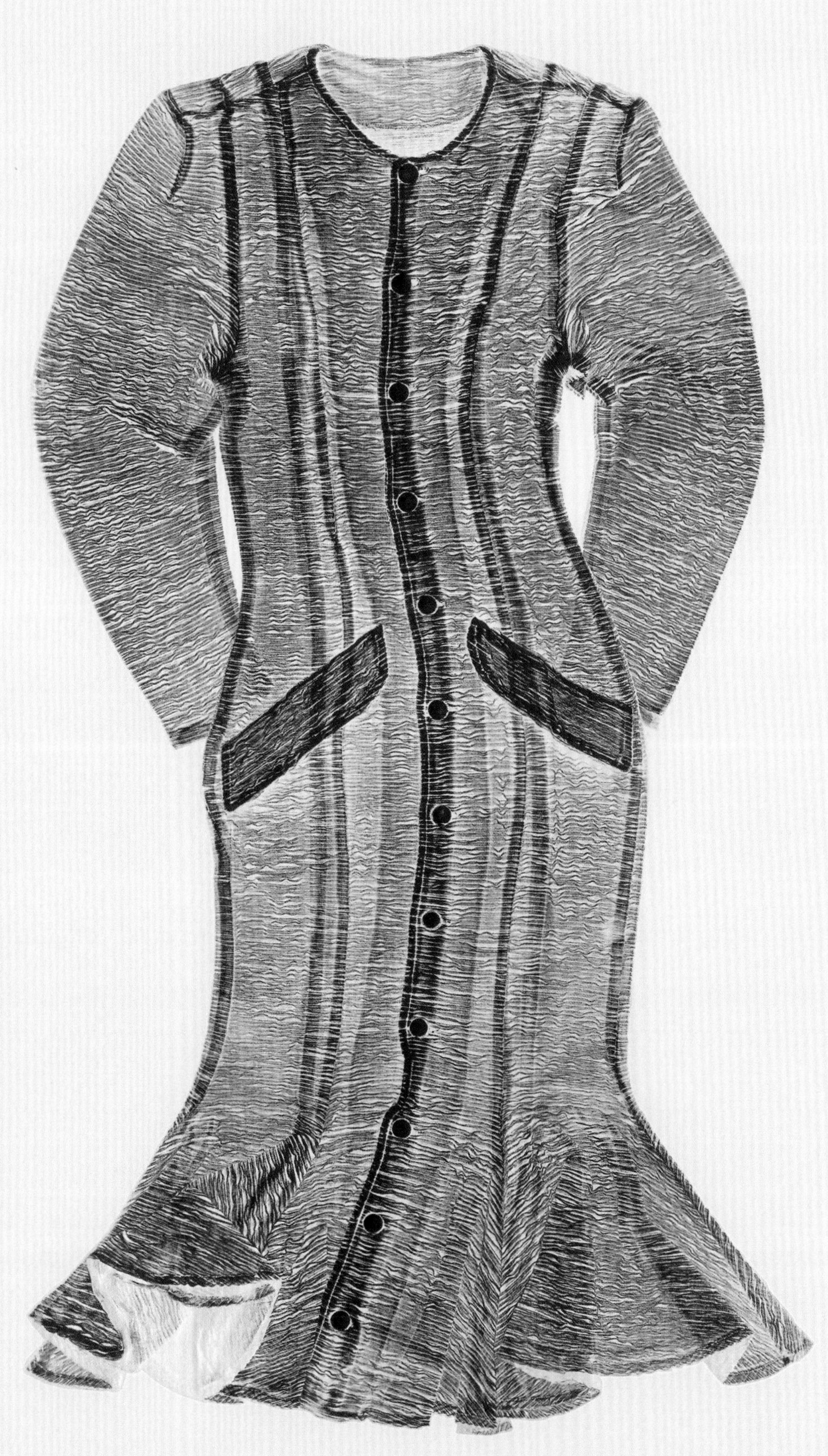

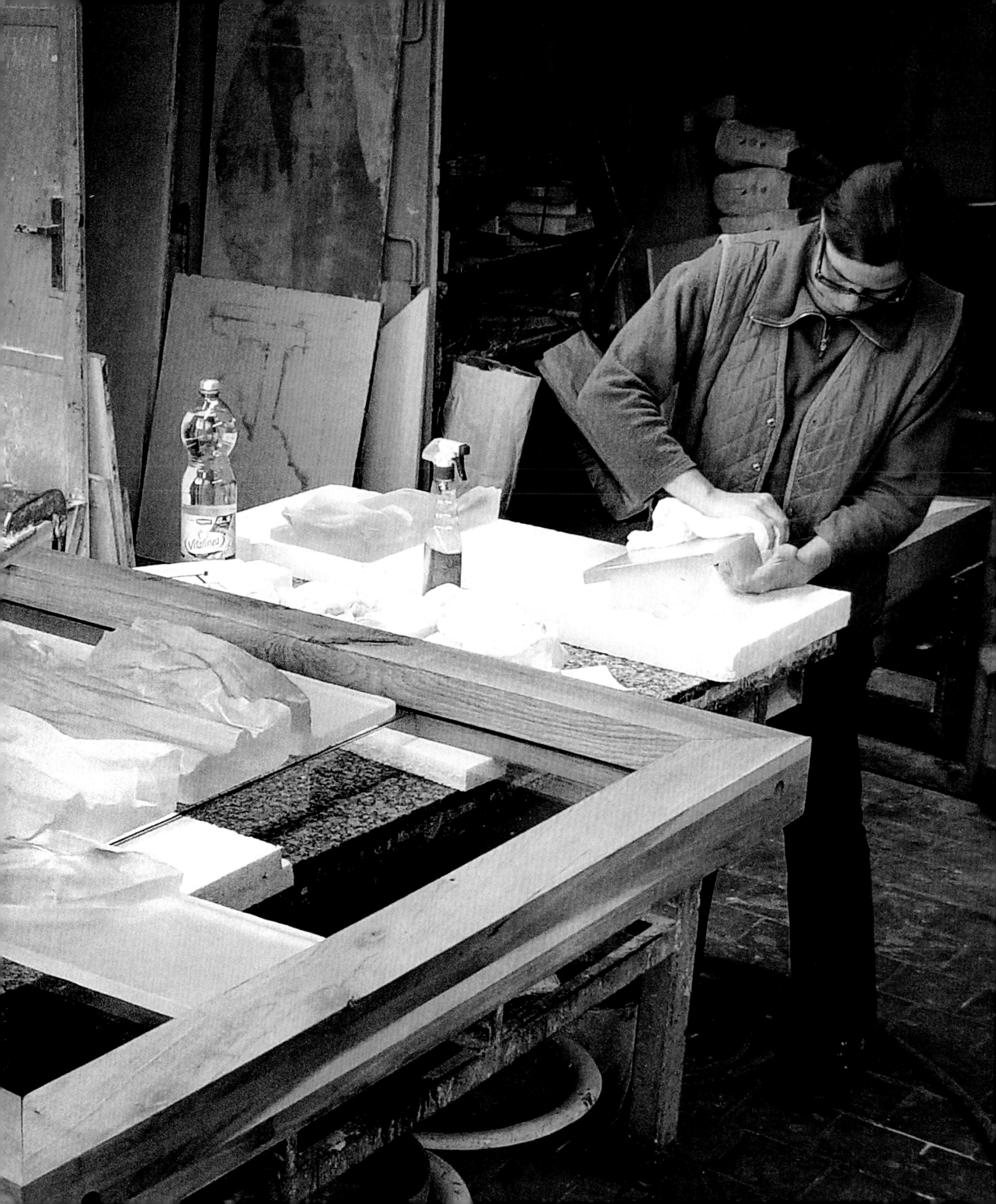

PREVIOUS
Assembling a cast glass bas-relief, 2002.

Remnant (Dress), 2002
Cast glass, 81½ × 51 × 5½ in. (207 × 130 × 14 cm)

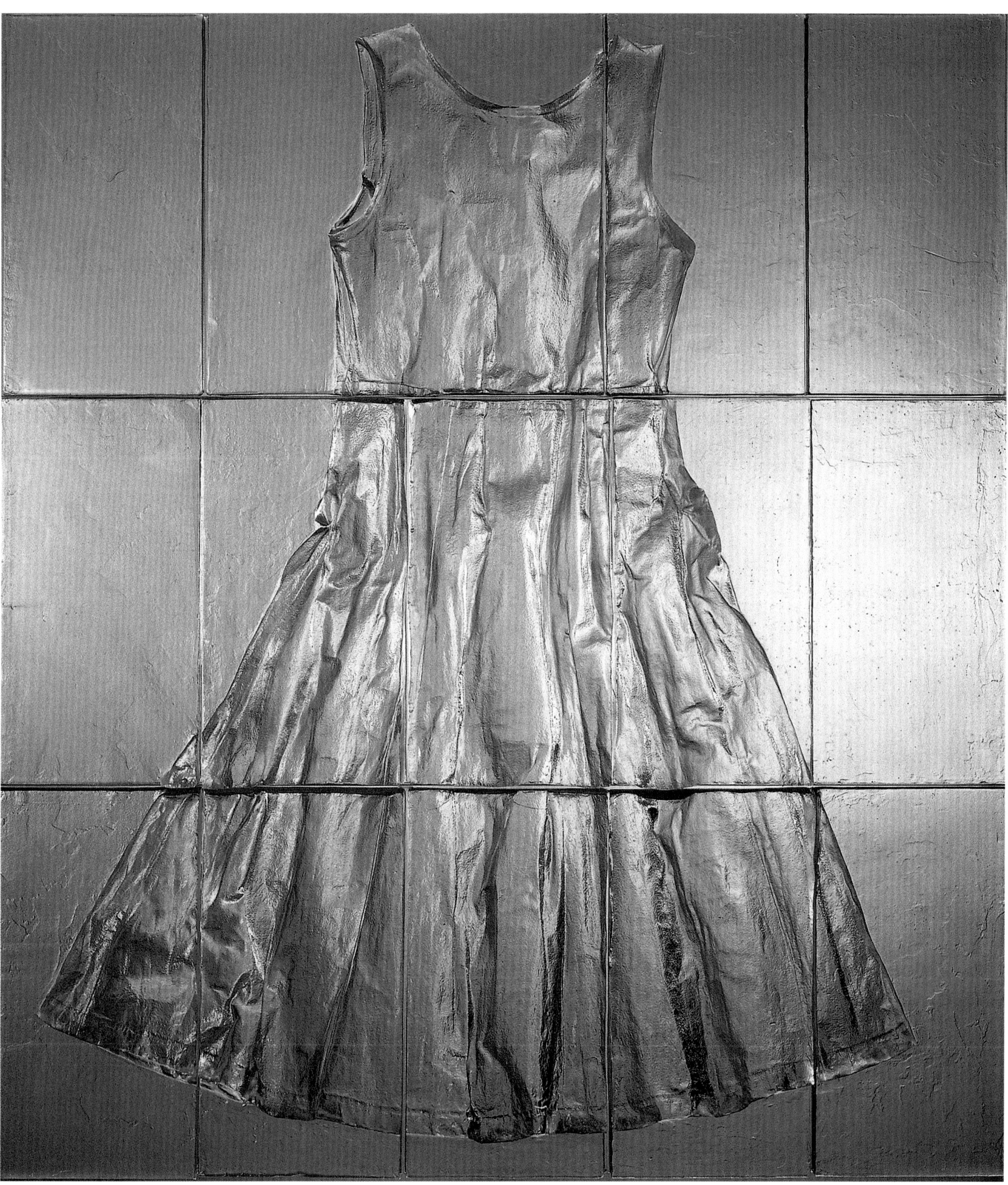

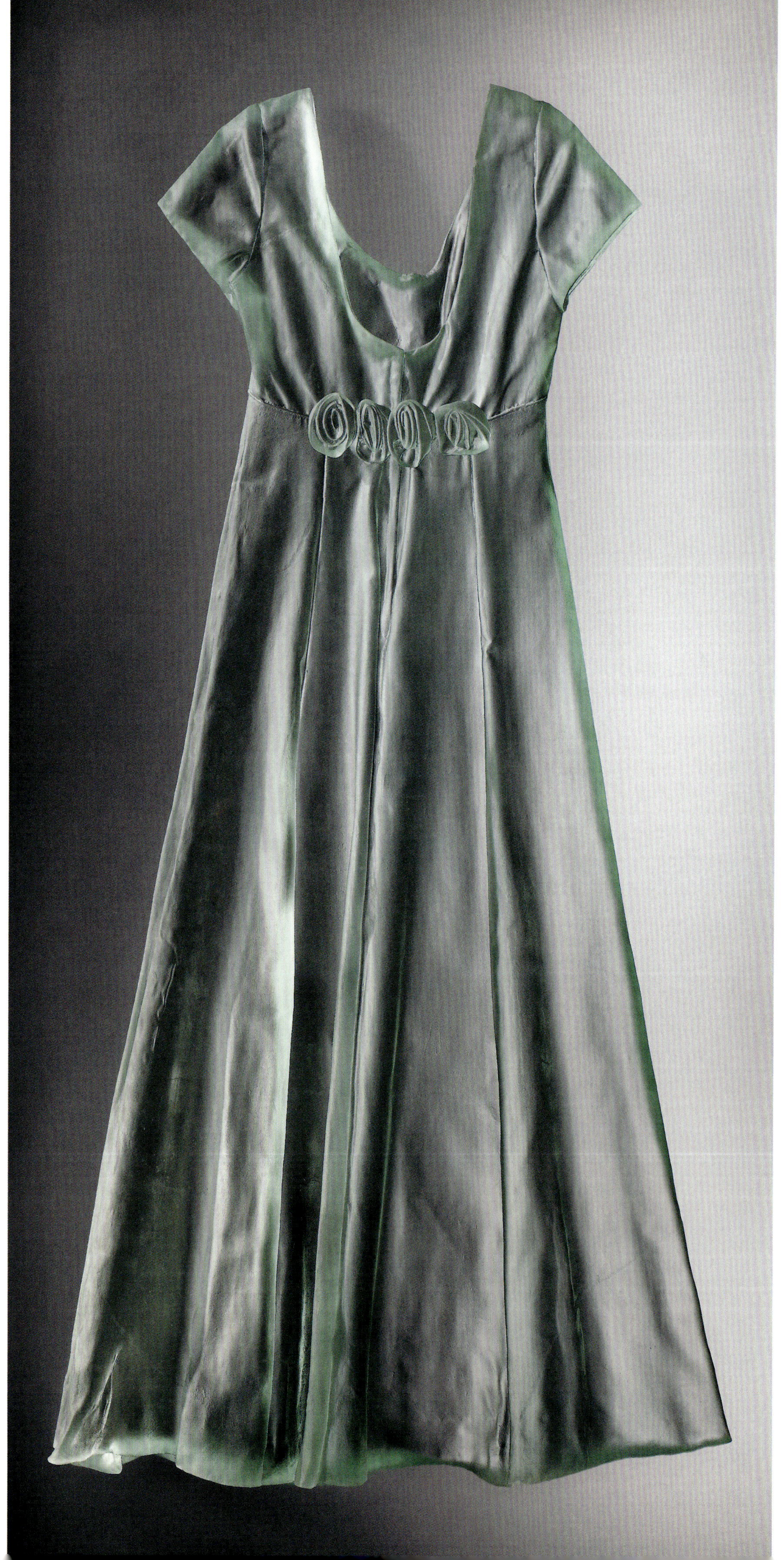

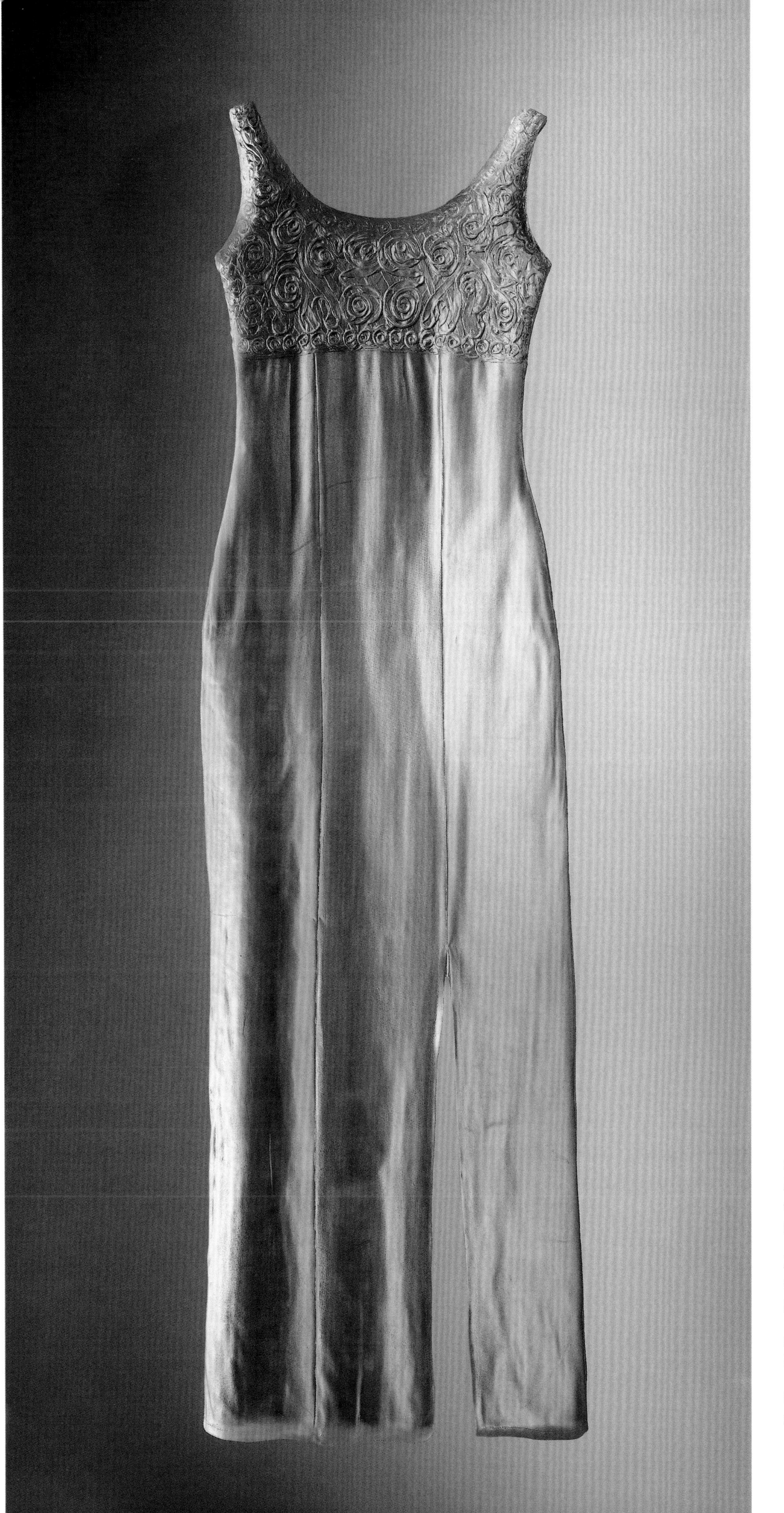

OPPOSITE
Remnant (Evening Rose Dress), 2005
Cast glass, 78½ × 35 × 4½ in.
(200 × 89 × 11 cm)

Remnant (Lace Dress), 2005
Cast glass, 78½ × 35 × 2 in.
(200 × 89 × 5 cm)

FOLLOWING
Preparing *Vestige* for casting, 2000.

Sculpting the inner shell of a dress casting, 2000.

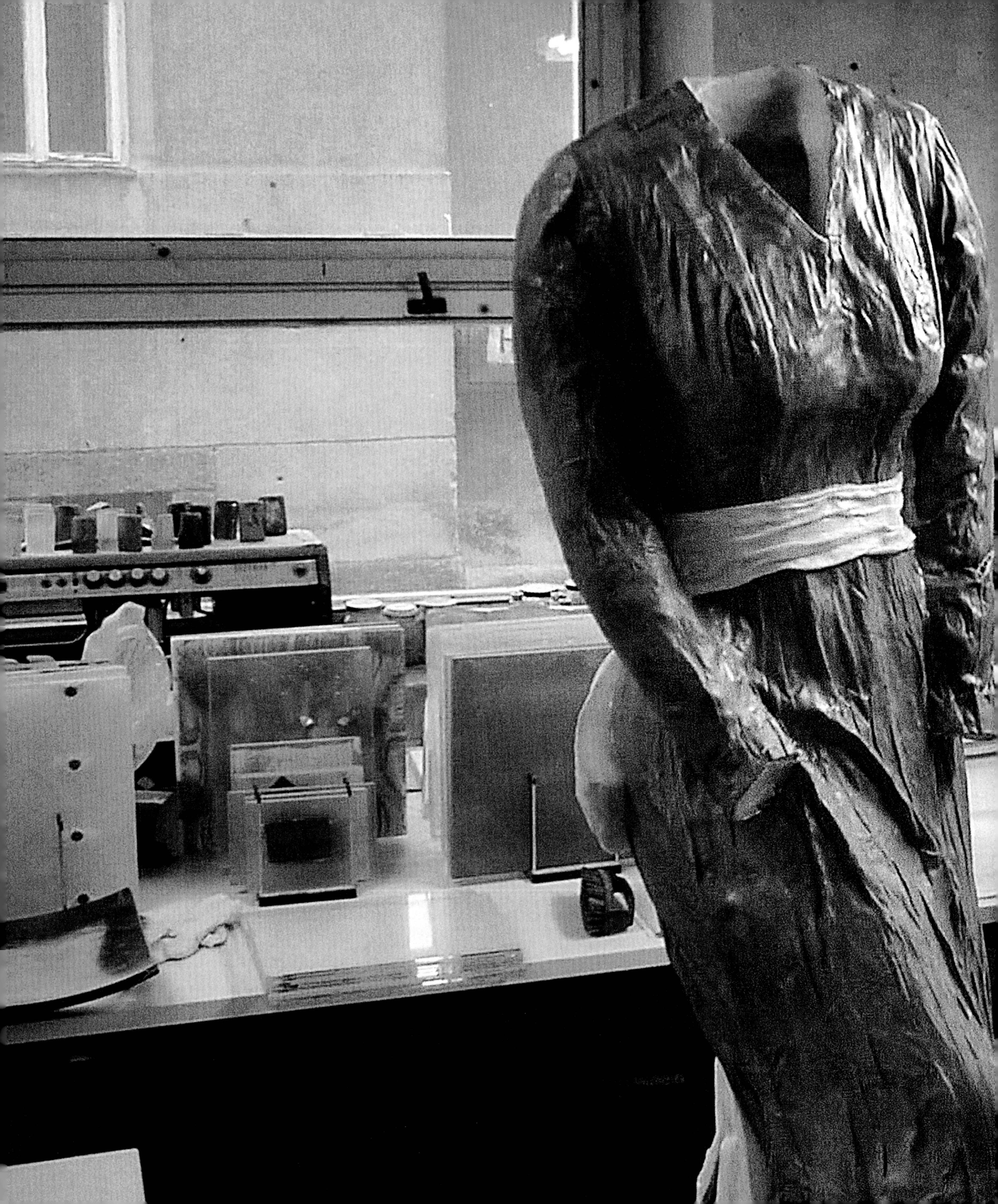

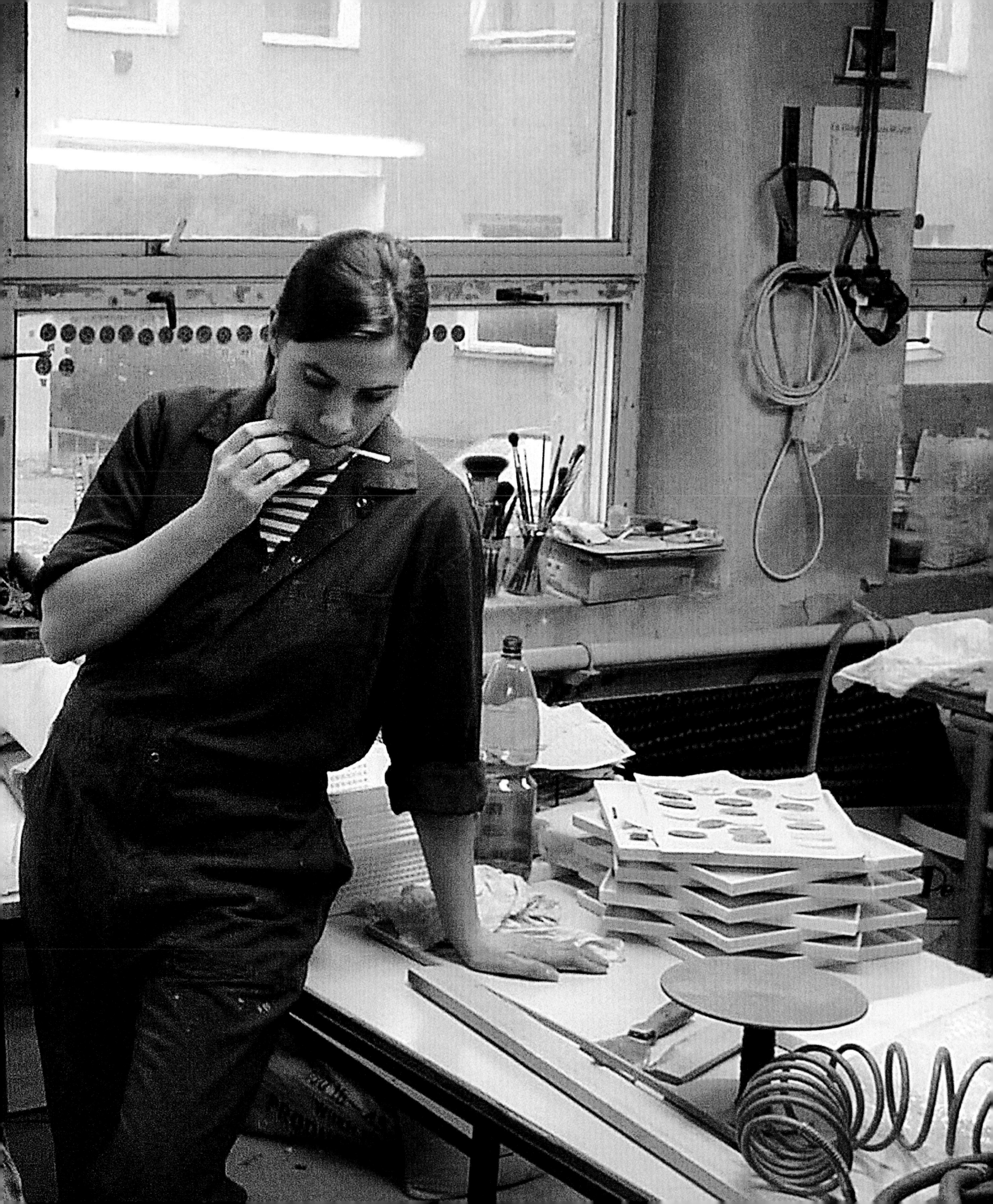

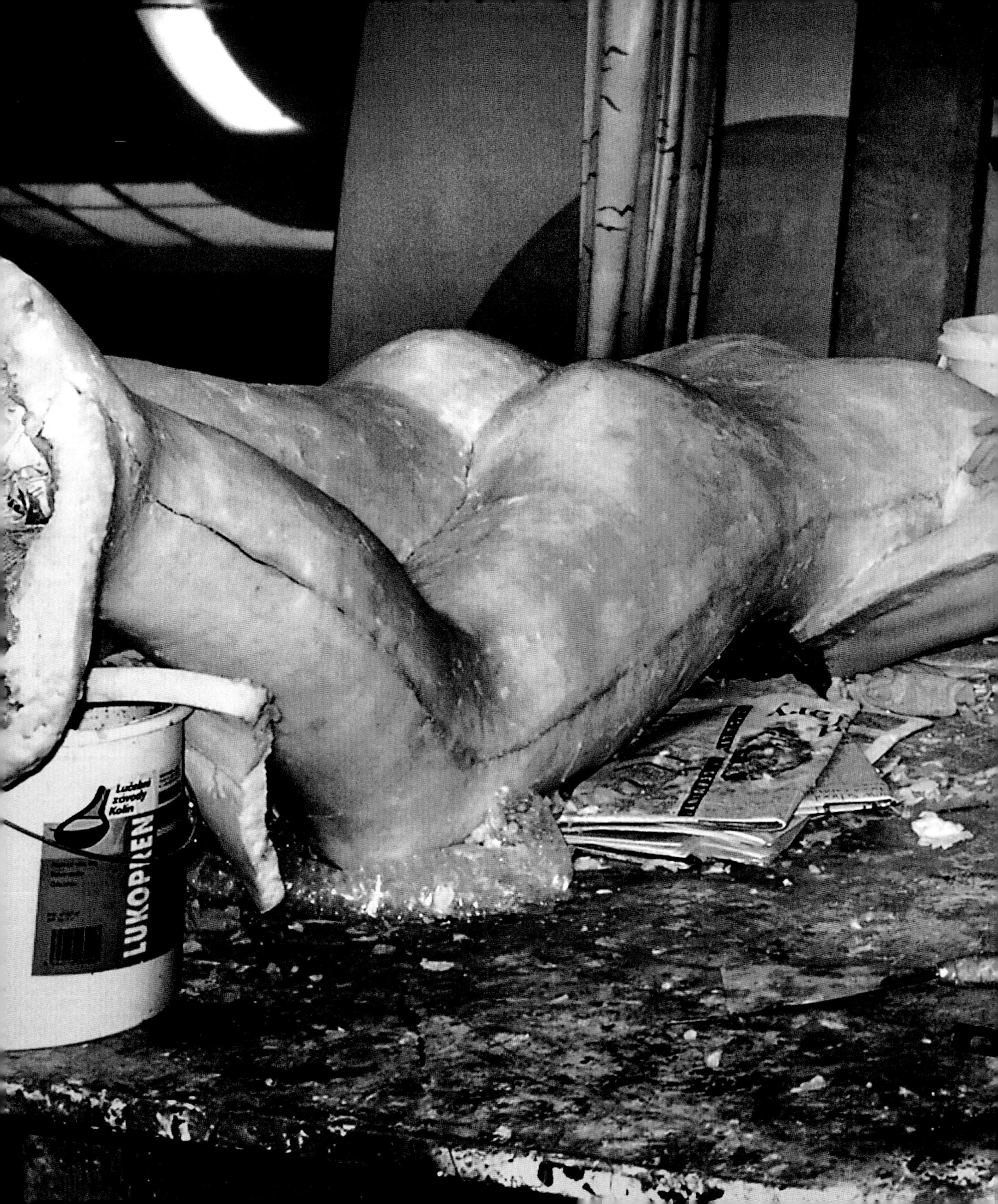
Lučební
závody
Kolín
LUKOPREN

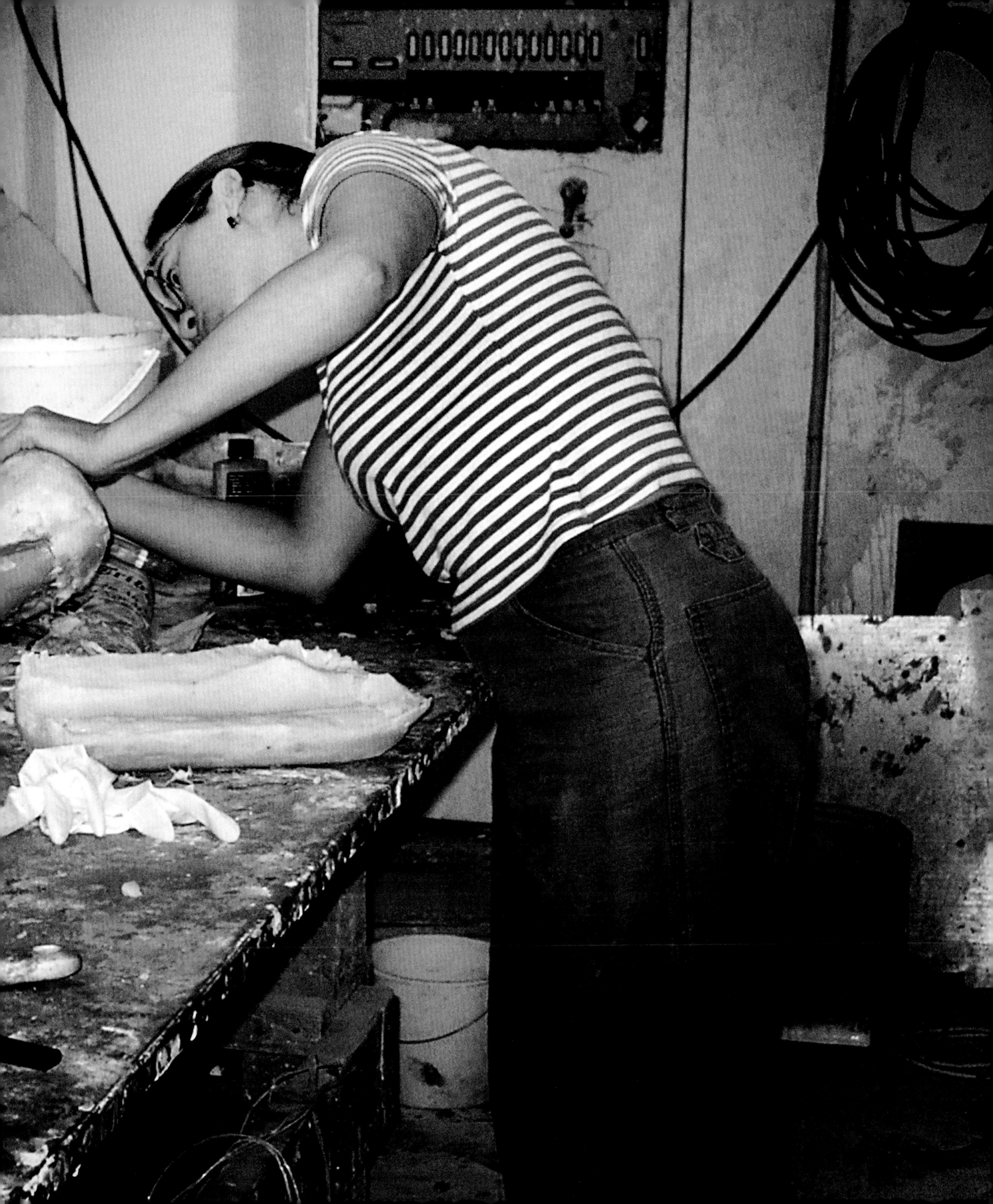

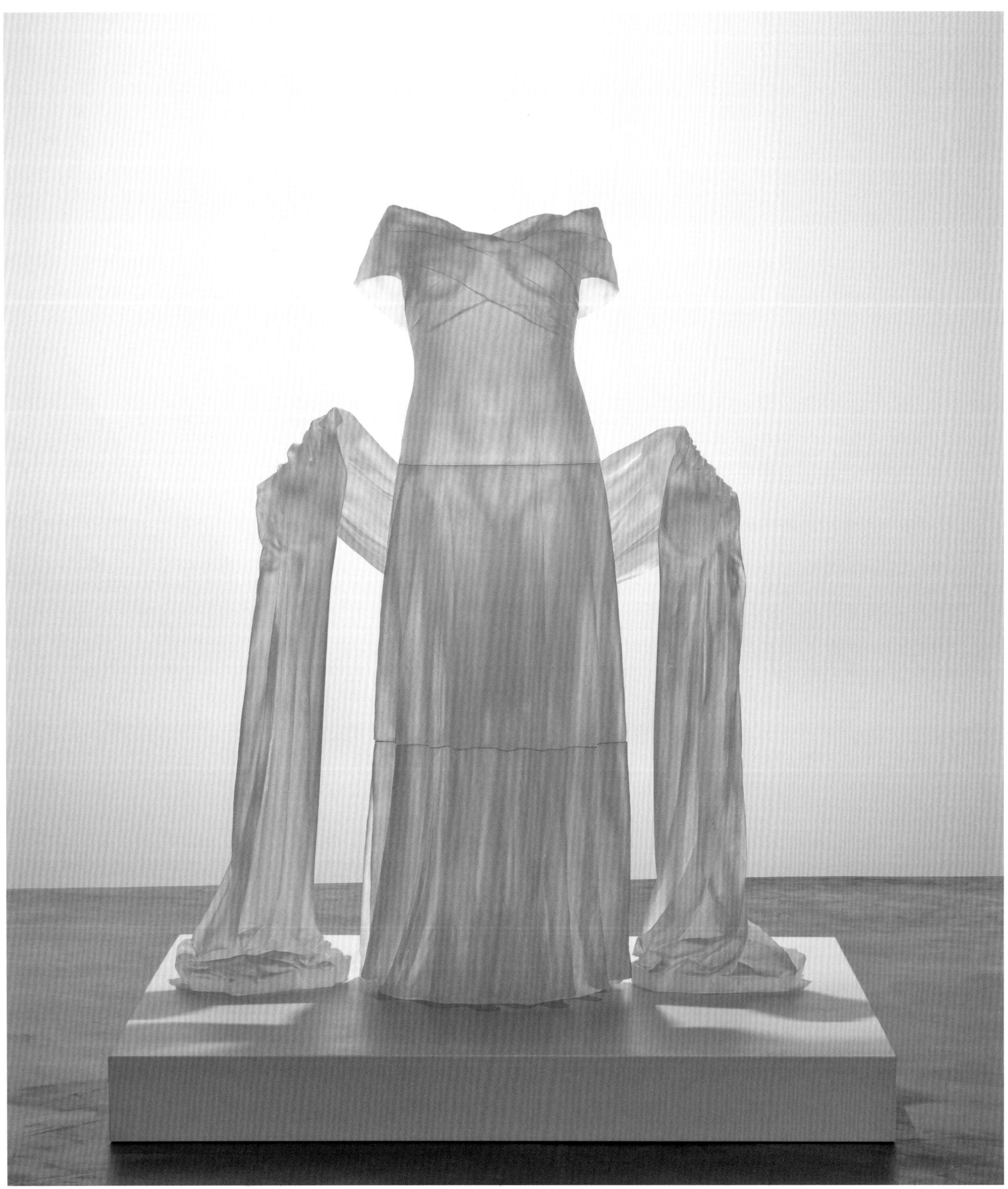

The Poetry of Meaning and Loss

Arthur C. Danto

When I became fascinated with the work of Karen LaMonte, my interest was in the genius of her vision. It was bestowed as a gift of the creative imagination, and transformed her into a very different artist than she would have been, had the vision not been granted her. LaMonte's pieces, whatever their weight, proclaim beauty and evanescence, fragility and delicacy, transparency and light, luxury and magic. Her decision to make the dress her central motif led to the kind of dress she chose for transubstantiation into glass, where the fragility of the glass augments the fineness and translucency of the fabric, and the lightness expressed by ornamentation of the garment—flounces, bows, ribbons, ruffles. At least initially, the dresses she chose were declarations of radical femininity on the part of their wearers—garments so constructed as to project an image of ideal grace. In her brilliant book, *Seeing through Clothes,* Anne Hollander argues that "the primary function of Western dress is to contribute to the making of a self-conscious image, an image linked to all other imaginative and idealized visualizations of the human body." The garments LaMonte worked with were not, except from a cynical perspective, working clothes—housedresses, business suits, uniforms. They were ornamental garments for special occasions, and they translated into visual terms the metaphor of the woman as herself an ornament, whose substance was aesthetic through and through.

Most of the dresses that LaMonte has cast in glass are as much vestiges of a vanished time as of an absent person. They are as dated as old photographs, found in the backs of drawers or forgotten between the pages of books. This brings me to one of the most interesting features of LaMonte's work. We can see through the fabric to the naked body of the women who wore it, as if the body left its imprint on the dress that concealed but alluded to it. It is as if the beauty of the wearer's body were preserved in her garment, and we see the navel, the nipples, the shadowed delta between her legs, her buttocks. I see this as adding a dimension of tragedy to the poetry of the work. The dress belonged to a moment when the wearer was, to use an expression of Proust's, *en fleur.* The dress belonged to a certain moment of history, which it preserves—it shows how women dressed for certain occasions at a certain

Evening Dress with Shawl, 2004
Cast glass, 59½ × 51 × 21 in.
(151 × 130 × 53.5 cm)
Collection of Corning Museum of Glass, Corning, NY. Gift in part of the Ennion Society.

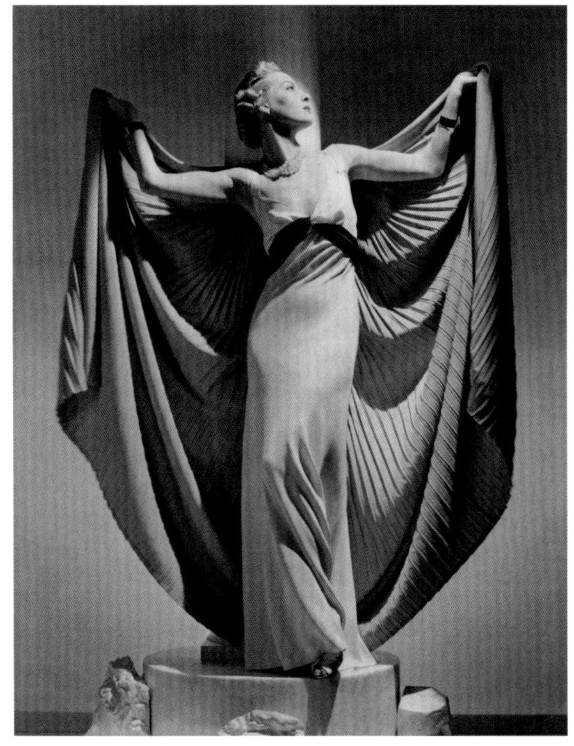

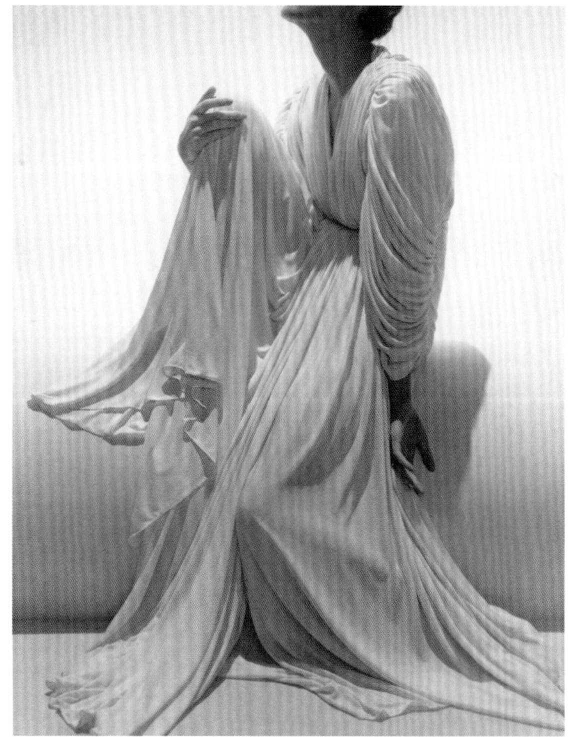

Helen Bennett in Cape Dress. Horst P. Horst, *Vogue*, 1936

Robe de Grès by Madame Grès. George Hoyningen-Huene. Fall 1936. Musée National d'Art Moderne, Centre Georges Pompidou, Paris

moment. The wearer will have aged. She looked like that then, but, if she is still alive, it is certain she will not look that way now. There is a double melancholy—the melancholy of fashion, and the melancholy of bodily change, from nubility to decrepitude. The breasts have fallen, the waist thickened, the skin has lost its transparency and luminescence. The poignancy of LaMonte's dresses is a product of two modes of change in which we participate as human beings, composed, as we are, of flesh and meaning. Their poetry is the poetry of beauty and loss.

Exhibition *Absence Adorned*, 2005
Museum of Glass International Center for Contemporary Art, Tacoma, WA

FOLLOWING
Reclining Drapery Impression, 2005
Exhibition *Réflexions Féminines*, 2010, Musée du Verre, Sars-Poteries, France

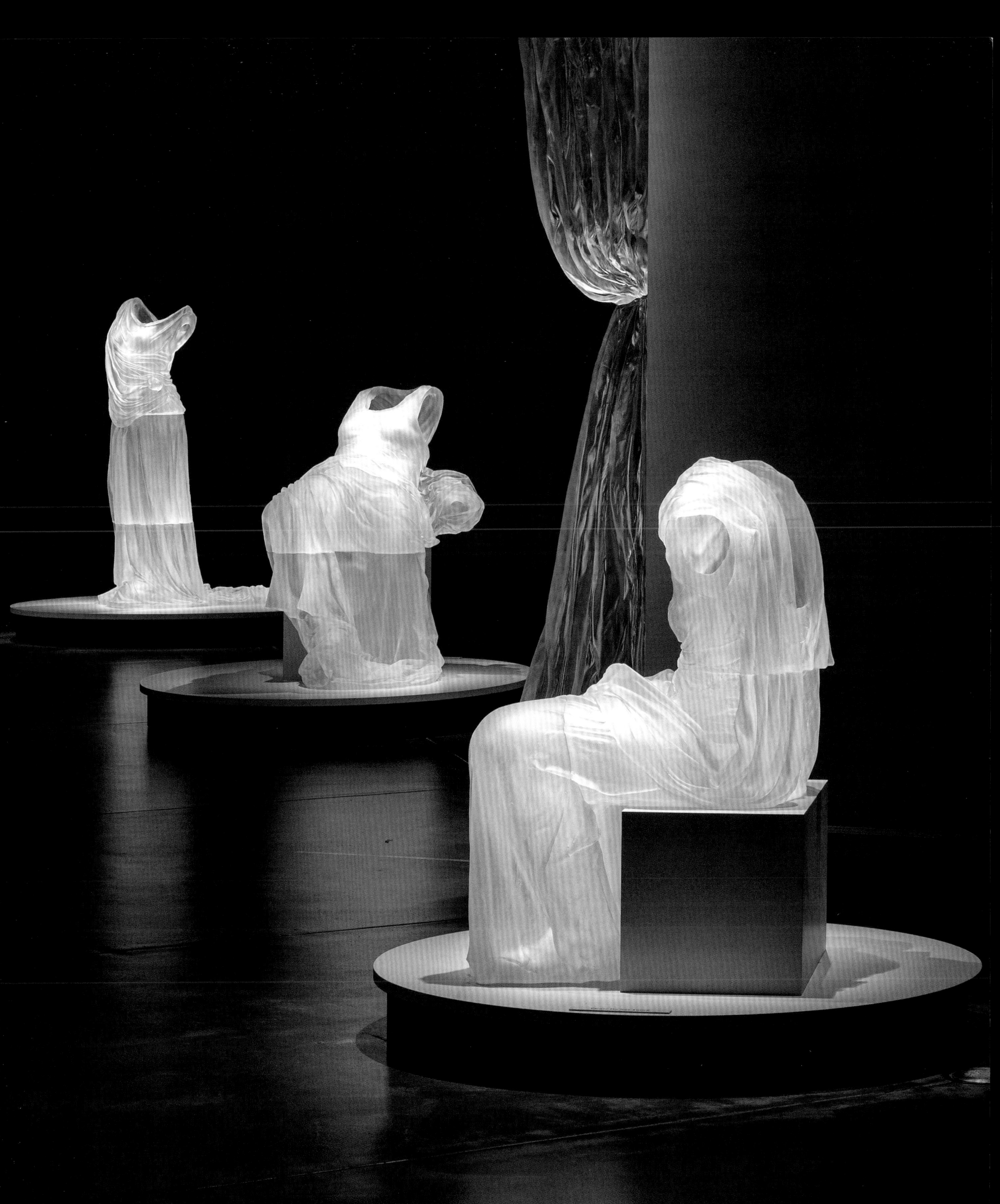

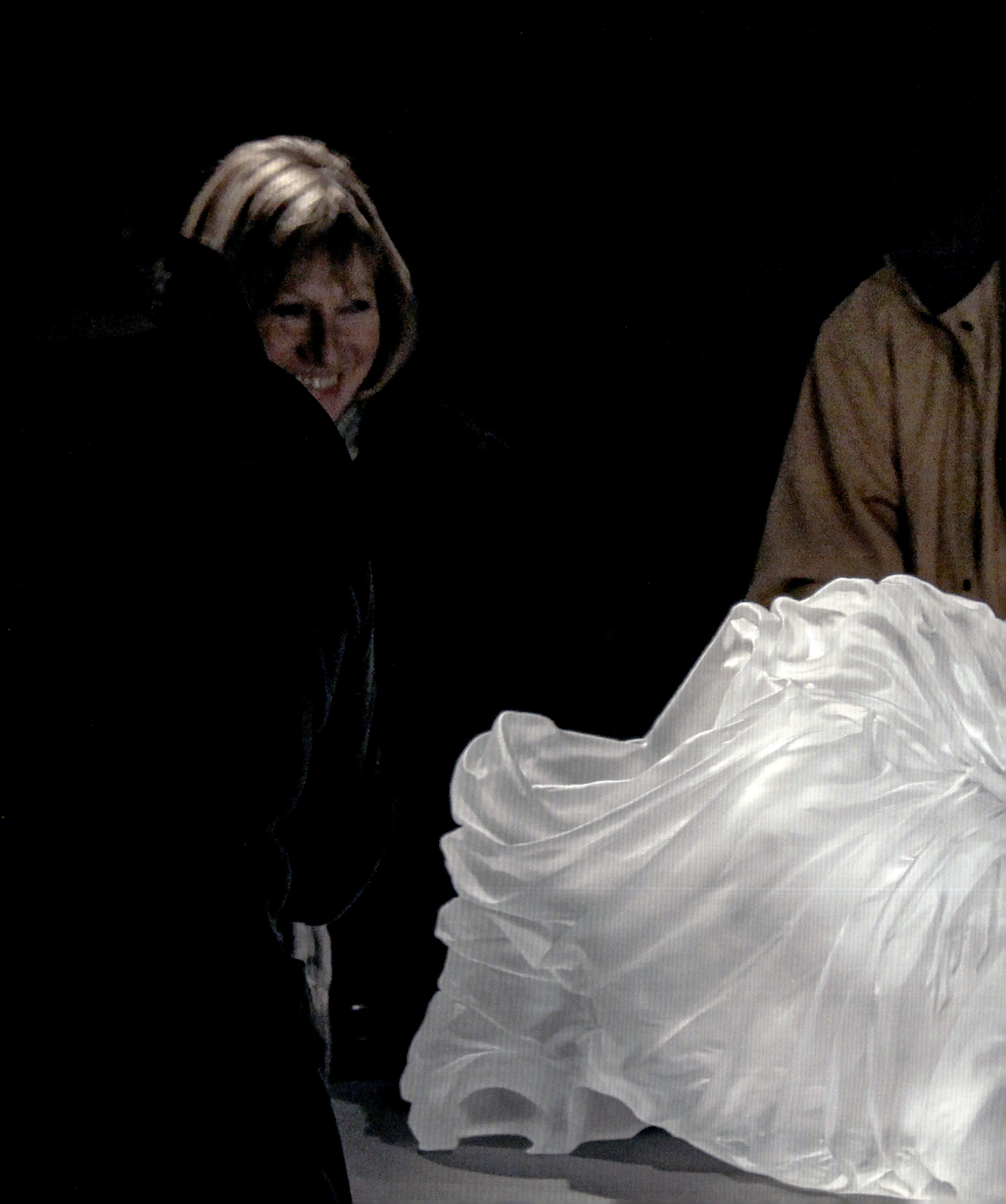

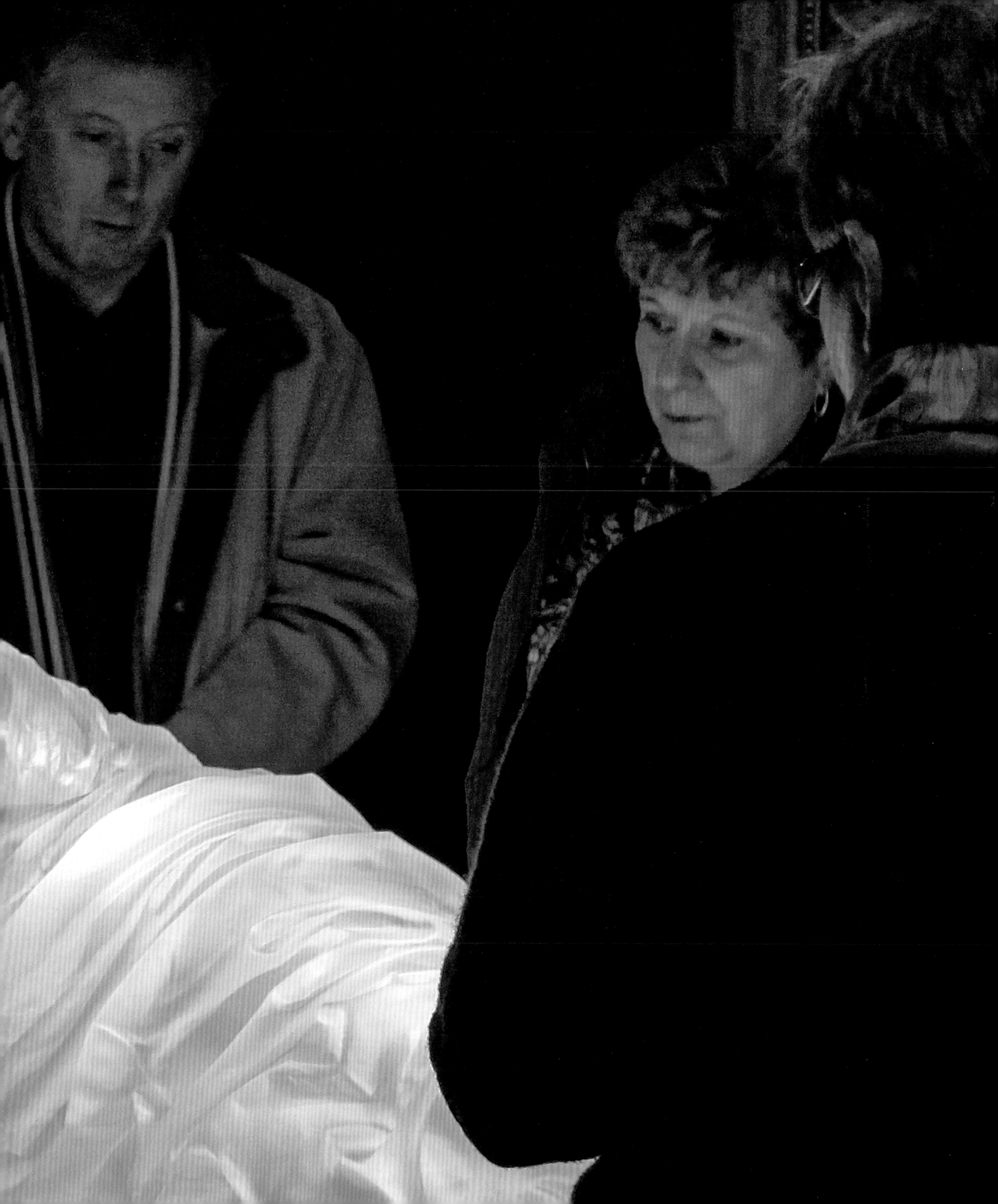

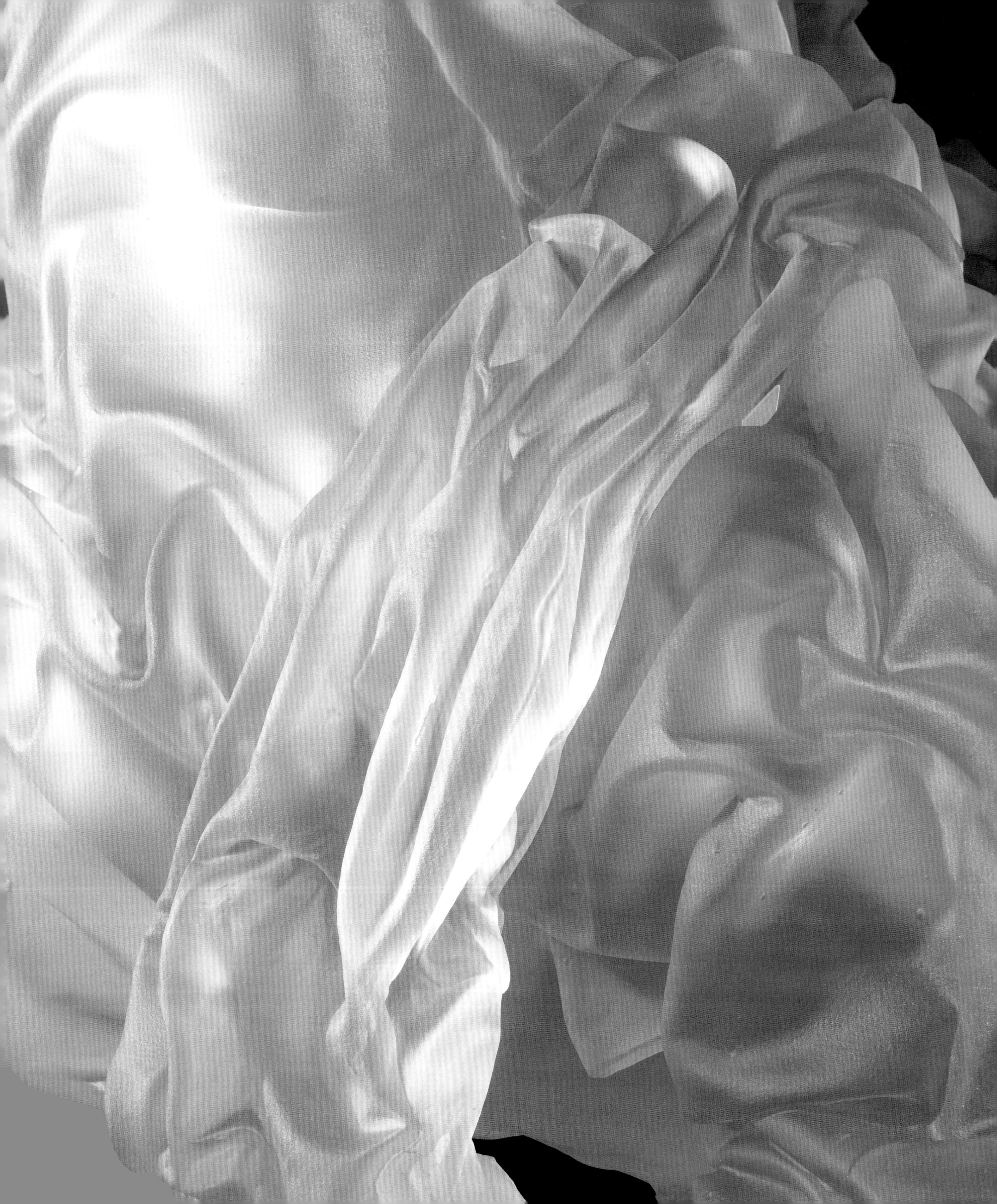

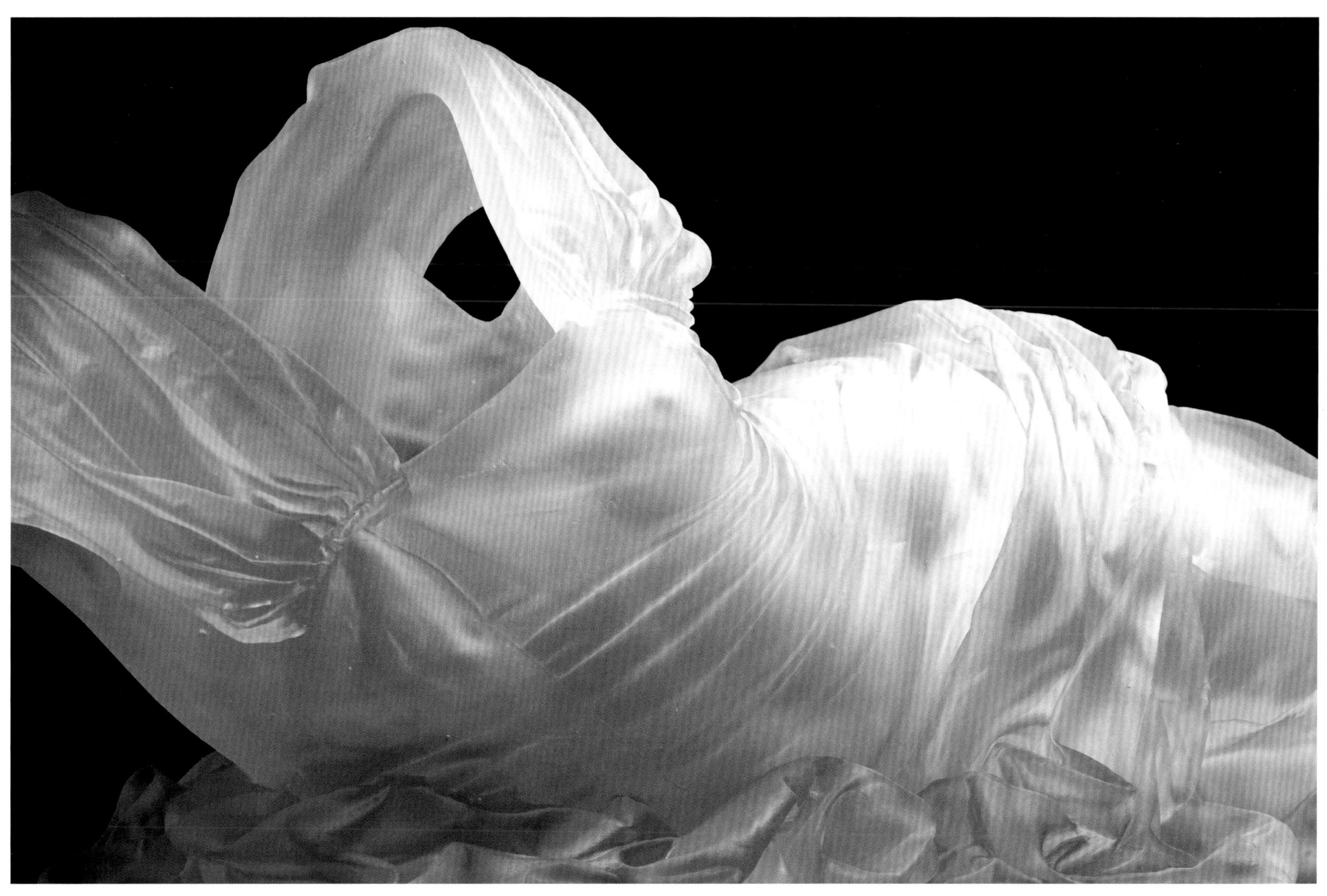

THIS AND FOLLOWING
Reclining Dress Impression with Drapery, 2006
Cast glass, 18½ × 61 × 23 in. (47 × 155 × 58 cm)
Collection of Smithsonian American Art Museum, Renwick Gallery, Washington, DC; Collection of Hunter Museum of American Art, Chattanooga, TN

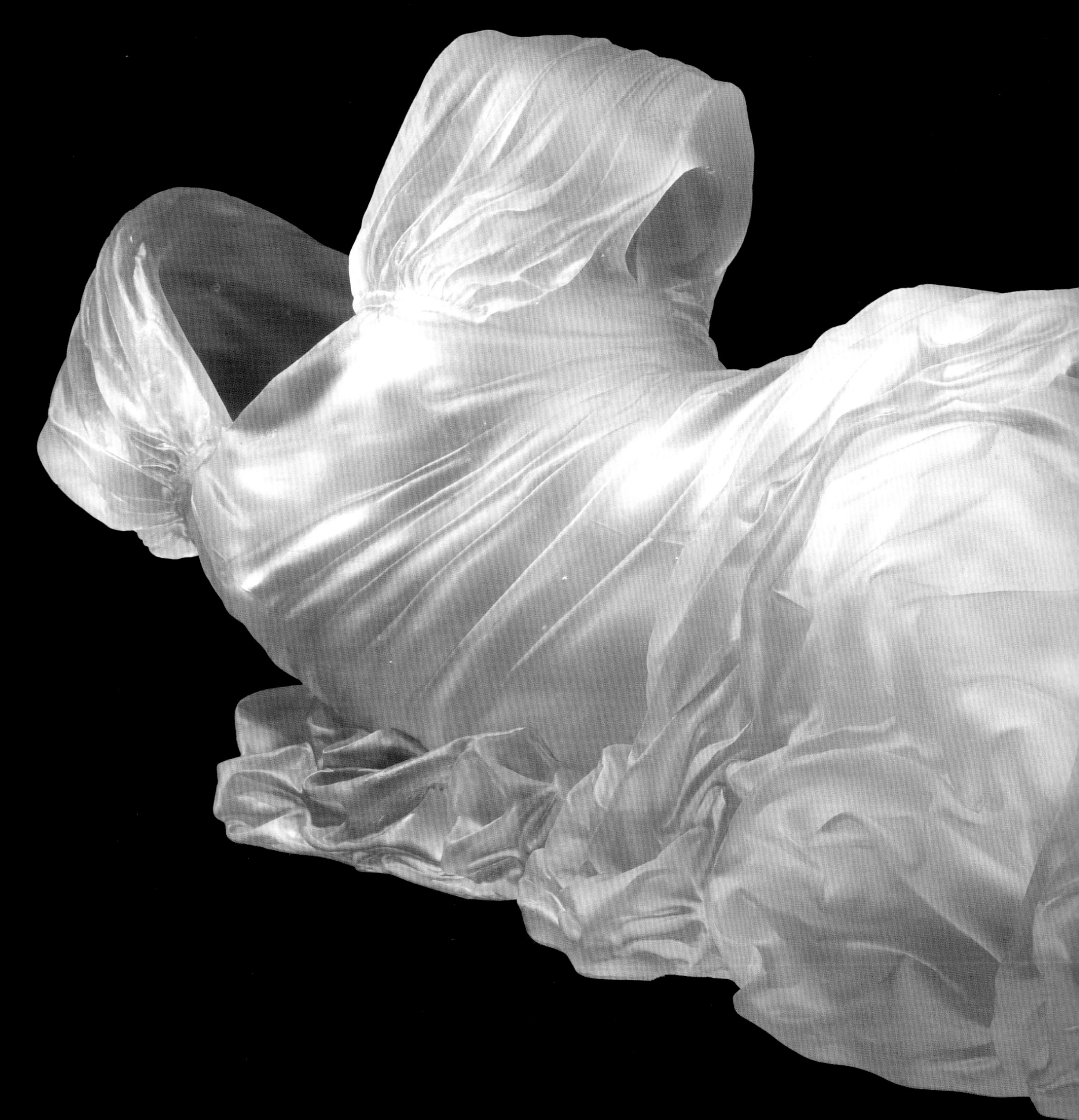

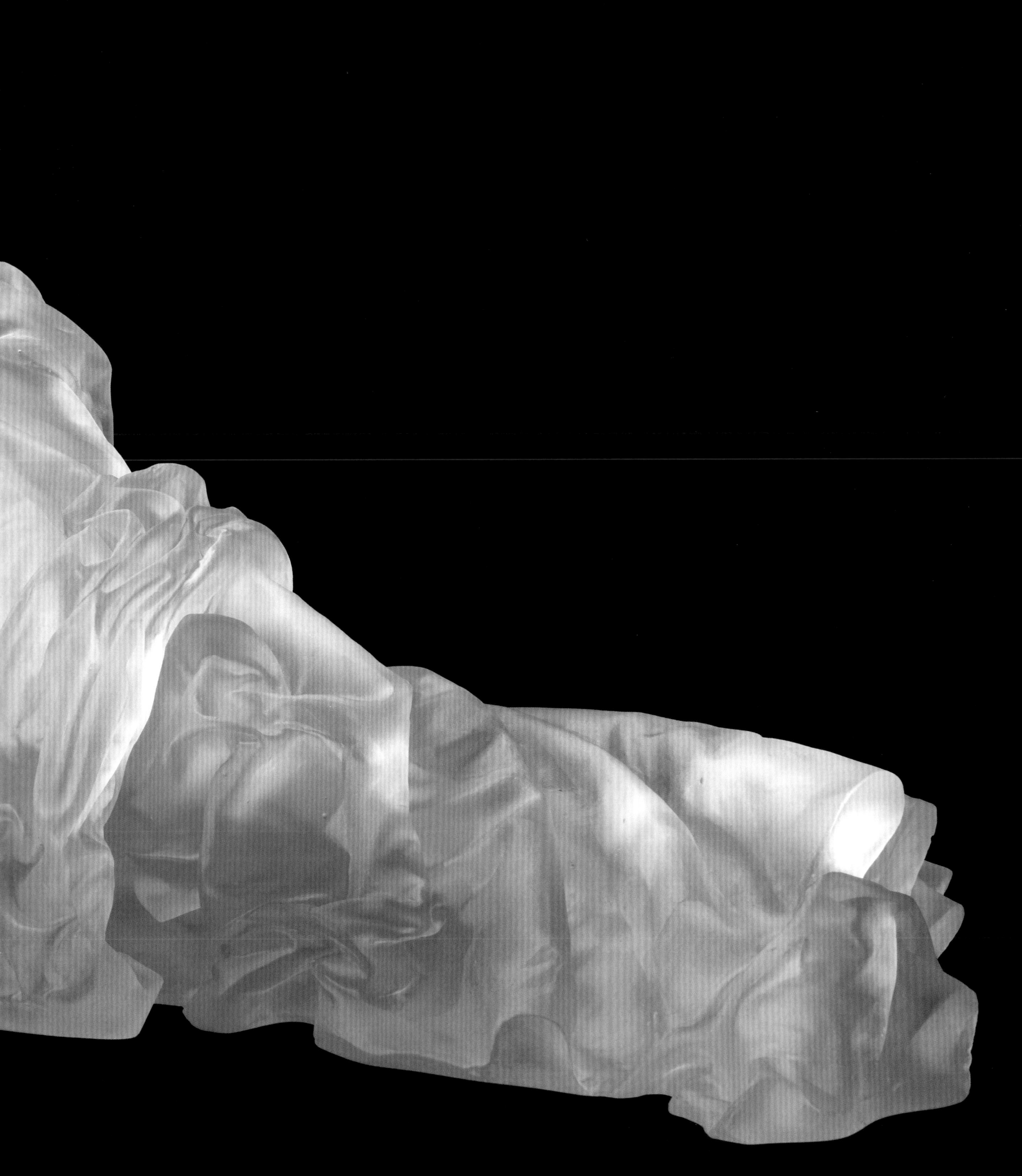

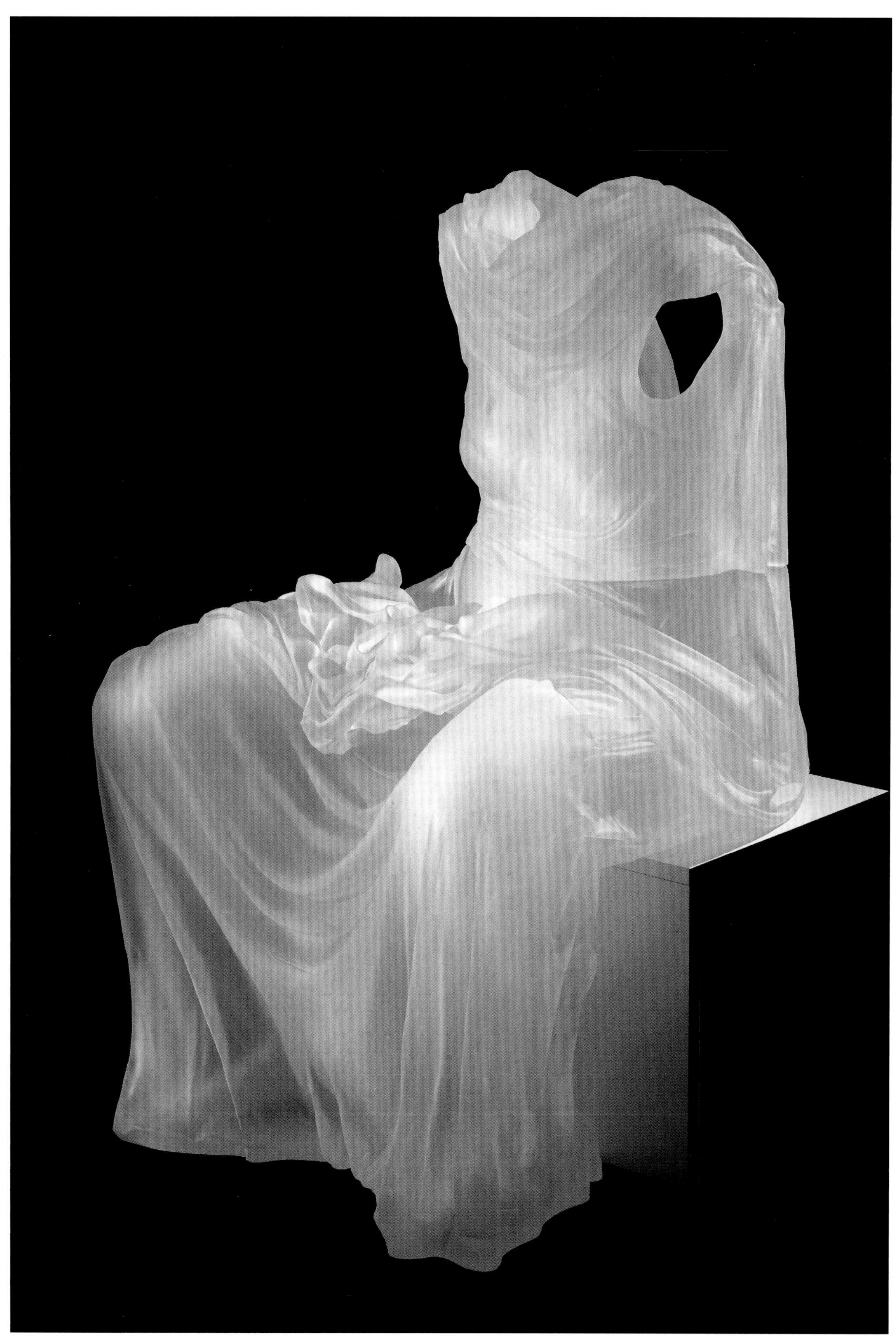

Seated Dress Impression with Drapery, 2005
Cast glass, 48½ × 29½ × 27 in.
(123 × 75 × 68 cm)
Collection of Cincinnati Art Museum, Cincinnati, OH;
Collection of Musée du Verre, Sars-Poteries, France

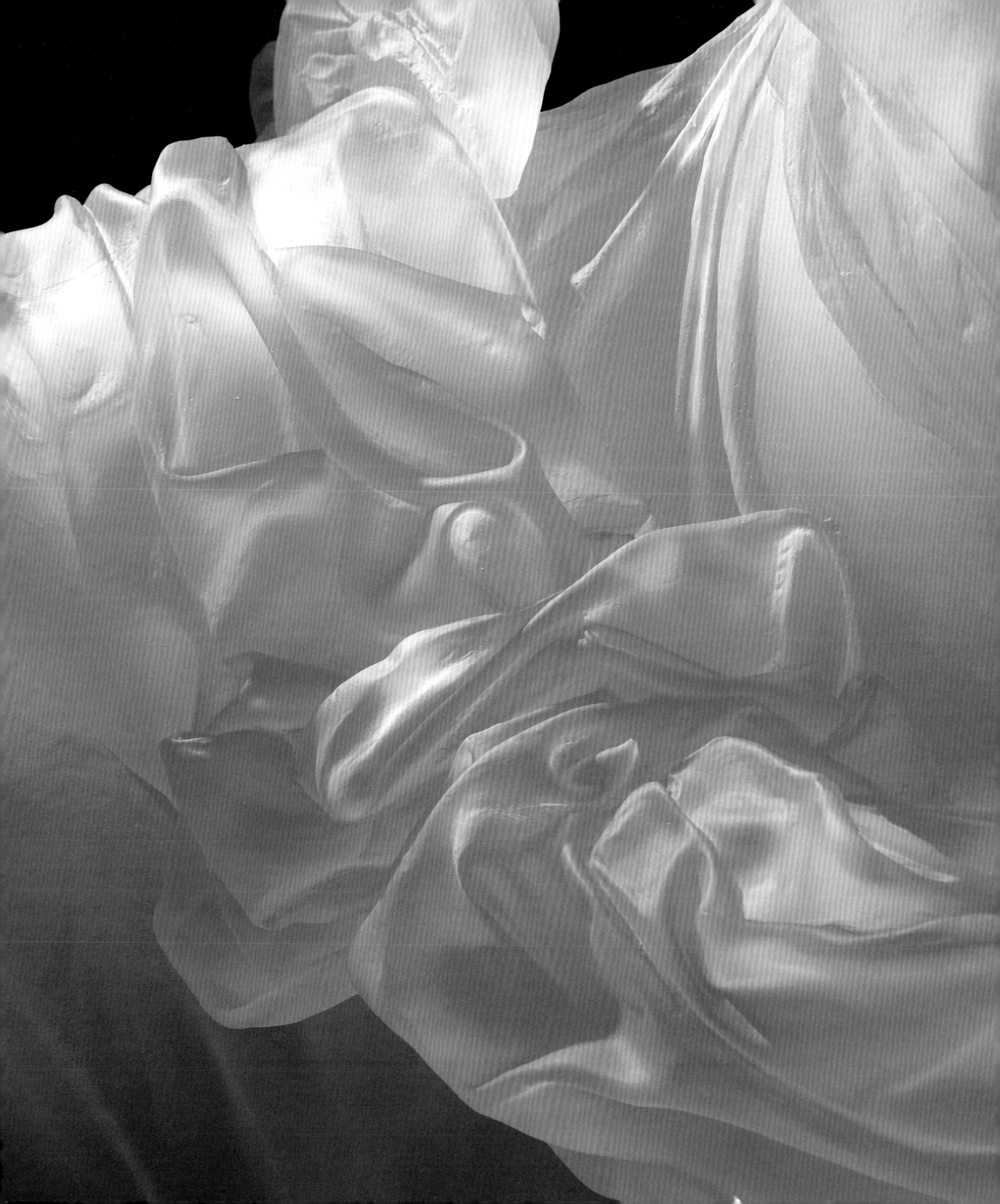

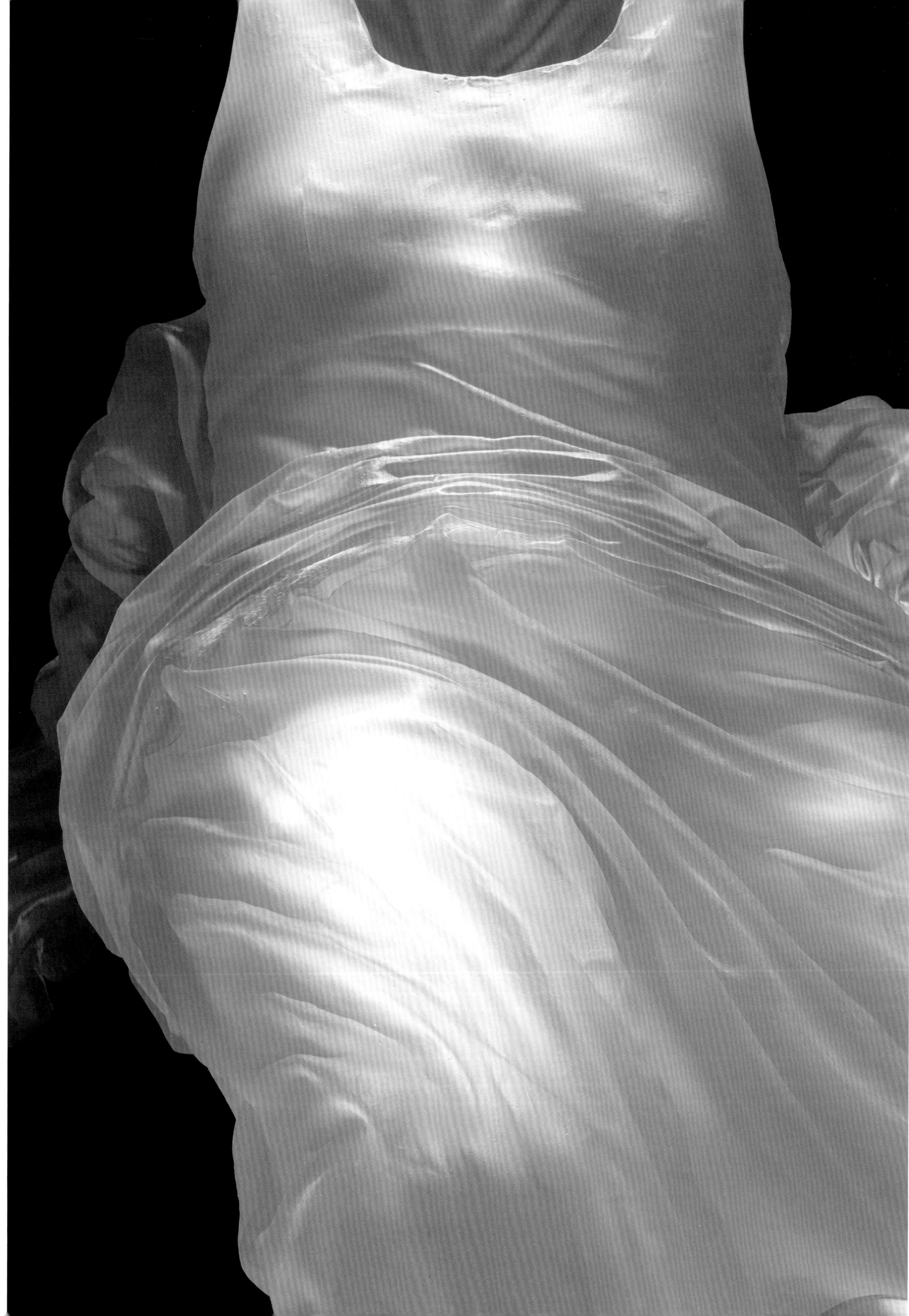

Semi-Reclining Dress Impression with Drapery, 2005
Cast glass, 42½ × 27½ × 39½ in. (108 × 70 × 100 cm)

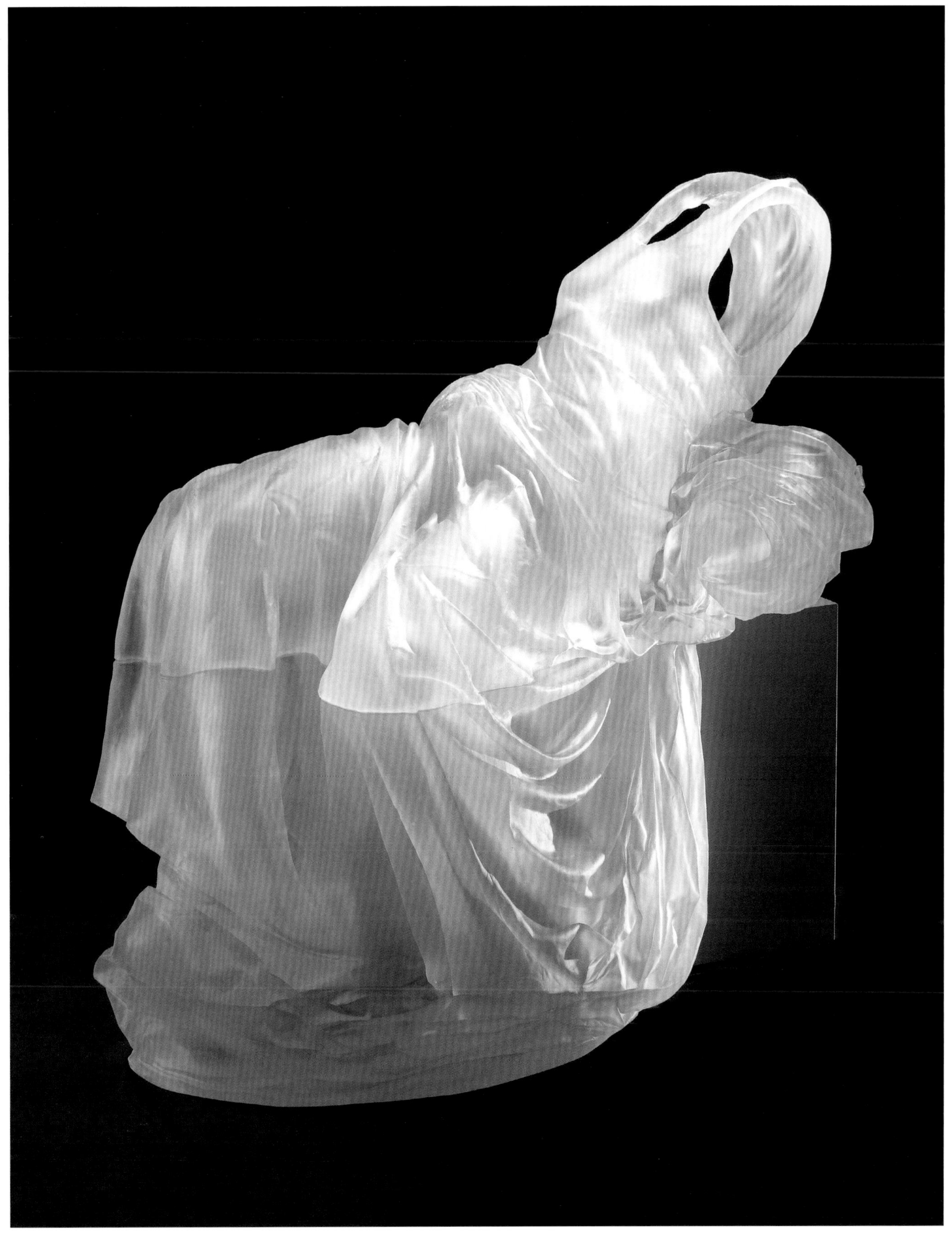

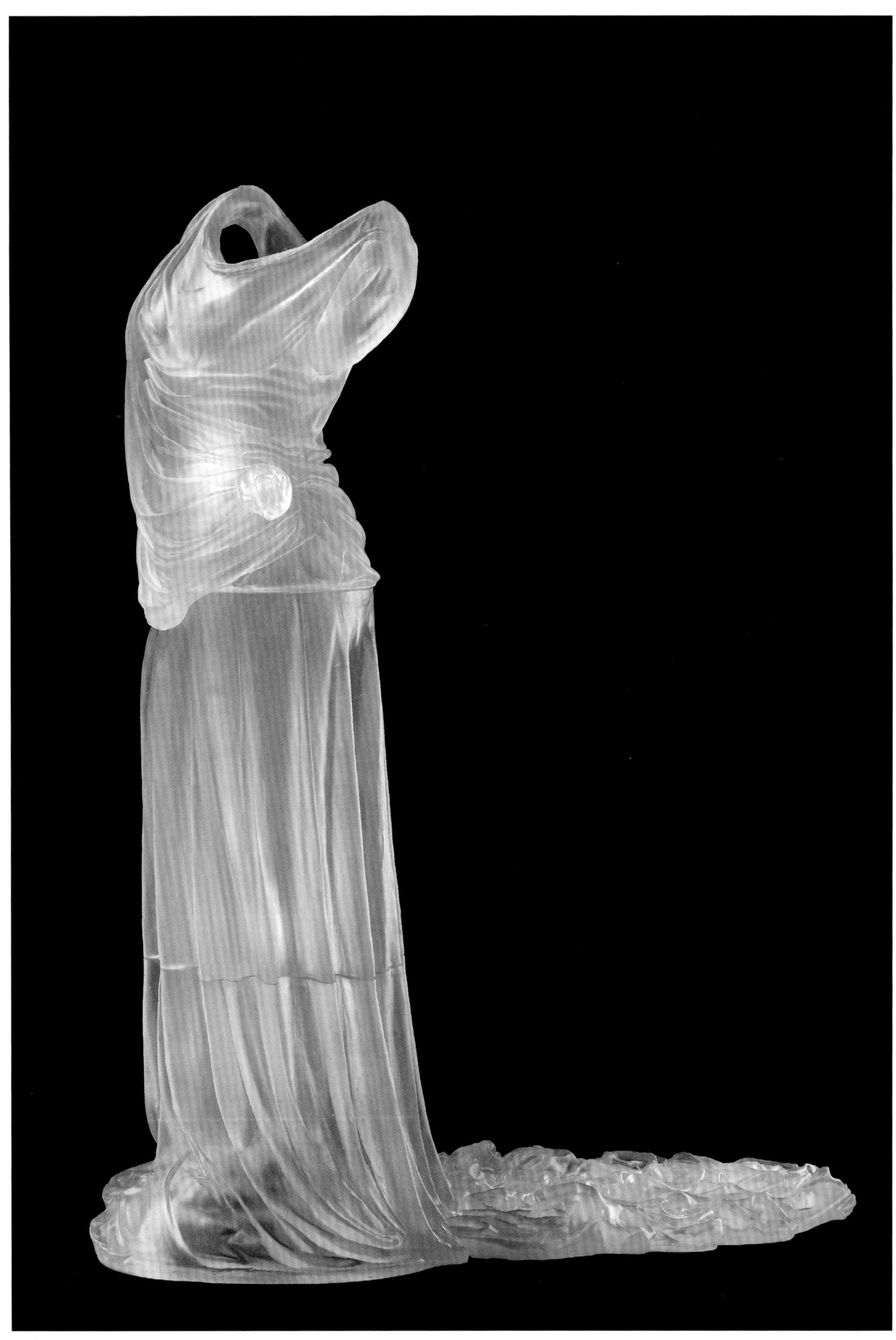

THIS AND FOLLOWING
Dress Impression with Train, 2005
Cast glass, 58½ × 22½ × 43½ in.
(148 × 57 × 110 cm)
Collection of Toledo Museum of Art, Toledo, OH; Collection of Flint Institute of Arts, Flint, MI

GERALD PETERS
CONTEMPORARY

24 East 78th Street
New York, NY 10075
212.628.9760

1011 Paseo de Peralta
Santa Fe, NM 87501
505.954.5800

gpgallery.com
@geraldpetersgallery

John Ravenal
Executive Director
deCordova Sculpture Park and Museum
51 Sandy Pond Road.
Columbus, OH, 43215

January 4, 2021

Dear Mr. Ravenal,

I hope you've been well over this very challenging past year. With any luck, 2021 will offer all of us some degree of a return to normal!

I'm writing to you today as the gallery's liaison to Karen LaMonte, a post of held since 2018. It's an incredible experience to have a rapport with an artist who is so wonderfully multifaceted; who always seems to have a new idea to pursue with single-minded gusto. I've learned that, in reality, Karen percolates and stews, and performs research and technical trials (sometimes to a nearly agonizing extent)—for years—in pursuit of those ideas, before turning them into fully developed bodies of work. The rest of us then have the great fortune to enjoy the fruits of all that labor when finally, she lets us see each new artwork.

So I am delighted to enclose Rizzoli's beautiful new monograph on LaMonte, which provides a rich view into her process and artistic career, beginning with her earliest works, examining her mid-career, and leaving off with a tantalizing glimpse of what she is working on in the studio right now: some of her most innovative and ambitious projects yet.

I hope that once all is returned to normal, I can welcome you to one of our galleries in New York or Santa Fe, to view some of Karen's more recent works. In the meantime, I send my best wishes for a happy and prosperous 2021!

Kind regards,

Alice Hammond
Cell: 303.885.5146
ahammond@gpgalleryny.com

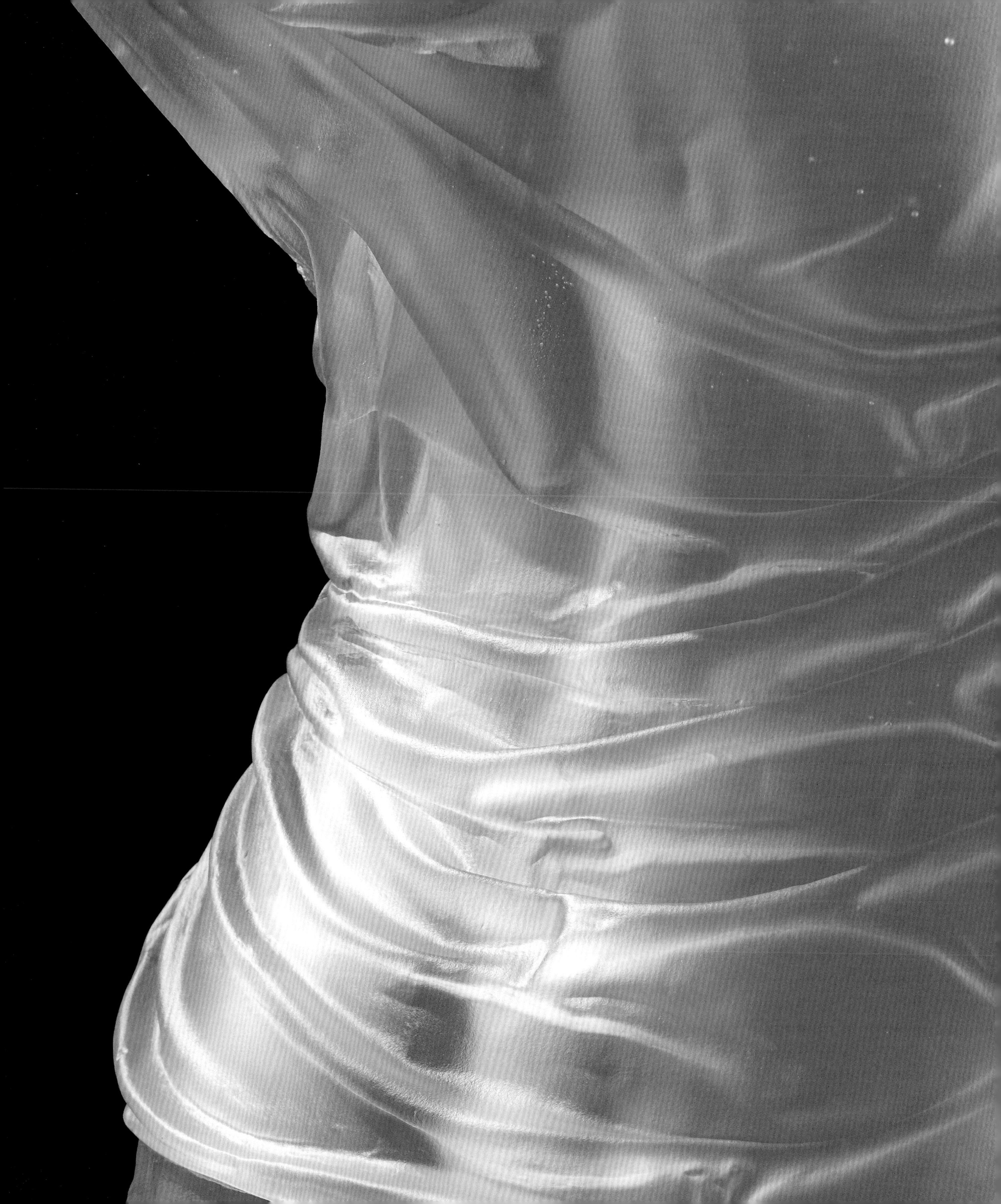

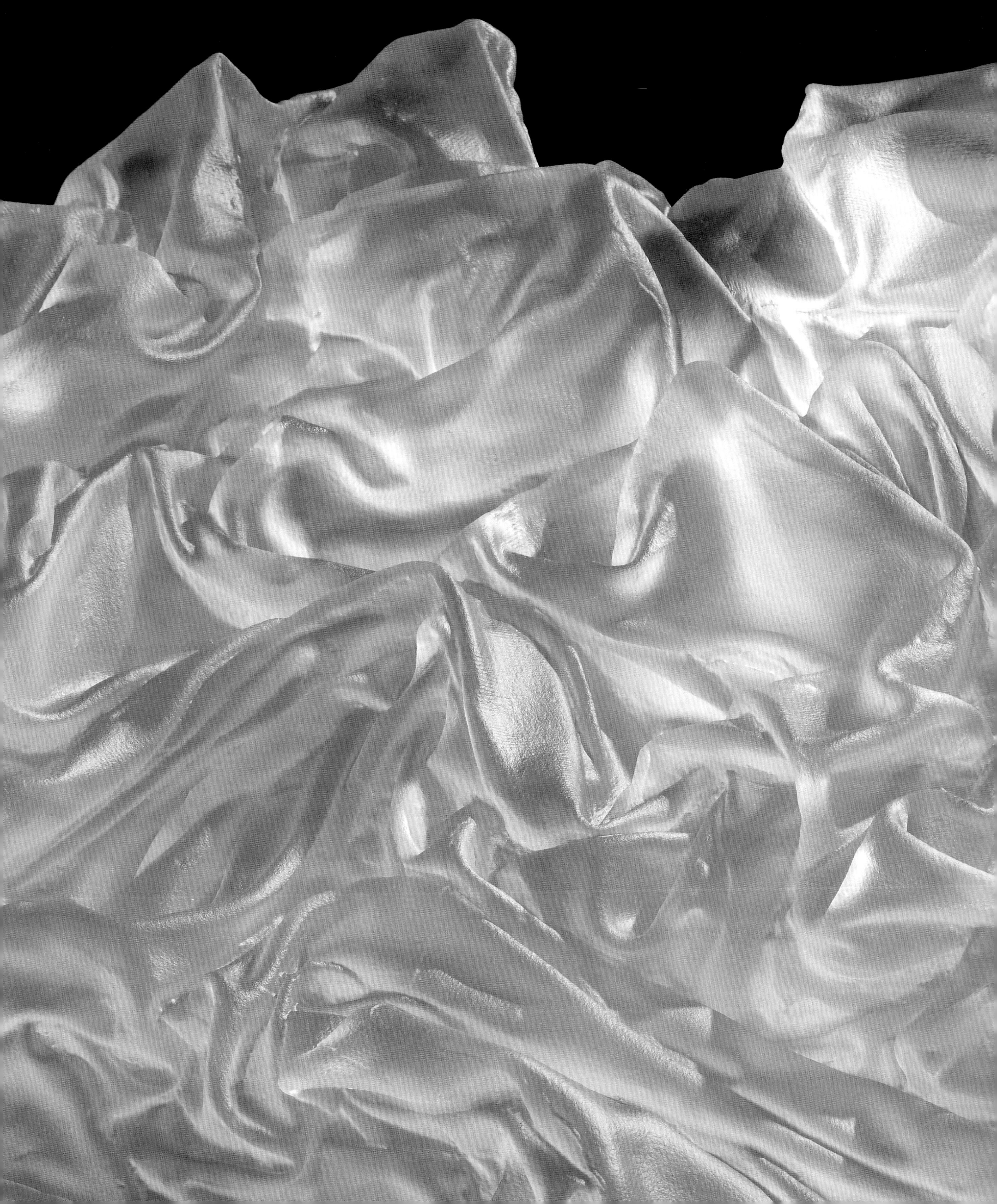

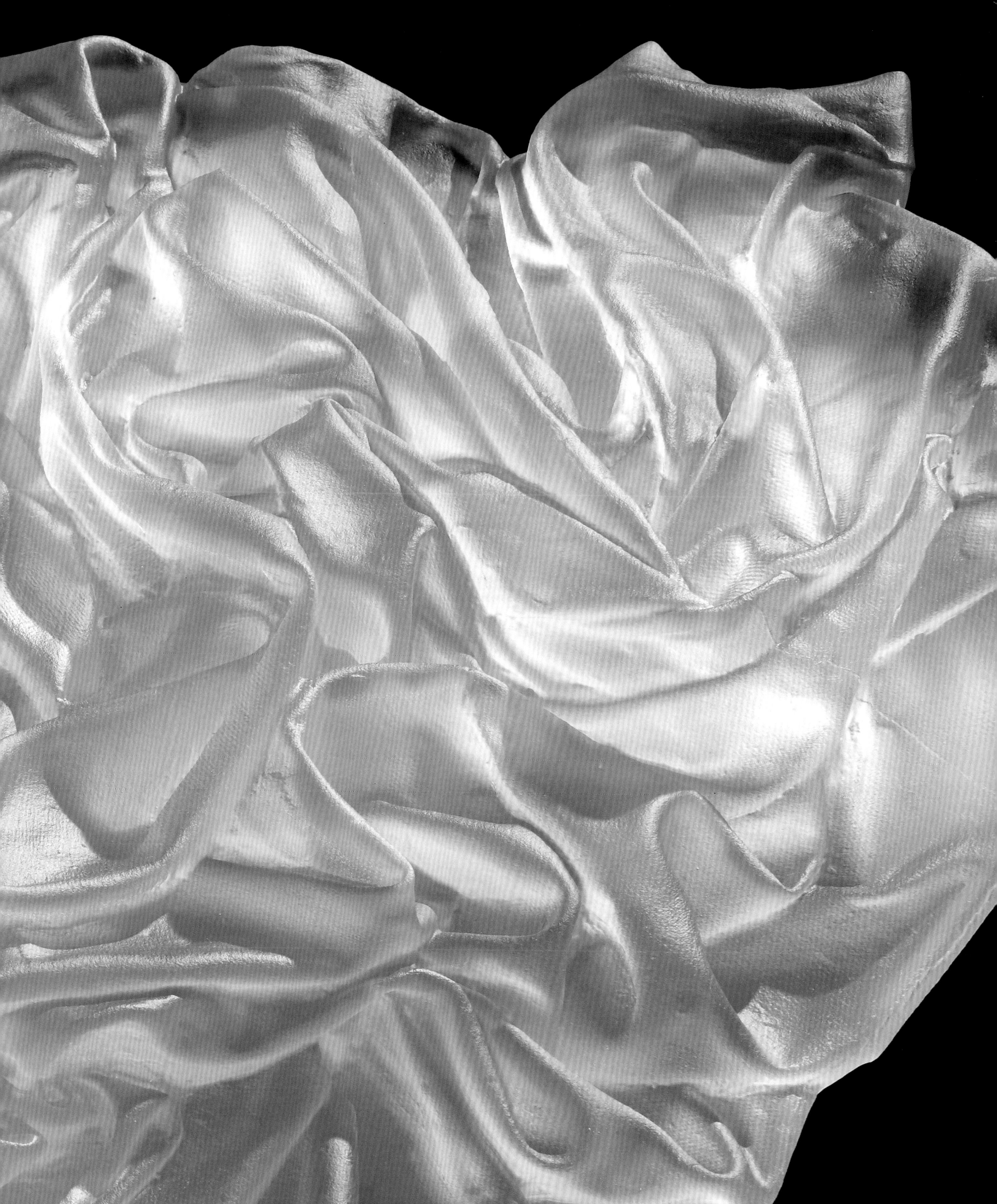

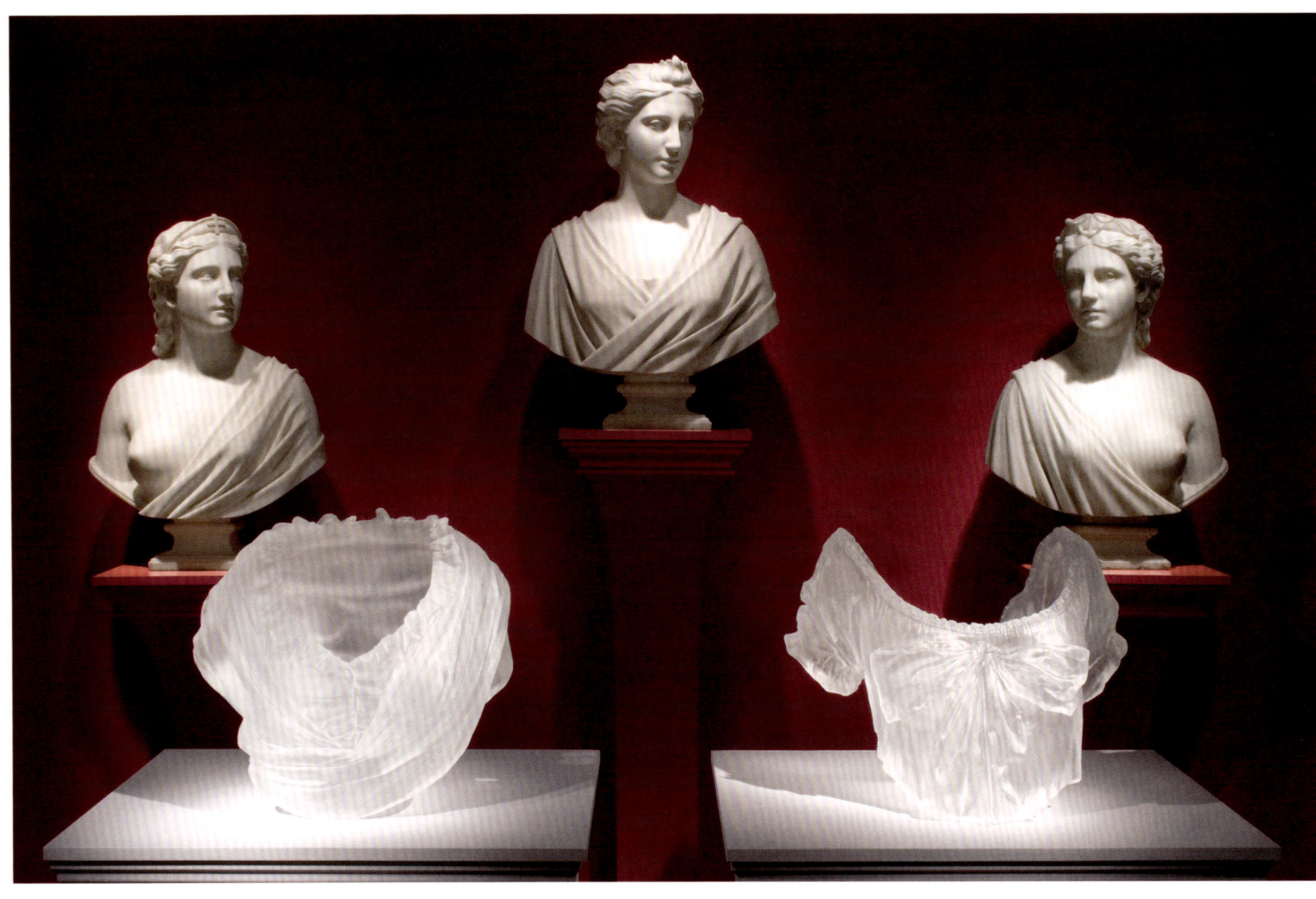

Exhibition *Contemporary Among the Classics*, 2009
Chrysler Museum of Art, Norfolk, VA

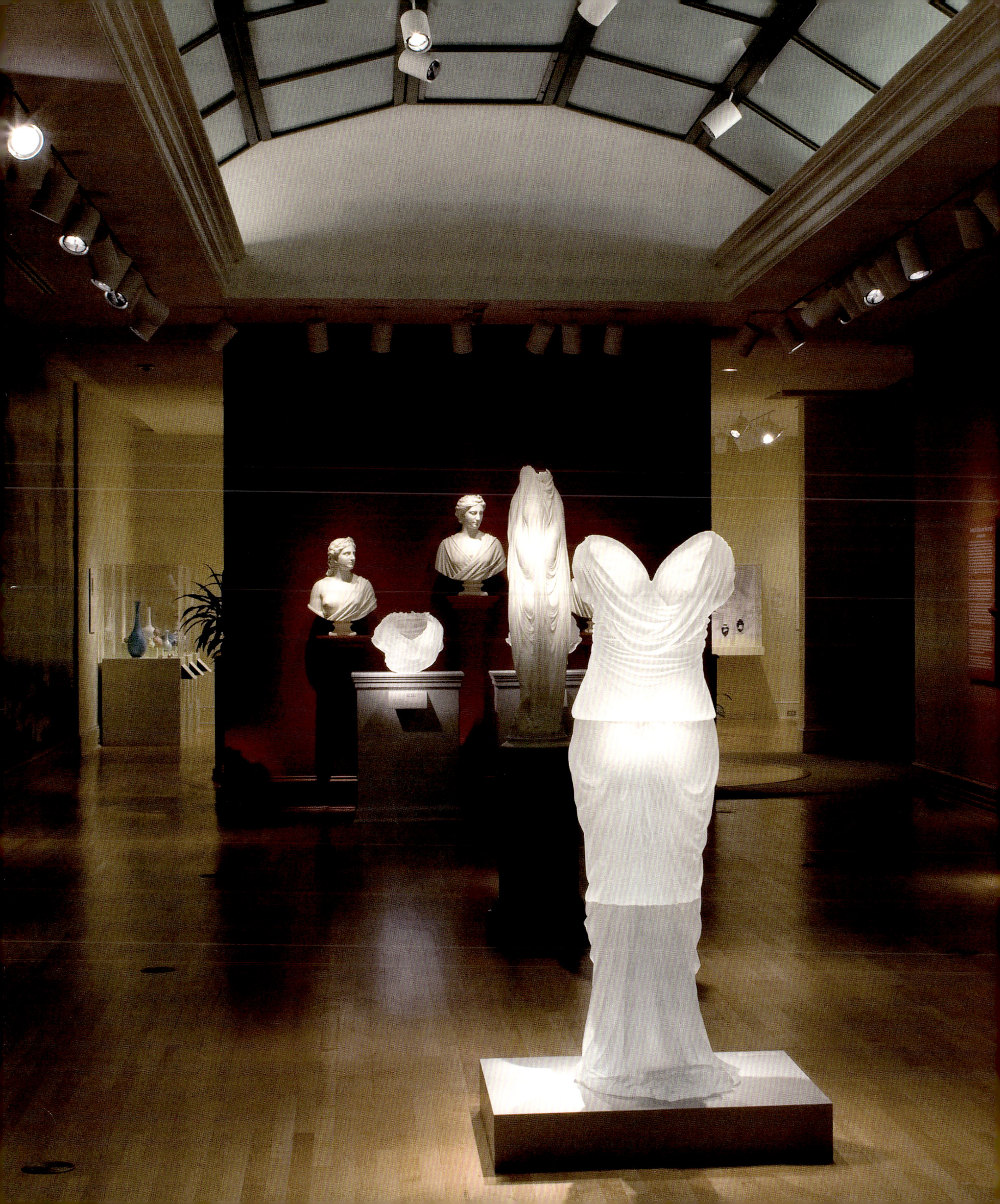

Taking a mold for the interior of a sculpture, 2004.

FOLLOWING
Dress 3, 2001
Cast glass, 59 × 26 × 21½ in. (150 × 66 × 55 cm)
Collection of de Young Museum/Fine Arts
Museums of San Francisco, San Francisco, CA

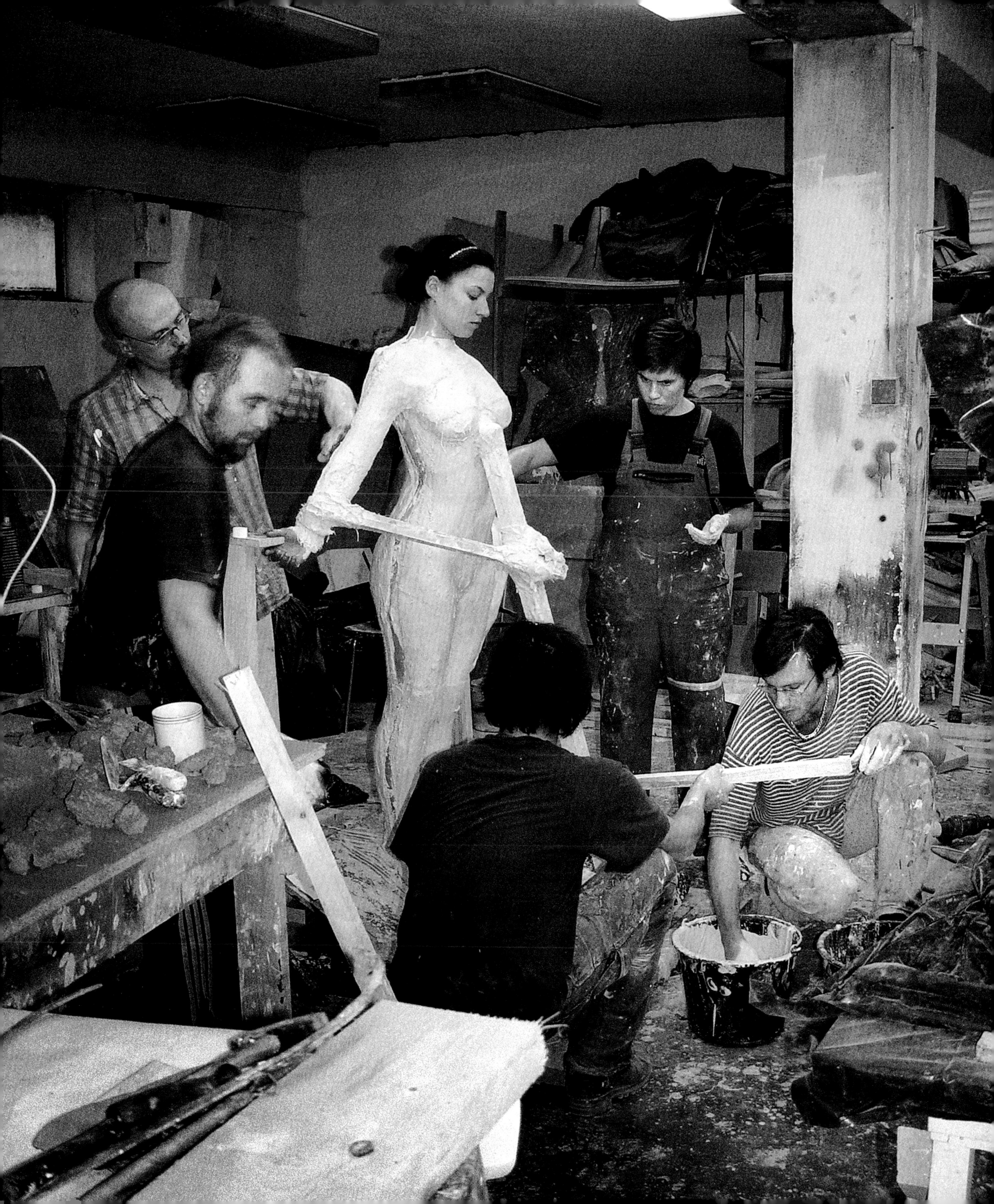

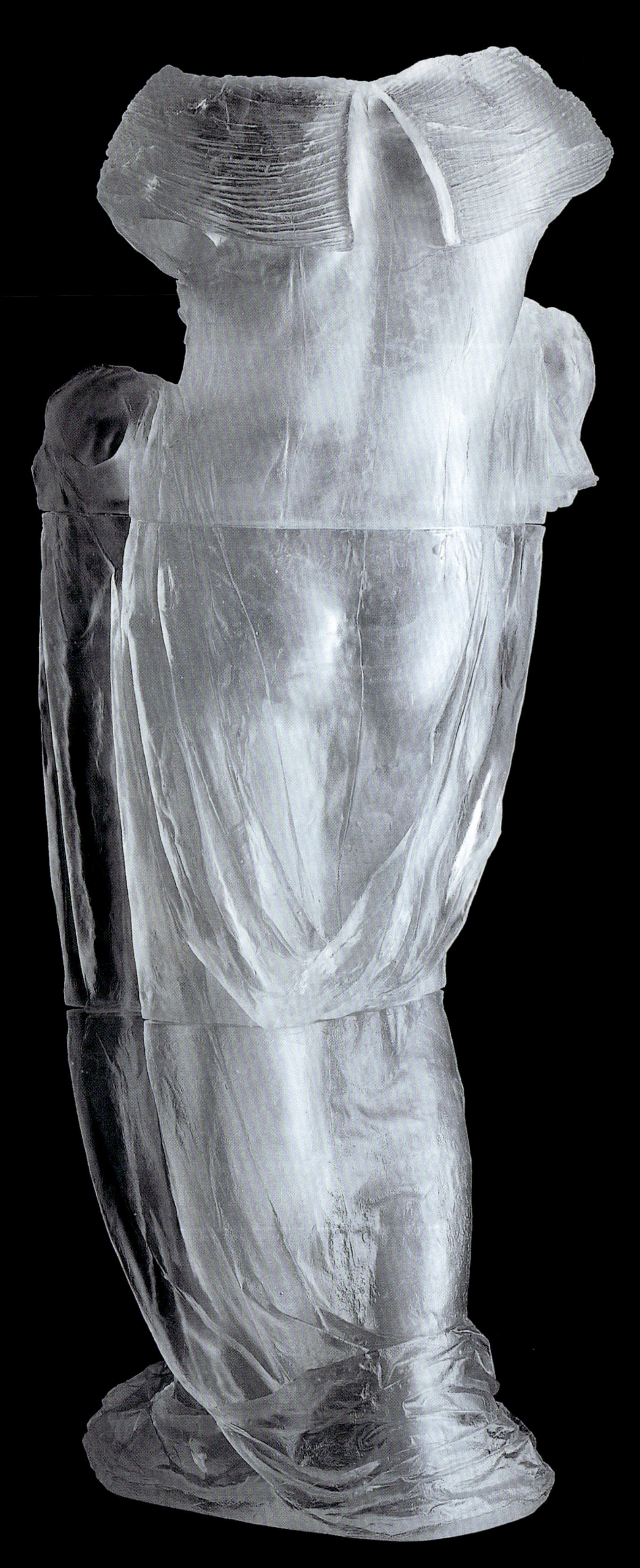

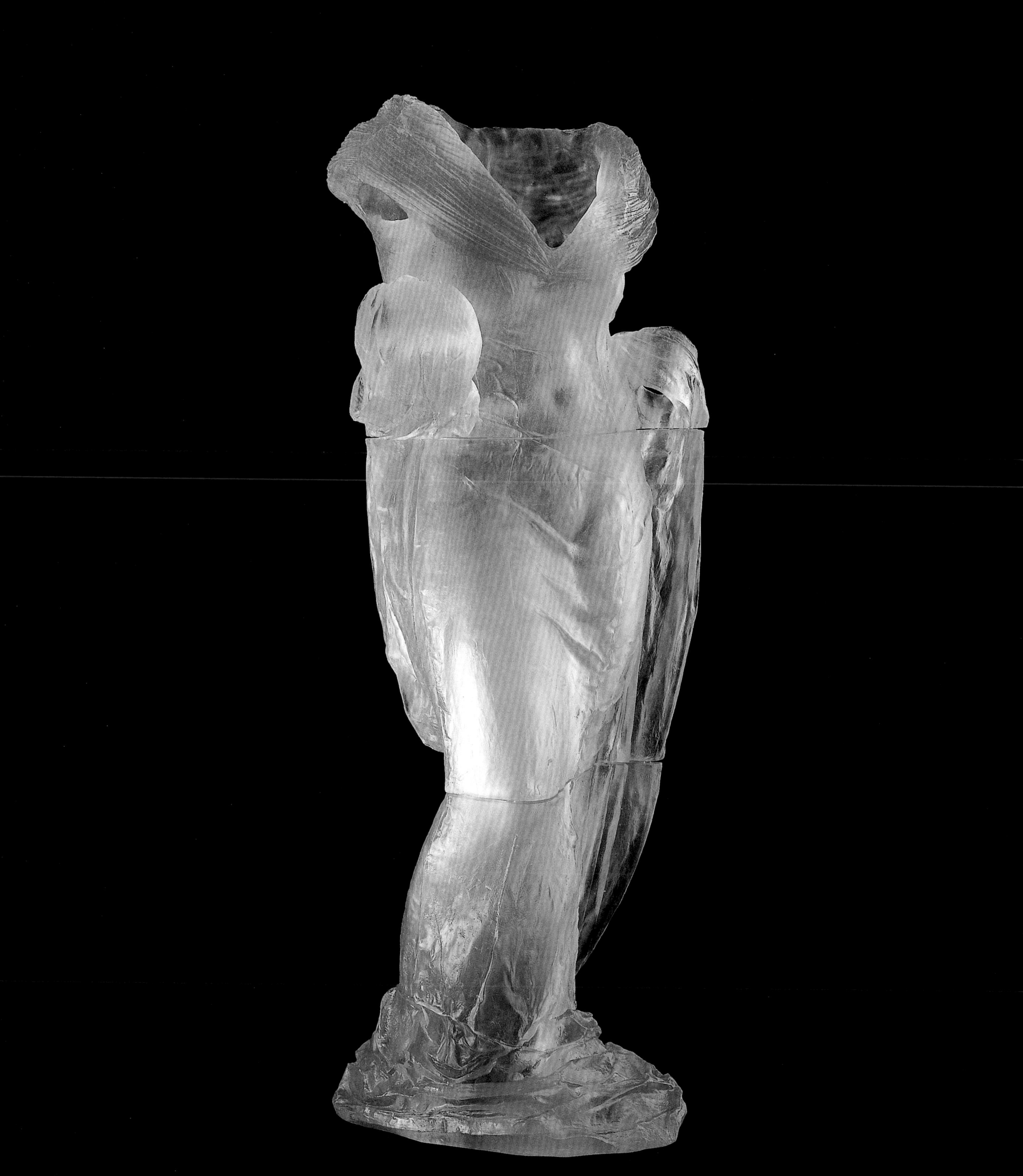

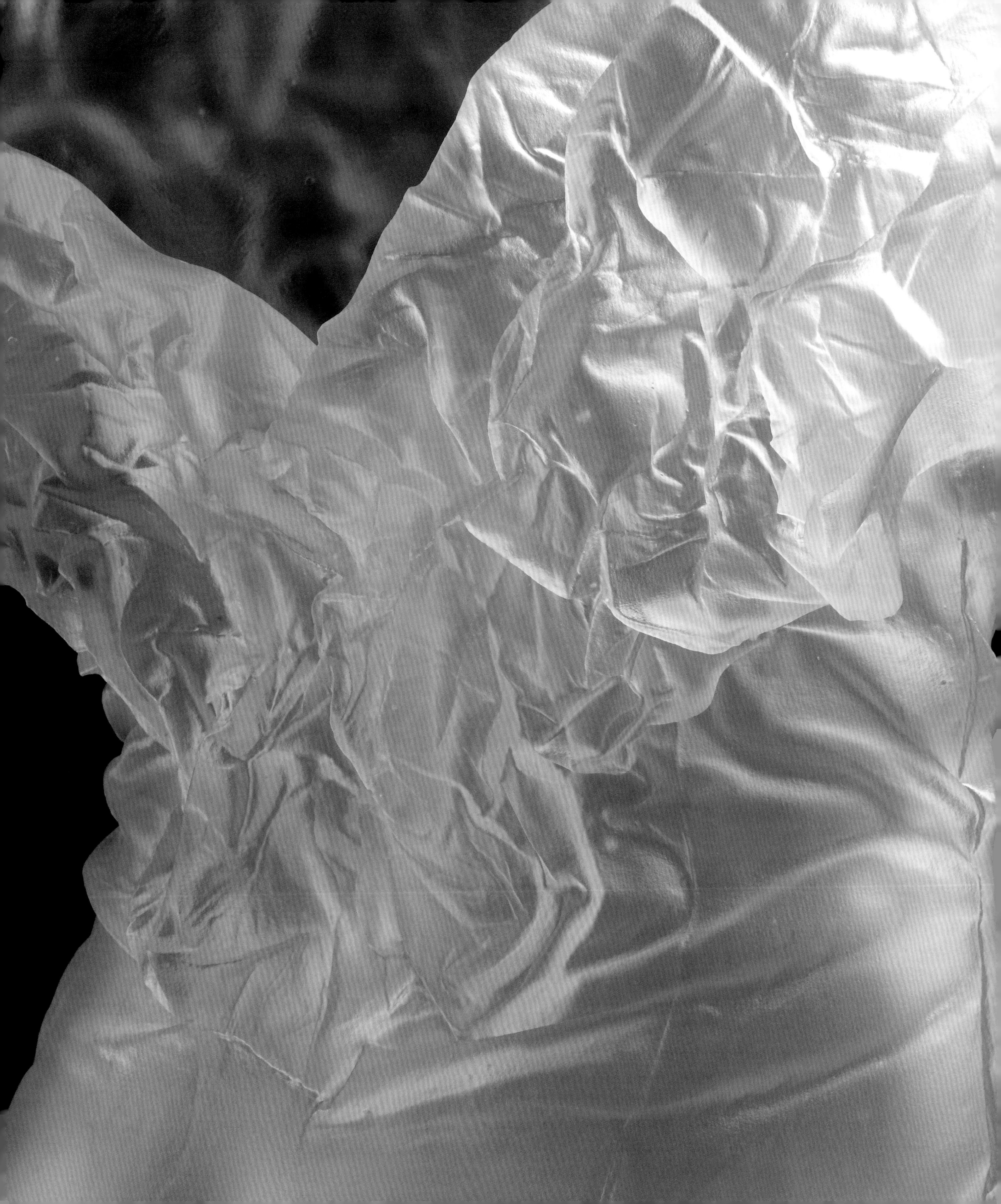

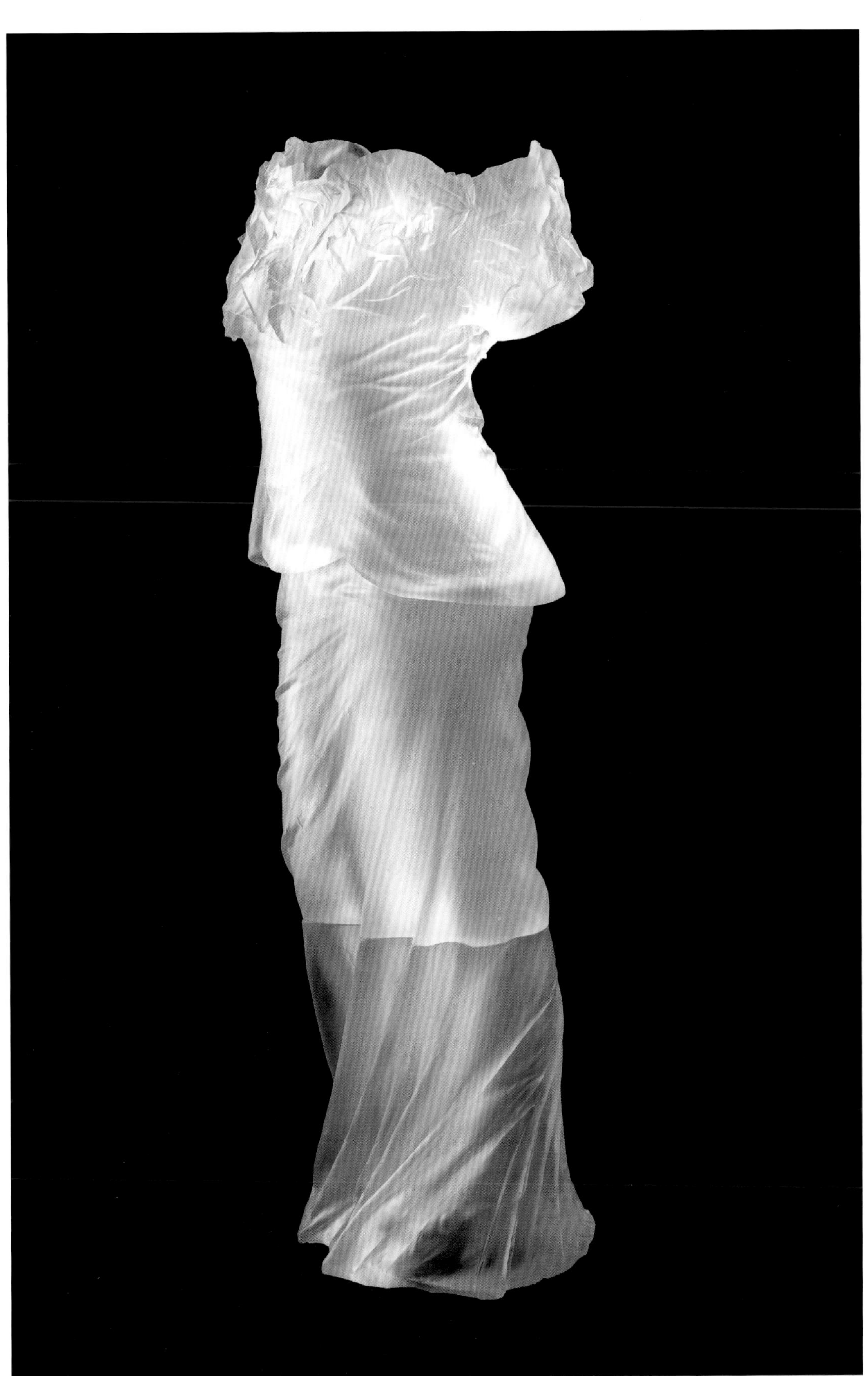

Dress Impression with Wrinkled Cowl, 2007
Cast glass, 56 × 21½ × 16½ in.
(142 × 54 × 42 cm)
Collection of Crystal Bridges Museum of American Art, Bentonville, AR

FOLLOWING
Undine, 2007
Cast glass, 61½ × 19½ × 24 in.
(156 × 49 × 61 cm)

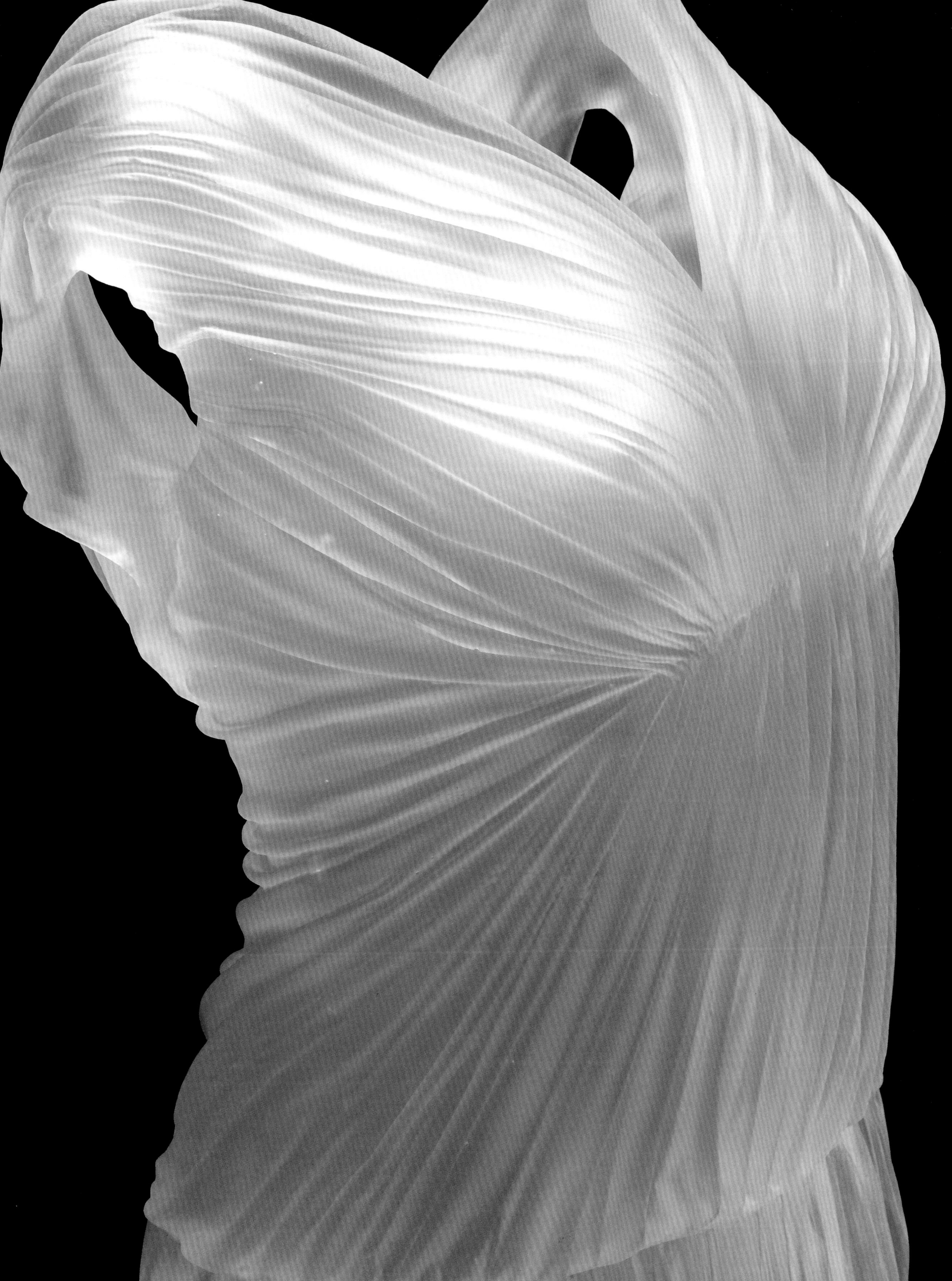

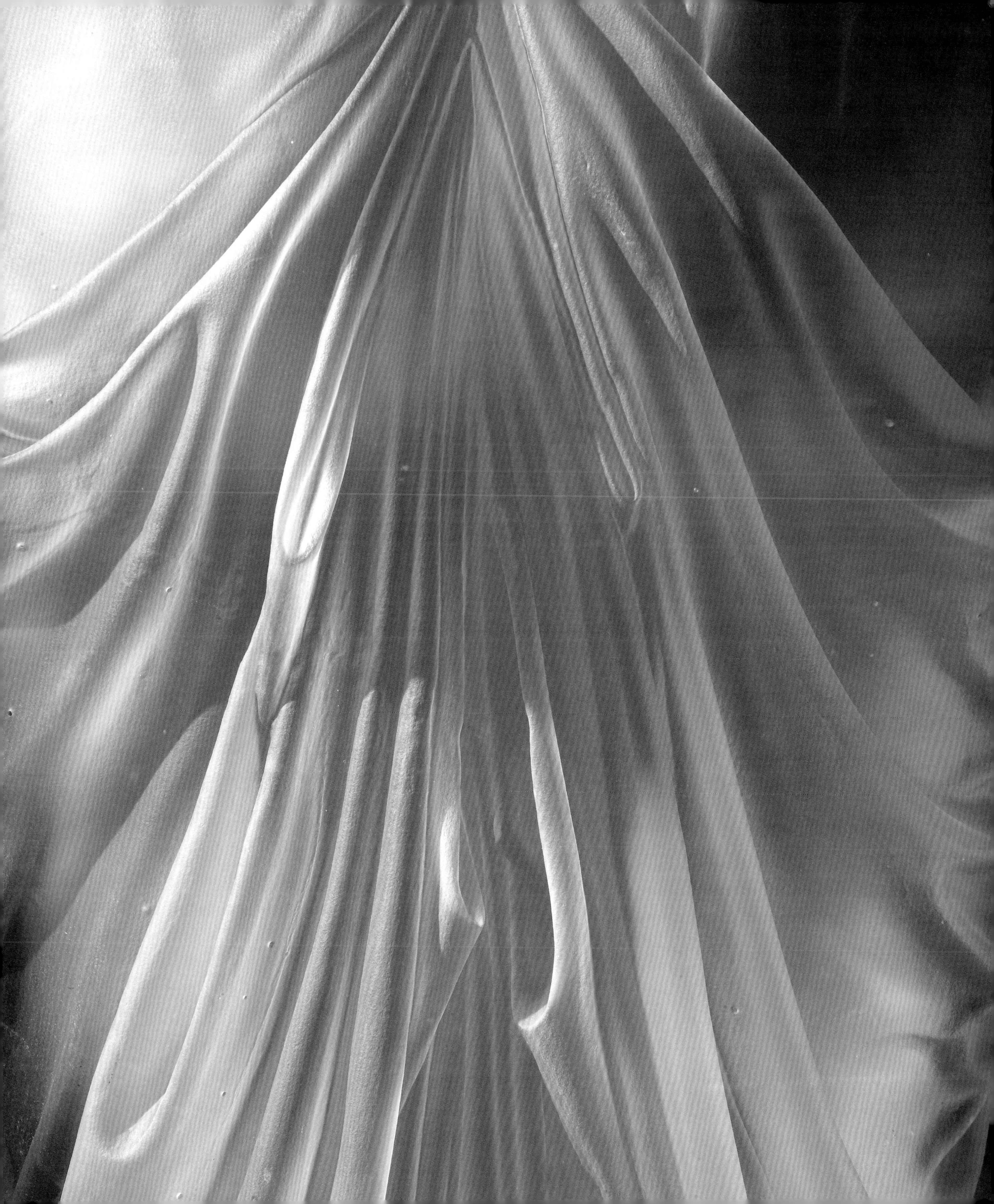

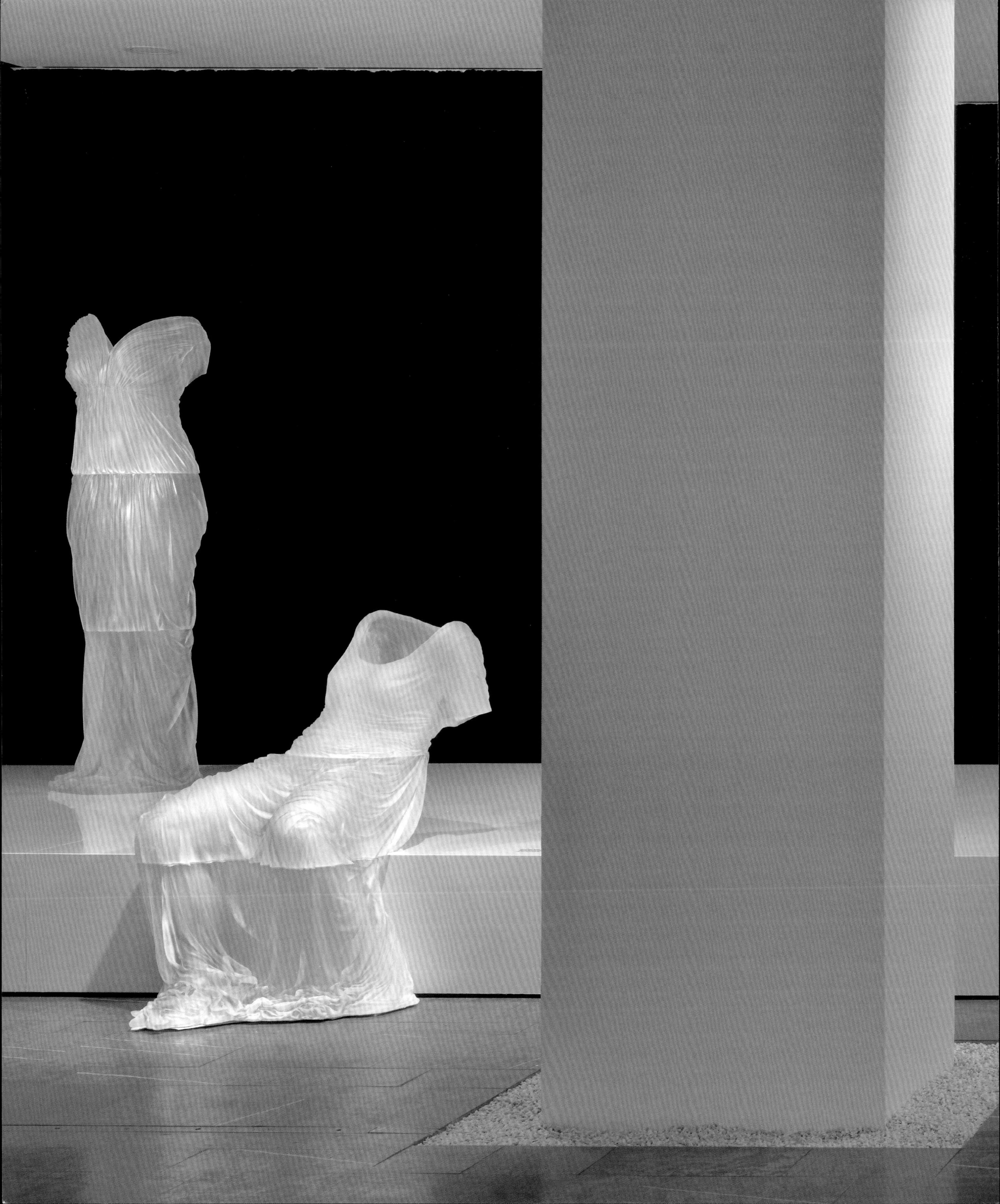

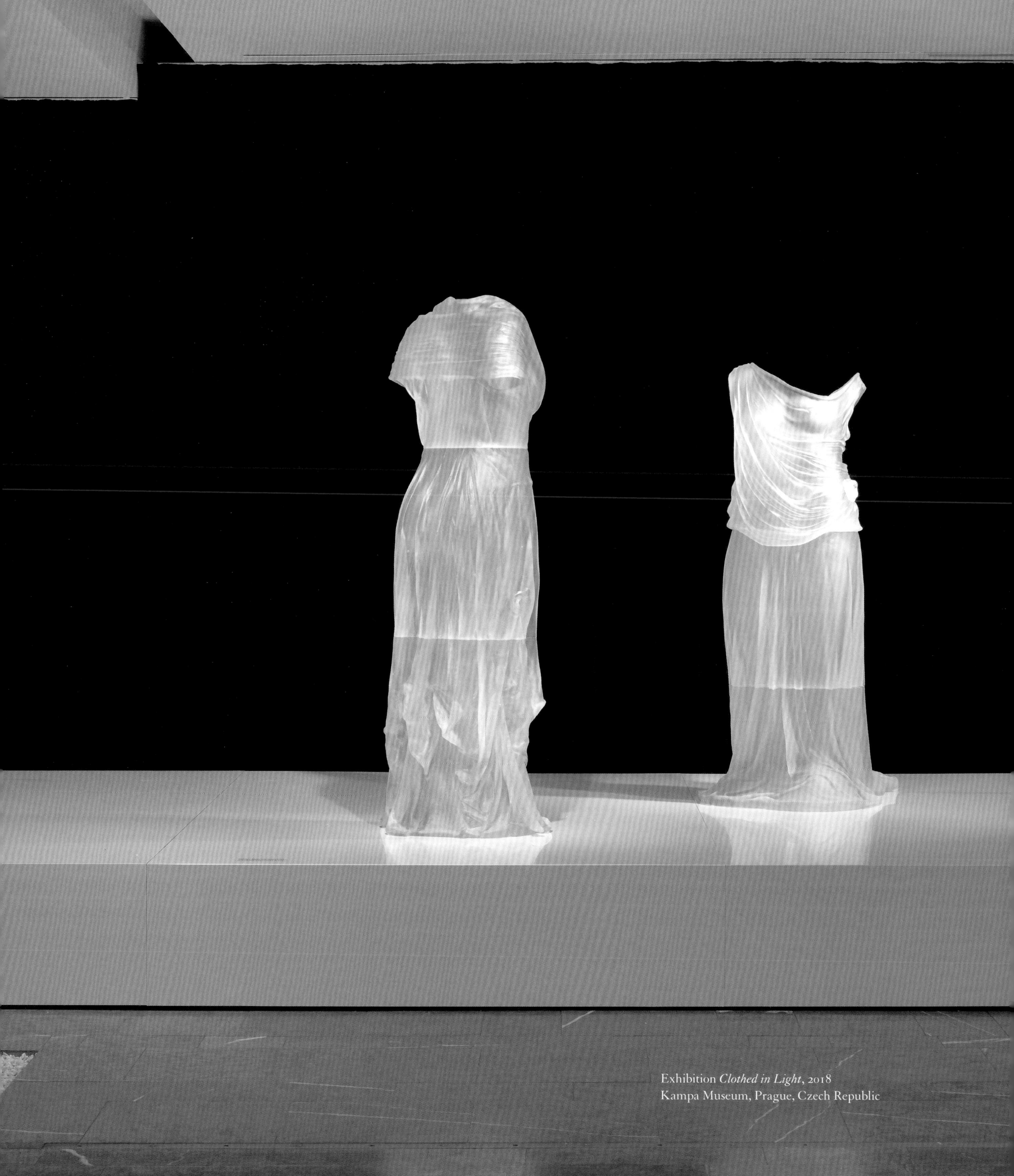

Exhibition *Clothed in Light*, 2018
Kampa Museum, Prague, Czech Republic

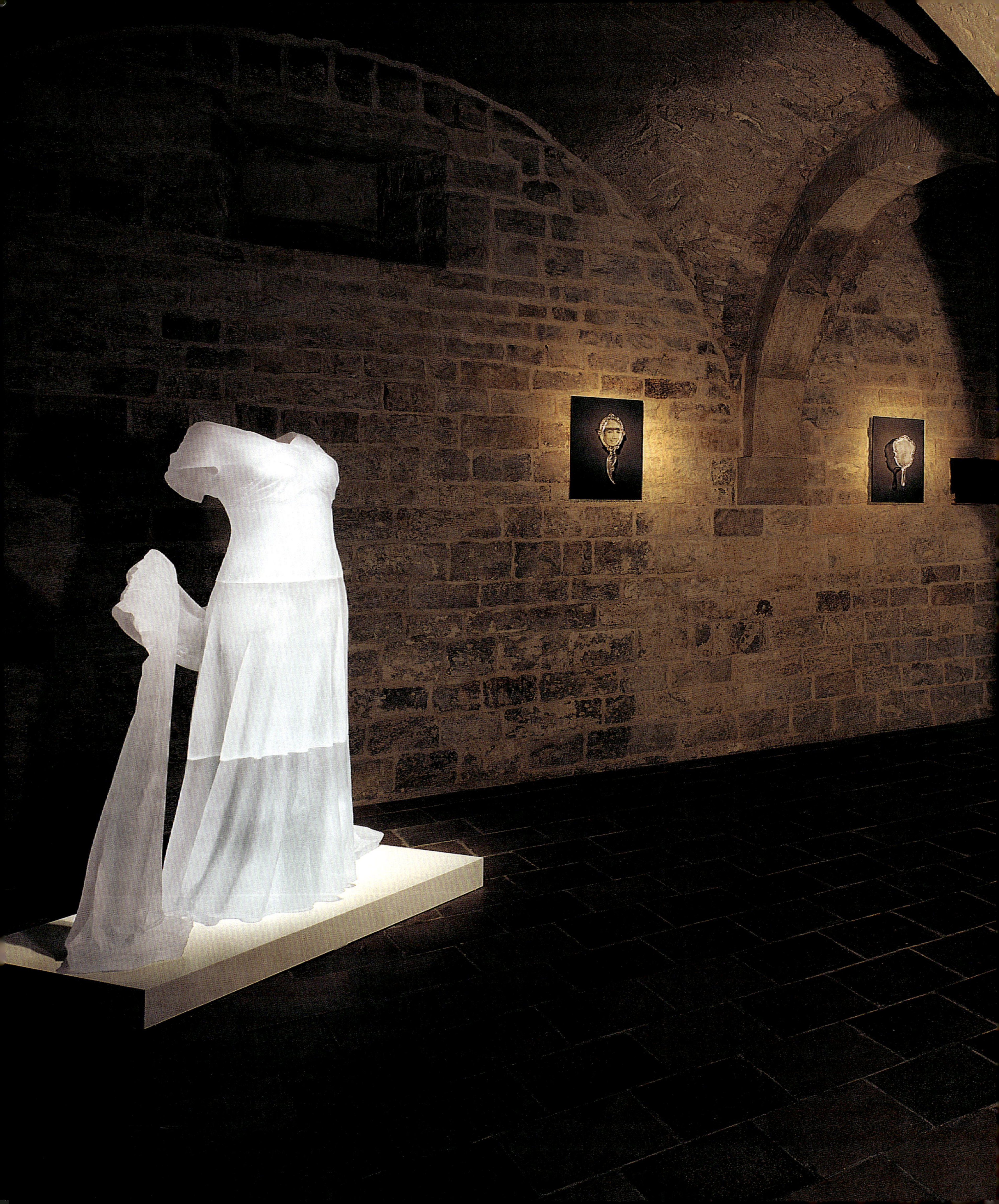

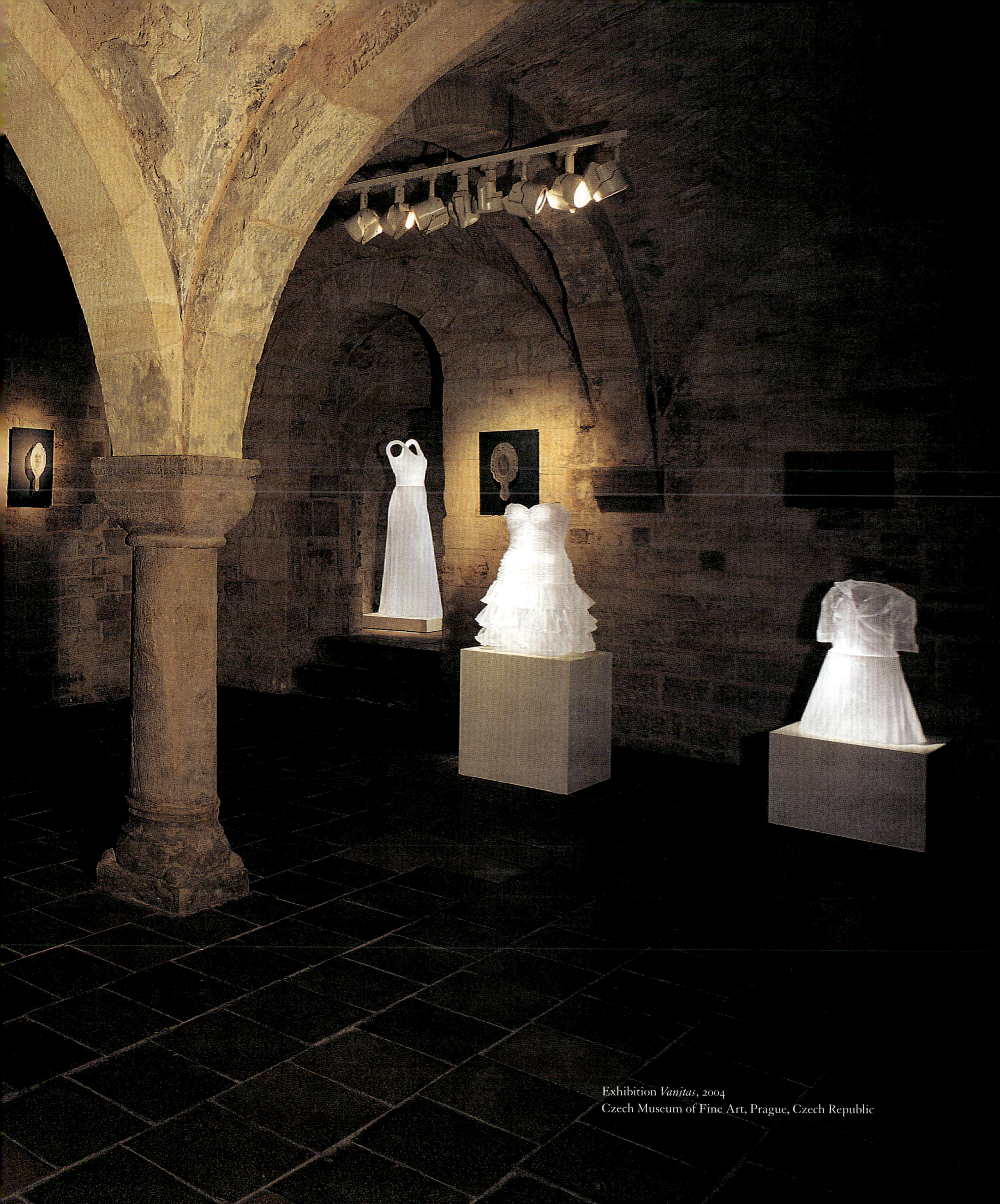

Exhibition *Vanitas*, 2004
Czech Museum of Fine Art, Prague, Czech Republic

Exhibition *Vanitas*, 2004
Czech Museum of Fine Art, Prague, Czech Republic

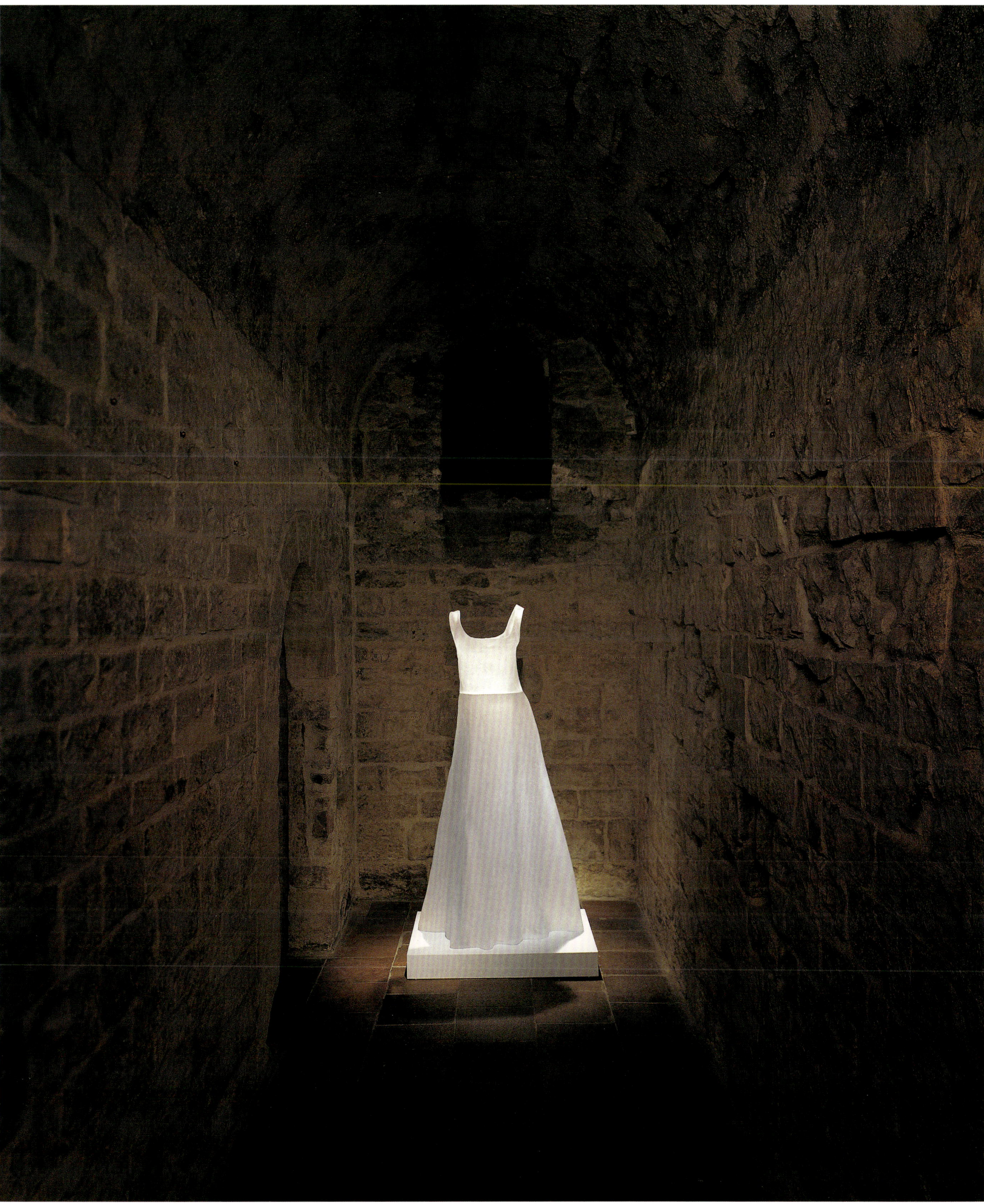

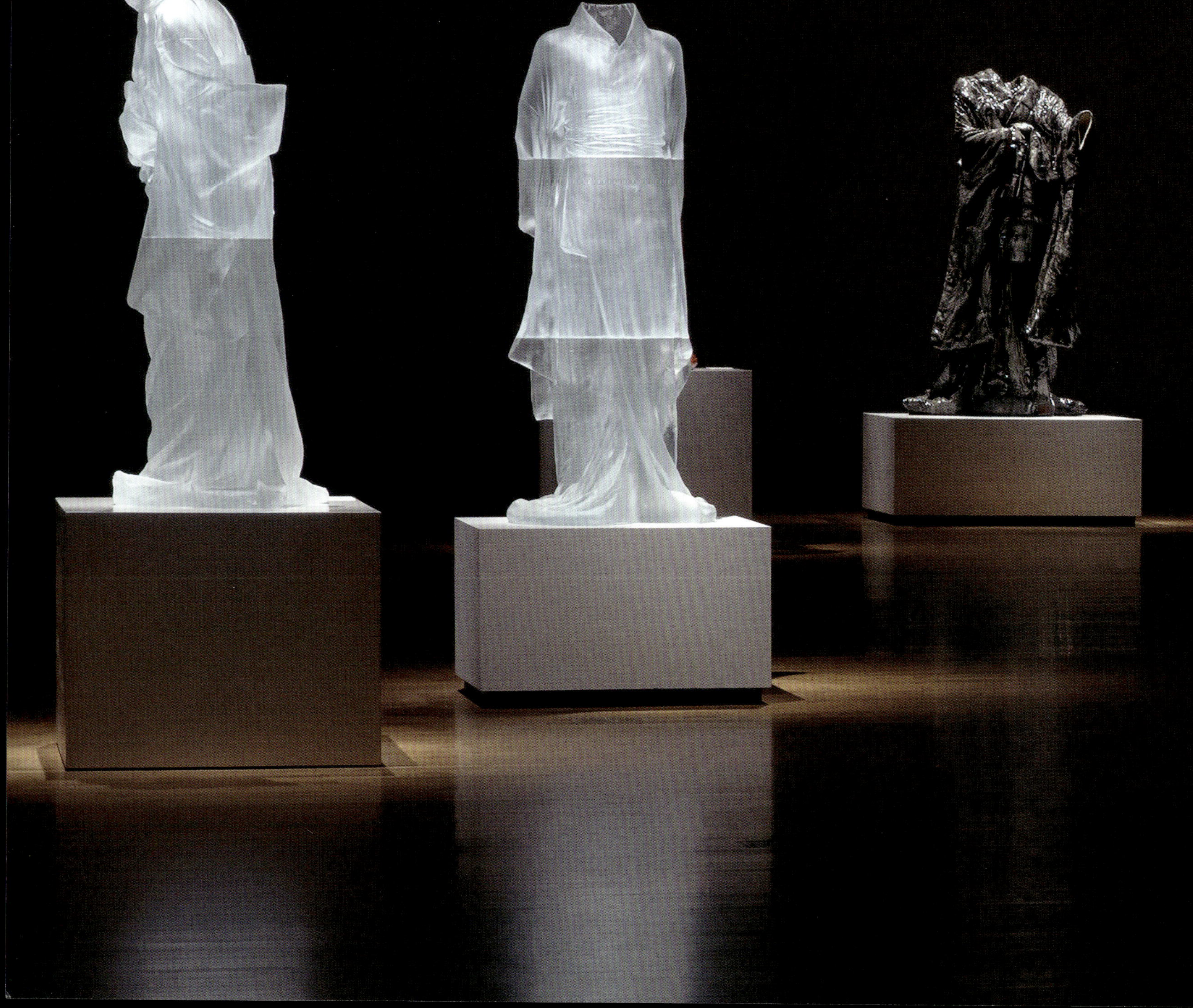

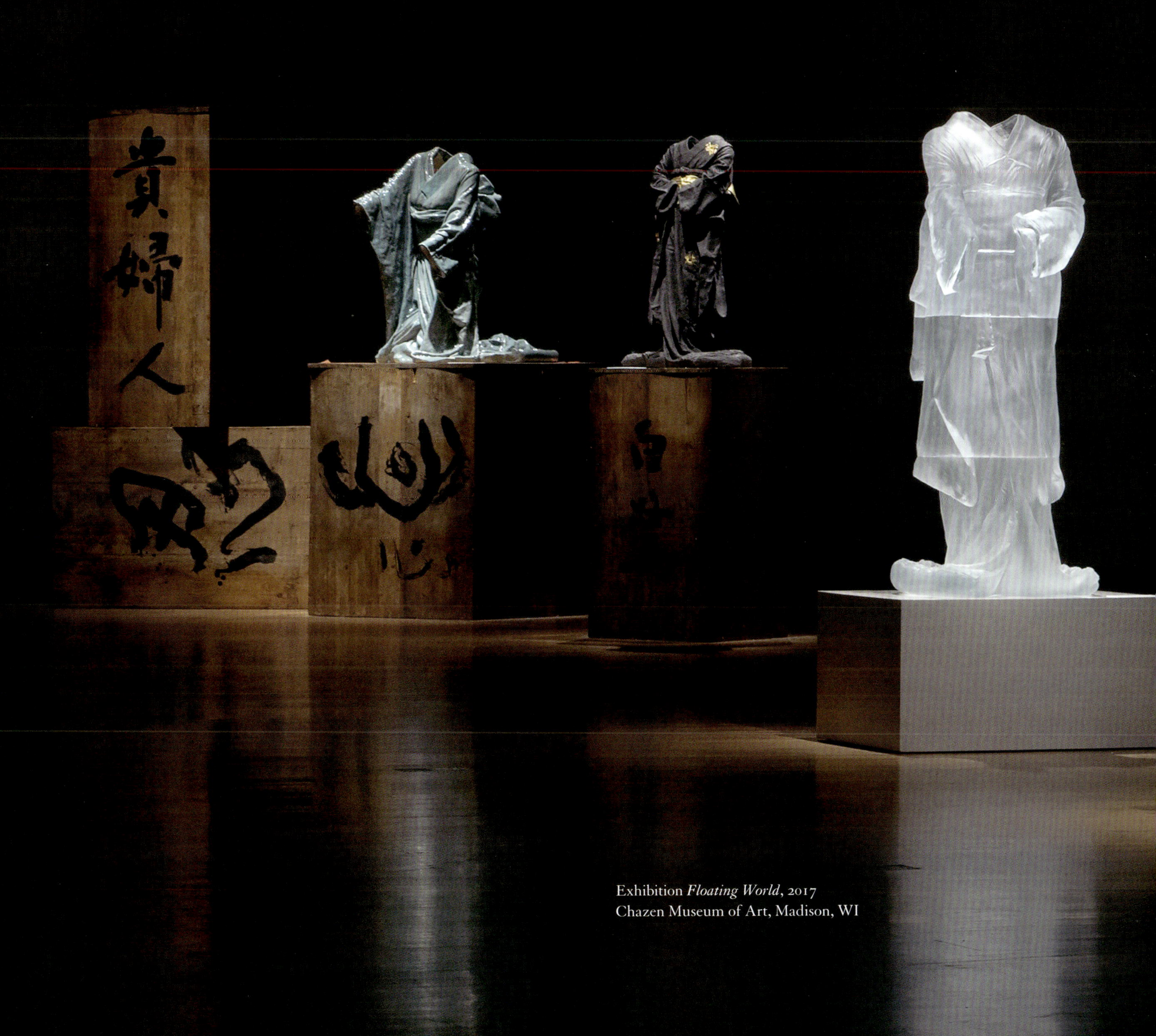

Exhibition *Floating World*, 2017
Chazen Museum of Art, Madison, WI

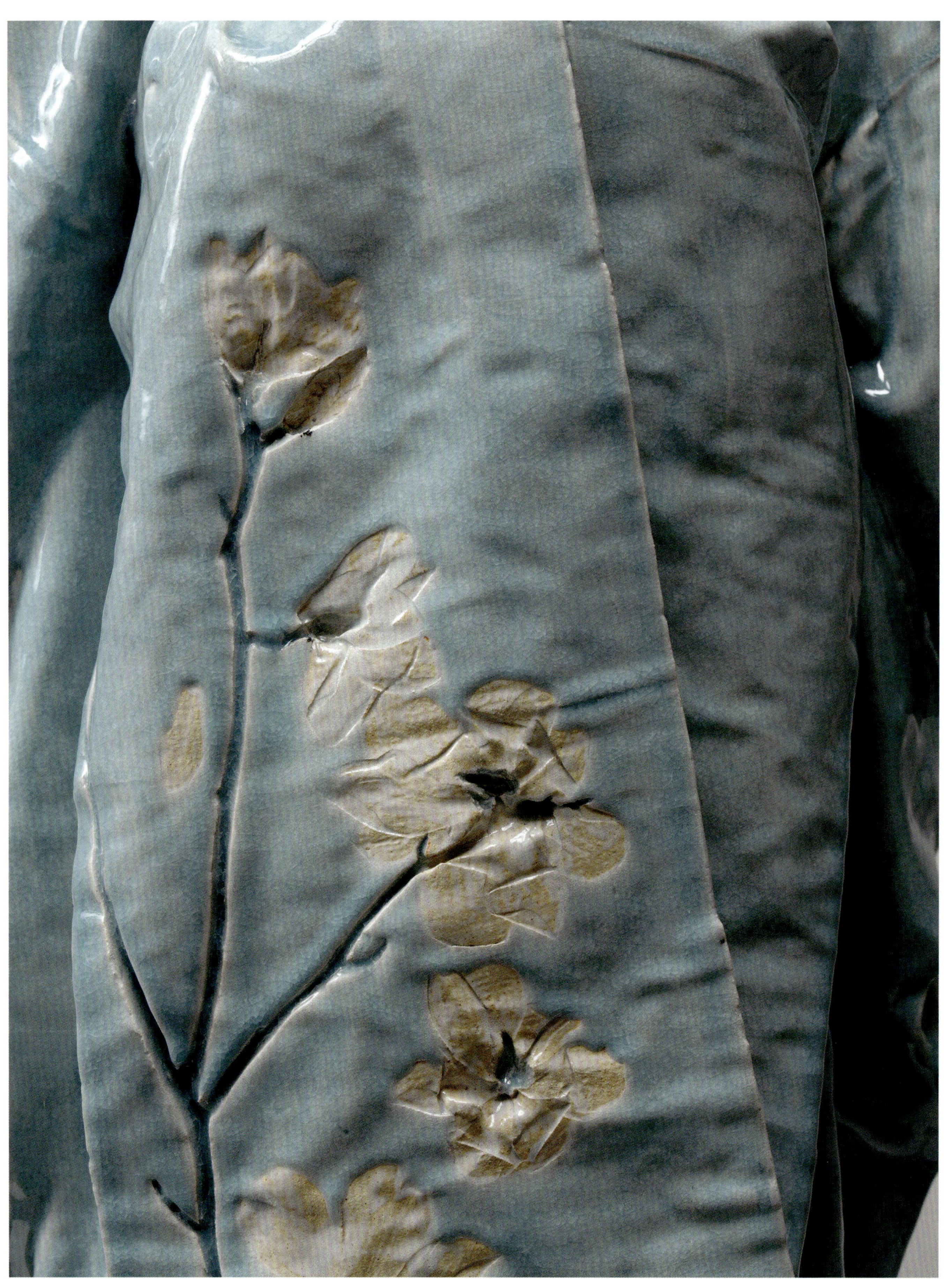

Hauntings in the Floating World

Laura Addison

Detail of *Maiko*, 2010
Ceramic, 48 × 28½ × 21 in.
(122 × 72 × 53 cm)

Since 1990, Karen LaMonte has explored figuration in glass through the motifs of marionettes, mirrors, and clothing as surrogates for the human. With her life-size, cast glass dresses for which she is widely known, LaMonte concentrates on two notions of skin. "I believe we have two skins that outline and define who we are," she has explained. "One of course is our natural skin, but we obscure and conceal it beneath clothing, which is a second skin, our social skin."[1]

EVERYWOMAN EMBODIED

In her *Floating World* series,[2] Karen LaMonte elaborates upon the notion of a "social skin"[3] by incorporating the cultural specificity of Japan and the material connotations of glass, ceramic, bronze, and rusted iron. The project offered LaMonte the opportunity to work the complex system of signification embedded in the archetypal garment of Japan: the kimono.[4]

LaMonte spent four years researching the kimono for this project, including a seven-month residency in Kyoto, funded by the Japan-U.S. Friendship Commission. While there, she educated herself about all aspects of the kimono—its production, form, function, symbolism. She learned about the rituals associated with wearing a kimono, and the complex endeavor of dressing in one. She even collaborated on a project with a master kimono maker, Minami-san. When she returned to her home and studio in Prague, LaMonte brought back more than 250 kimonos. LaMonte's work with the kimono has echoes of Japonisme, and the legacy of the Western gaze upon the Japanese subject, which can be seen in the subject matter and compositional devices used by European avant-garde artists such as Édouard Manet, Edgar Degas, Claude Monet, James Abbott McNeill Whistler, and Vincent van Gogh. However, LaMonte's interest was not in compositional devices and fantasy—or even gender, for that matter—but an exploration of the language of the kimono, beauty, and the social dynamics that are reflected in clothing.

Quite distinct from the sensuous curves and baroque drapery of her European-American dress sculptures, LaMonte's kimono sculptures reflect a different cultural norm, one in which the human form is depleted of all curves to become an idealized cylindrical form. "How the kimono is worn parallels the relationship between Japanese individuals and their society," LaMonte explains. "Putting on a kimono is literally about erasing the individual's identity and joining the group."[5]

This notion is at the heart of LaMonte's kimono project: "the erasure of the individual."[6]

The intent to "erase" the individual in deference to the group is even reflected in LaMonte's casting process. For the *Floating World* series, the artist built a mannequin based on the biometric data of the Japanese population compiled by NASA. She selected the measurements for the fiftieth percentile of forty-year-old Japanese women in the year 2000 at 1 gravitational force. That is, LaMonte created an average female—"the exact everywoman or no-woman," as she describes it.[7] The figure is not individual, but the median of a collective. The kimono are embodied—the clothing appears occupied, inhabited, and perhaps even haunted. Yet the lack of visible skin, flesh, limbs, head, and facial features denies the figure an individual identity.

(IM)MATERIALITY

LaMonte's exploration of different materials—glass, ceramic, bronze, and rusted iron—endows each subject with different degrees of presence. Glass has the disordered molecular structure of a liquid but the physical state of a solid. It is neither one nor the other, but rather both simultaneously. Moreover, glass has metaphorical associations with light, the ethereal, the immaterial. LaMonte describes her work in cast glass as an effort to "negotiate the visible and invisible."[8] The combination of all of these factors allows all of LaMonte's glass sculptures to give the impression of being apparitions. The glass kimono sculptures give the viewer the sense that this Japanese everywoman is a specter that persists in spite of her immateriality. She may well dematerialize into pure light.

For an artist so celebrated for her glass sculpture, working with ceramic, bronze, and rusted iron offered LaMonte entirely new sets of material symbolism to explore. She refers to clay as "our universal corpus,"[9] extending a corporeal metaphor from unformed earth to formed sculpture. To create a kimono in clay is a reverential nod to Japan's rich history of ceramics.

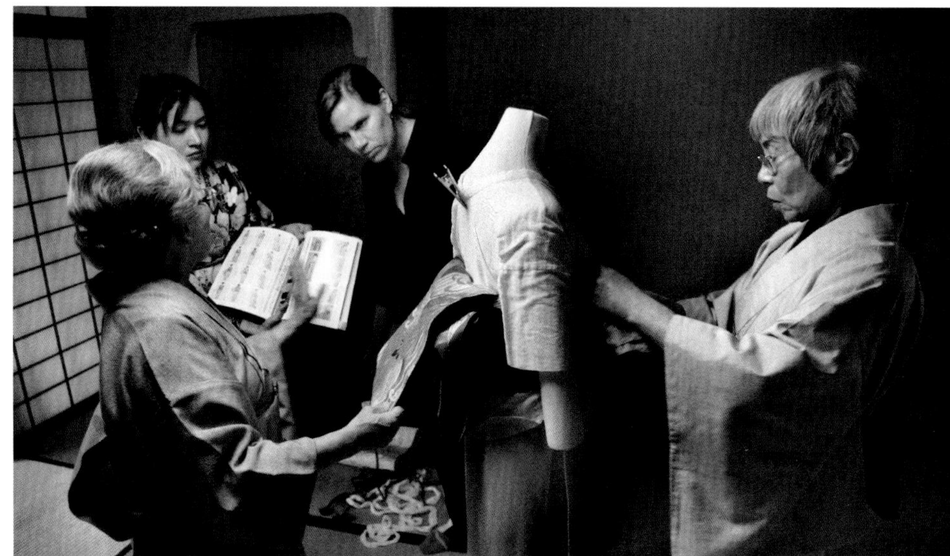

Studying how to tie an obi, Kyoto, Japan, 2007

The ceramic kimono sculptures also introduce color to LaMonte's repertoire, whether sumptuous green celadon glaze, black or white unglazed clay, or the reddish-orange of terra cotta. The opacity of the ceramic kimono provides an earthy yin to the spiritual and translucent yang of glass.

LaMonte's castings in metal play longevity against vulnerability. The kimono in bronze and rusted iron also enable the greatest exploration of surface decoration—a fact that aligns LaMonte's sculptures beautifully with the patterning that is so important in *ukiyo-e* (woodblock) prints. Relief impressions on the kimono are an opportunity for LaMonte to include some of the iconography characteristic of these Japanese garments.

"Bronze," the artist notes, "celebrates effort and achievement. We cast our heroes in bronze."[10] To cast the Japanese everywoman in the medium once reserved for men in positions of authority is a way to value her as much as her male counterpart. At the same time, bronze busts of national leaders focus attention not on the body but on the individual identity and likeness of the subject. These are precisely the elements intentionally rejected by LaMonte in her sculptures of the Japanese everywoman. Bronze memorializes and has a durability not characteristic of the more vulnerable materials of glass or ceramic. To memorialize is to acknowledge the "having been there"[11] of the memorialized—the ghosts who, in LaMonte's sculptures, are simultaneously present and absent.

Iron, like bronze, is significant in industry, peace, and war. It is the material of African currency, of weaponry, and of farming implements. LaMonte associates it with temporality and ephemerality by virtue of its intentional rusting, giving it a sense of age and neglect. Iron itself is haunted by the ghosts of agricultural life, when the blacksmith occupied a pivotal role in small-town life, salvaging iron from worn implements and re-forming another by melting the old one down in the forge.[12] In other words, iron denotes a nostalgia for bygone days and traditions of the past, an impression underscored by the rusting stains that belie the fact that these sculptures were made in 2012, not centuries ago. Rusted iron also signifies how the kimono has lost its standing as a daily garment as a result of the Westernization of postwar Japanese culture. Today, kimonos are primarily worn only for ceremonial occasions.

HAUNTINGS AND TRANSFORMATIONS

Regardless of her chosen medium, LaMonte enacts a transformative process that involves a cast and formation by fire. Casting itself is a process that uses a negative to create a positive. Hence, it is a process whereby there is a loss of the "original" physical presence—the model (real or fabricated)—whose body is used to create a mold. There is a subsequent recuperation of that former presence when the casting is done in the mold. The fact that LaMonte will create the same figure in each of the four mentioned mediums underscores the significance of repetition, replication, and reproduction to this particular series.

Each material—ceramic, bronze, iron, glass—records the details of the fabrics differently. LaMonte's repetitions of the same posture or gesture in various mediums are an insightful melding of material and content, form and iconography. The nuances of meaning that haunt glass, ceramic, bronze, and iron provide an interpretive lens through which we may better understand LaMonte's cultural and aesthetic explorations of the kimono. Through her sculptural hauntings in a floating world, LaMonte proposes a modern- day Japonisme that is informed by history and sociology, not fantasy and desire.

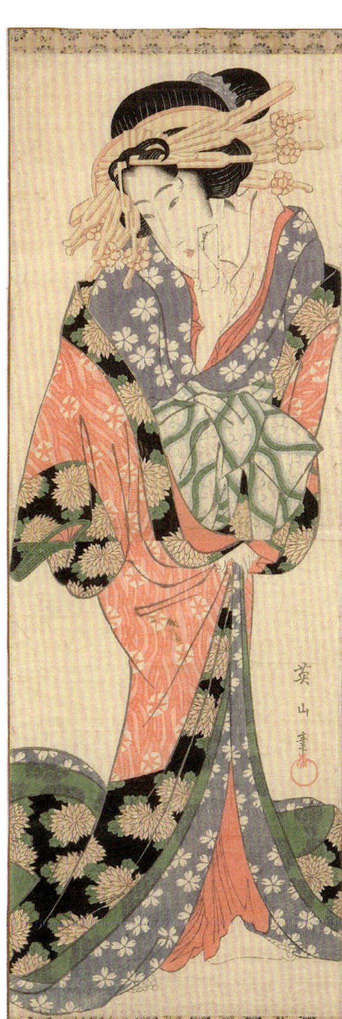

Kikugawa Eizan (1787–1867). *Courtesan Holding a Letter*, 1810–20. Color woodcut. Chazen Museum of Art, Madison, WI

NOTES

1 Karen LaMonte, "Artist Talk" (untitled lecture given at the Renwick Gallery, Smithsonian American Art Museum, February 26, 2010), accessed at https://americanart.si.edu /videos/artist-talk-karen-lamonte-154347.

2 The term *floating world* (*ukiyo*) is a reference to Edo-period Japan (1615–1868), which was marked by social changes such as urbanization, the rise of a middle class, and—significantly—a lifestyle in pursuit of earthly pleasures. This period also saw the development of *ukiyo-e* (pictures of the floating world), or woodblock prints that depicted *bijin* (beautiful women), courtesans, folk tales, landscapes, and kabuki actors.

3 See Terence S. Turner, "Social Skin," *HAU: Journal of Ethnographic Theory* 2, no. 2 (2012): 486–504. Reprint of 1980 article.

4 Throughout this essay, the author refers to research done for an exhibition at the New Mexico Museum of Art, *Kimono: Karen LaMonte and Prints of the Floating World*, June 24–November 6, 2011, as well as to an article written on the exhibition: Laura Addison, "On Exhibit: Kimono: Karen LaMonte and Prints of the Floating World," *El Palacio* 116, no. 2 (Summer 2011): 58–61.

5 Karen LaMonte, "Artist Talk."

6 This cultural value placed on the group over the individual is illustrated by the Japanese saying, "The nail that sticks out gets hammered down."

7 Addison, "On Exhibit," 61.

8 Karen LaMonte, email correspondence with author, January 3, 2013.

9 Ibid.

10 Ibid.

11 See Roland Barthes, *Camera Lucida: Reflections on Photography*, trans. Richard Howard (New York: Hill and Wang, 1981), 63–89.

12 See Tom Joyce, *Life Force at the Anvil: The Blacksmith's Art from Africa* (Asheville, NC: University of North Carolina at Asheville, 1998).

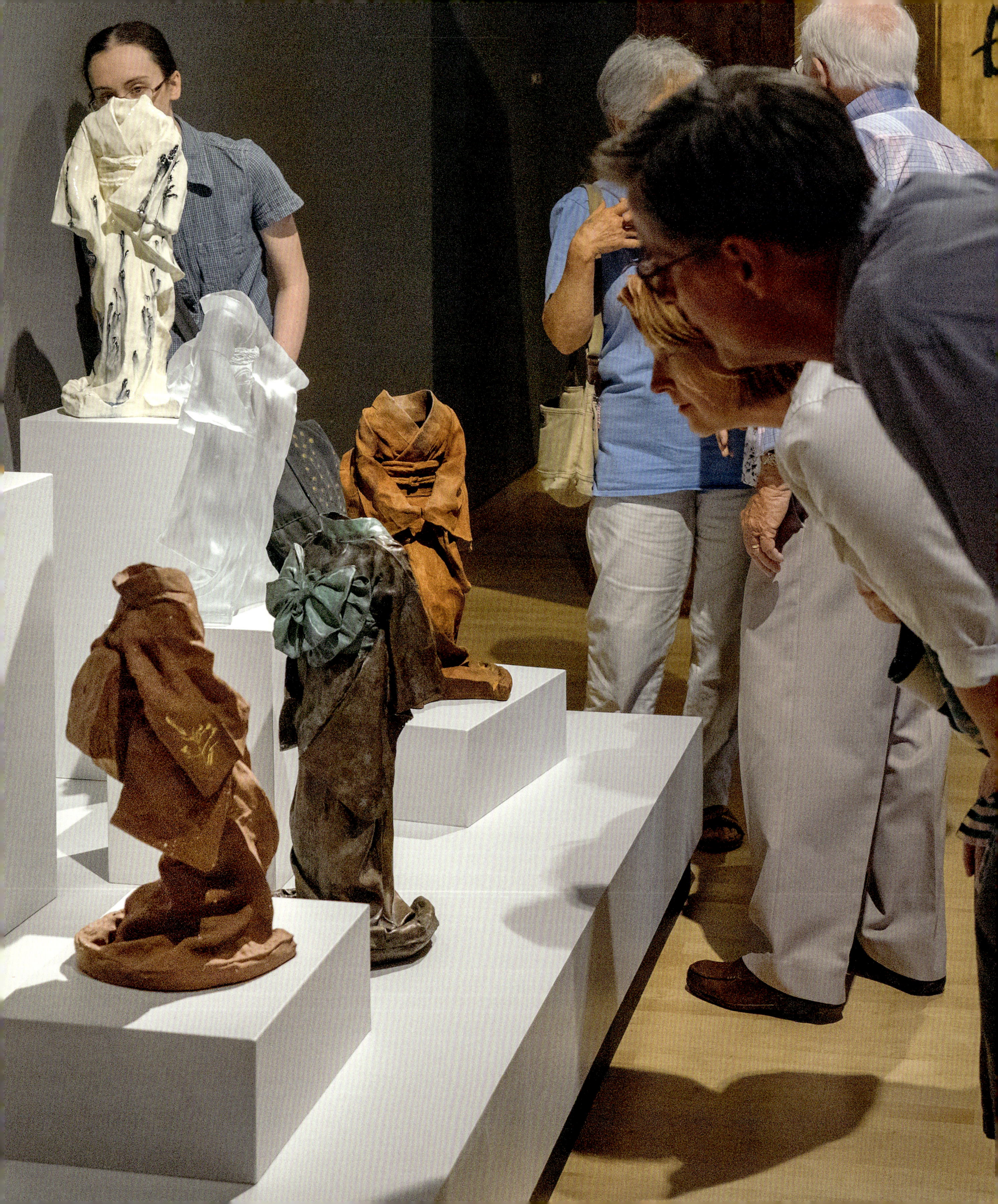

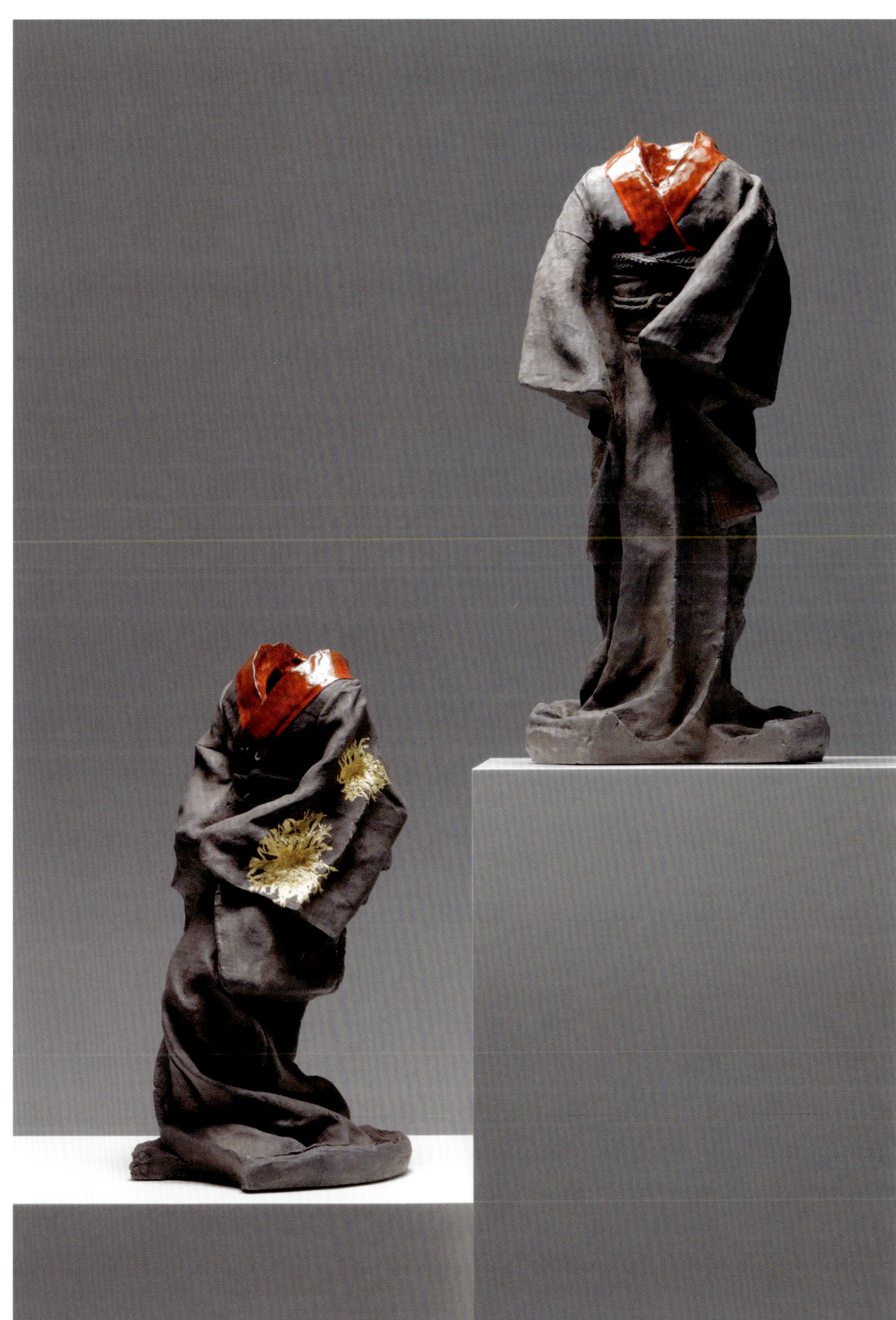

OPPOSITE

Exhibition *Embodied Beauty*, 2018
Hunter Museum of Amercan Art,
Chattanooga, TN

LEFT TO RIGHT

Kimono Maquette, 2014
Ceramic, 18 × 10 × 10 in.
(46 × 25 × 25 cm)

Kimono Maquette, 2014
Ceramic, 21½ × 10½ × 9 in.
(55 × 27 × 23 cm)

Exhibition *Floating World*, 2017
Chazen Museum of Art, Madison, WI

FOLLOWING LEFT TO RIGHT

Exhibition *Embodied Beauty*, 2018
Hunter Museum of Amercian Art, Chattanooga, TN

Young Maiko, 2010
Ceramic, 36 × 18½ × 15½ in. (92 × 47 × 39 cm)

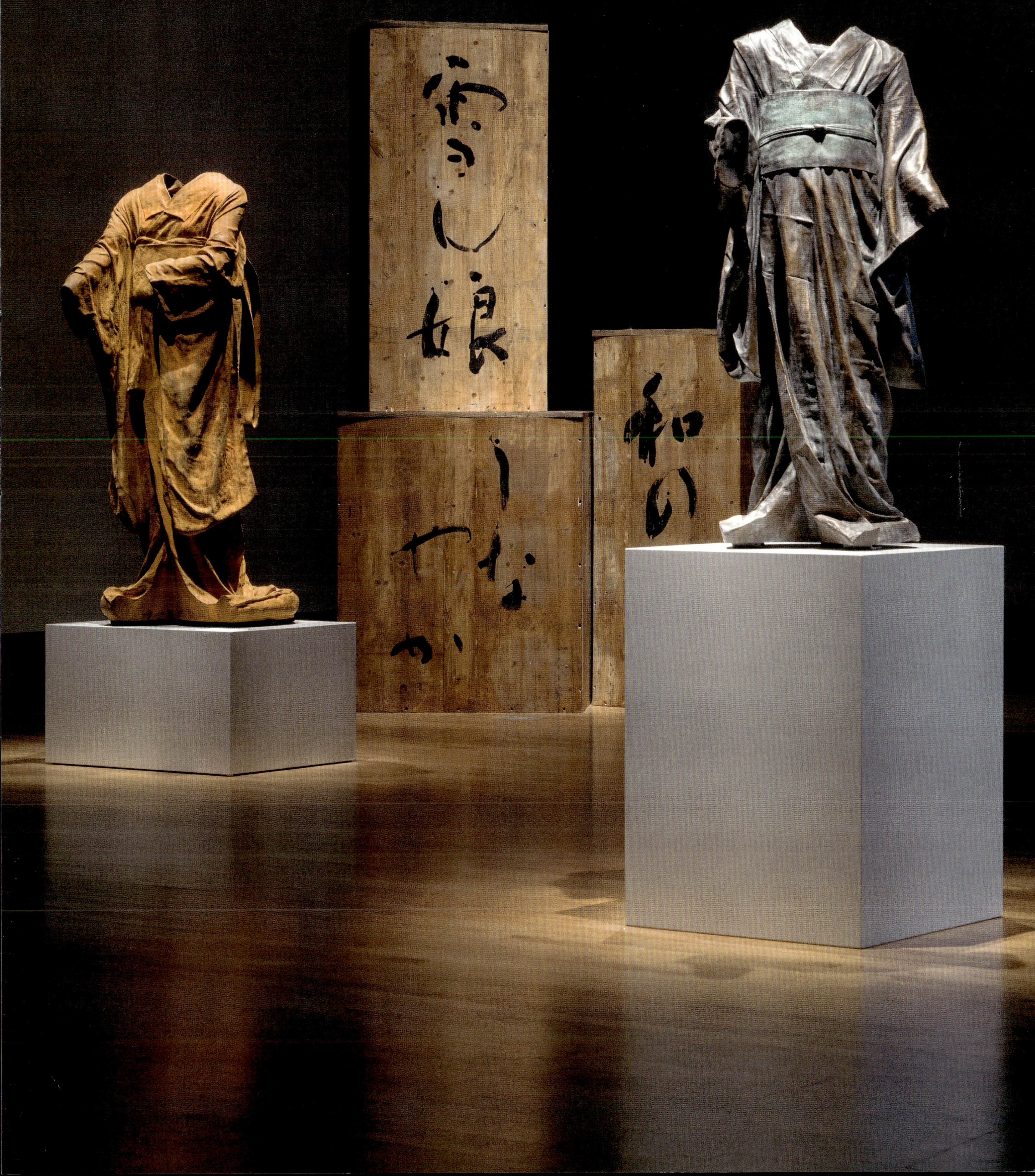

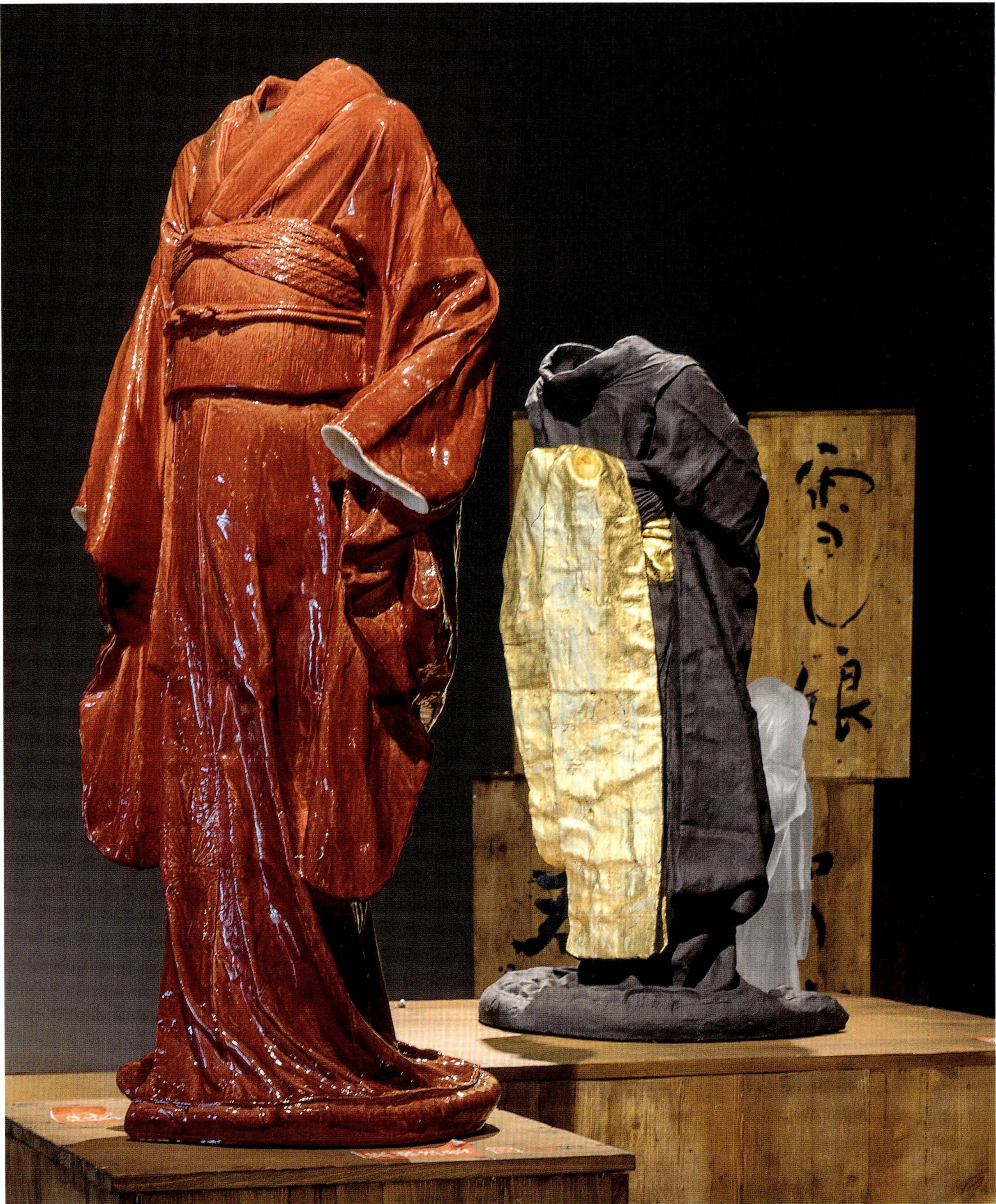

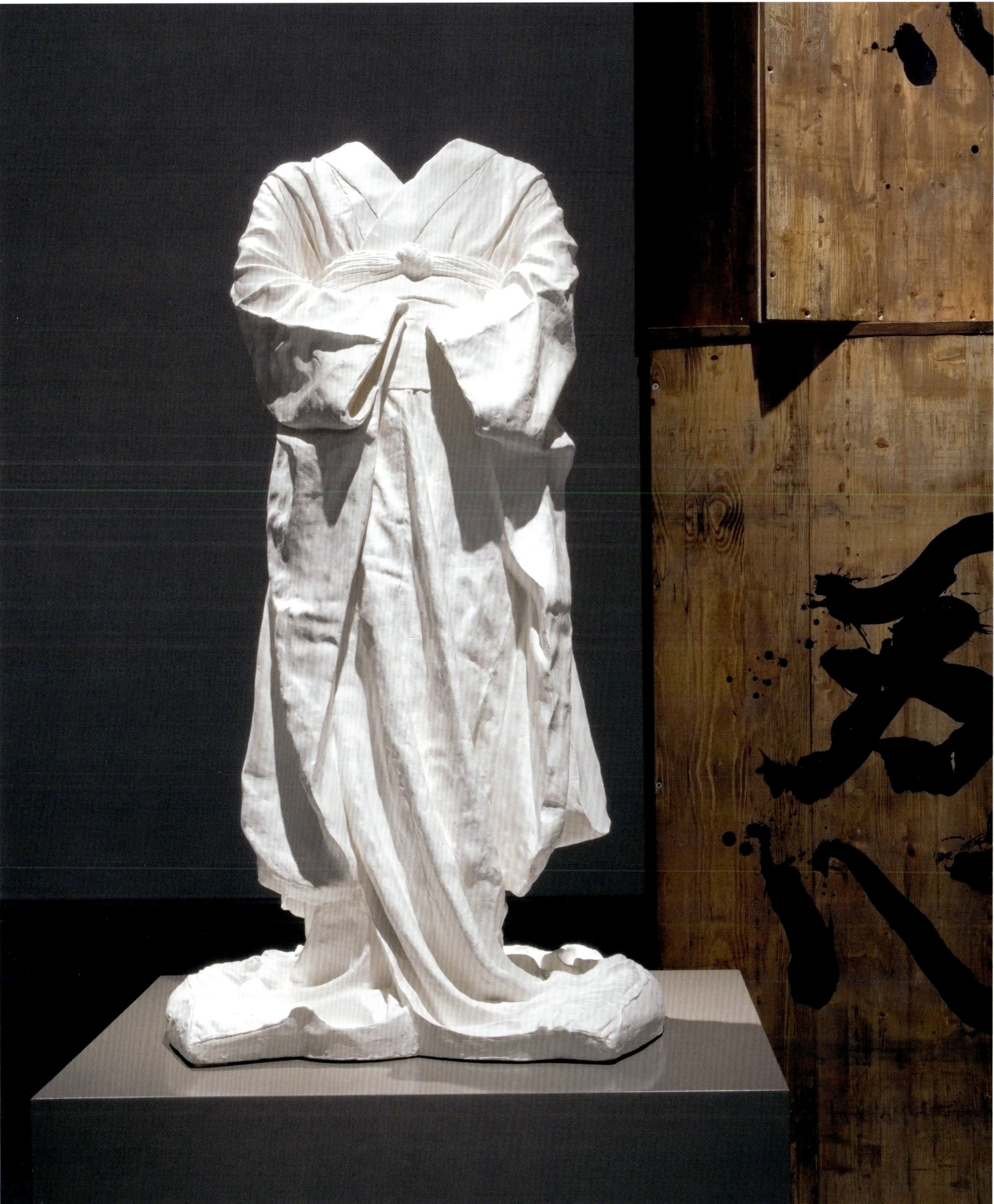

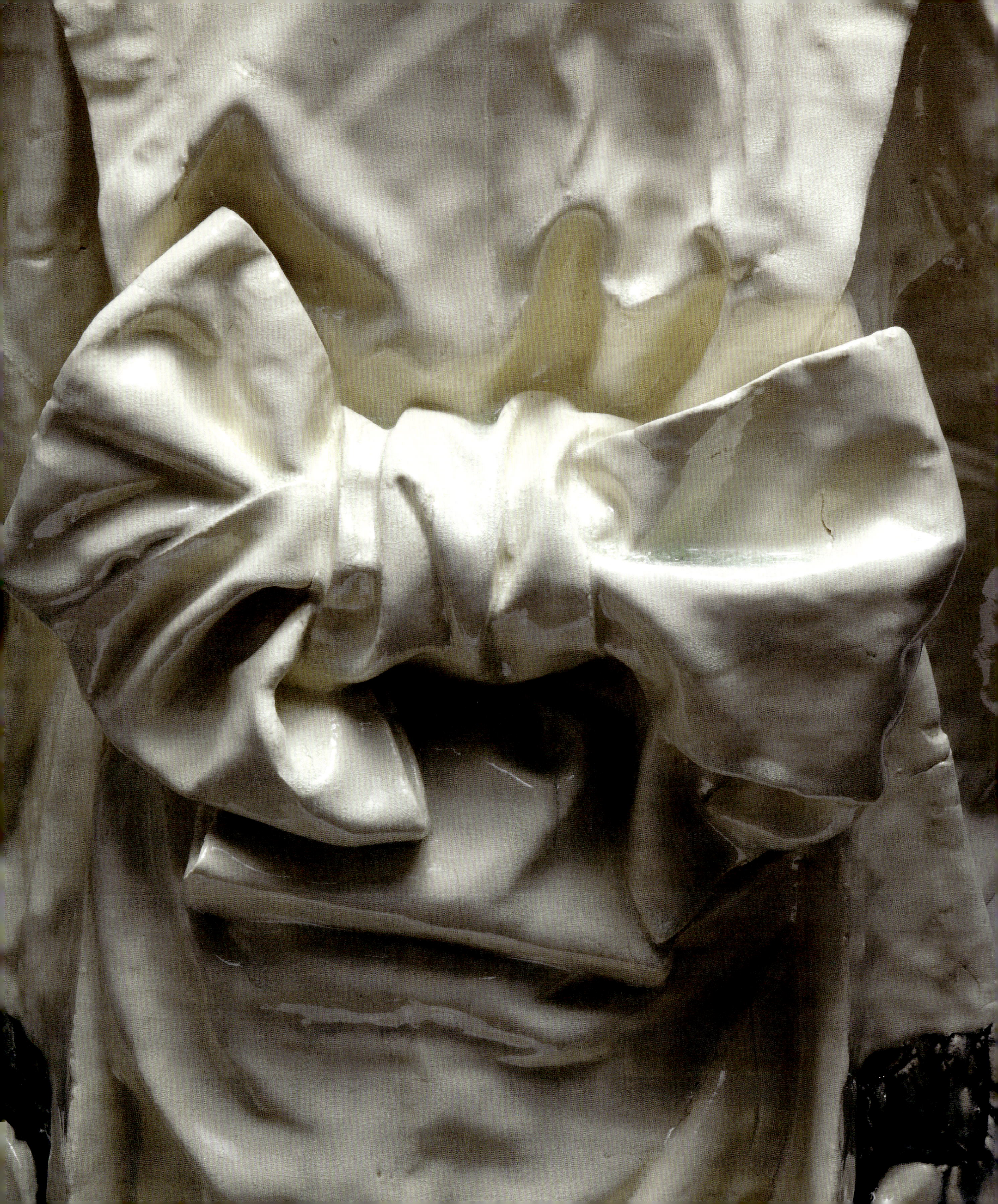

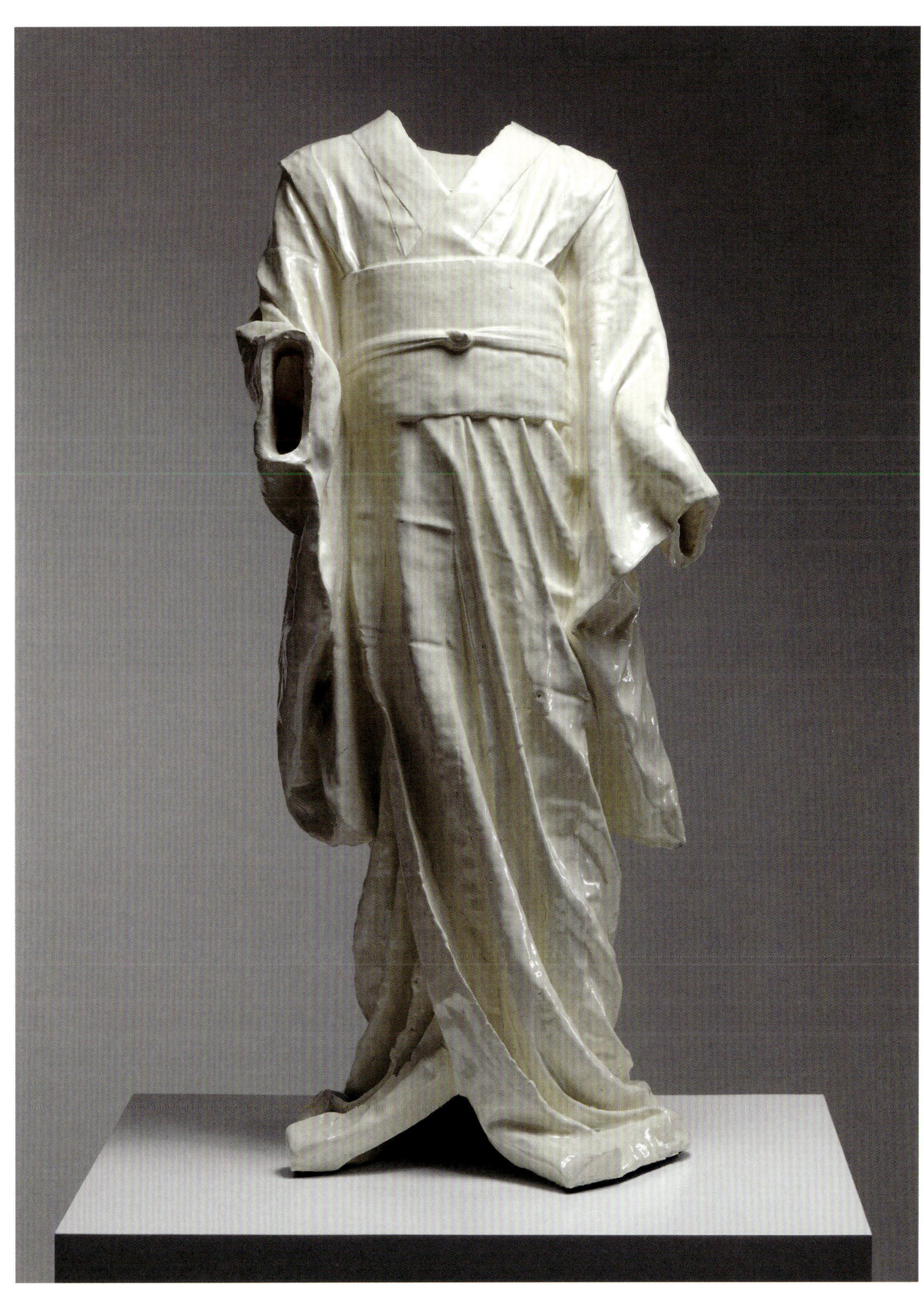

THIS AND FOLLOWING LEFT
Child's Kimono, 2011
Ceramic, 38½ × 18½ × 14 in.
(98 × 47 × 35 cm)

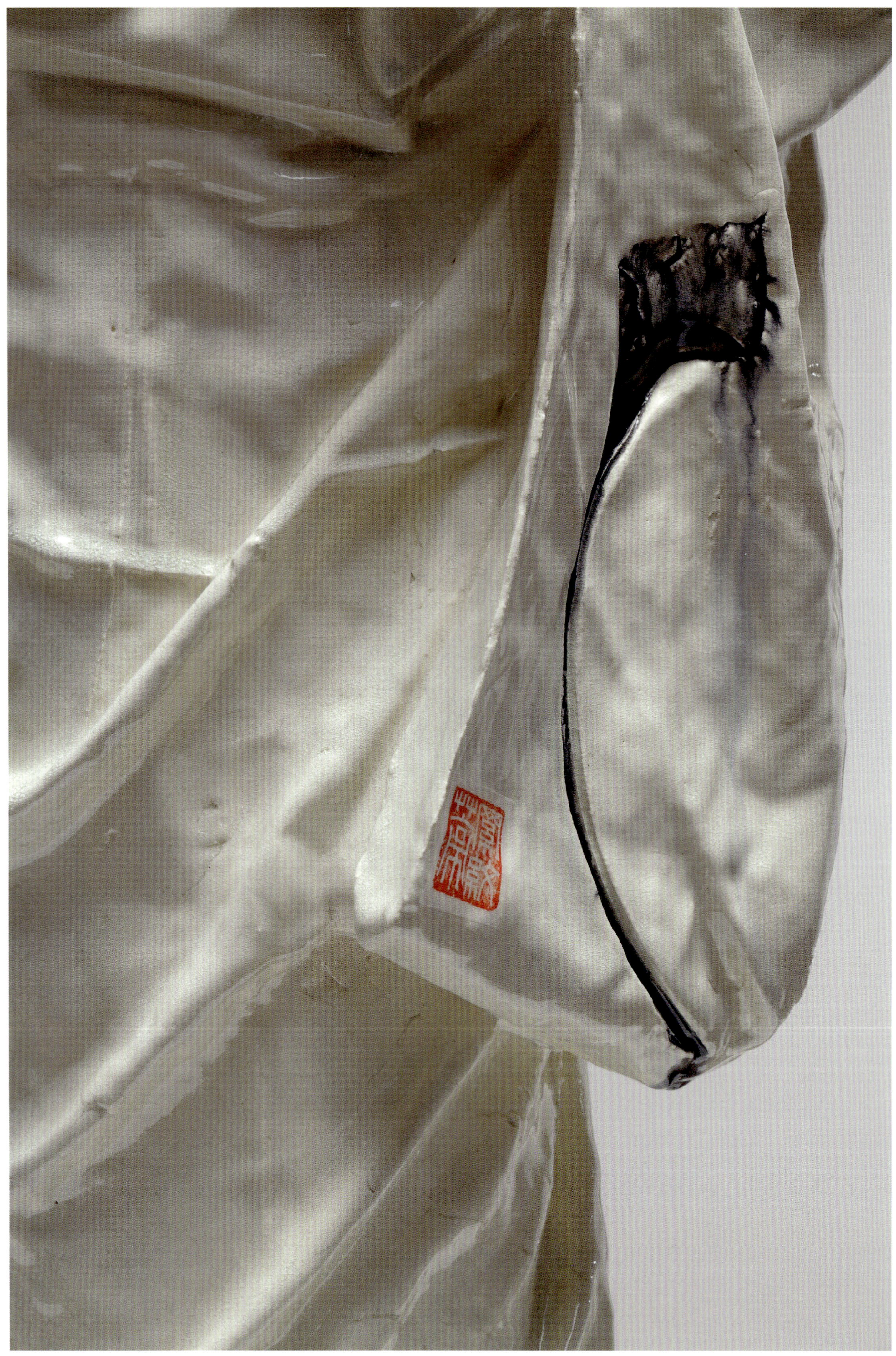

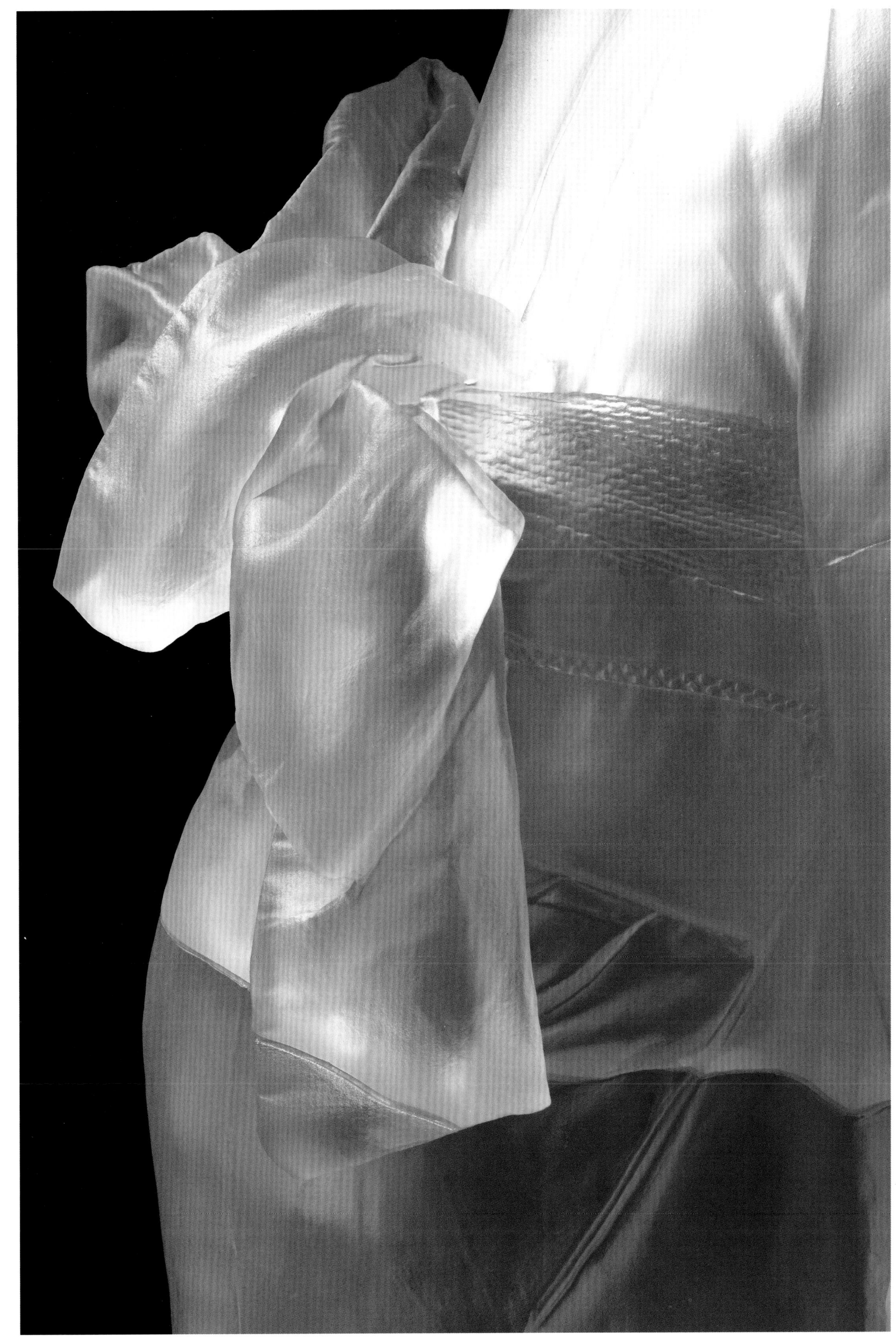

RIGHT AND FOLLOWING
Ojigi, 2010
Cast glass, 52 × 25 × 18 in.
(132 × 63 × 46 cm)
Collection of Montgomery
Museum of Fine Arts,
Montgomery, AL

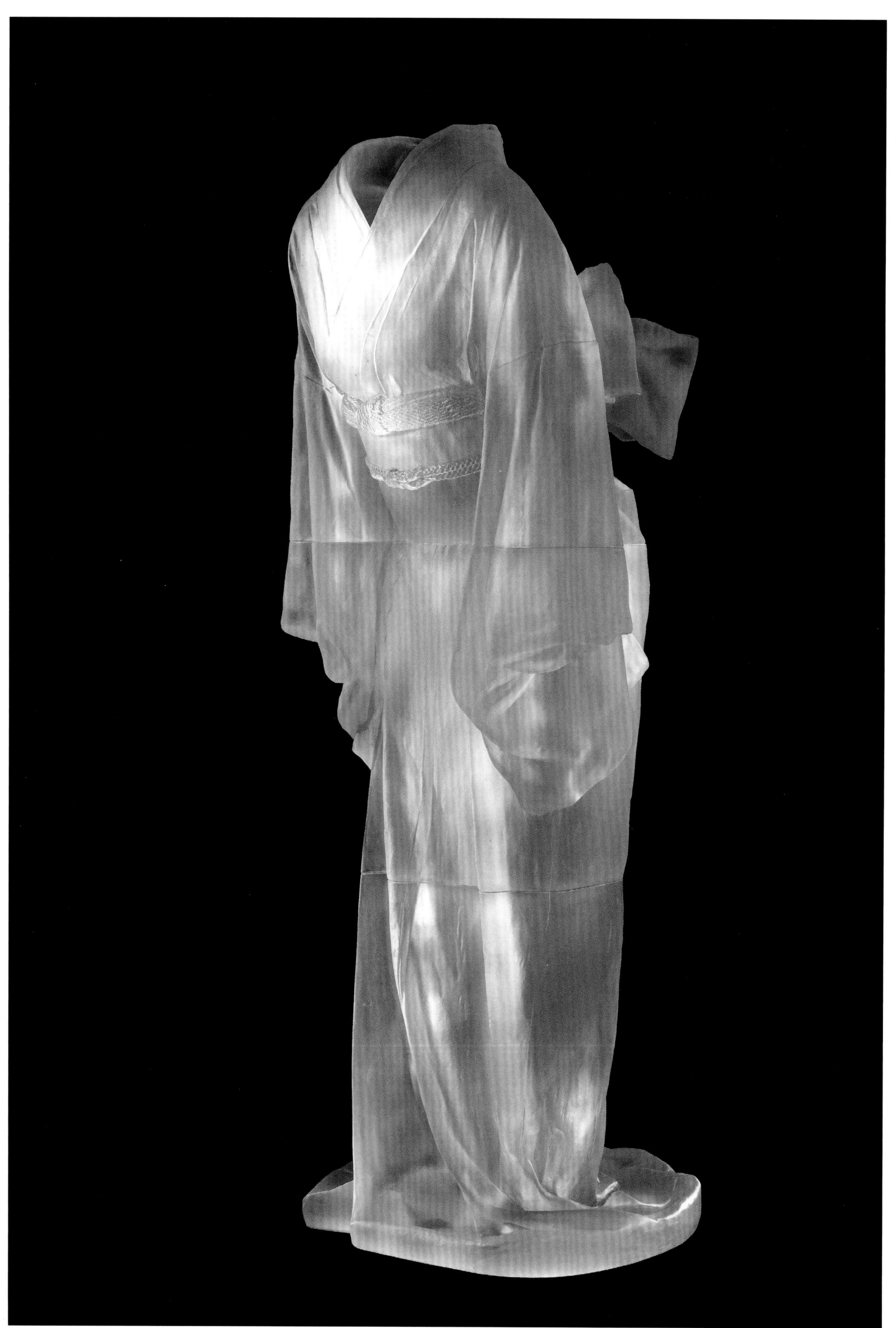

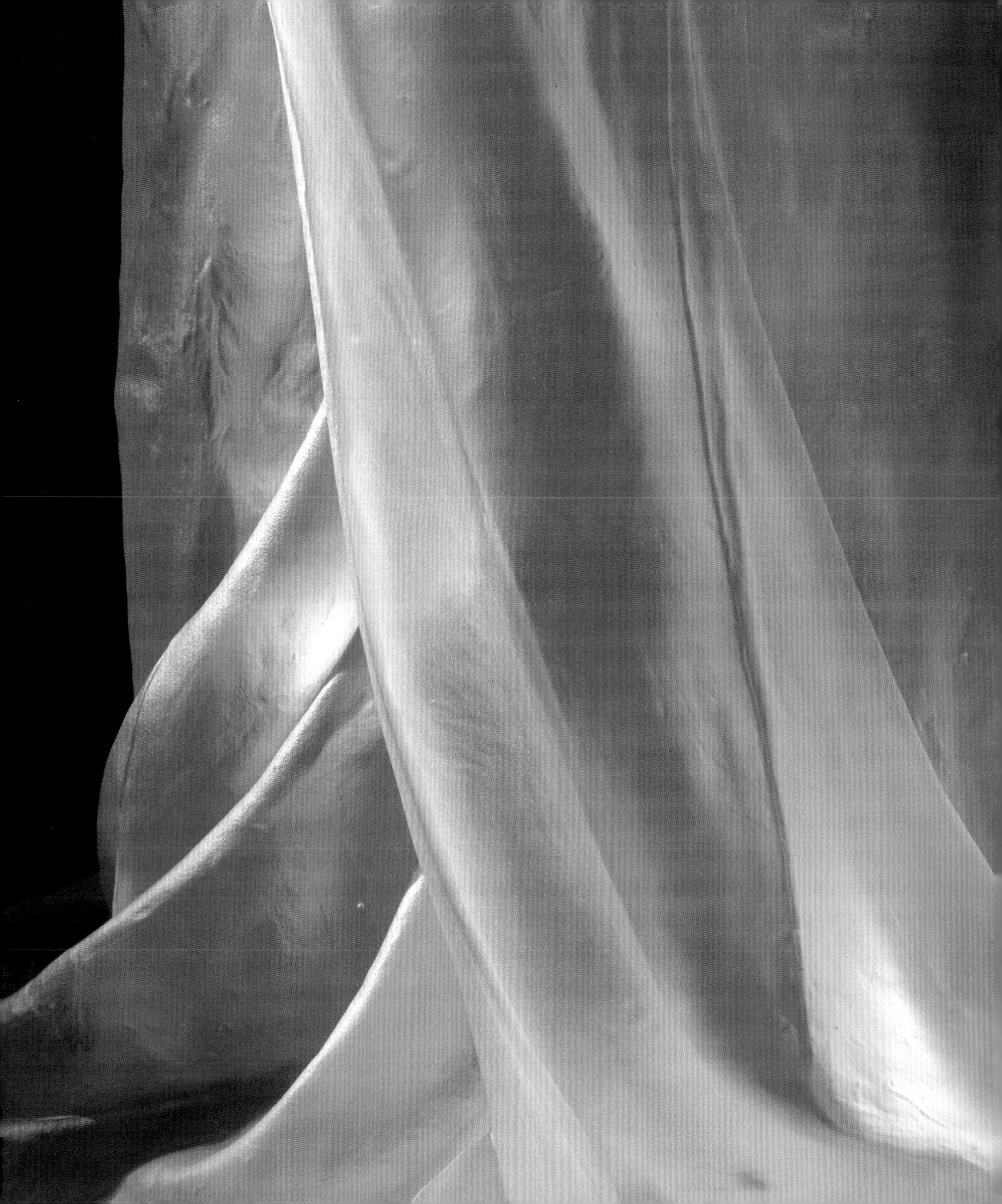

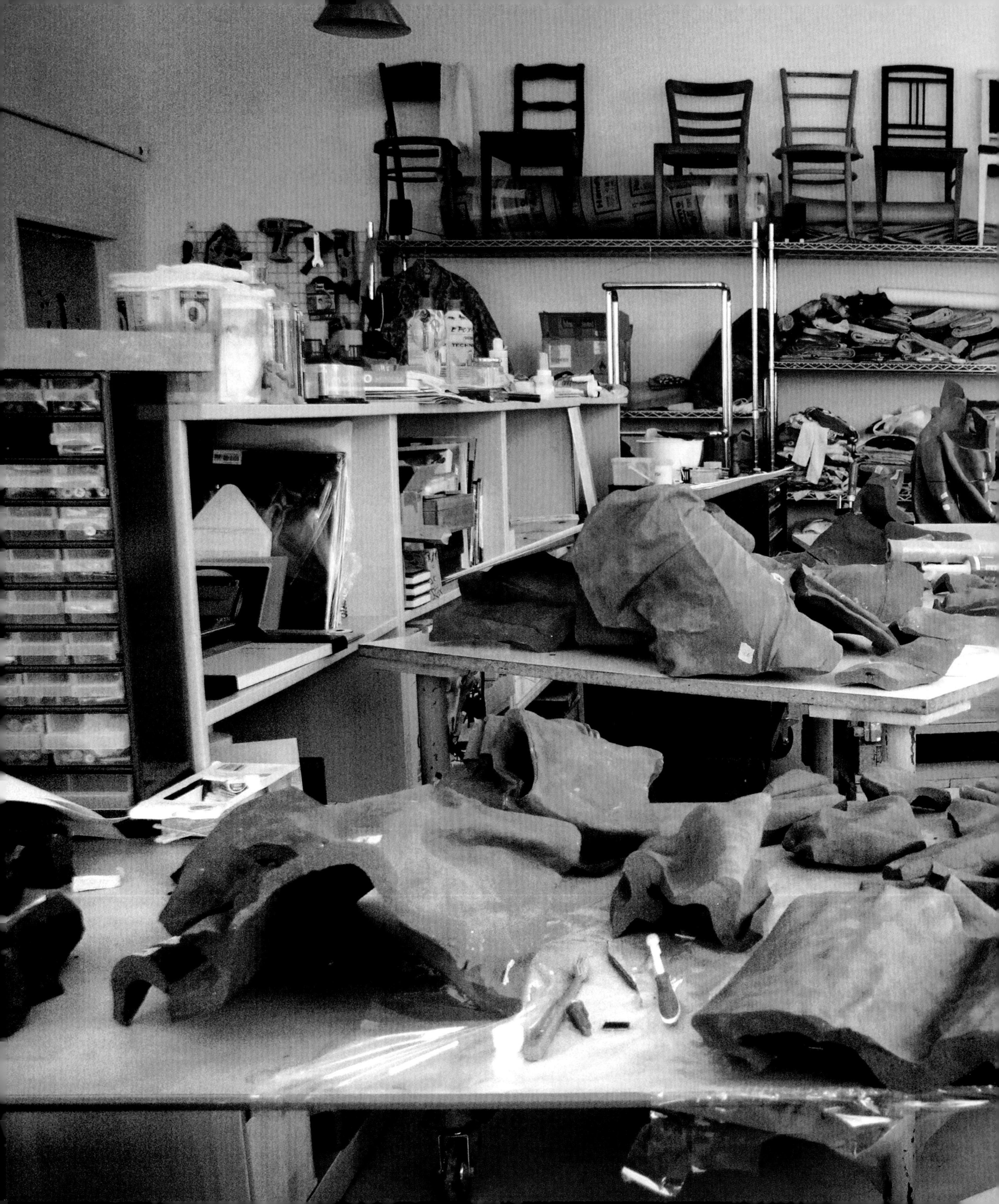

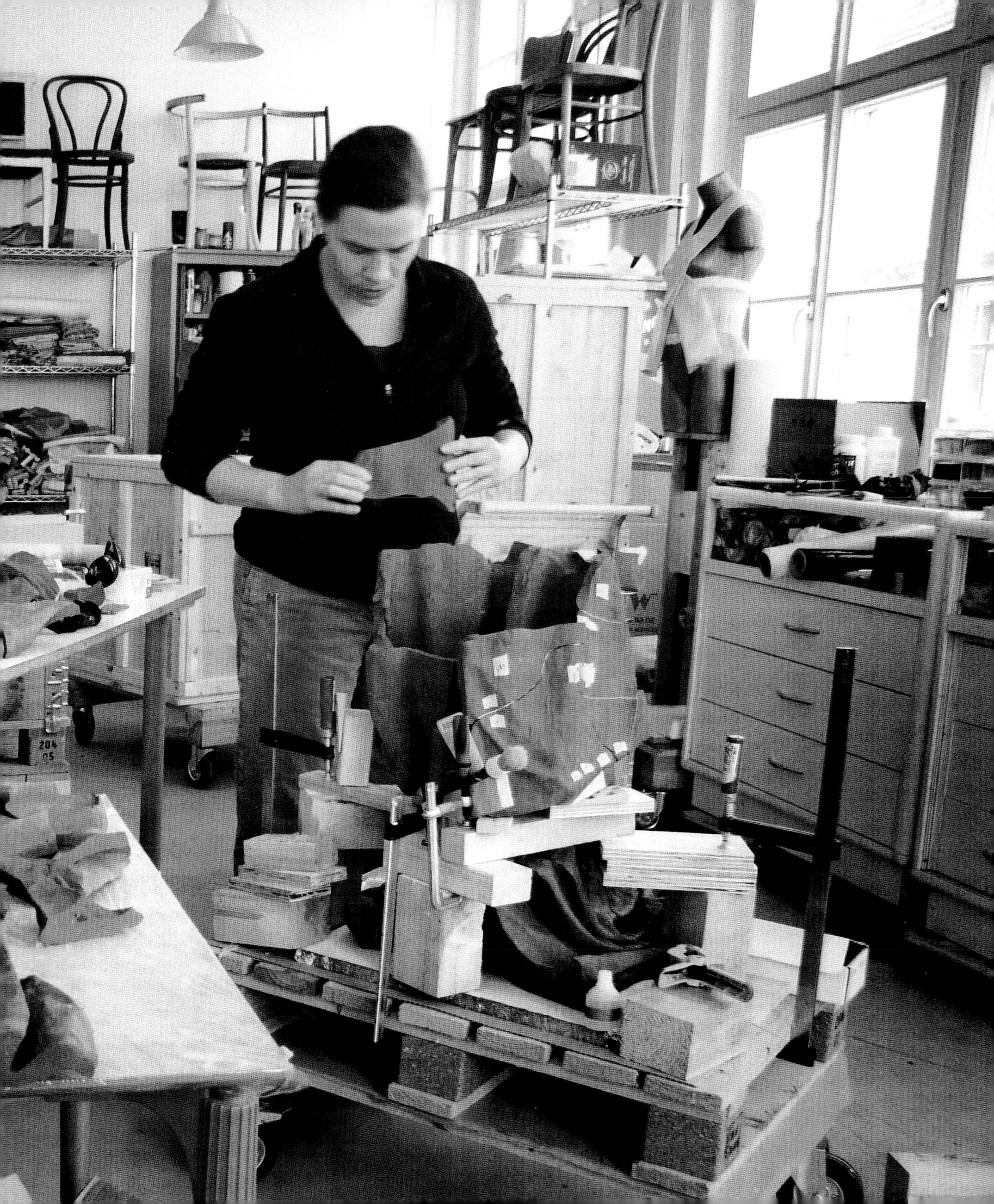
204
05
WADE

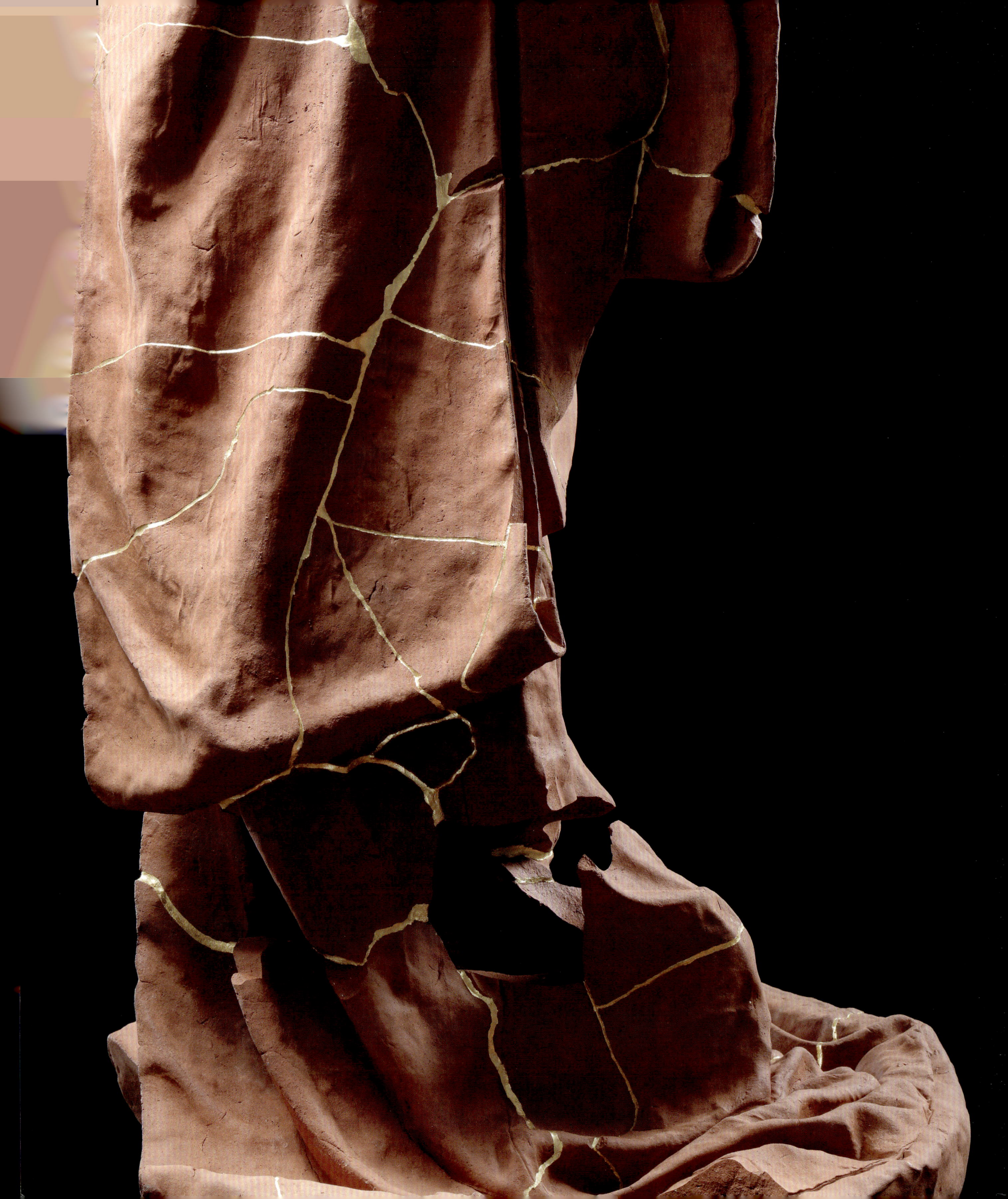

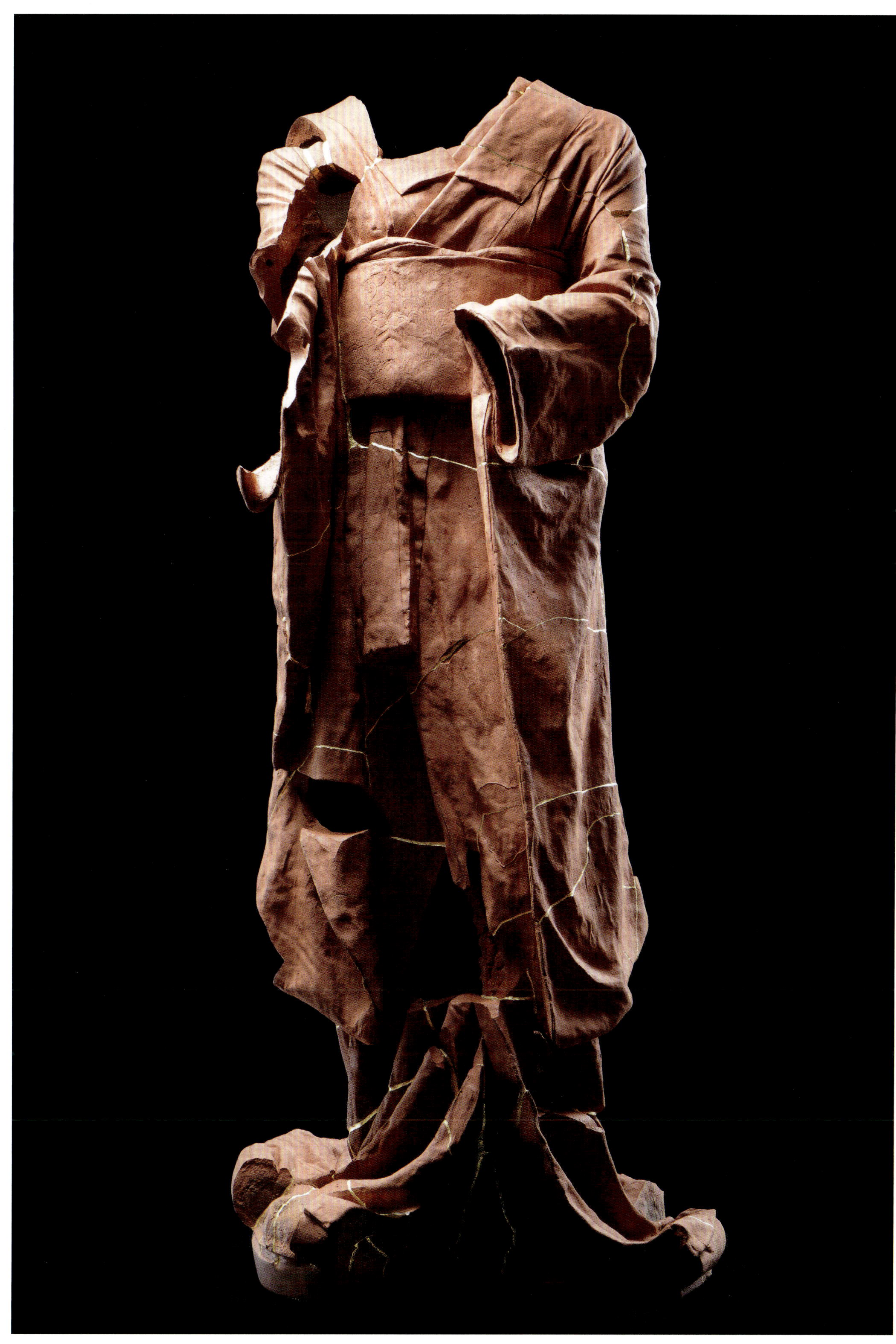

PREVIOUS
Repairing ceramic sculptures using *kintsugi*, 2012.

Bijin (Kintsugi), 2011
Ceramic, 49 × 20½ × 24 in.
(124 × 51.5 × 61.5 cm)

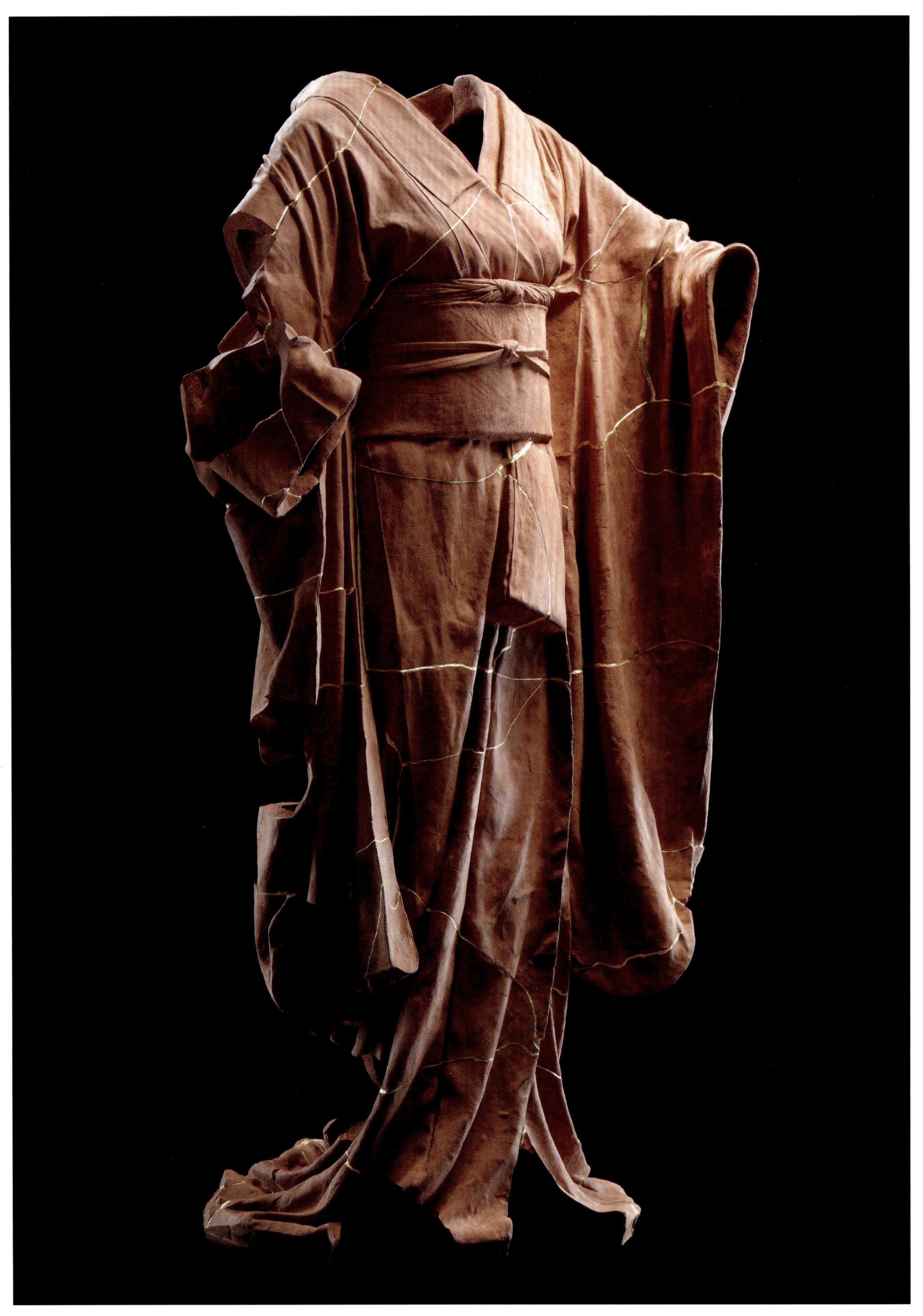

Odoriko (Kintsugi), 2011
Ceramic, 49½ × 27 × 17½ in.
(126 × 68 × 44 cm)

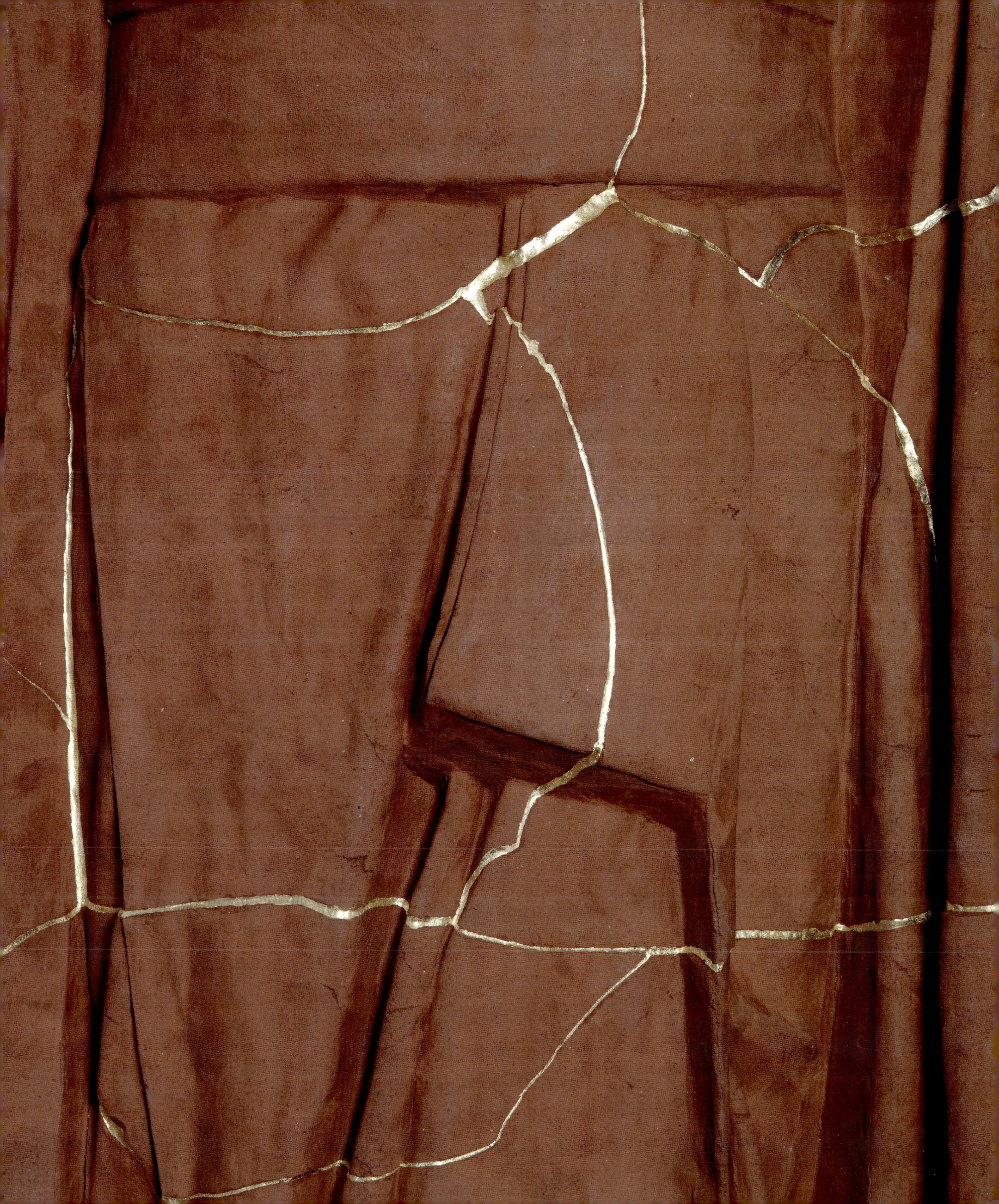

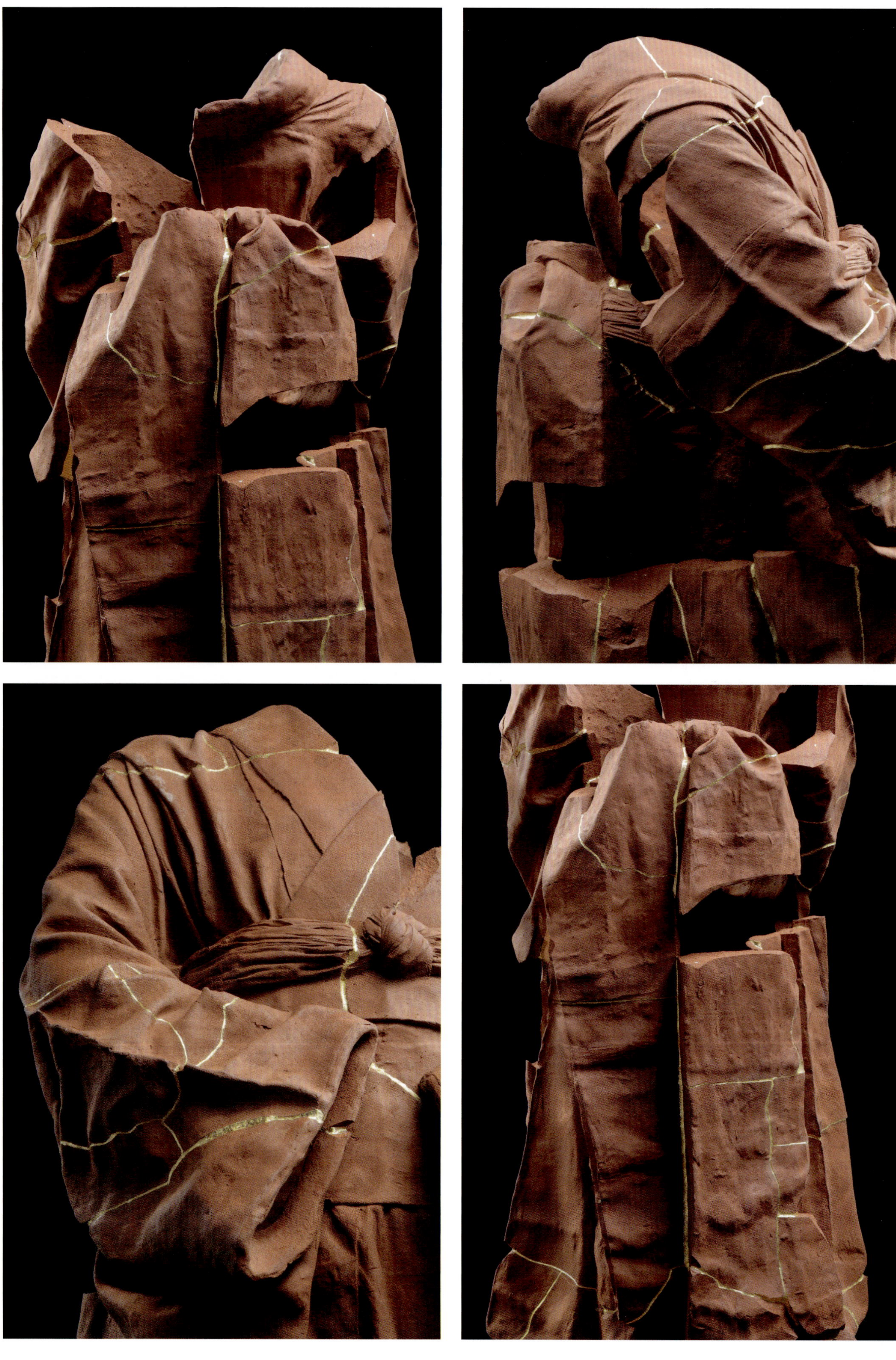

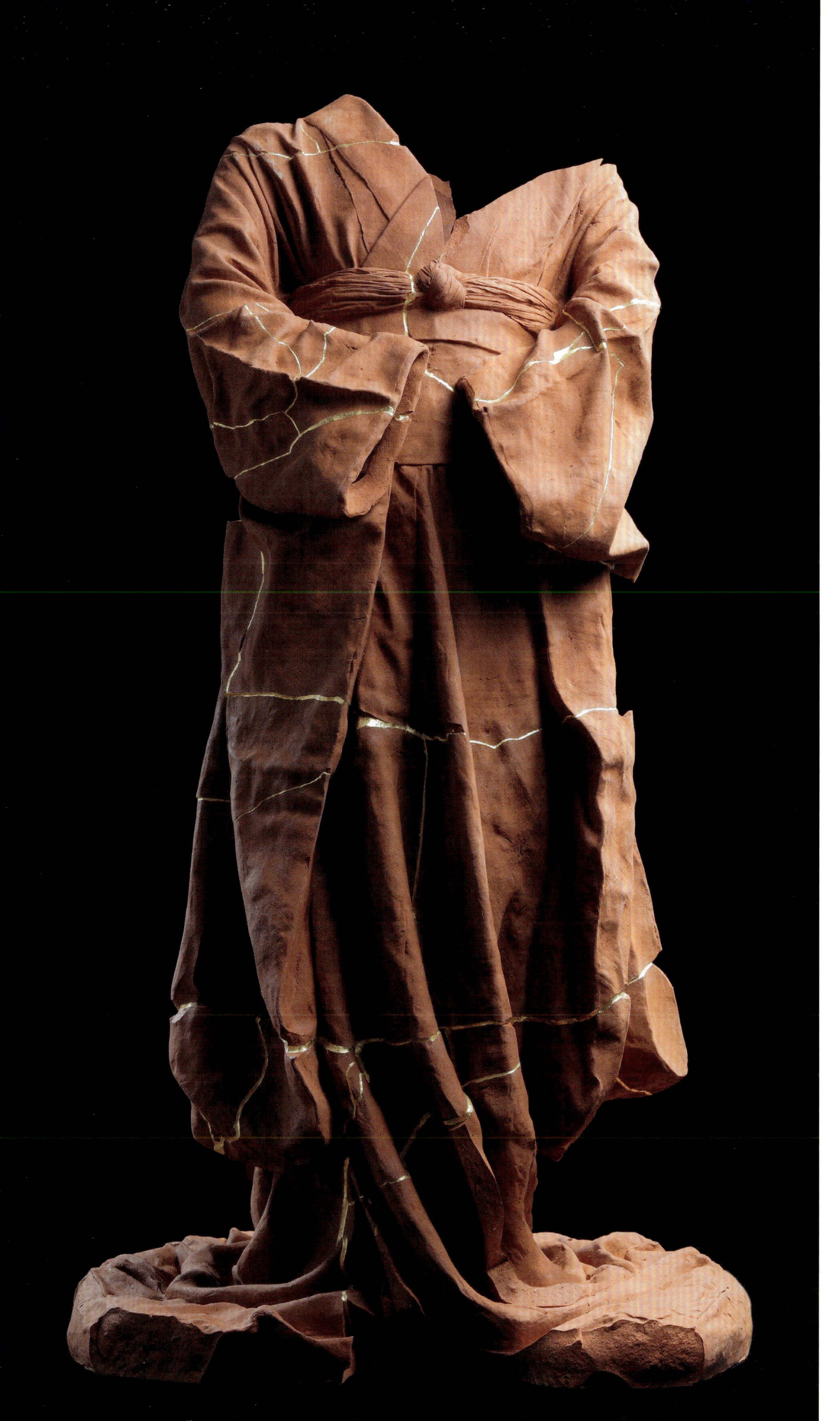

Young Maiko (Kintsugi), 2011
Ceramic, 35½ × 18½ × 15½ in.
(90 × 46.5 × 39 cm)

FOLLOWING
Installation of rusted iron
kimonos, 2013

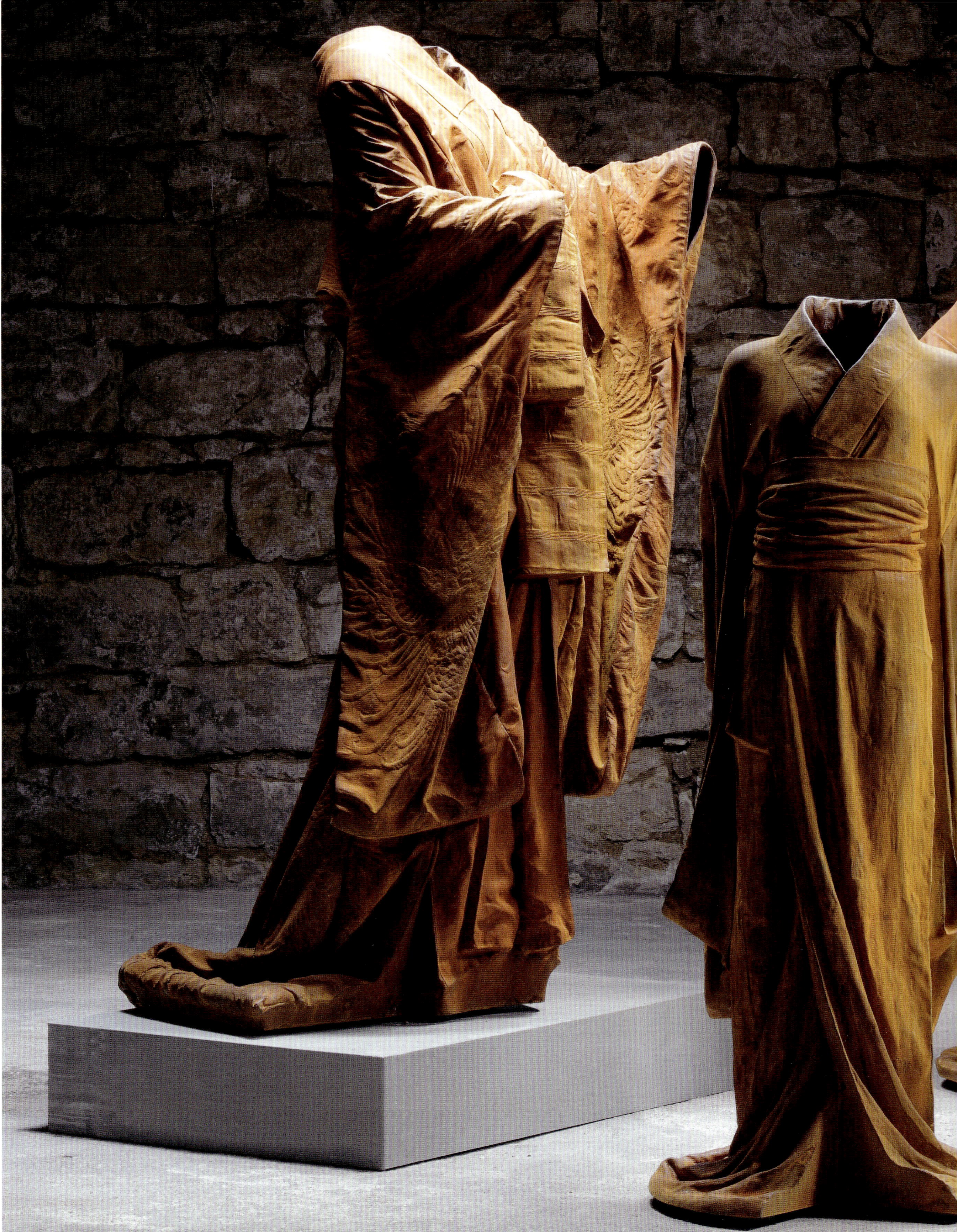

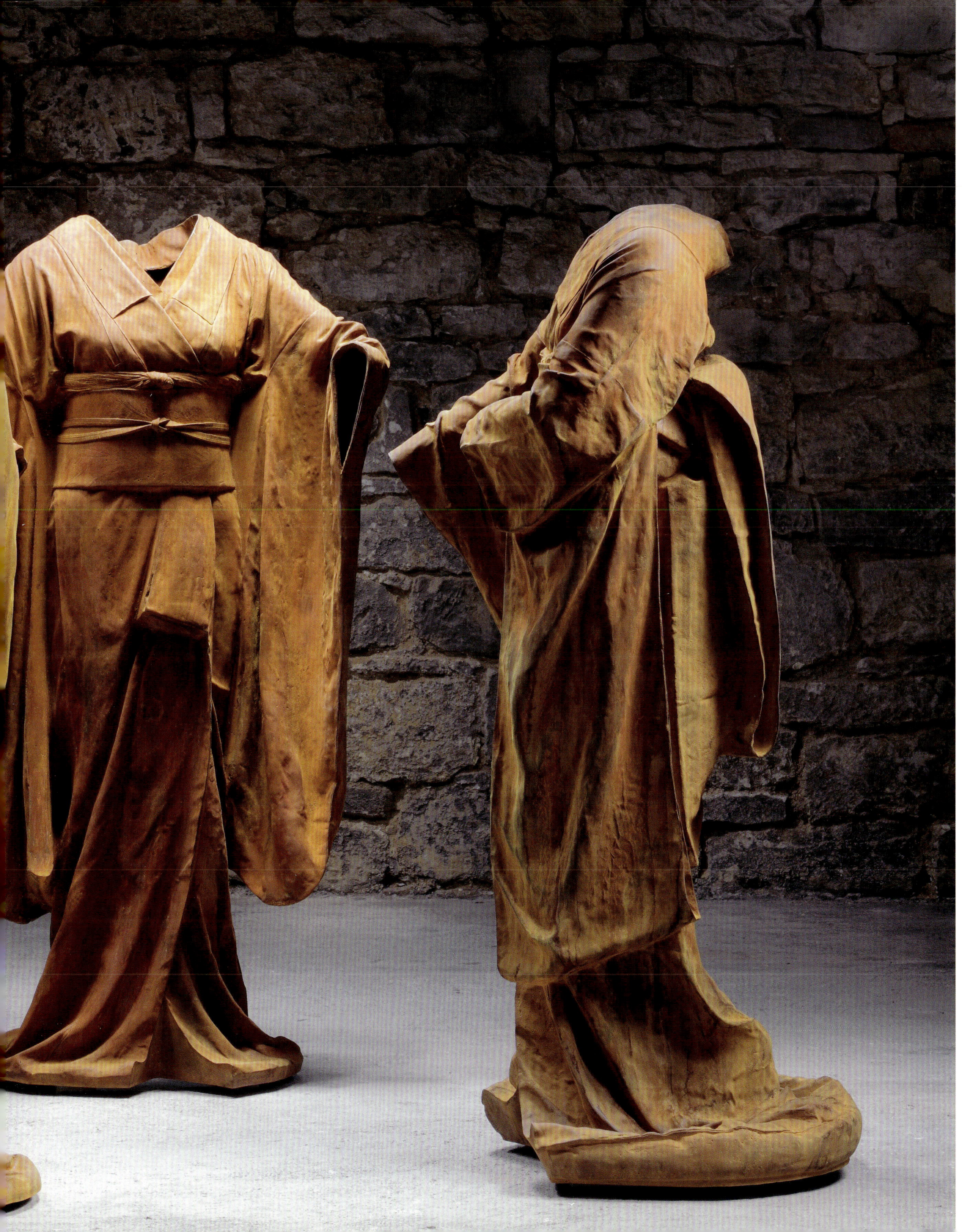

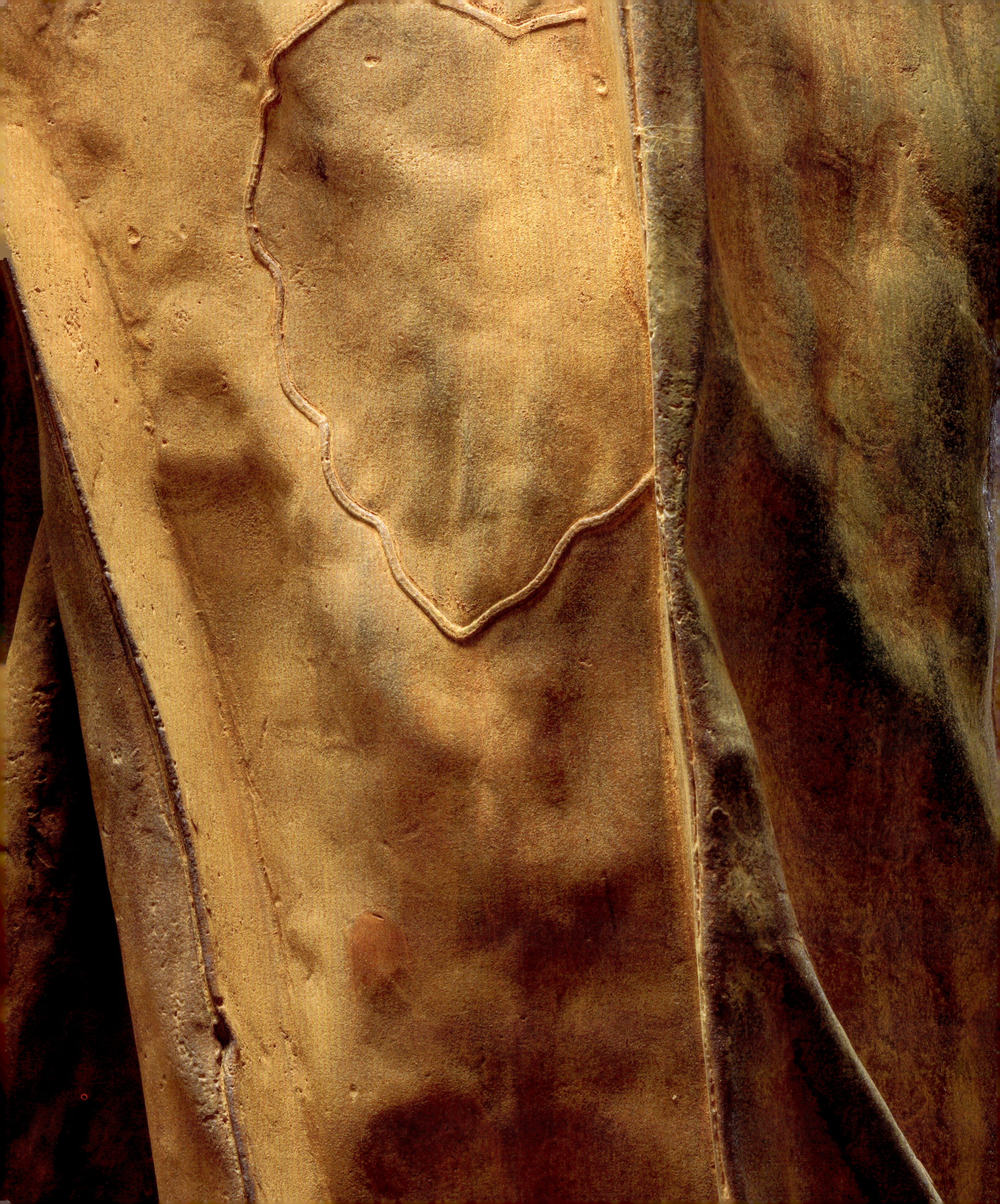

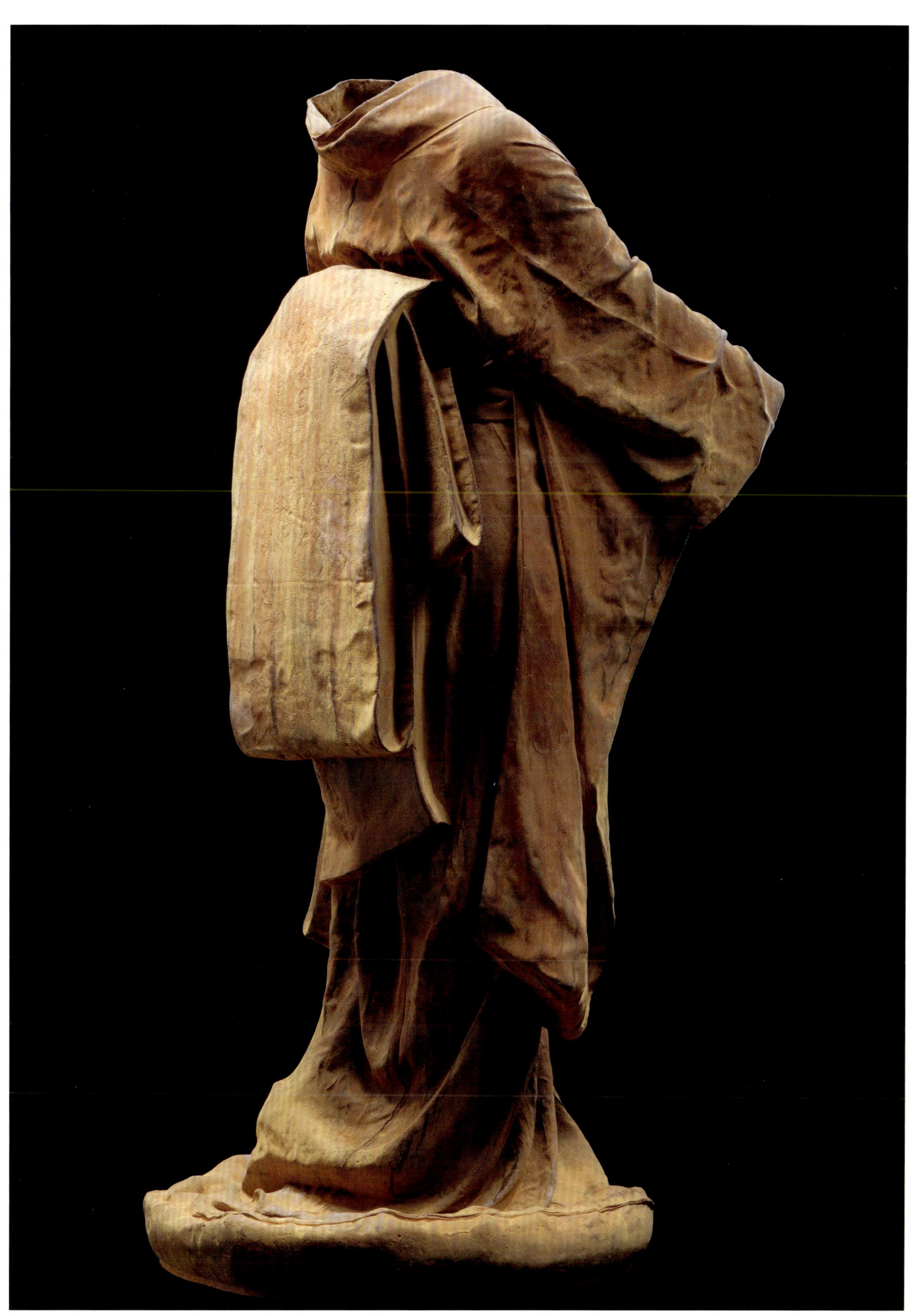

Bijin, 2012
Rusted iron,
53 × 21½ × 26½ in.
(134 × 55 × 67 cm)

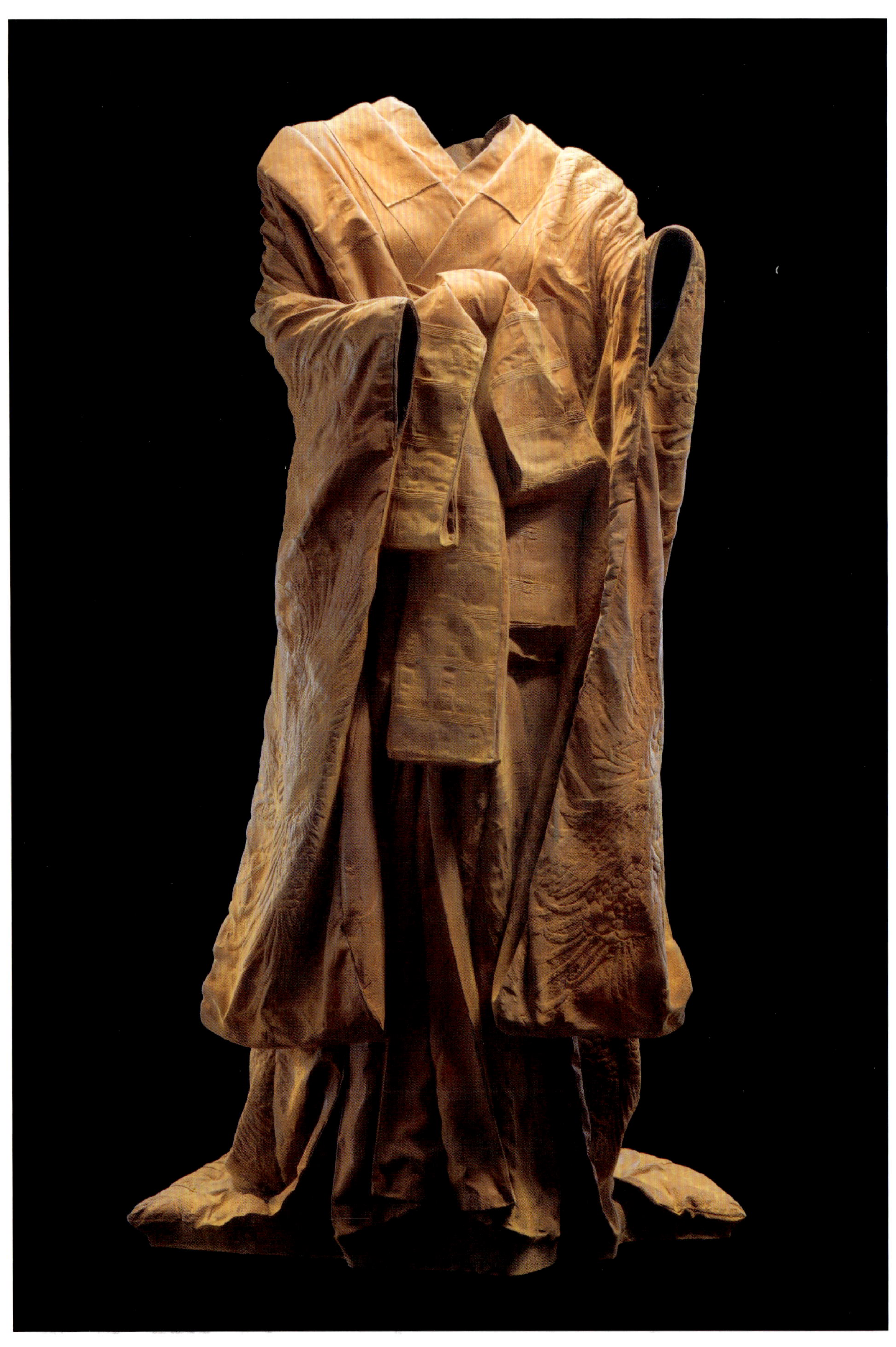

Kabuki, 2012
Rusted iron, 60 × 32 × 32½ in.
(152 × 81 × 83 cm)
Collection of Imagine Museum,
St. Petersburg, FL

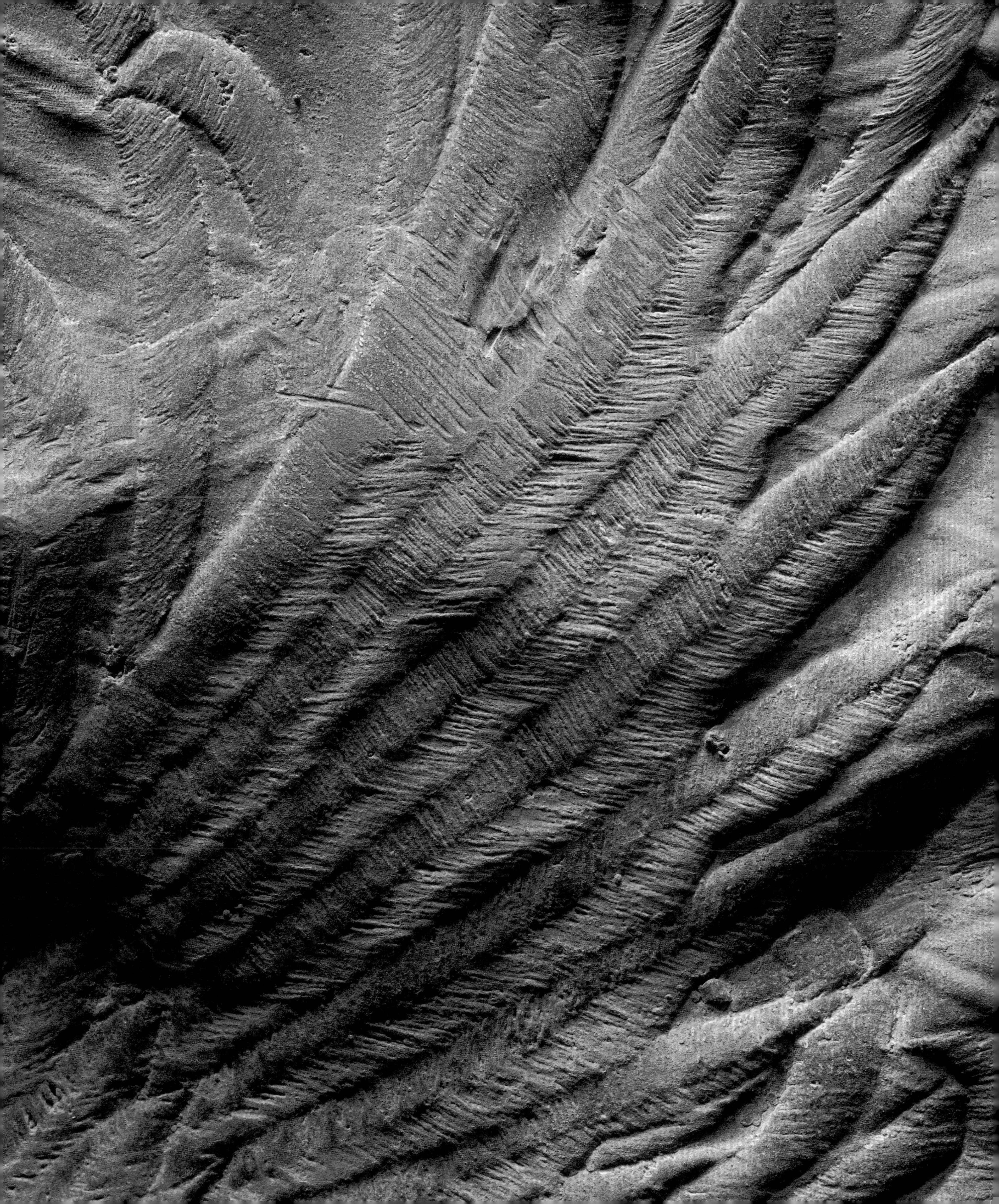

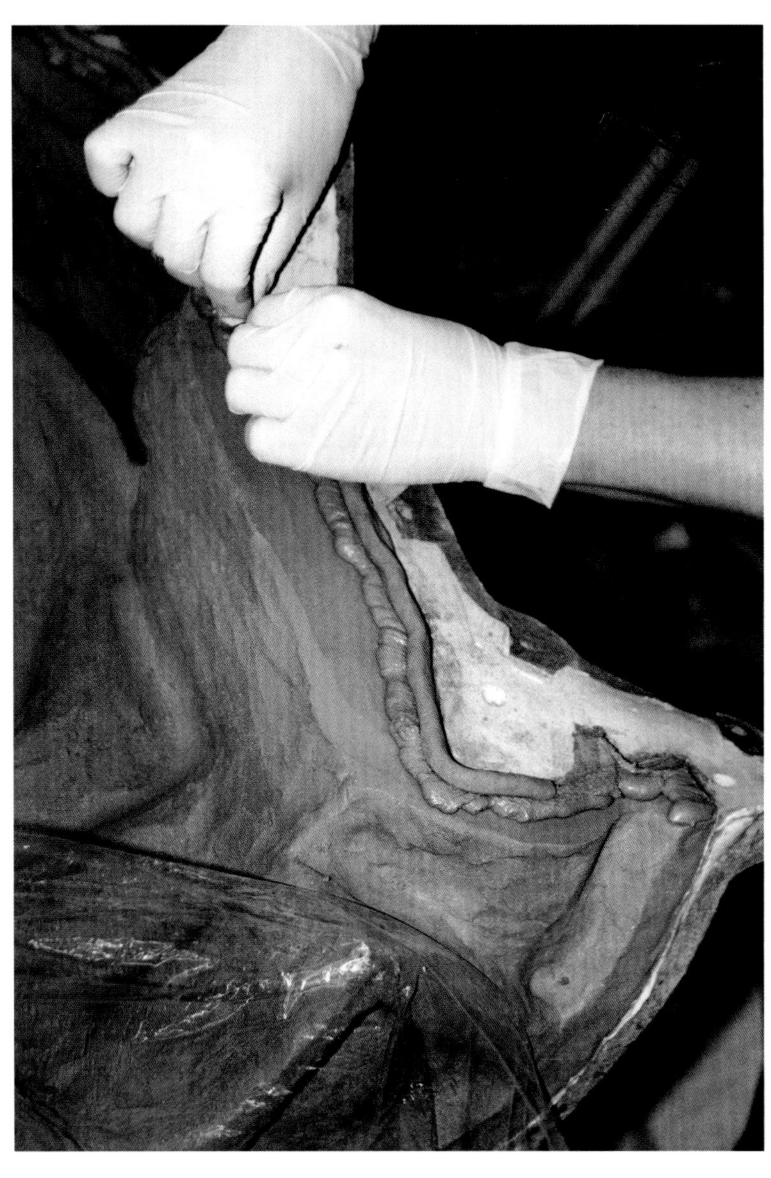

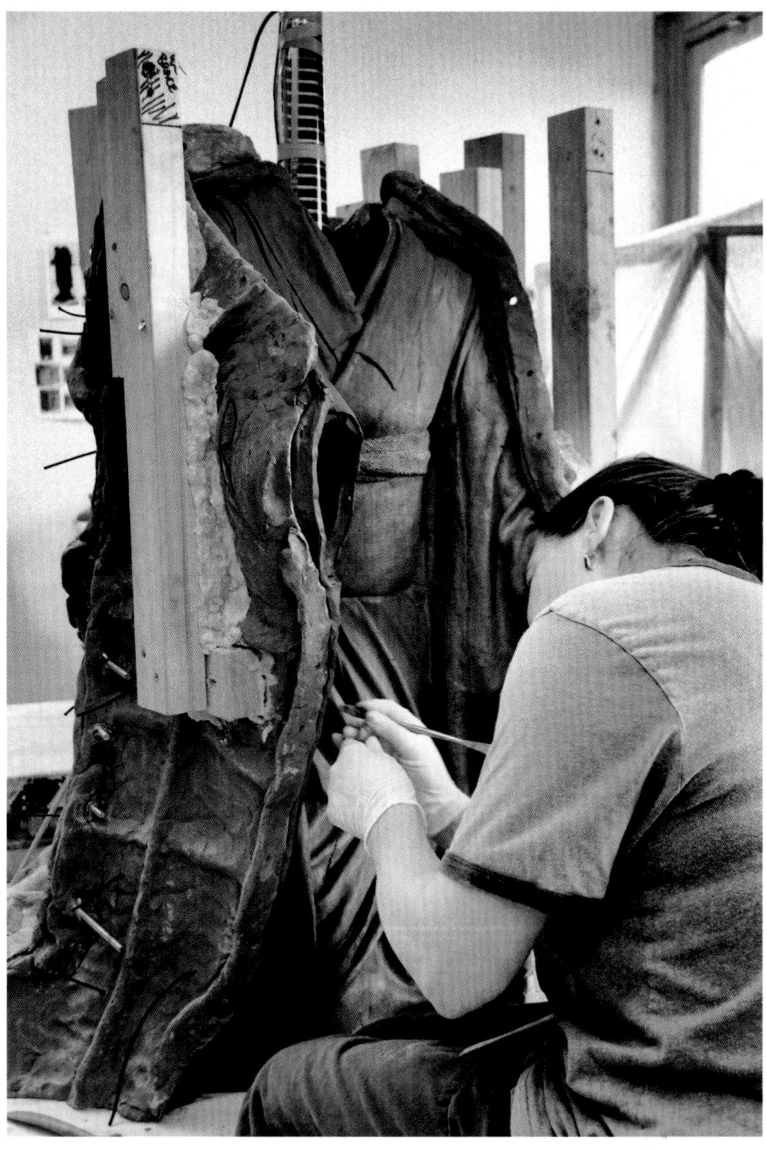

Sculpting in clay, 2010.

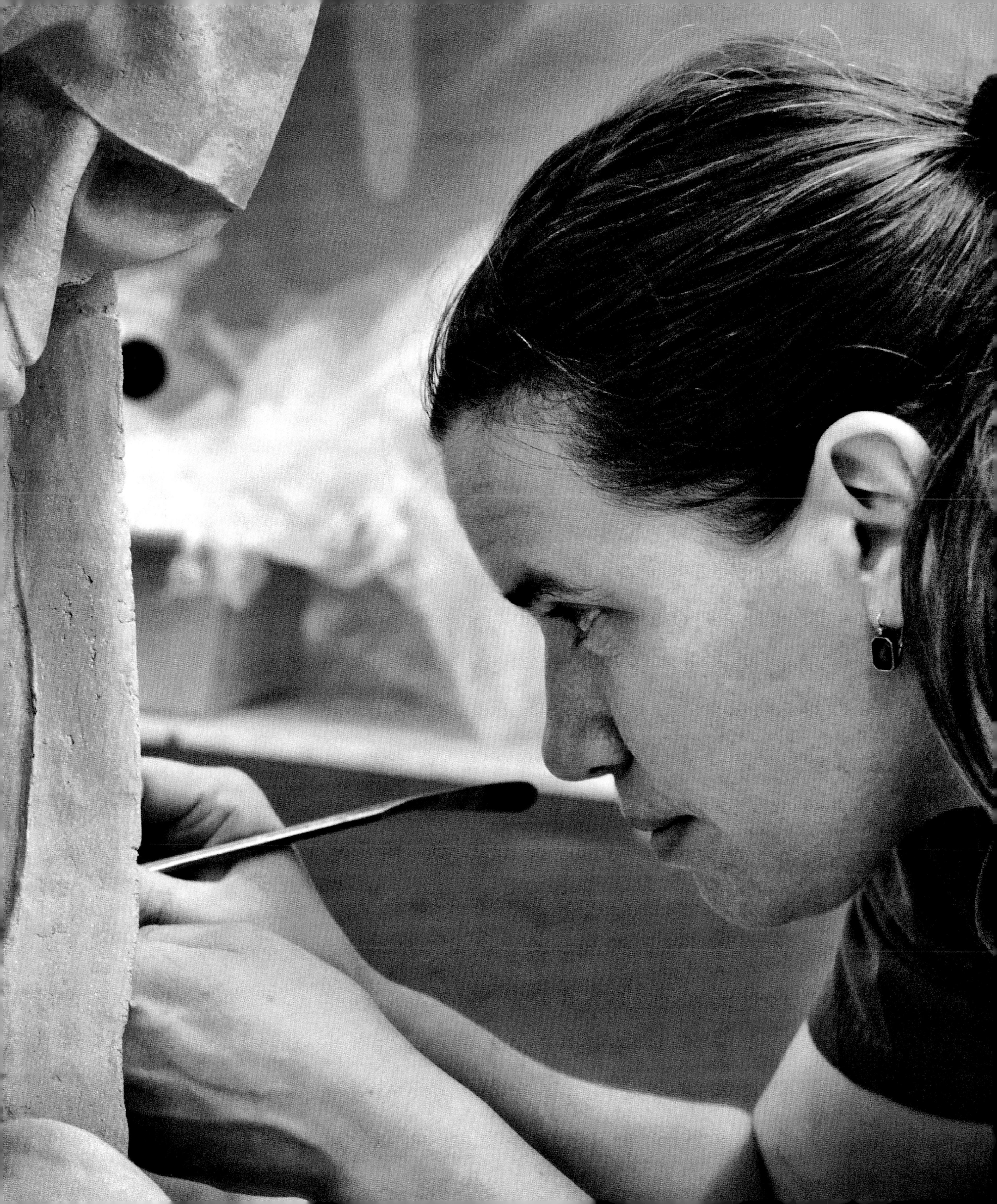

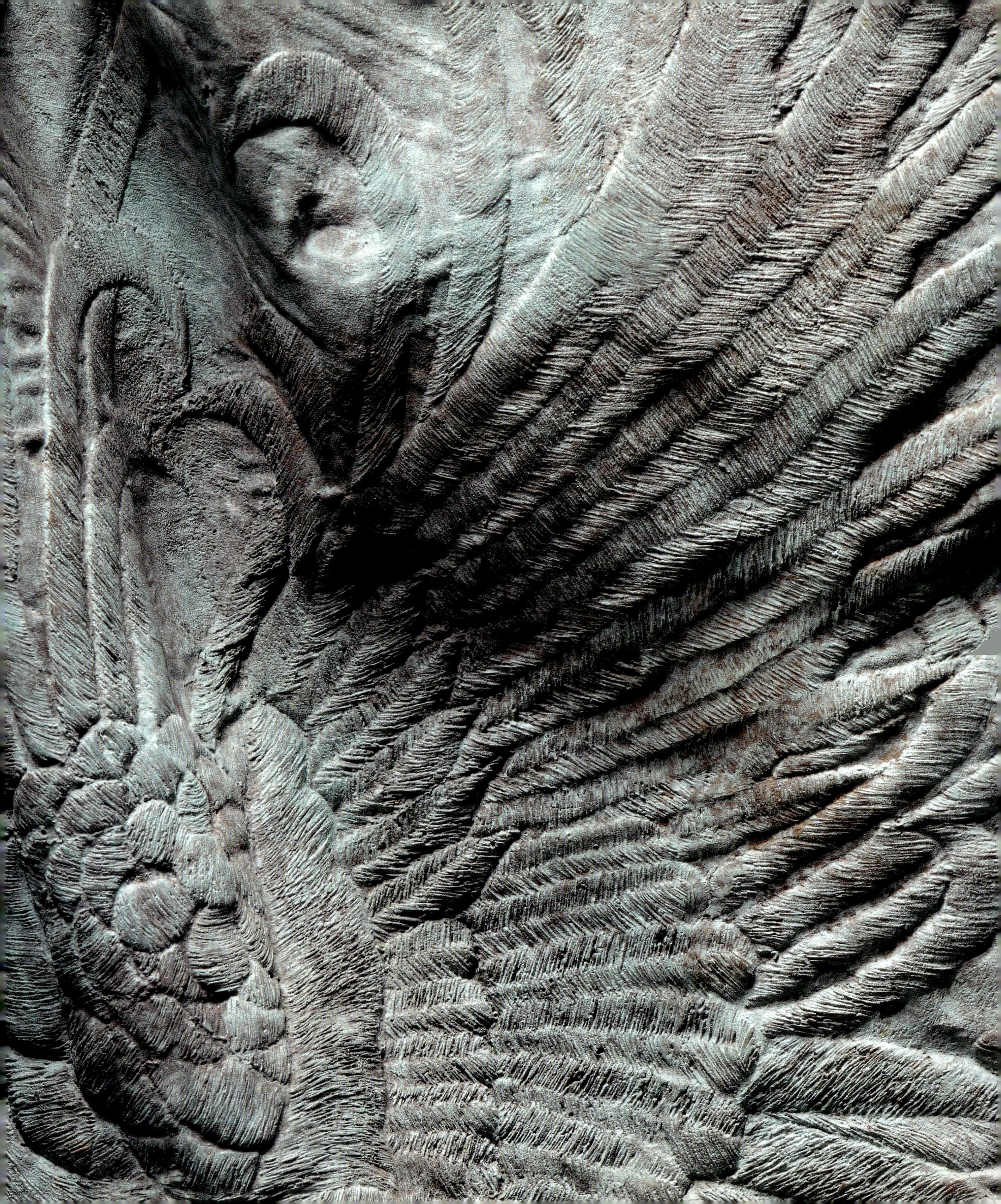

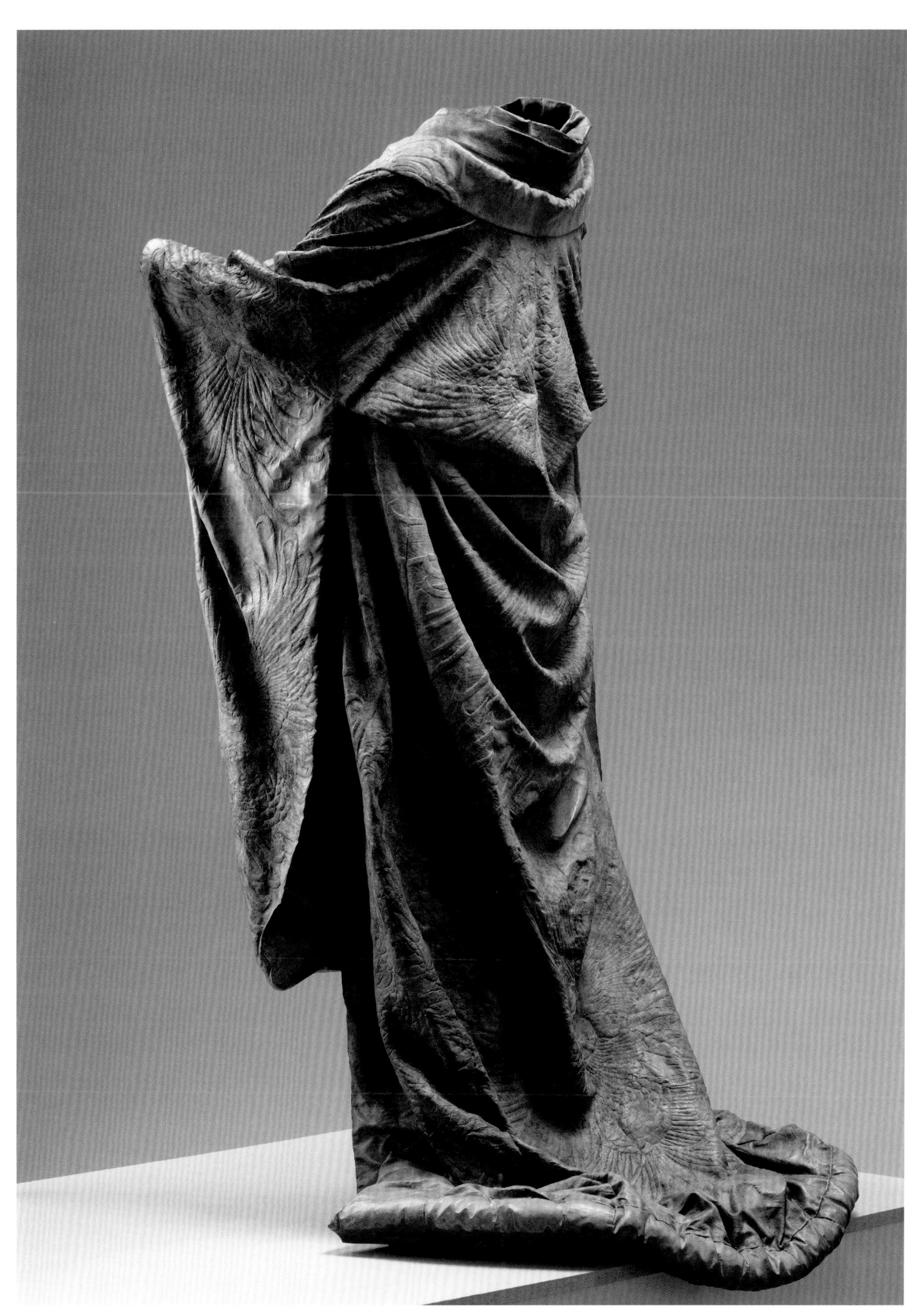

Kabuki, 2012
Bronze, 60 × 32 × 32½ in.
(152 × 81 × 83 cm)
Collection of Imagine
Museum, St. Petersburg, FL

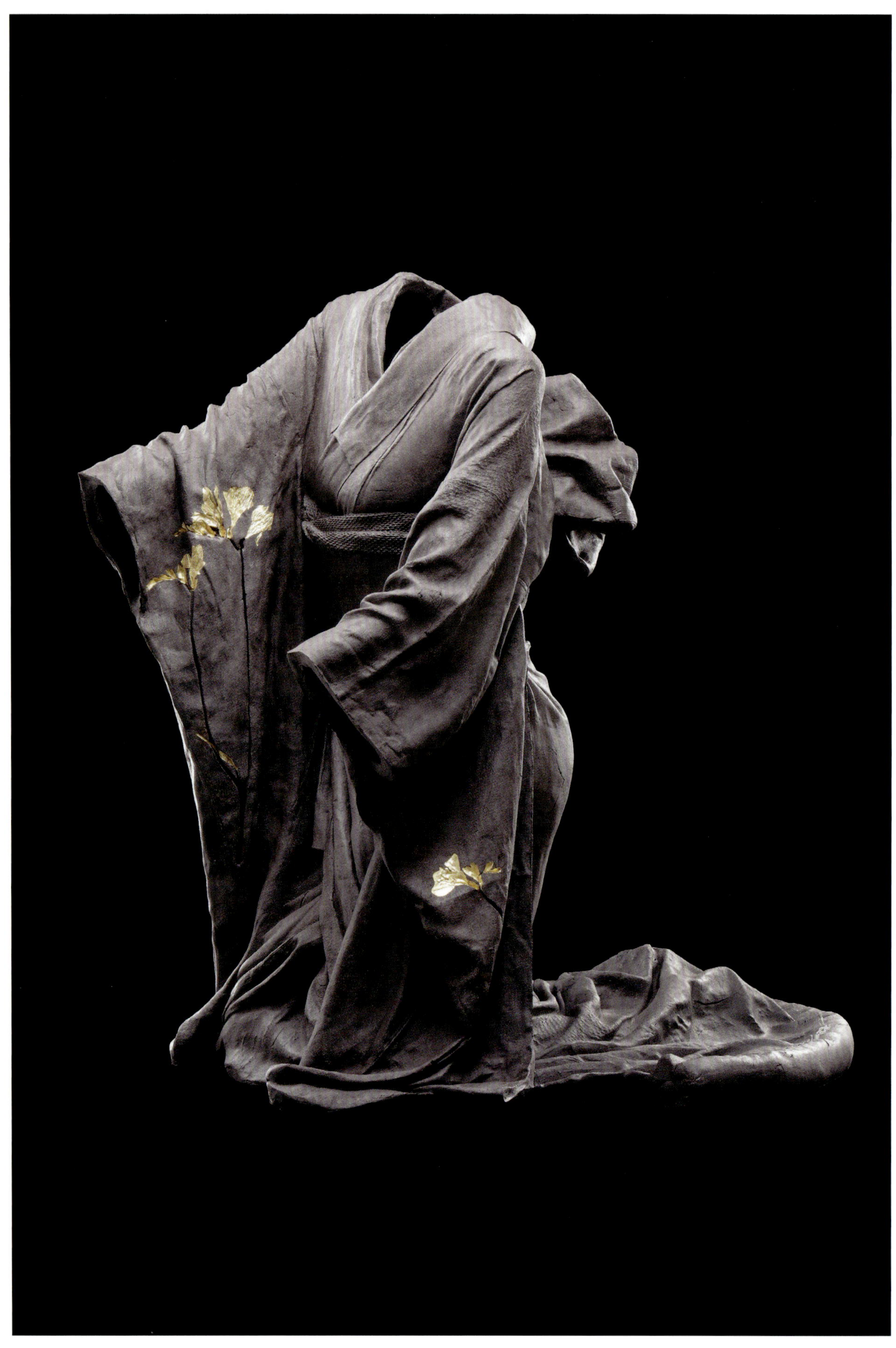

Chado, 2010
Ceramic, 39 × 33½ × 32½ in.
(99 × 85 × 82 cm)

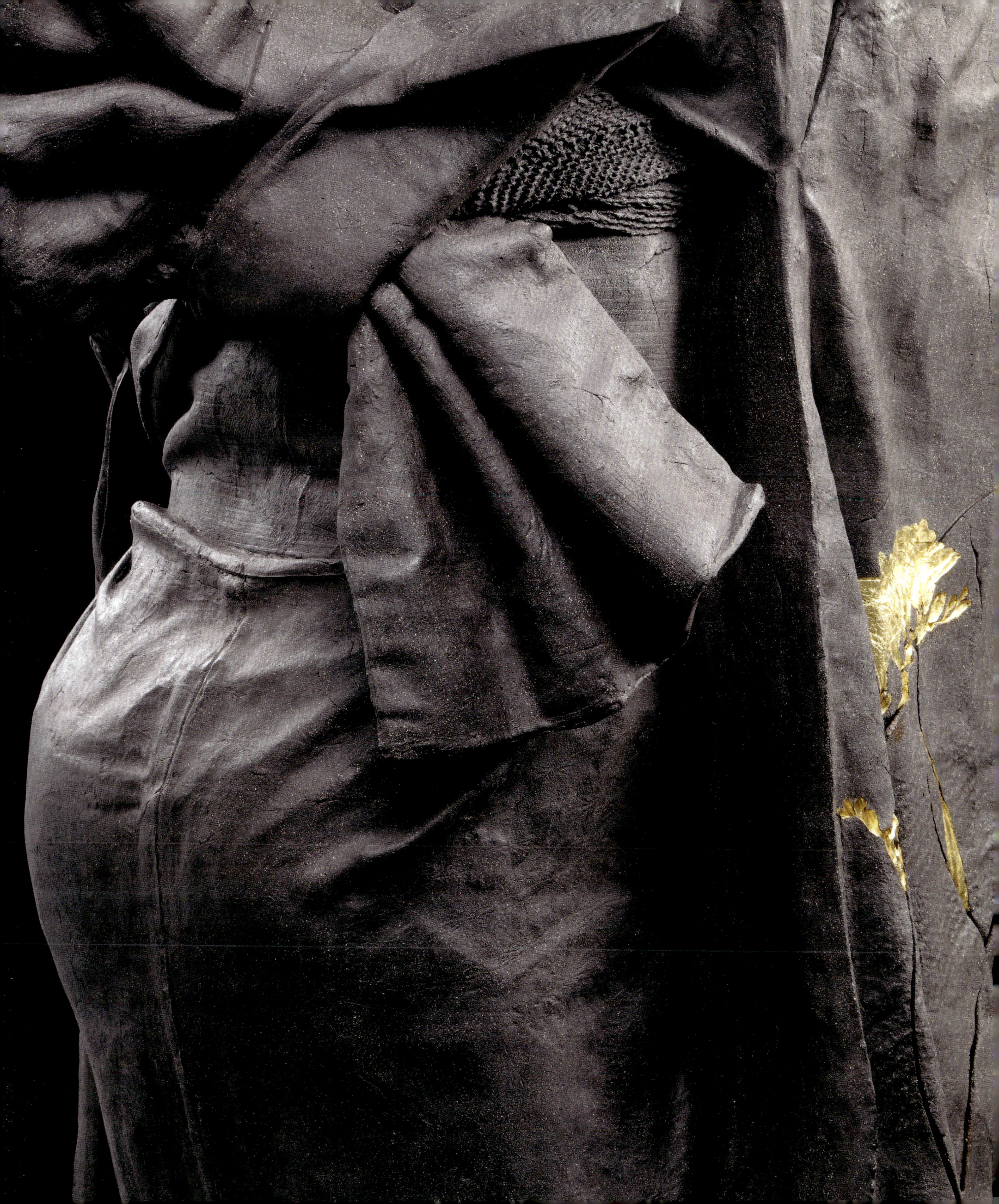

Odoriko, 2012
Bronze, 53½ × 30 × 17 in. (136.5 × 76 × 43.5 cm)
Collection of Chazen Museum of Art, Madison, WI

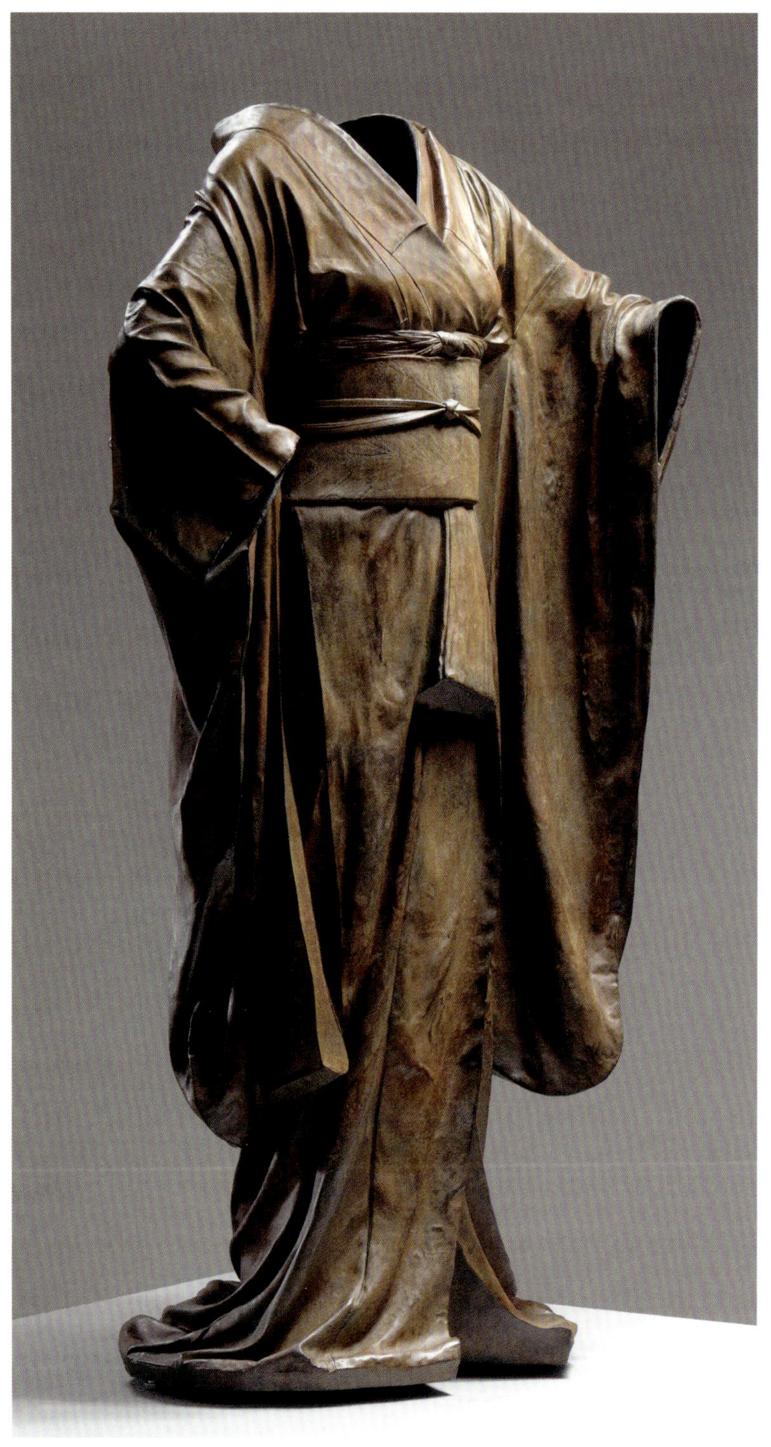

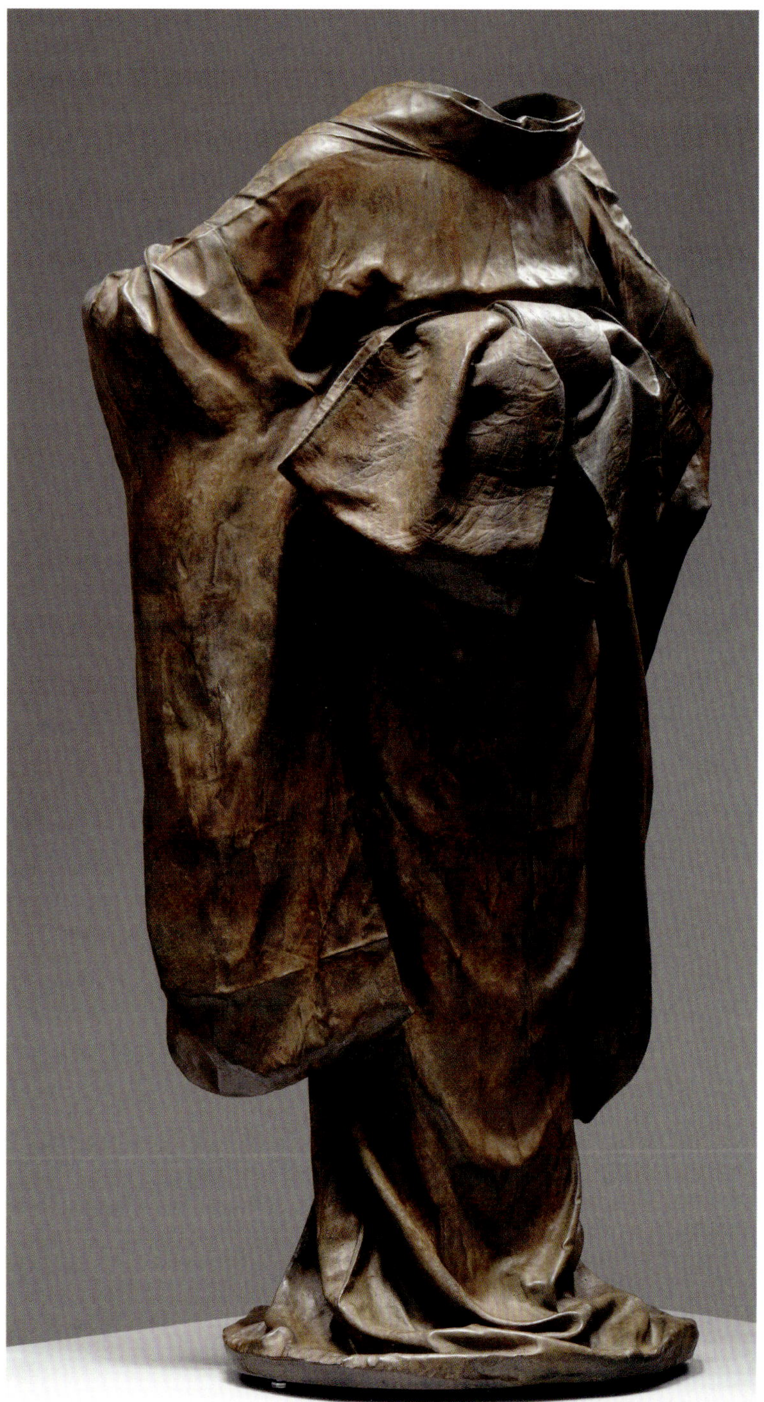

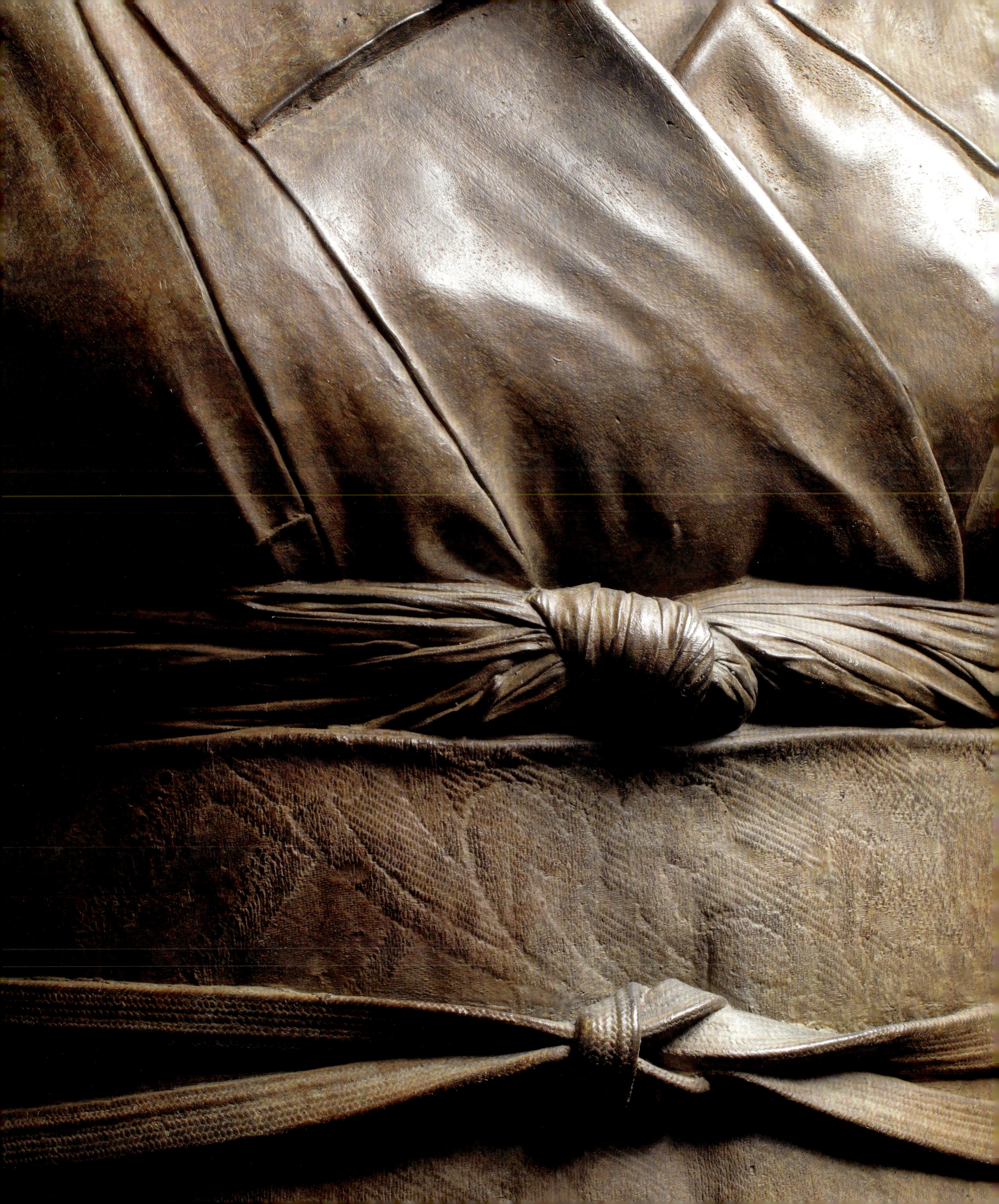

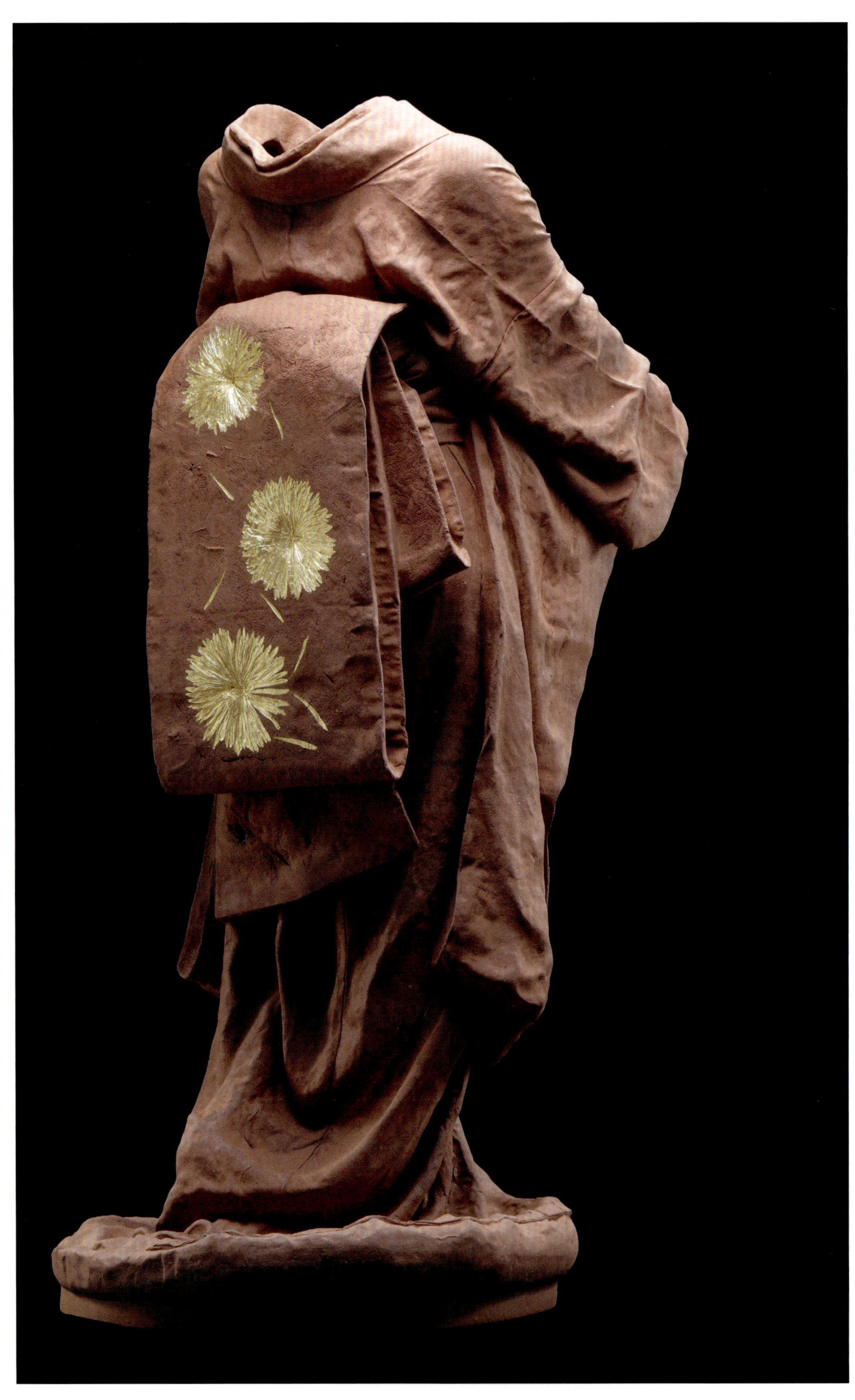

Bijin, 2011
Ceramic, 48½ × 19½ × 23½ in.
(123 × 50 × 60 cm)

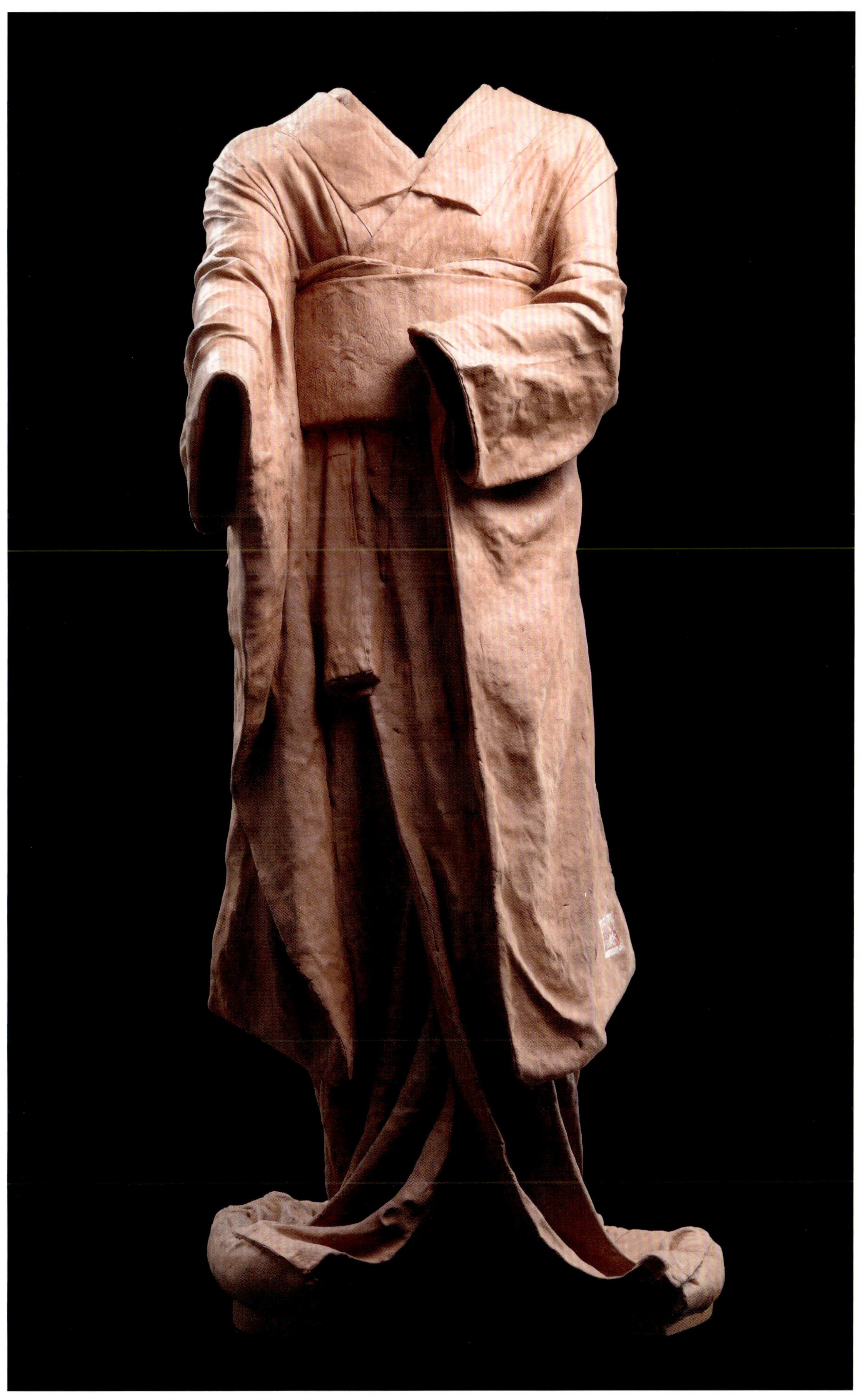

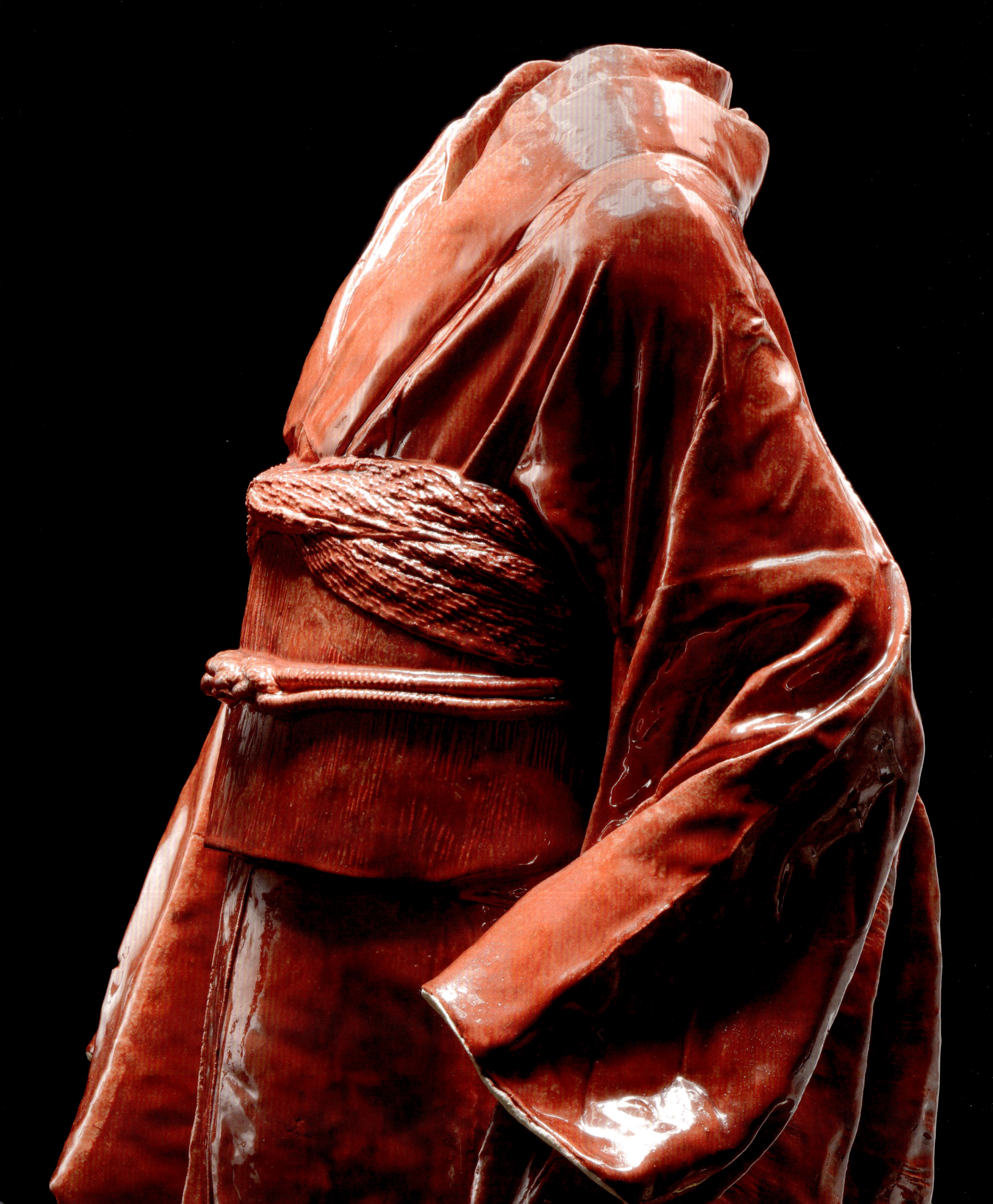

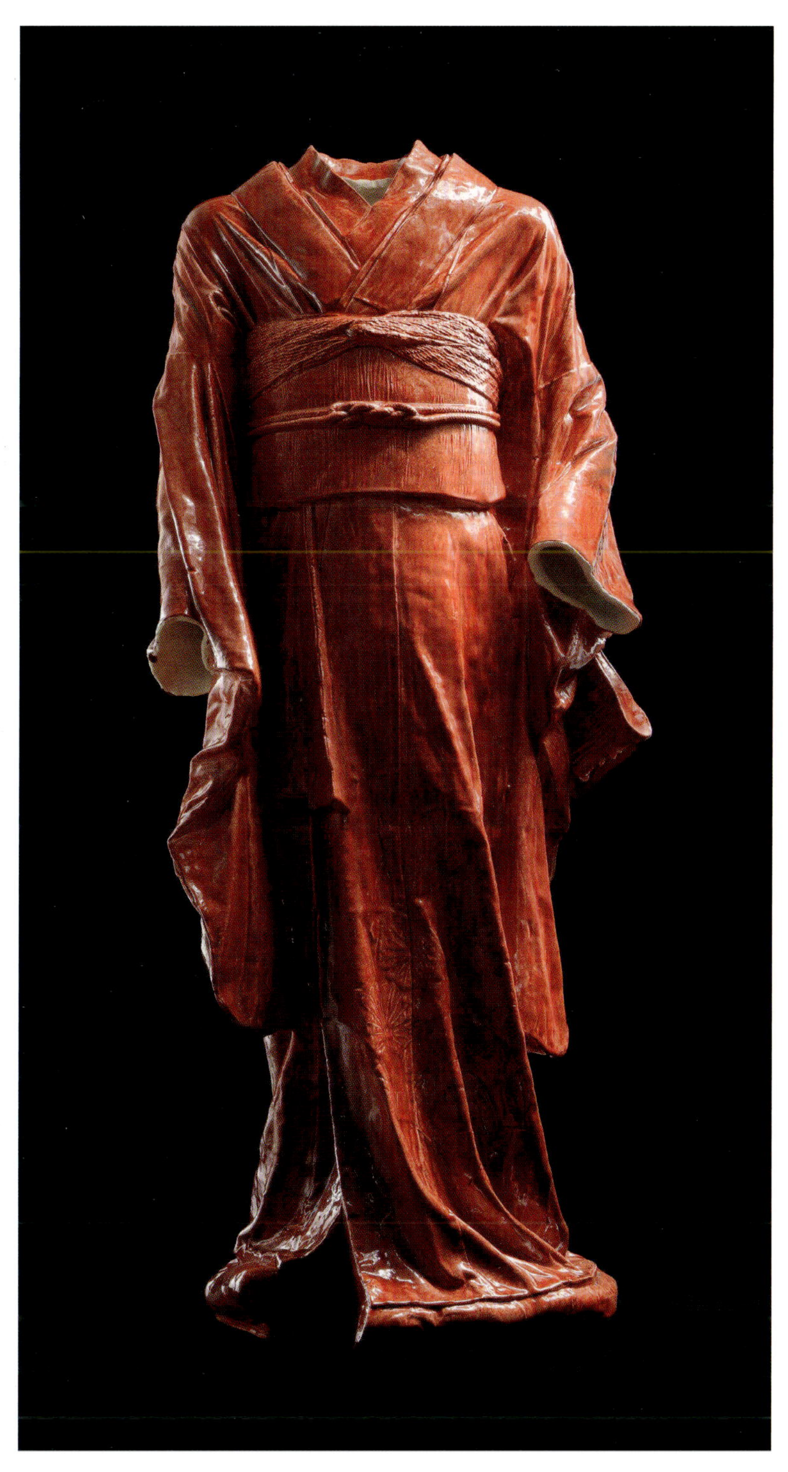
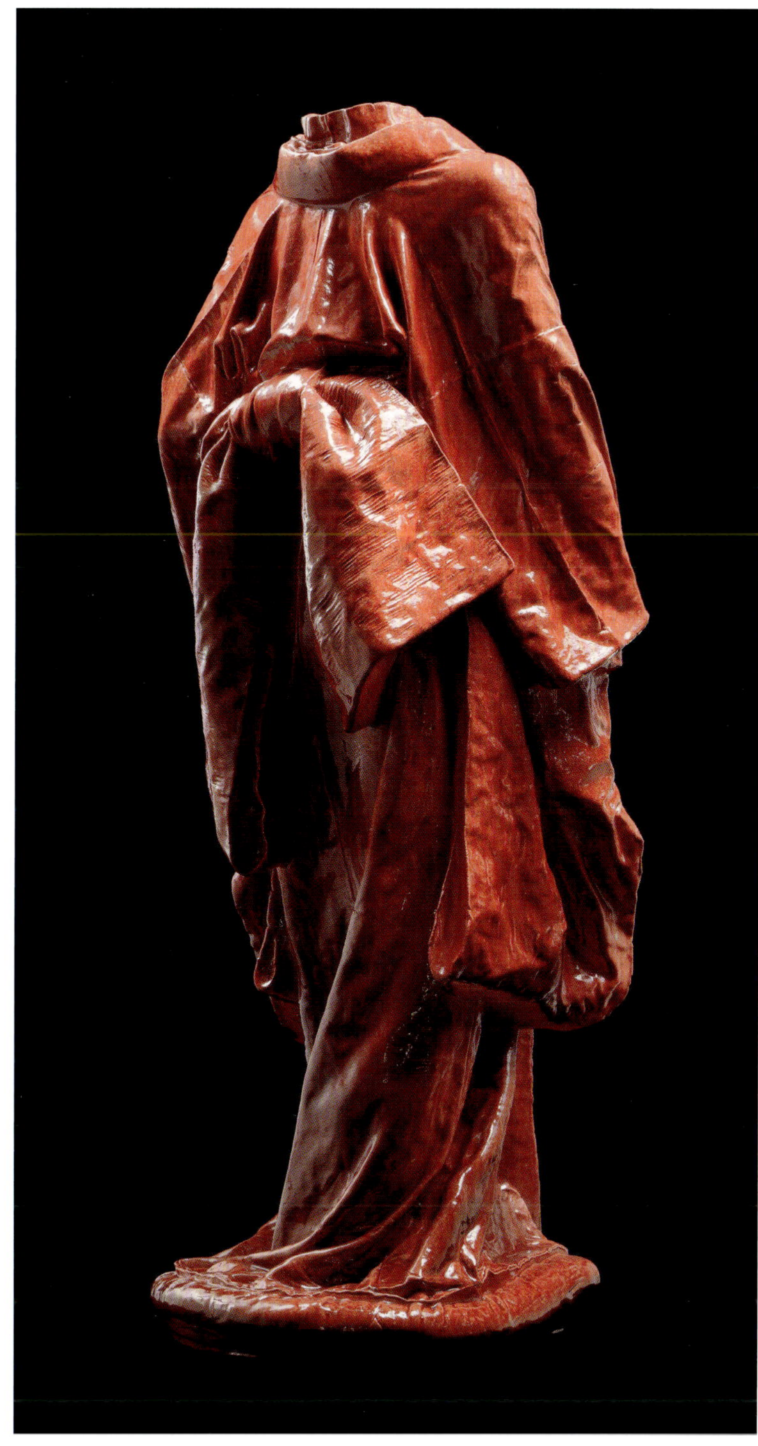

THIS AND FOLLOWING
Young Bijin, 2012
Ceramic, 42 × 17½ × 16 in.
(107 × 44 × 40 cm)

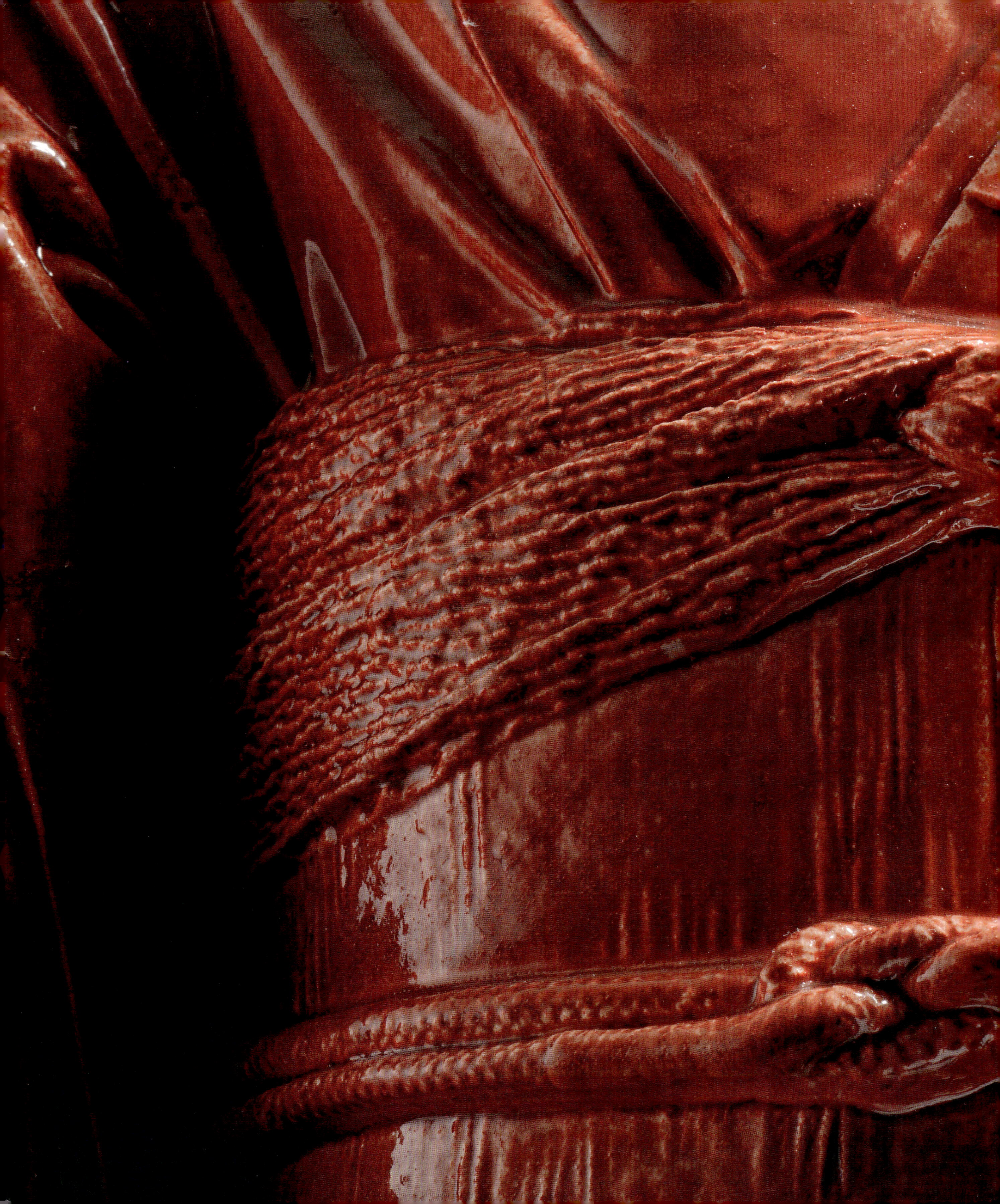

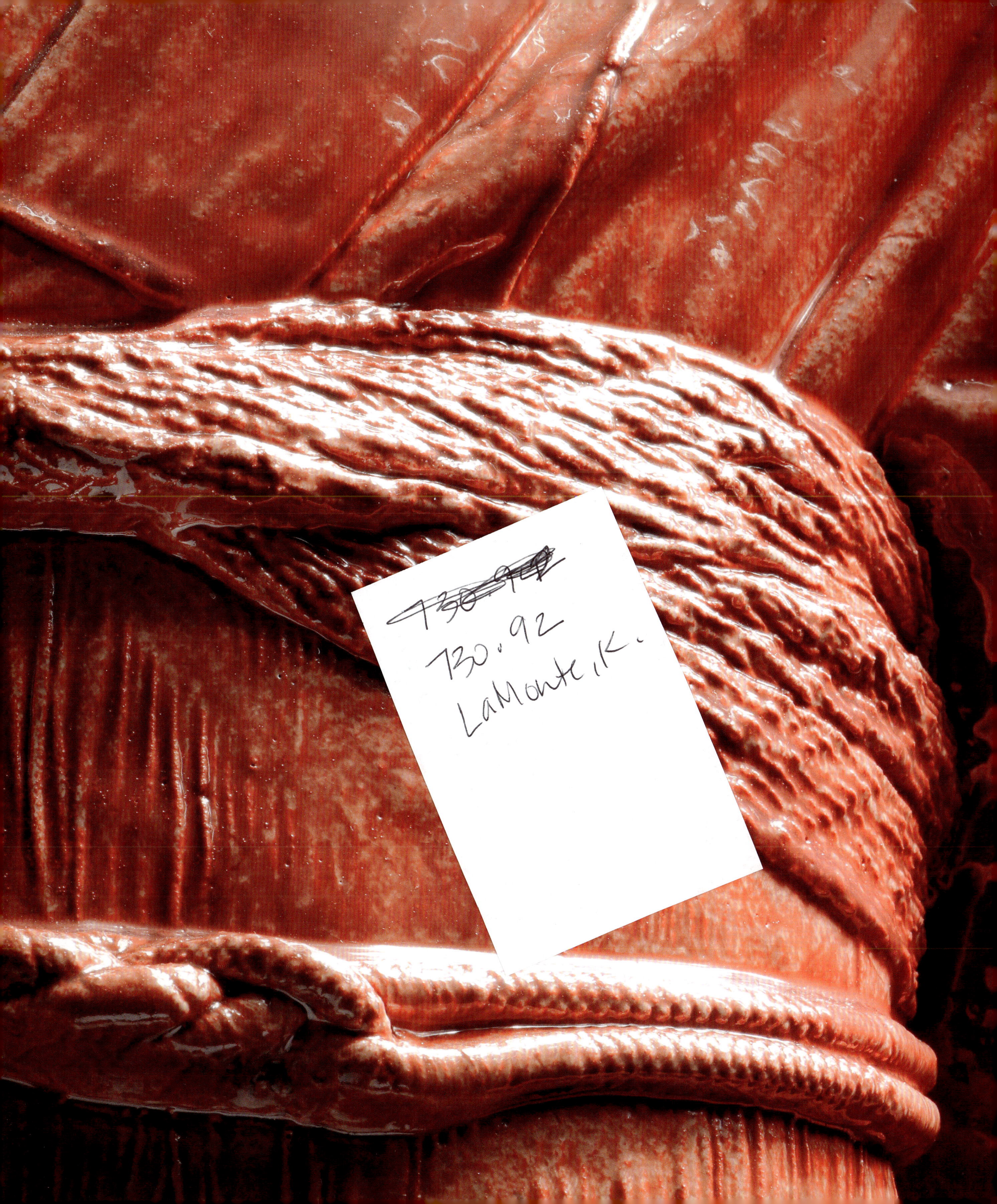

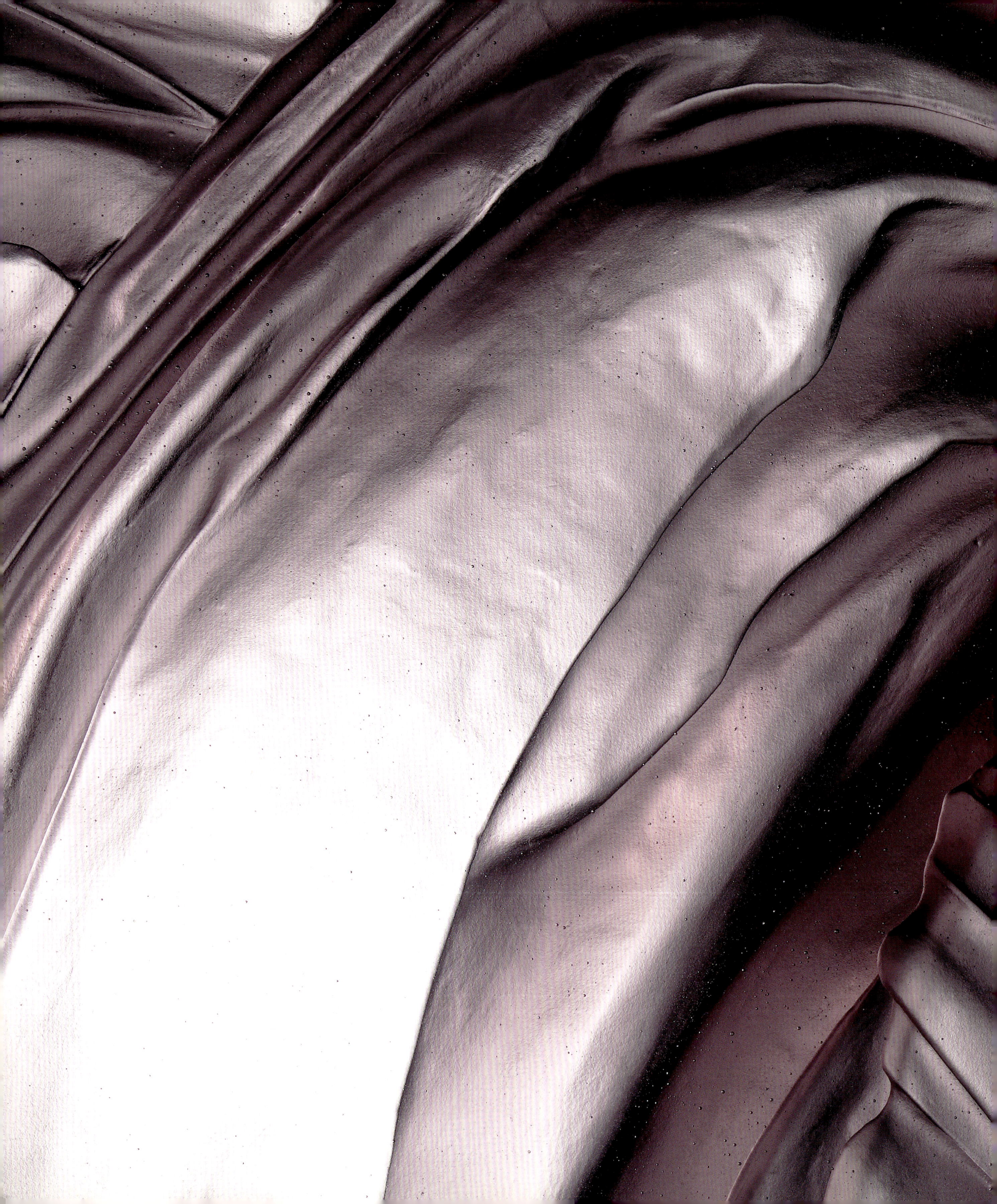

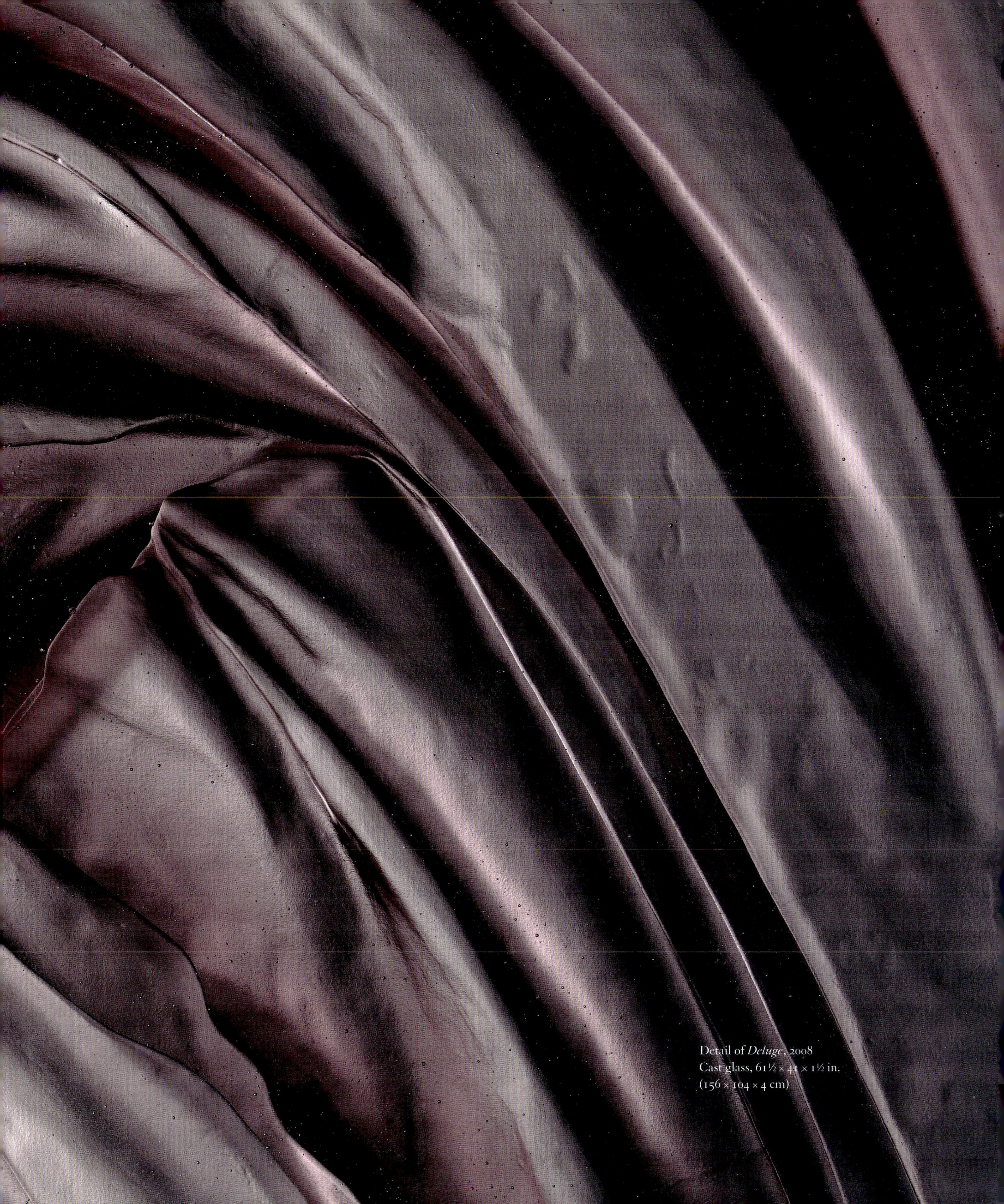

Detail of *Deluge*, 2008
Cast glass, 61½ × 41 × 1½ in.
(156 × 104 × 4 cm)

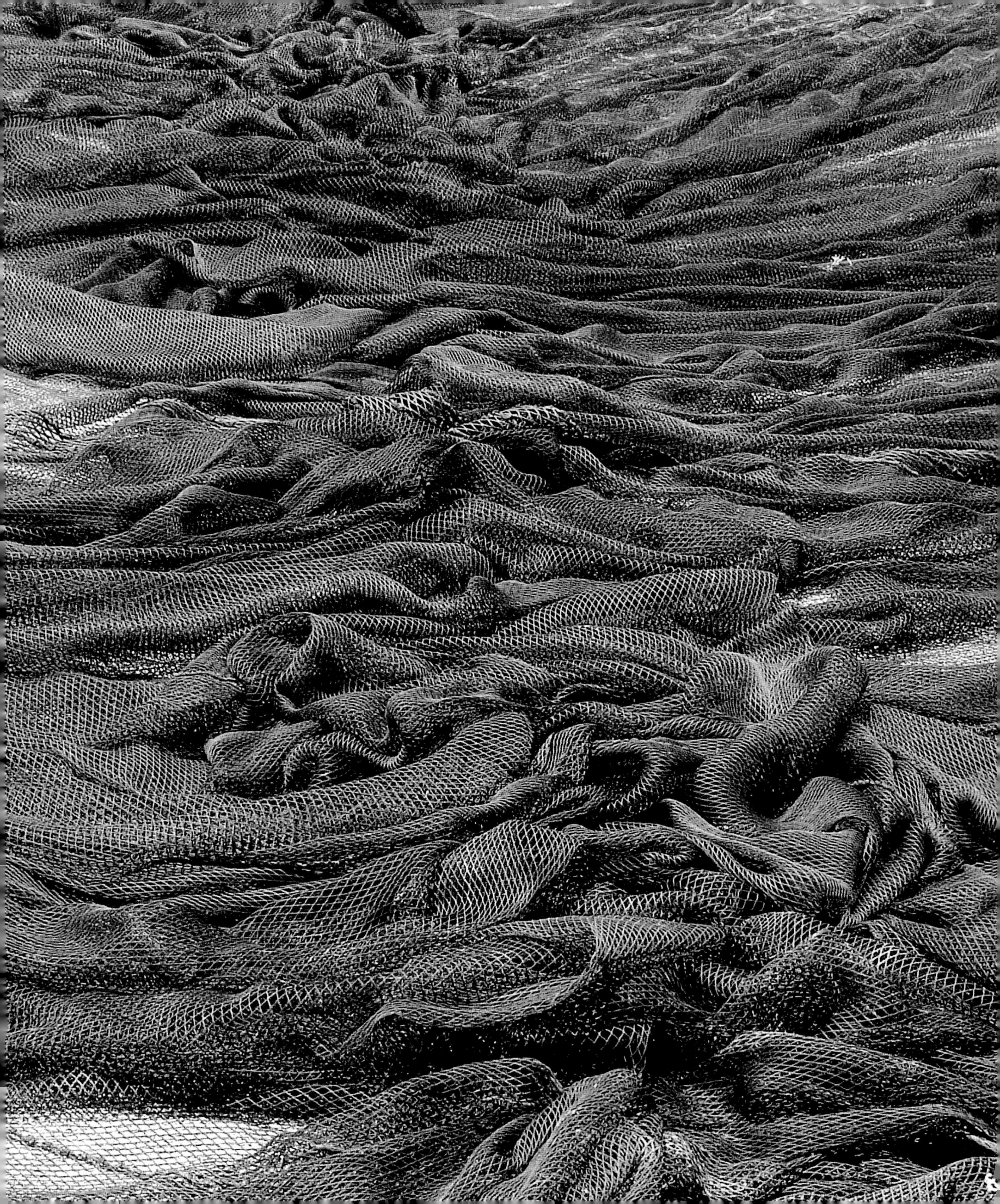

Charting the Iconography of Desire

Tina Oldknow

DRAPED BODIES

In her references to beauty, pleasure, loss, and identity, Karen LaMonte raises themes that have become a significant part of contemporary art discourse in a post-9/11 world. In an essay published in conjunction with the Hirshhorn Museum's 1999 exhibition *Regarding Beauty: A View of the Late Twentieth Century*, Olga Viso related that, "According to contemporary psychologist James Hillman, the demystification of nature through science and the contemporary awareness of the Earth's fragile, expiring ecology have made late 20th-century society immune to the world's complex magnificence. . . . The results of such a view, argues Hillman, have contributed to the 'repression' of beauty in our time. . . . In his view, [this] . . . has created a disinterested, narcissistic, self-referential culture that mistrusts beauty and the senses."[1] What is striking about this observation, to me, is that I can remember when it rang true. Now, I believe, there is a vast cultural shift toward the reclamation of this "magnificence" as the aftermath of loss (terrorism, war, and global warming) and scientific and technological discovery (the mapping of the genome).

Fishnets in Toyama, Japan, 2006.

Concepts of beauty and the sublime are central to LaMonte's work. She notes, "From beauty, I have become fascinated with the sublime. For me, the heart of the sublime is a sense of longing and desire. Unlike beauty, which we can control, the sublime defines a boundary between what we understand and that which lies beyond our power of reason. We are not in control of sublime experiences."[2]

LaMonte's notion of beauty as something symmetrical and physically harmonious—and thus representing "good" as opposed to "evil"—makes reference to the ancient Greek and Roman canons of beauty that are the foundations of Western art and culture. The investigation of the sublime, and its differentiation from beauty, was famously addressed by the philosopher Immanuel Kant in his *Critique of Judgment* (1790). The Kantian interpretation of the sublime, as something great, boundless, and distinct from beauty, became a cornerstone of nineteenth- and twentieth-century aesthetic theory. Given the entrenched suspicions about beauty and the "aura" of the object[3] in recent years, the reemergence of—and the reassertion of the credibility of—the sublime in art has profound implications.

JAPAN

In 2006, LaMonte was awarded a Creative Artists Exchange Fellowship from the Japan-U.S. Friendship Commission and the National Endowment for the Arts to study the kimono as an investigation into the Japanese use of clothing as social language. One day as she was exploring the coast near Toyama, she walked by mounds of fishing nets piled on a dock. Under her gaze, the nets transformed into a mountain landscape, and she was thunderstruck. "Immediately, it hit me," LaMonte remembers. "I had this realization, this discovery of the connection between drapery and landscape. I had to stop everything and work with the nets."

She began to move the tangle of nets around, shaping them, and extending the "landscape" from the dock into the adjacent parking lot. "It was like this wide road opened up for me out of nowhere," LaMonte says, "one that I could go down, that was unexplored." The gray mounds also made her think of *sumi-e* (ink-wash painting), a practice she was also studying at the time: the nets were like a physical, malleable version of ink. There were faint, openwork nets in some areas, and in other areas, the nets were piled up and dark, appearing solid. In their juxtapositions of dark and light, opaque and transparent, the nets behaved like ink and also like smoke.

When LaMonte went back to her studio, she started arranging her yards of kimono cloth on the floor. "I was thinking constantly about kimonos, and I was looking at the light and shadow of the massed fabric," she recalls. "I was thinking kimono, kimono, kimono, but it was really about the massing of fabric, color, light and shadow."

DRAPED EARTH

After her return to Prague, LaMonte continued making her figural sculpture while ruminating on how she might move away from it. For a reclining figure made in 2007,[4] LaMonte extended the drapery into a pool around the figure. This, for her, became a figure lying in a landscape. Then, she understood the profile of the figure to refer to landscape as well: "My two topographies of body and dress became joined in a third: the landscape. Where the human figure is an object of beauty, the landscape inspires the sublime."

In 2008, LaMonte formulated a strategy to work exclusively with drapery. In a series of cast glass bas-reliefs, she played with massing the drapery, as she had massed her fishing nets, creating contrasting areas of transparency and opacity that read as light and dark. In 2009, LaMonte

Emulating fishnets with kimono silk, Kyoto, Japan, 2006.

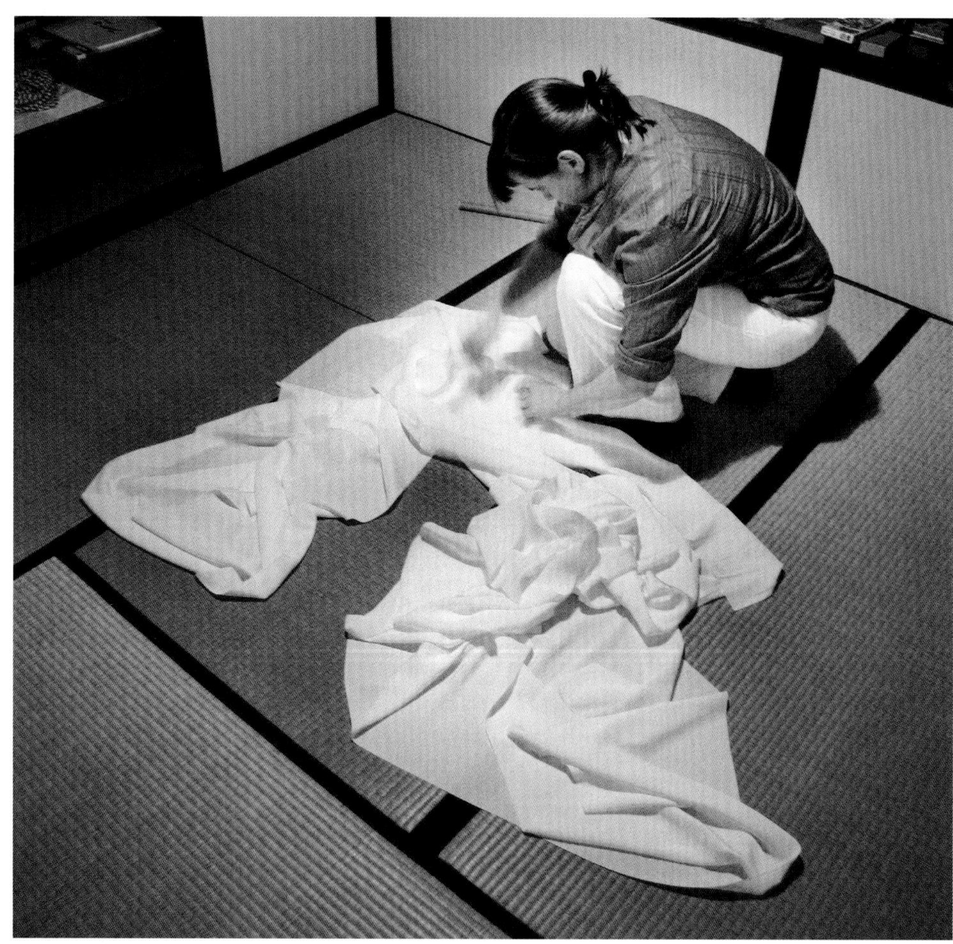

Casting vitreous china at the Kohler factory, Kohler, WI, 2009.

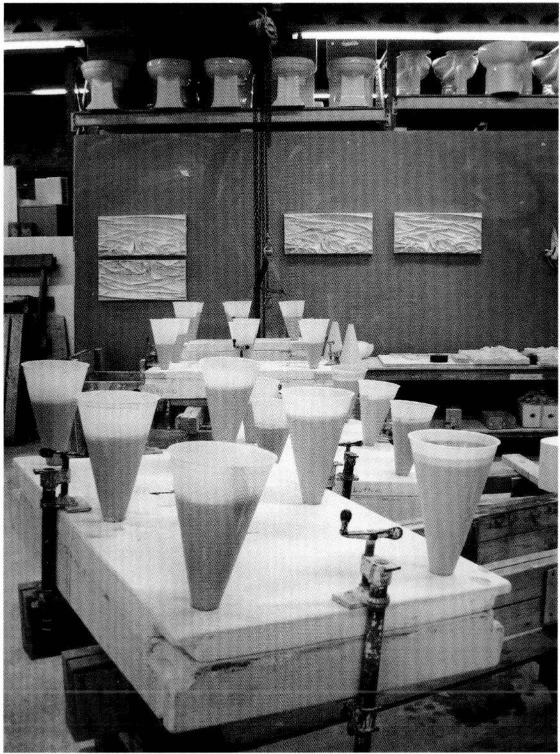

received a Corning Museum of Glass/John Michael Kohler Arts Center joint residency for working with ceramic and glass.[5] The residency began at the Kohler factory in Wisconsin, where LaMonte explored her drapery studies in ceramic. "In thinking about the landscape, I was inspired to work with ceramic—a literal draping of the earth," she notes. "In contrast to my sculptures in glass, which are about opacity and transparency, with ceramic, I am exploring light and shadow."

In Victorian symbolism, the draped object refers to sorrow, loss, and mourning, and LaMonte recognizes these themes, as well as those of impermanence and longing, in her work. It is the tension between beauty, representing love, safety, good, and immortality, and the fearful awareness of the destructive forces of nature, time, and mortality that results in the frisson of the sublime.

"Folds of fabric rendered in marble speak of beauty and loss, yet fabric can be as sumptuous and provocative as human flesh," says LaMonte. "In exploring the expressive potential of fabric, I see sensuality. The attraction of draped flesh, draped earth, alludes to this seductive quality of nature." In LaMonte's view, perhaps, it is our yearning to perceive the magnificence of nature as well as the mystery and beauty of the body—and to find a meaningful connection between the two—that will be our ultimate consolation. In her work, the notions of beauty and the sublime speak to the same concern, which is charting the iconography of desire.[6]

NOTES

1 Olga Viso, in Neal Benezra et al., *Regarding Beauty: A View of the Late Twentieth Century* (Washington, DC: Hirshhorn Museum & Sculpture Garden in association with Hatje Kantz Publishers, 1999), 119.

2 All quotes by Karen LaMonte are taken from Karen LaMonte, "Meet the Artist: Karen LaMonte" (lecture, Corning Museum of Glass, Corning, NY, February 28, 2008); conversations with the author in November 2009 and June 2010; and Karen LaMonte (lecture, New Mexico Museum of Art, Santa Fe, NM, July 8, 2010).

3 This refers to Walter Benjamin's essay "The Work of Art in the Age of Mechanical Reproduction," in which his theory of the effect of mechanical reproduction on the traditional art object turns on the issue of authenticity, because, he argues, only the authentic object (and not a secondary copy) can work the magical, healing effects of the original, cult object. This unique power Benjamin calls "aura," arguing that "what withers in the age of mechanical reproduction is the aura of the work of art." Rosalind Krauss, "Objet petit a," in *Part Object Part Sculpture*, ed. Helen Molesworth (Columbus, OH: The Wexner Center for the Arts, Ohio State University; and University Park, PA: Pennsylvania State University Press, 2006), 88–89.

4 Karen LaMonte (b. 1967, New York), *Reclining Dress Impression with Drapery*, 2007, glass, 19 x 61 x 22 1/2 in., Smithsonian American Art Museum, Gift of the James Renwick Alliance and Colleen and John Kotelly, 2009.24.

5 This residency is part of the Arts/Industry Program at Kohler, a leading American manufacturer of kitchen and bath fixtures. In its factory, artists are invited to utilize slip-cast ceramic and ironworking facilities. The Corning Museum of Glass residency is one of several residencies offered each year in glass.

6 Dave Hickey, *The Invisible Dragon: Four Essays on Beauty* (Los Angeles: Art Issues Press, 1993), 12. Hickey stumbled onto the topic of beauty when replying to a question at a seminar. Stating that beauty would be the issue of the 1990s in contemporary art, he concluded his remarks by saying, "I direct your attention to the language of visual affect—to the rhetoric of how things look—to the iconography of desire—in a word, to *beauty*!"

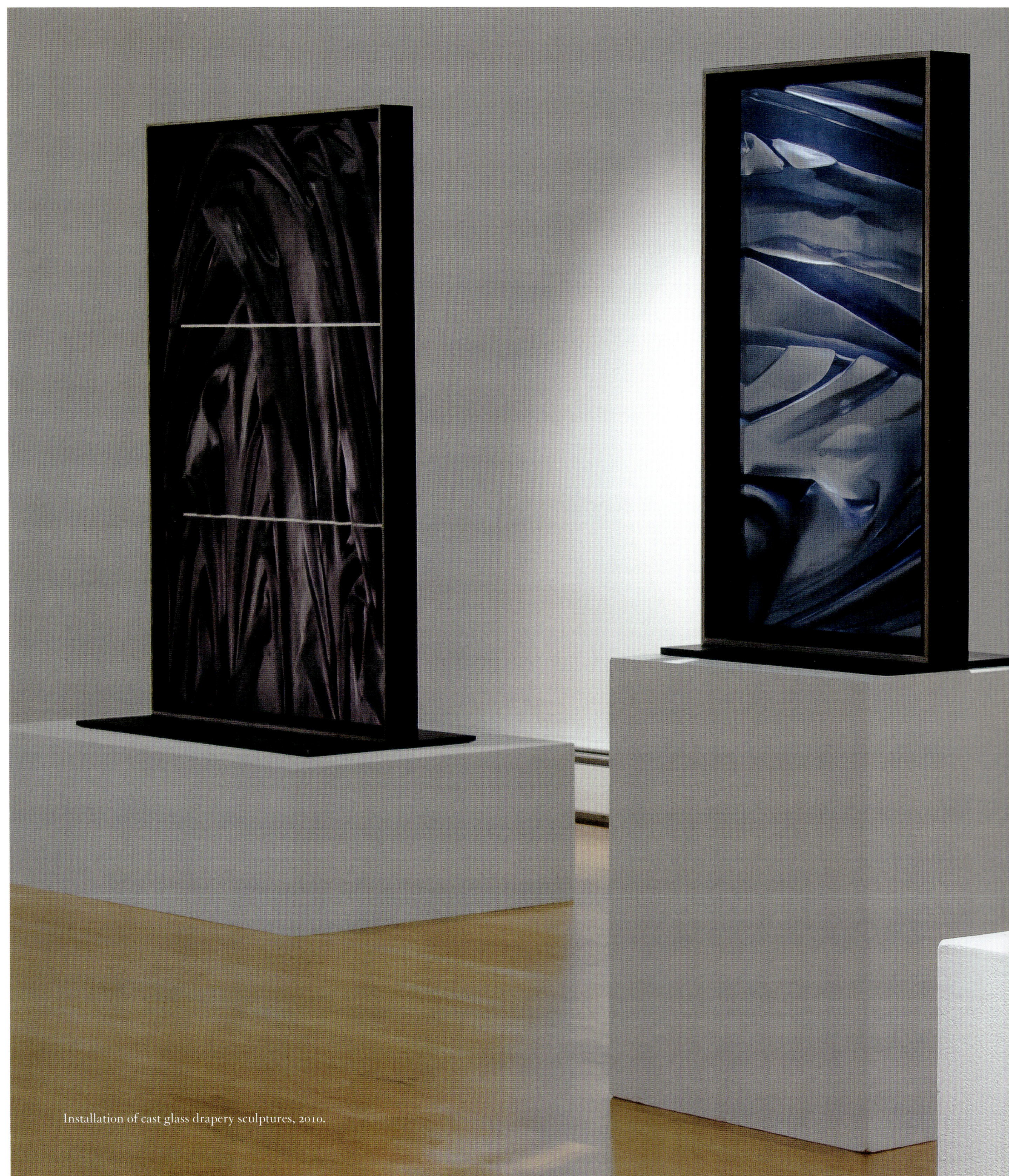

Installation of cast glass drapery sculptures, 2010.

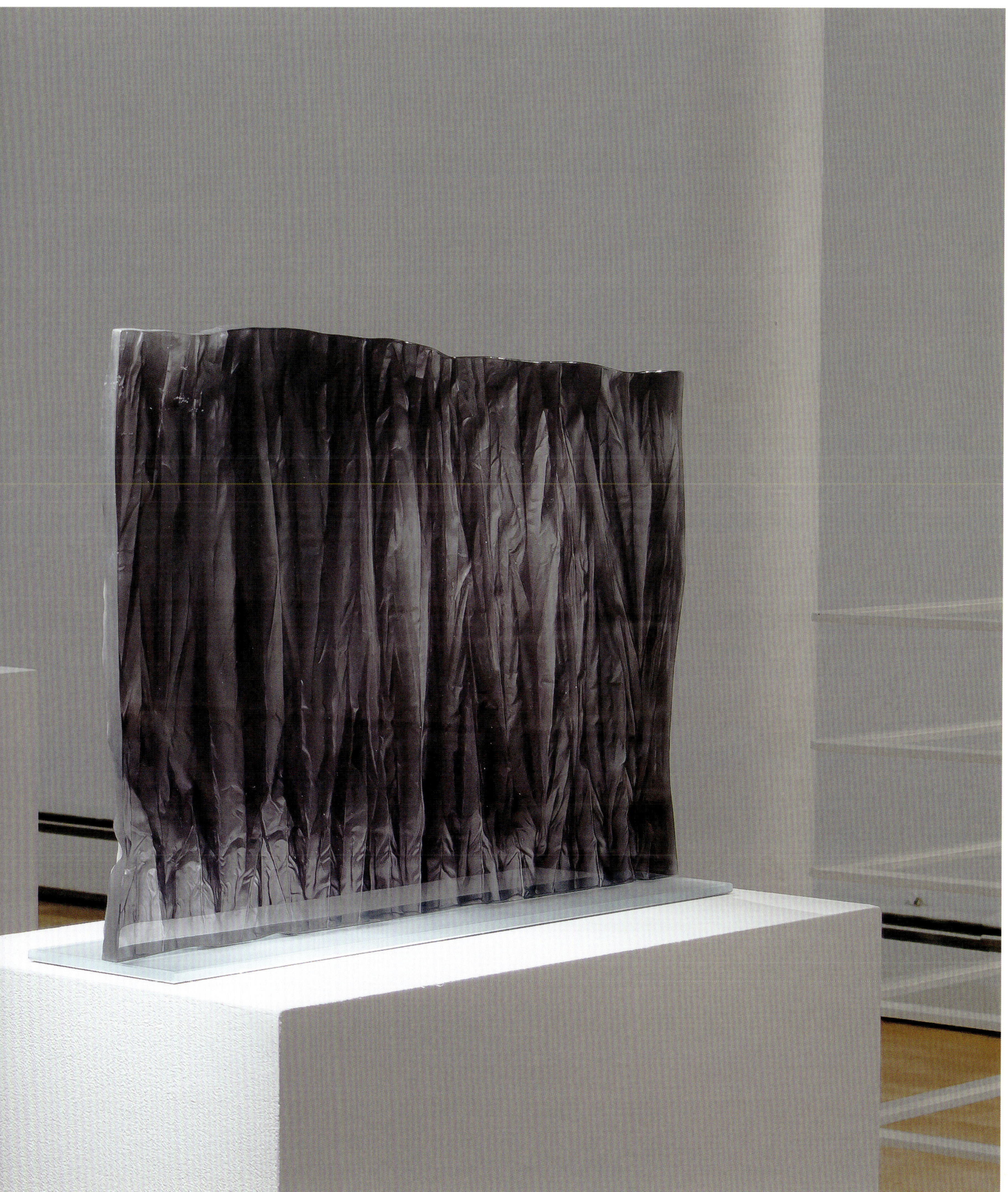

Deluge, 2008
Cast glass, 61½ × 41 × 1½ in. (156 × 104 × 4 cm)

FOLLOWING LEFT TO RIGHT
Detail of *Strata*, 2008.

Detail of *Curtain*, 2008.

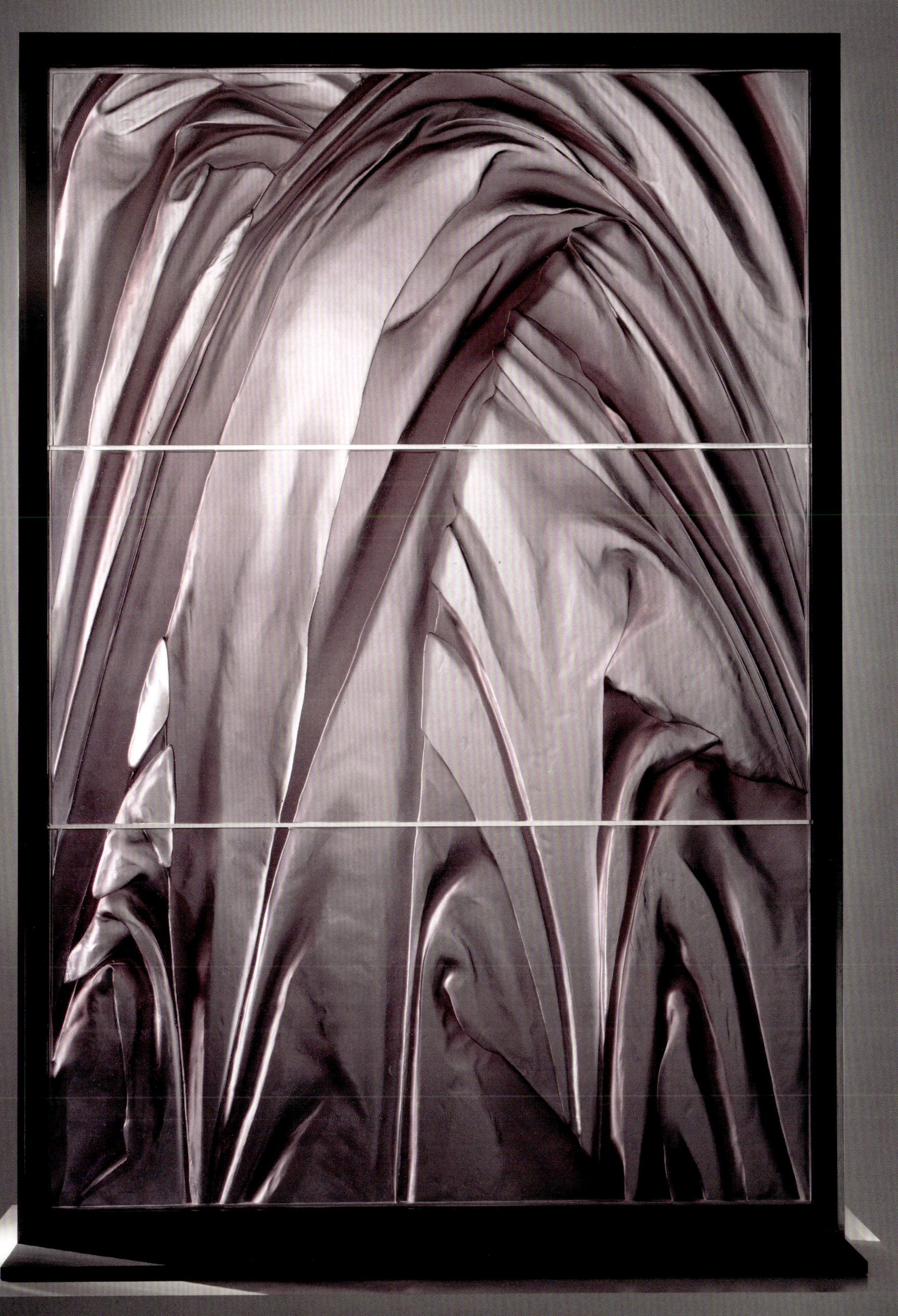

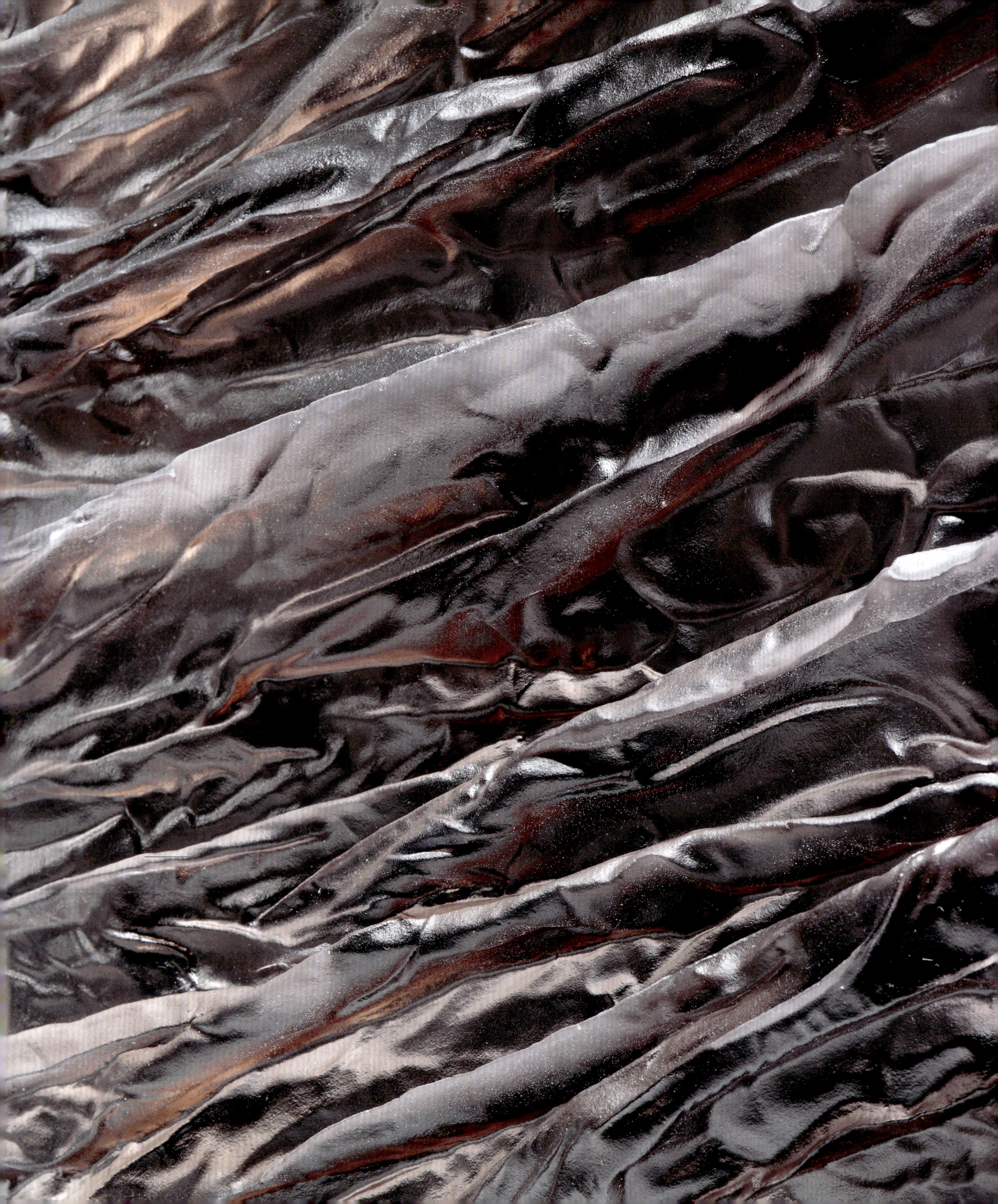

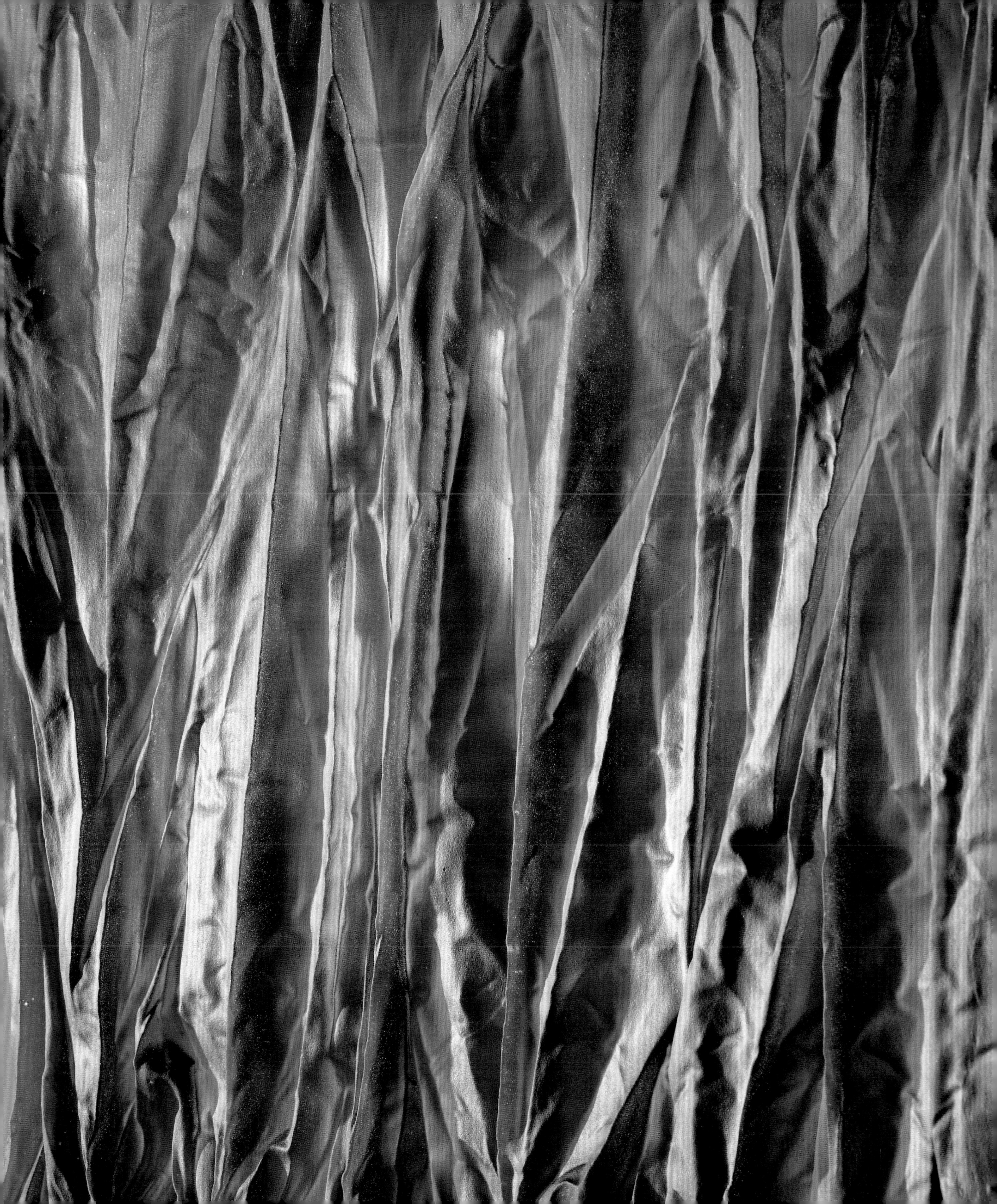

Strata, 2008
Cast glass, 14½ × 29 × 5 in. (37 × 73.2 × 13 cm)

OPPOSITE
Curtain, 2008
Cast glass, 22½ × 33 × 7 in. (57 × 84 × 18 cm)
Collection of Musée du Verre, Sars-Poteries, France

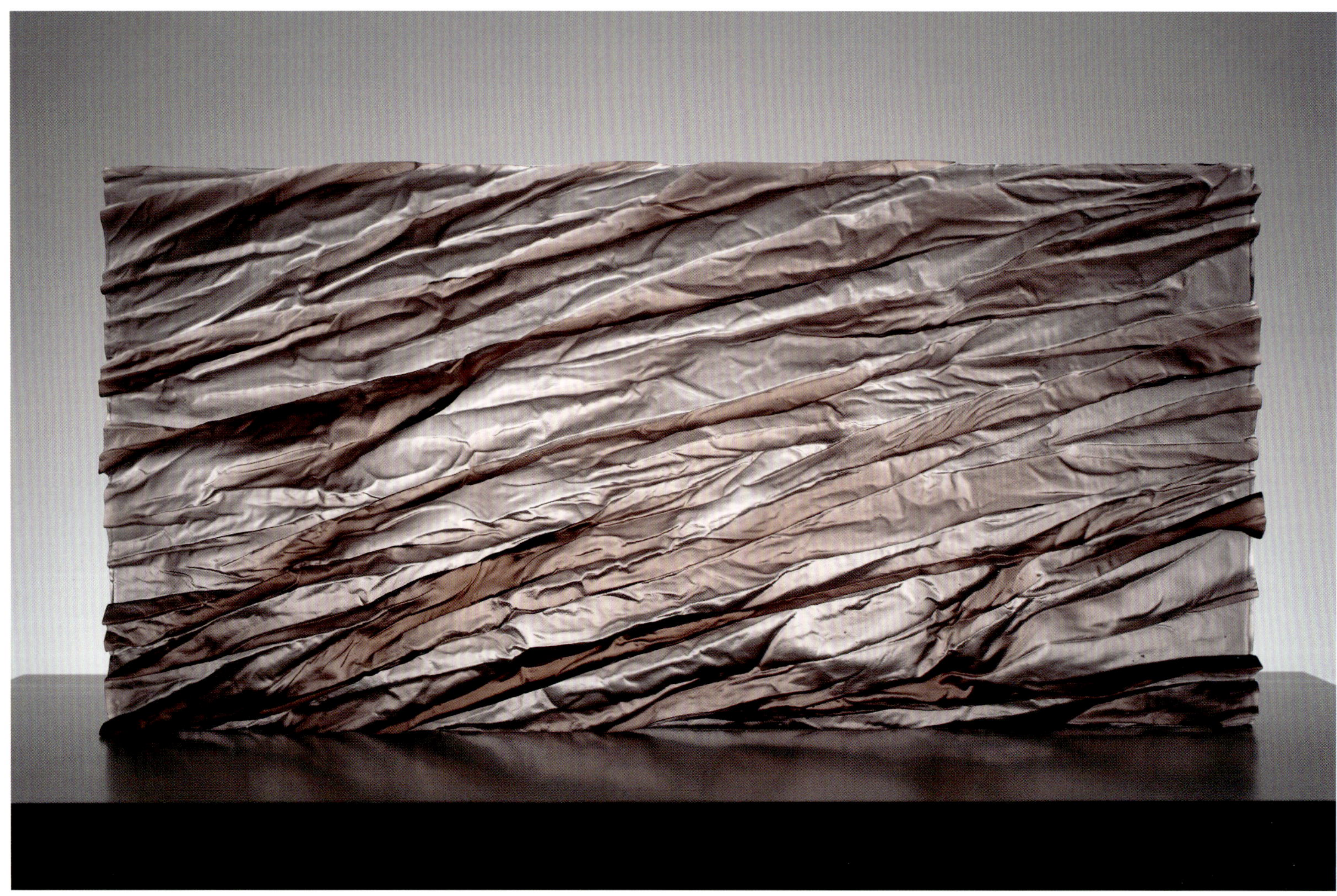

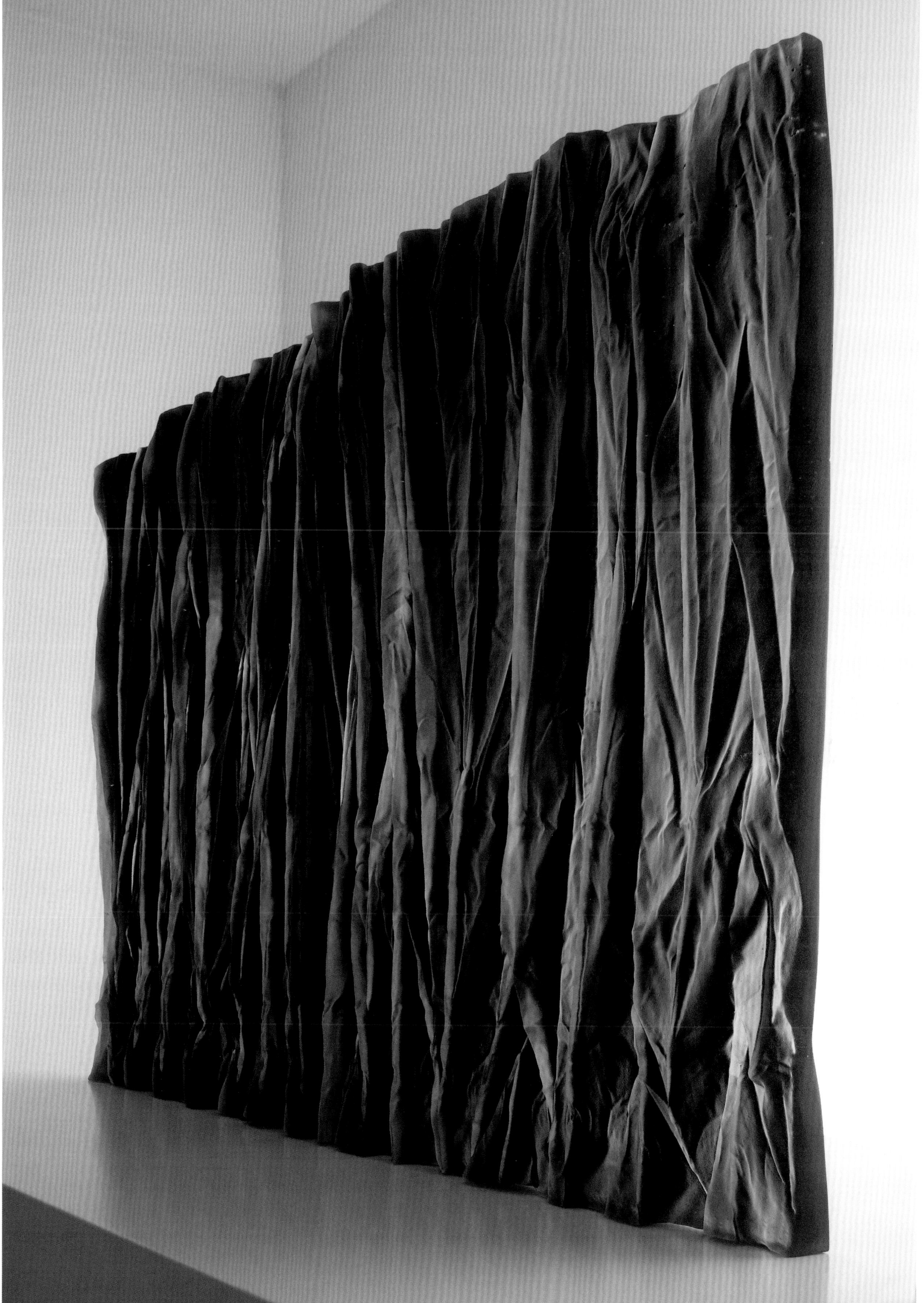

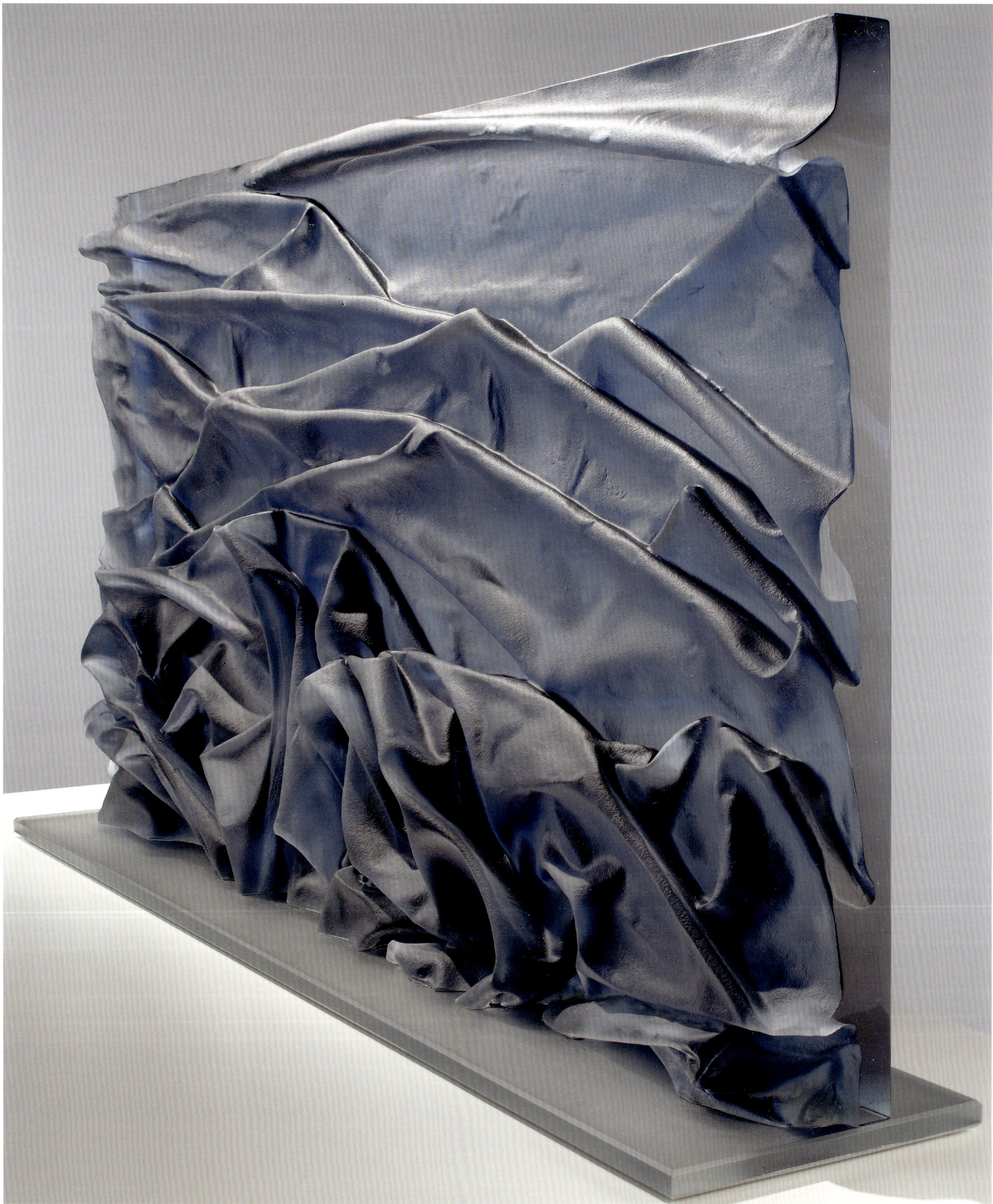

Landscape, 2008
Cast glass, 15 × 28 × 5 in. (38 × 71.6 × 13 cm)

FOLLOWING
Finishing cast ceramic at the European Ceramic Workcentre, 's-Hertogenbosch, Netherlands, 2009.

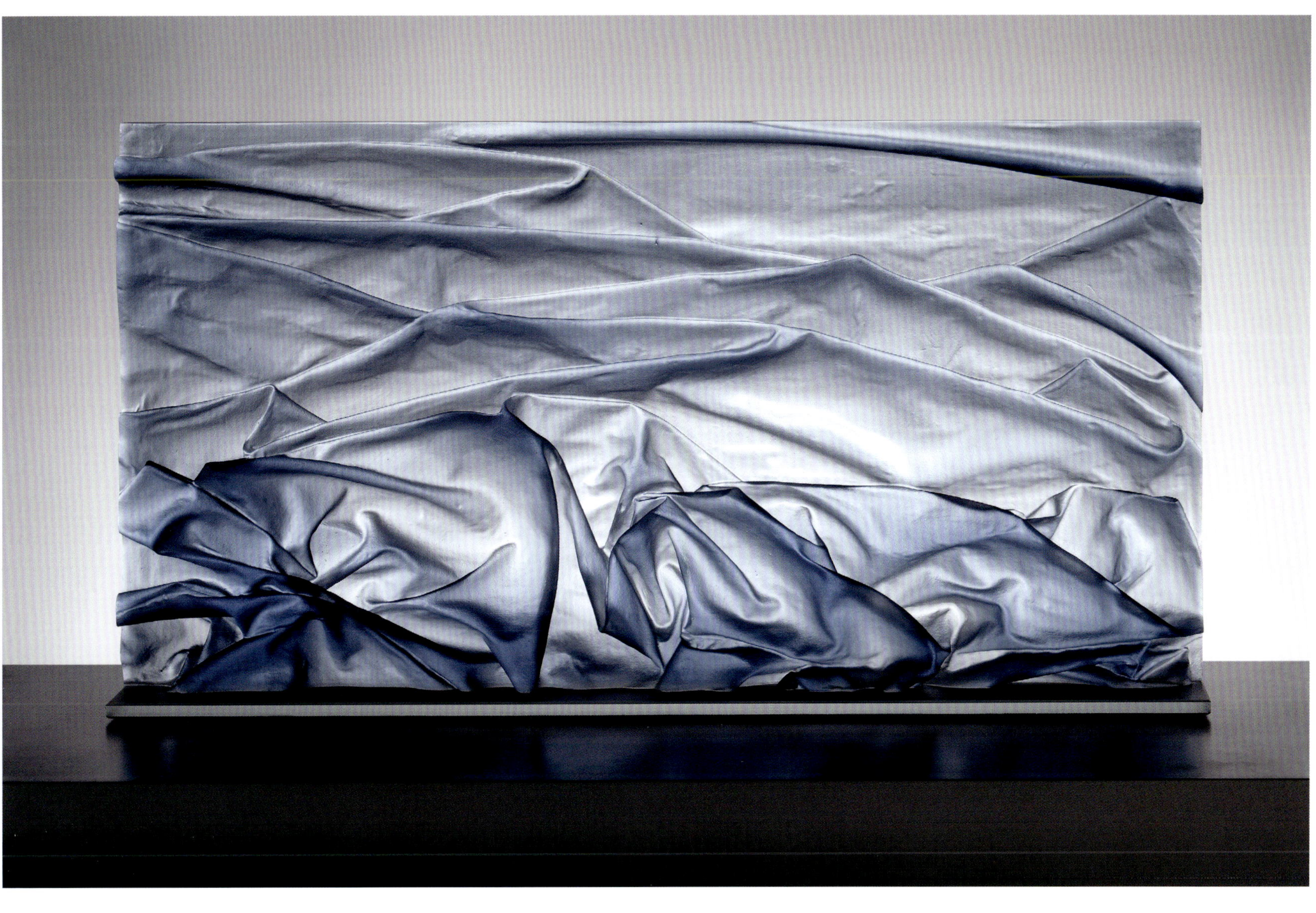

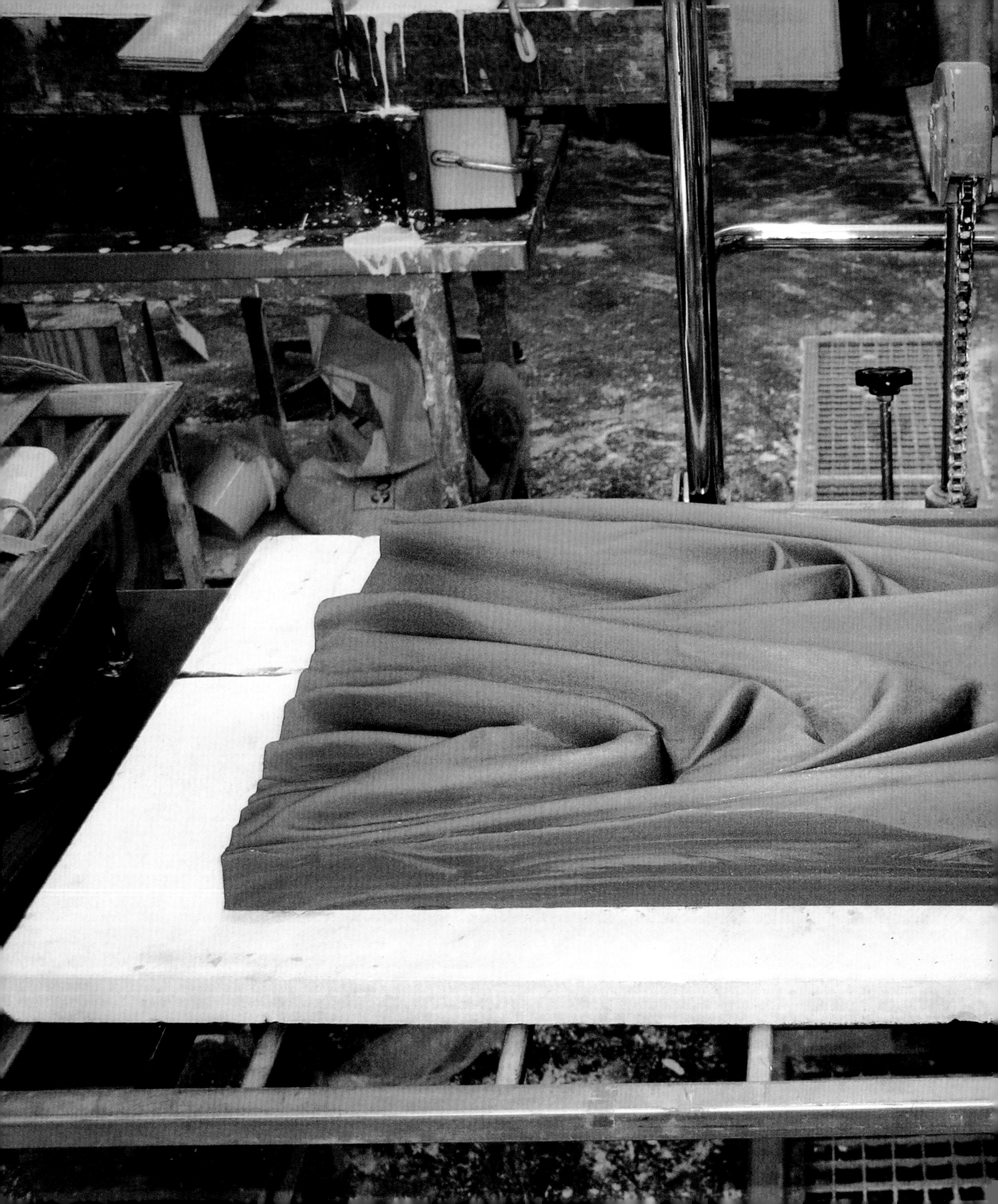

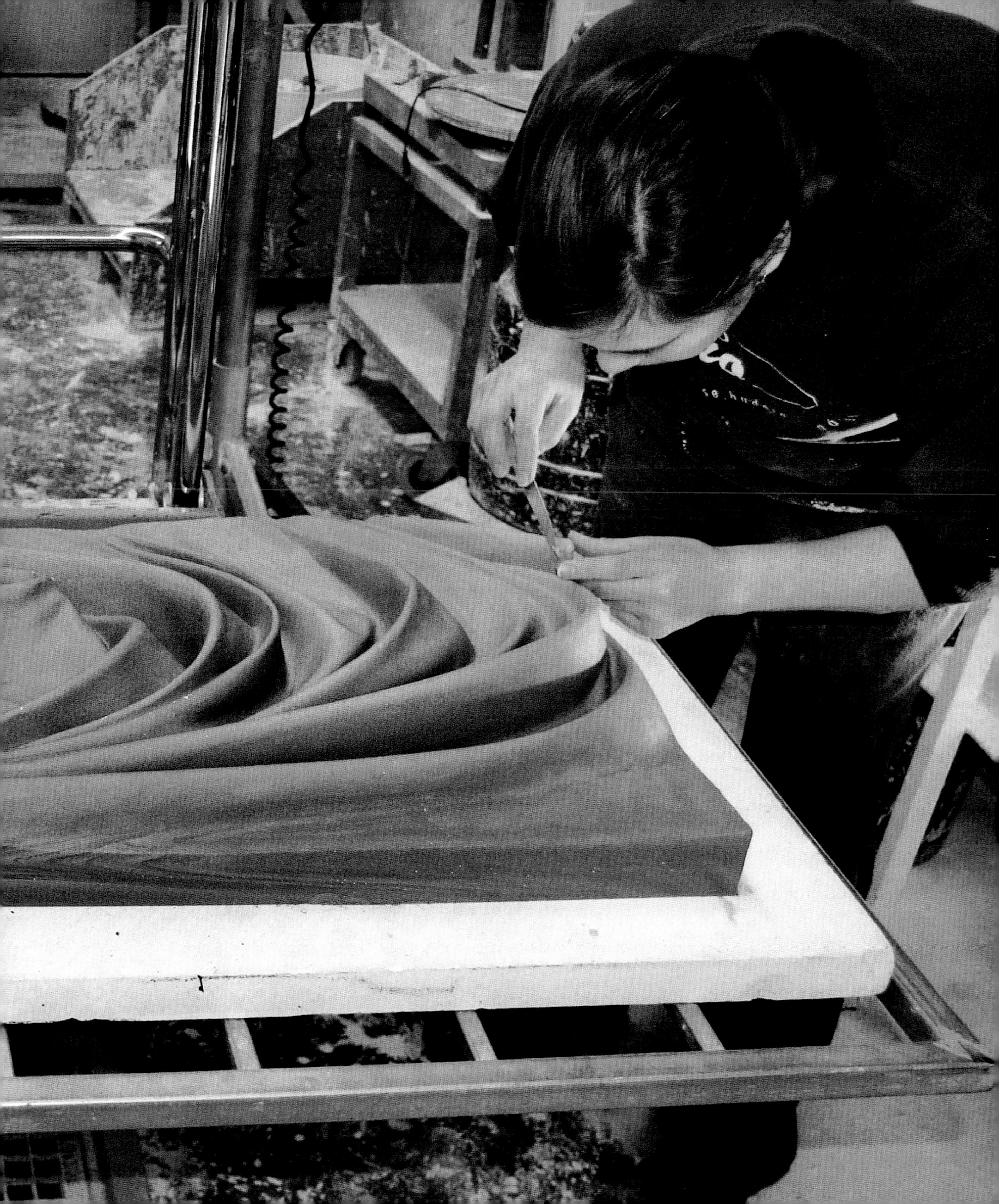

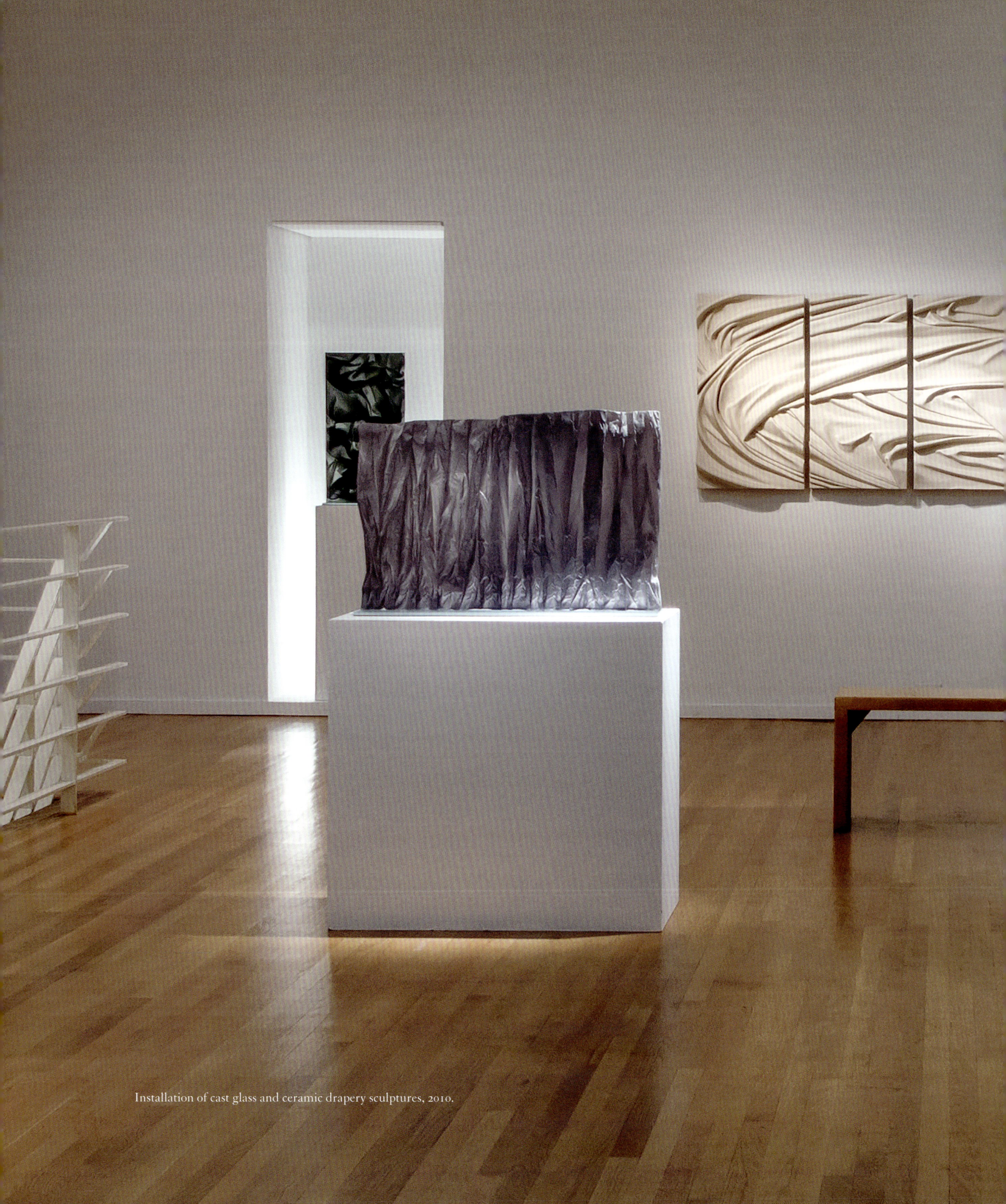

Installation of cast glass and ceramic drapery sculptures, 2010.

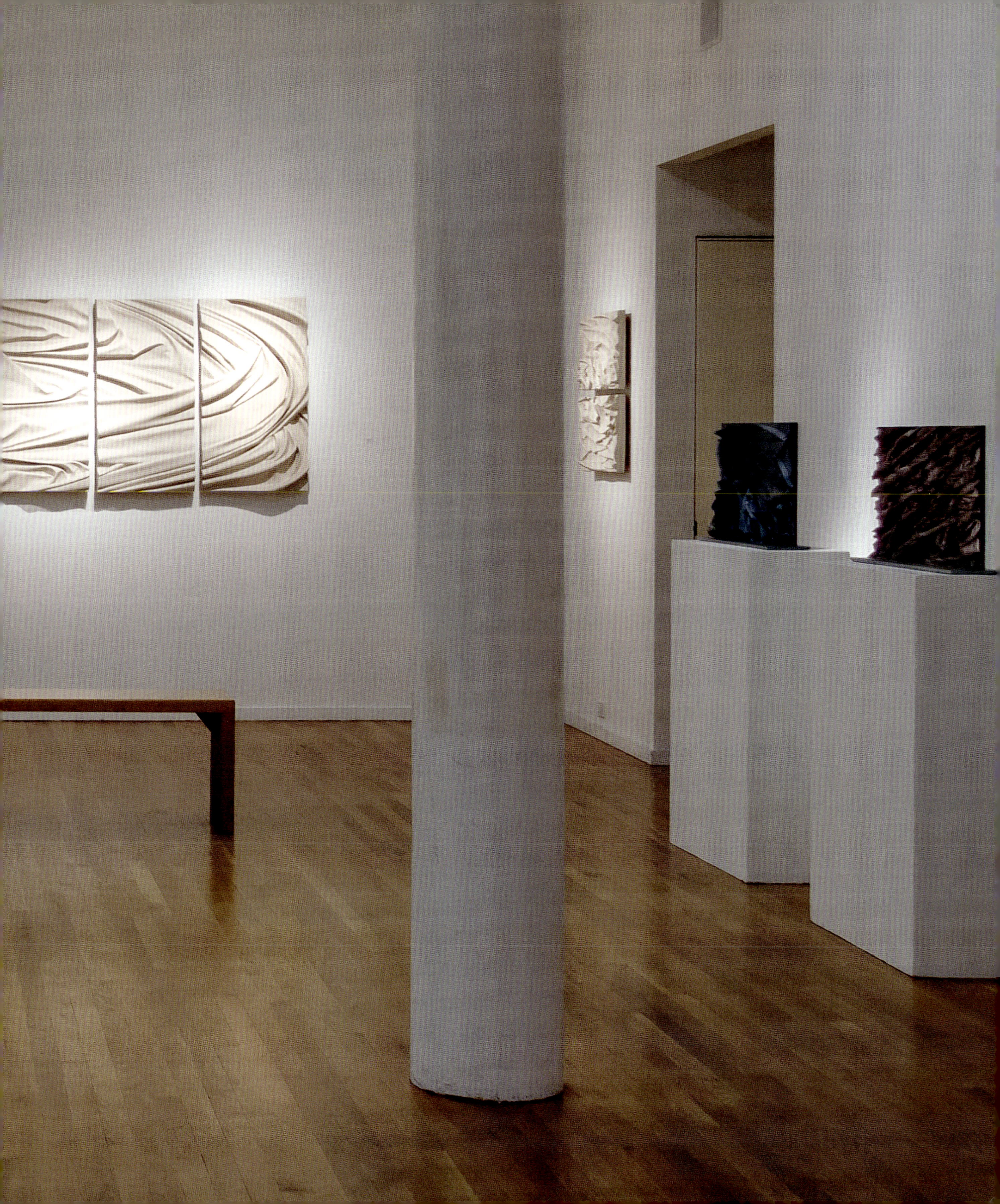

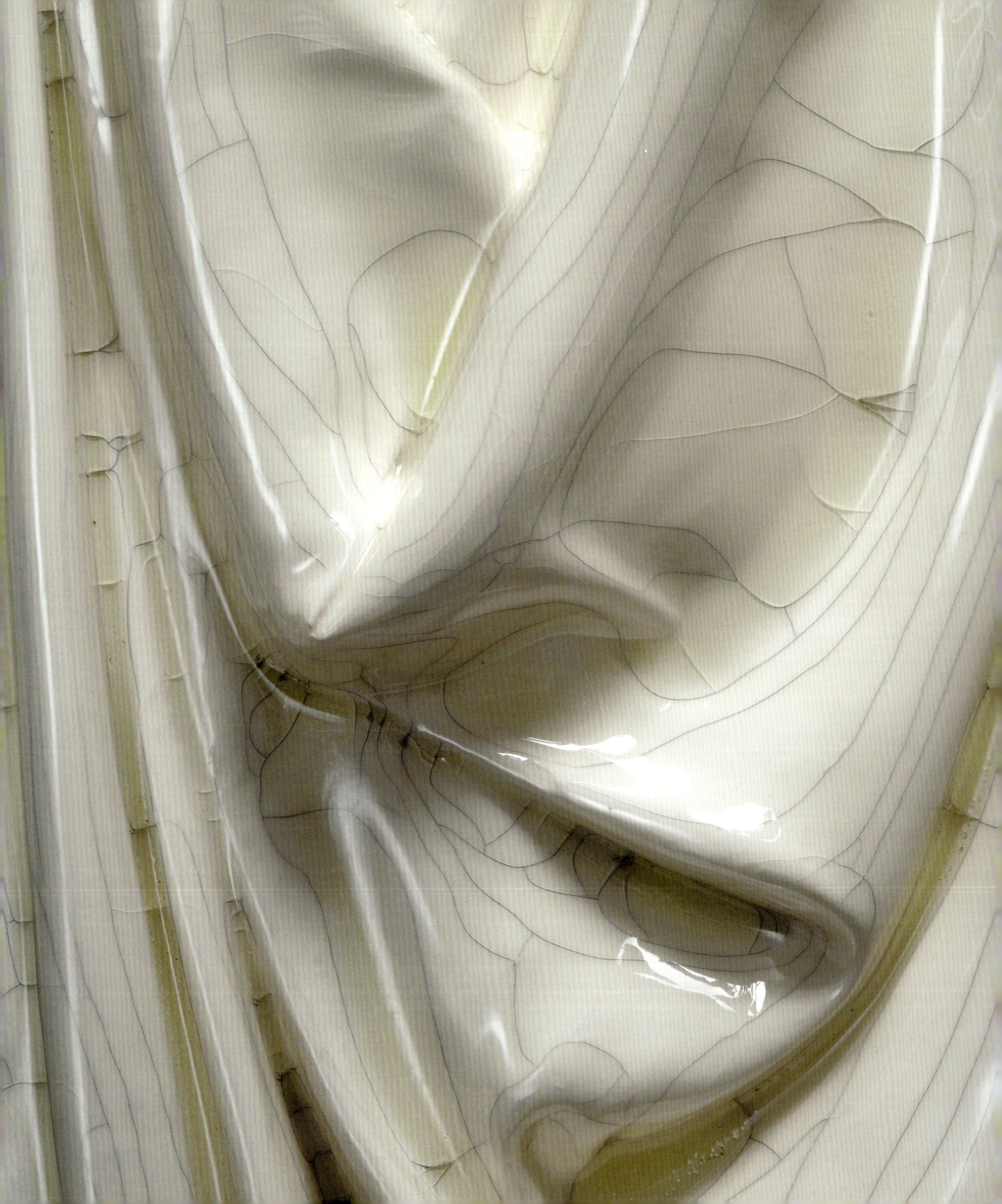

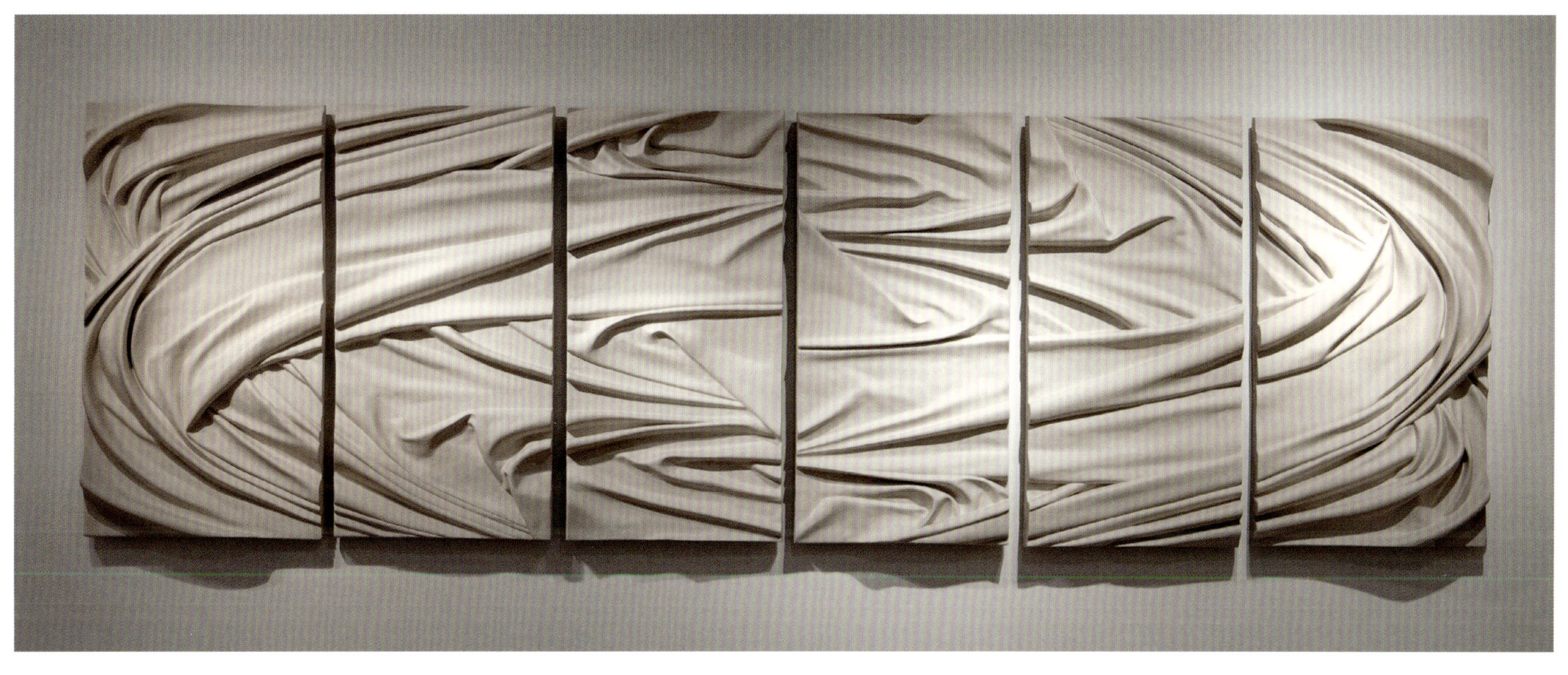

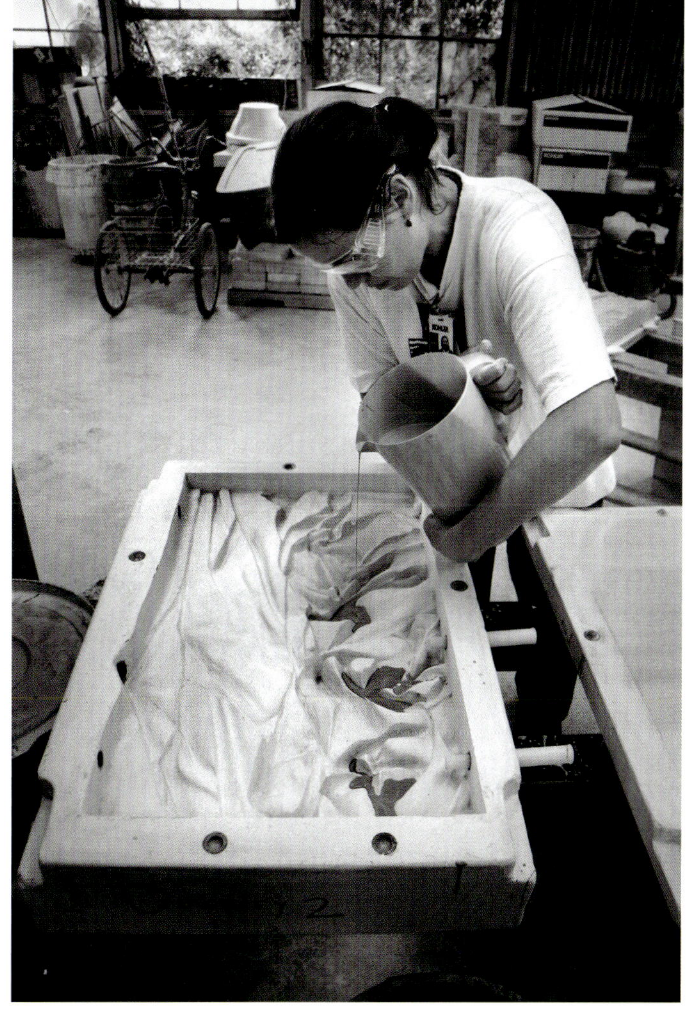

OPPOSITE
Detail of *Drapery*, 2009
Ceramic, 36 × 17 × 4 in. (91 × 43 × 10 cm)

ABOVE
Vortex, 2009
Vitreous china, 36 × 130 × 4 in.
(91 × 330 × 10 cm)

RIGHT
Pouring slip at the Kohler factory,
Kohler, WI, 2009.

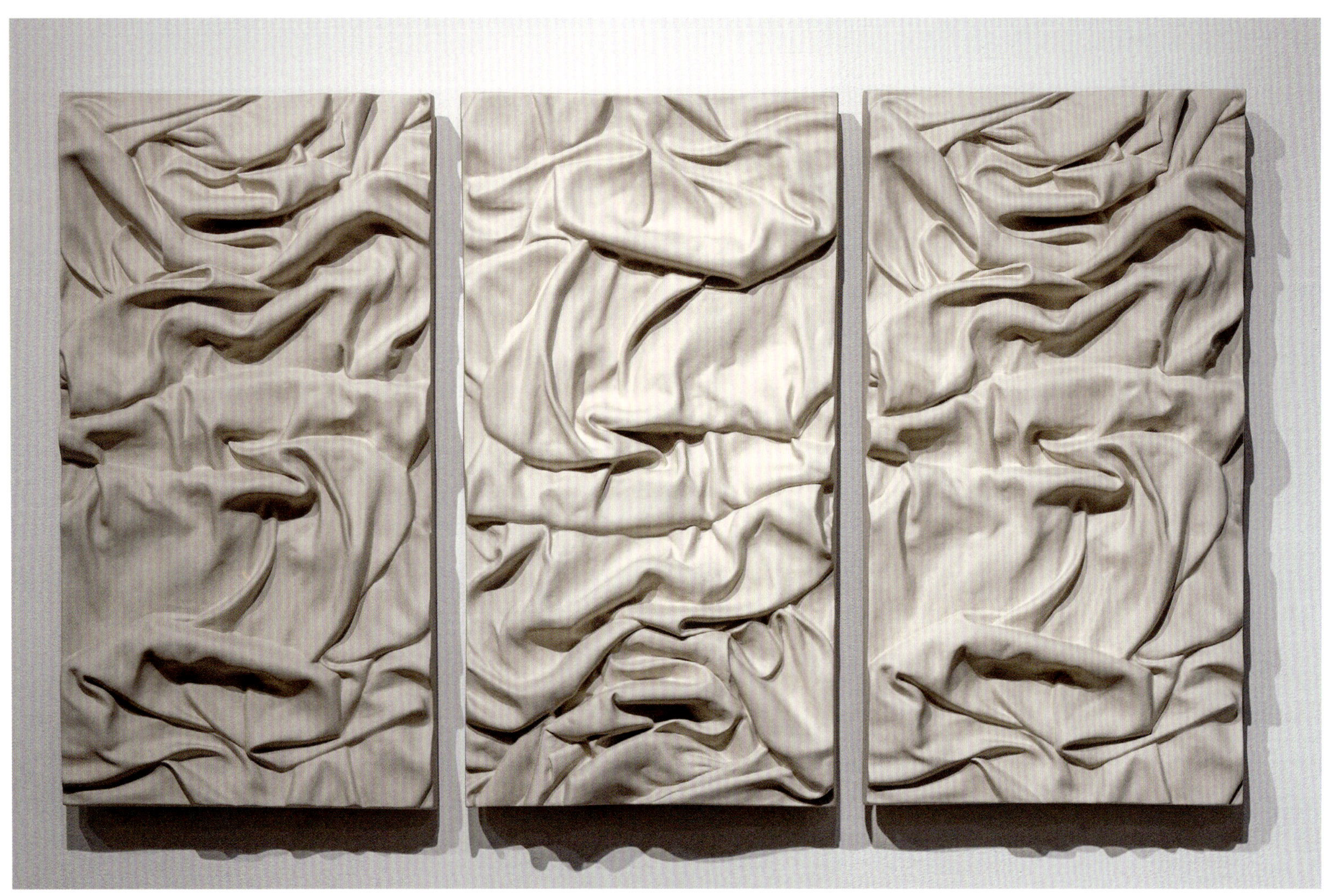

Smoke Triptych, 2009
Vitreous china, 25 × 41½ × 3 in. (64 × 105 × 8 cm)

OPPOSITE
Filling a drapery mold with ceramic at the European Ceramic Workcentre, 's-Hertogenbosch, Netherlands, 2009.

FOLLOWING
Detail of *Vortex*, 2009
Vitreous china, 36 × 130 × 4 in. (91 × 330 × 10 cm)

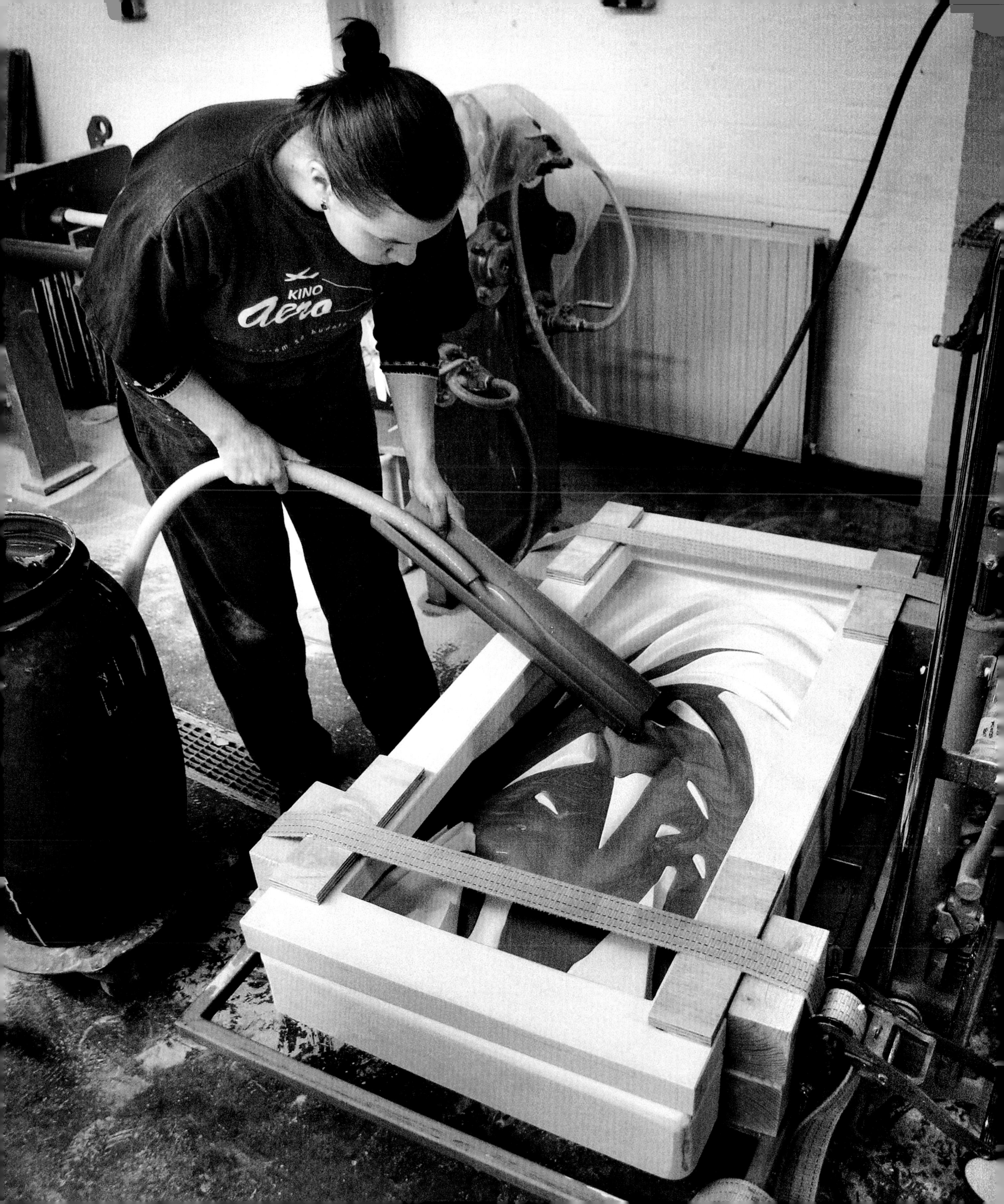
KINO
aero

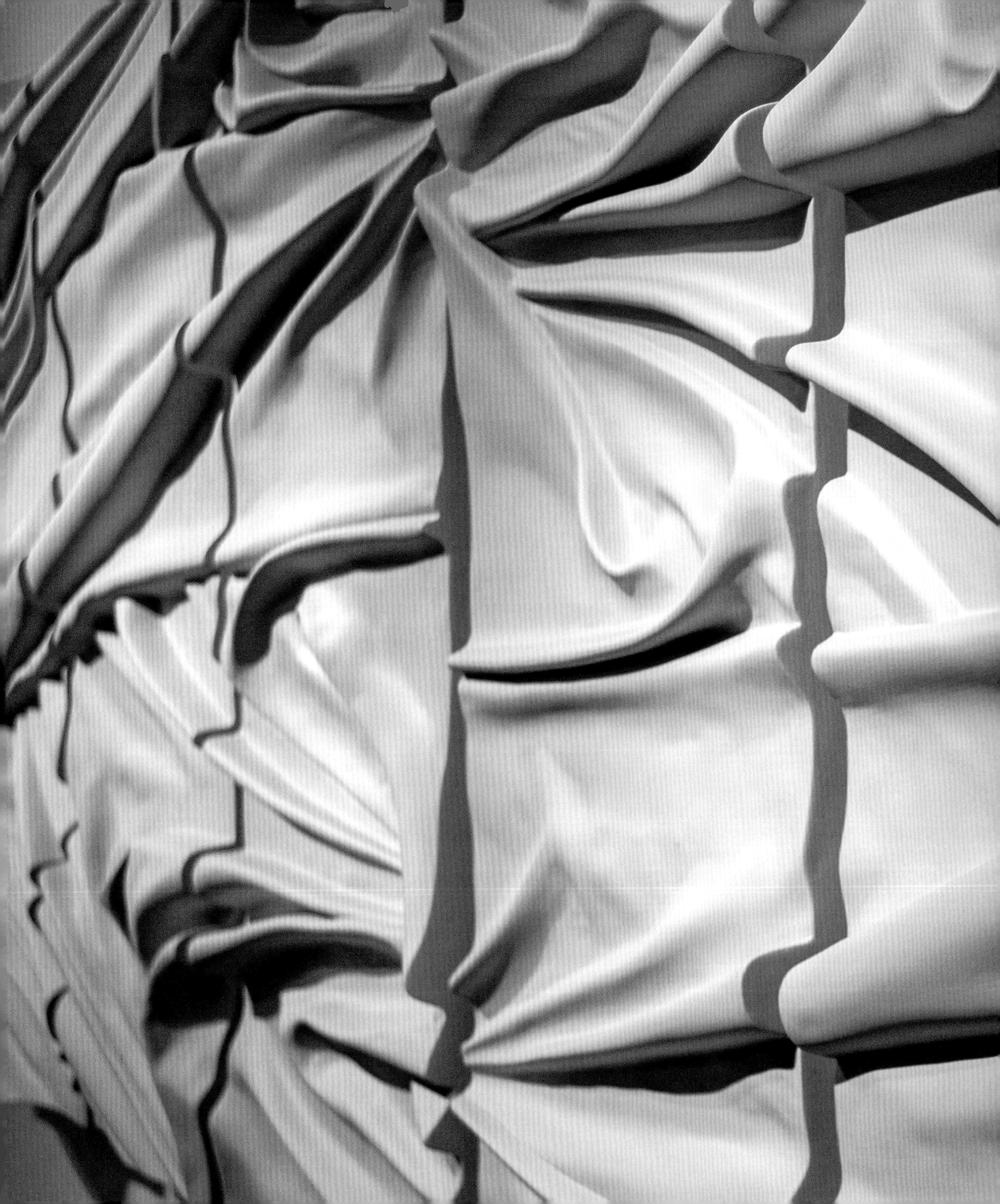

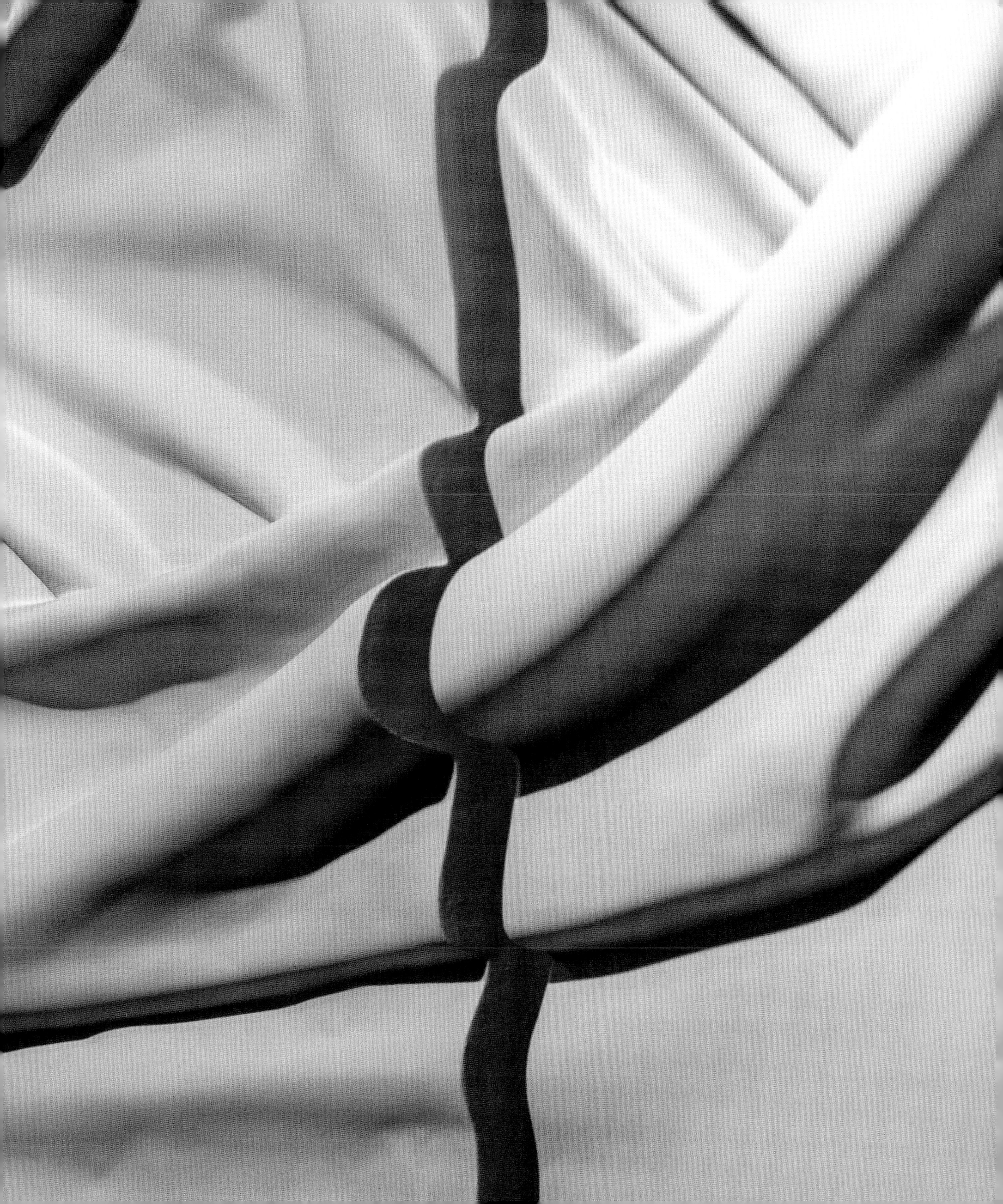

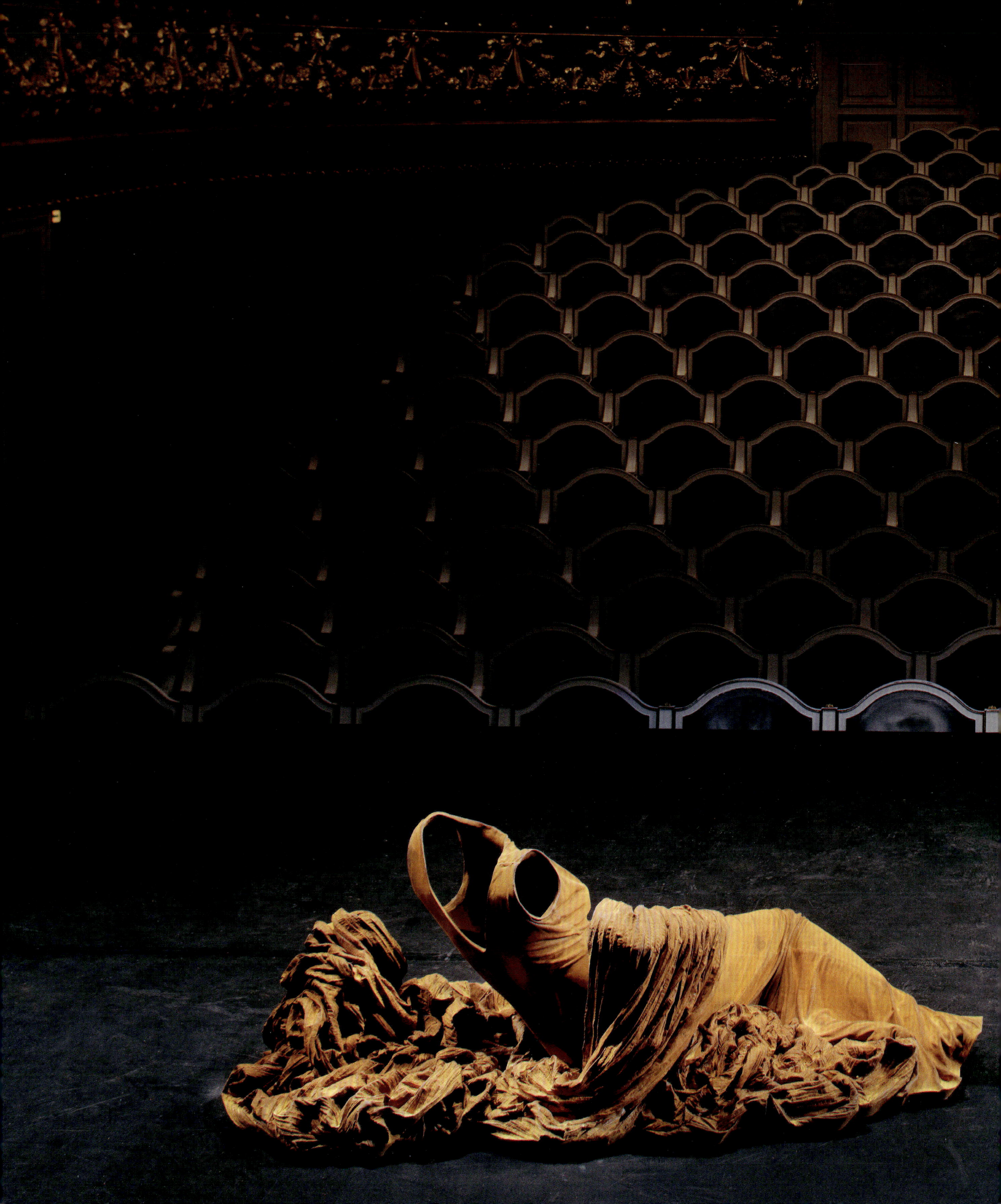

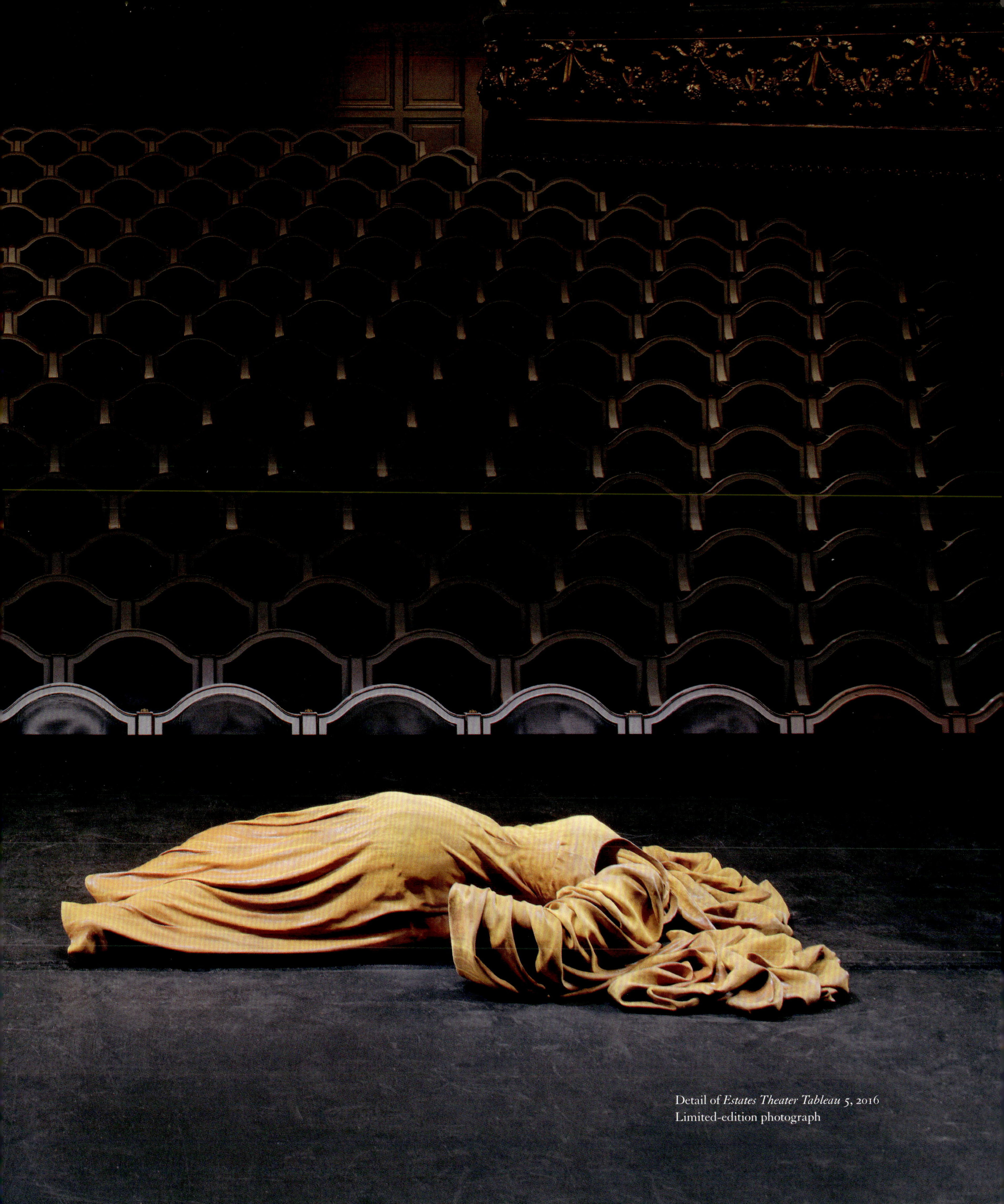

Detail of *Estates Theater Tableau 5*, 2016
Limited-edition photograph

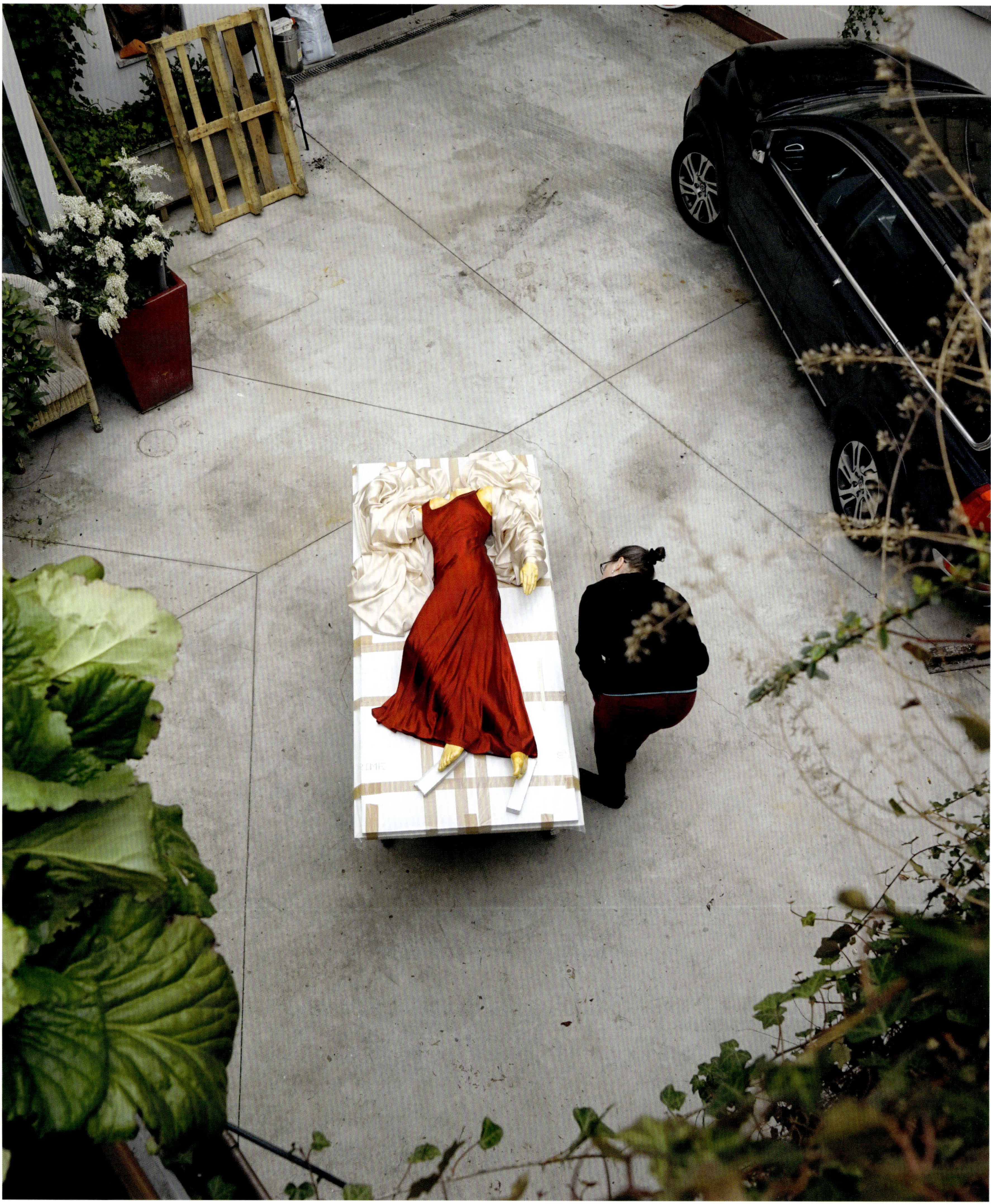

Night Becomes Her
Nocturnes, Etudes, and Tableaux

Steven A. Nash

Composing *Suspended Nocturne*, 2015.

Karen LaMonte's *Nocturne* sculptures, and their expression as *Etudes* and *Tableaux*, have dominated a major portion of her career, from approximately 2012–13 to the present. They continue, but also expand upon, themes basic to her work since her early formative years, including the interaction of drapery and the female figure in conceptions of beauty, light as an element of form, the interplay of solid and void, and the inherent physical and optical character of different materials. These works, however, venture into new territory both visually and emotionally. As LaMonte herself has put it, "Inspired by the beauty of night, I call these sculptures *Nocturnes*—dark, seductive, and sublime. They are absent female forms rising from penumbral garments as figurations of dusk."[1]

In fact, the *Nocturnes* represent a distinctively different stage in LaMonte's artistic trajectory, referencing key aspects of earlier work but also introducing new attributes of materiality and poetic expression. Their extended seriality hints at a special fascination for the artist, and they continue even as LaMonte ventures into new sculptural ideas, such as her recent carvings in marble of cumulus clouds. This vital role that they play in her overall productivity makes an exploration of their development and meanings all the more significant.

DARKNESS EMBODIED

As with the earlier clear glass sculptures, LaMonte presents in the *Nocturnes* a multilayered interrogation of physical beauty, asking us to consider the appeal of the dresses themselves, the allure of the women within (recorded through the imprint of their bodies on the interior surfaces of the hollow casts), and the phenomenon of how clothes influence perceptions of the sensuality and identity of the wearer.

But the iconographic nature of the *Nocturnes* is markedly different. LaMonte has commented eloquently about her intentions:

> In 2009 I became focused on night and began to think about the human body in a much larger and more abstract context. . . . I became interested in making female figurations of night . . . [and] focused on atmosphere over narrative. [Figures were] simultaneously emerging from and merging with night. . . . I wanted to wrap the female figure in dusk, exploring both beauty and darkness.[2]

The achievement of this ambitious program began with an introduction of both color and new materials into her casting process. In her *Floating*

World kimonos she had expanded her repertoire of sculptural media by adding bronze, iron, and ceramics to her practice. In the *Nocturnes*, she focused on glass, bronze, and iron as her media of choice, capitalizing on different properties than she did in earlier work. For her glass casts, she worked with German scientists to develop a formula for additive color that produced the right tonalities and light absorption to yield her desired penumbral effects. For the bronzes, she started working with a different alloy—known as white bronze—to create lustrous, silver-gray surfaces. The iron casts were allowed to weather slowly, resulting in powdery cinnamon patinas representing for the artist, due to the temporality of the process, the idea of transition and transformation.[3]

Light obviously responds much differently to the *Nocturnes* than it does to earlier glass works. Gone is the spectral luminescence of the clear glass dresses, in which light refracts through sculptures and blurs the intersections between solid edges and surrounding space, thus helping to dematerialize the forms. The *Nocturnes*, in contrast, seem to dimly trap light within them, giving the figures a mysterious and languorous quality, as if they were controlled by reverie or nostalgia. This shadowy coloration creates an aura that signifies the artist's desire to relate in three-dimensional form to the nighttime visions and meditations of such composers and artists as Frédéric Chopin, John Field, and James Abbott McNeill Whistler.

At the same time, LaMonte's investigations of glass, steel, and iron stress their inherent physical nature and tactility—one is always tempted to touch the works to better understand their beautiful physicality—helping to give them a strong sculptural presence and a weighty displacement of space. LaMonte's interest in texture, weight, and the natural properties of materials recalls distantly such "truth-to-materials" sculptors as Jacob Epstein and Constantin Brancusi, who once opined famously that "Matter must continue its natural life when modified by the sculptor."

MAKING OBJECTS OF DESIRE

As with all her works, the *Nocturnes* invite contemplation as much for their formal qualities as their iconographic implications. LaMonte strives for sculptural rigor, with an honesty and clarity of form-making that produces objects complete unto themselves, articulate in structure, and confident in their interaction with space. Always apparent is their connection across time with ancient Greek and Roman sculpture, which is appreciated for its formal strength and composure.

Unique to LaMonte's work is the dialogue that hollow casts create between solid and void, interior and exterior, active and calm surfaces. They both push against space and contain it. Her enduring theme of absence is carried further in the *Nocturnes*, with its appeal to imagine the displaced figures, but is heightened by the shadowy constitution of the forms. Her nocturnal dresses simulate in effect the glow of moonlight with shades that range from steely gray to tints of green and violet. Women represented only by their formal attire become more elusive and mysterious than ever, taking, so to speak, the objects of desire farther out of reach and increasing the sense of longing.

Many sculptors before her have rendered such nighttime themes as dreaming, mourning, and terror through narrative devices including pose and facial expression (consider, for example, Constantin Brancusi's *Sleeping Muse* and Auguste Rodin's *Night* and *The Three Shades*), but it is a different matter to absorb that experience into the very essence of the sculptures.[4] Medardo Rosso came close, through his impressionistic use of translucent wax to achieve the atmospheric effects championed by Tonalist painters, but LaMonte's *Nocturnes* are more holistic in approach.[5]

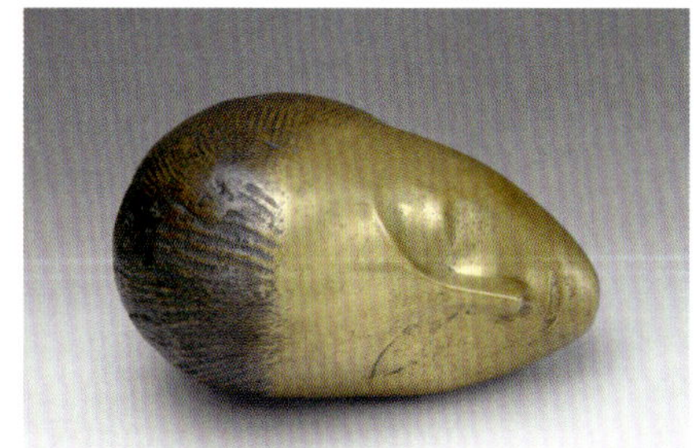

Constanin Brancusi (1876–1957). *Sleeping Muse*, 1910. Bronze. The Metropolitan Museum of Art, New York

James Abbott McNeill Whistler (1834–1903). *Nocturne: Blue and Gold – Old Battersea Bridge*, c. 1872–75. Oil on canvas Tate Gallery, London

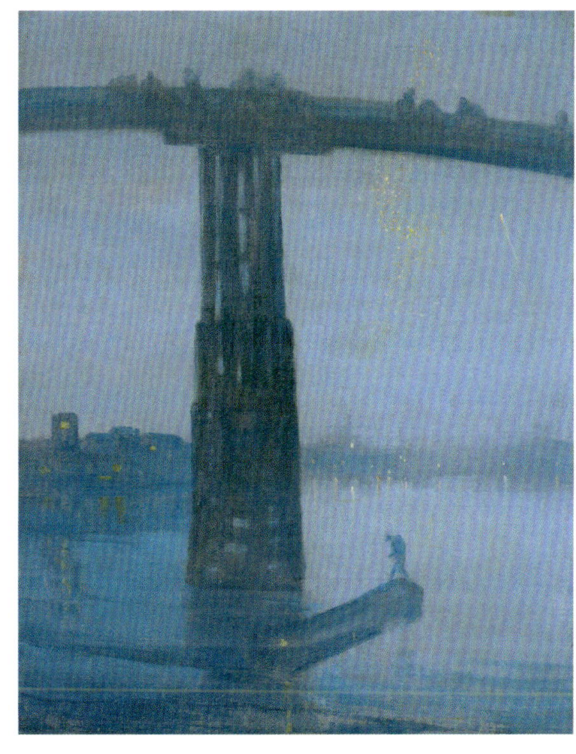

ETUDES AND *TABLEAUX*

The *Etudes* and *Tableaux* represent sizeable subsets of the *Nocturnes*. The former, more recent in chronology, are so named because of associations with concepts in Tonalist and Symbolist music and art involving ideas of materials that are unfinished, insubstantial, and ephemeral. They are essentially small-scale versions of the large sculptures—approximately one-third the scale—and sometimes relate very closely to larger works. But they do not serve the purpose of maquettes or preliminary studies. LaMonte thinks of them instead as independent works and is particularly focused on the difference of aesthetic effects produced by dramatic changes of scale and small adjustments of composition. All of them are created from scratch using small mannequins (produced sometimes by scanning models and making three-dimensional prints) that are costumed with the same care and precision as their larger relatives and then solid-cast with the same painstaking techniques.

Scale is a critical consideration in sculpture. Whereas some artists such as Auguste Rodin and Henry Moore freely made the same work in multiple scales, other sculptors conceive of works in a certain scale that they consider to be most correct or effective for the composition. Maquettes exist but are studies and not independent works. In LaMonte's case, there is, as noted, a specificity of purpose with the two distinct sizes, although the precise effects conjured are hard to put one's finger on. For this writer, the *Etudes* seem more delicate, refined, and precious. Their delicacy provokes memories of old master finely crafted silver and gold figurines. In a contrary sense, however, the miniaturization of form seems to concentrate the energy of effusive drapery, giving a sense of pent-up power. This conjunction of increased precision and enlivened drapery helps endow these works with a distinctive design language.

Behind the *Etudes* exists the very strong influence of the *Théâtre de la Mode*, an exhibition of small figurines dating from the close of World War II that were dressed by well-known French fashion designers and displayed within sets created by contemporary artists, including Jean Cocteau and Christian Bérard. Quickly becoming very popular through its tours in Europe and America, this miniature theater was both a sign of renewed national pride and an impetus for economic revival. LaMonte has said of it: "The small scale of the work with its large intention and effect mesmerized me, as it did the world in March 1945. It was a declaration of the importance of beauty and culture particularly during difficult and confusing times and reminded me of the many stories of creation in which light is born from darkness."[6] In summing up the importance of the *Etudes* in her practice, she noted that they are "much more than studies for larger works. They celebrate the power of human optimism and our enduring need for beauty."[7]

The *Tableaux* were also inspired in no small part by the *Théâtre de la Mode*. LaMonte has long been interested in the theater as a conjunction of life and art, and study of the mise-en-scènes of the miniature costume theater encouraged her to install life-size *Nocturnes* in historic theaters with the goal of photographing them, capturing the impact of her "stories without bodies" and the resonance between her timeless couture and timeless theater. The resultant images, with their sense of nostalgia and even mystery, match the aura of her sculptures.

Opportunities to create the *Tableaux* came first in 2016 and then again in 2017 at two remarkable theaters in the Czech Republic: the Prague Estates Theater, dating from 1783, and the Baroque Litomyšl Castle Theater, founded in 1797. LaMonte considers these two presentations to be among the most moving of all the installations of her work, commenting on the emotional experience of the first installation in a theater where Mozart conducted the premiere of *Don Giovanni* in 1787: "I felt an overwhelming sensation of the past colliding with the present."[8] The theater in Litomyšl is immaculately preserved, including furnishings and original sets. Designed as a space for small-scale productions, it brought the hollow-cast dresses—now seen in a particularly intimate and lush environment—even more to life.

The artist has likened these photographs of the theatrical installations to living *tableaux* popular in the nineteenth century, in which models, in various states of undress, struck poses for photographers in large ensembles that relate historical narratives or different moral or religious messages. Other more high-art analogies also exist with moralizing history painting in a classical tradition that was rampant in nineteenth-century academic art, including, for example, Thomas Couture's famous, but also much maligned, *Romans during the Decadence* from 1847. No other installations of this kind have followed, but these two mark special moments in LaMonte's career. The *Tableaux* allowed her to expand her work beyond the boundary of art museums and galleries into a real-life context that is both artful and instructive of her interest in endowing her work with meanings outside pure formalism, connecting it to the world beyond.

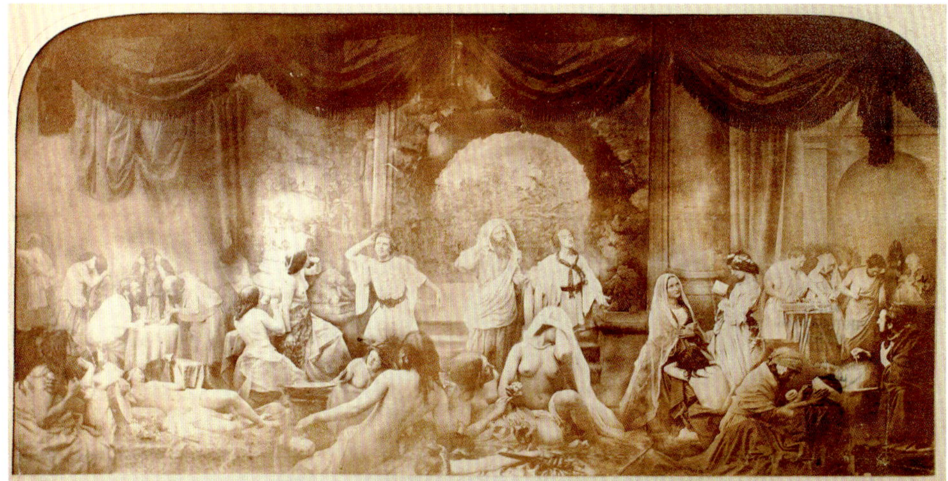

Oscar Gustav Rejlander (1813–1875). *Two Ways of Life* (second version), 1857. Photograph

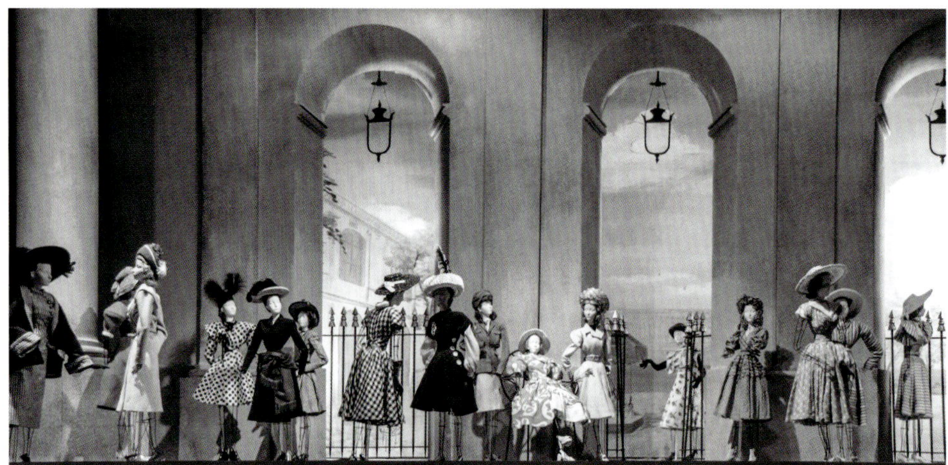

Théâtre de la Mode. Maryhill Museum of Art, Goldendale, WA

LAMONTE AND HISTORY

It would be hyperbolic to compare Gian Lorenzo Bernini to any of our contemporary artists, but it can be said that LaMonte's attitude toward and formal treatment of drapery invokes distantly the potent historical precedent of Bernini's seventeenth-century marble carvings, such as the great *Tomb of Blessed Ludovica Albertoni* in the Church of San Francesco a Ripa in Rome. Her draperies are a constituent part of the figures beneath them yet also take on a life of their own (as with the cascading folds of Albertoni's habit). And both artists take delight in exposing the

Gian Lorenzo Bernini (1598–1680). *Tomb of Blessed Ludovica Albertoni*, 1671–75. Marble. Church of San Francesco a Ripa, Rome

innate qualities of their materials with seductive textures, soft modeling, and tonal ranges that impart luminescence to drapery and skin.

Interesting if coincidental affinities also exist with two acclaimed works from the Neoclassical period. In one of LaMonte's *Nocturne* installations in Czech theaters in 2016–17, a reclining figure was placed on an Empire-style chaise longue, forming a composition related to portraits by both Italian sculptor Antonio Canova and French painter Jacques-Louis David. With Canova's *Pauline Bonaparte as Venus Victoria* (1805–8), it shares not just roots in ancient depictions of reclining figures but also an eroticism amplified by the visual tease of bodies at once revealed and concealed. David's portrait is exemplary of the kind of social and cultural attributes of dress that interest LaMonte deeply. The unfinished *Portrait of Madame Récamier* was painted shortly after the French Revolution when, during the Directory, social strata and the importance of commerce and luxury were being reconstructed. As emblematic of a new fashion wave that succeeded revolution-era austerity and Rococo flamboyance, it proclaimed social status, fashionable taste, and consciousness of a new national order. Self-expression, self-confidence, social standing, and seductiveness are combined in one very telling fashion statement.

CONTEMPORANEITY

Despite these associations with the past, LaMonte's sculptures are very much of our own time. They take their place in the resurgence of figurative art following Minimalism's banishment of the human figure in favor of elemental abstract forms and help underline the importance that sculpture has played in that development. Many contemporary sculptors have adopted the human body as an important vehicle for study of different aspects of the human condition, including Kiki Smith, Jaume Plensa, Thomas Schütte, Huma Bhabha, Juan Muñoz, and Georg Baselitz. LaMonte's contributions in this arena involve both her inventive treatment of materials and form and her investigations of female identity and self-expression, which, as we have seen, strike us in both sensuous and abstract ways. Each sculpture is an individual construction of visual, haptic, and intellectual experience, totally integrated. As the acclaimed British painter Cecily Brown has opined, "Painting is very good at saying more than one thing at once."[9] LaMonte's *Nocturnes* affirm that sculpture is as well.

NOTES

1 *Karen LaMonte: Nocturnes*, video, "Artist Talks & Videos," accessed December 1, 2018, karenlamonte.com.

2 Ibid.

3 The ten large-scale *Nocturne* forms for glass have been cast in different shades, and certain of the metal forms have been cast in both iron and bronze. The glass forms are distinct from the metal forms, despite the fact that the glass and metal works share the same numbering system. (For example, the titles for the glass and metal forms utilize "No. 1s.")

4 For Brancusi's *Sleeping Muse*, see, among many sources, *Constantin Brancusi 1876–1957*, exh. cat. (Philadelphia: Philadelphia Museum of Art, 1995), cat. nos. 15 and 16. For the two works by Rodin, see Albert Elsen, *The Rodin Collection of the Iris and B. Gerald Cantor Center for Visual Arts at Stanford University* (New York: Oxford University Press, 2003), cat. nos. 34 and 43.

5 On Rosso's exploitation of the malleability and translucency of wax for such effects, see Harry Cooper and Sharon Hecker, *Medardo Rosso: Second Impressions*, exh. cat. (Cambridge, MA: Fogg Art Museum, 2003), passim.

6 Karen LaMonte, "Fashioning Darkness," in *Karen LaMonte: Nocturnes* (Prague, Czech Republic: ArtWorks Publishing, 2019), 127.

7 Ibid.

8 Karen LaMonte, "Tableaux," in *Nocturnes*, 221.

9 Quoted in Hilary M. Sheets, "Cecily Brown's Paintings Are at the (Other) Met," *New York Times*, September 20, 2018.

Building wax interiors for *Nocturnes*, 2014.

FOLLOWING
Molding figure for interior of a *Nocturne*, 2012.

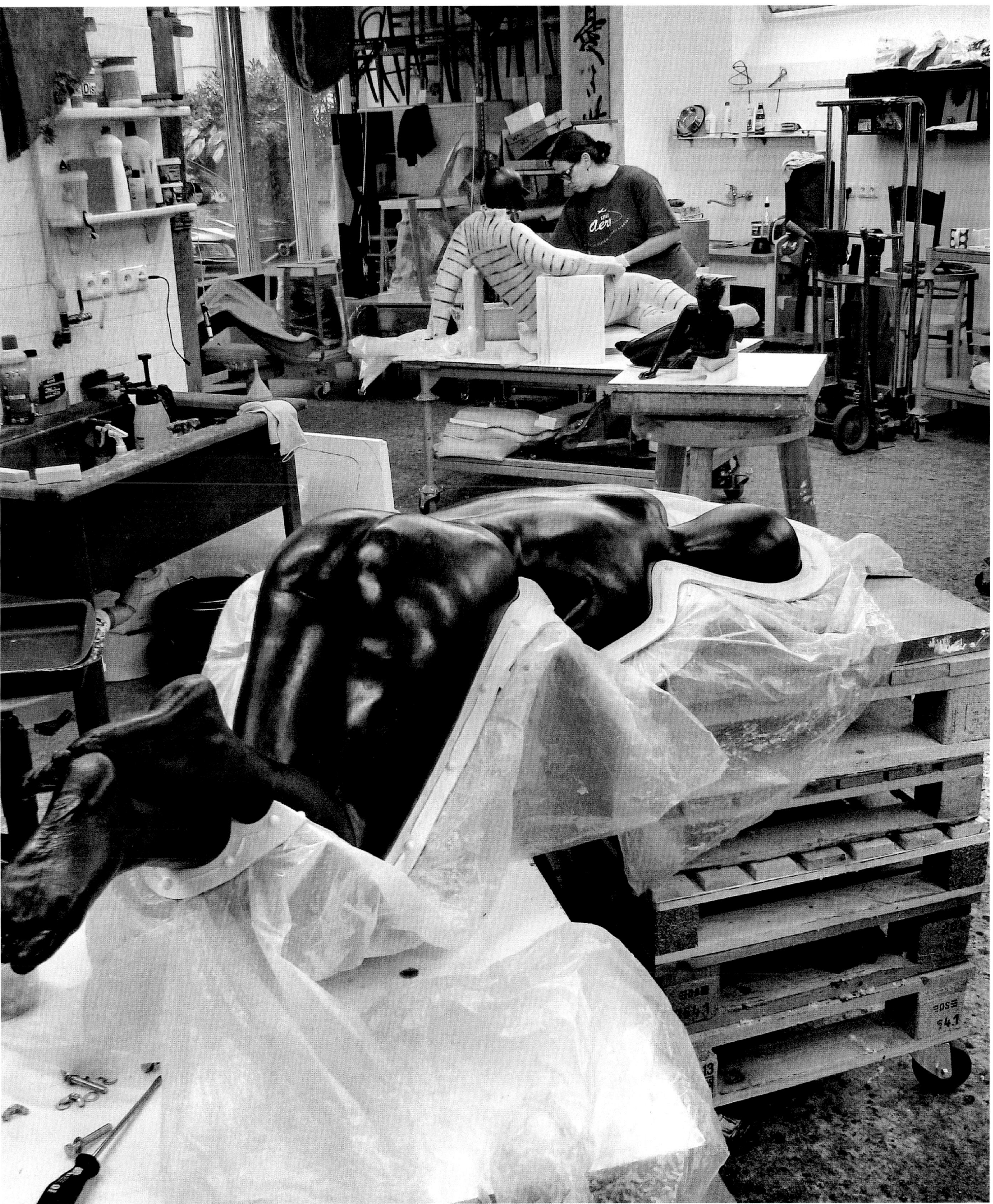

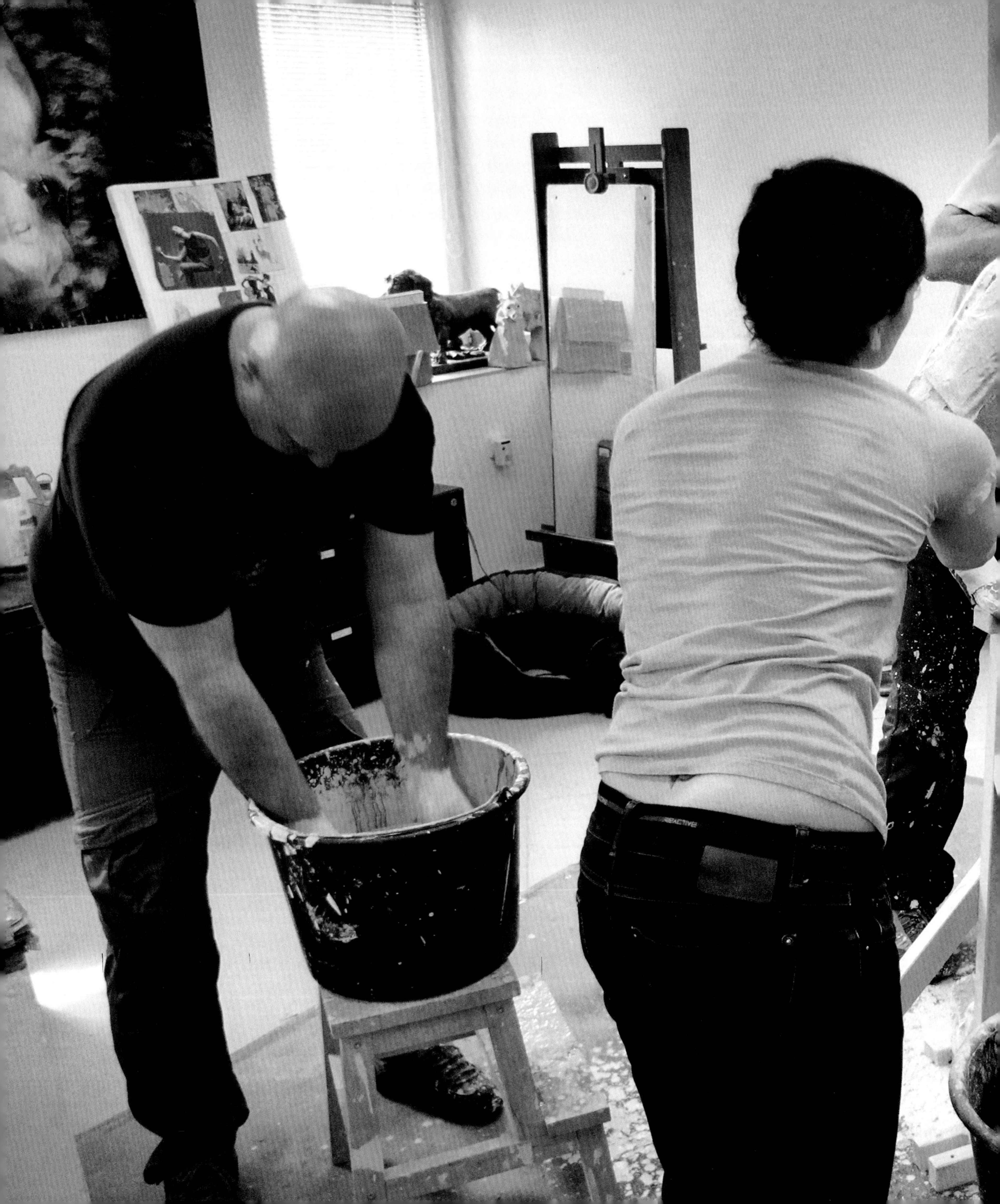

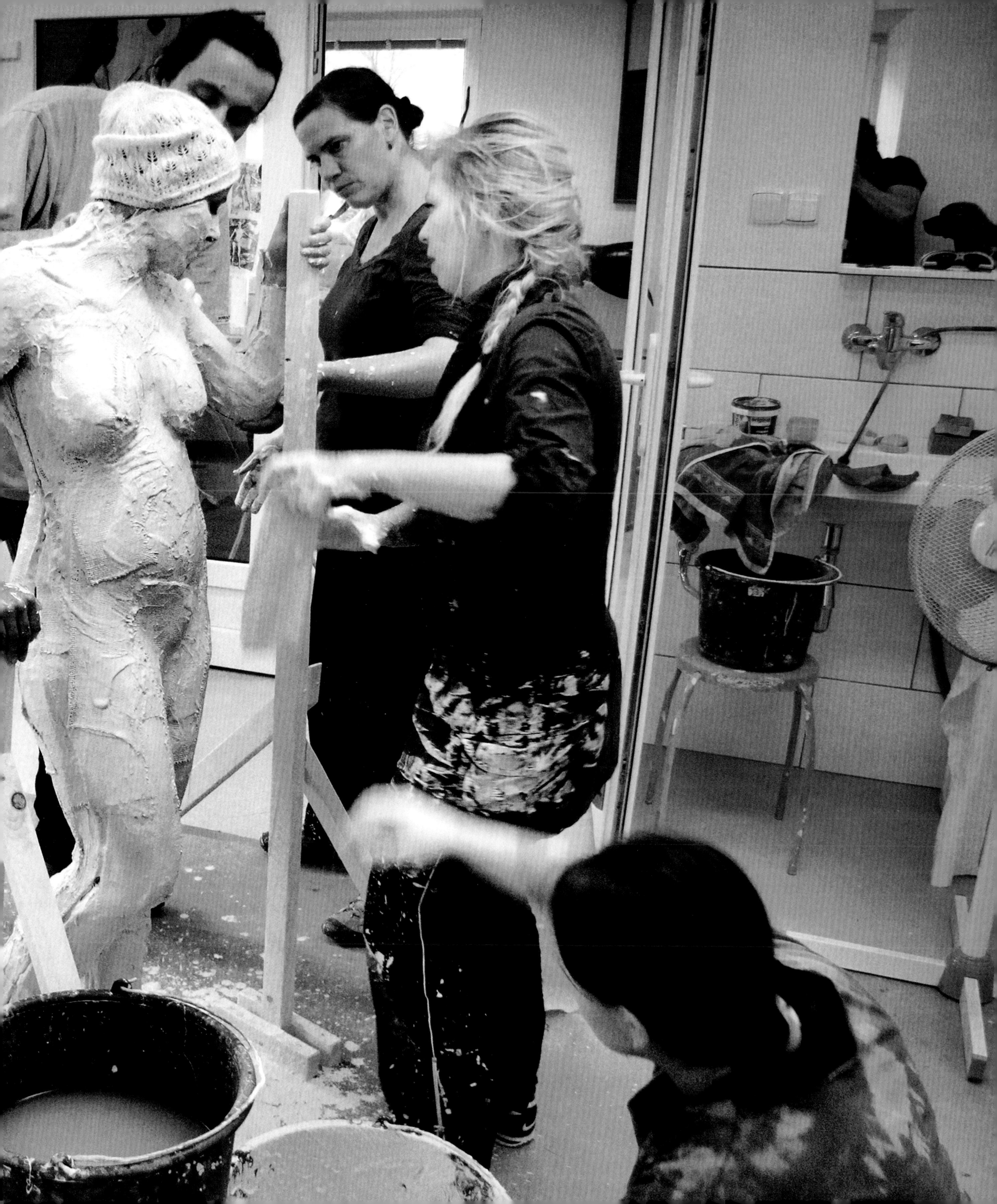

Fashioning *Reclining Nocturne 2*, 2014.

FOLLOWING

Installation of white bronze *Nocturnes*, 2015.

Installation of white bronze, rusted iron, and cast glass *Nocturnes*, 2019.

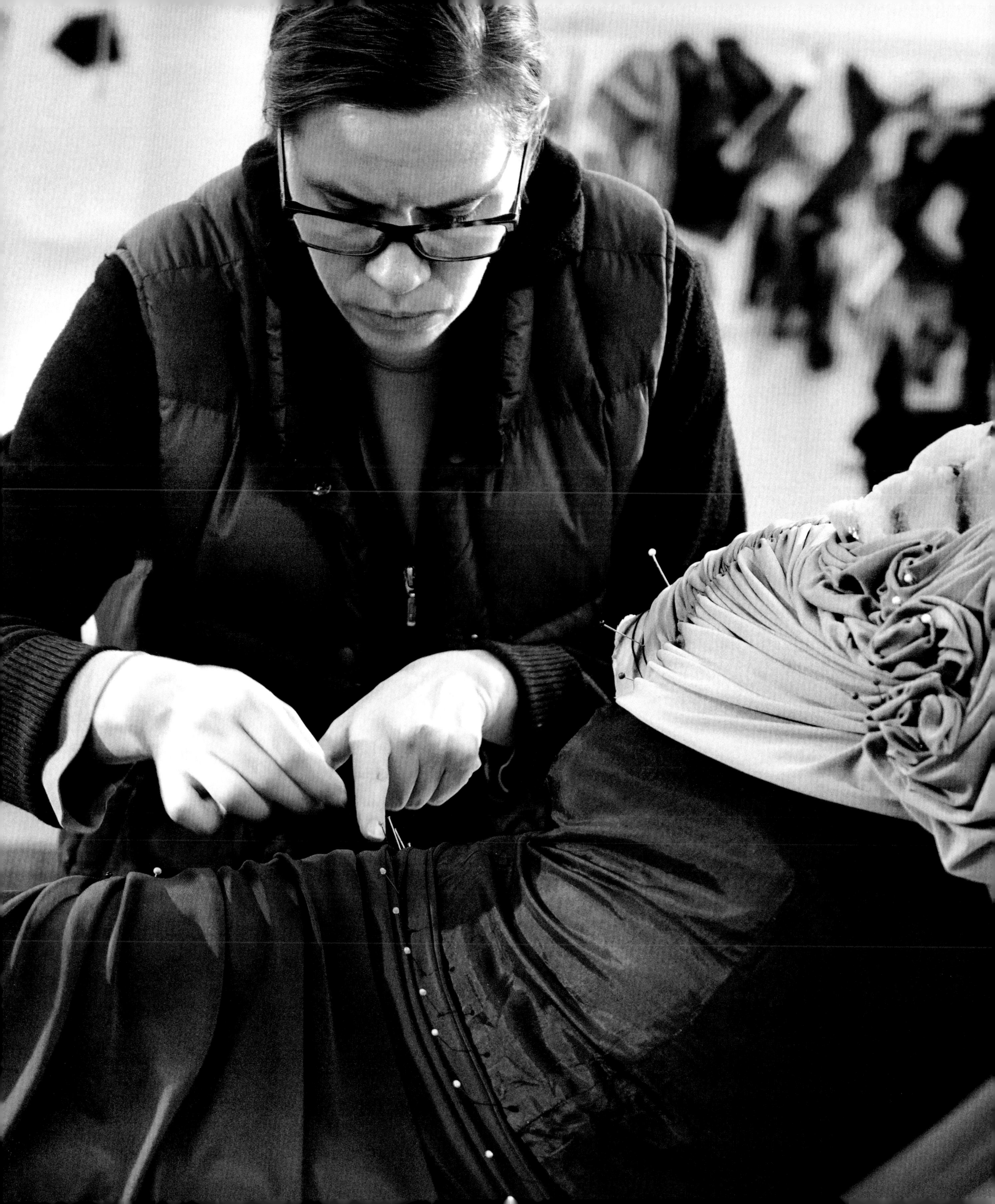

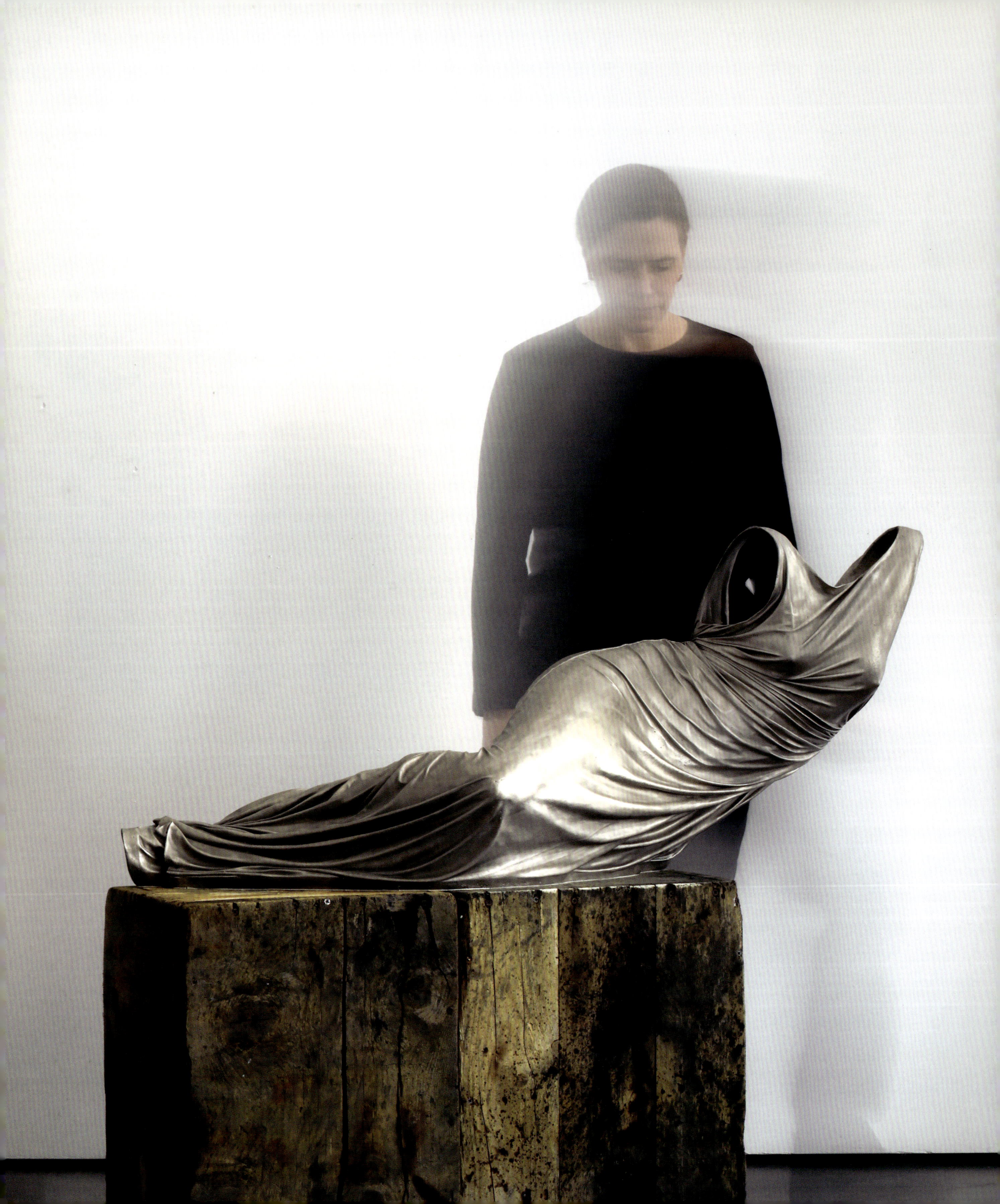

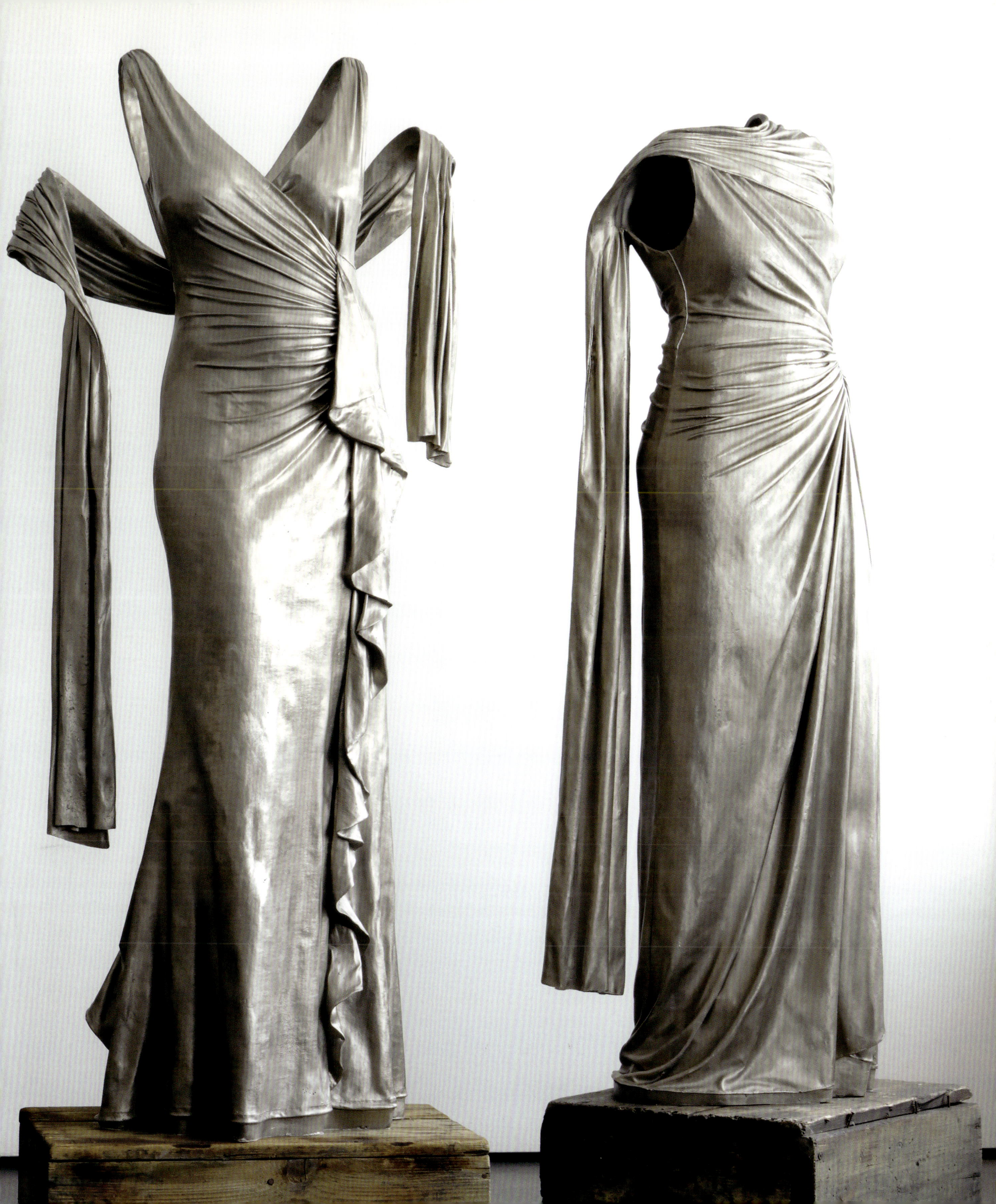

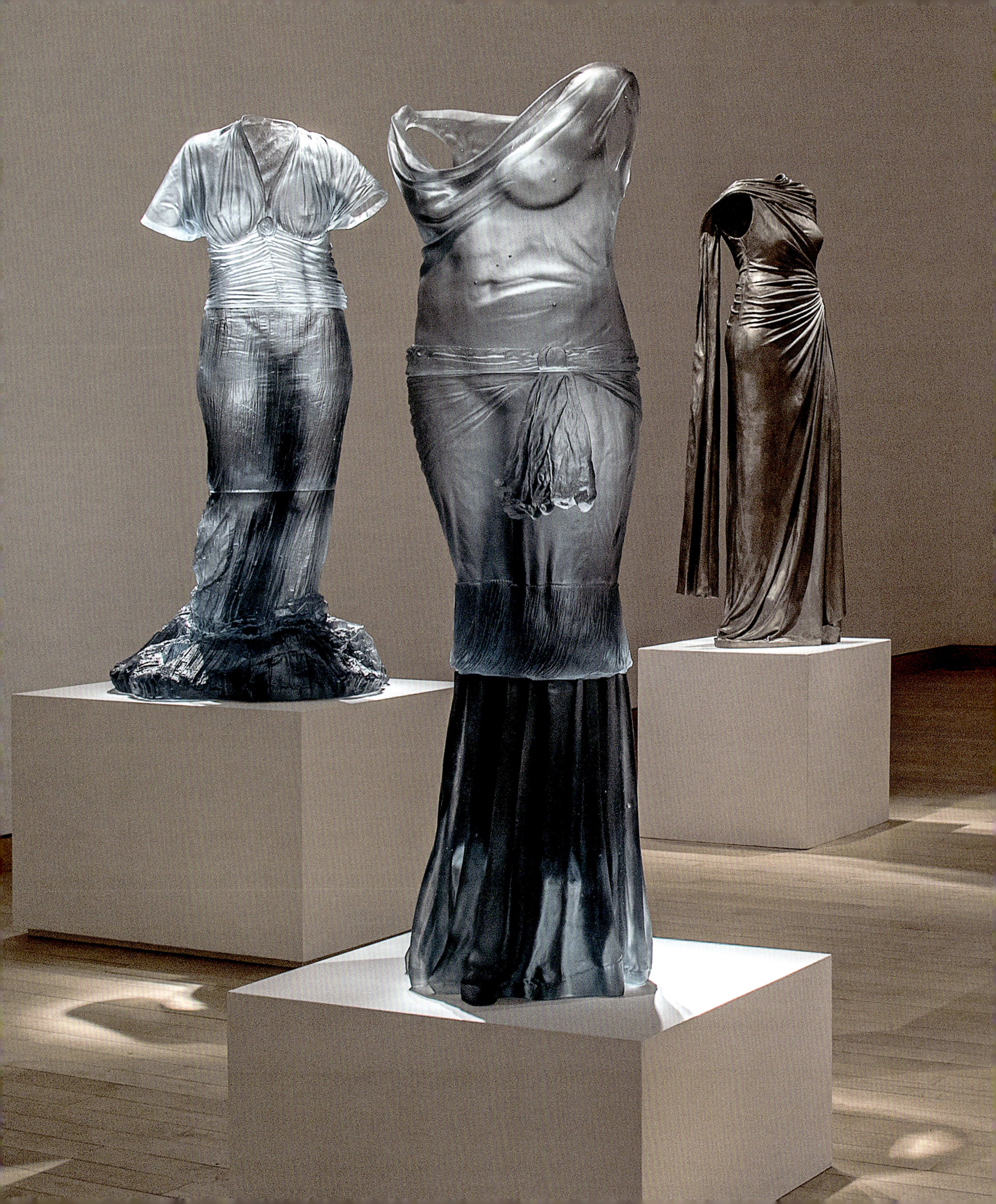

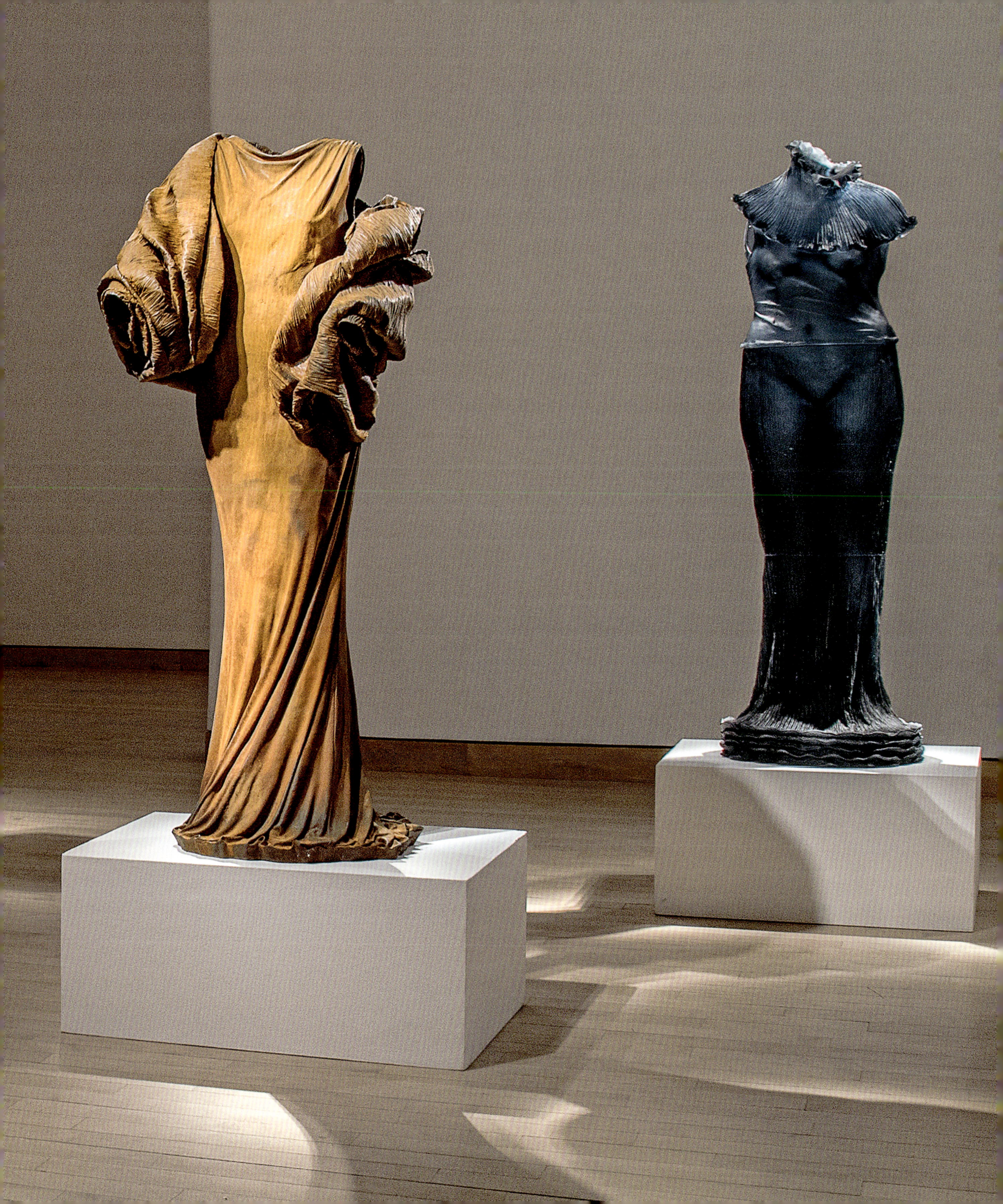

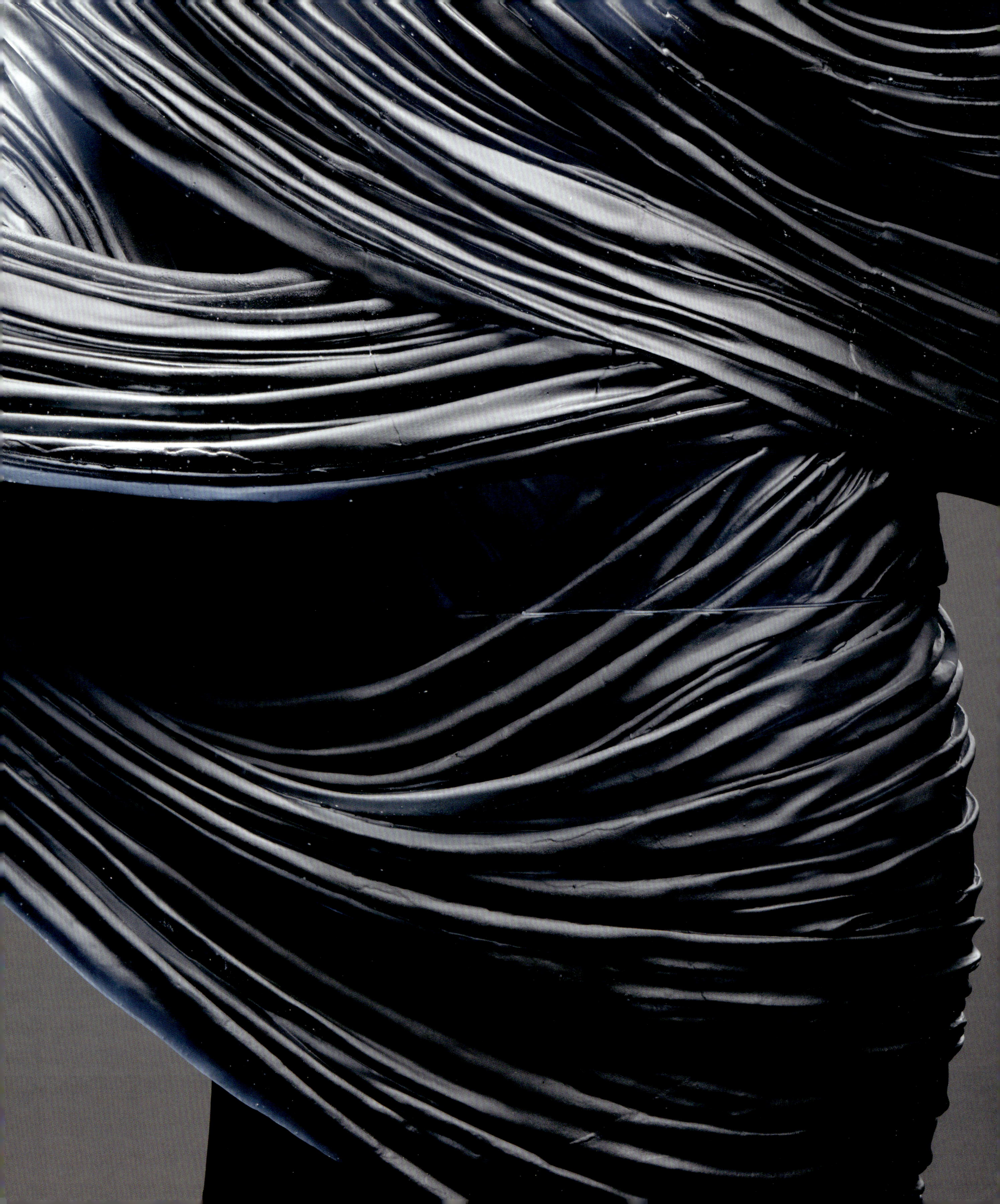

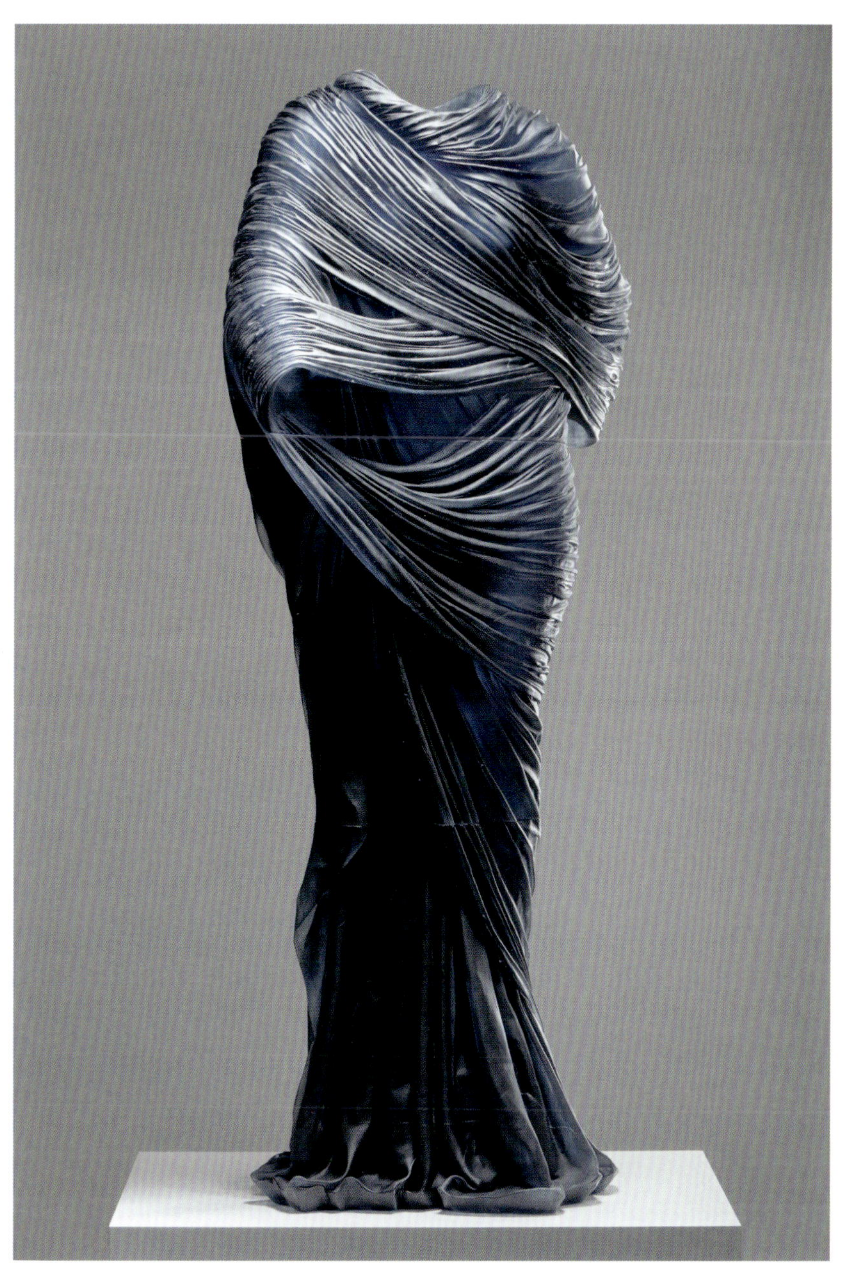

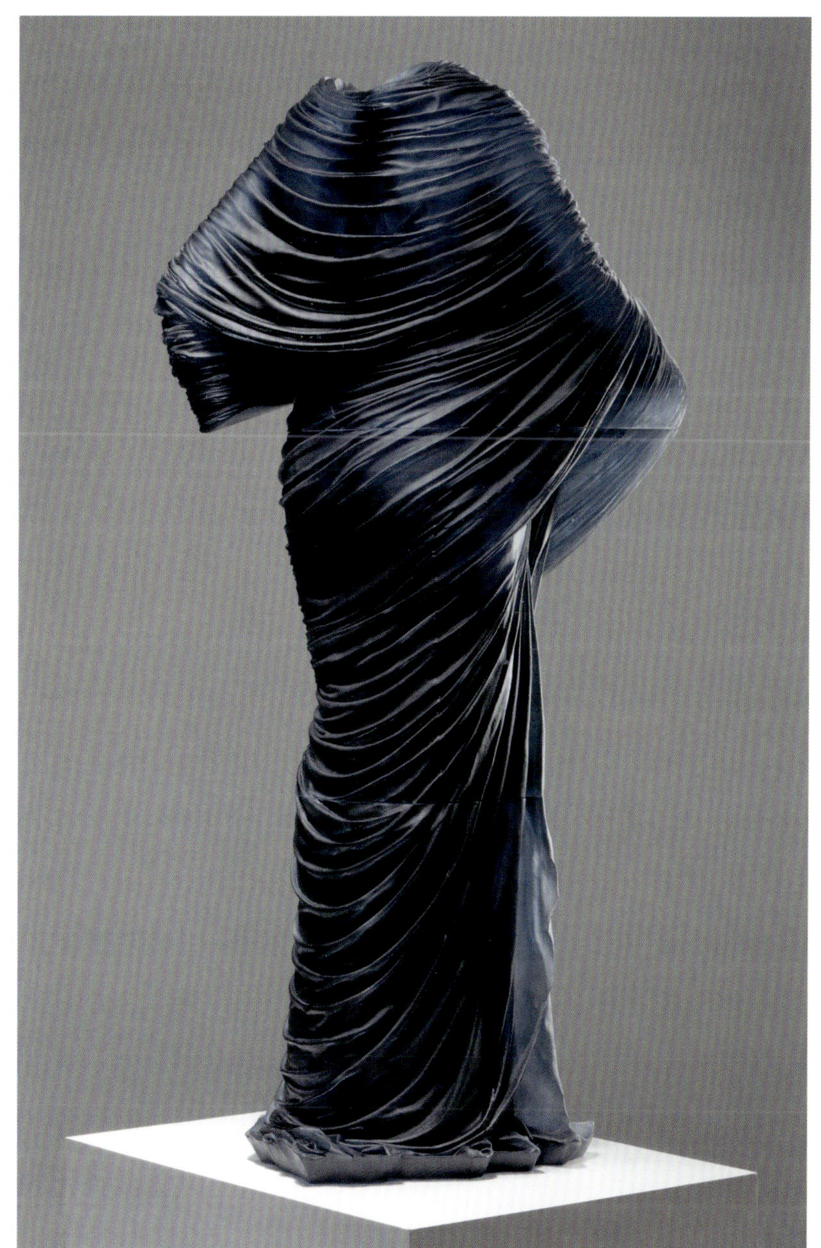

Nocturne 5, 2015
Cast glass, 60½ × 28½ × 22 in. (153.5 × 73 × 56 cm)
Collection of Corning Museum of Glass, Corning, NY

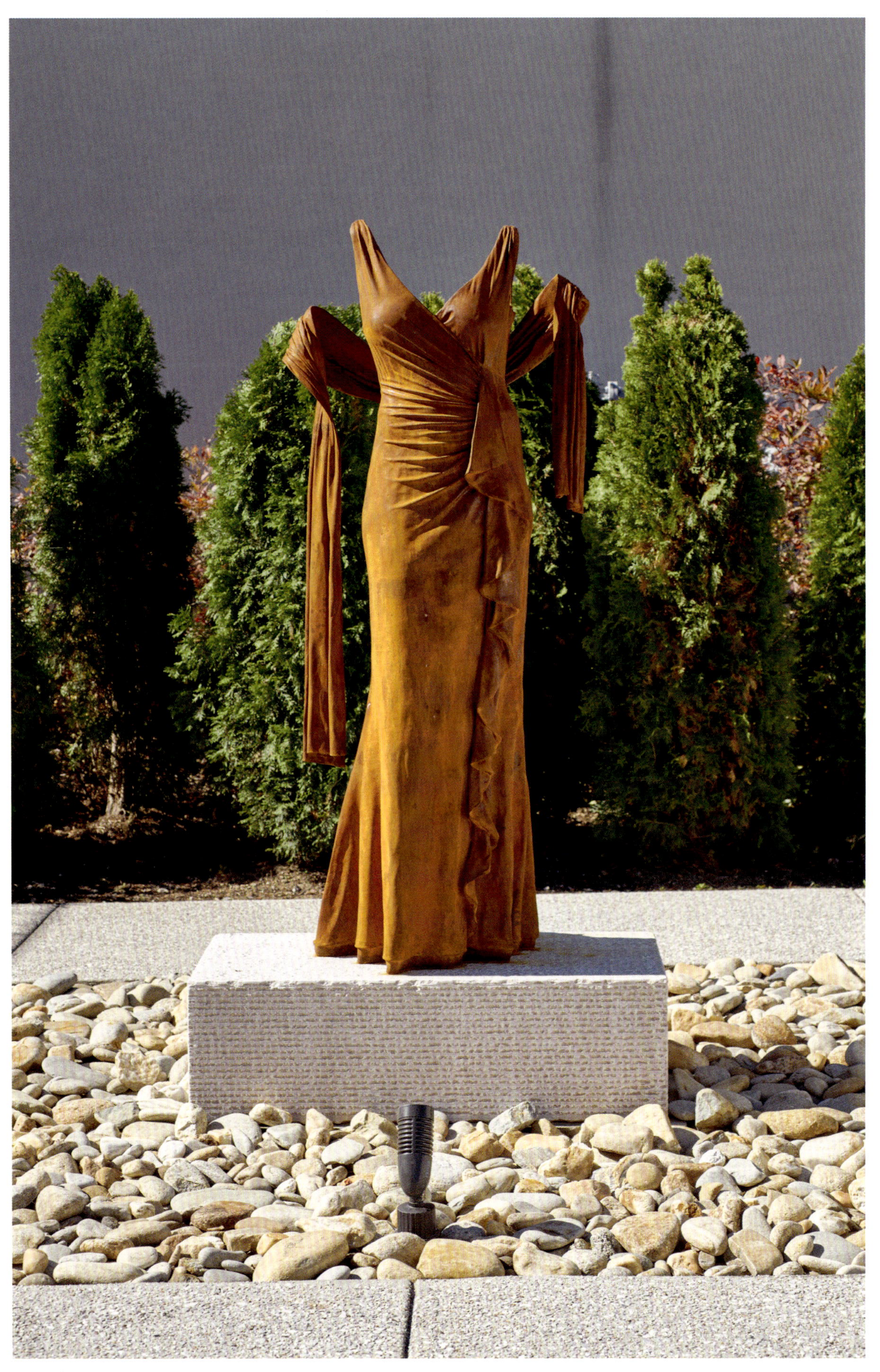

Nocturne 1, 2018
Land Family Sculpture Garden, 2019
Knoxville Museum of Art, Knoxville, TN

OPPOSITE
Nocturne 1, 2018
Rusted iron, 60 × 26½ × 18½ in.
(153 × 67 × 47.5 cm)
Collection of Knoxville
Museum of Art, Knoxville, TN

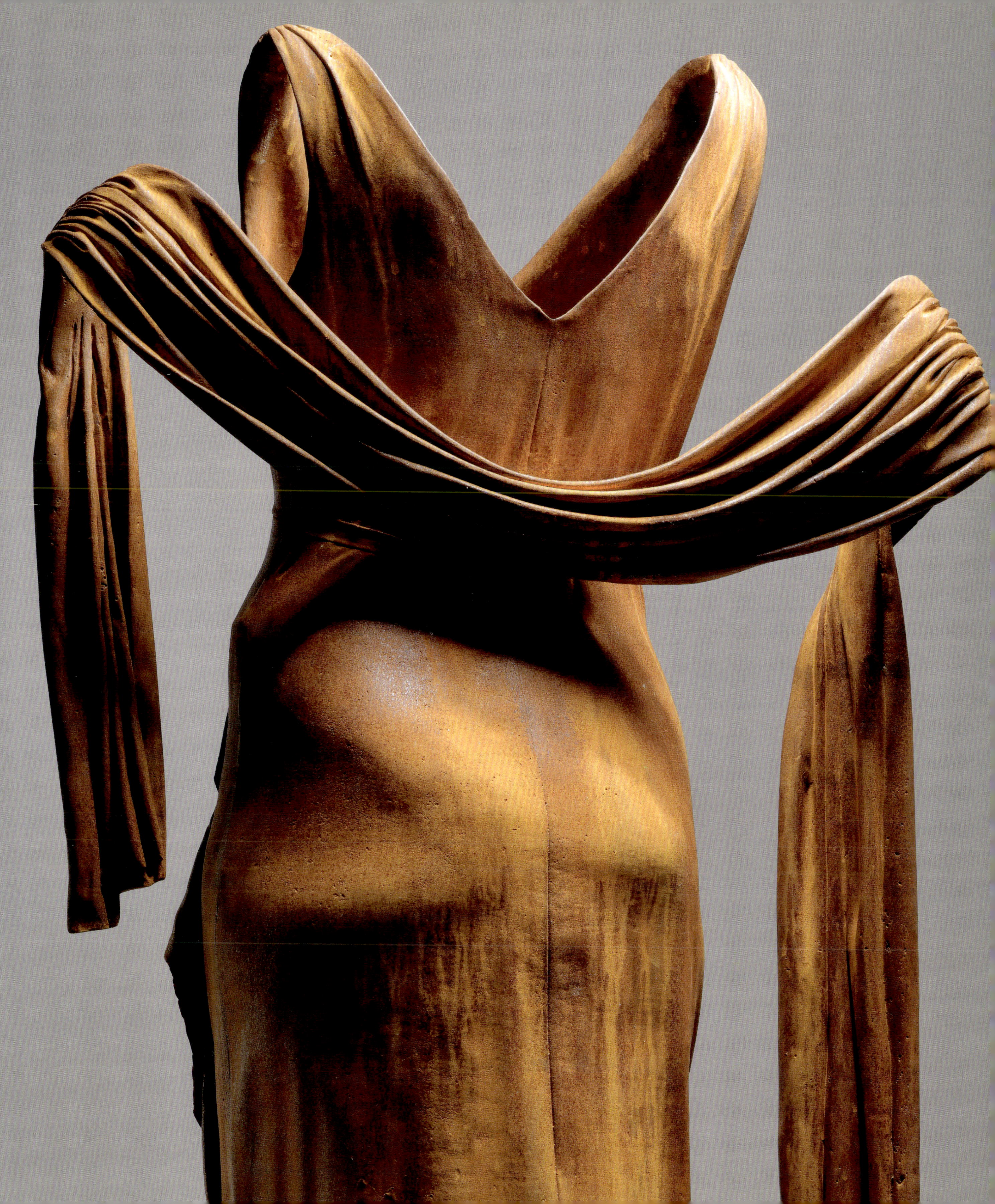

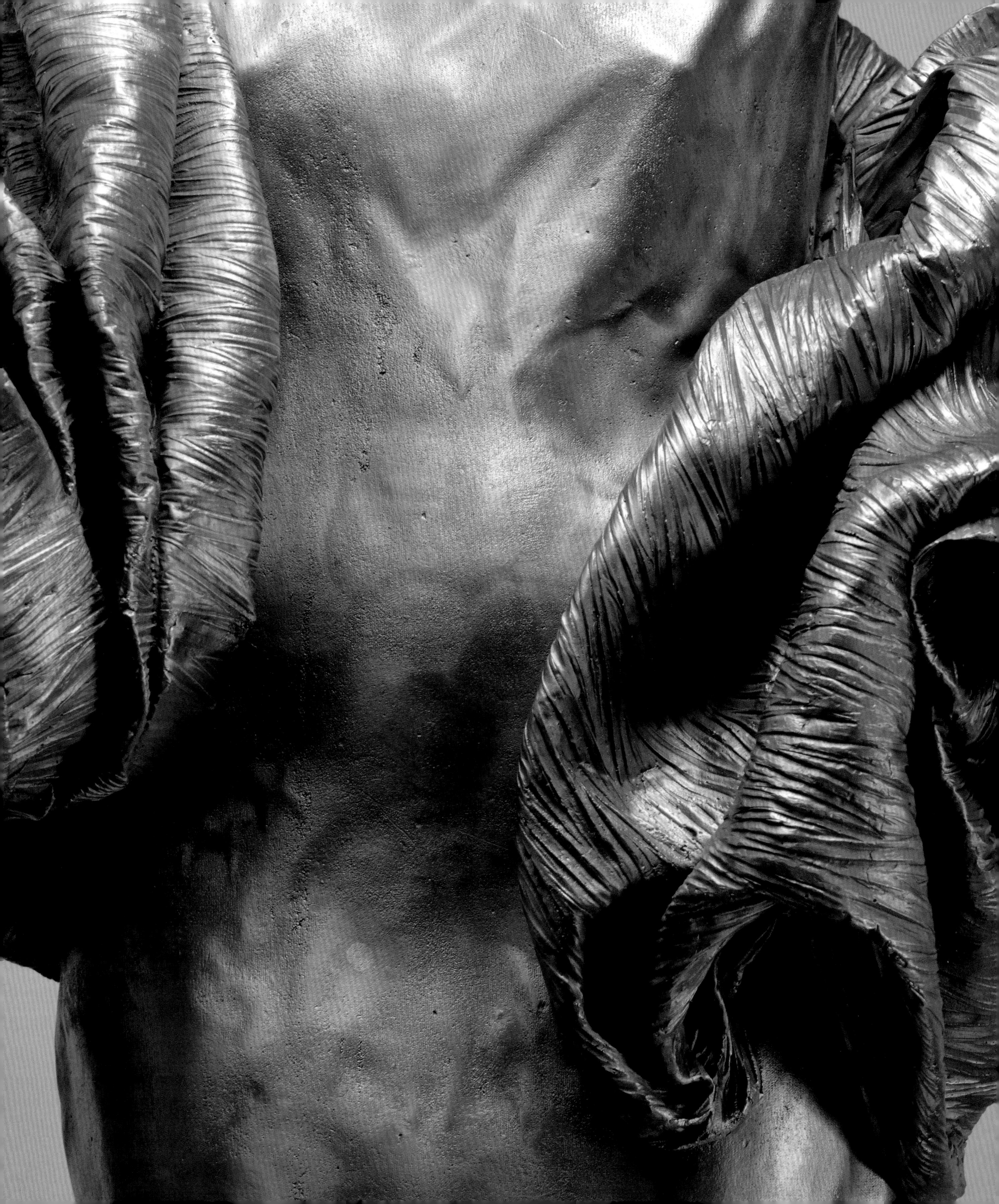

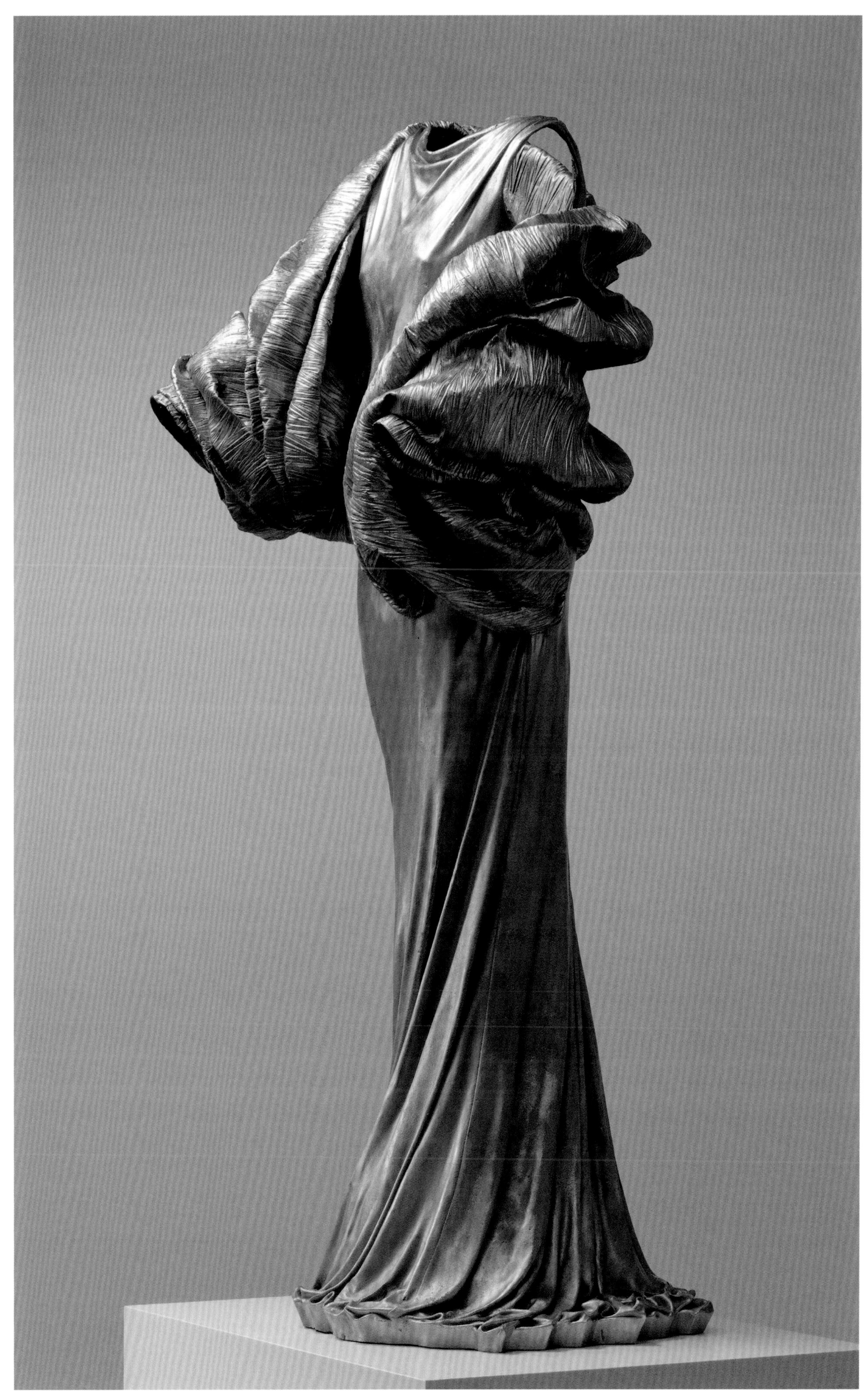

Nocturne 3, 2015
White bronze,
59½ × 25½ × 25½ in.
(151.5 × 64.5 × 65 cm)

Nocturne 2, 2015
White bronze, 59½ × 19½ × 15½ in.
(150.5 × 49 × 40 cm)

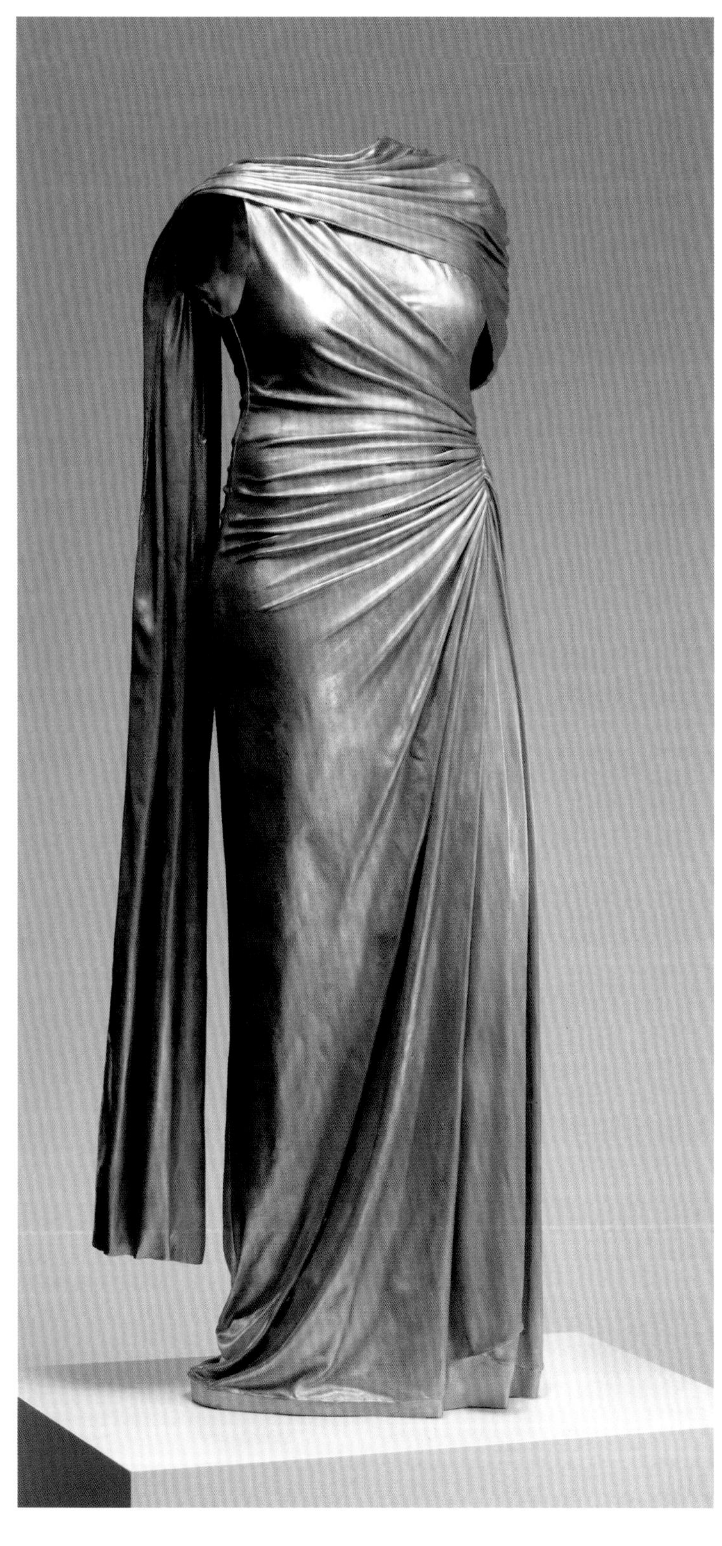

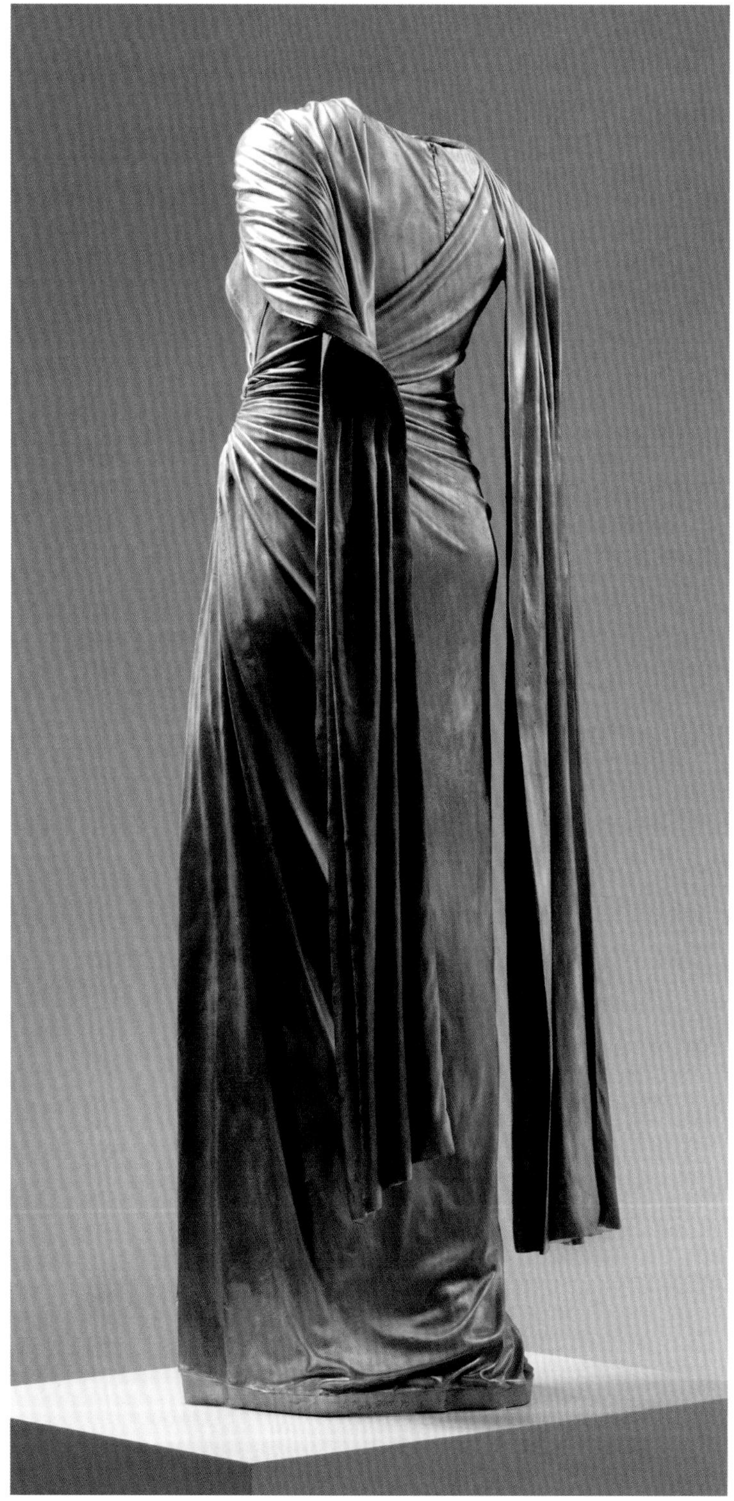

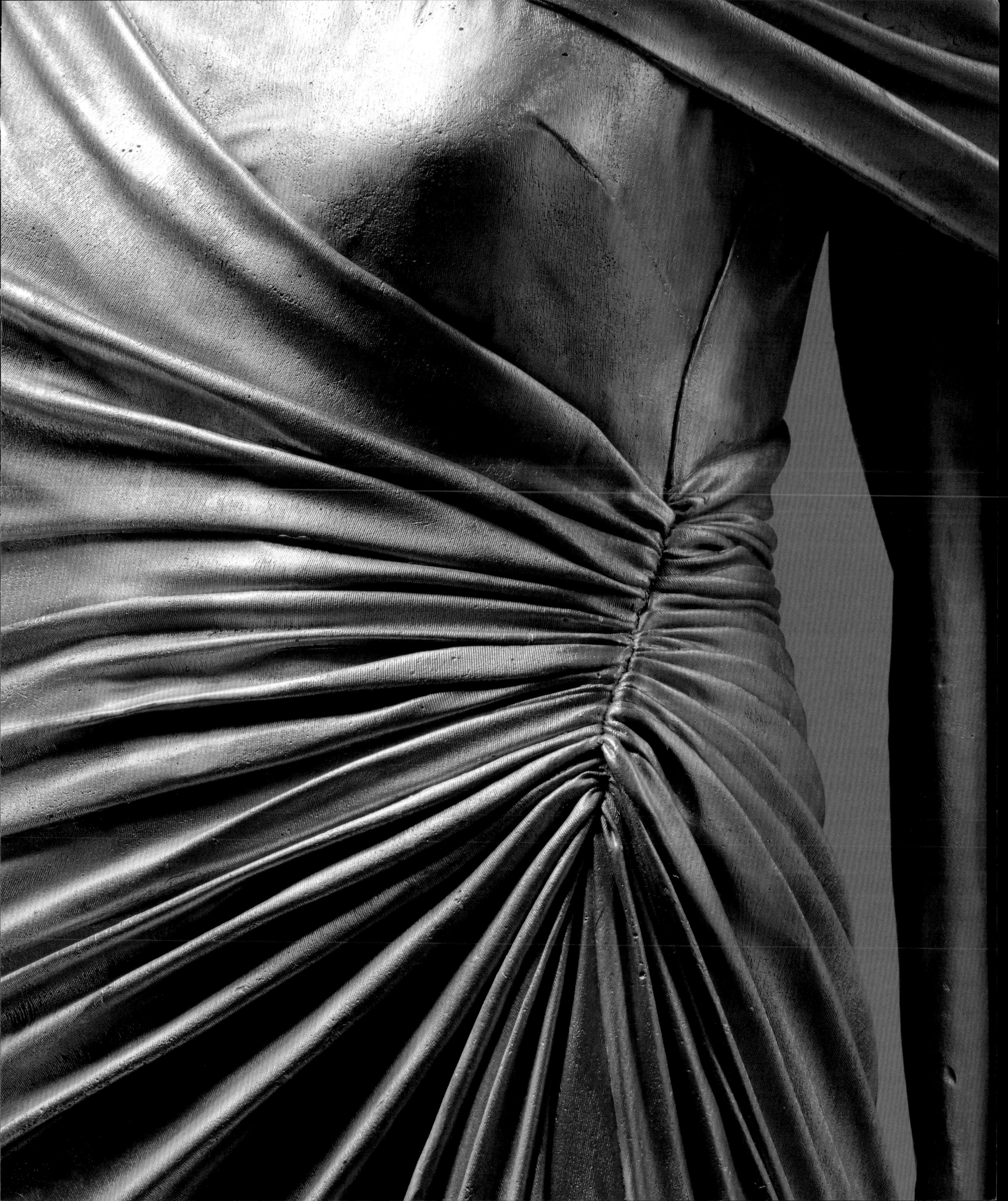

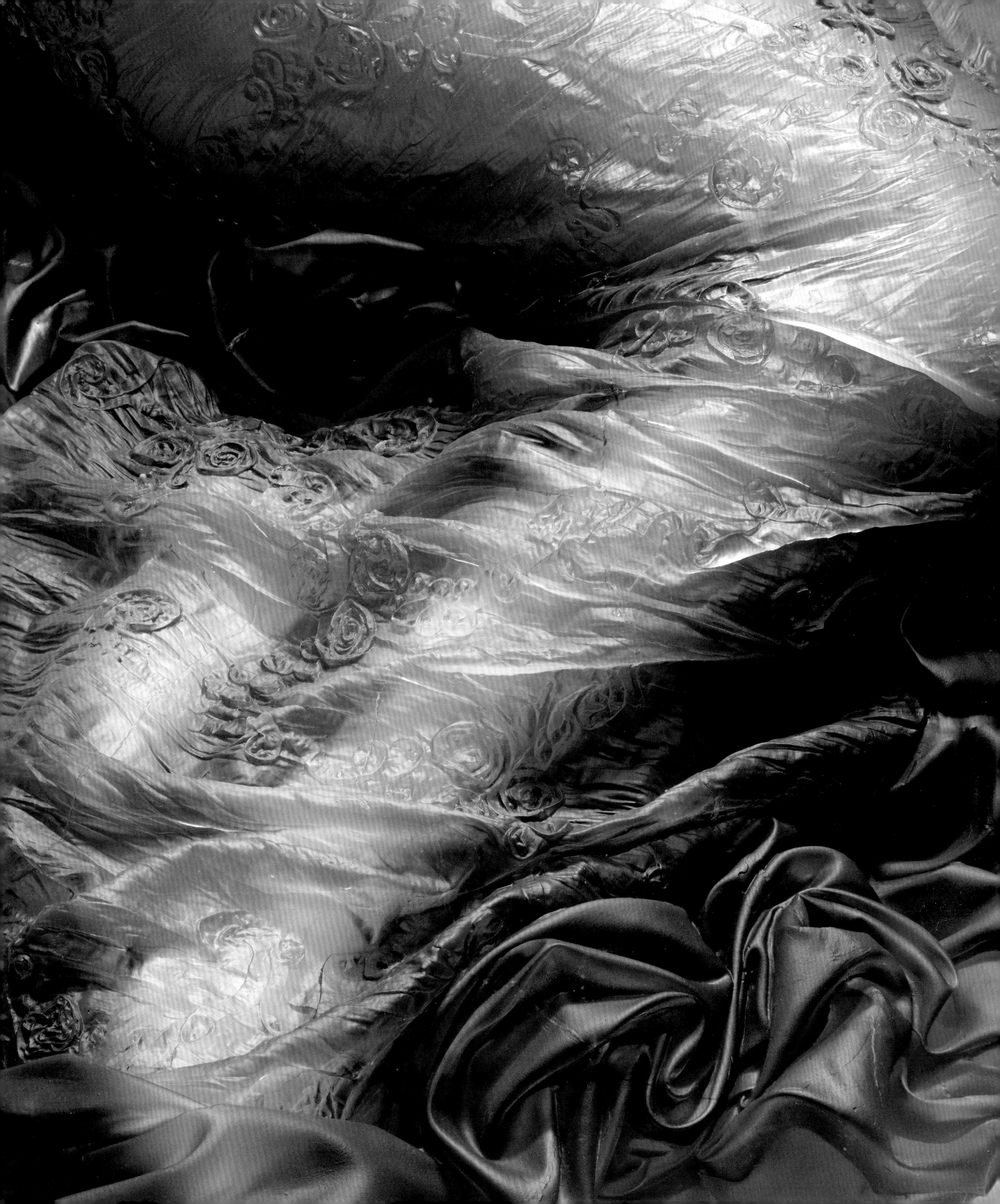

Reclining Nocturne 1, 2015
Cast glass, 21½ × 53 × 32½ in. (55 × 135 × 82 cm)

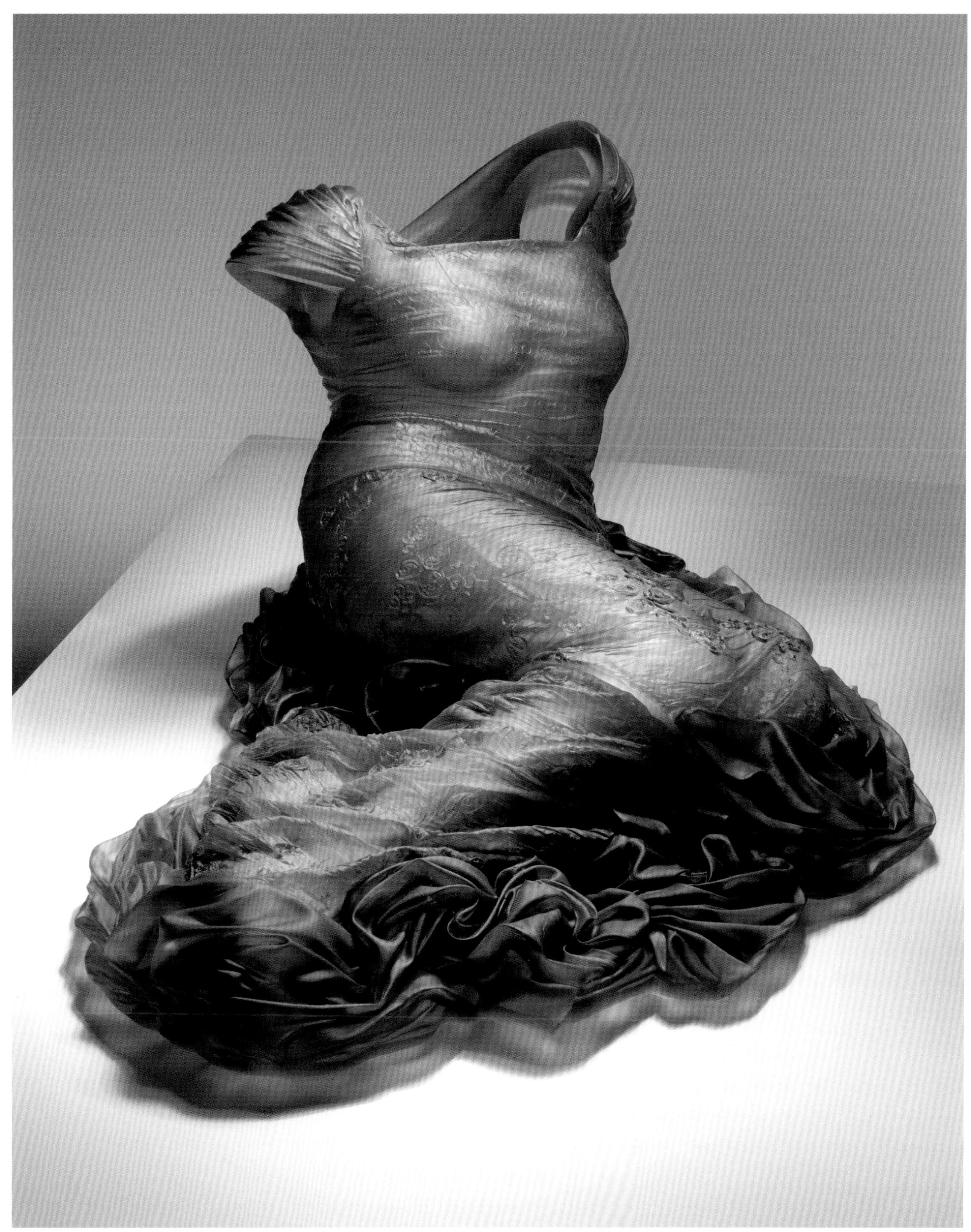

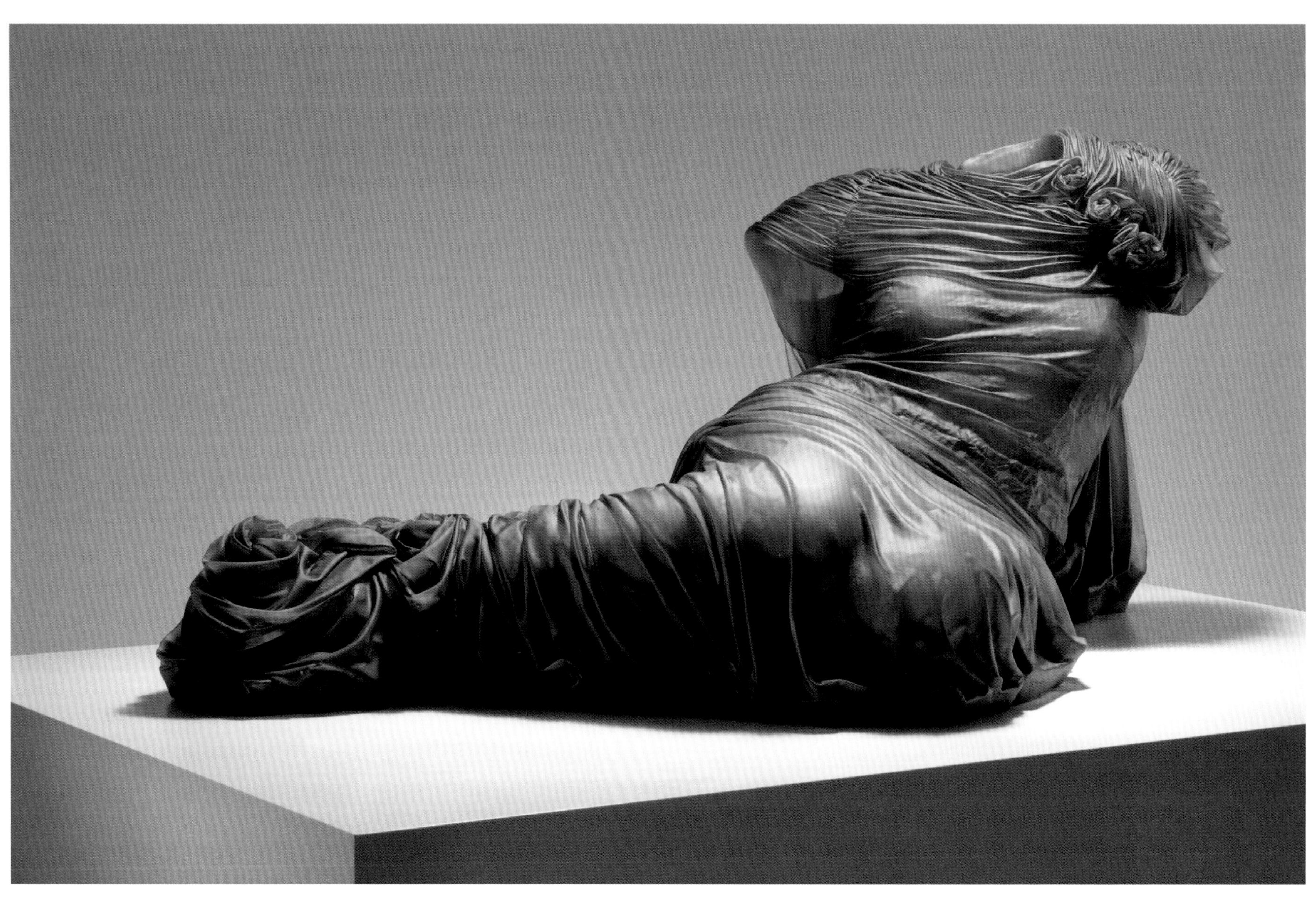

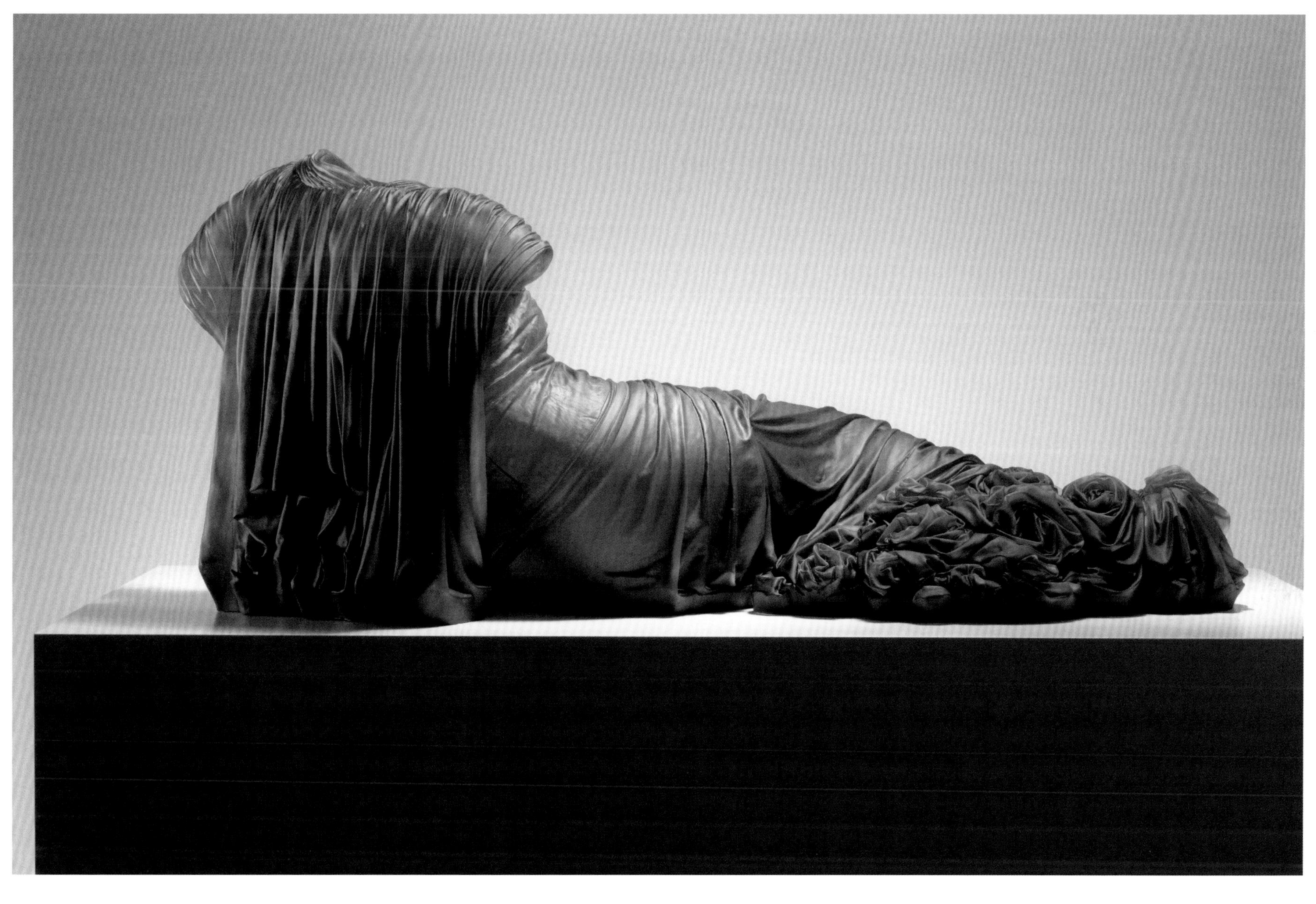

Reclining Nocturne 2, 2019
Cast glass, 22 × 53 × 26½ in. (55.5 × 134.5 × 67.5 cm)

FOLLOWING
Reclining Nocturne 3, 2017
Cast glass, 20½ × 60 × 26 in. (51.5 × 153 × 65.5 cm)

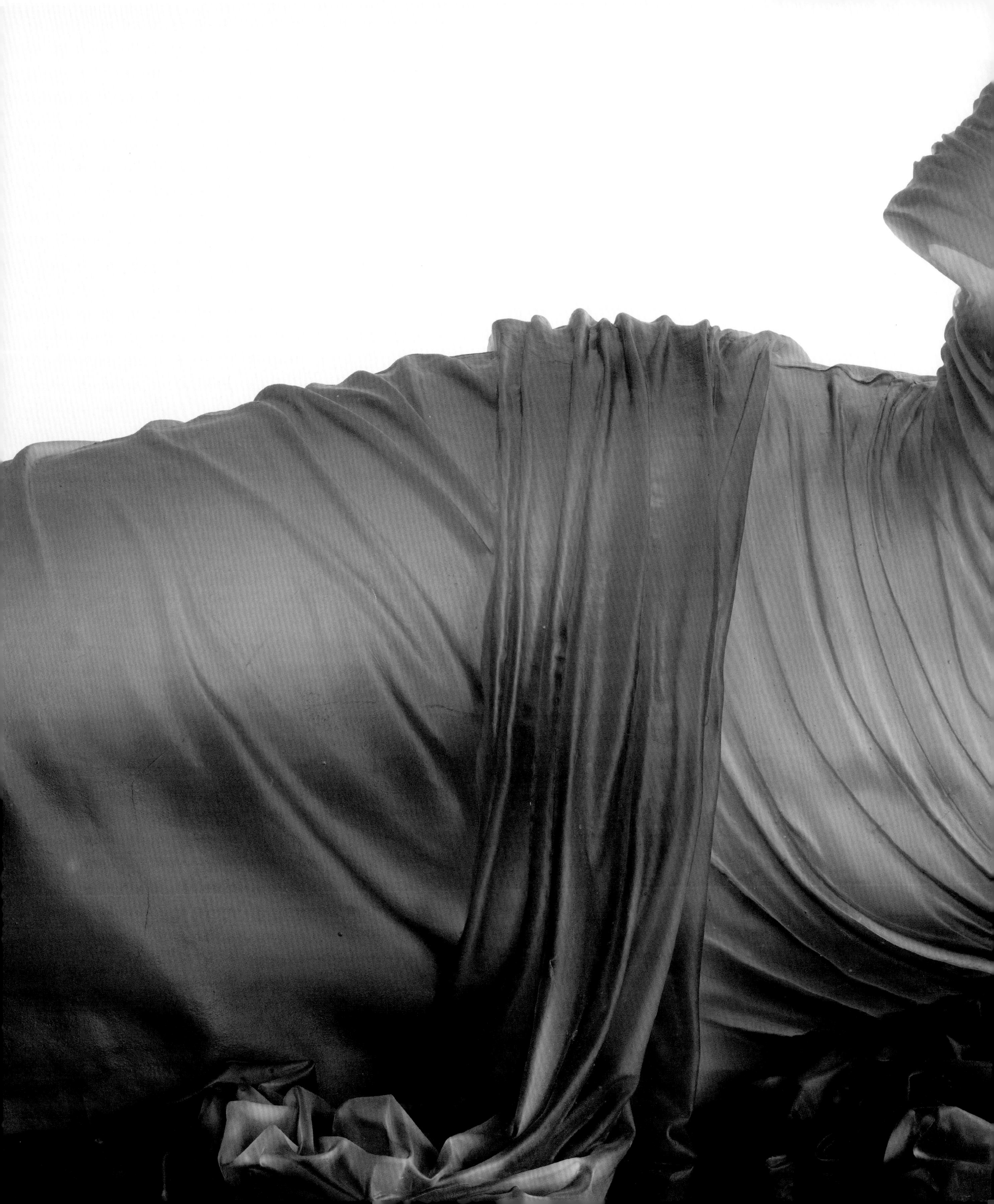

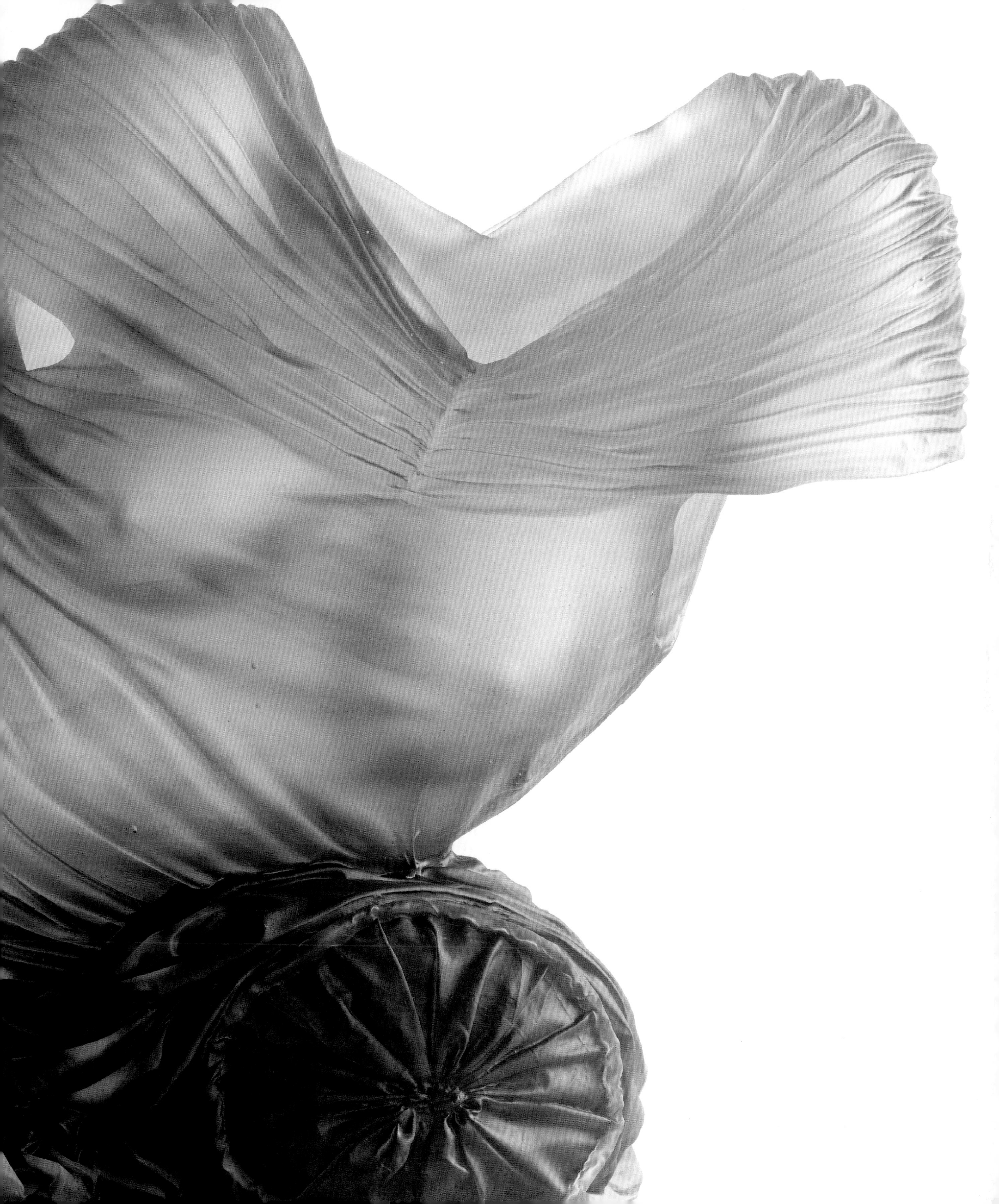

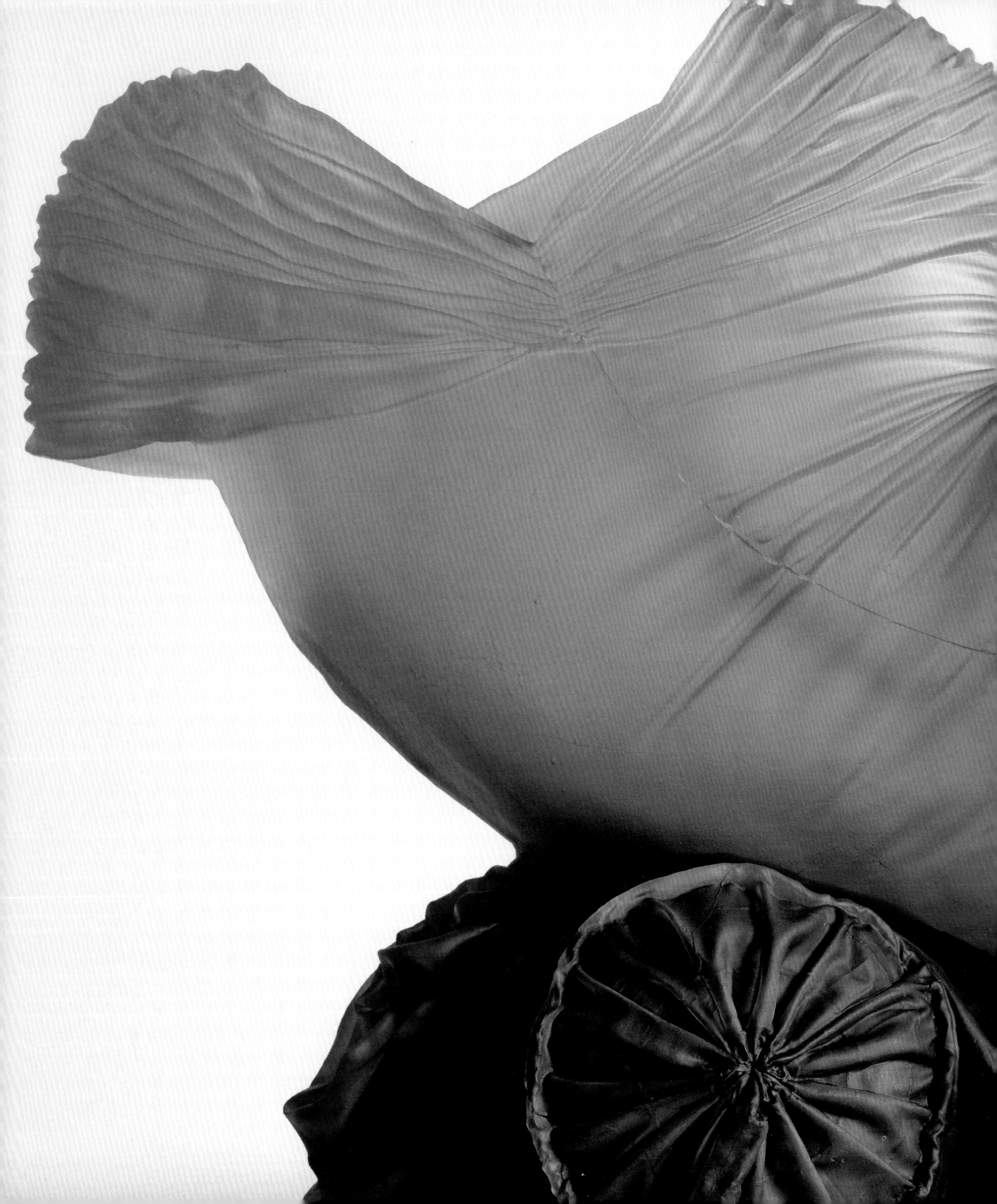

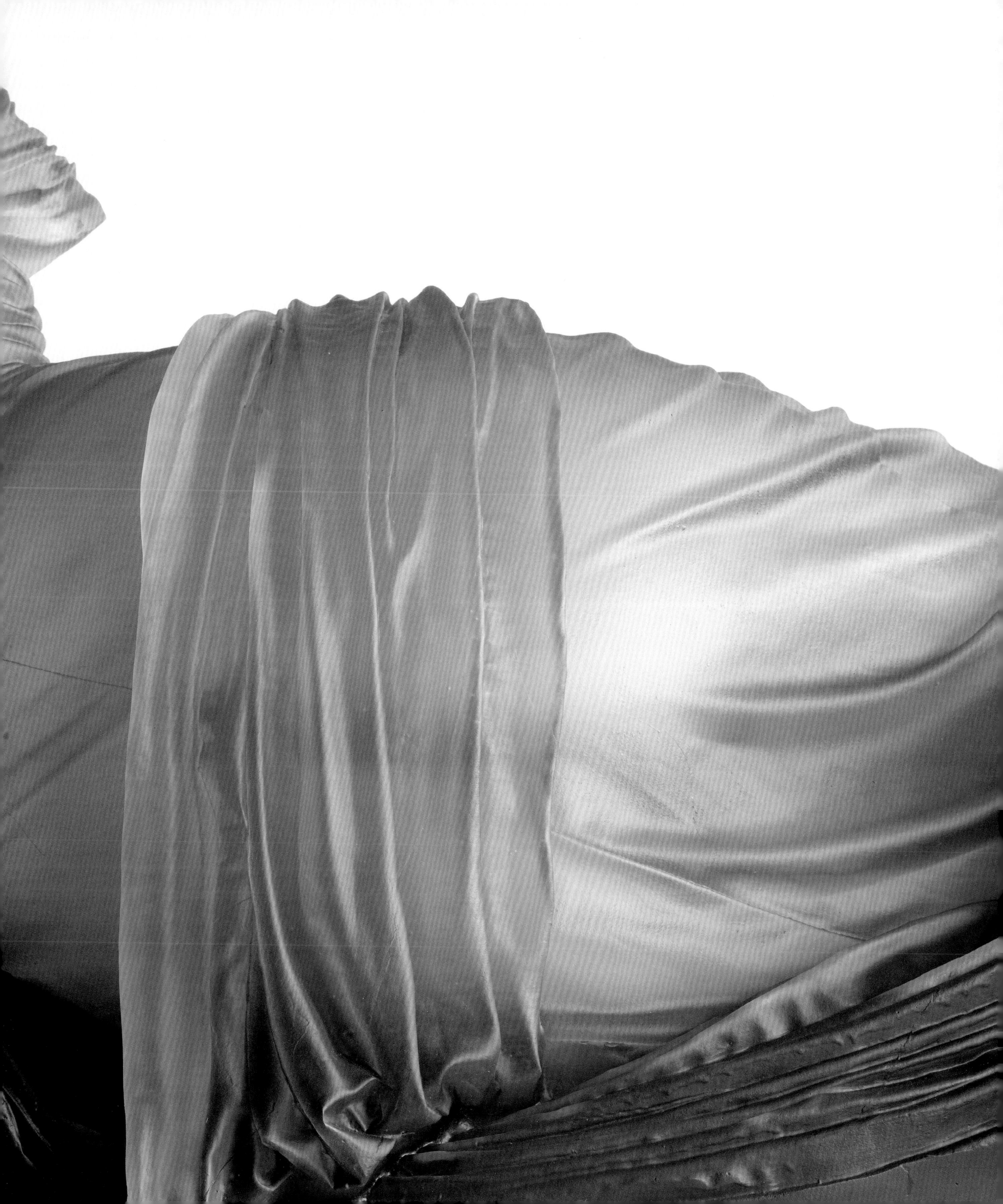

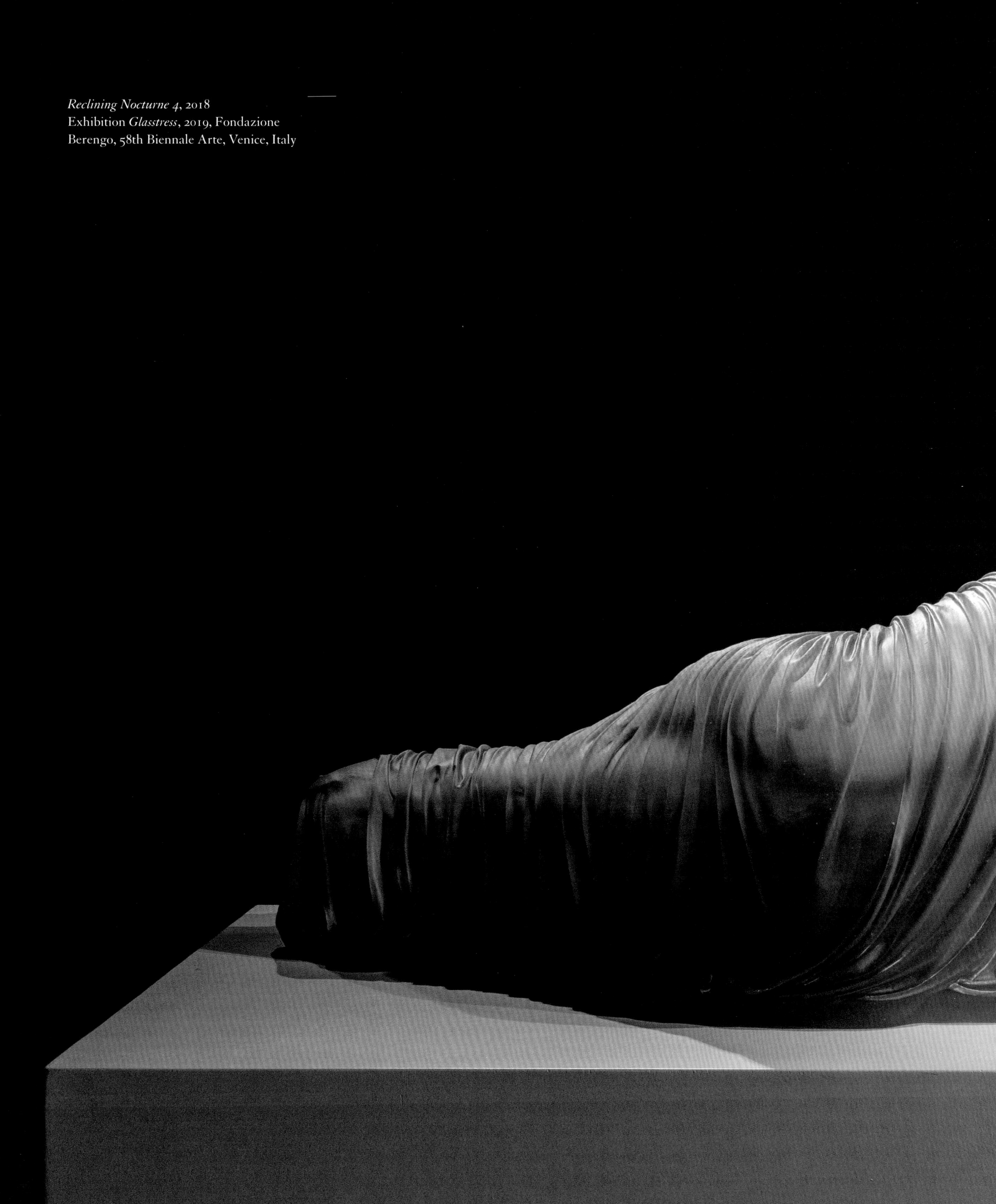

Reclining Nocturne 4, 2018
Exhibition *Glasstress*, 2019, Fondazione Berengo, 58th Biennale Arte, Venice, Italy

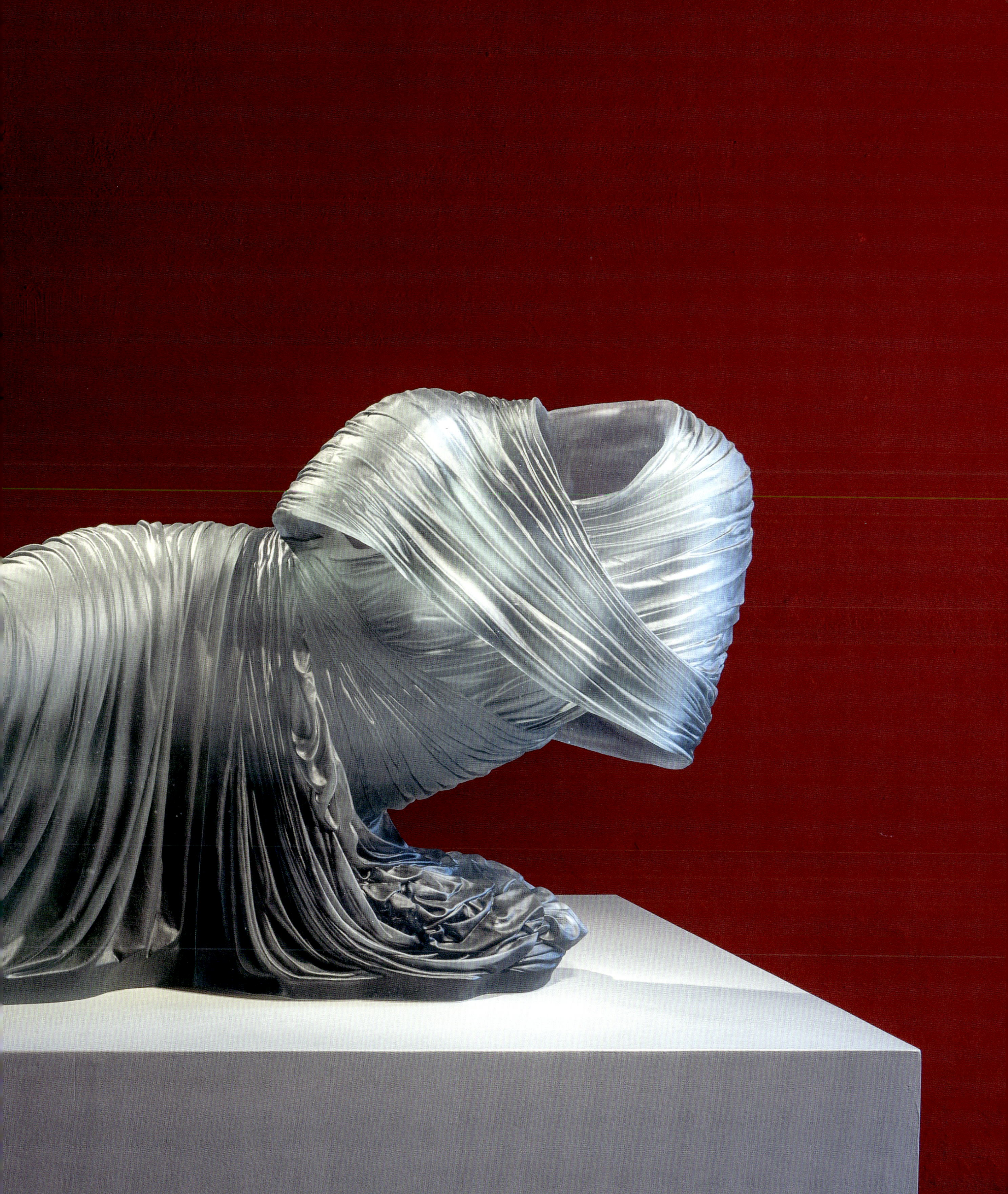

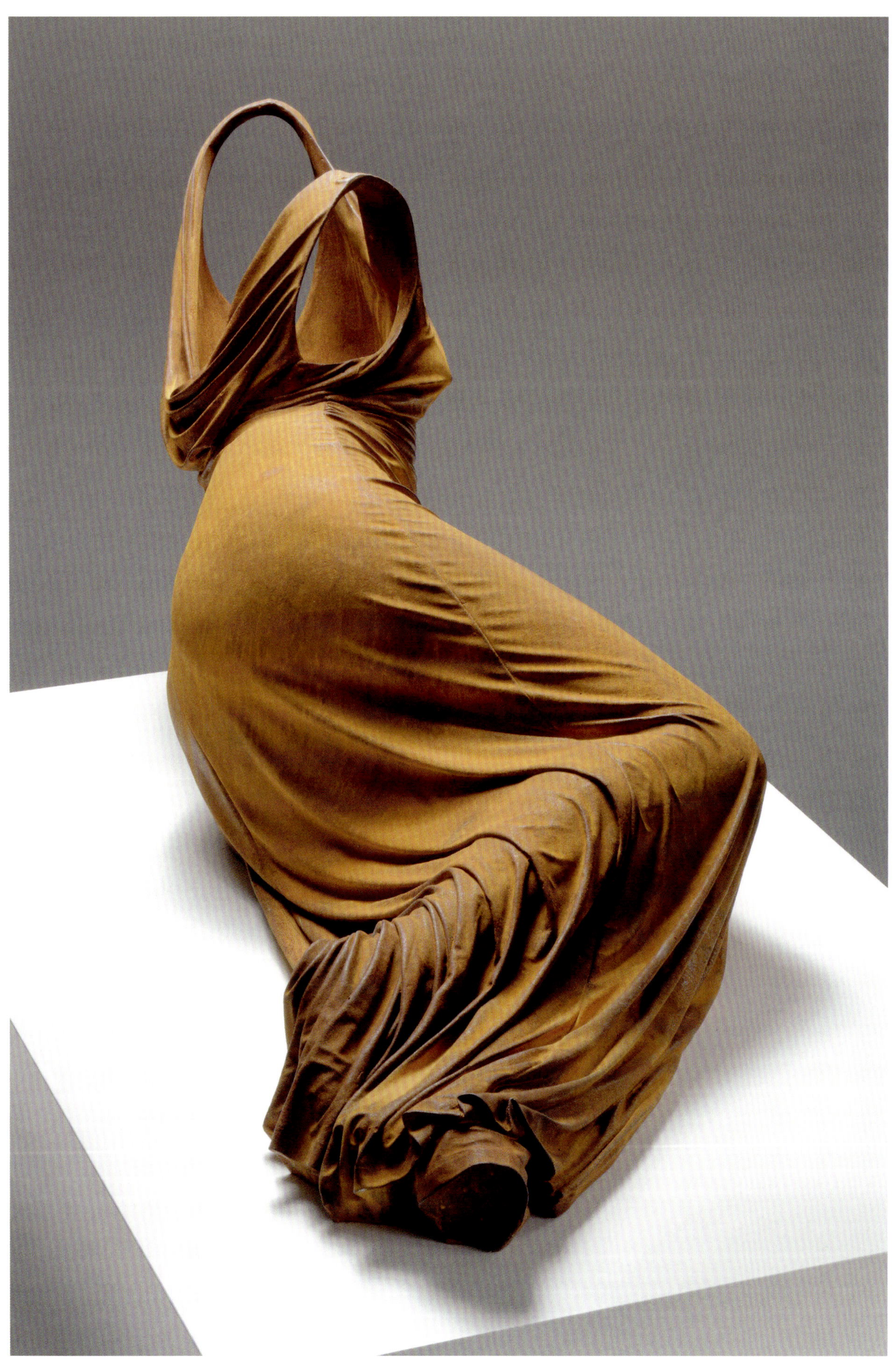

Reclining Nocturne 1, 2015
Rusted iron, 21½ × 49 × 19½ in.
(55 × 124 × 50 cm)

FOLLOWING
Exhibition *Glasstress*, 2017
Fondazione Berengo
57th Biennale Arte, Venice, Italy

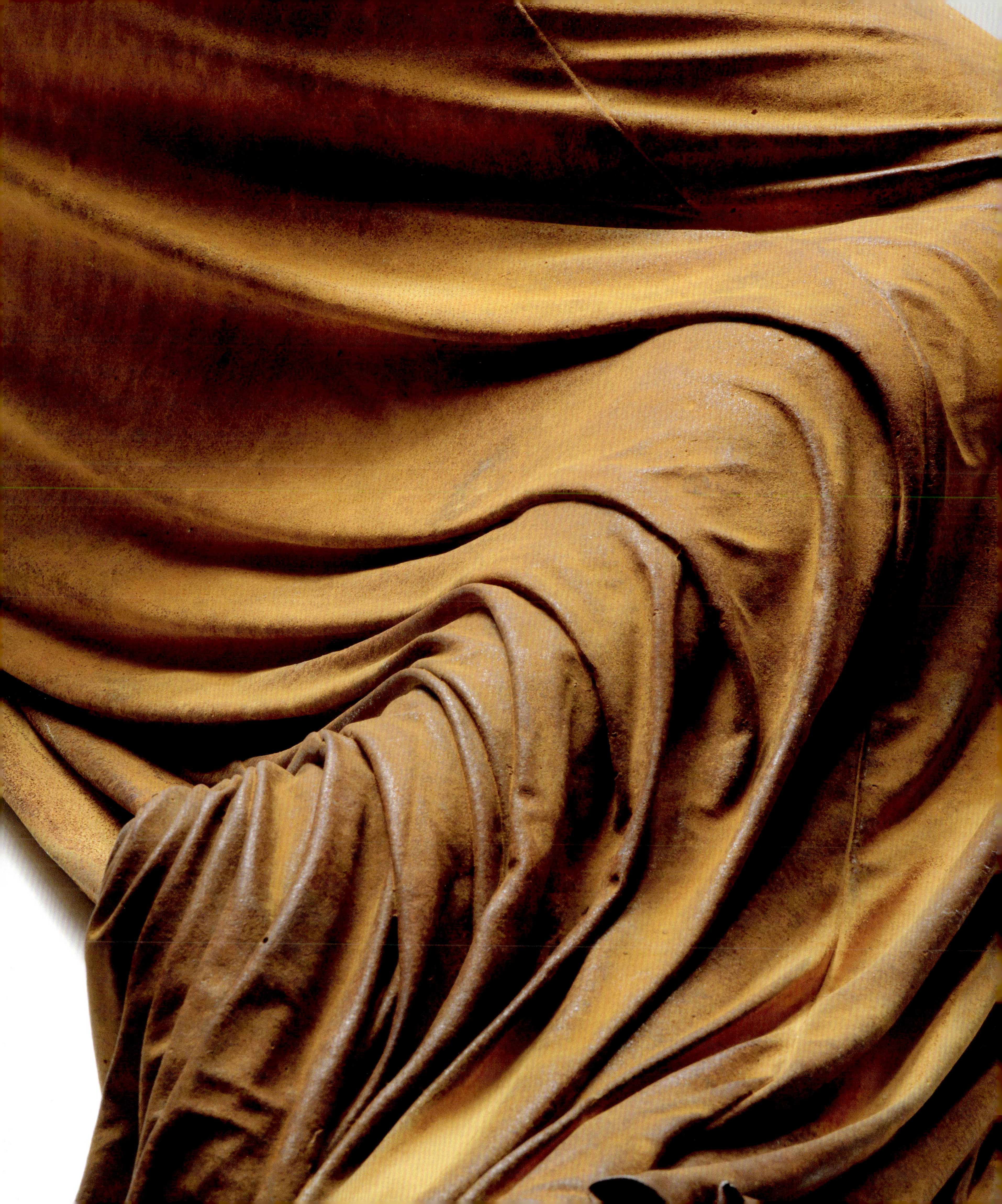

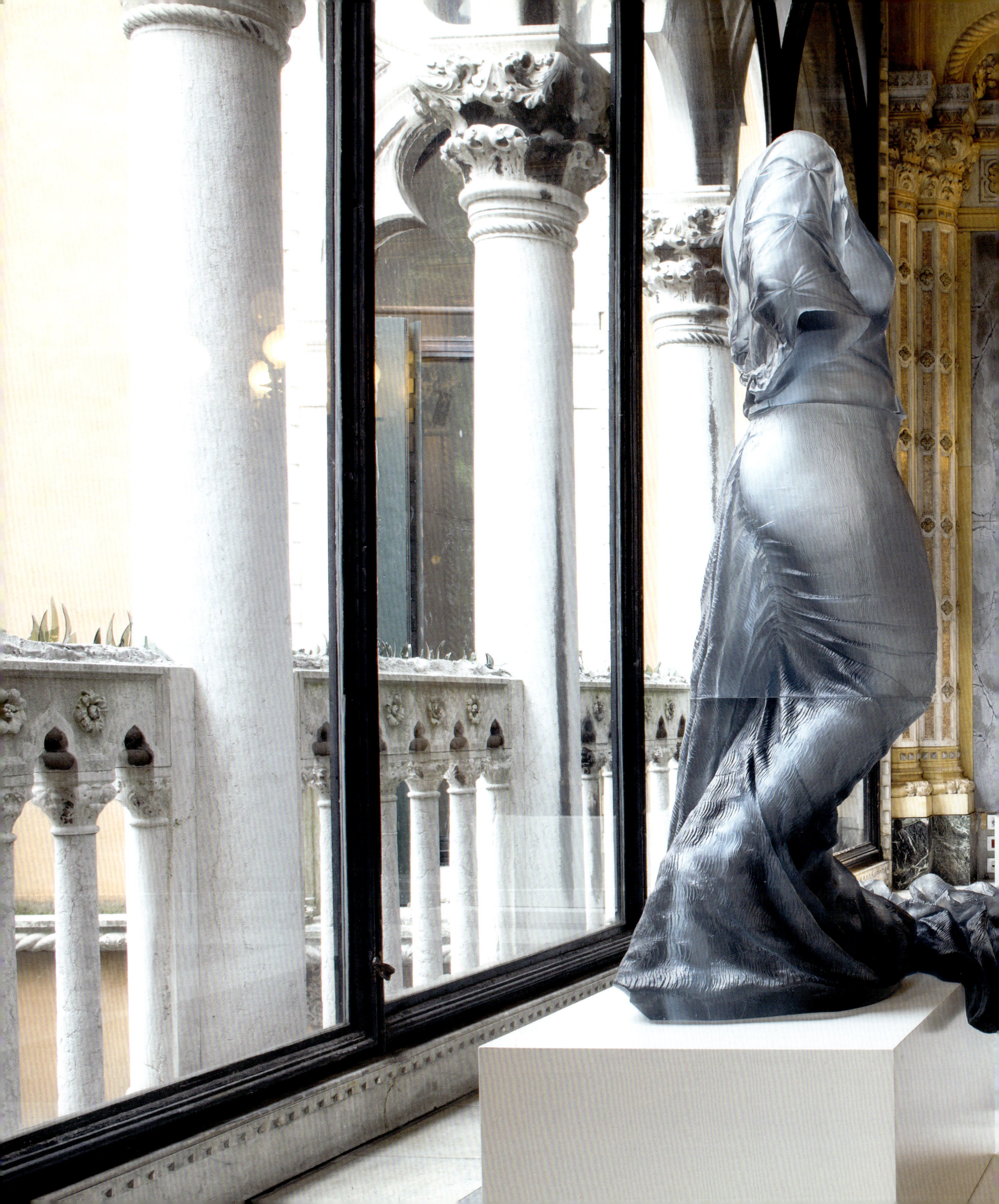

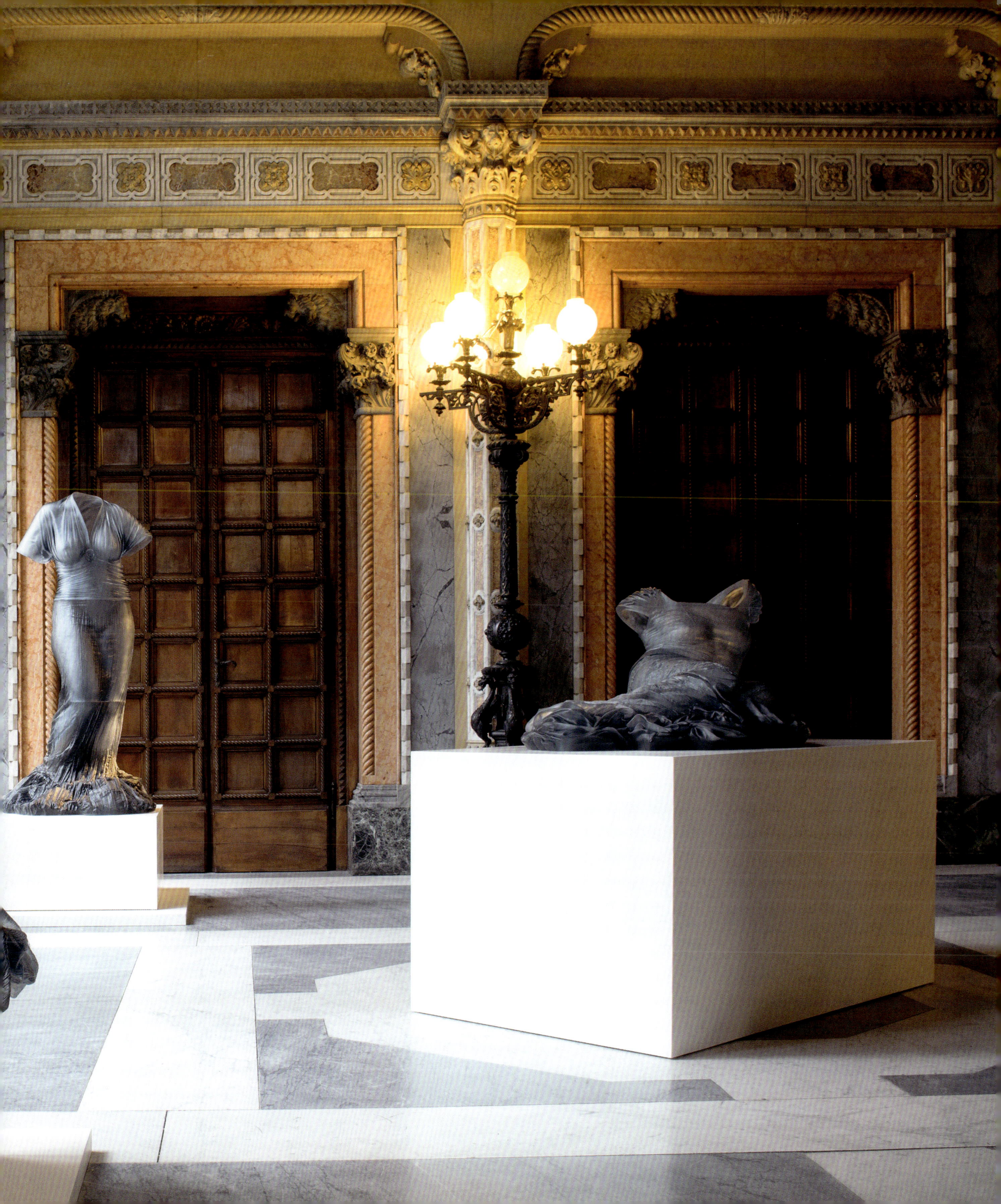

Installation of rusted iron, white bronze, and cast glass *Etudes*, 2014.

FOLLOWING
Reclining Etude 3, 2015
White bronze (left), rusted iron (right), each 6½ × 24 × 13 in.
(17 × 61 × 32.5 cm)

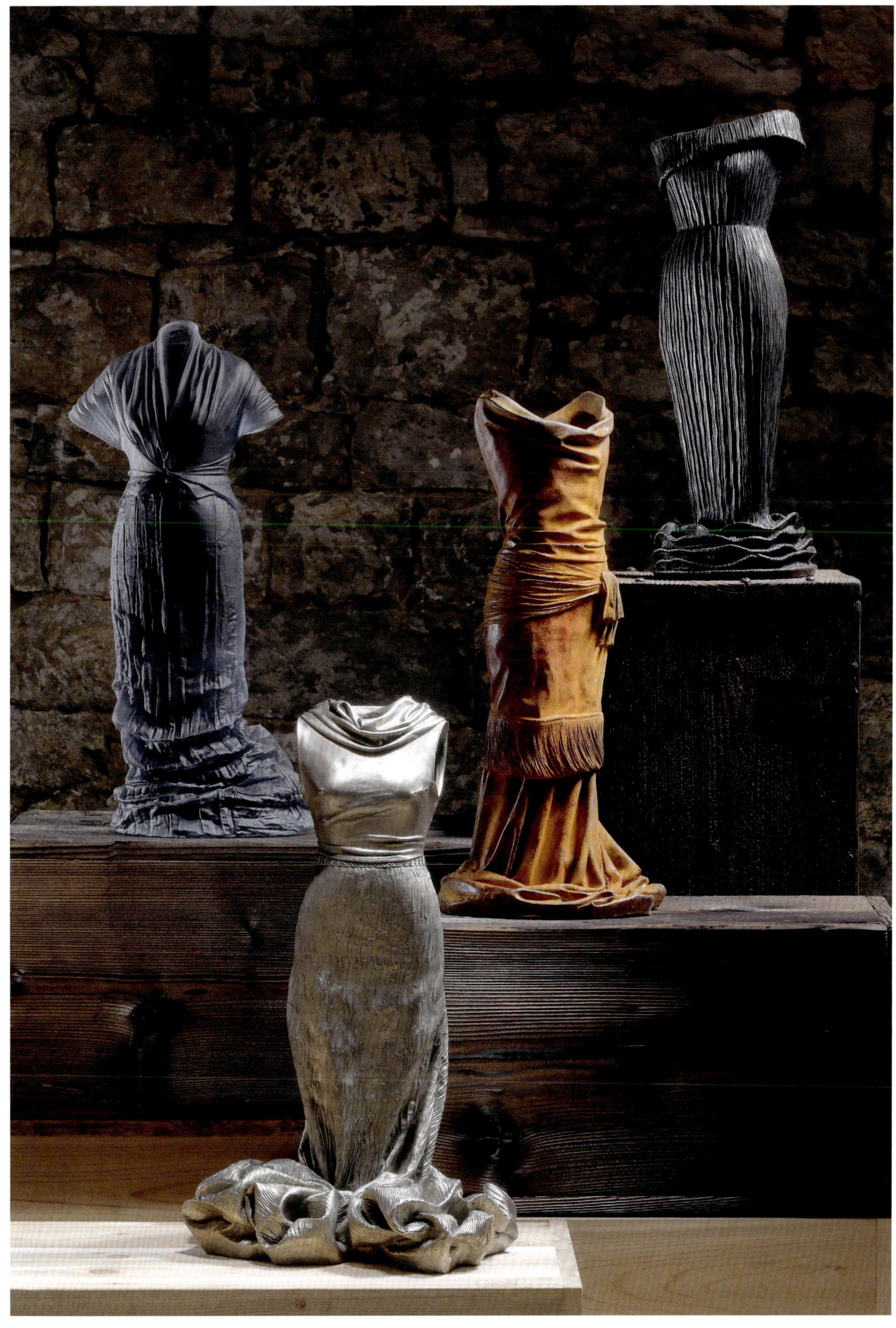

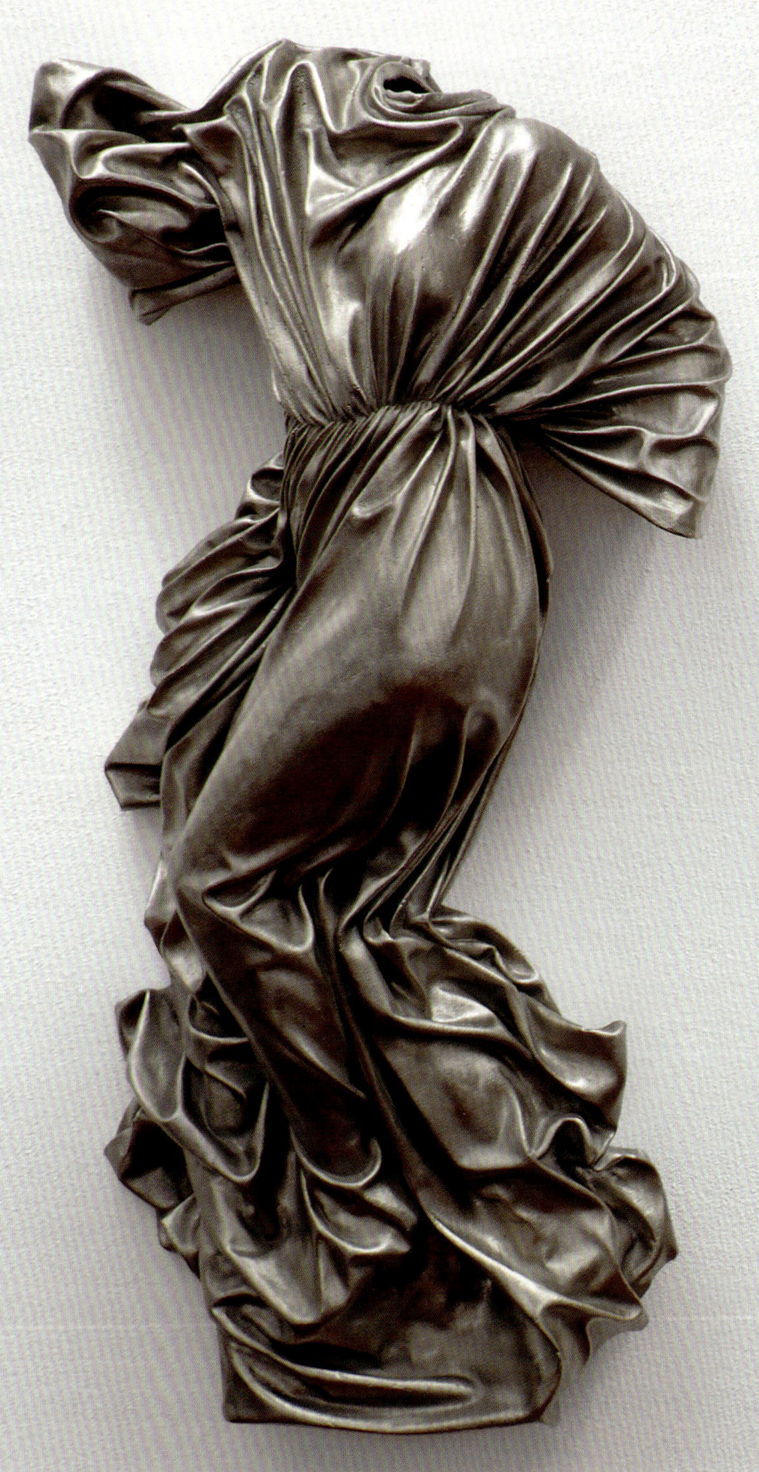

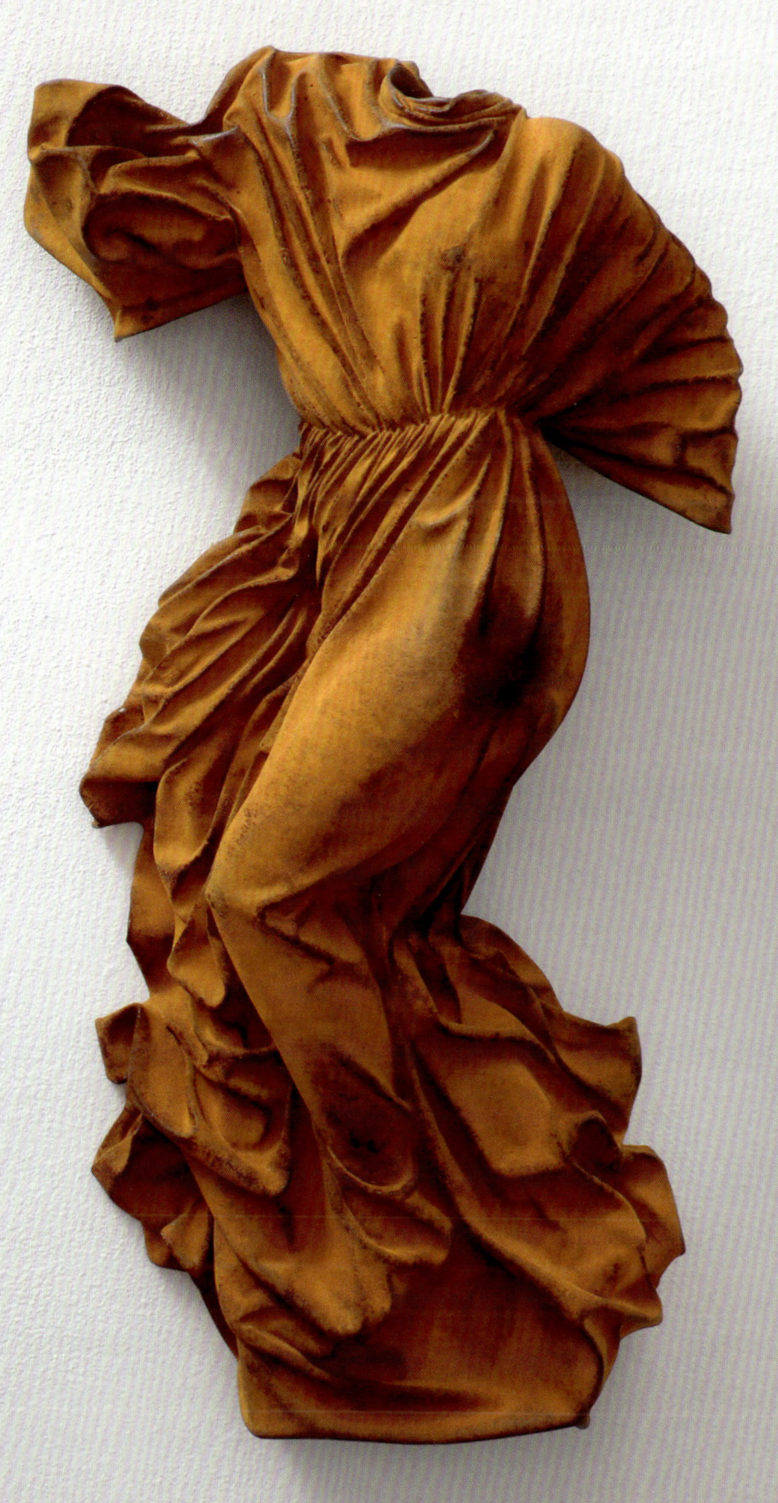

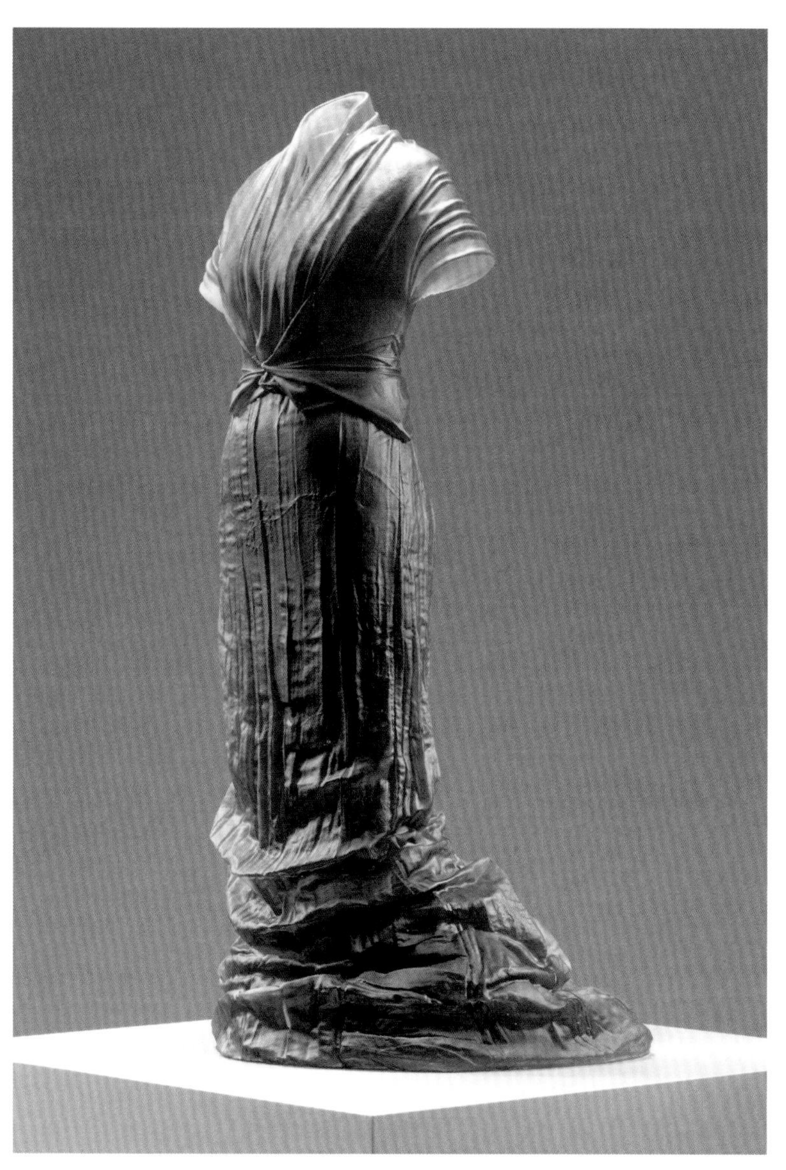
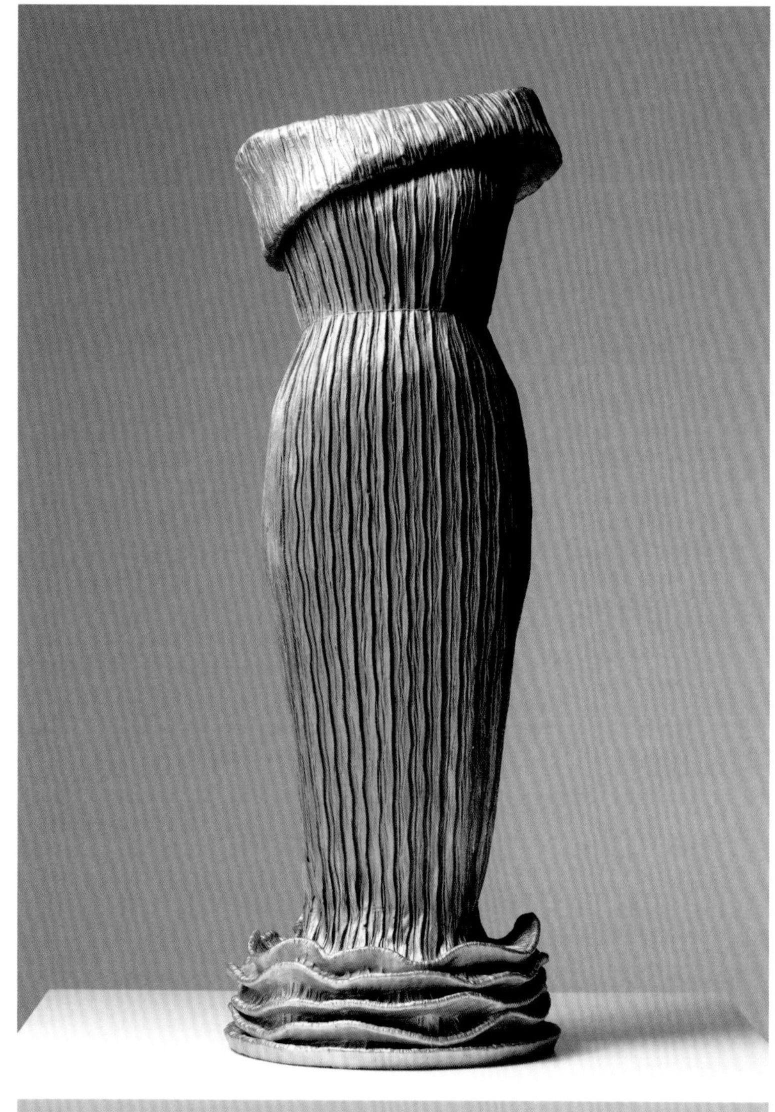

LEFT TO RIGHT
Etude 1, 2013
Cast glass, 24½ × 10½ × 10 in. (62 × 27 × 25.5 cm)

Etude 2, 2015
White bronze, 22½ × 8 × 8½ in. (57.5 × 20.5 × 22 cm)

Etude 5, 2014
Rusted iron, 24 × 11 × 11 in. (60.5 × 28.5 × 27.5 cm)

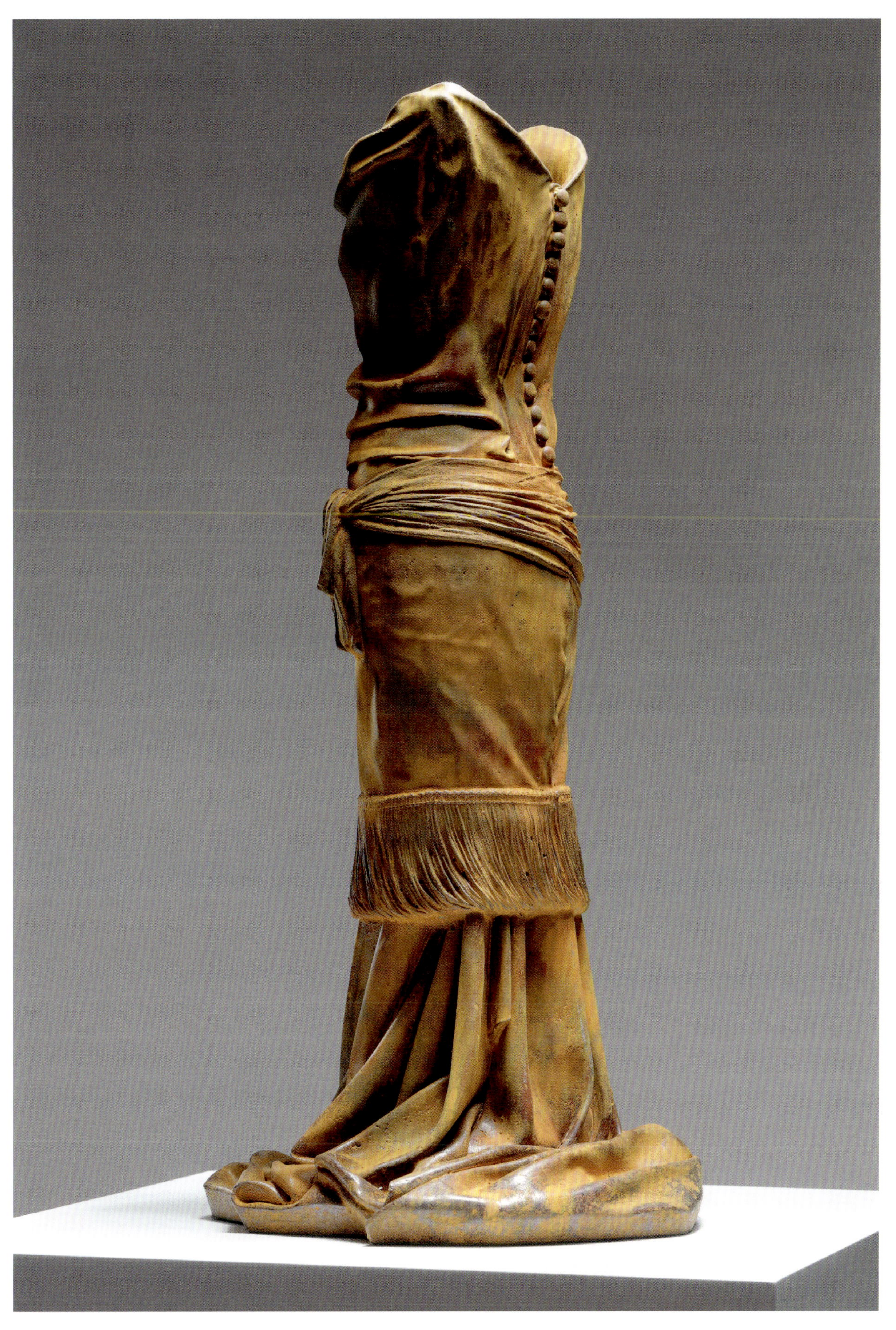

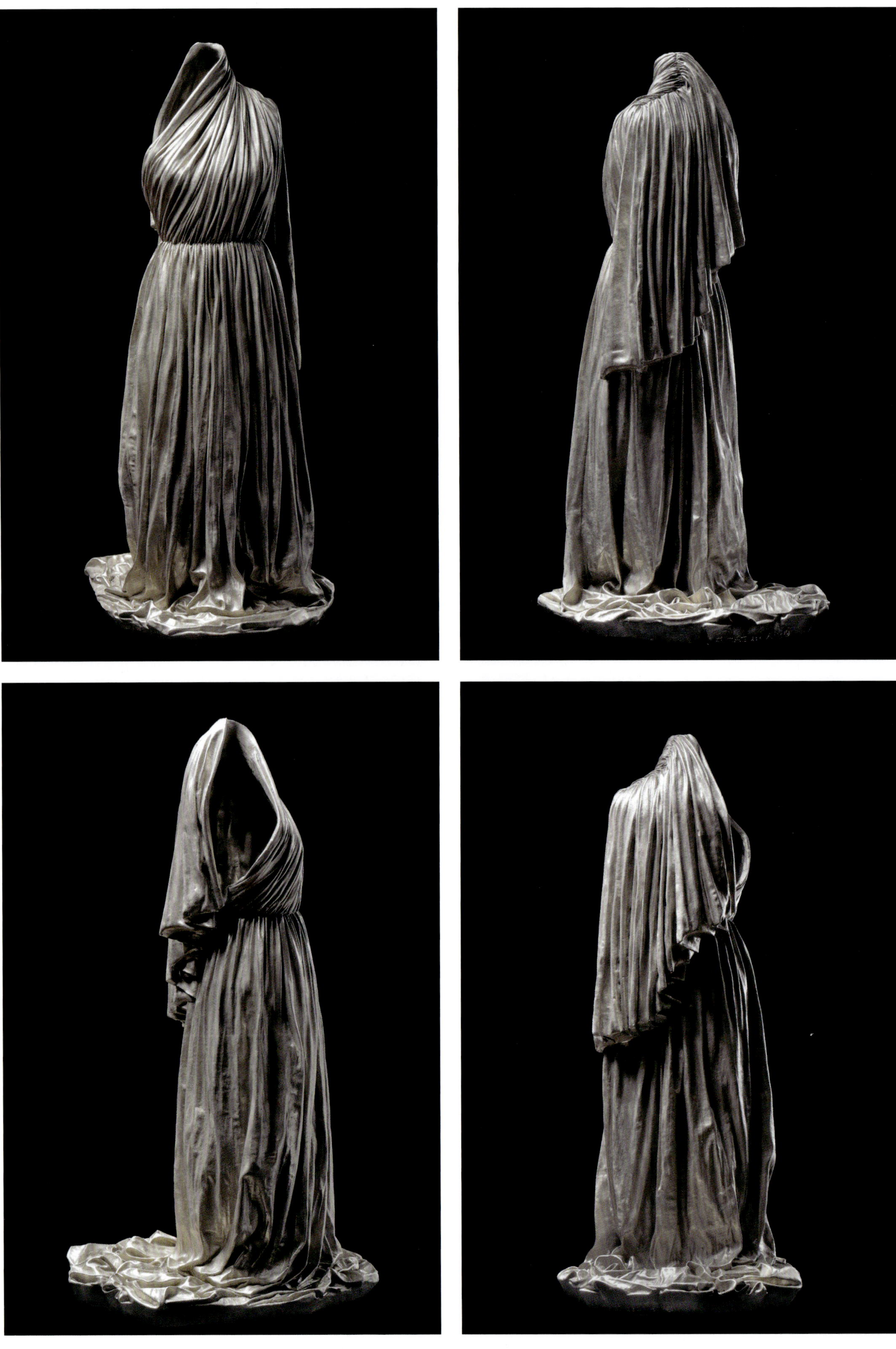

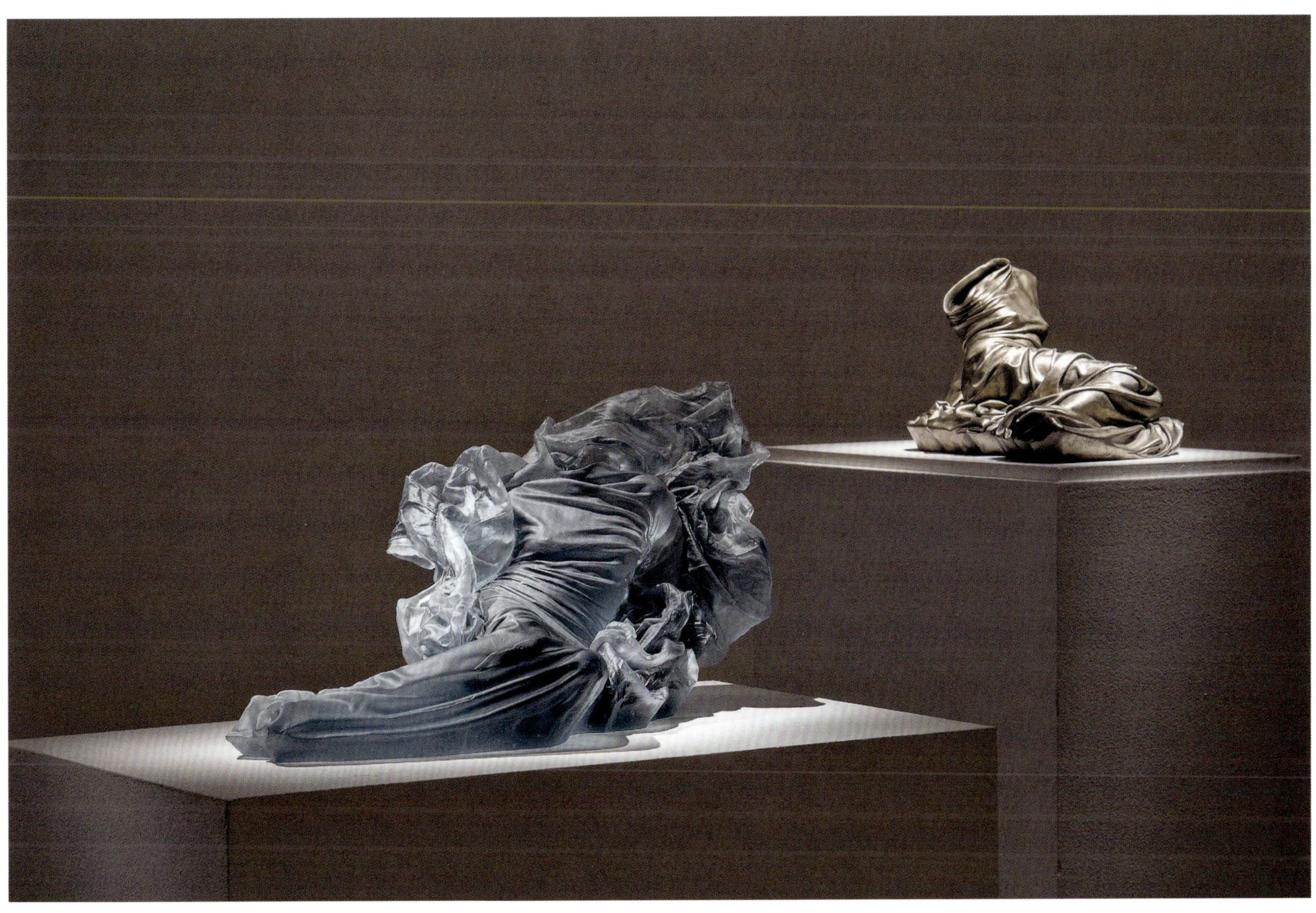

OPPOSITE
Etude 7, 2014
White bronze, 27 × 11 × 14½ in. (68 × 28.5 × 36.5 cm)

Installation of cast glass and white bronze *Etudes*, 2019.

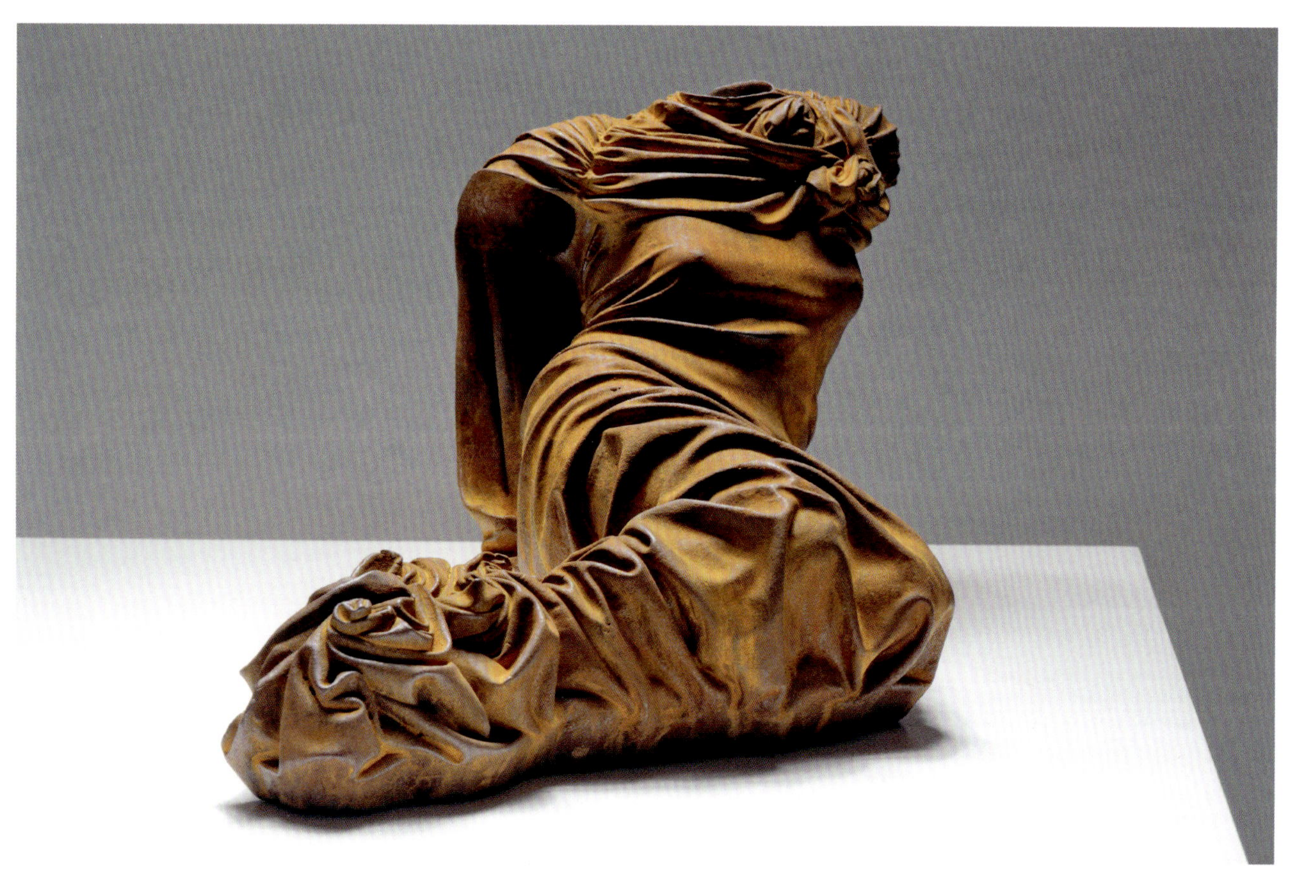

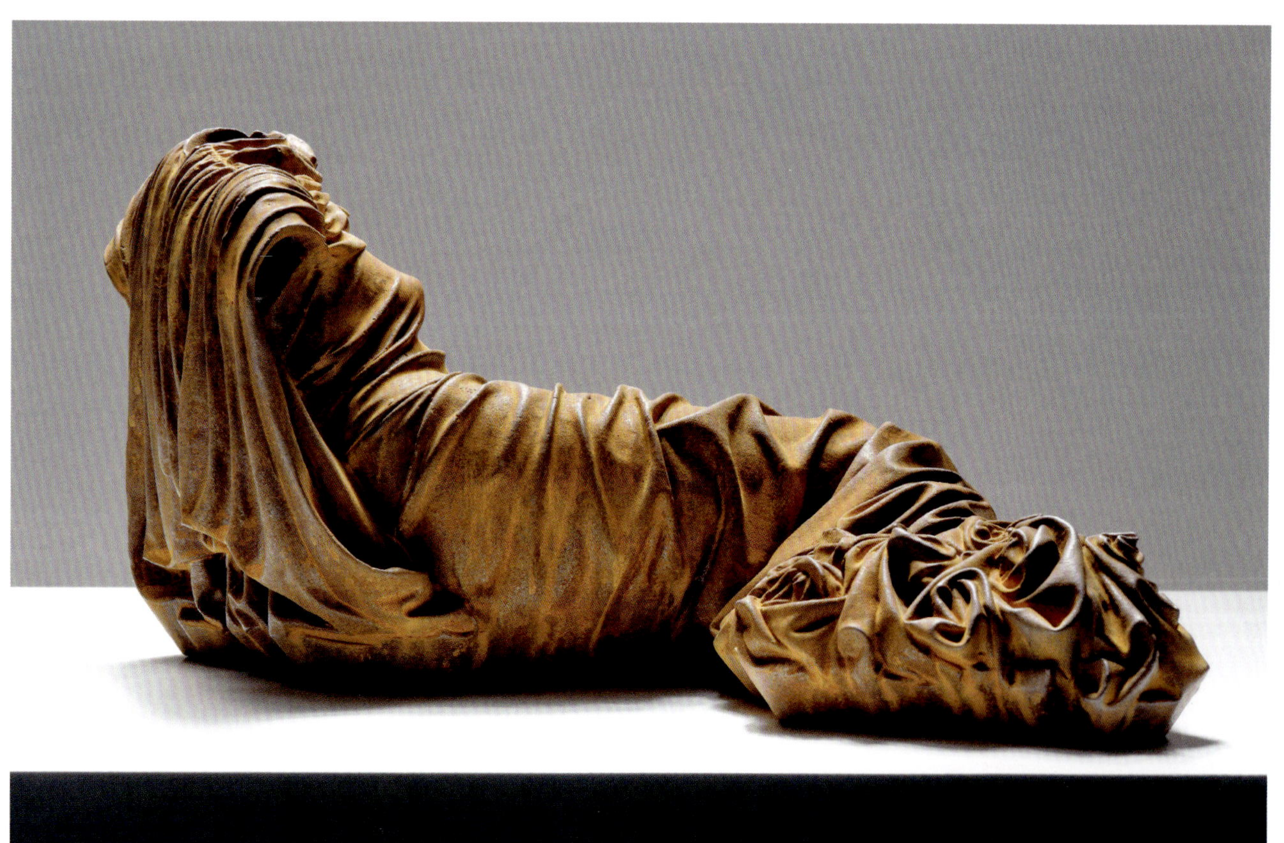

OPPOSITE
Reclining Etude 7, 2015
Rusted iron, 8½ × 19½ × 10 in. (22 × 50 × 25 cm)

Reclining Etude 2, 2015
White bronze, 9 × 23 × 11½ in. (23 × 58 × 29.5 cm)

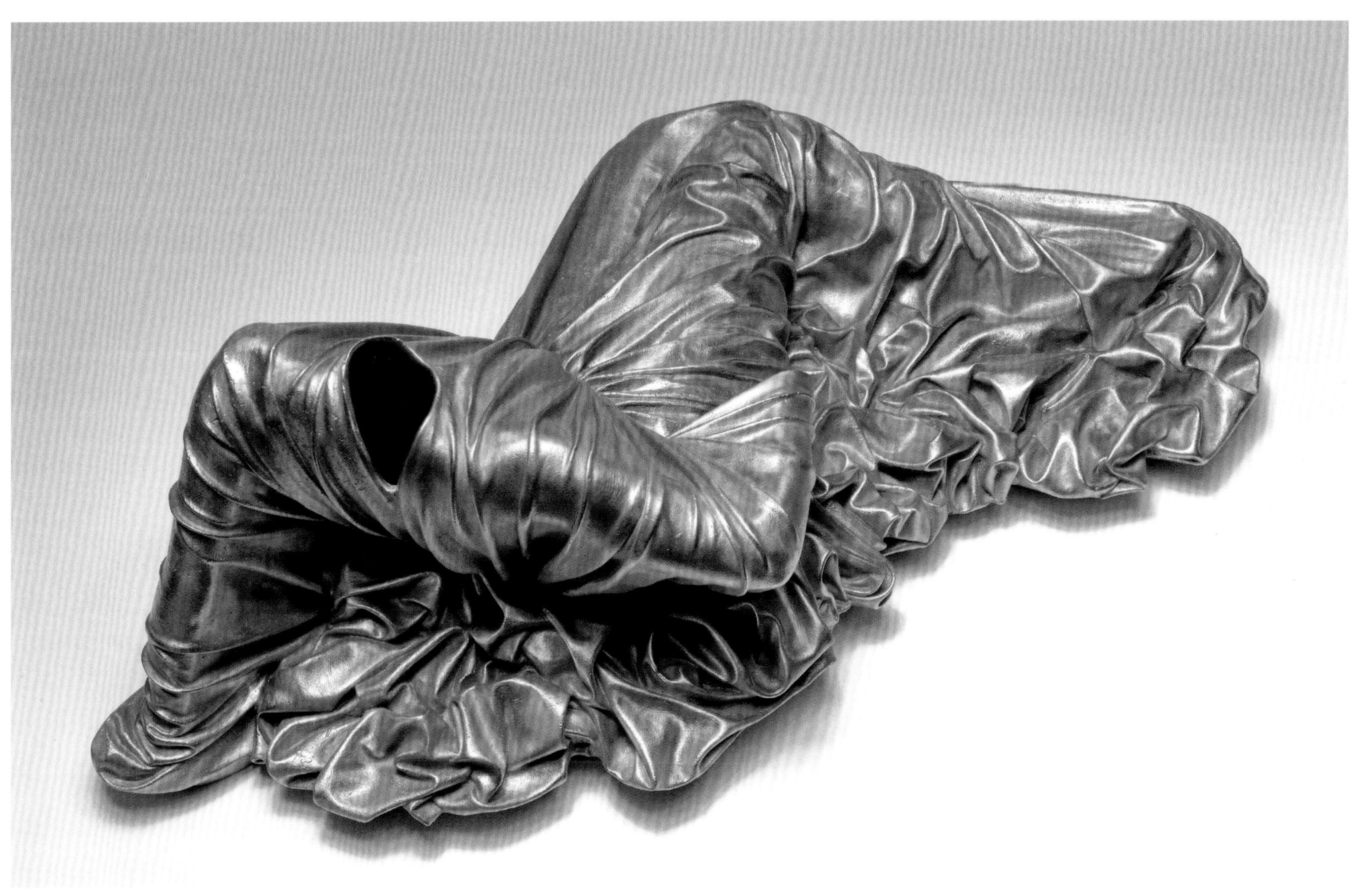

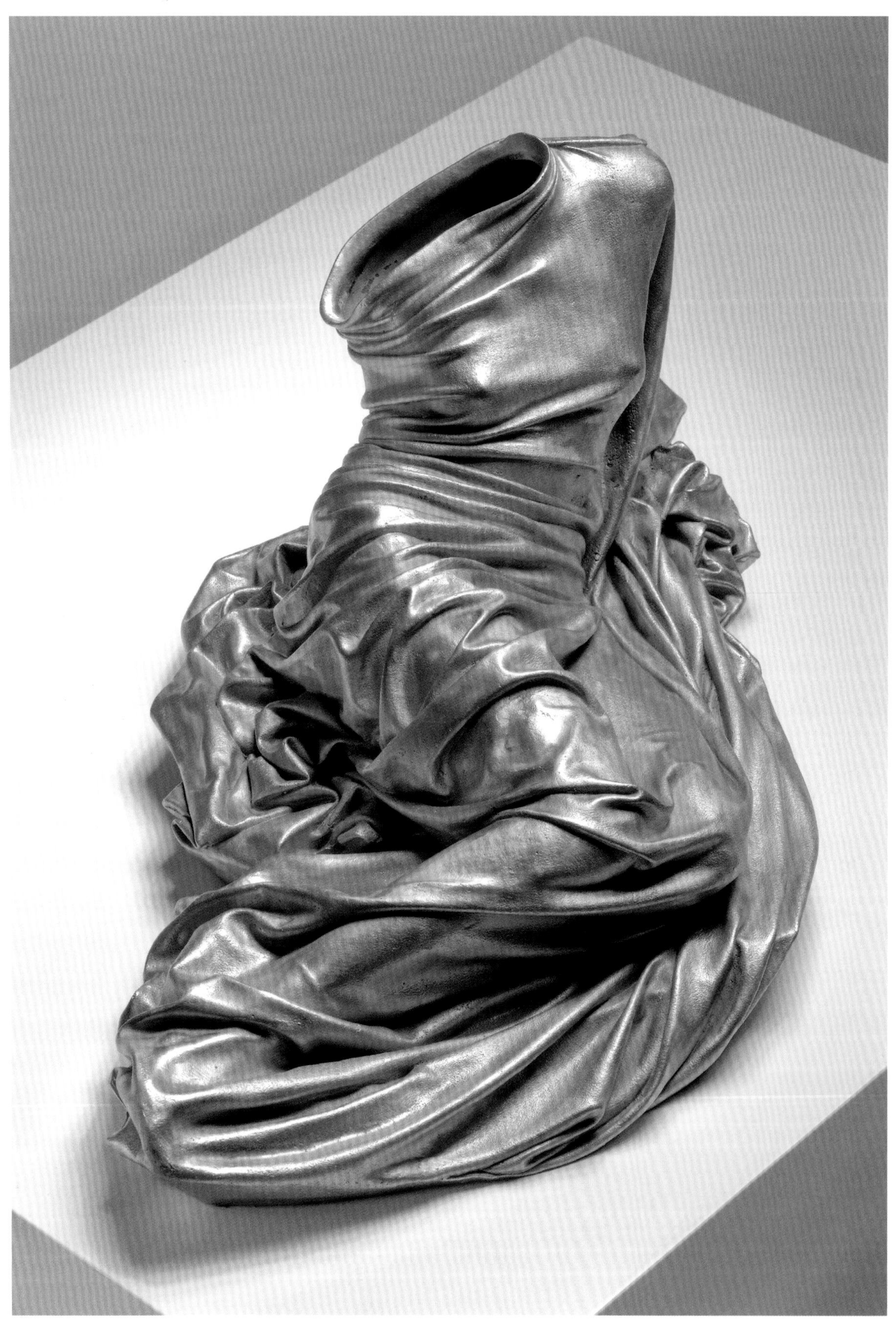

Reclining Etude 1, 2015
White bronze, 9½ × 23½ × 11 in.
(23.5 × 59.5 × 28.5 cm)

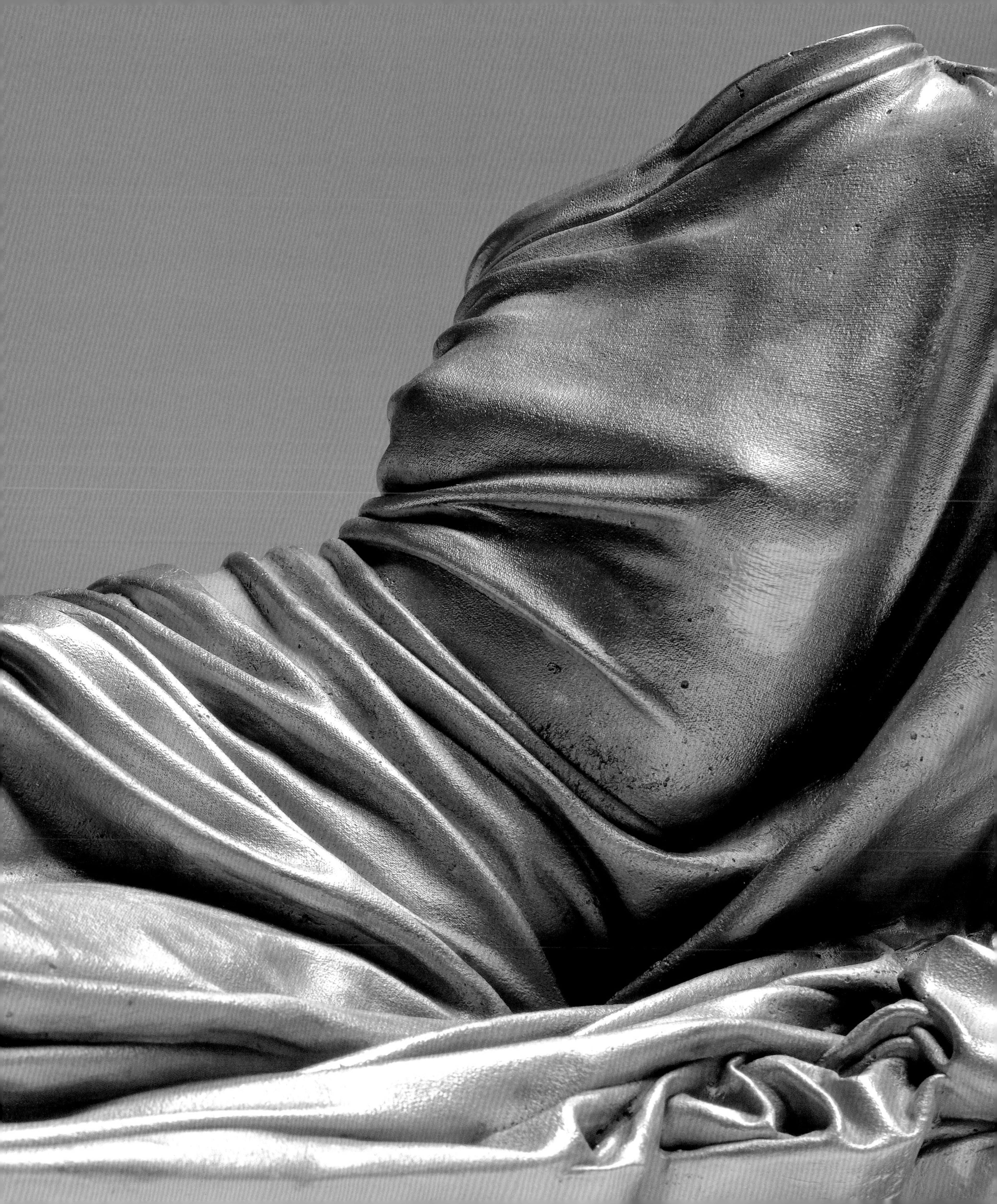

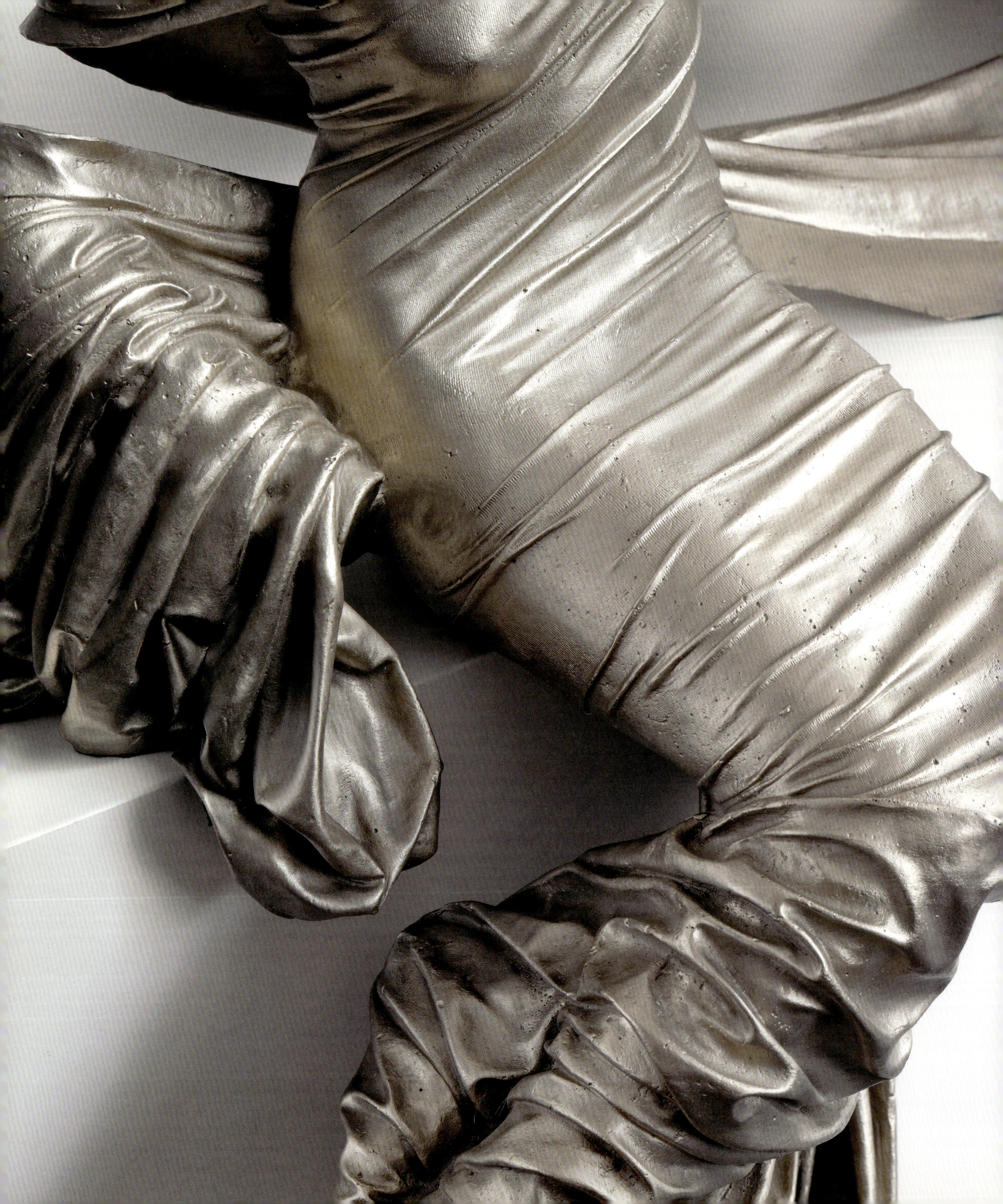

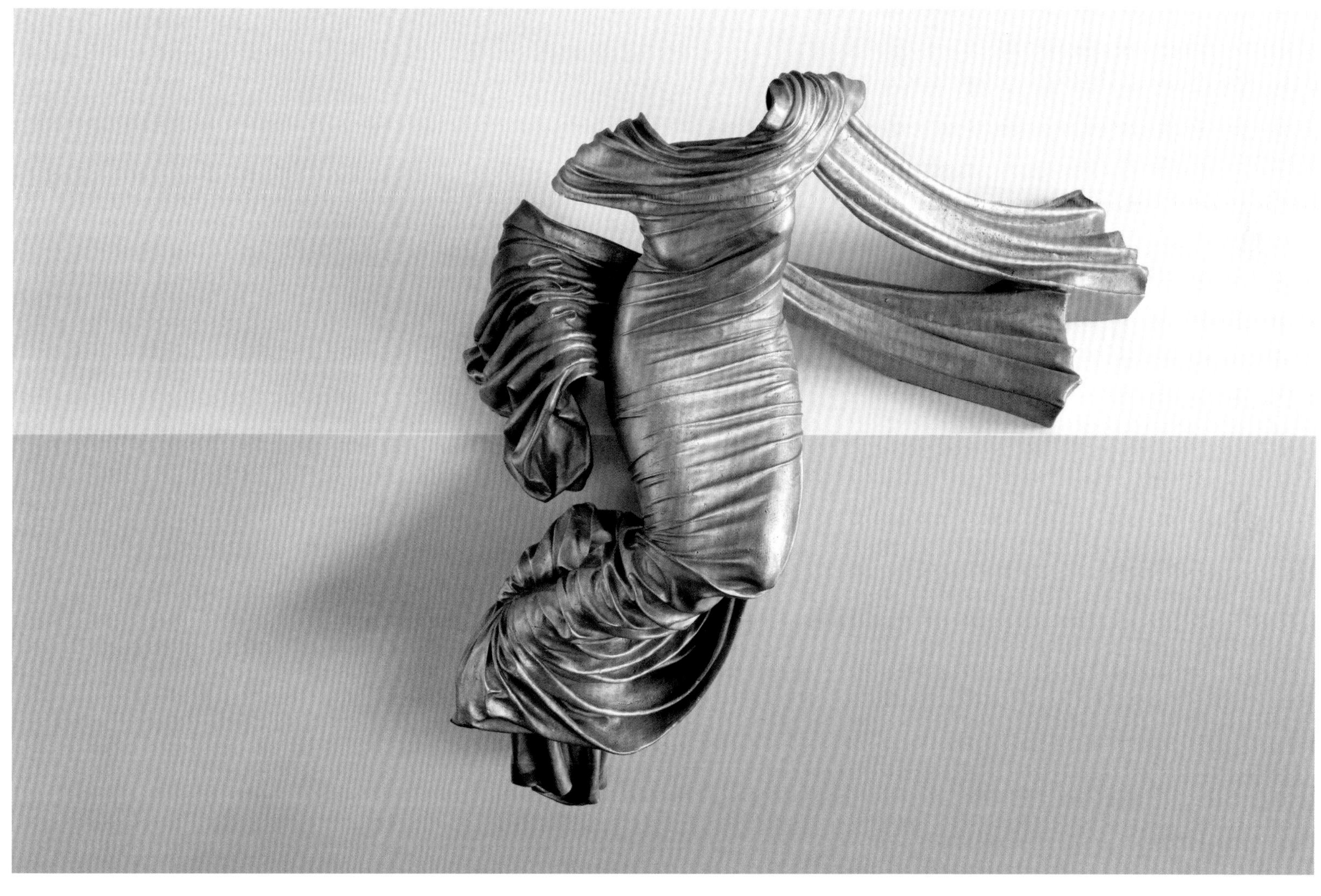

Reclining Etude 13, 2017
White bronze, 25 × 20 × 15 in.
(63 × 51 × 37.5 cm)

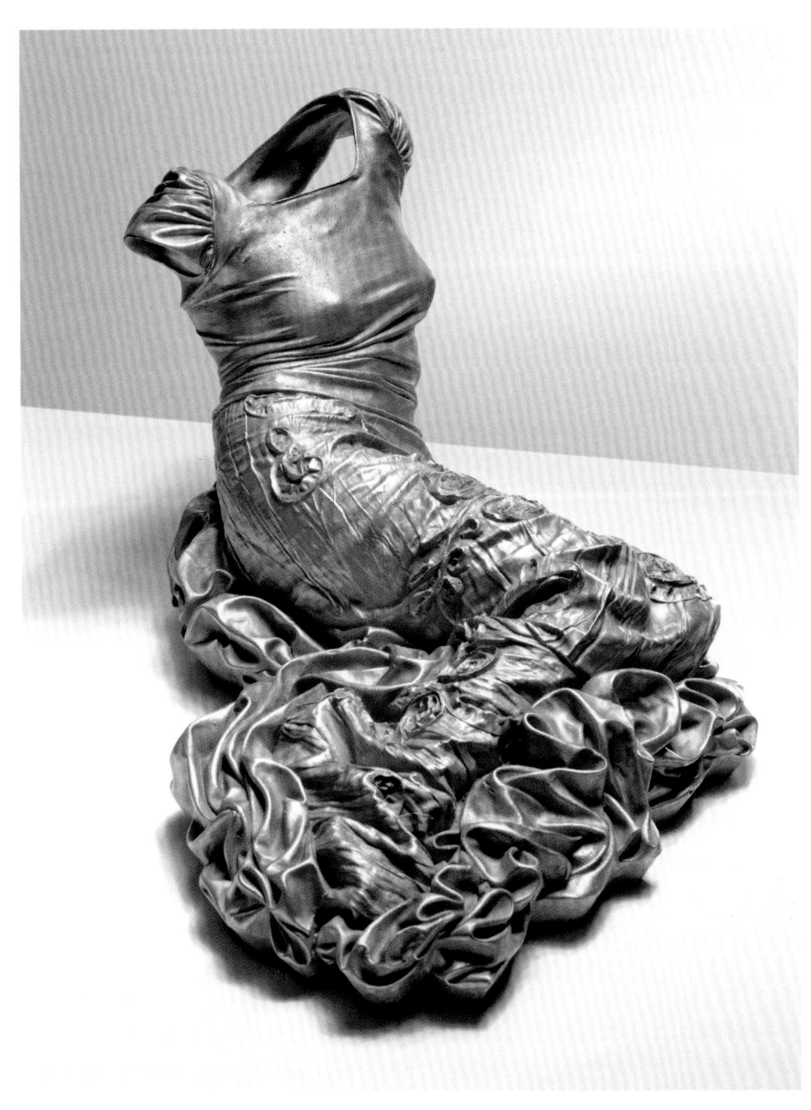

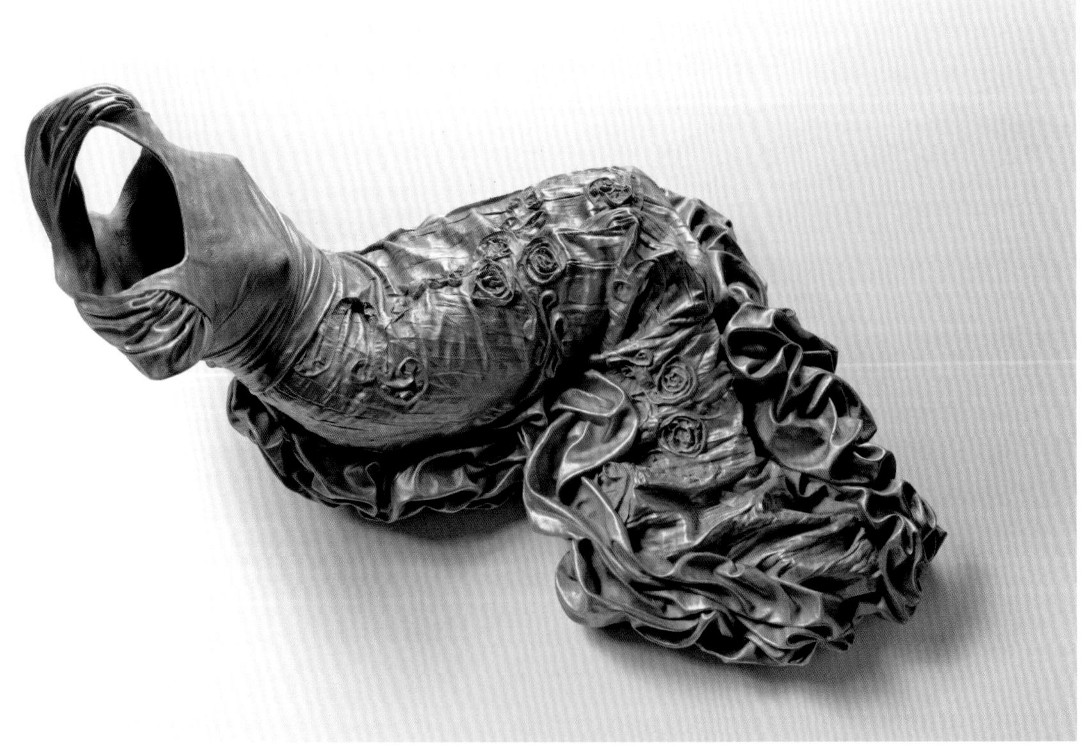

Reclining Etude 6, 2015
White bronze, 9 × 20½ × 11 in.
(22.5 × 52 × 27.5 cm)

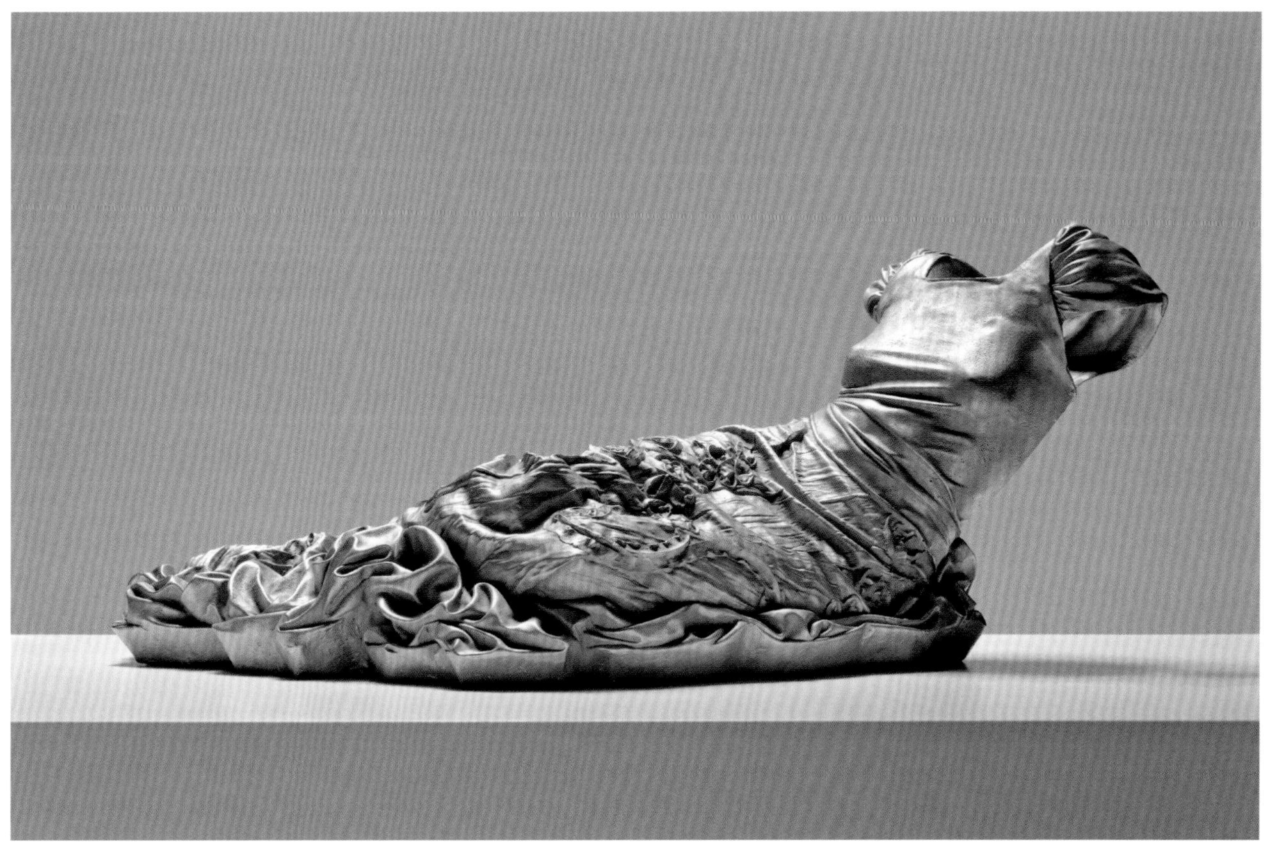

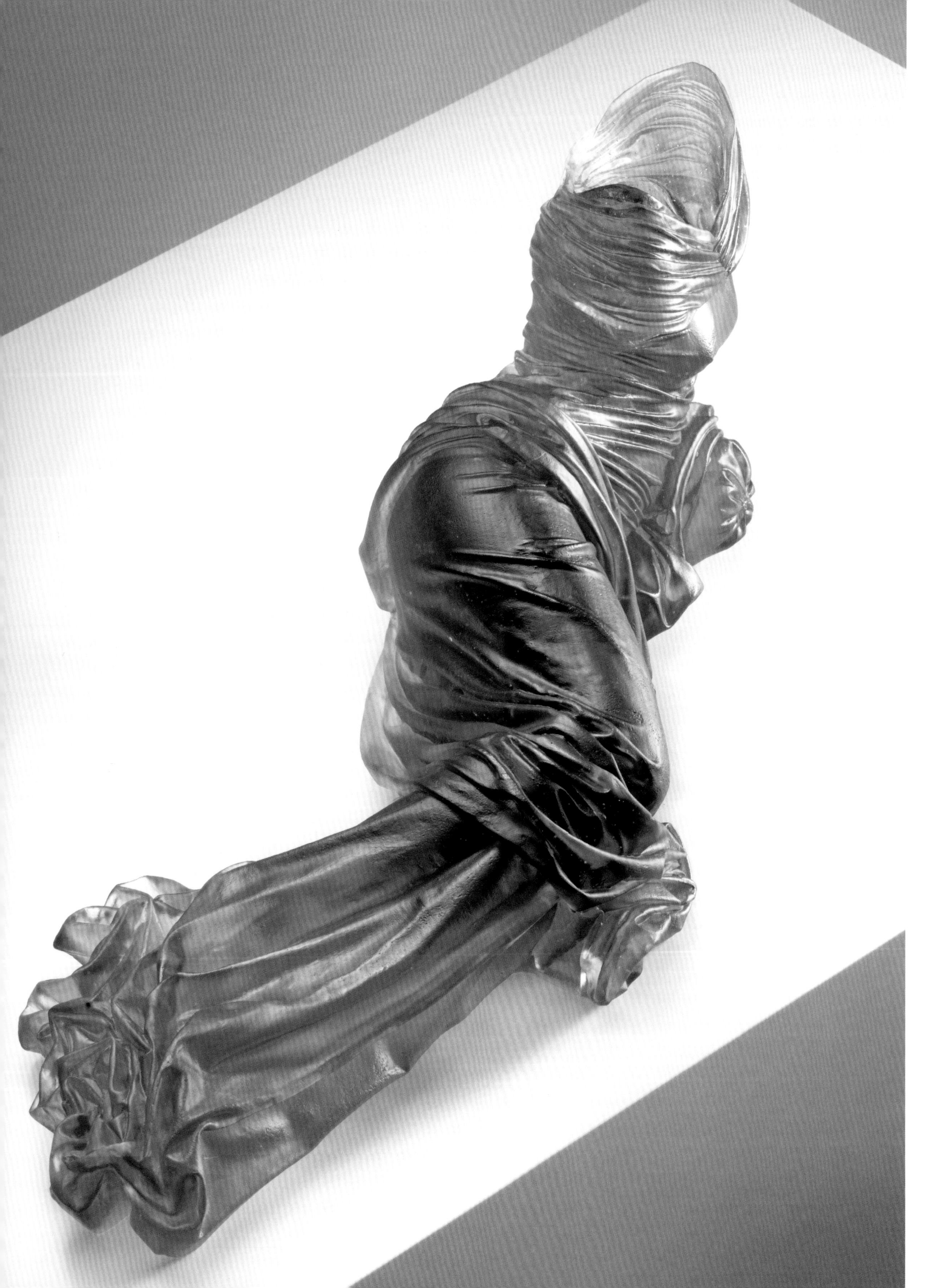

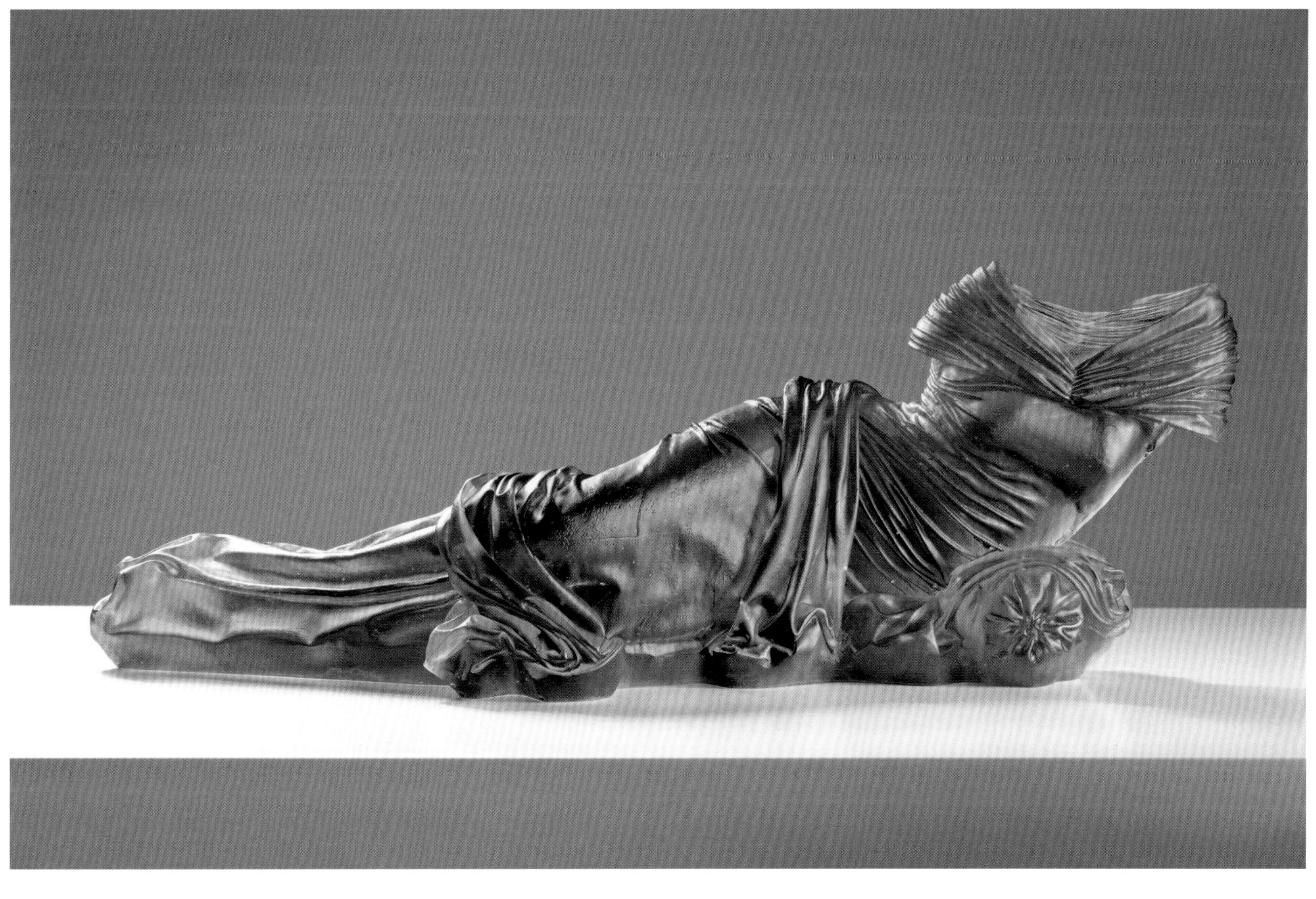

Reclining Etude 10, 2016
Cast glass, 8½ × 23 × 10½ in. (21.5 × 59 × 26.5 cm)

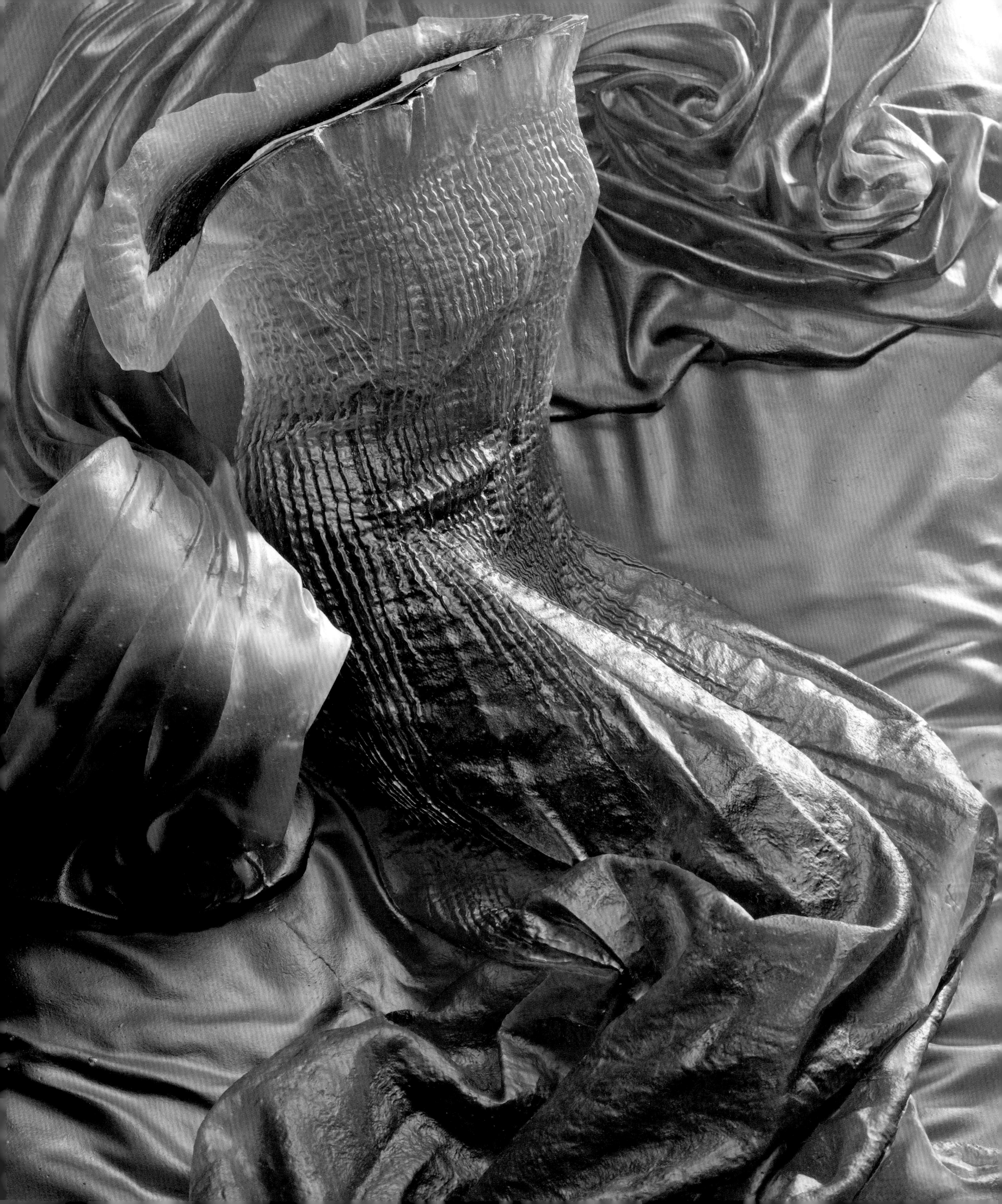

Reclining Etude 11, 2016
Cast glass, 10 × 29½ × 16½ in. (25 × 75 × 42 cm)

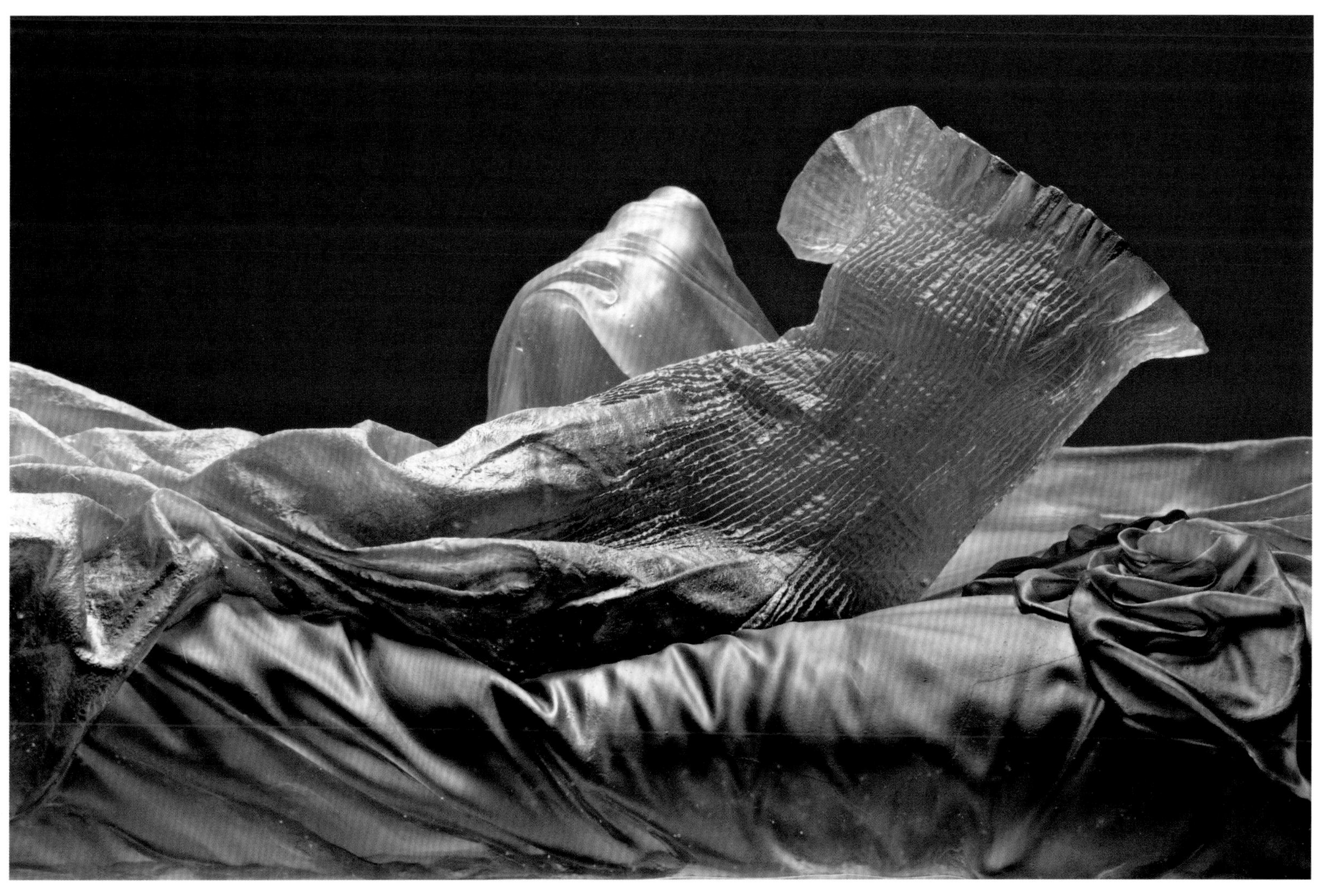

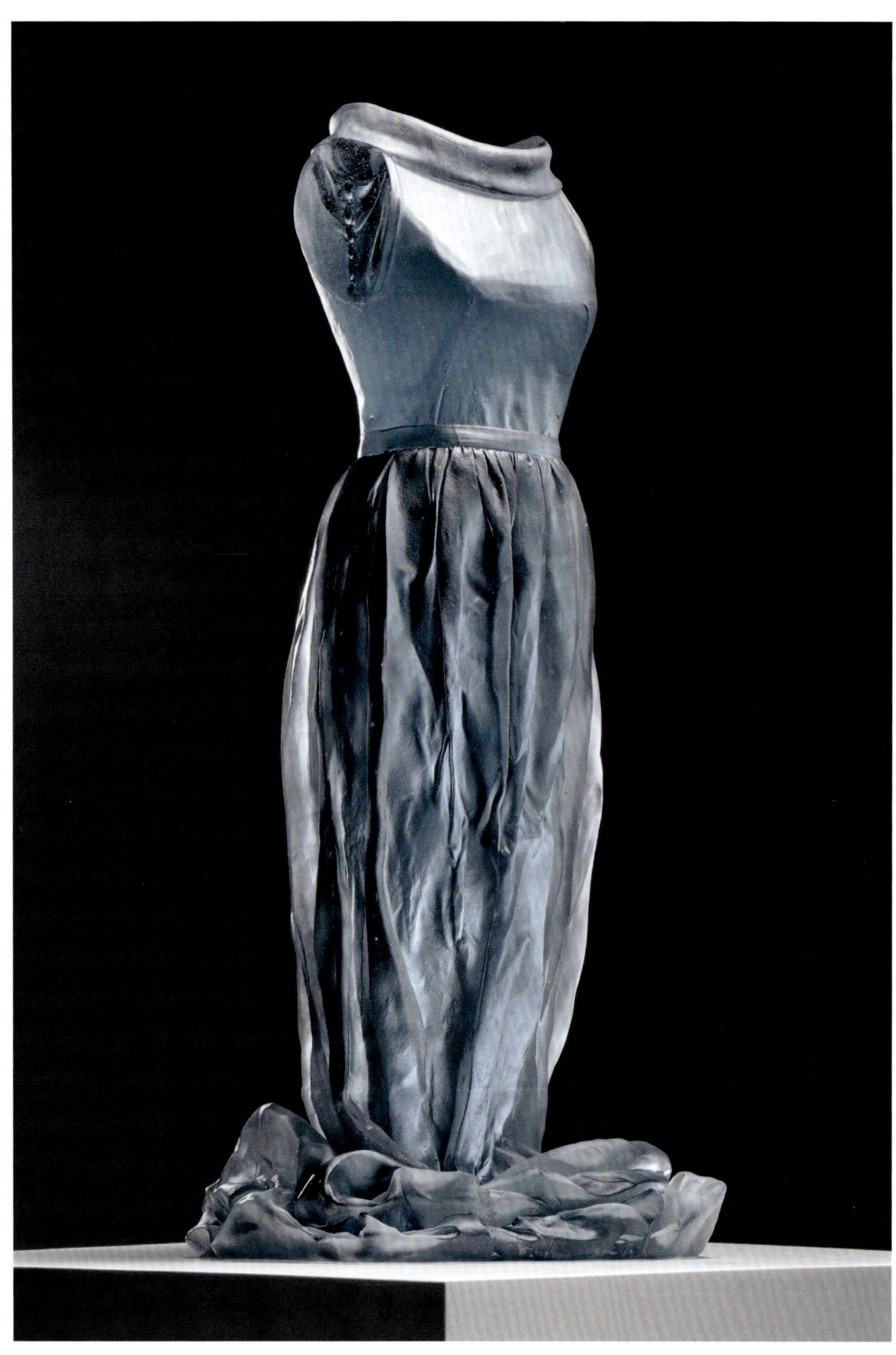

Etude 8, 2015
Cast glass, 23½ × 11 × 10½ in.
(60 × 28.5 × 26.5 cm)

FOLLOWING LEFT TO RIGHT
Etude 8, 2014
White bronze, 23½ × 11 × 10½ in.
(60 × 28.5 × 26.5 cm)
Collection of Jordan Schnitzer Family Foundation

Etude 8, 2014
Rusted iron, 23½ × 11 × 10½ in.
(60 × 28.5 × 26.5 cm)

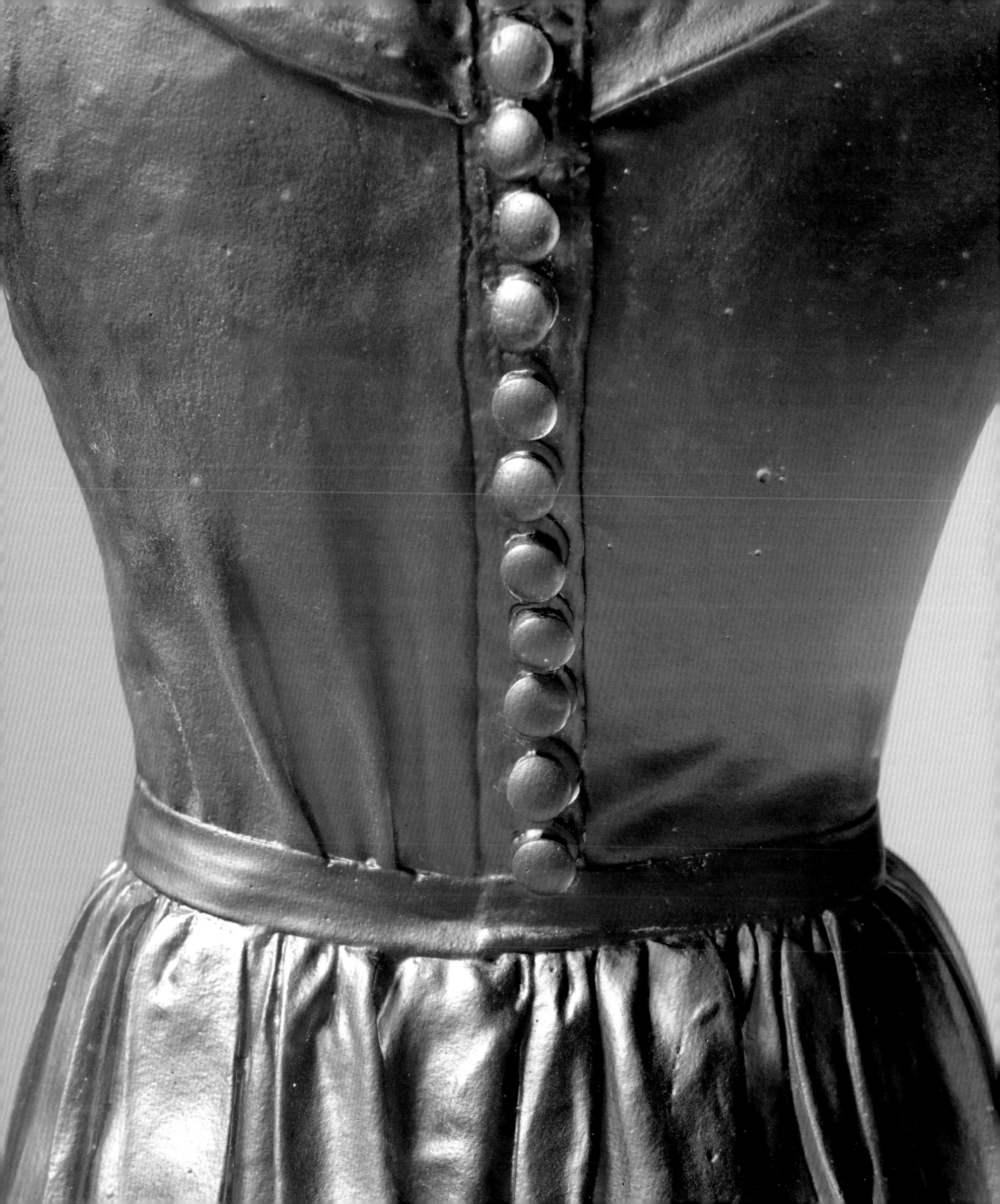

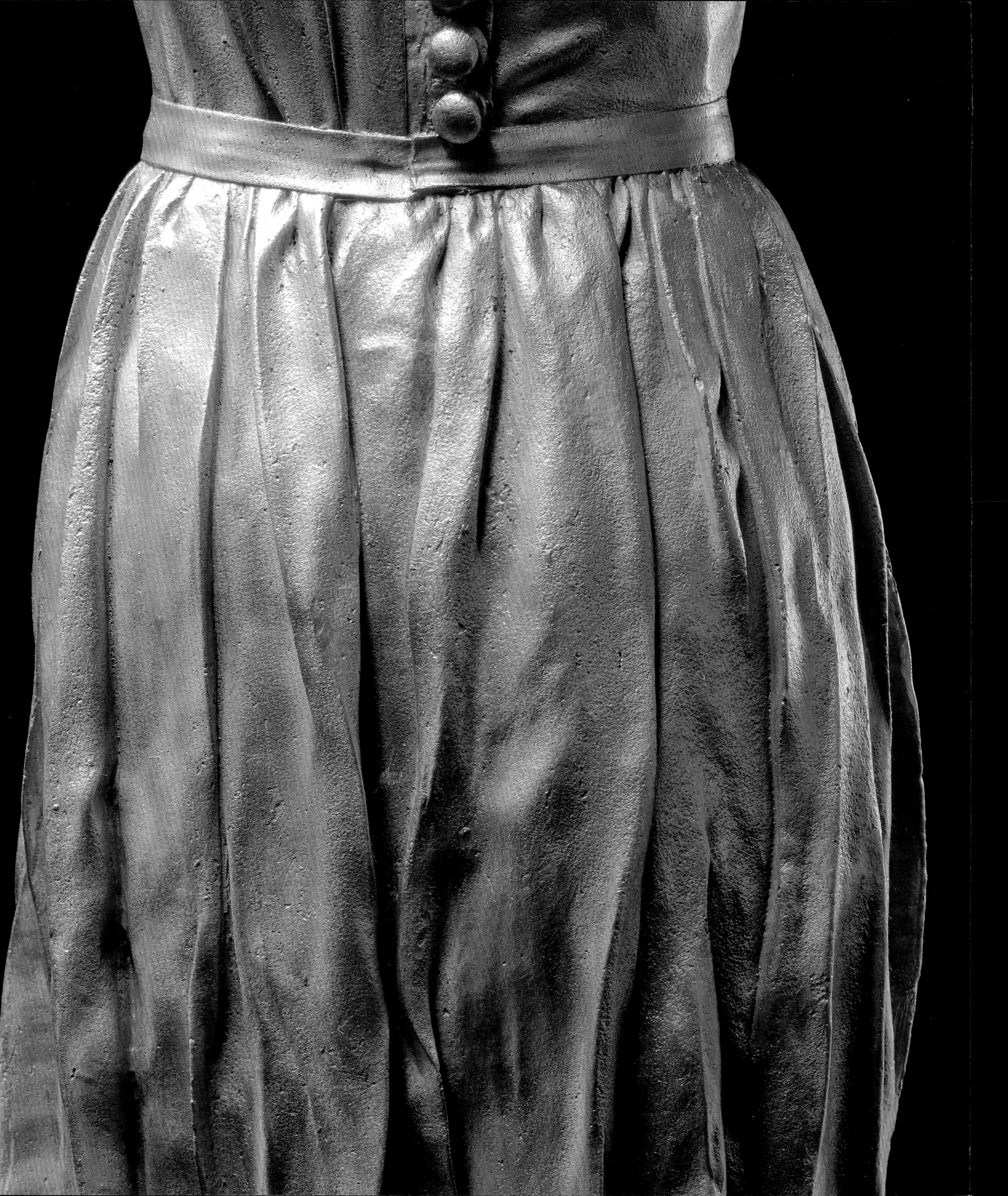

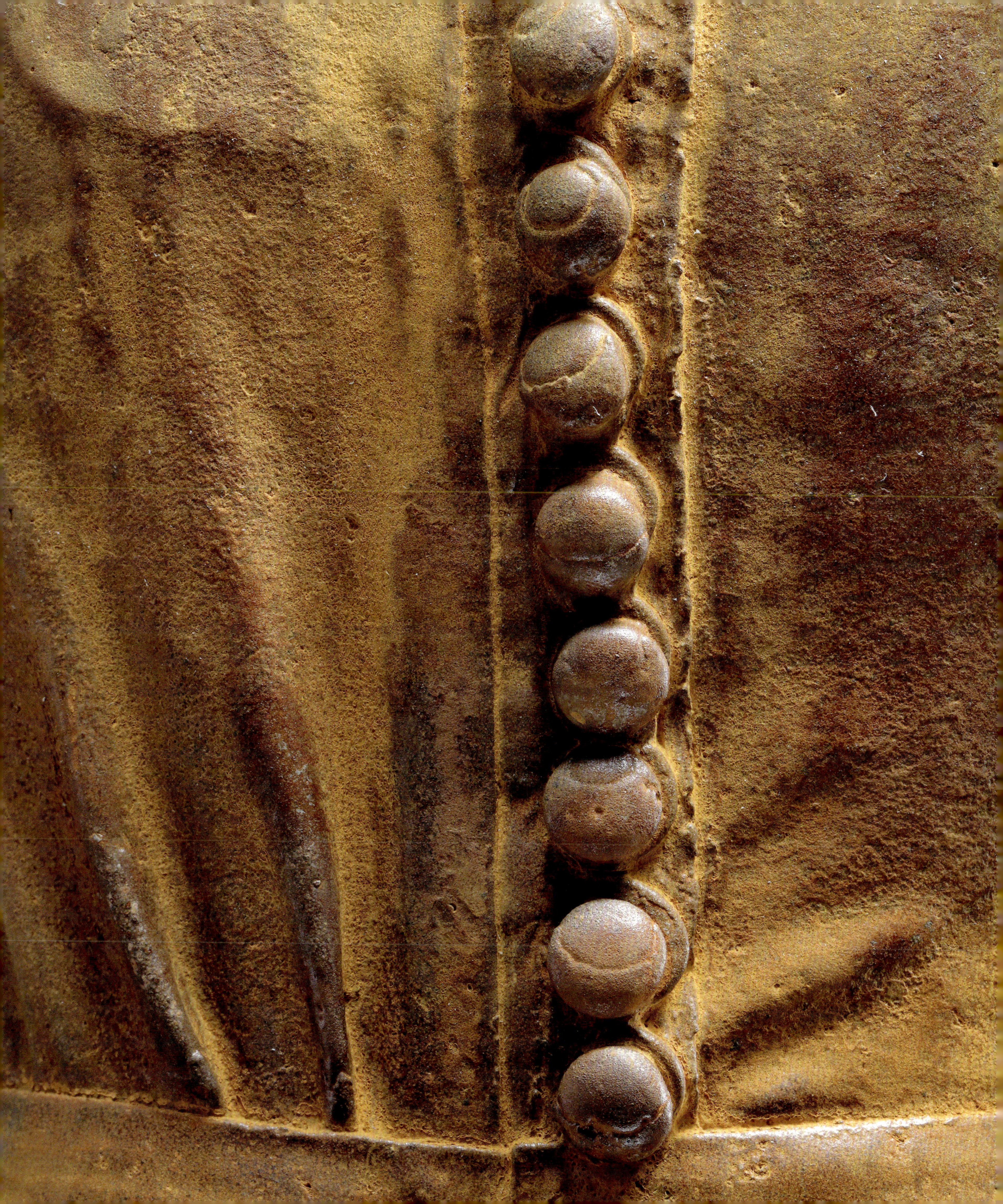

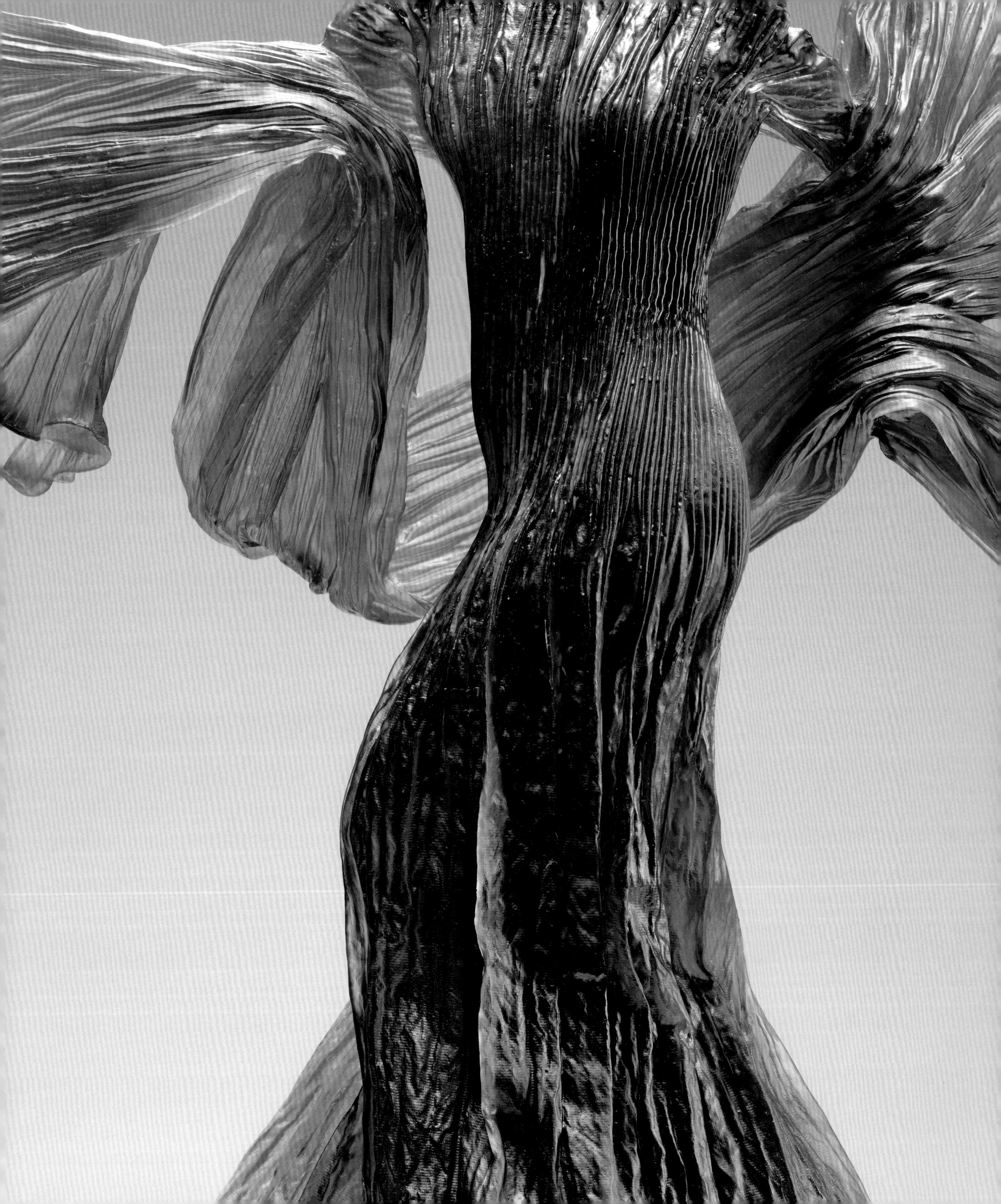

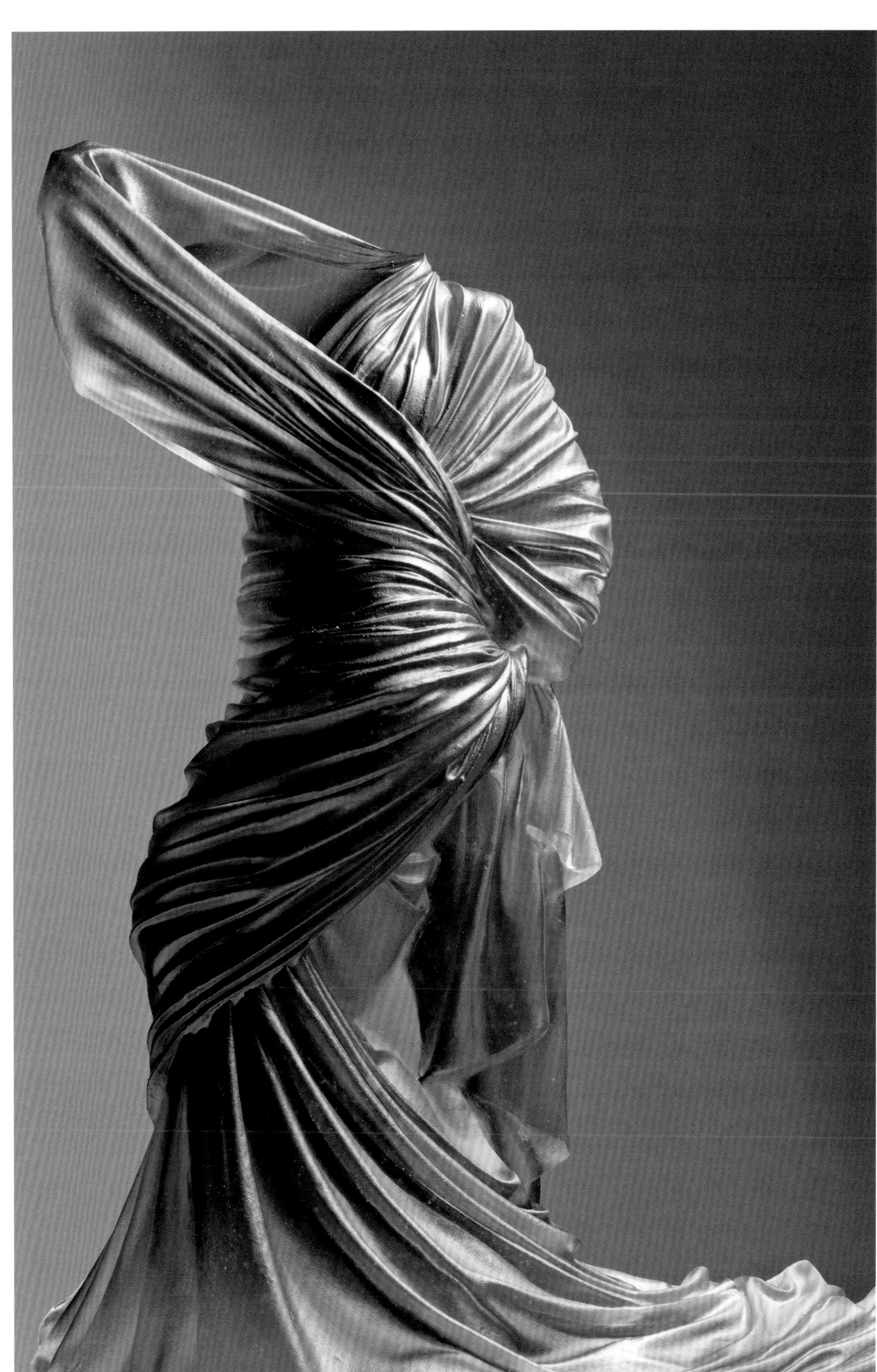

OPPOSITE
Etude 12, 2017
Cast glass, 24 × 22½ × 8½ in.
(60.5 × 57 × 22 cm)
Collection of Imagine
Museum, St. Petersburg, FL

RIGHT
Etude 13, 2017
Cast glass, 26 × 19 × 7½ in.
(66 × 48 × 19 cm)

FOLLOWING
Litomyšl Tableau 6, 2017
Limited-edition photograph

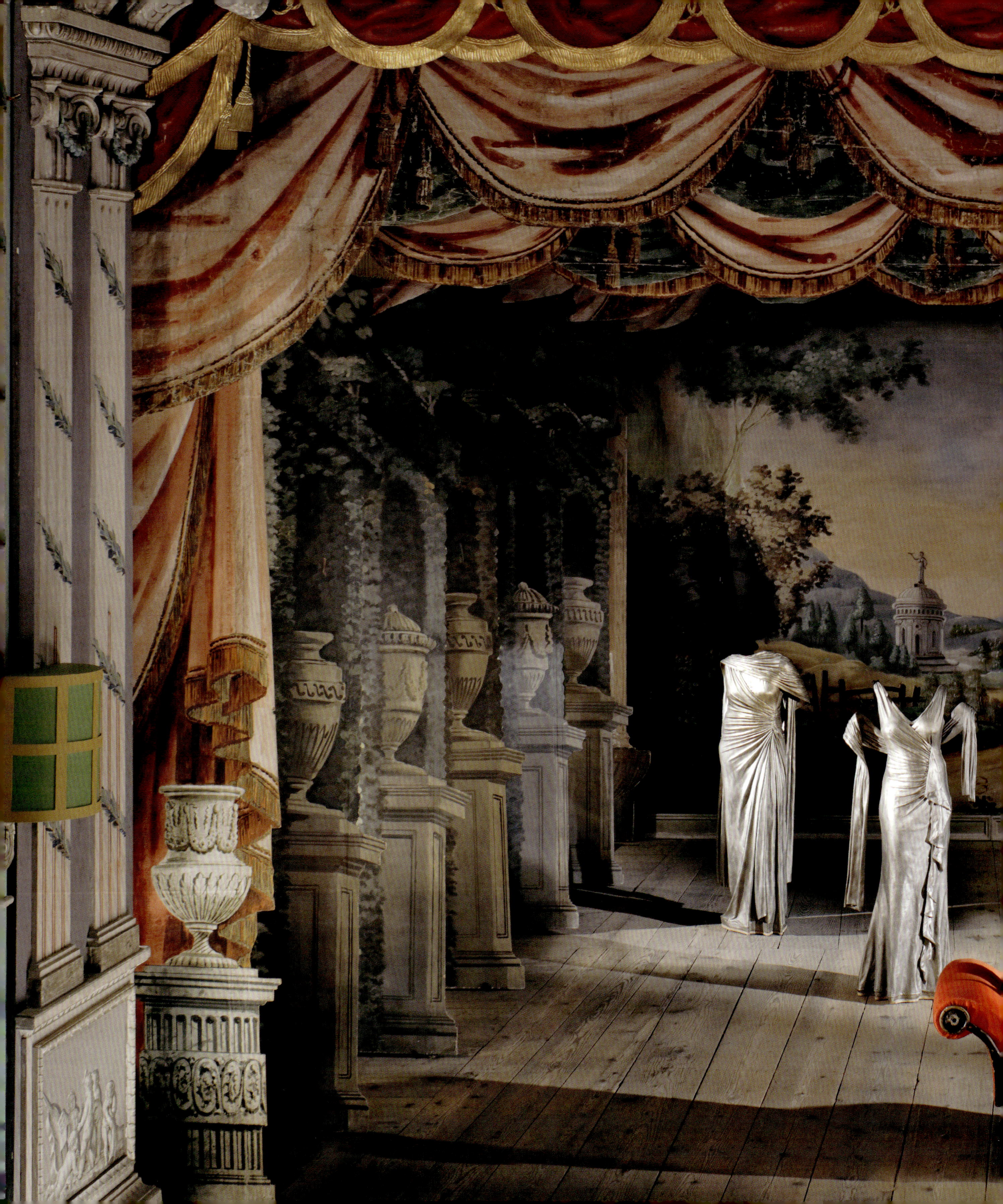

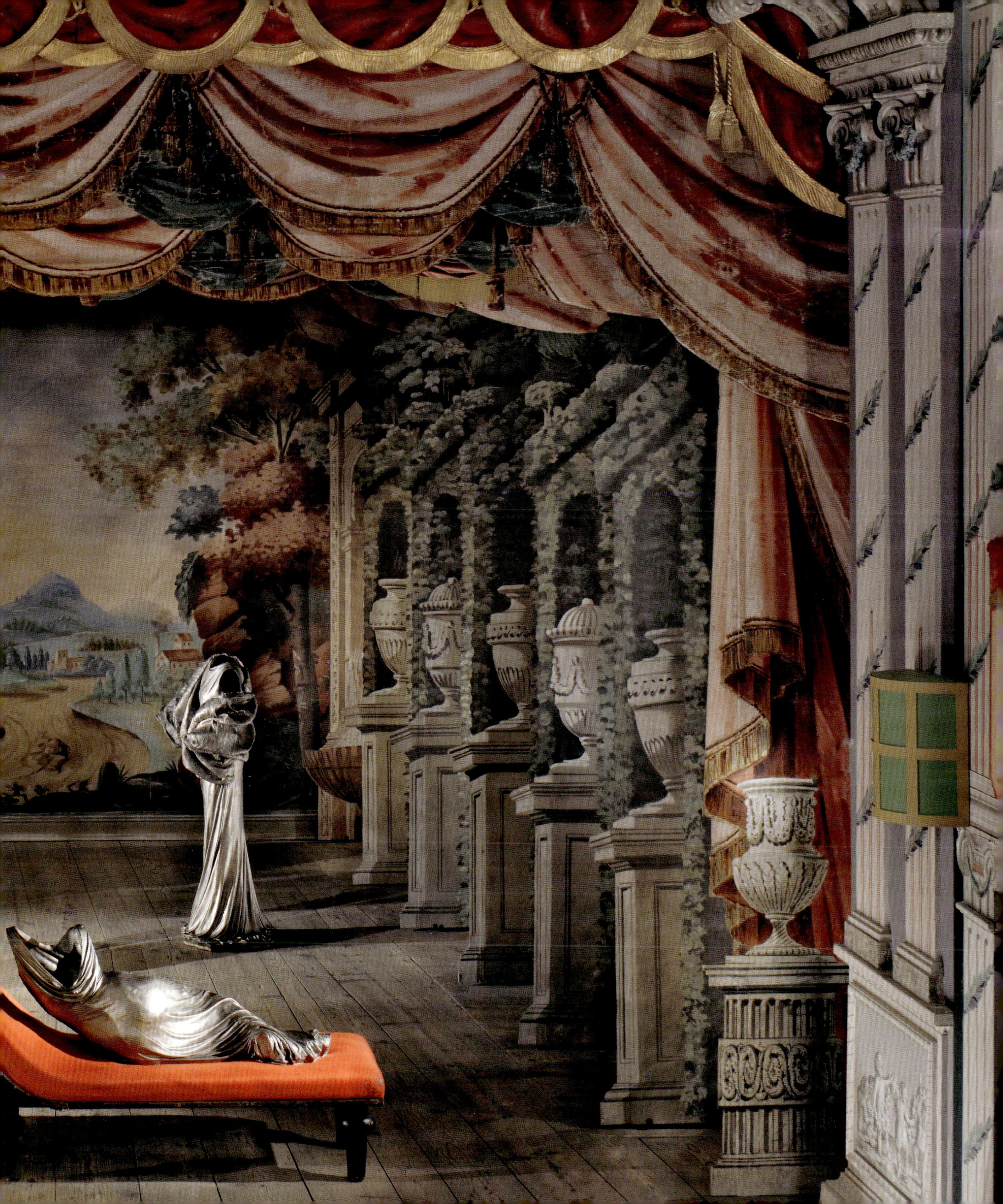

Litomyšl Tableau 7, 2017
Limited-edition photograph

OPPOSITE
Estates Theater Tableau 1, 2016
Limited-edition photograph

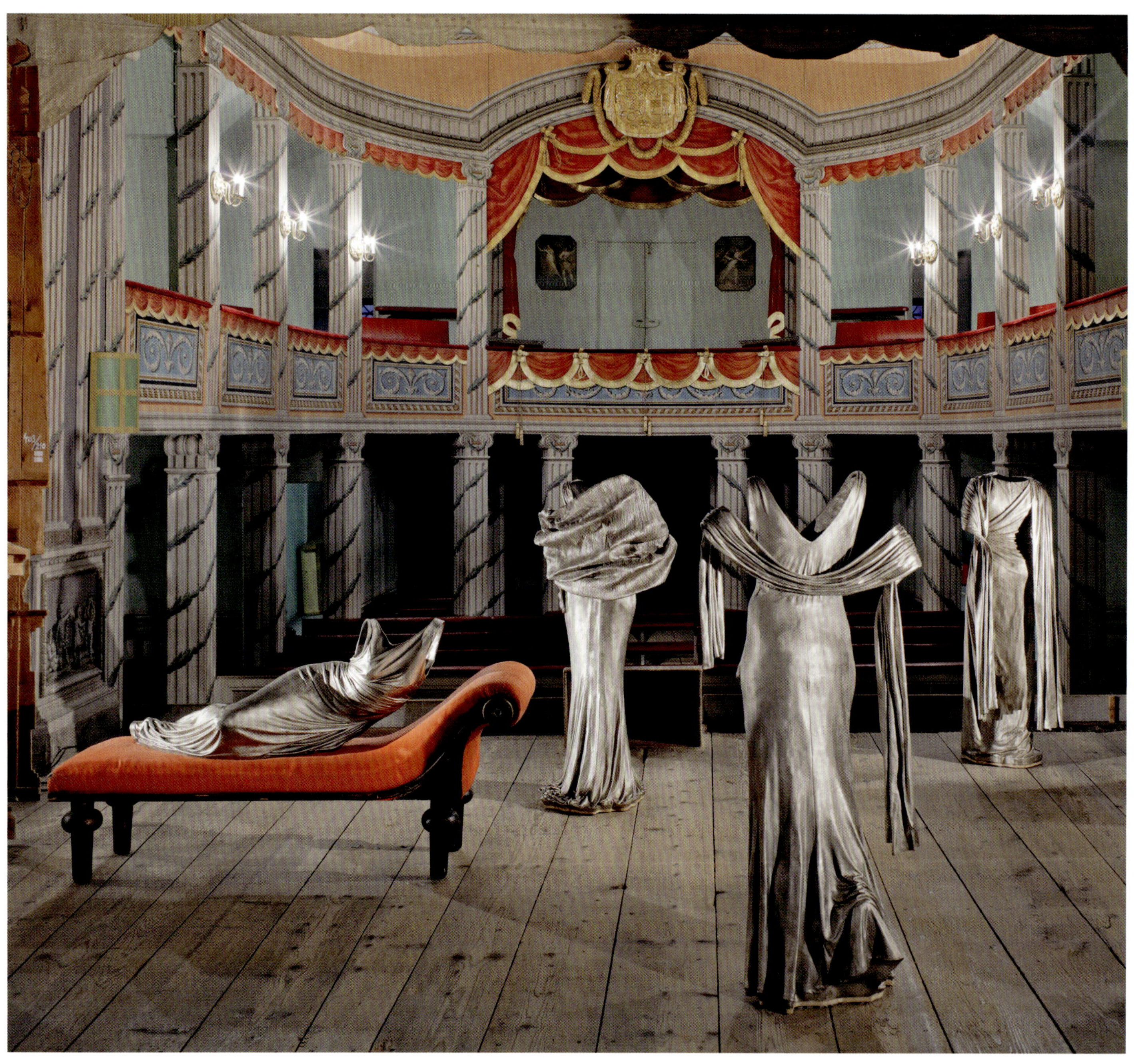

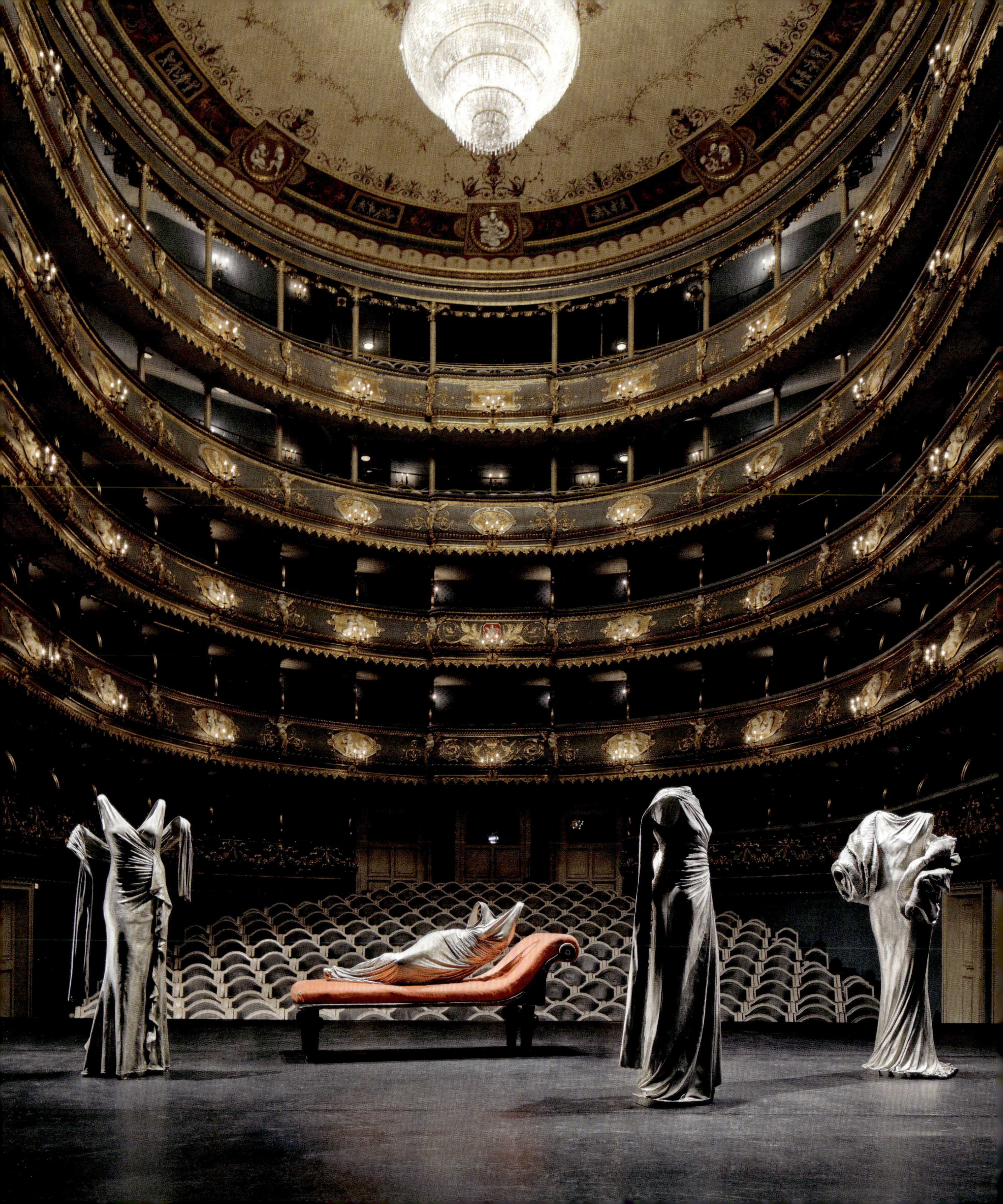

Detailing a wax positive for *Nocturne 3* in cast glass, 2014.

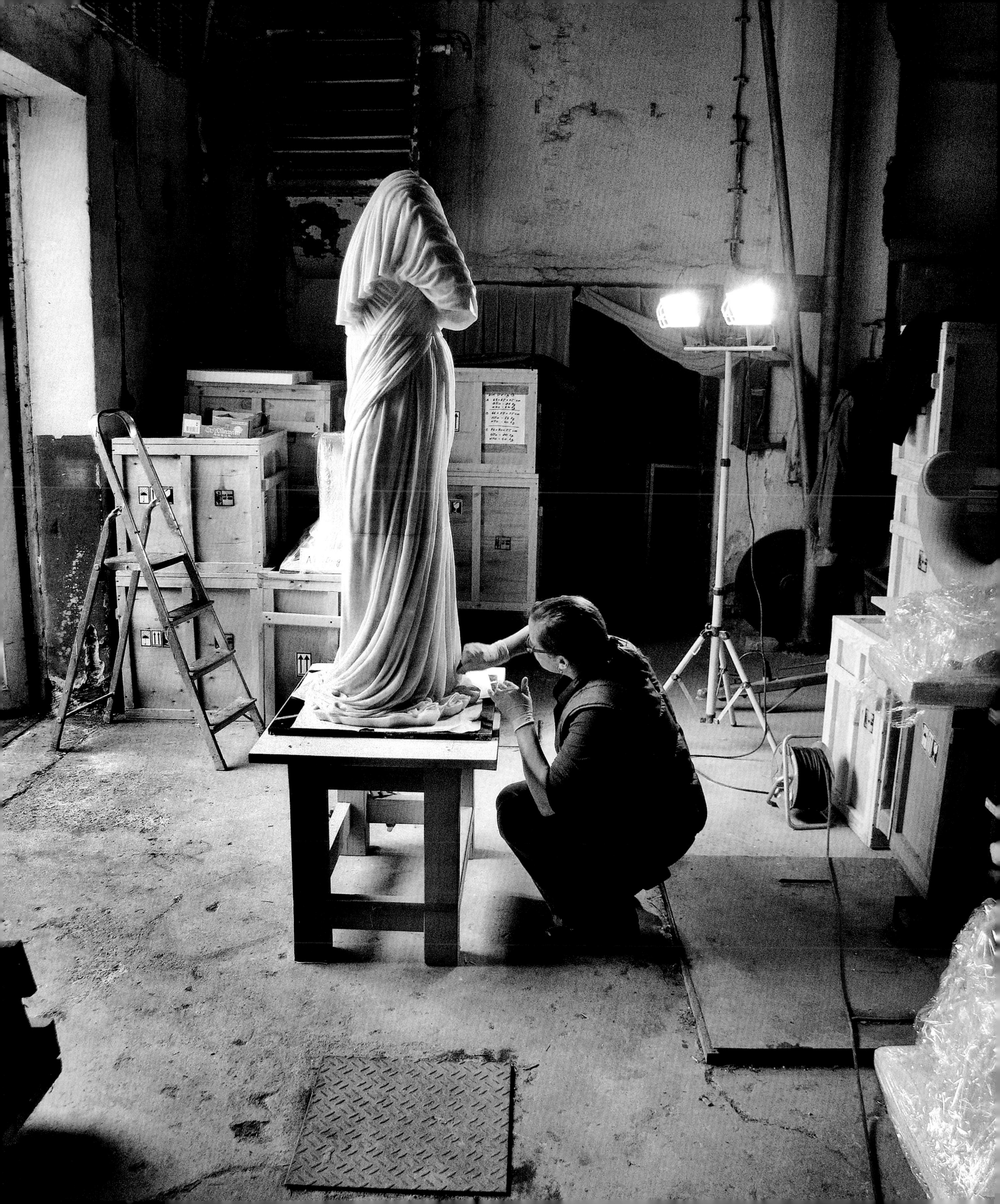

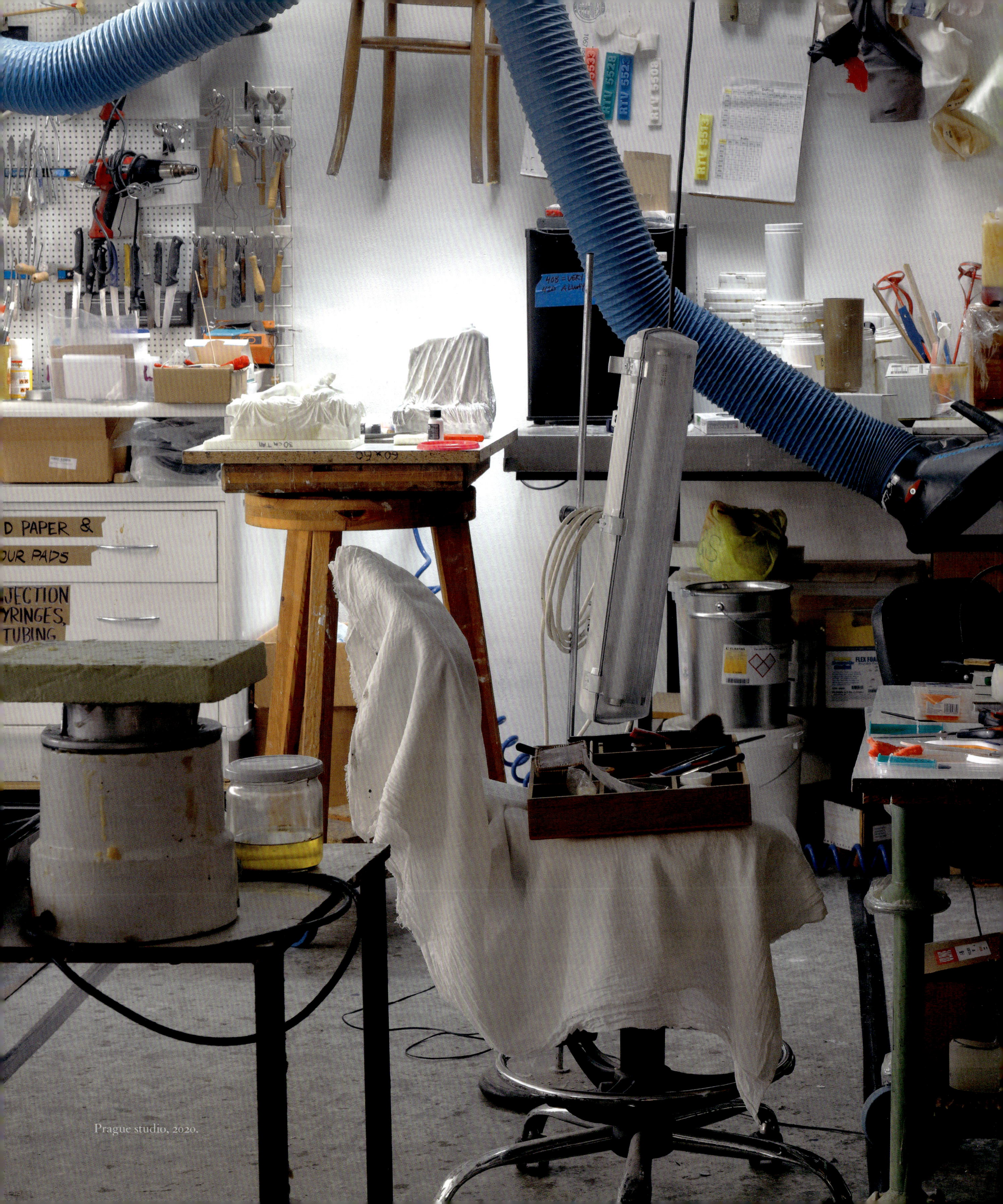

Prague studio, 2020.

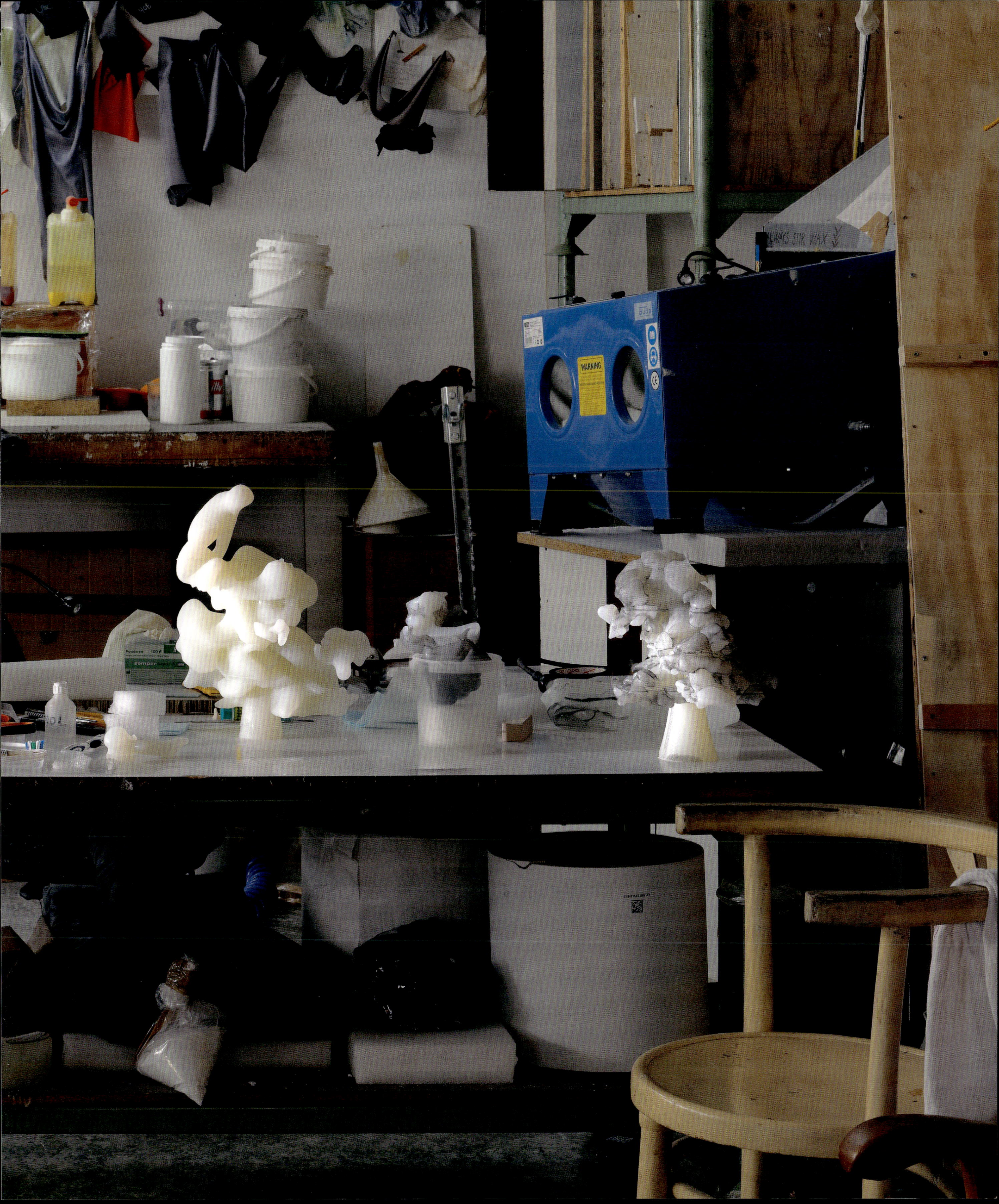

ALWAYS STIR WAX
WARNING

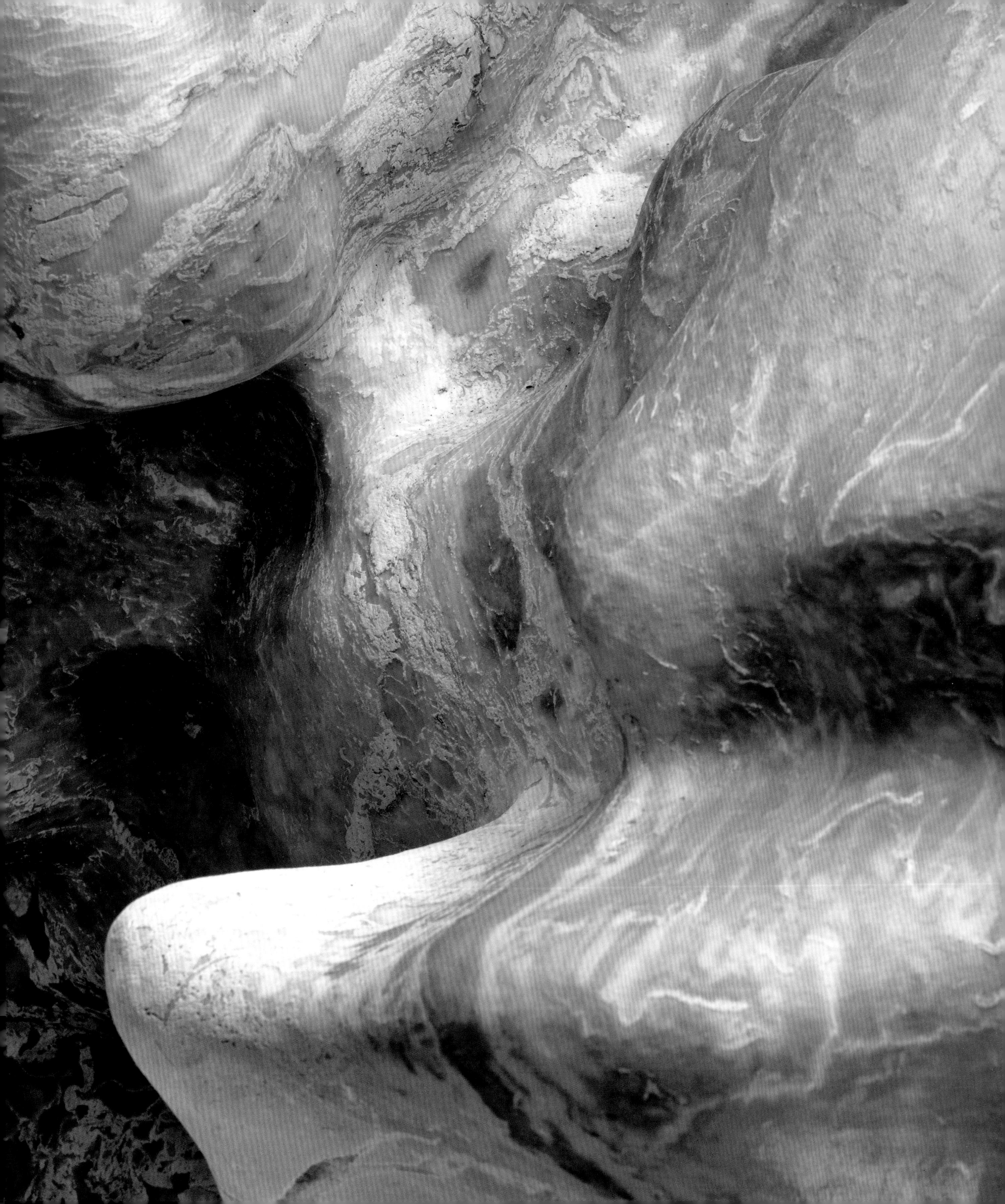

On the Origin of Ideas
Artist as Explorer

Karen LaMonte

Detail of *Cumulus 1:2*, 2017

For me, being an artist is about being curious, about constantly examining and responding to the world around me. Given the world we live in, it is no surprise that my newest explorations involve as much science and technology as they do art history.

Over the past several years, I have returned to the human figure and the landscape, but I am now working with scientists and inventors in my search for methods and materials to make sculpture.

Just as the *Floating World* series looked at my earlier themes of body and beauty, and presence and absence, but through a different cultural lens, my new work with figurines is a reexamination of the body through the lens of new technologies and materials that mimic human biology. I am also revisiting clouds and climate, which I had investigated in my early works and the *Drapery Abstractions* series, but this time I am doing so in collaboration with climatologists, material scientists, and roboticists.

Although I have been working on these projects for several years, I feel I am still at the beginning. What follows are snapshots of explorations mid-step, down paths with unknown destinations.

BEAUTY AND BIOLOGY: THE FIGURINES

Around 2014, I became interested in going beyond the veneer of culture and looking under clothing at the figure on a more primordial level. The body is our common denominator—it transcends culture, gender, and time. I started thinking about the figure in its purely physical manifestation and asking questions about biology and being in the twenty-first century.

My studio in Prague, Czech Republic, is three hundred miles away from the cave in Germany where the oldest-known depiction of a human being was discovered: the Venus of Hohle Fels. Standing just two and a half inches tall, this diminutive carving in mammoth ivory is forty thousand years old. She fascinates me.

We do not know why the carving was made or how it was used. Some anthropologists believe it is about fertility, sex, and reproduction—the power of the female essence. Maybe, like the Roman goddess of love and beauty we named her after, she represents the divine.

I am drawn to her because she embodies the enduring impulse to create art in our own image. I am also intrigued by questions she raises about gender and perception: Why are the majority of figurines made over the next ten thousand years female? And, since three-quarters of the handprints in prehistoric cave drawings were female, were the first artists mostly women?

As I embarked on making modern figurines, I wanted to acknowledge the history but reflect the times in which they are made. When the Venus of Hohle Fels was carved, daily life was perilous; we would probably have categorized ourselves as an endangered species. Yet the times that we live in now are perhaps just as perilous. As a species, we are abundant, but our activities are destroying the environment that we need to sustain ourselves. The threat of our extinction is once again a possibility.

We live in an age of synthetic biology—a time, more than any era before, when we can alter our bodies. As a figurative sculptor, I had been working metamorphically with materials to talk about being human. But once I began exploring the figurines, I felt it important to work with materials that mimic human biology.

I learned about biomimetic materials by studying the field of regenerative medicine. This first led me to Dr. Joseph Vacanti, a preeminent researcher in the field, whom I visited in his lab at Harvard University. I was looking for a sculpting material that was whitish and semitranslucent. He showed me astonishing decellularized organs and three-dimensional printed collagen, but nothing I felt I could use. I turned my attention to making *Nocturnes,* but the idea of working with biomimetic materials never left my mind.

Several years later, when I was the artist in residence at Corning Incorporated's research facility in Sullivan Park, I learned about biomedical glasses. There are many types ranging from bioactive glasses, which dissolve in contact with body fluids providing raw materials that the body uses to heal, to tough stable glass-ceramics used as permanent replacements for tooth and bone.

I wanted to utilize biomimetic materials to explore the tension between our desire for eternal physical perfection and the reality of our faults, aging, and death. Bioactive glasses seemed perfect because they are designed to be unstable and impermanent. When implanted in the body, they transform and become part of the person.

I came to think of the glass ceramic used for bone and tooth replacement as biomimetic ivory. It offered a link back to the mammoth tusk of the Venus of Hohle Fels. Using it to make my figurines gave me a vocabulary to explore the timeless commonality that binds us together.

The motif of small-scale figurines—the Venuses, netsuke, porcelain from the nineteenth century, even action figures—springs from the instinct to re-create ourselves. To make a figurine for the twenty-first century, I wanted to use the same tools that we are beginning to use in regenerative medicine to repair and modify our bodies. The work started in my studio where I composed still lifes with fabric, furniture, and live models. Then, I used a device that 3-D scans body parts for the manufacture of custom prosthetics to capture the compositions and reduce the scale.

My investigation into the Venus of Hohle Fels began me thinking about how we define ourselves by the materials we use. We define the epochs of prehistory by material: the Stone, Bronze, and Iron Ages. I had been focused on biomimetic materials, but I started to expand my experiments, seeing other materials as an interesting way to connect our present to our ancient past, and linking my figurines to the earliest endeavors of modern humans. I had already been experimenting with glass—what the

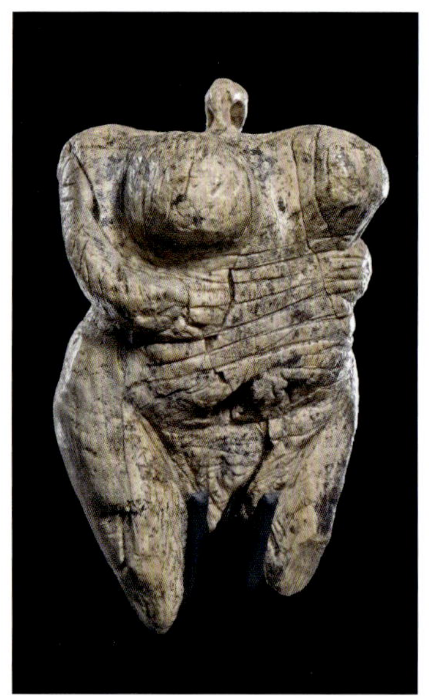

Venus of Hohle Fels, 38,000 BCE. Urgeschichtliches Museum/ Prehistory Museum, Blaubeuren

ancient Egyptians called "the stone that flows." I began using bronze, which embodies timelessness and human intervention, and pewter, which dates to the Bronze Age but evokes Victorian toy soldiers. And, finally, I utilized rusting iron, which I had used in *Floating World* and *Nocturnes* to speak to transience and transformation. It is a perfect vehicle to communicate time and change.

In thinking about the idea of Venus in the twenty-first century, I am also compelled to look at the broadest manifestation of the feminine, including not only cisgender females of every body type, race, and religion but also transgender and non-binary people. To me, exploring this expansive expression of inherent beauty is one of the most exciting aspects of reinventing an ancient icon.

A PERFECT STORM
WEATHER AS METAPHOR

As a kid, I thought clouds were made in a nearby power plant. From my bedroom window in New York City, I would watch billowing steam climb from its chimneys into the sky. My fascination with clouds has never ended.

Clouds intrigue me because they make visible the invisible forces of the natural world. They pepper the sky with transition, becoming being and not being, speaking universally to human impermanence, which Johann Wolfgang von Goethe called "constancy in change." John Ruskin wrote that "between the heaven and man came the cloud."[1] Perhaps this is why cumulus clouds are the choice for religious imagery in both the East and the West. In traditional Chinese art, the female earth essence is manifested in the clouds; as a fusion of the elements of water and air, sky and earth, they are considered the union of yin and yang. In Western religious art, clouds are the domain of saints and gods. In Islamic esotericism, the cloud is the primordial state of Allah.

With much simpler thoughts in mind, I started making my own clouds when I was twenty-three years old. After graduating from Rhode Island School of Design, I made sculptures capturing weather under bell jars, and I enameled clouds on the surface of glass flowers and blown glass dresses. Inspired by the Surrealist works of René Magritte, I planted the flowers in the Black Rock Desert on the edges of Burning Man in 1995.

Over the next decade, the small dresses evolved into monumental sculptures. As I worked with increasingly exaggerated drapery, such as in *Reclining Drapery Impression*, I started to see the body as a landscape shaping the mountains of fabric tumbling across the figure. Eventually, drapery, landscape, and weather merged in my glass and ceramic abstractions.

Untitled early works in glass and bronze, 1995–96

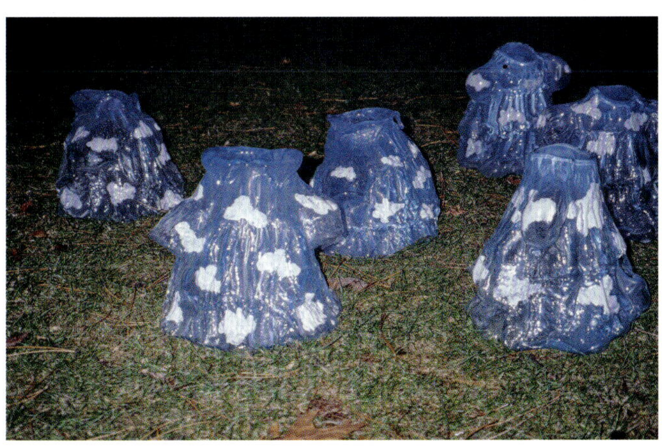

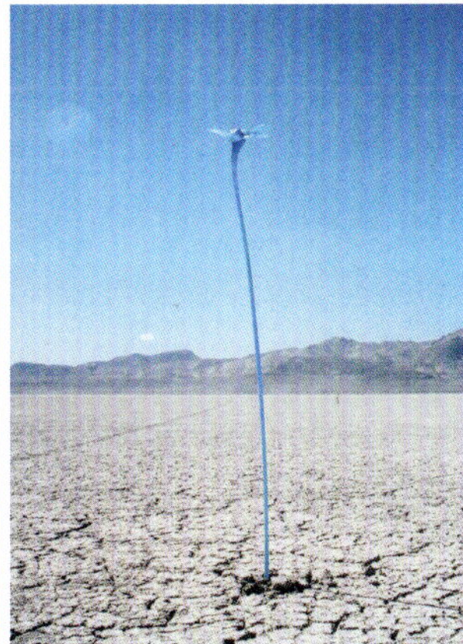

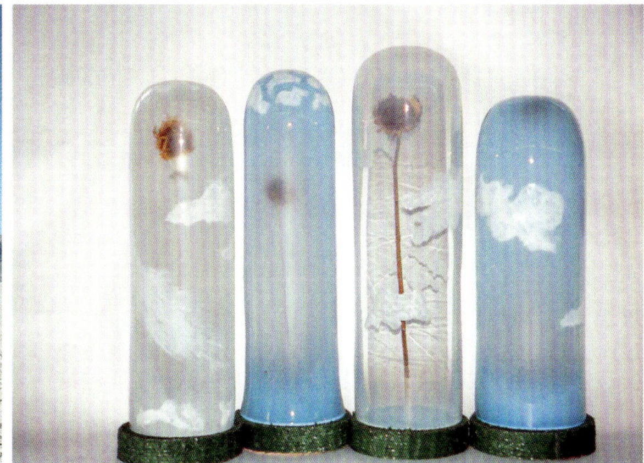

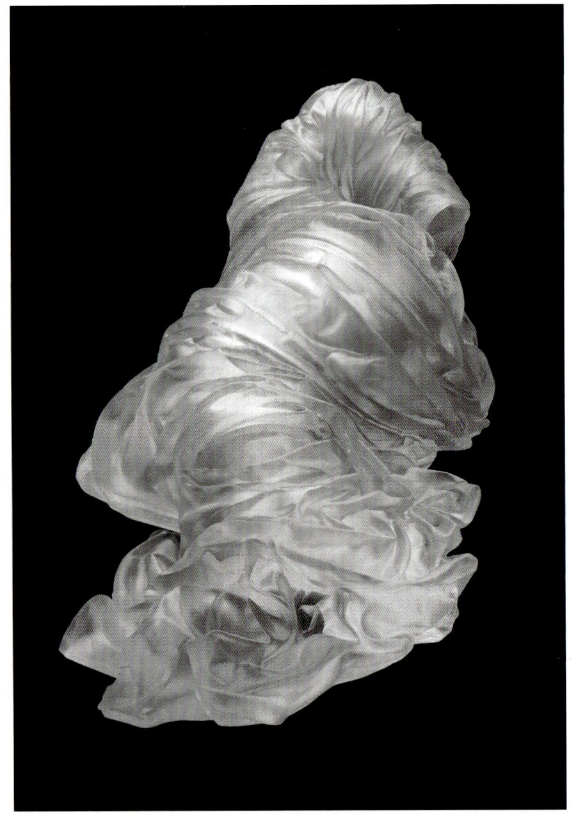

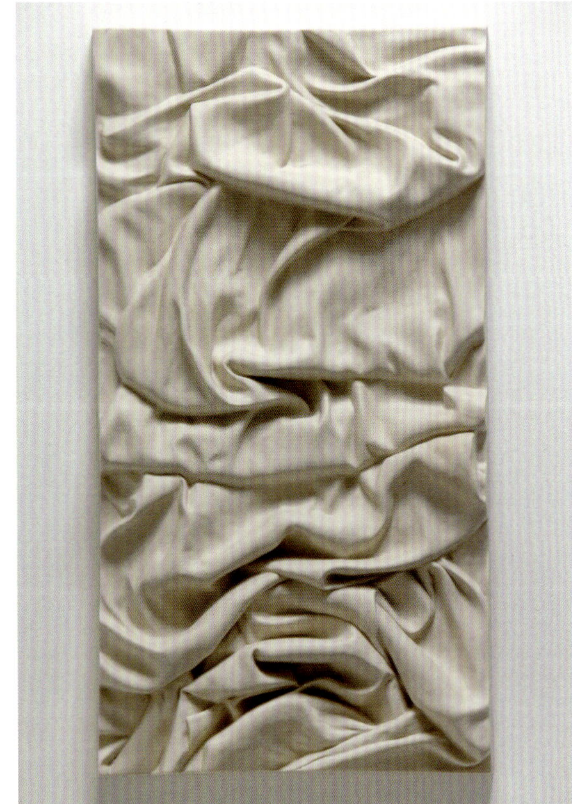

Reclining Drapery Impression, 2005
Cast glass, 18 × 61½ × 23 in.
(46 × 156 × 58 cm)

Smoke, 2009
Vitreous china, 25 × 14½ × 3 in.
(64 × 36 × 8 cm)

In 2015, I returned to clouds, focusing on their embodiment of contradiction. The largest cumulus clouds can weigh up to 220 tons yet float effortlessly. I became inspired to make a cloud in stone that would be equivalent in weight to the real cloud on which it was based—a meditation on the paradoxes of weight and weightlessness, the material and immaterial, and presence and absence.

I like to challenge the boundary between representation and reality, so like my dresses and kimonos, my cloud needed to be real, not just a visual representation. This pursuit of realism led me to the Climate Dynamics Group at the California Institute of Technology, where scientists and engineers study climate change. I worked with Tapio Schneider and Kyle Pressel, who are experts in atmospheric dynamics. They fed data into a supercomputer and ran a weather simulation program for days to create a vast virtual block of weather filled with clouds formed according to the laws of nature—as close to real clouds as I could get.

Every aspect of the project forced me to engage with new technologies. I needed data to divine the form, a supercomputer to model the weather, scientists to calculate the water weight of the cloud, and the precision afforded by robots to transfigure a real cloud into marble with an exact weight equivalency.

Although based on a real cloud, the sculpture *Cumulus* looks decidedly biomorphic, like a mountain of nude figures. Baroque in its physicality, it suggests folds of flesh or fabric tumbling through space.

The painter John Constable referred to the sky as the "organ of sentiment."[2] I see clouds as a powerful mirror for inner activity—a barometer of human feeling expressing the transience of emotion with muscular visuality.

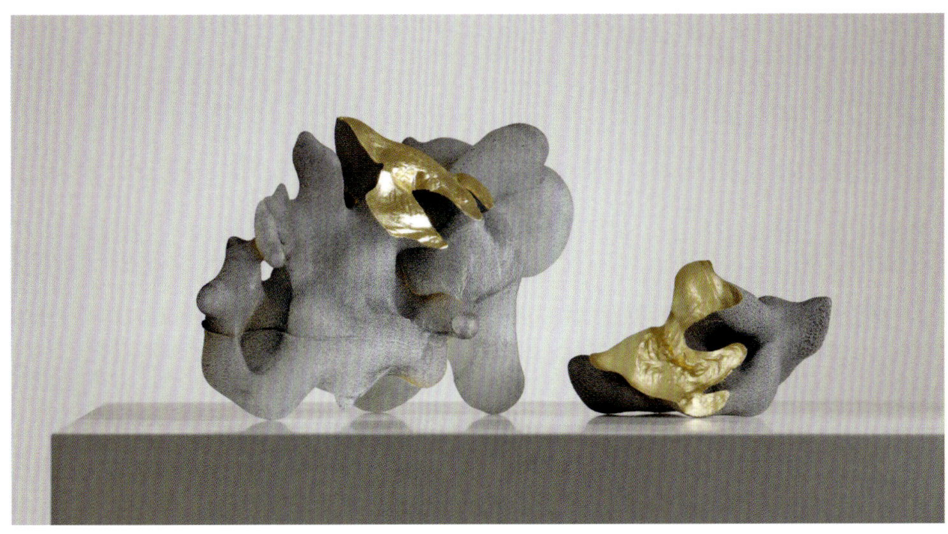

Cloud in progress, 2019
Cast bioglass-ceramic, gold leaf,
6 × 14 × 11 in. (15 × 35 × 27 cm)

Clouds also fascinate me because of how they interact with light—a dynamic that is not only beautiful and mystical, but also at the center of the research on global warming. I have been using light as sculptural material for thirty years in my earlier works, but clouds required a new approach. Wanting to use materials that physically related to clouds, I focused on opal glass, which gets its milky rainbow appearance by refracting light in a similar way to clouds and the atmosphere.

I had learned about glass ceramic during my residency at Corning Incorporated's research facility. It starts as a glass, but when treated with a secondary thermal cycle, it forms nucleating agents—like little seeds—that are sites for the growth of ceramic crystals. This is exactly how clouds form! The atmosphere is a solution of water dissolved in air. When the conditions are right, the moisture nucleates around airborne particulates (little seeds), forming water droplets creating a cloud.

Armed with new materials, my first experiment was to make sculptures of stratocumulus, a cloud that is in danger of extinction from climate change. I also worked with the cumulus shape, whose complex form led to uneven cooling of the material and irregular crystal growth, resulting in variations of clear and opaque glass—the creation of a cloud within a cloud frozen in time.

As with all experiments, sometimes things did not go as planned and several castings cracked—a blessing of sorts, because I had wanted to work with broken clouds but lacked the resolve to break a perfect casting. Thinking back to my broken kimonos of the *Floating World* series, which I repaired with gold using the ancient *kintsugi* technique, I gold-leafed the cracked planes. Broken clouds seem like an apt symbol for our times.

Although not complete, these experiments are important milestones that mark the beginning of a whole new phase, one that allows me to integrate both artistic and scientific knowledge and tools. In a way, I feel as though I am returning to earlier modes of exploring the world—when science was "natural philosophy" and not a separate discipline from the creative arts. When artists were equal part observers, inventors, and creators.

NOTES

1 Johann Wolfgang von Goethe, "Dauer im Wechsel" (Constancy in Change), 1803; John Ruskin, "The Cloud-Balancings," in "Of Cloud Beauty," *Modern Painters*, vol. 5 of 5, 1843–60.

2 Charles Robert Leslie, *Memoirs of the Life of John Constable, Esq. R.A. Composed Chiefly of His Letters*, 1845.

Works in progress, 2019
Cast bioglass-ceramic

FOLLOWING
Figurines in progress, 2019
From left: Cast bioglass-ceramic, white bronze, rusted iron, pewter, each approx. 5 × 10 × 5 in. (12 × 25.5 × 12 cm)

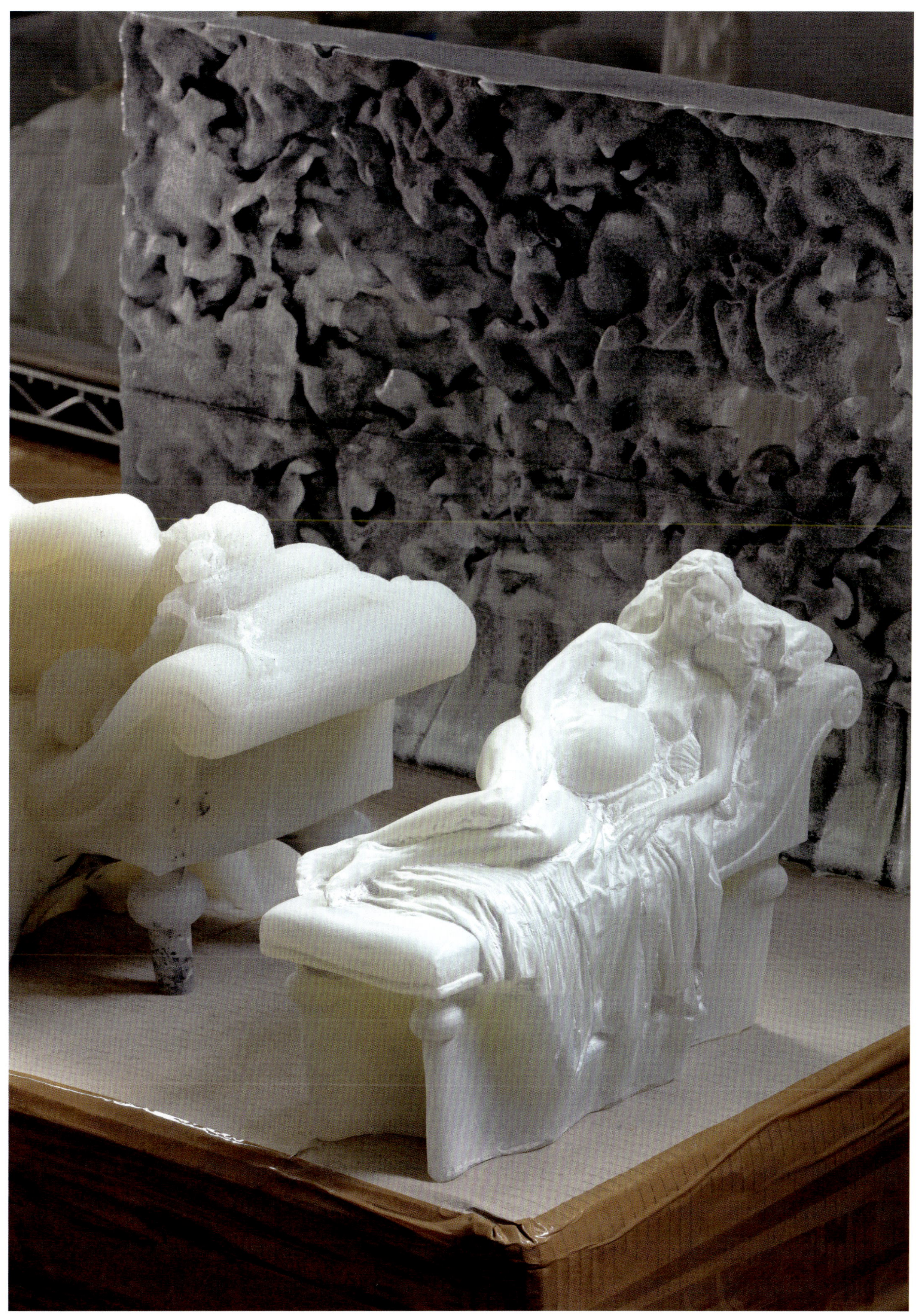

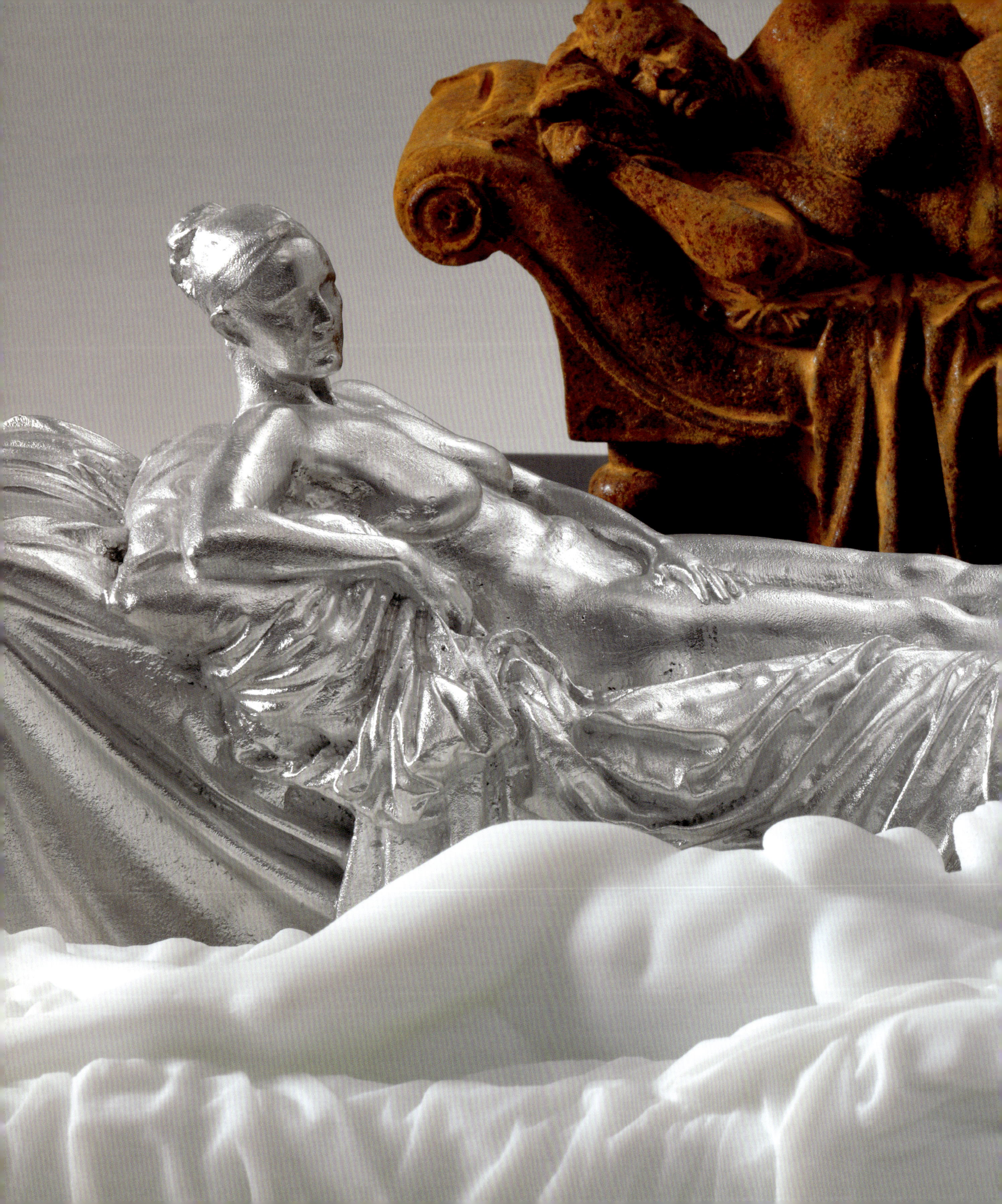

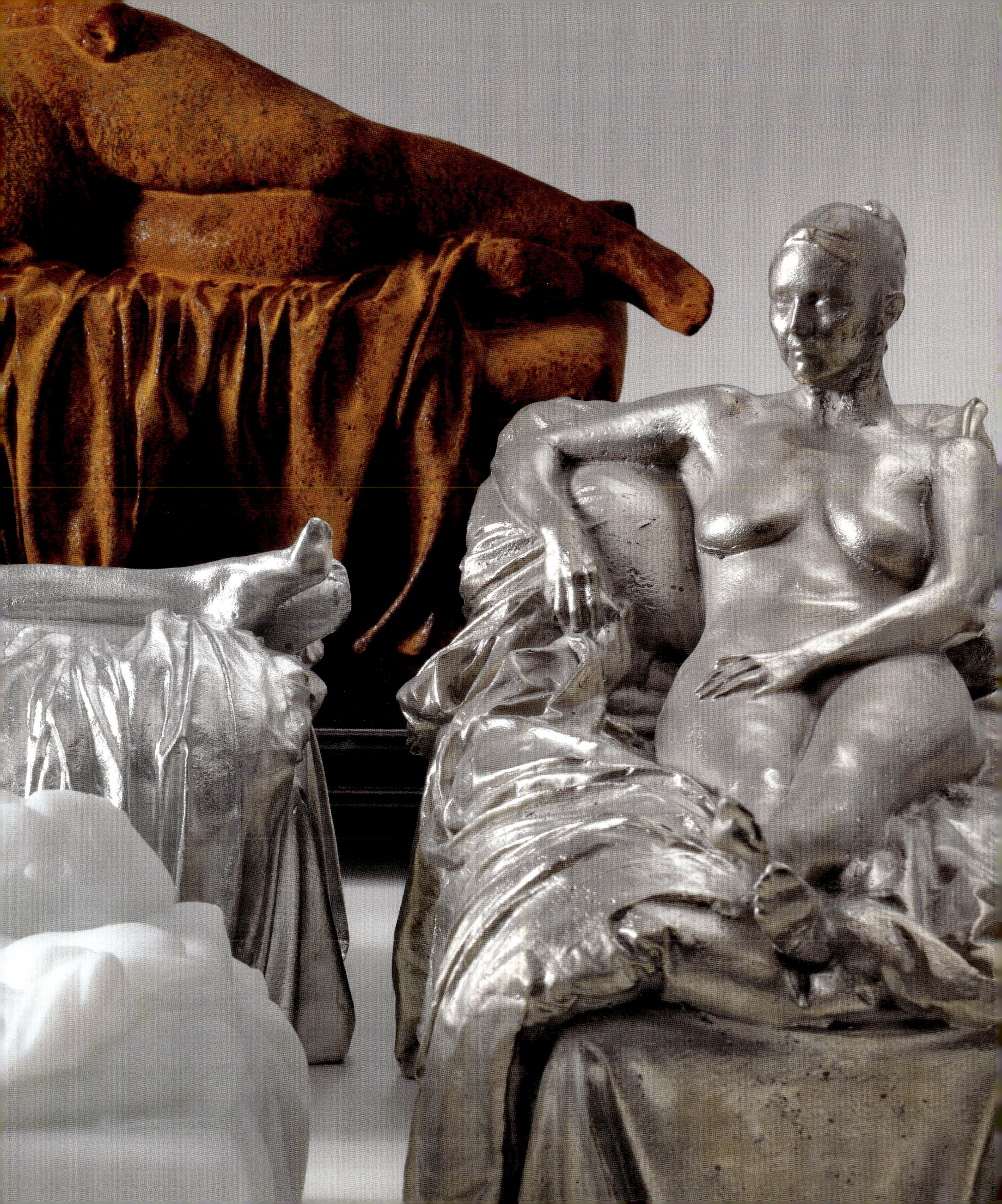

Figurines in progress, 2019

Rusted iron, 5 × 10 × 5 in. (12 × 25.5 × 12 cm)

Bioglass-ceramic, 8 × 3 × 5 in. (20 × 8.5 × 12.5 cm)

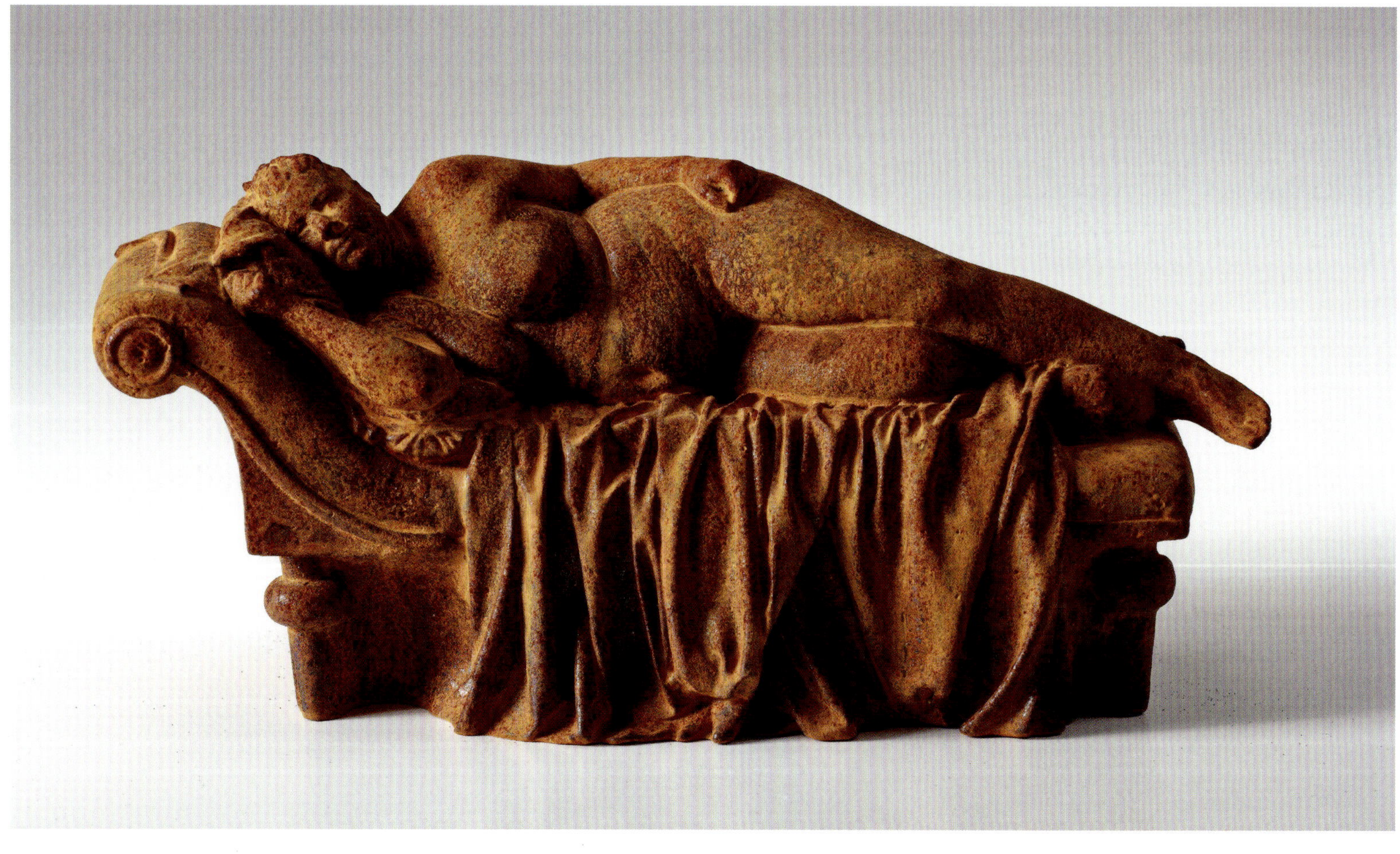

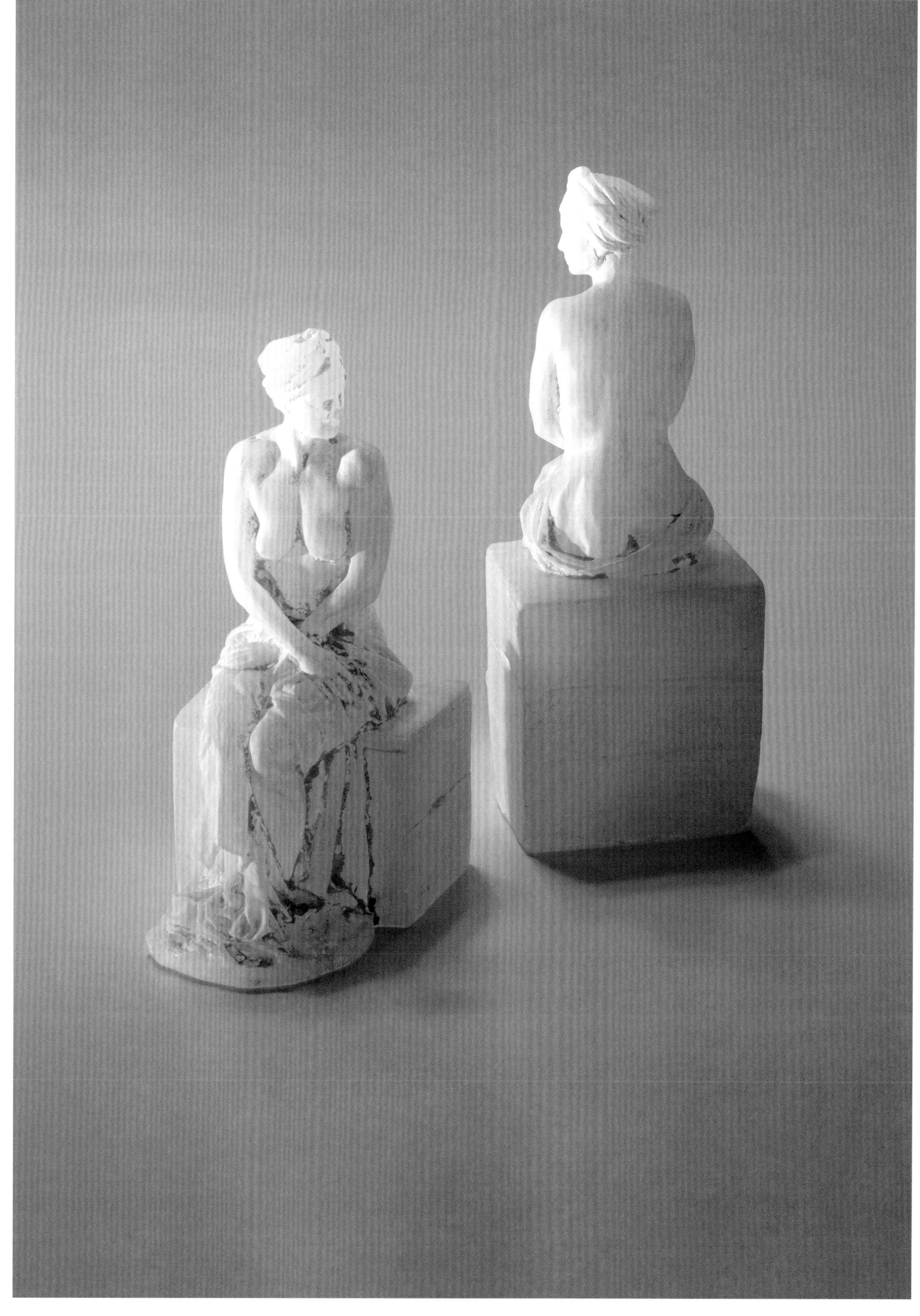

Works in progress, 2019

Rusted iron and bioglass-ceramic, each approx. 5 × 10 × 5 in. (12 × 25.5 × 12 cm)

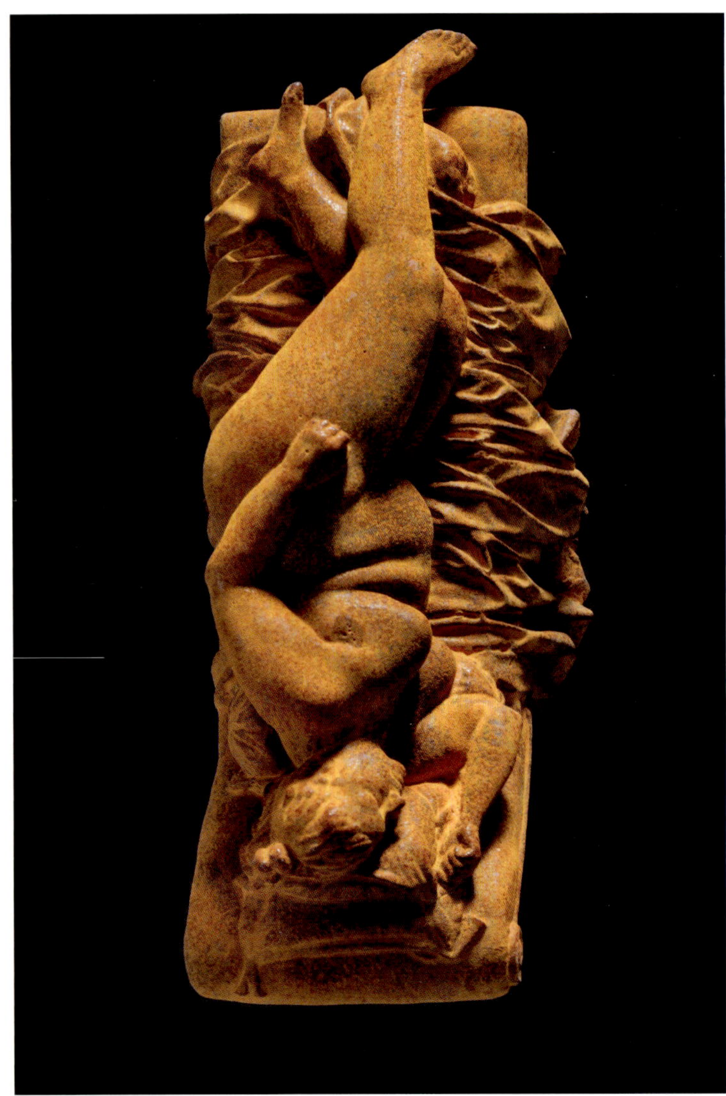

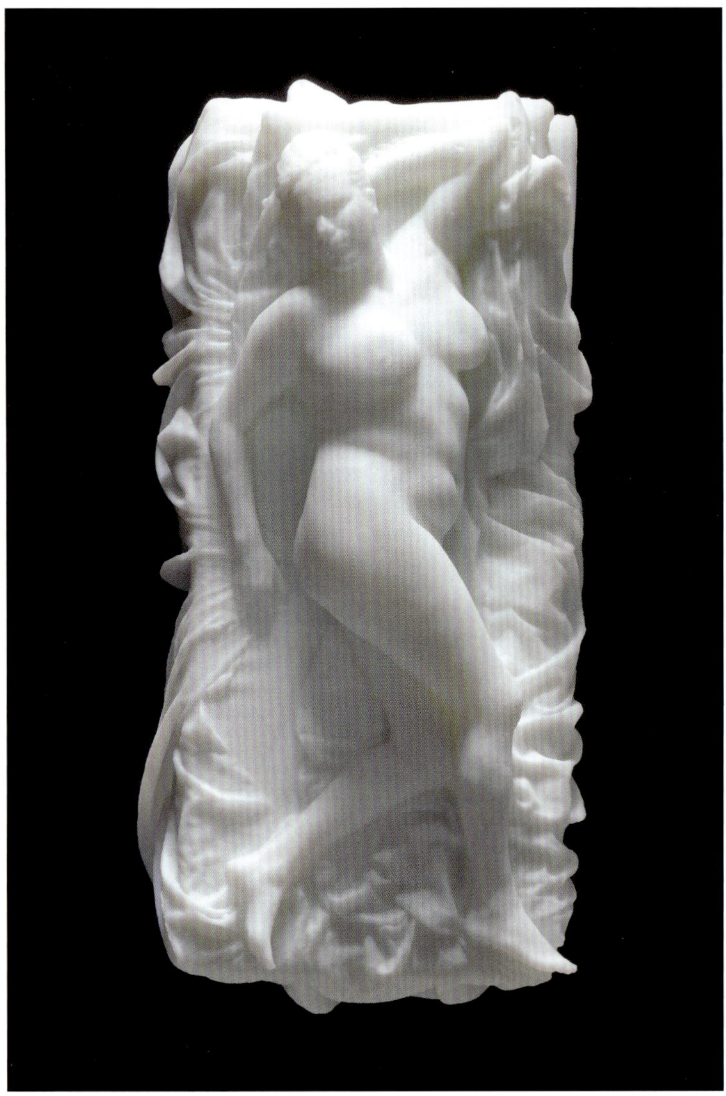

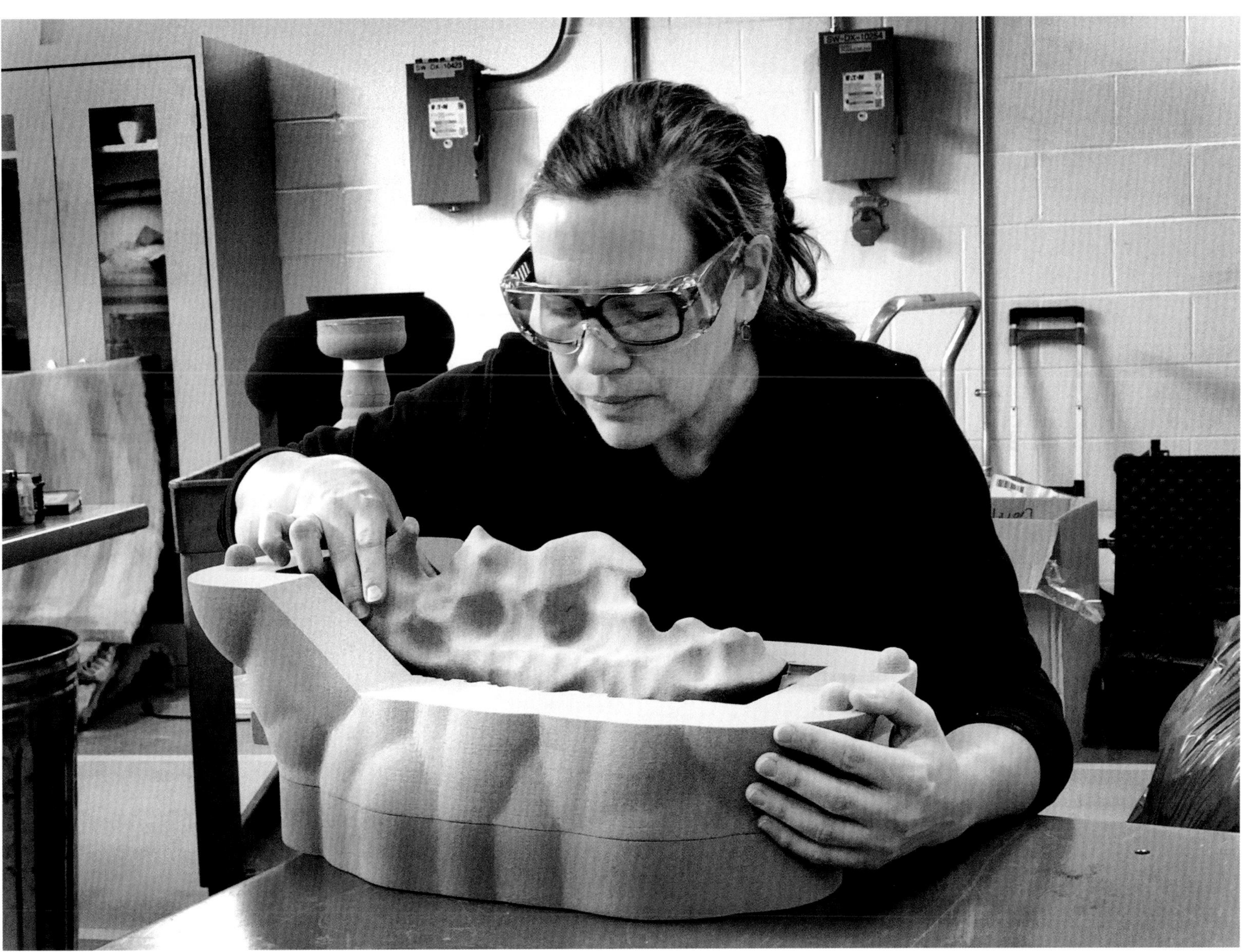

In residence at Corning Incorporated Sullivan Park research facility, Corning, NY, 2018.

FOLLOWING

At work with robotic carving arm on *Cumulus 1:2*, 2017.

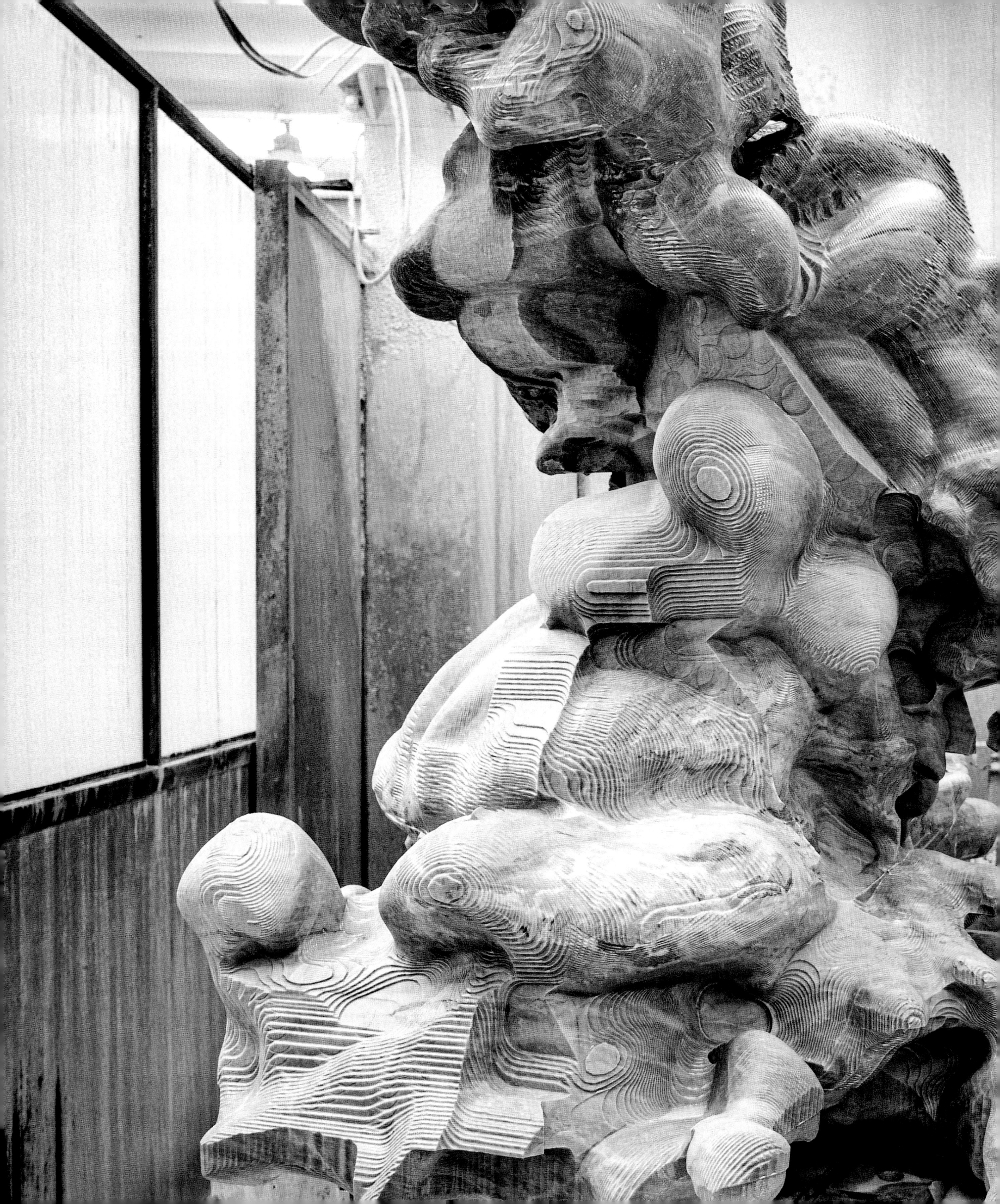

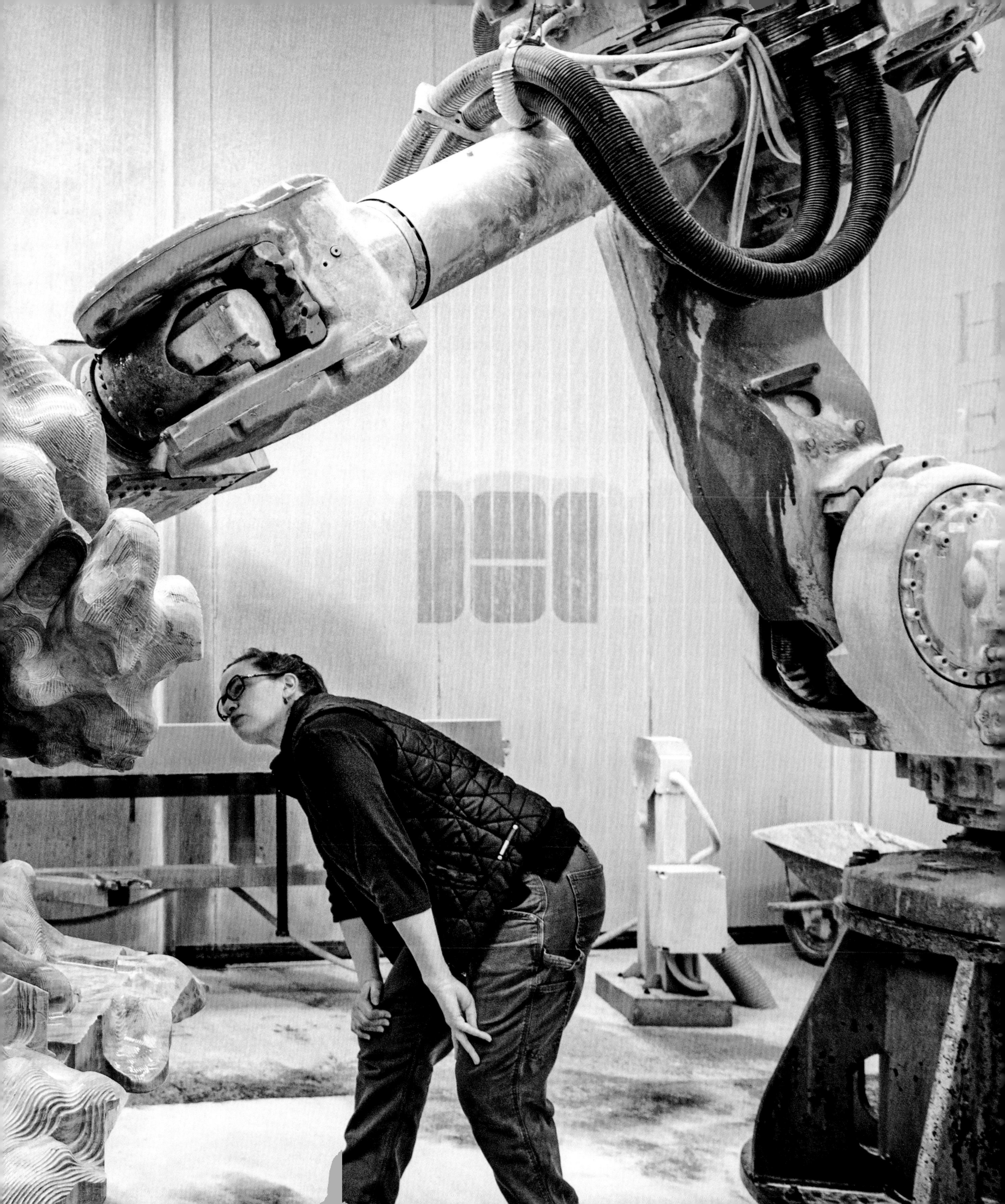

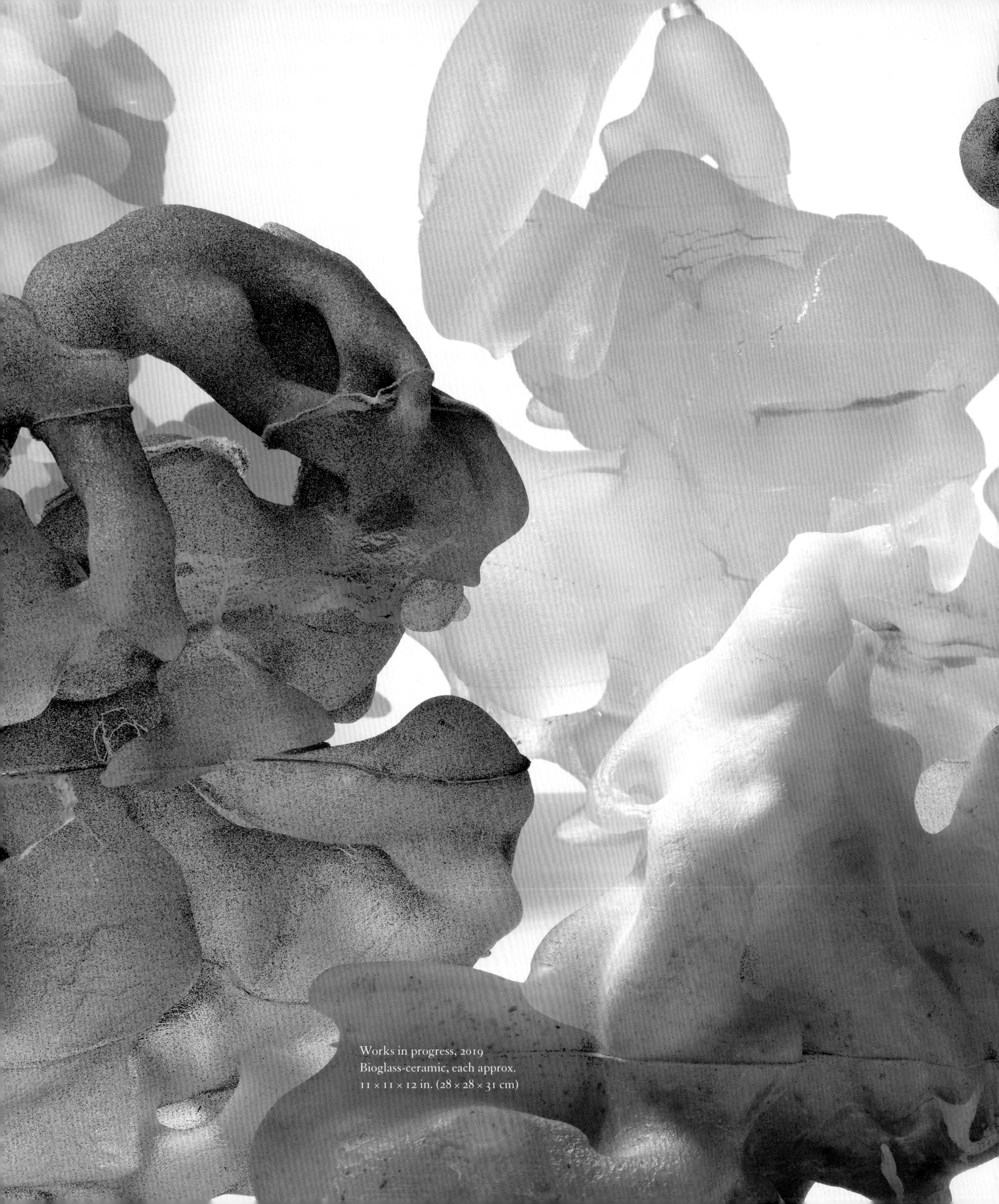

Works in progress, 2019
Bioglass-ceramic, each approx.
11 × 11 × 12 in. (28 × 28 × 31 cm)

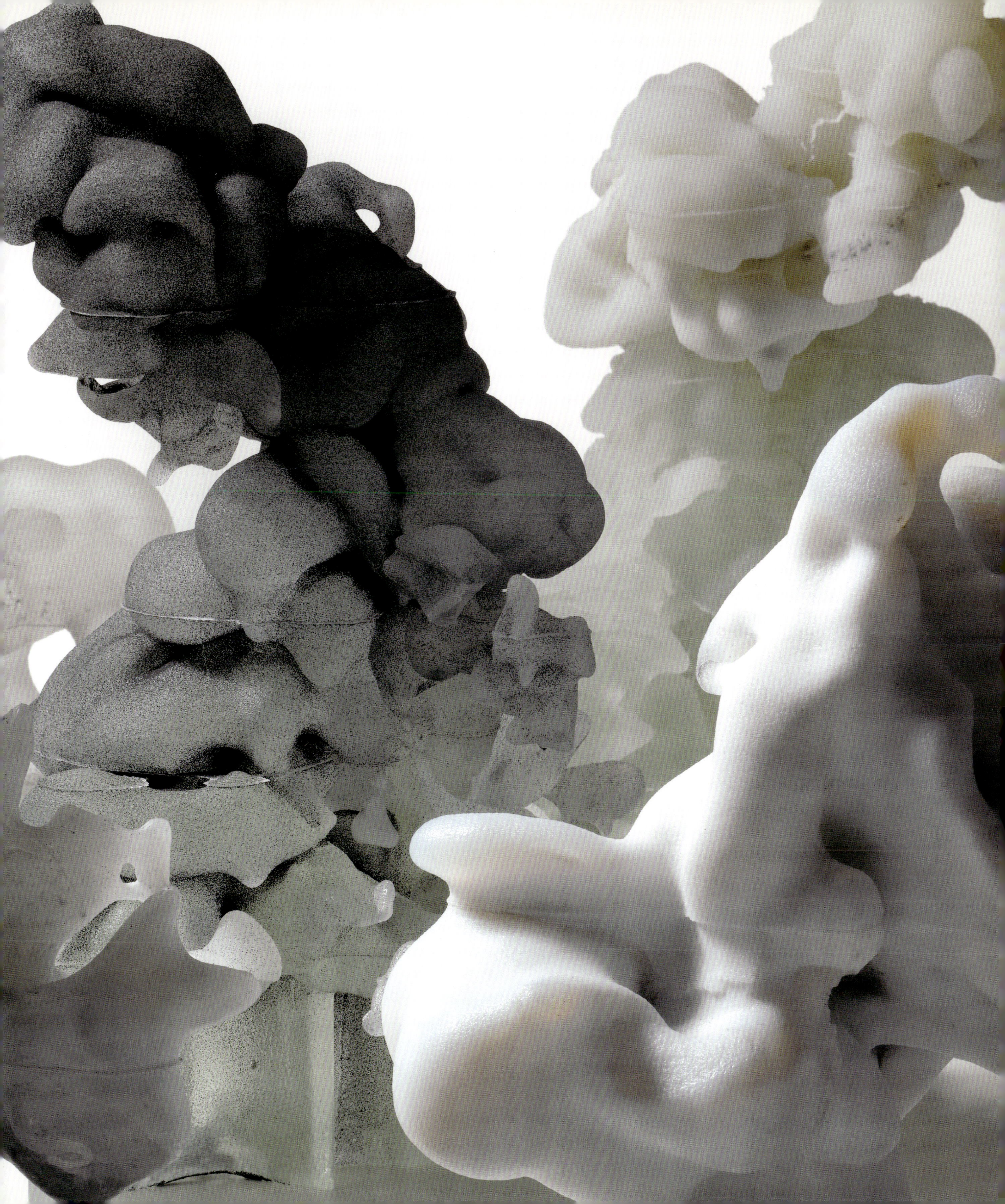

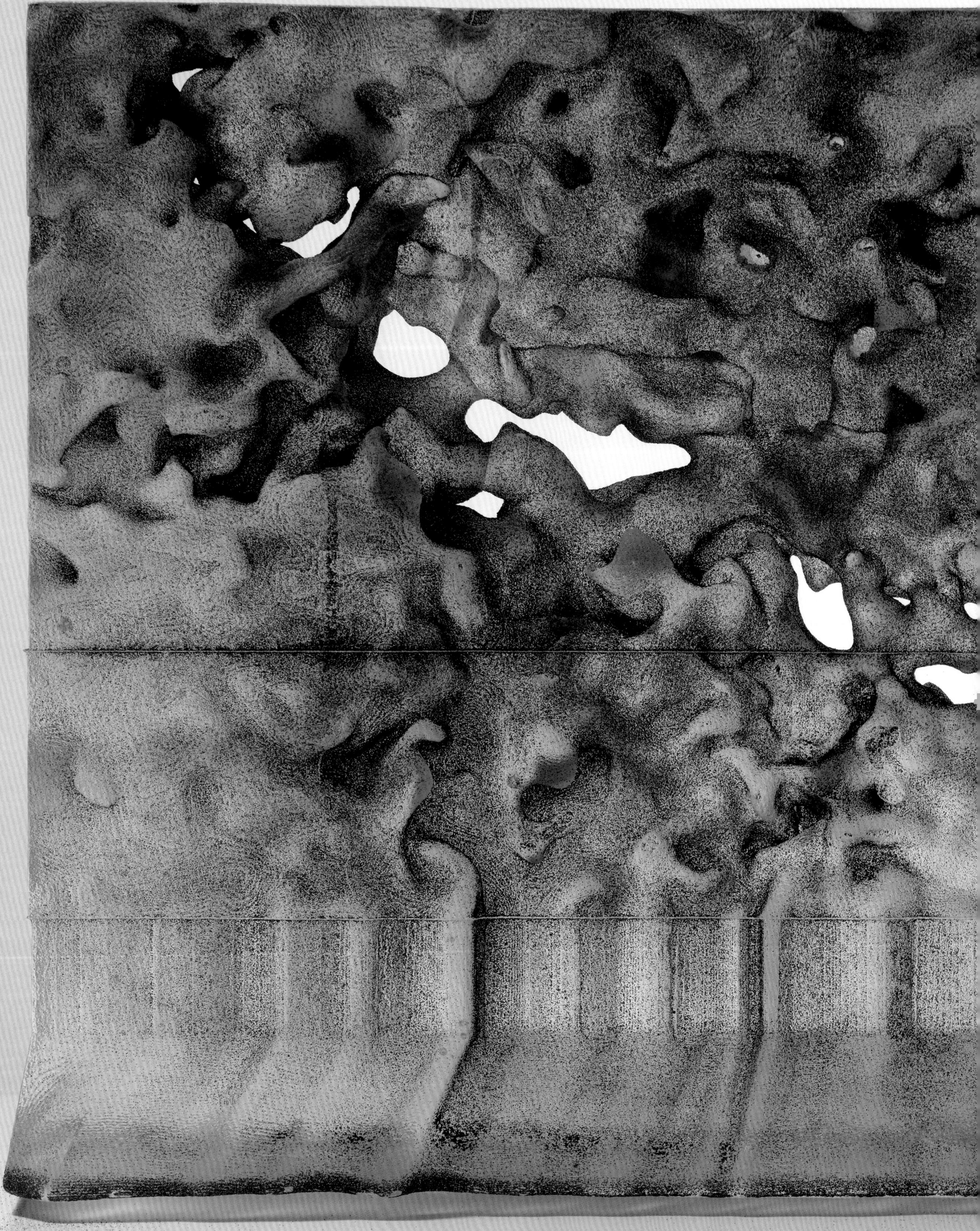

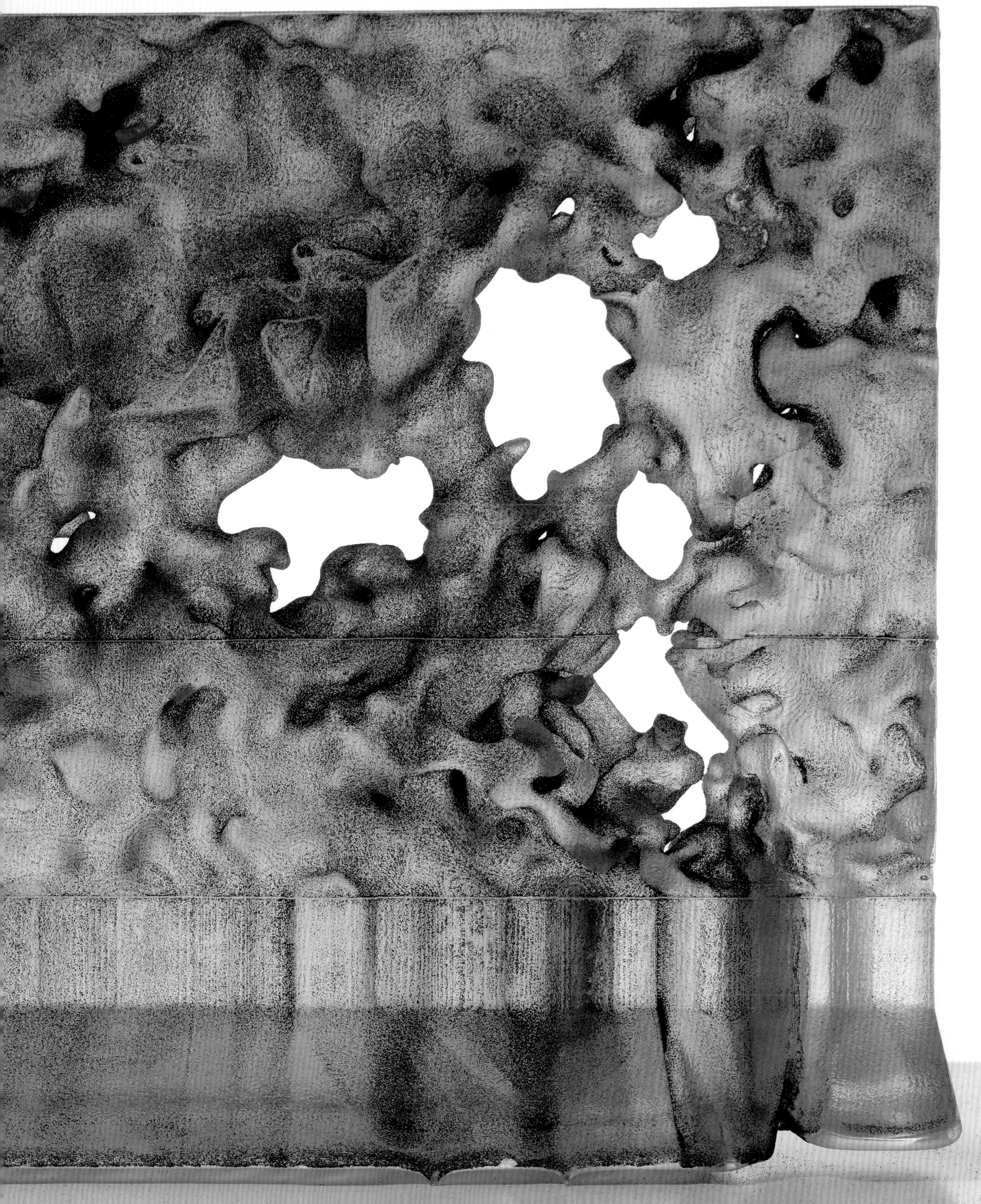

Work in progress, 2019
Bioglass-ceramic, 9½ × 20 × 2 in. (24 × 50 × 5 cm)

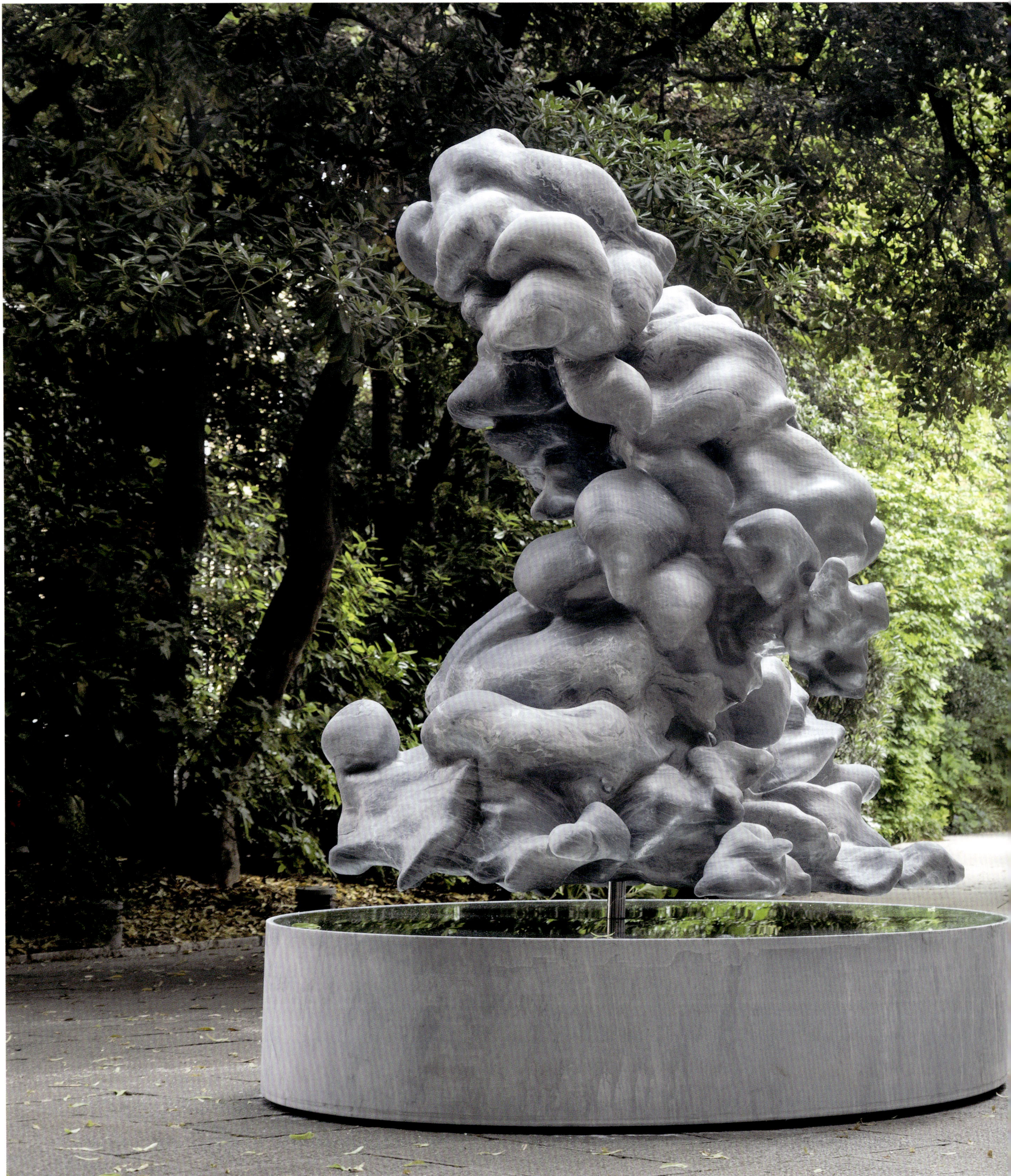

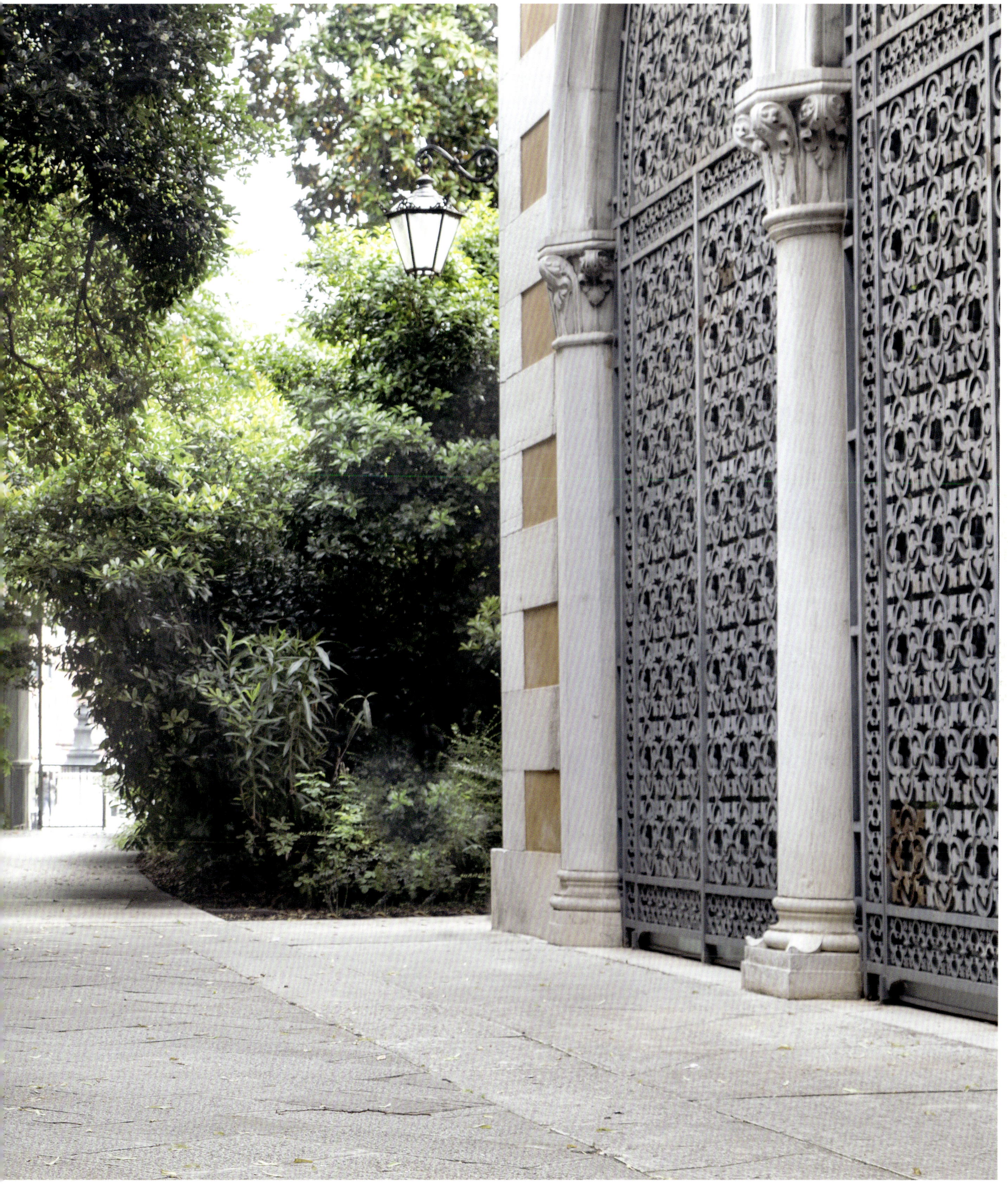

PREVIOUS AND BELOW
Cumulus 1:2, 2017
Exhibition *Glasstress*, 2017, Fondazione Berengo
57th Biennale Arte, Venice, Italy

OPPOSITE
Detail of *Cumulus 1:2*, 2017
Collection of Imagine Museum, St. Petersburg, FL

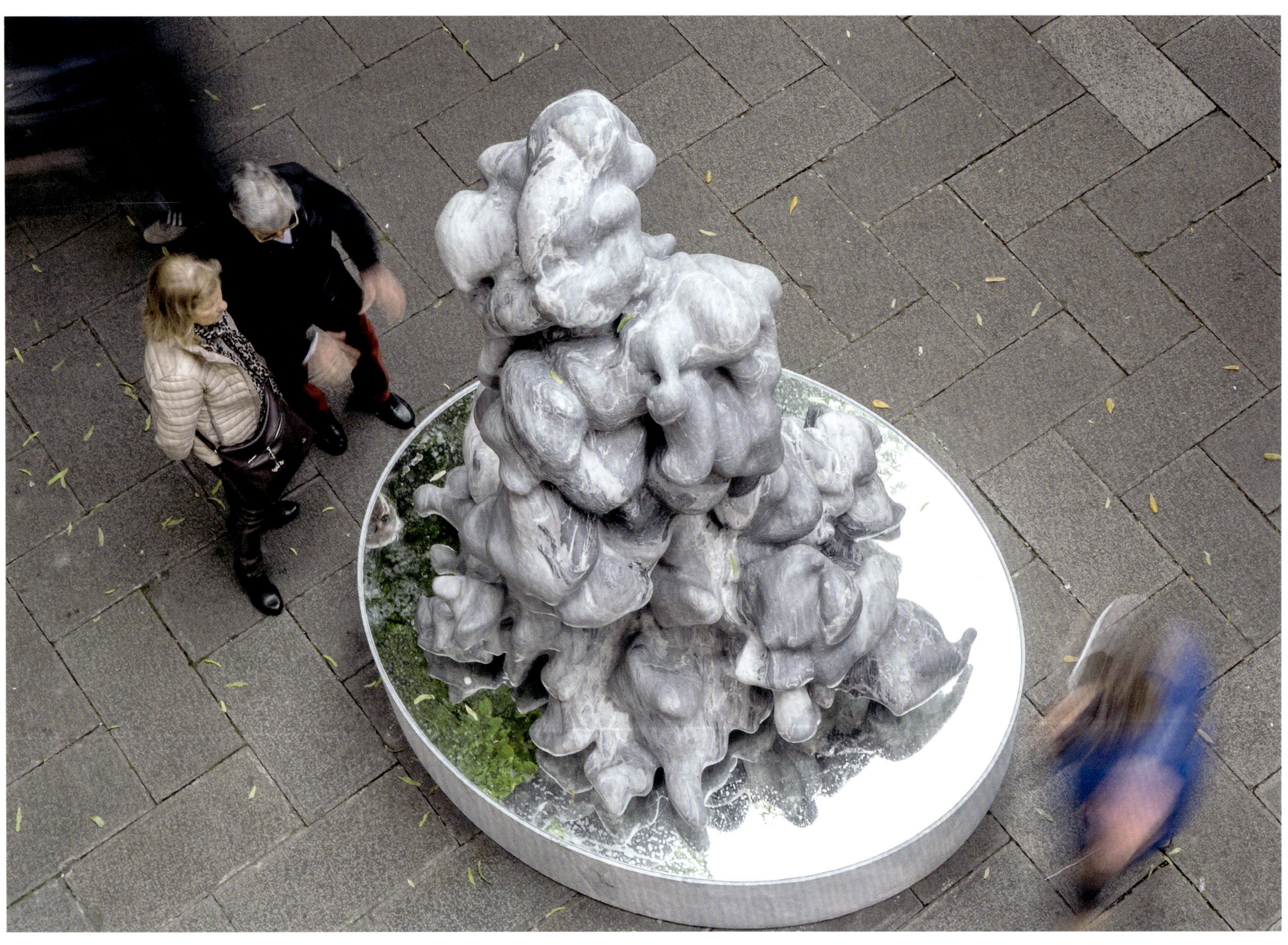

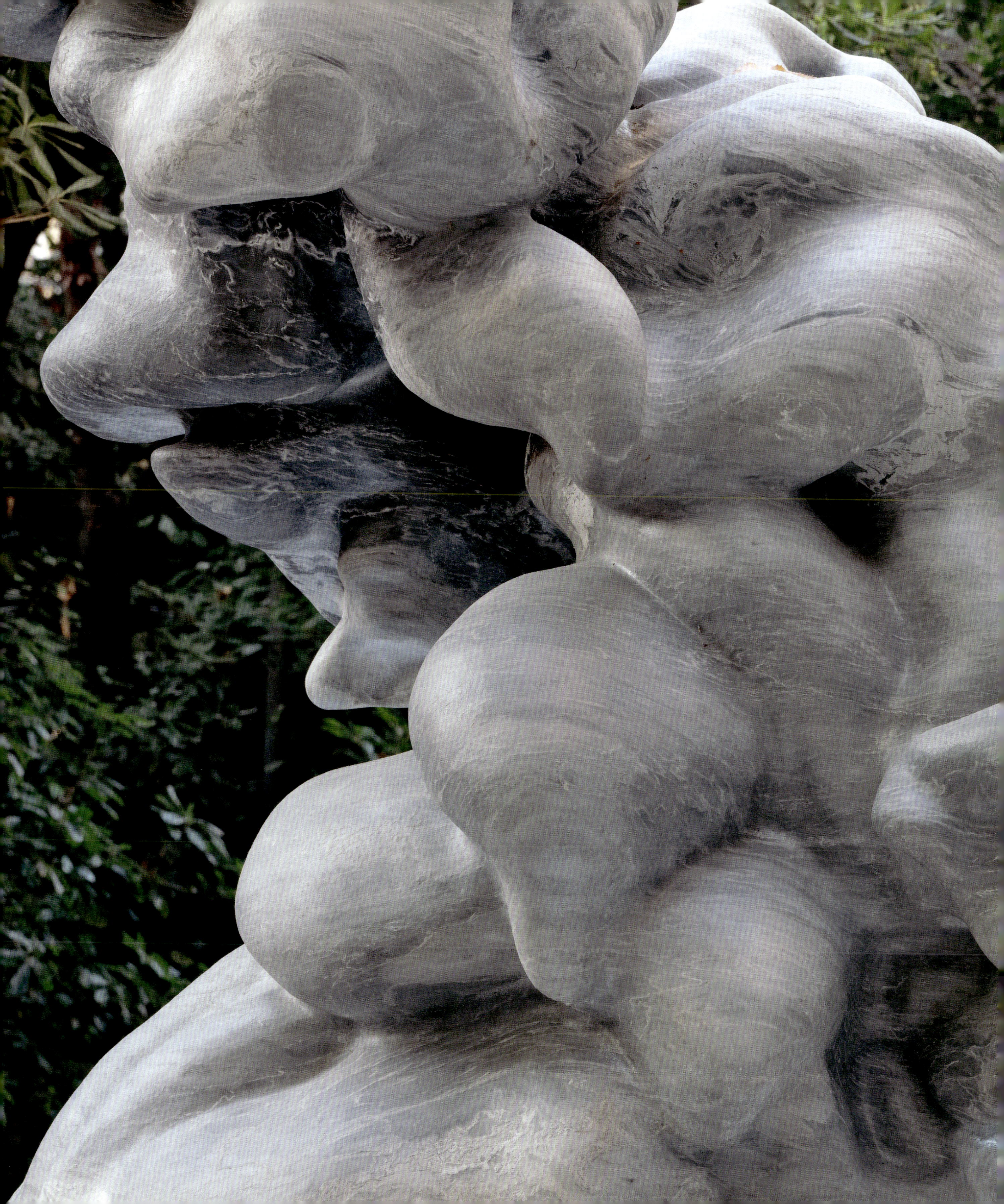

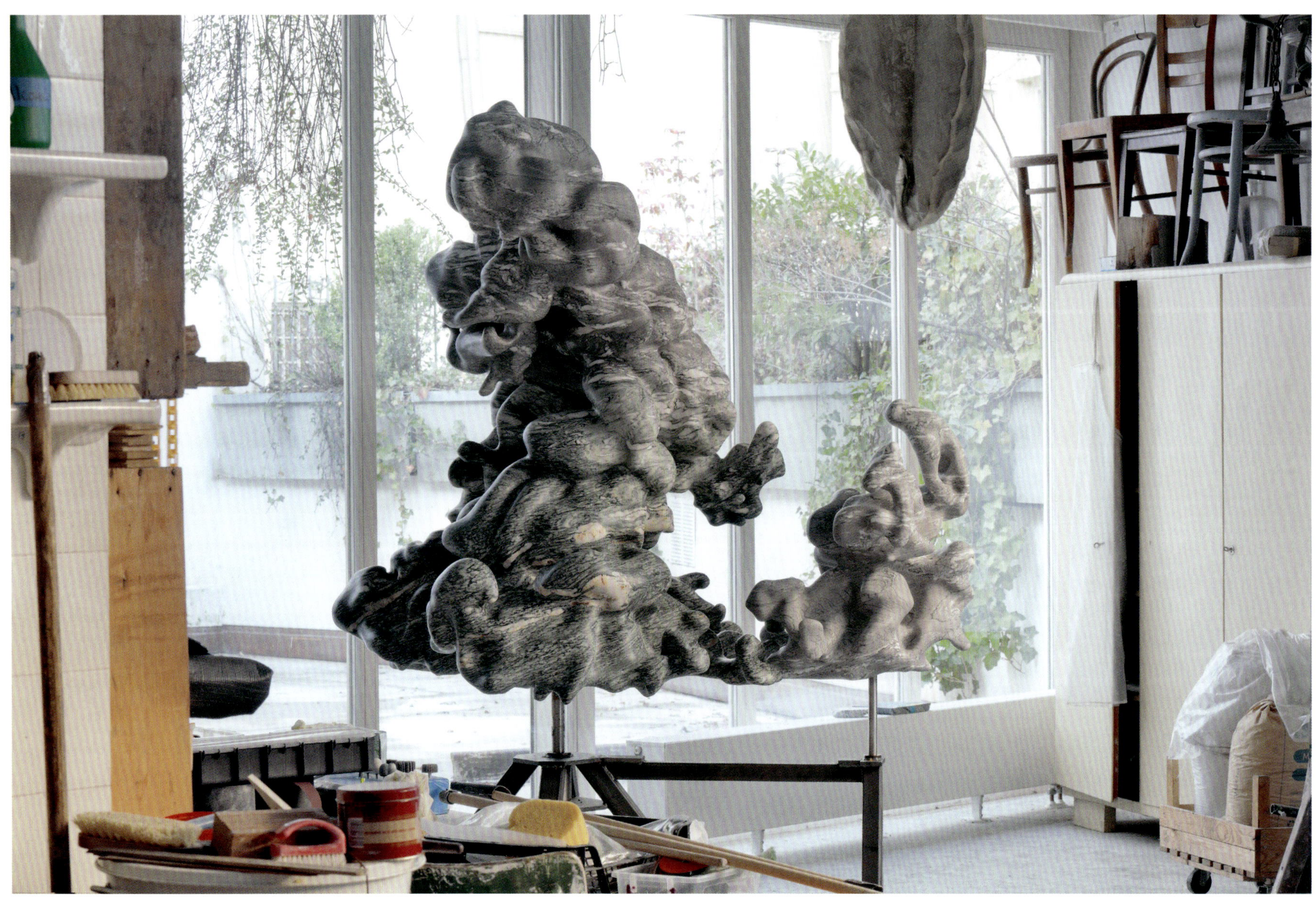

Cumulus 1:3, 2019
Marble, 82½ × 59 × 45 in. (210 × 150 × 114 cm)

OPPOSITE
Polishing *Cumulus 1:3*, 2019.

FOLLOWING
Hand carving *Cumulus 1:2*, 2017.

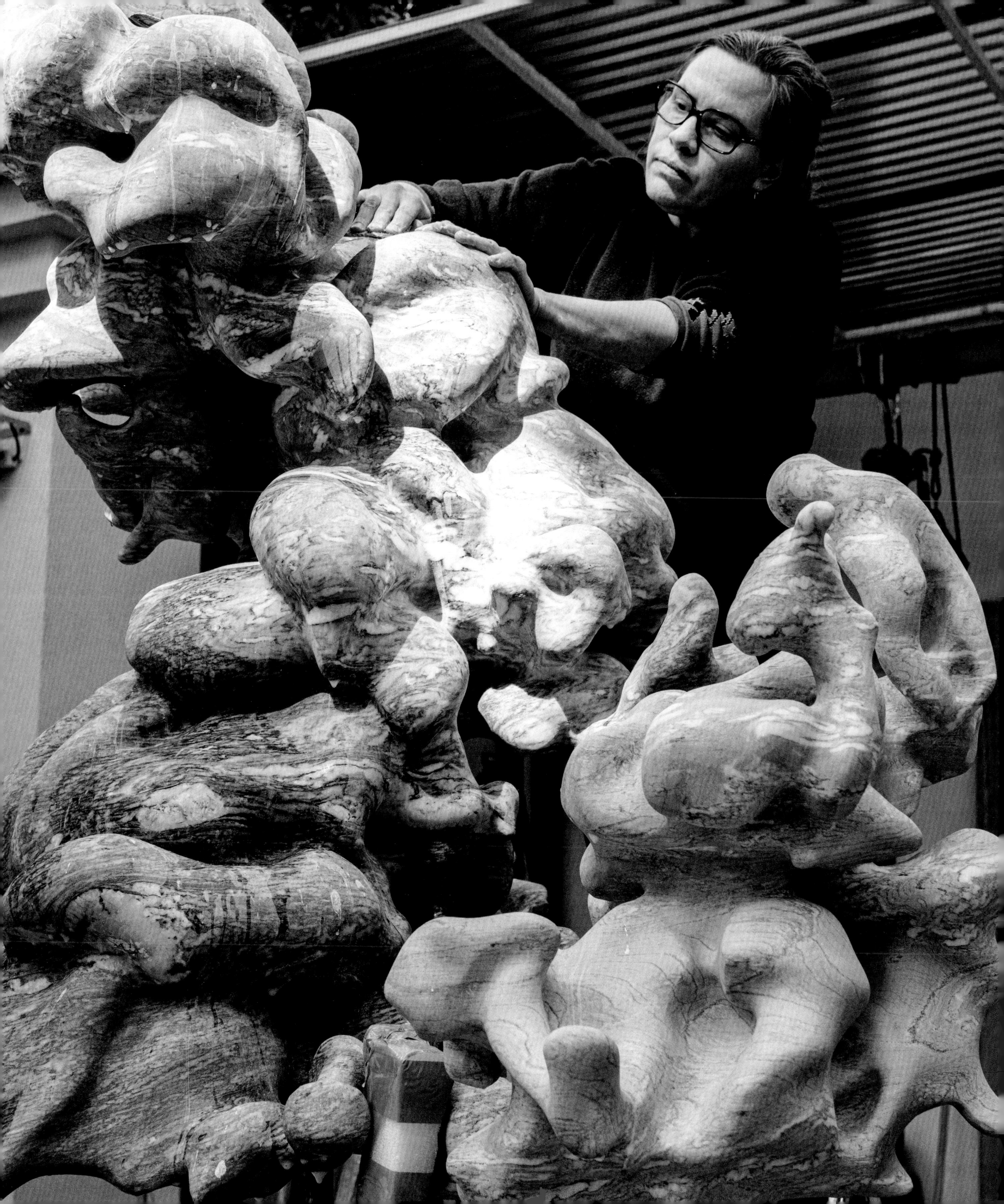

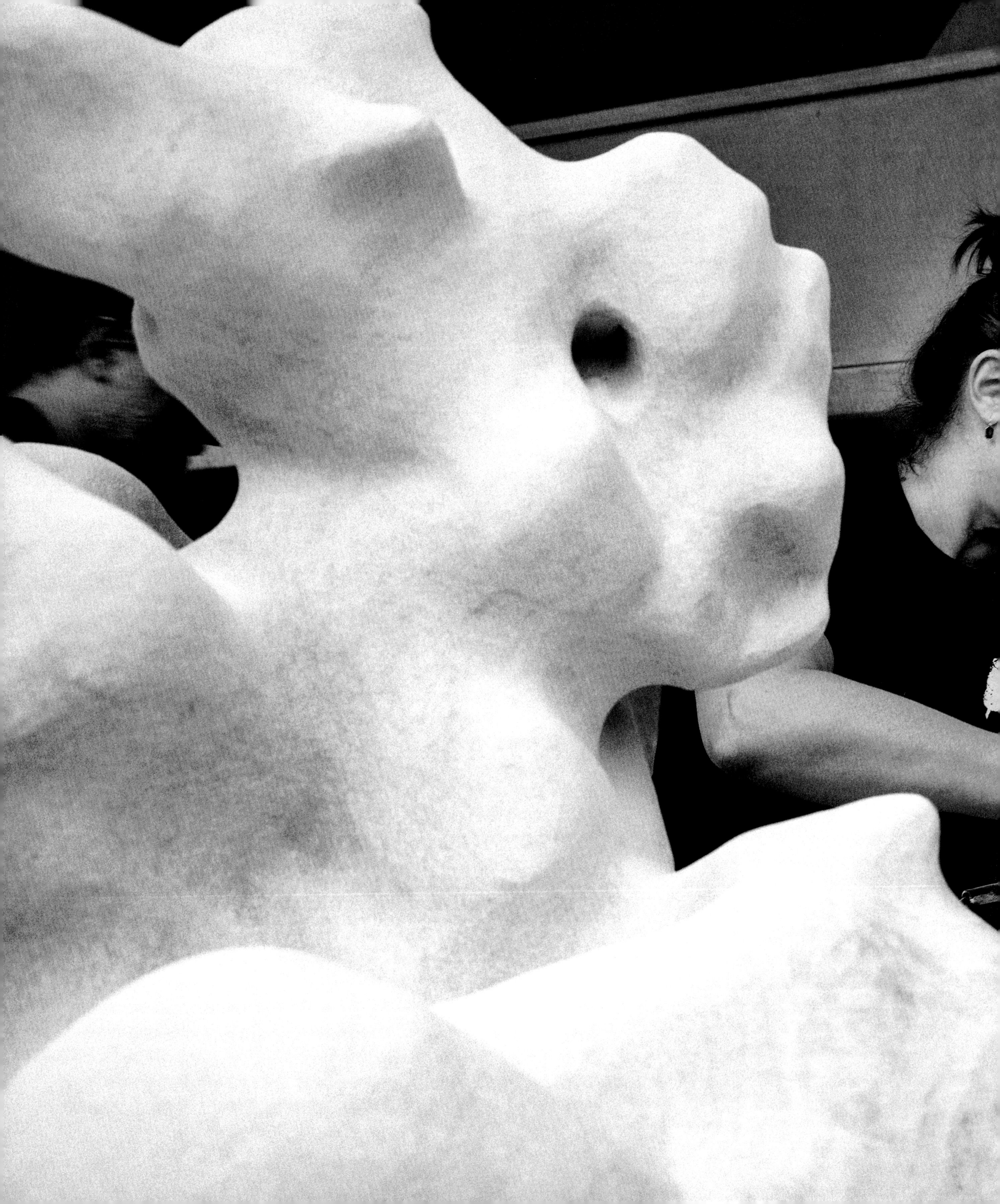

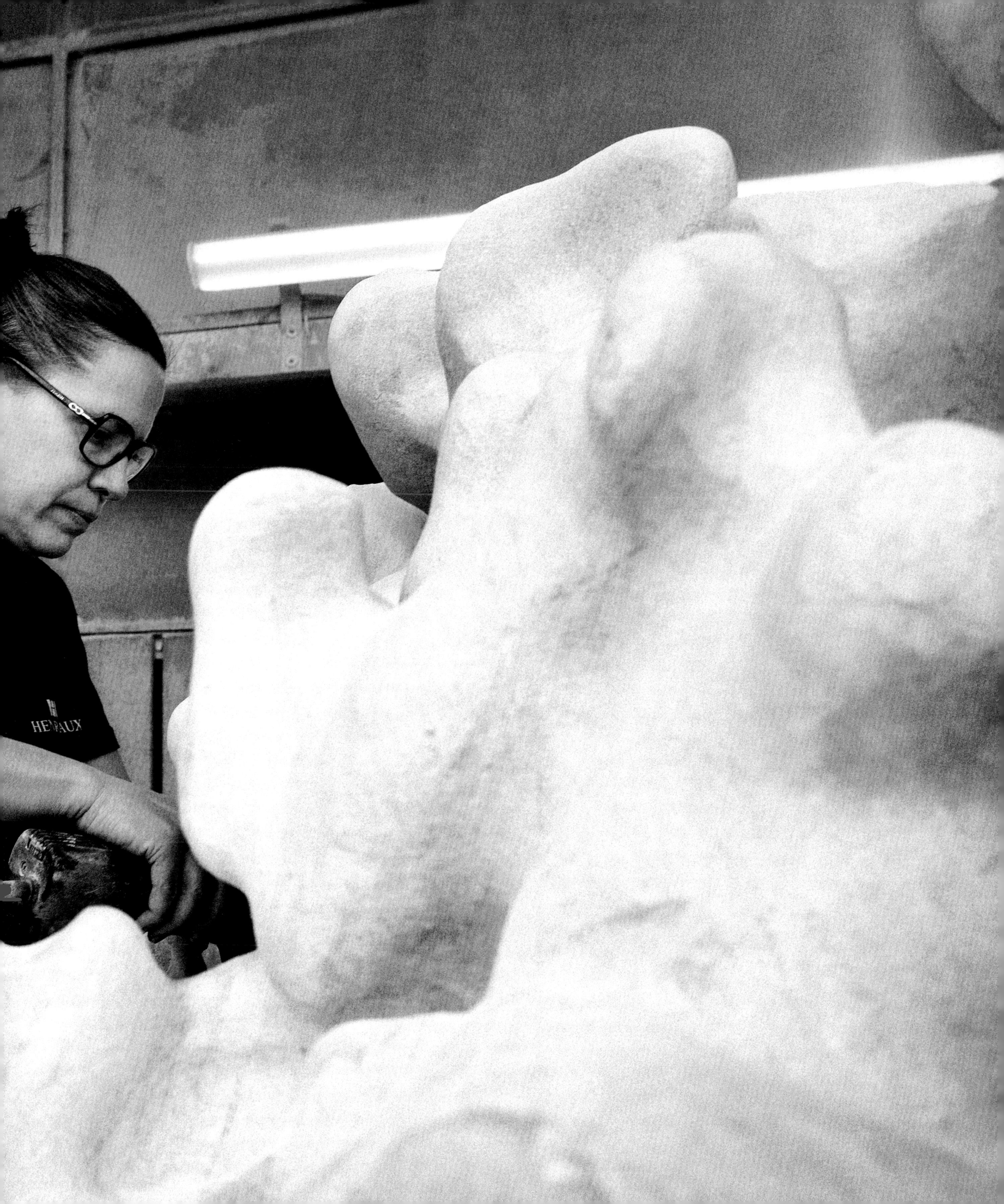

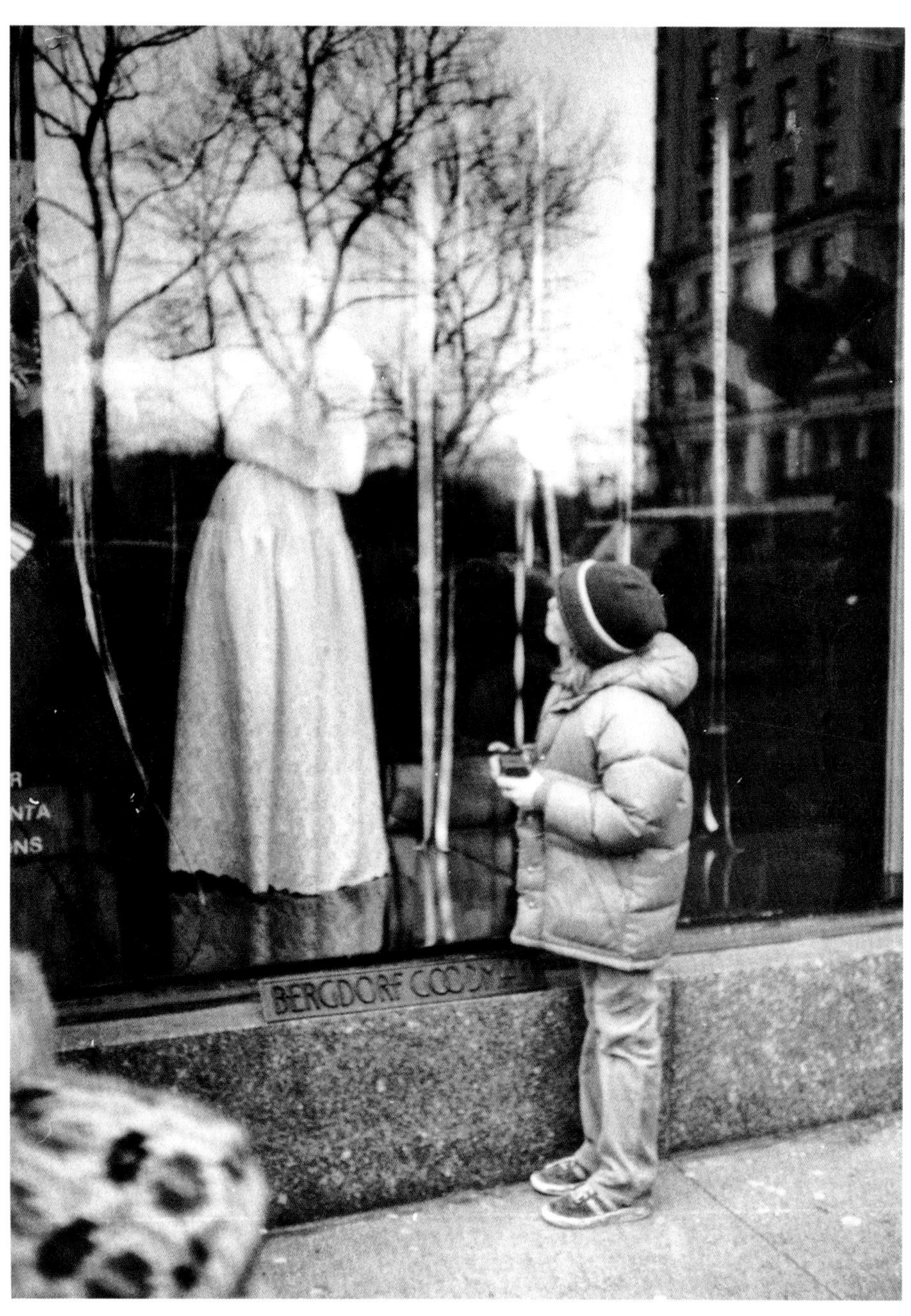
BERGDORF

Chronology

Born 1967 in New York City
Lives and works in Prague, Czech Republic

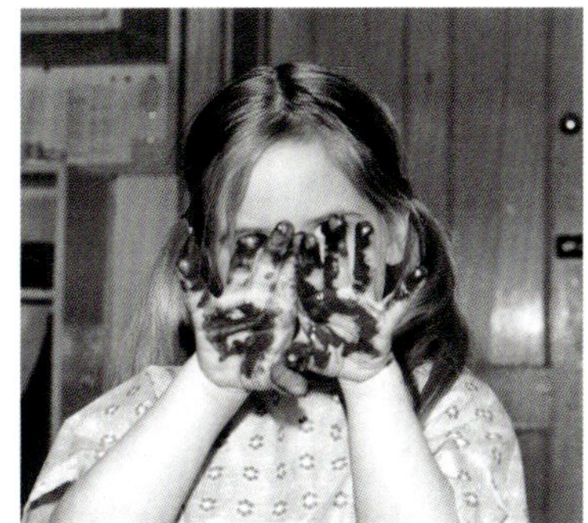

1973

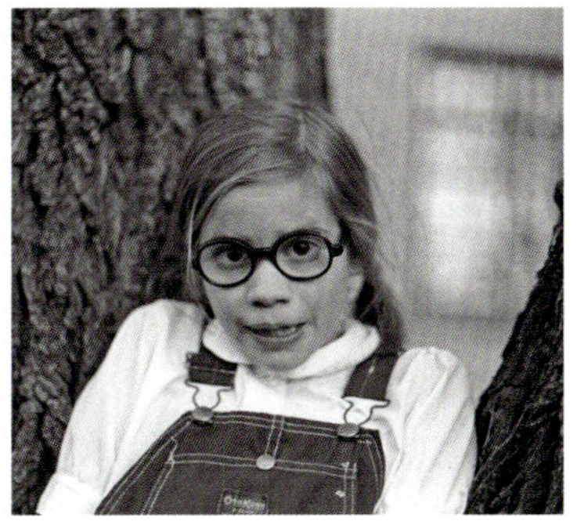

1974

1638

Colony of Massachusetts Bay. Lawrence Southwick, a direct ancestor of Karen LaMonte, owns the first glassworks in the Thirteen Colonies. The first glass made at the works was probably cast.

1692

Province of Massachusetts Bay. LaMonte's ancestors Giles and Martha Corey are accused of witchcraft during the Salem witch trials. Martha is convicted and hanged, and Giles dies from injuries sustained while being crushed with rocks. As portrayed in Arthur Miller's 1953 play *The Crucible*, his last words were "more weight."

1967

New York. Karen LaMonte is born at Lenox Hill Hospital in New York City. Her sister, Hilary, is three years old and not thrilled.

1971

New York. Growing up next to a power plant, LaMonte thinks the billowing smokestacks are cloud makers, igniting a lifelong fascination that later blooms into weather-based artworks. The three-year-old LaMonte observes several older children bullying her sister, Hilary, then seven. The aggressors disperse after LaMonte confronts them, hands on hips, proclaiming, "You leave my sister alone!"

1972

New York. The Bronx is burning and the city is bankrupt, but Mrs. LaMonte's inability to drive keeps the LaMonte family in the city. The family migrates from Stuyvesant Town to 94th Street. The new apartment suffers from a plague of cockroaches, which hide under kitchen cabinets and in clothing drawers, trunks, closets, shoes, paper bags, and boxes. LaMonte develops a strong aversion of all members of the Blattodea order, which stays with her throughout adulthood.

1973

New York. During the fourth-longest heat wave in recorded history, Mrs. LaMonte teaches her daughters the broad benefits offered by cultural institutions by taking them swimming in the fountains of the Metropolitan Museum of Art.

1974

New York. LaMonte's first-grade teacher identifies her as dyslexic. Dr. Hirst and her ever-present Mr. Red Pencil take on LaMonte as a special project. LaMonte remains under their tutelage for years, saving Mr. Red Pencil's curly hair (pencil shavings) in plastic bags.

1977

New York. In another heat wave so hot you could cook an egg on the sidewalk, the LaMontes, who do not have air conditioning, spend days in museums, which do.

Unable to afford babysitters, Mrs. LaMonte brings the children to an art history class at Hunter College. When asked to pick a favorite, the ten-year-old LaMonte chooses *The Scream* by Edvard Munch over *Le déjeuner sur l'herbe* by Édouard Manet.

1980

New York. The LaMontes take their daughters to the Thalia, a tiny Upper West Side art house theater, for viewings of black-and-white foreign films such as Alain Resnais's *Hiroshima mon amour* (1959) and Hiroshi Teshigara's *Woman in the Dunes* (1964). Butterless popcorn in white paper bags (salt optional) and subtitles leave lasting impressions on the dyslexic LaMonte.

At thirteen years old, LaMonte decides to be an artist. She starts dressing in black and spending time in Greenwich Village.

1984

Brooklyn. LaMonte and her sister resolve to be leftist intellectuals and attempt the five-hour performance of Philip Glass's *Einstein on the Beach* at the Brooklyn Academy of Music. She spends most of the time at a Greek coffee shop, which later becomes her hangout when working as the director of education at UrbanGlass.

LaMonte starts figure drawing classes at the Art Students League of New York.

1985

New York. LaMonte writes her application to Rhode Island School of Design (RISD) in the VIP lounge of the Limelight nightclub in Chelsea. A college counselor advises her family that art school is a waste of time.

LaMonte finishes high school, leaving a worn vinyl Kraftwerk album, *Computer World,* in the art room where she had played it ceaselessly for two years. Diane Martin, the art teacher, ceremonially breaks the album in half over her knee.

In her graduating yearbook, classmates choose LaMonte's male counterpart Bella [*sic*] Lugosi.

1986

Providence, Rhode Island. LaMonte begins coursework at RISD in the painting department. For the first time, she is in an educational environment with members of the opposite sex. She is disappointed.

The department is crowded and figurative art is out of fashion, so LaMonte switches to the smallest department in the school: the glass department, which has only five students.

1990

Providence, Rhode Island. LaMonte graduates from RISD with a Bachelor of Fine Arts with honors.

Homer, Alaska. After school, she stays in a tent city on the Homer Spit with a friend who is working at the canneries and ponders the world while experiencing a temporarily expanded state of consciousness.

1991

Millville, New Jersey. LaMonte is awarded a fellowship at the Creative Glass Center of America. She starts working with surrogates for the human form, like puppets and clothing and anything that implies an absent body. Over the following years, this exploration results in her first sculptures acquired by museums: *Clothesline* (1995), *Carousel* (1995), *and Seven Deadly Sins: Sloth* (1997).

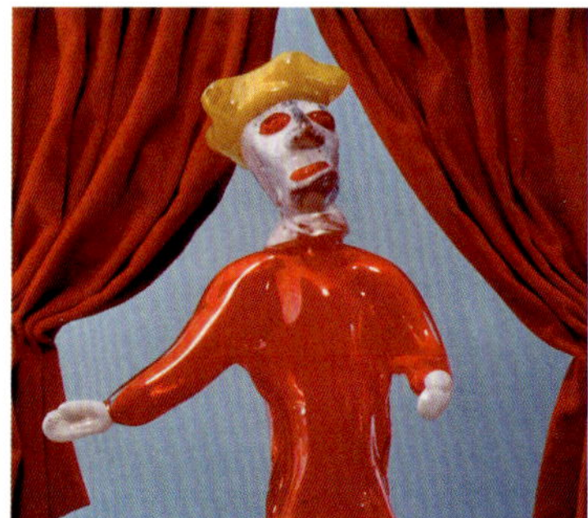
1994

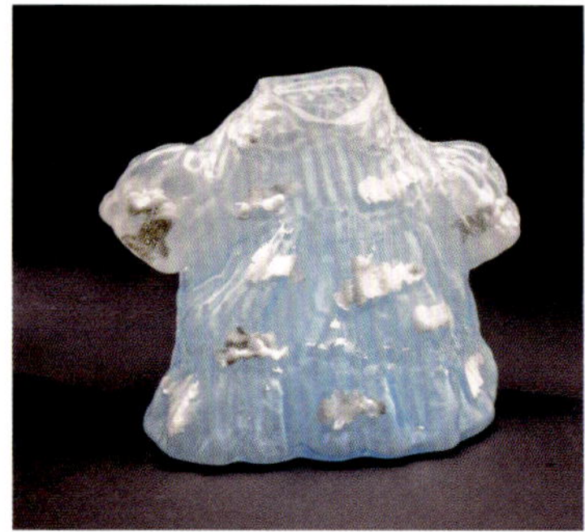
1995

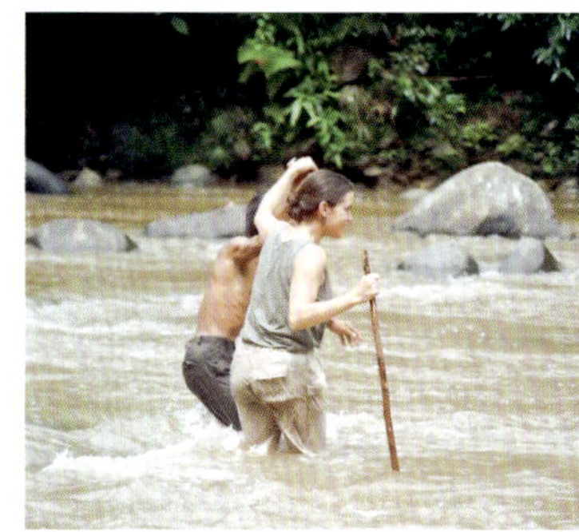
1997

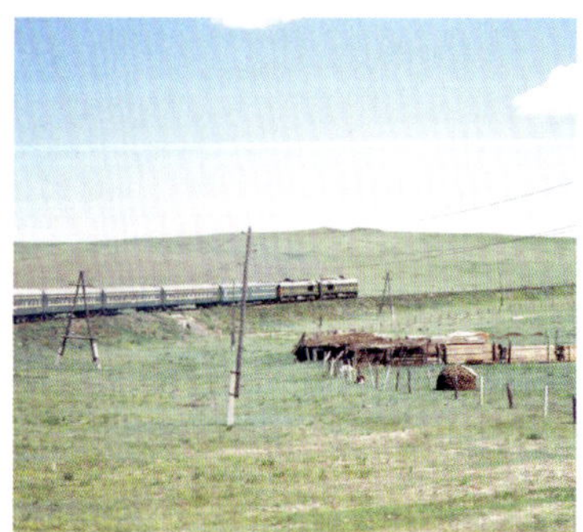
1997

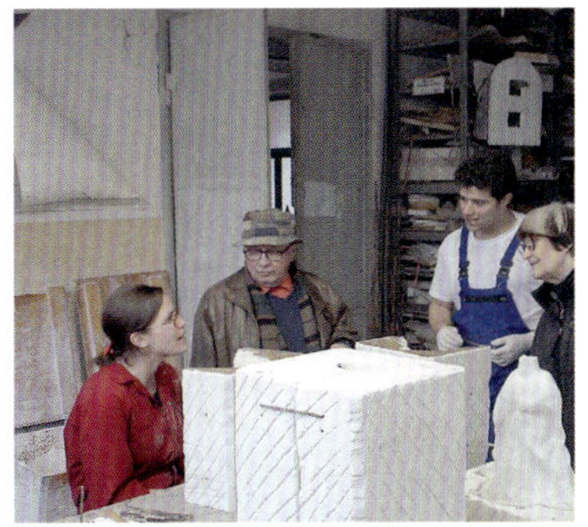
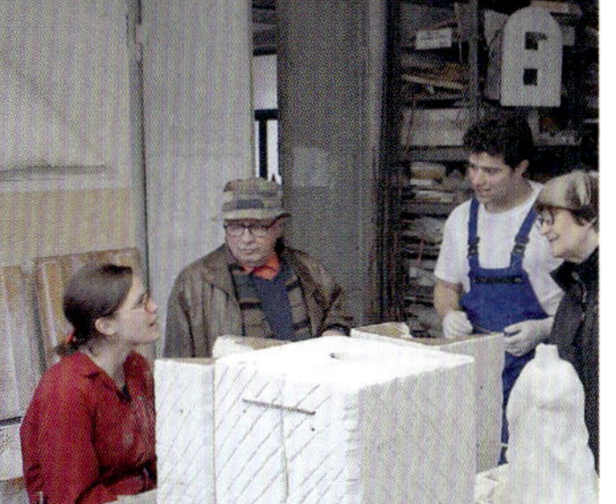

1997

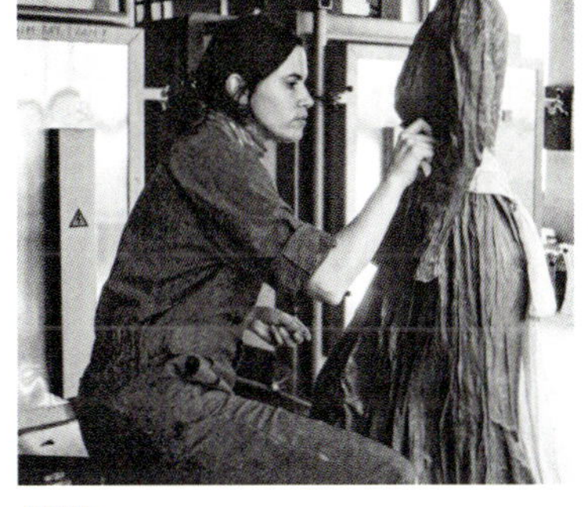

1999

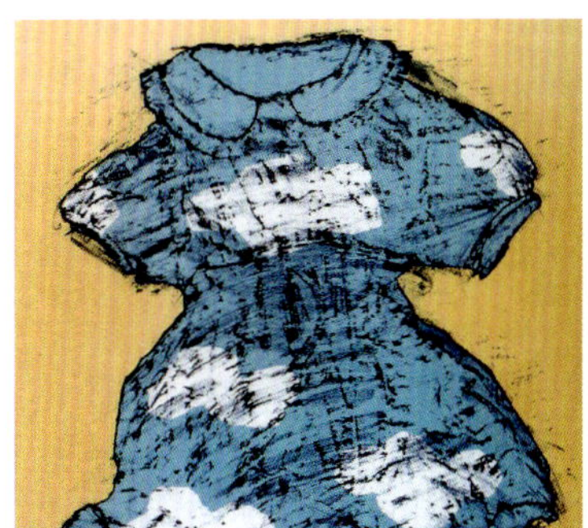

1999

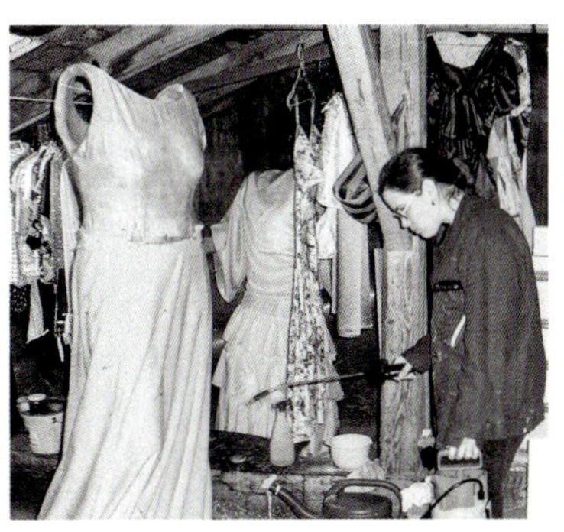

2000

Brooklyn. LaMonte rents a cheap studio in Williamsburg, where she sleeps illegally without heat or a proper bed. She retreats to other accommodations only after rats eat her toothpaste. Decades later, the building becomes luxury apartments.

1994

New York. Thinking of clothing as costume and life as a theater, LaMonte photographs her glass puppets with red theater curtains.

While riding a bike in Lower Manhattan through the intersection of Worth Street and Avenue of the Strongest, LaMonte is hit by a car traveling forty miles per hour. She suffers ruptured bursae in both knees and massive contusions, and the pavement grinds through her helmet. LaMonte realizes for the first time that she is mortal.

1995

Pilchuck, Washington, and Brooklyn. LaMonte starts investigating weather, making *Atmospheres* —bronze and glass flowers contained under bell jars or enameled with clouds—which she installs in the Black Rock Desert during Burning Man. She also combines her interest in weather and clothing for the first time by painting clouds onto blown glass dresses—none of which survive the collapse of a shelving unit in 1999.

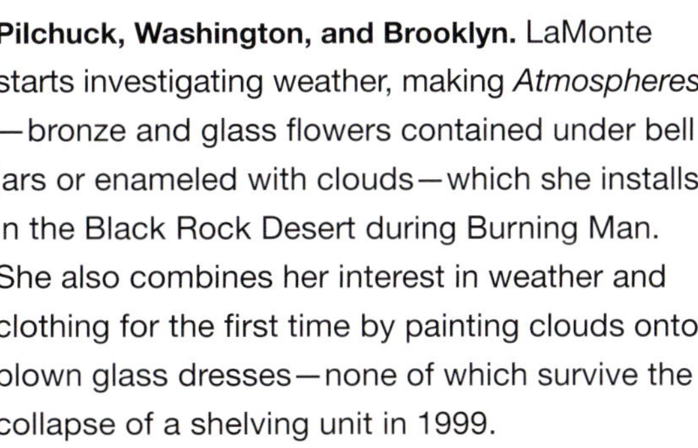

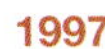

1997

Borneo, Malaysia, Brunei, and Indonesia. After flying to the wrong city, LaMonte and her partner Steve Polaner take an unplanned three-week trek across the island of Borneo. A childhood on the streets of Manhattan leaves LaMonte poorly prepared for jungle walking. Because of her slow pace, the party runs out of food and the guide discloses his theory that LaMonte is blind.

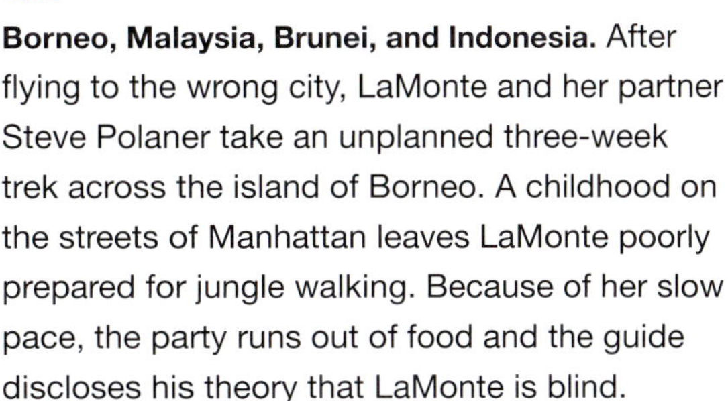

Asia and Europe. As LaMonte and Polaner continue their journey from Asia to Europe by land, LaMonte develops an innate understanding that humans share universal experiences like their bodies and weather, but concepts of beauty are bound to culture.

Czech Republic. Having experimented with casting glass at RISD, and to make *Carousel* (1995), *How Deep Is the Water* (1996), and *The Robbers* (1998), LaMonte decides her dress sculptures need the realism, weight, and detail that casting affords. She is drawn to the Czech Republic, where the inspirational artists Jaroslava Brychtová and Stanislav Libenský pioneered monumental casting for art. She applies for a Fulbright Fellowship to explore the glass-casting foundries.

1999

Prague, Czech Republic. During her Fulbright Fellowship, LaMonte makes small castings in preparation for her first life-size sculpture of a dress, *Vestige*, which takes nine months to complete. LaMonte learns to speak Czech by drinking beer and overhearing words like *katastrofa* and *ne* at the glass foundry.

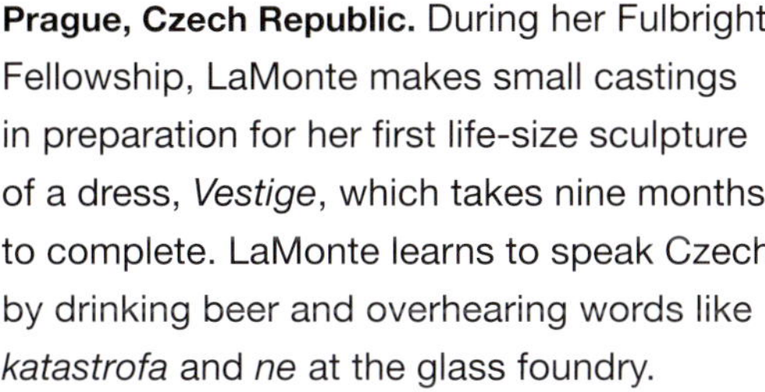

LaMonte stretches the Fulbright stipend by eating cabbage, but still goes into debt to cast *Vestige*. As soon as she sees it completed, she knows that she needs to make a sculpture with the absent impression of a body on the inside.

Returning to weather and clothing, LaMonte makes *Dress Print*, a lithograph of a dress with clouds.

New York. She marries Polaner at City Hall. The newlyweds open a bottle of champagne on the middle of the Brooklyn Bridge and meander for hours through Chinatown and Little Italy before spending the night at the wrong hotel.

2000

Prague, Czech Republic. Working in an uninsulated attic with a black tar roof, LaMonte alternately sweats and freezes for eighteen months while making life-size cast glass dresses for her first solo gallery exhibition in New York. Making these works is a critical period in the five-year journey that leads to the exhibitions *Vanitas* and *Absence Adorned*.

2001

New York. The Louis Comfort Tiffany Foundation grants LaMonte its biennial award.

Prague, Czech Republic. Despite the gray winter, LaMonte endeavors to make cyanotype photographic prints by coating paper at home with light-sensitive emulsion, then sneaking it into a tanning parlor to expose it to ultraviolet light. Observing her wan complexion, the attendant refuses to rent her the sun bed for more than fifteen minutes, forcing her to trudge to five different parlors to complete the project.

North Adams, Massachusetts. Depressed by the absurdly long and risky process of glass casting, LaMonte searches for a faster way to work with implied bodies. She travels three thousand miles to an enormous, deserted mill building that houses a jerry-rigged monster press. She invents the sartoriotype—a monotype print made by using dresses as printing plates—which become an integral part of *Absence Adorned.*

2002

Prague, Czech Republic. LaMonte's attic studio is within the evacuation zone of the most devastating flood in one thousand years. LaMonte and her husband decide to stay in the studio despite the interruption of electrical and water utilities. On the second day, realizing the toilet does not work, they flee to a friend's house. The contents of the entire studio need to be moved out without an elevator.

2004

Campbeltown, Scotland. Ten years before the word *selfie* was included in the Oxford English Dictionary, LaMonte becomes fascinated with lark mirrors. Originally a bird trap with a mirror for a lure, a lark mirror has become a metaphor for a fatally attractive illusion. She creates her own lark mirrors by etching portraits onto the back of cast-mirror sculptures, creating the illusion of breath on glass, like an image left behind for an instant that becomes trapped for eternity.

Prague, Czech Republic. The curator of the Czech Museum of Fine Arts asks LaMonte to a morning meeting to discuss a solo exhibition. He starts by pouring shots of whiskey. LaMonte proposes *Vanitas*, an exhibition of cast glass dresses and lark mirrors, while surreptitiously dumping her whiskey into the potted plant when he is not looking.

New York. Arthur Danto interviews LaMonte in his Upper West Side apartment for the book *Absence Adorned*. Years later, she still has fond memories of his kindness, his wife's glasses, and the sculpture of Modesta on their mantel.

Prague, Czech Republic. LaMonte installs the *Vanitas* exhibition in the thousand-year-old, crypt-like, Romanesque basement of the Czech Museum of Fine Arts. It causes her to focus on elements of transience and mortality in her artwork.

2005

Tacoma, Washington. Returning to thoughts of theater, LaMonte installs the *Absence Adorned* exhibition at the Museum of Glass as an abandoned tableau vivant where viewers cross into a surreal world inhabited by vacant costumes and become part of the installation.

2006

Železný Brod, Czech Republic. Driven by a profound belief that ideas can be expressed visually through well-made objects, LaMonte continues to push the technical boundaries of cast glass, making increasingly ambitious sculptures in the *Absence Adorned* series. At times, the breakage rate surpasses 50 percent.

Kyoto, Japan. The Japan-U.S. Friendship Commission grants LaMonte a seven-month research fellowship, during which she studies the kimono and Japanese aesthetics of transience and imperfection known as *wabi-sabi*. Her time in Kyoto will have far-reaching impact on her artwork, including a radical rethinking of materials.

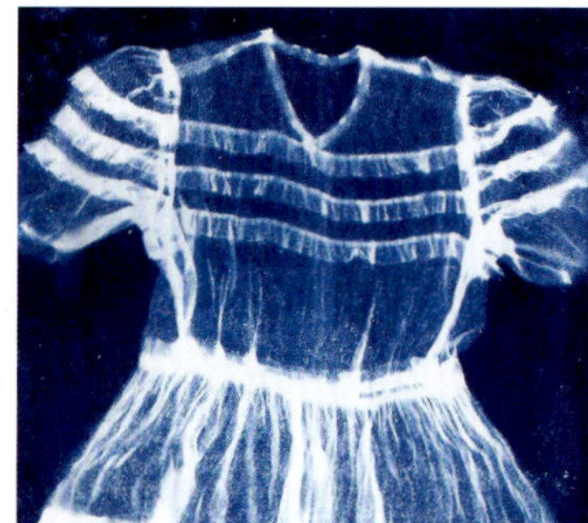
2001

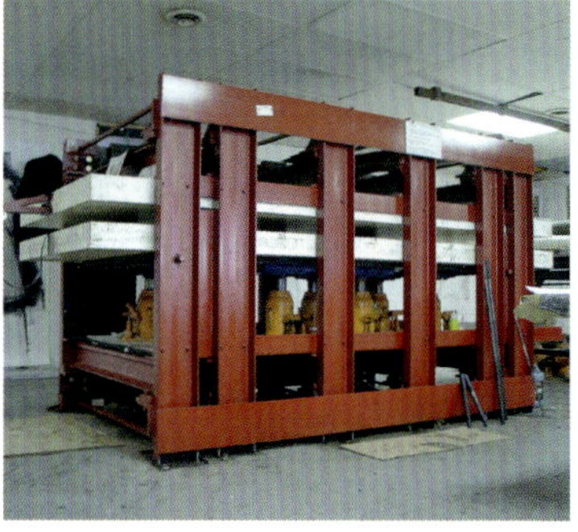
2001

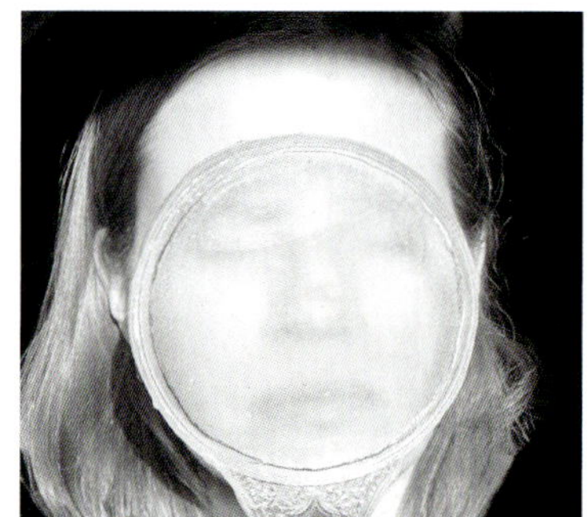
2004

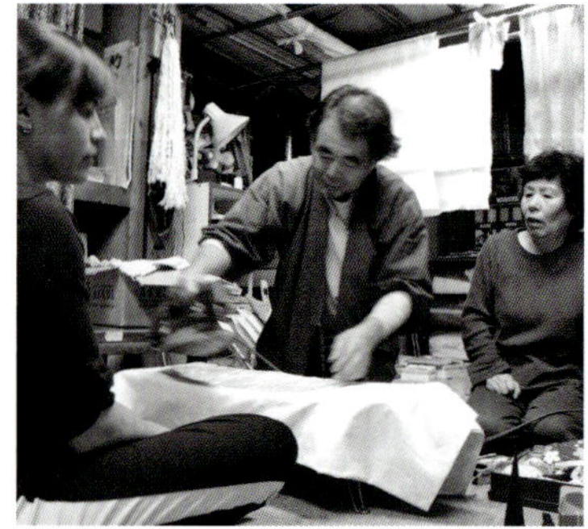
2006

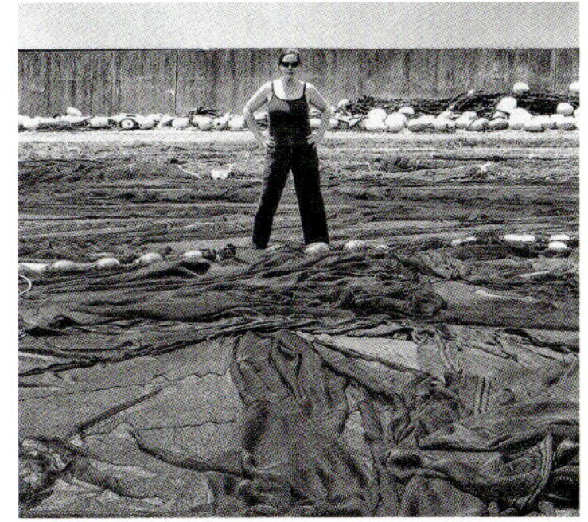
2006

Toyama, Japan. Exploring the western coast of Japan, LaMonte happens upon a vast parking lot filled with fishing nets and has a transcendental experience. To the dismay of the fishermen, she plays with the nets for hours, using them to draw on an unimaginable scale. In her mind's eye, the nets are transfigured into drapery rendering the landscape as a body. Eventually, the experience leads to a series of works in ceramic and glass in which drapery is transformed into elemental landscapes suggesting the earth, the ocean, and cloud formations.

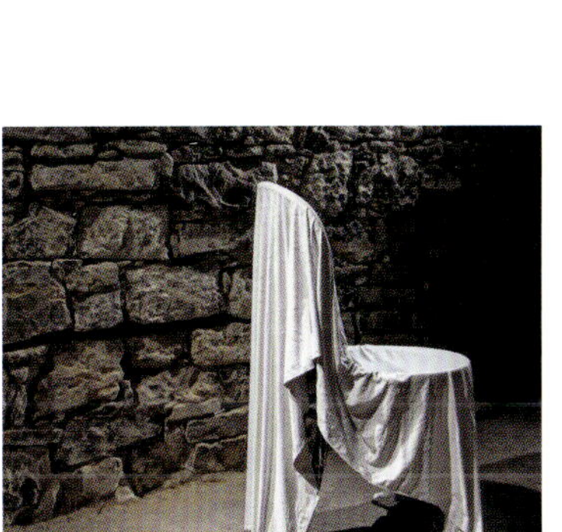
2008

2008

Düsseldorf, Germany. LaMonte receives the Jutta Cuny-Franz Memorial Award.

Prague, Czech Republic. Having spent more than a decade thinking about dresses and kimonos as a surrogate for the figure, LaMonte wants to find a surrogate for her surrogate. Looking for something that would imply human presence by making obvious its absence, she starts draping chairs in the basement.

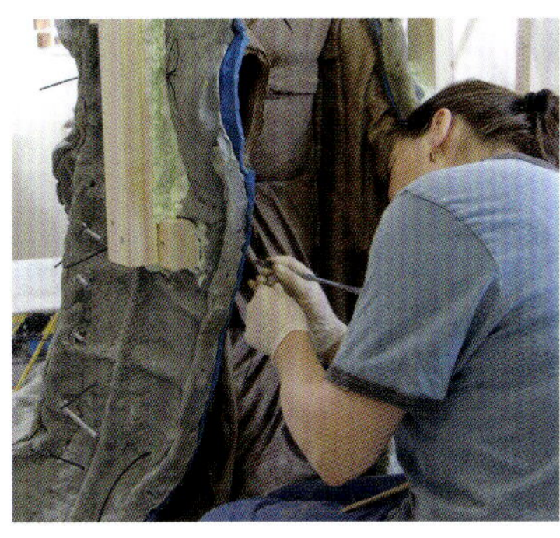
2009

2009

's-Hertogenbosch, Netherlands. After years of research, LaMonte begins building the sculptures for the *Floating World* series. Drawn to ceramics for the medium's ability to convey humility and imperfection, she goes to the European Ceramic Workcentre (EKWC). In a three-month residency, LaMonte pioneers the technique for making her life-size sculptures. It is an exciting and groundbreaking time of experimentation.

Kohler, Wisconsin. LaMonte spends two months in a toilet factory as a recipient of the Corning Museum of Glass/Kohler Arts Center Joint Artist-in-Residence Program. With the unflagging support of the factory workers, she adapts toilet-casting technology to make sculptures about weather and landscapes by rendering drapery compositions in vitreous china.

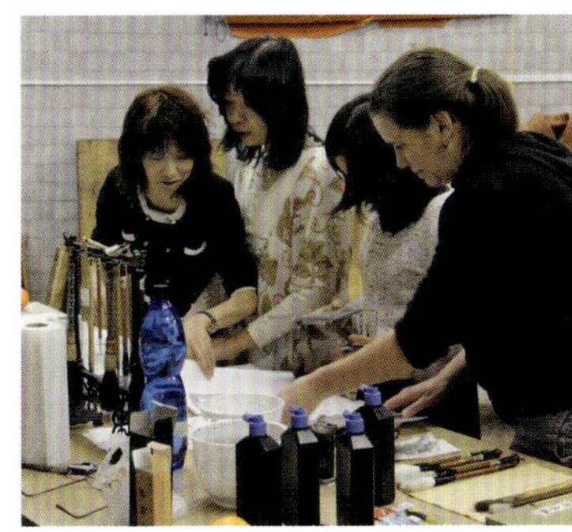
2010

2010

's-Hertogenbosch, Netherlands. After one year of preparation, sculpting, and mold making, LaMonte returns to EKWC for an intense work session making life-size ceramic kimono sculptures for the *Floating World* series.

Inspired by the Japanese tradition of *tomobako*—calligraphed crates for historic ceramic works—LaMonte buys stacks of distressed wood from a Dutch cheese manufacturer. The mold residue and odor prove much more resilient than expected.

New York. LaMonte assembles a large installation of ceramic drapery abstractions into a sculpture called *Vortex*, using fabric to explicitly represent clouds for the first time.

Sars-Poteries, France. The local community is so moved by LaMonte's exhibition *Réflexions Féminines* at the Musée du Verre that they organize a public subscription to raise money to acquire her *Seated Dress Impression with Drapery* (2005) and *Curtain* (2009).

Prague, Czech Republic. Two months before the opening of the first exhibition of *Floating World*, fate guides LaMonte to two master calligraphers from Japan, Shizue Morioka and Kohro Yonemoto, who happen to be in Prague. For a magical morning, together they draw the calligraphy on the *tomobako* crates, which become an integral part of the installation.

2012

Tommerup, Denmark. A kiln malfunction causes three terra-cotta kimono sculptures to explode into hundreds of pieces. In the catastrophe, LaMonte sees the beauty of imperfection and the grace of death and rebirth. She spends months gluing the sculptures back together using *kintsugi,* the ancient Japanese technique in which objects are repaired using gold to highlight the join lines.

Prague, Czech Republic. While still working on the *Floating World* series, LaMonte becomes obsessed with night as a metaphor for the transition from known to unknown, from conscious to unconscious, from reality to dream, and from material to immaterial. She starts researching night, beginning an investigation that will eventually lead to her *Nocturnes* series.

Pietrasanta, Italy. Delving deeper into her investigation of materials to express concepts of beauty and transience, LaMonte begins working with rusted iron to make life-size sculptures of kimonos.

Washington, DC. LaMonte is the youngest person interviewed for the Smithsonian Archives of American Art Oral History Program.

2013

Prague, Czech Republic. LaMonte starts experimenting with different glasses and metals to find the right materials for *Nocturnes.*

2014

Železný Brod, Czech Republic. Two year's work is loaded into giant kilns for glass casting. Several months later, she opens the kilns and discovers all the glass devitrified into a crystalline state, rendering the castings unusable. Unbeknownst to LaMonte, the cloudy appearance of the glass plants the seeds for her to return to weather and atmosphere as subject matter in 2016.

Boston, Massachusetts. LaMonte visits the Laboratory for Tissue Engineering and Organ Fabrication at Massachusetts General Hospital to meet with director Dr. Joseph Vacanti to start research on new works using biomaterials from regenerative medicine to make figurative sculptures.

2015

Czech Republic and Germany. LaMonte continues experimenting with the glass composition for *Nocturnes*, eventually making more than thirty test formulations in her drive to capture the shade and optical density that most perfectly express the essence of night.

Prague, Czech Republic. Thinking of absence as a dissipating echo, LaMonte returns to her draped chairs. She makes three-dimensional scans of the opulent forms, then starves them of visual information by intentionally decimating the data files. Working at the Institute of Cryptoanarchy to print three-dimensional protypes, she has to pay in bitcoin. Later, as the value of bitcoin skyrockets, making the amount that she spent on the prints equivalent to US$25,000, she ponders what would have happened if she had kept the bitcoin instead.

Washington, DC. LaMonte receives the Master of the Medium award from the James Renwick Alliance. She is stricken silent by severe laryngitis, and her husband gives the speech in her stead. In the photograph commemorating the event, the organizers photoshop her head onto her husband's body.

Prague, Czech Republic. On August 11, LaMonte and her husband adopt a fur-child from the pound. Named Lucy, she bears a shocking resemblance to LaMonte's childhood dog, Puff.

Pennsylvania. LaMonte visits several manufactures of biomedical materials but is stymied by the materials' microscopic size and instability.

Europe. LaMonte starts searching for theaters to install her sculptures on empty stages to create new photographic works called *Tableaux.*

2016

Gramolazzo, Italy. Nine years after starting to experiment with draped chairs, LaMonte makes *Dissipations*, her first sculptures in marble.

Corning, New York. LaMonte thinks that she has "made it" because the Corning Museum of Glass's gift shop sells a fridge magnet and temporary tattoo based on her artworks.

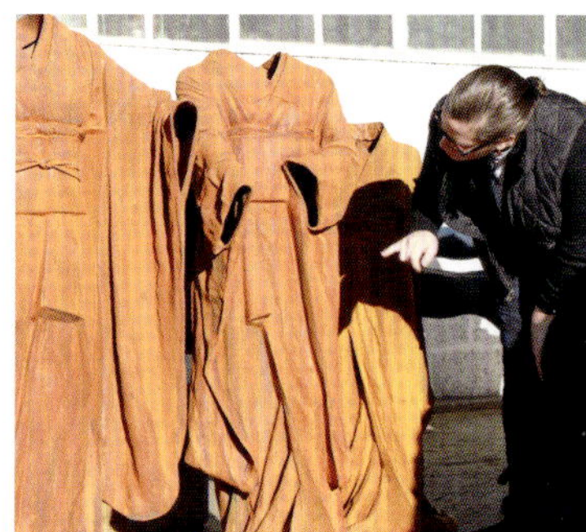
2012

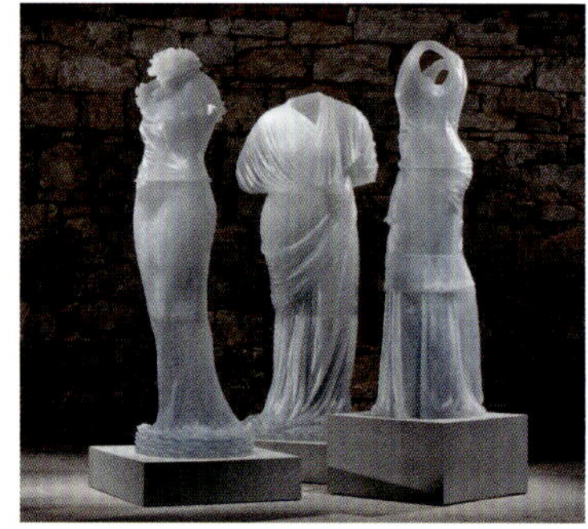
2014

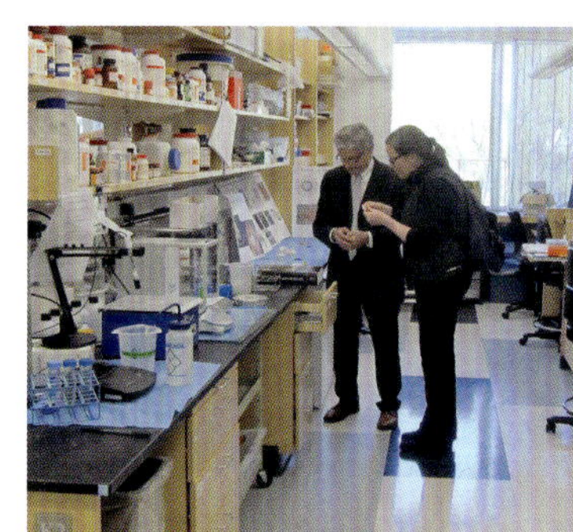
2014

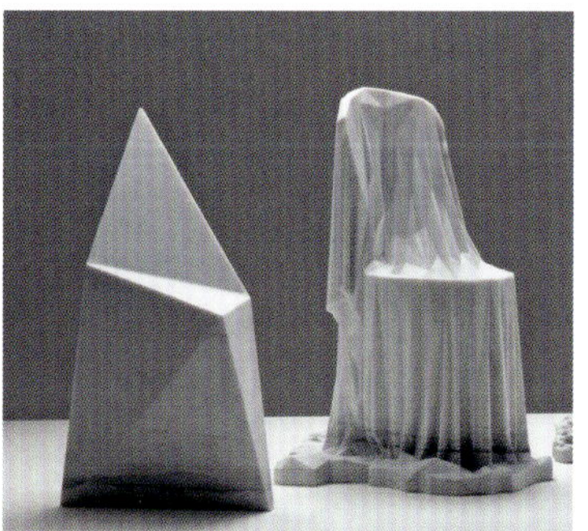
2016

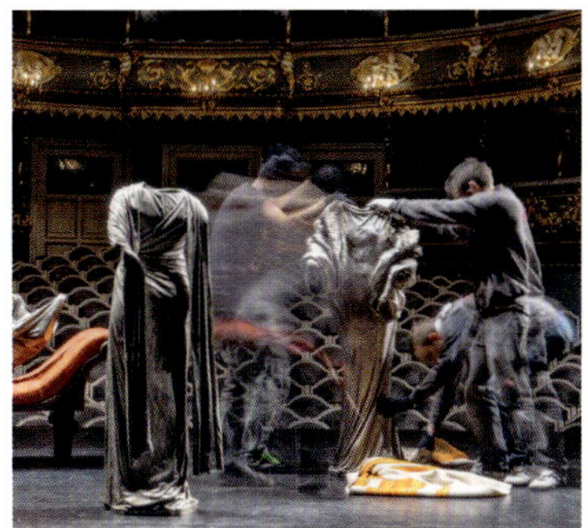
2016

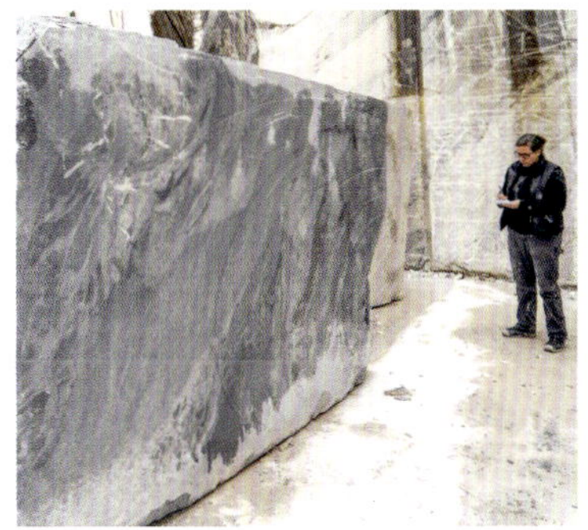
2017

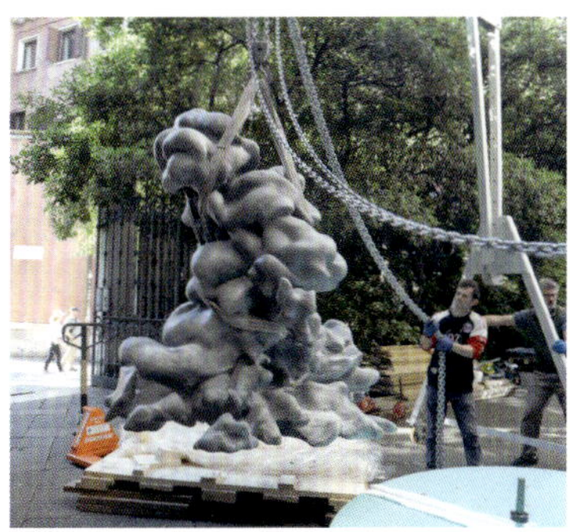
2017

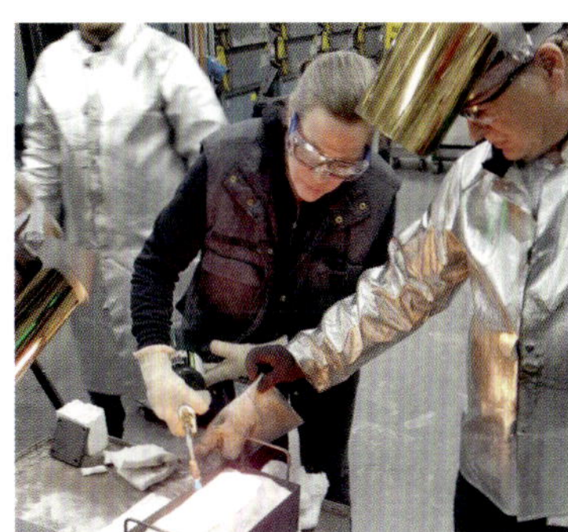
2018

Prague, Czech Republic. A months'-long drought prevents an iron sculpture from rusting according to plan. Dipping into a reserve of Tuscan rain that LaMonte collected in five-gallon jugs, she creates a downpour using tubing and roller clamps from intravenous bags.

To create her first photographic works, called *Tableaux*, LaMonte installs *Nocturnes* on the stage of the Estates Theater, where Mozart conducted the premiere of *Don Giovanni*. The rhythm of the empty chairs echoes in the absent bodies of the dresses.

LaMonte's desire to digitally scan clouds using drones goes nowhere because clouds have no edge or defined form, and they are constantly in motion. However, her attempts lead her to the weather-modeling atmospheric scientists at Caltech's Climate Dynamics Group.

2017

Litomyšl, Czech Republic. During a snowstorm, LaMonte photographs the second *Tableau* in the unheated Baroque theater of the Litomyšl Castle. The kind castle director offers shots of 100-proof slivovice, a plum brandy. This time, LaMonte drinks the alcohol.

Apuan Alps, Italy. LaMonte starts her first monumental sculpture in marble—a cumulus cloud developed from her collaboration with climatologists Tapio Schneider and Kyle Pressel. Standing in the quarry to choose the eighty-ton block from which her sculpture will be cut, LaMonte realizes that Michelangelo engineered the road and she could well be standing in the actual footsteps of artists like Henry Moore and Jean Arp. Her husband reassures her that there is no pressure. "Just don't mess up," he warns.

Venice, Italy. The six-ton marble sculpture *Cumulus 1:2* (2017) is installed during the 57th Biennale Arte in the garden of Palazzo Cavalli-Franchetti by a team of ten using manual hoists and muscle. LaMonte finds the process nerve-wracking.

Venice, Italy. *Cumulus 1:2* is de-installed in a torrential downpour, lifted a hundred feet into the air without a crate, and loaded onto a barge. LaMonte finds the process even more nerve-wracking than its installation.

2018

Prague, Czech Republic. In preparation for LaMonte's residency with scientists at Corning Incorporated's restricted-access research facility, the science liaison reads her tarot cards. LaMonte draws the High Priestess.

Corning, New York. LaMonte spends the year working with biomimetic and bioactive glasses to make figurative sculpture and with nucleated glass-ceramics to make cloud-based environmental works.

Los Alamos, New Mexico. While visiting the Bradbury Science Museum, LaMonte rests her hands on copper plates to measure how electrifying she is. She redlines the voltmeter pinning the needle.

2019

Reichenbach, Germany. LaMonte makes biomimetic glass ceramic billets for experimental kiln casting.

Venice, Italy. LaMonte feels a karmic closing of a circle as her *Reclining Nocturne* (2018) is permanently installed in the St. Regis Hotel, the former Grand Hotel Britannia, where J. M. W. Turner, John Singer Sargent, and Claude Monet stayed and close to where James Abbott McNeill Whistler painted his *Nocturnes*.

St. Petersburg, Florida. LaMonte is introduced to virtual reality through an experiential VR program at the Imagine Museum while there for a weekend honoring her work. Recognizing it as an incredible new technology for communication and aesthetics, LaMonte feels happy to be alive in such interesting times.

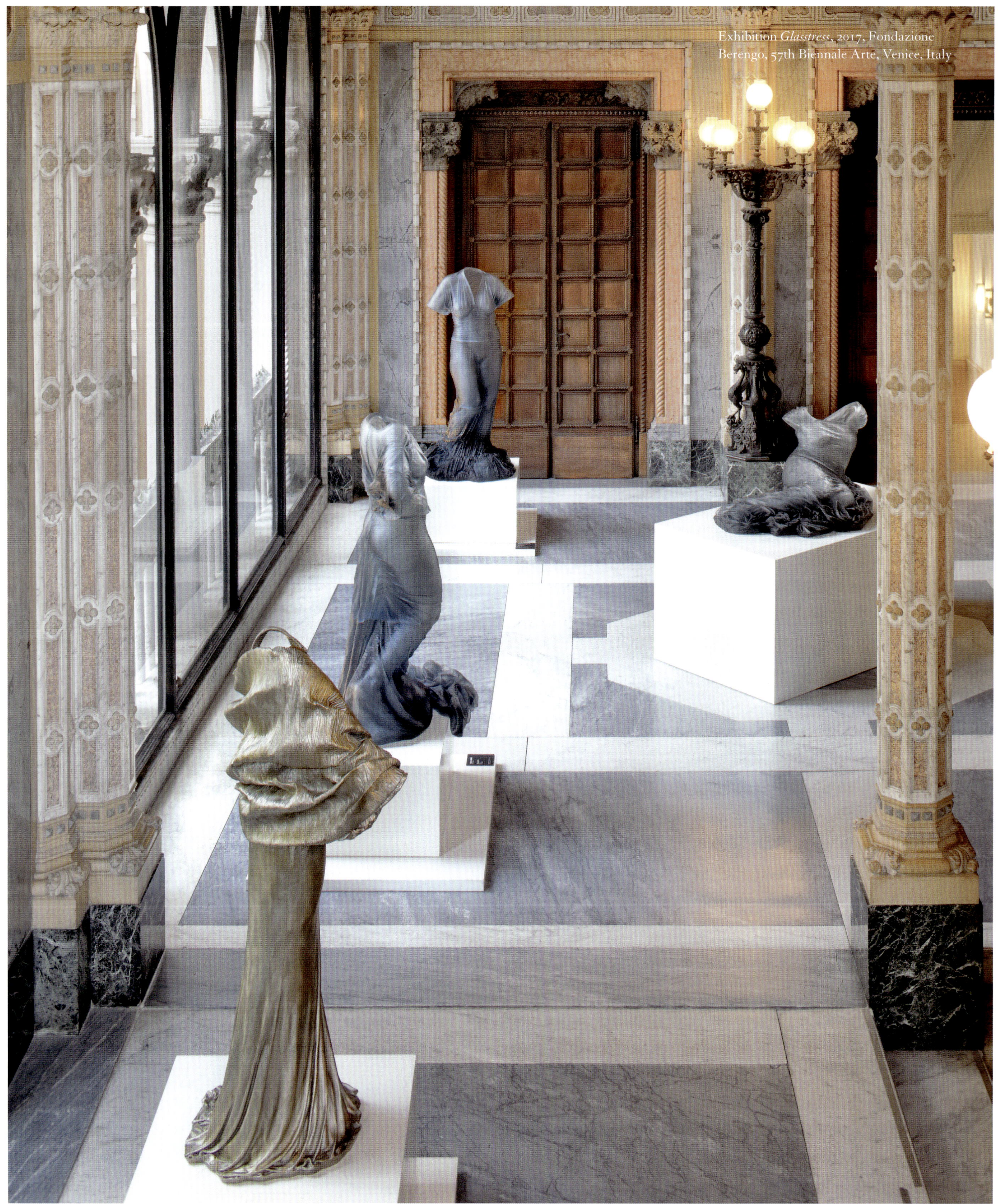

Exhibition *Glasstress*, 2017, Fondazione Berengo, 57th Biennale Arte, Venice, Italy

Museum Collections
Selected

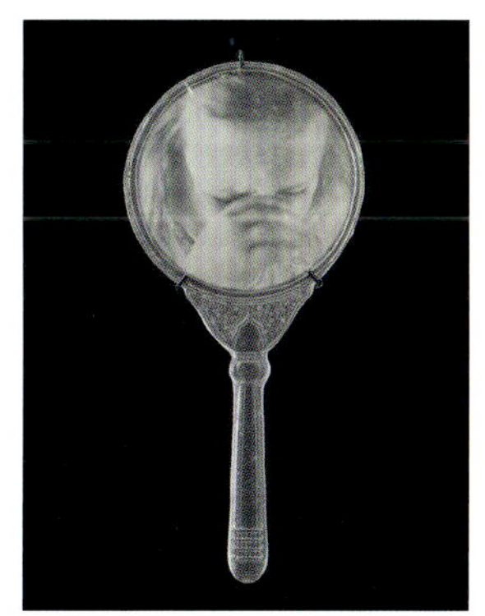
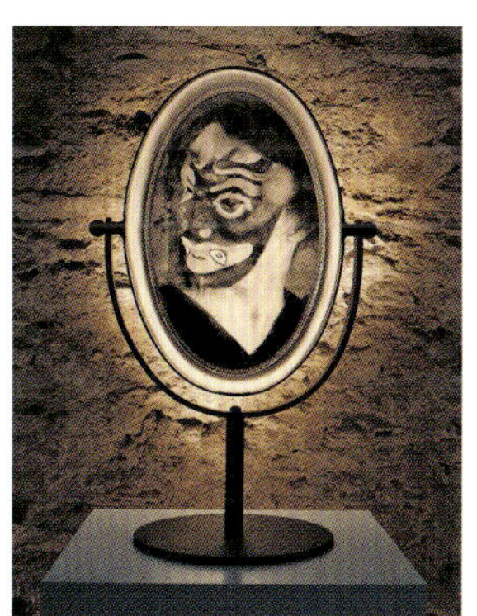
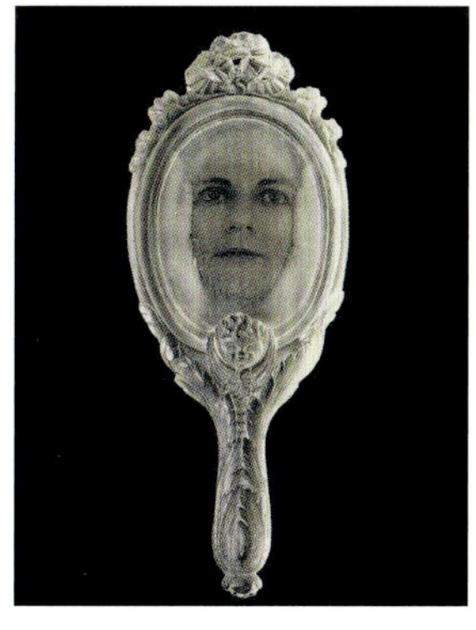

ALEXANDER TUTSEK-STIFTUNG
Munich, Germany

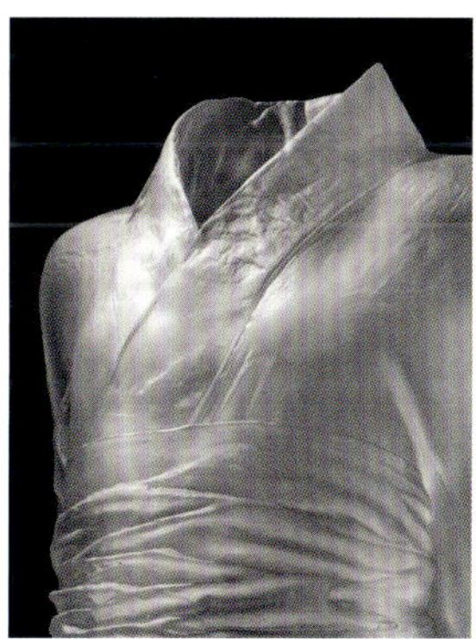
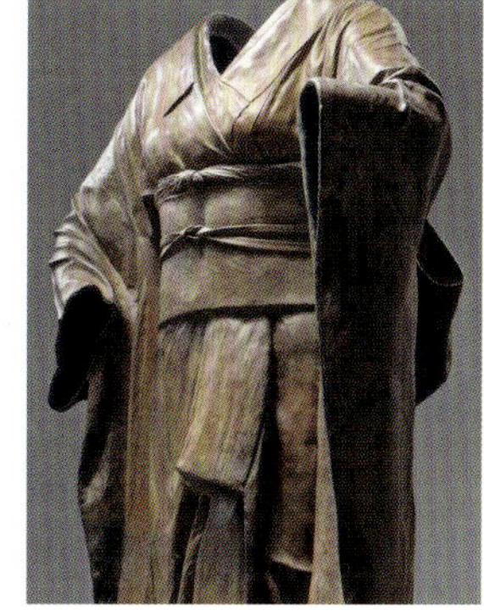
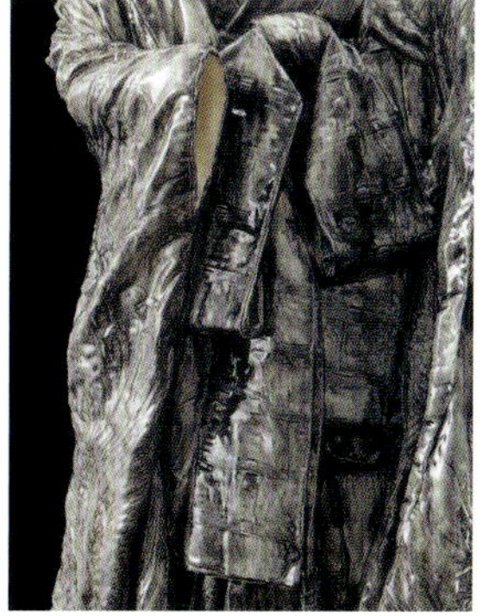

CHAZEN MUSEUM OF ART
Madison, Wisconsin

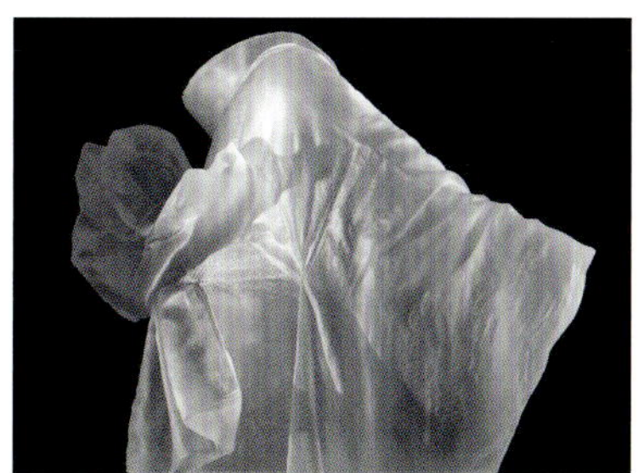

ALTURAS FOUNDATION
San Antonio, Texas

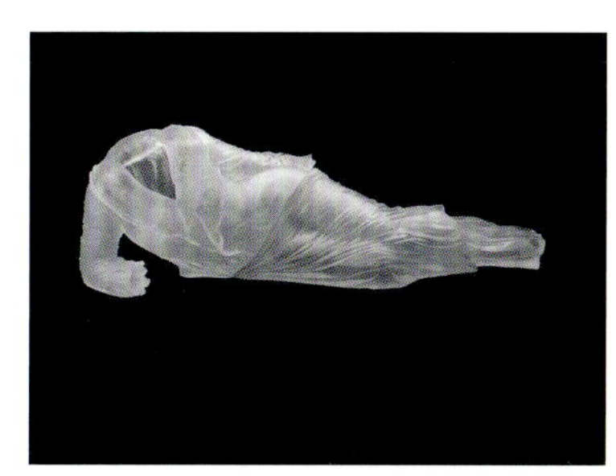

CHRYSLER MUSEUM OF ART
Norfolk, Virginia

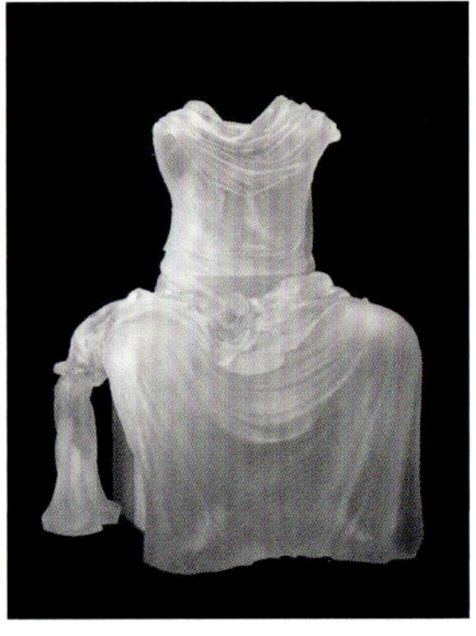

CINCINNATI ART MUSEUM
Cincinnati, Ohio

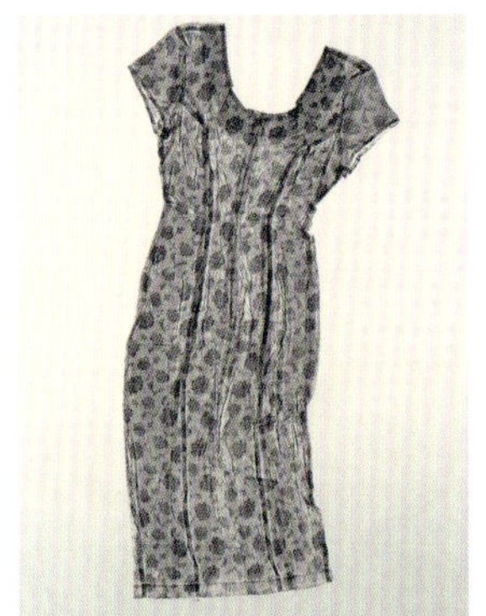

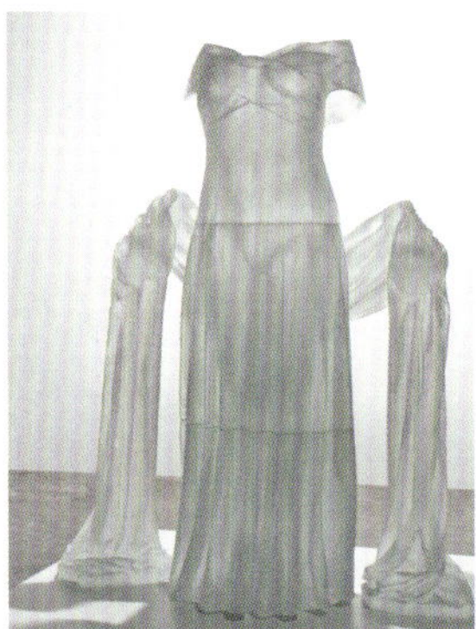

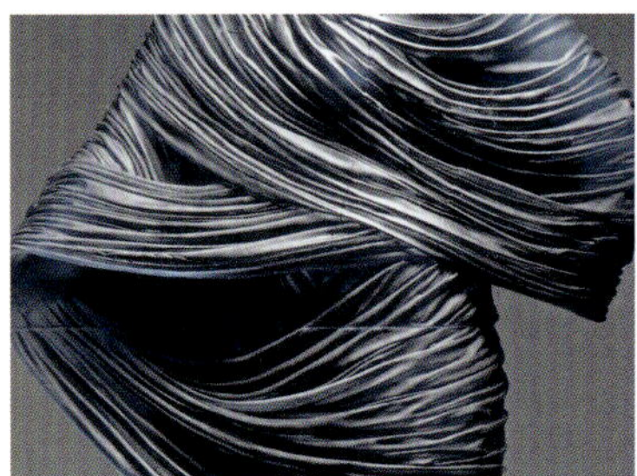

CORNING MUSEUM OF GLASS
Corning, New York

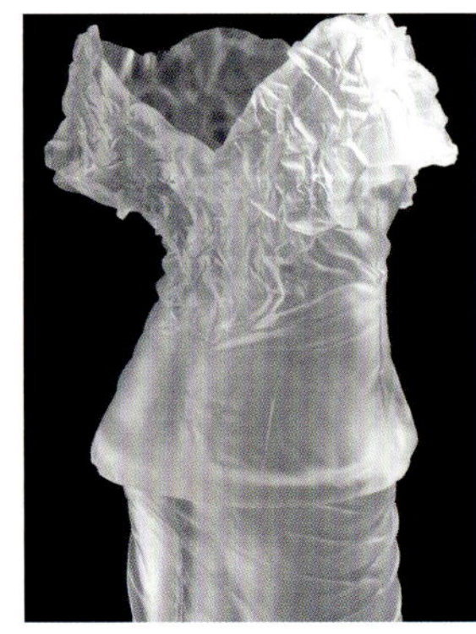

CRYSTAL BRIDGES MUSEUM OF AMERICAN ART
Bentonville, Arkansas

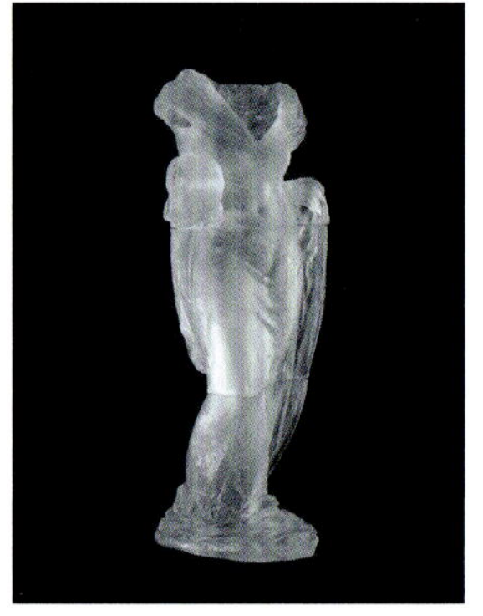

DE YOUNG MUSEUM/FINE ARTS MUSEUMS OF SAN FRANCISCO
San Francisco, California

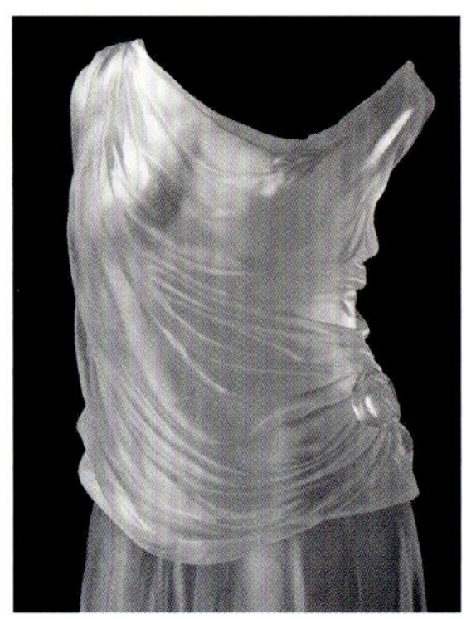

FLINT INSTITUTE OF ARTS
Flint, Michigan

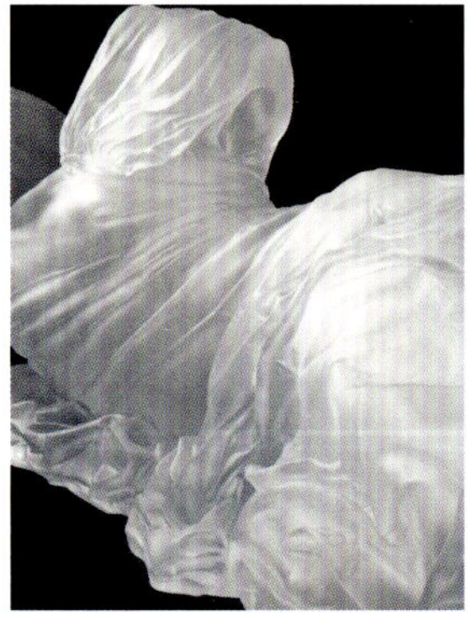

HUNTER MUSEUM OF AMERICAN ART
Chattanooga, Tennessee

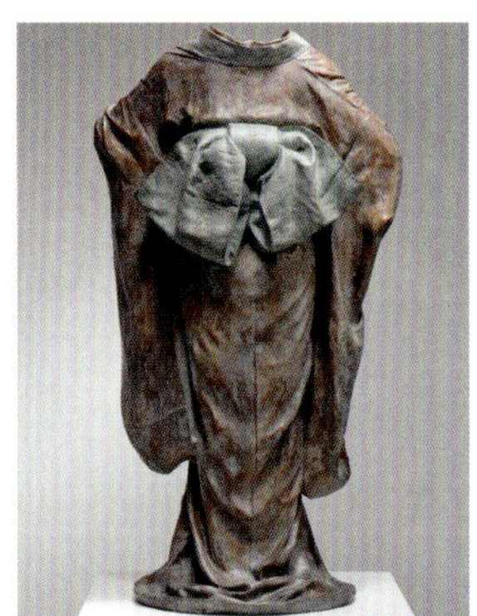

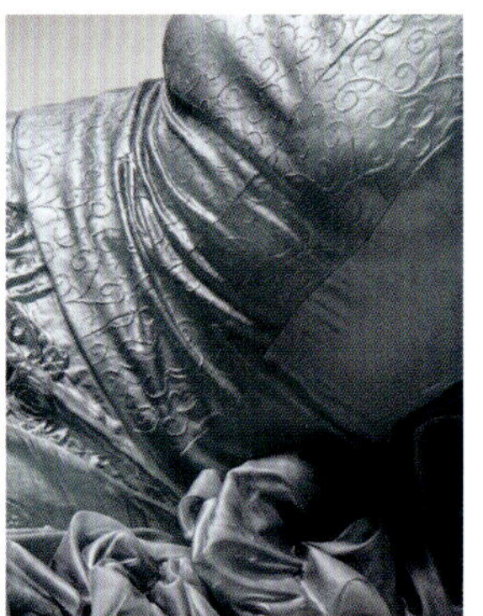

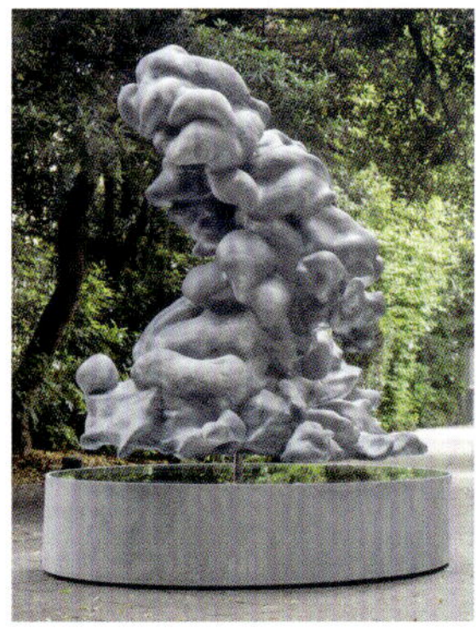

IMAGINE MUSEUM
St. Petersburg, Florida

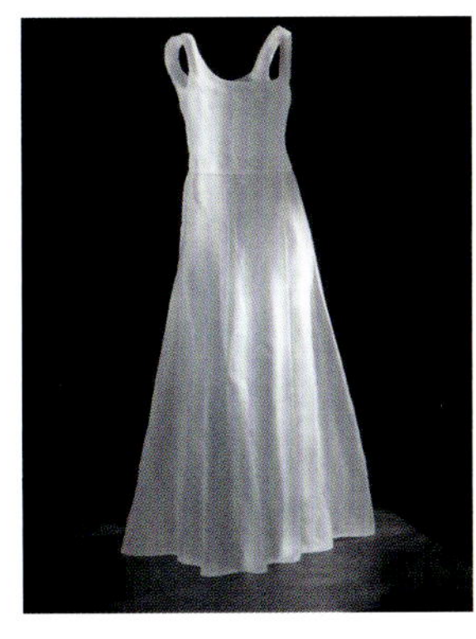

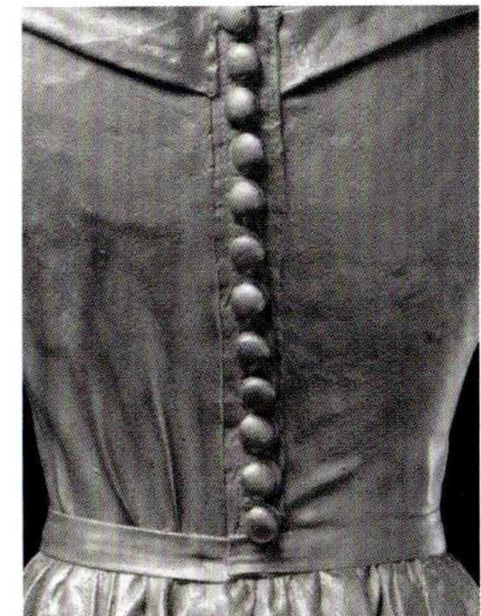

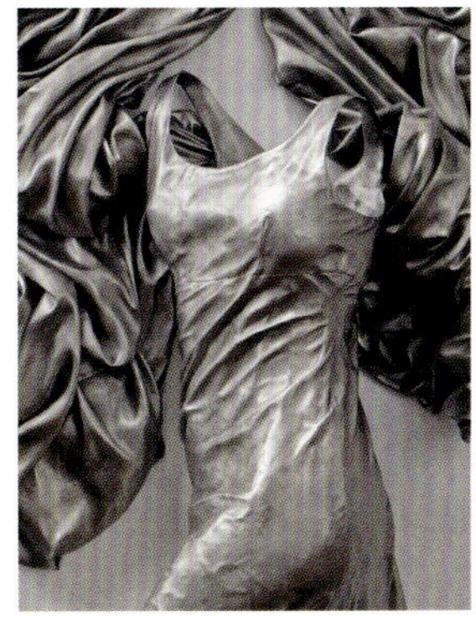

JORDAN SCHNITZER FAMILY FOUNDATION
Portland, Oregon

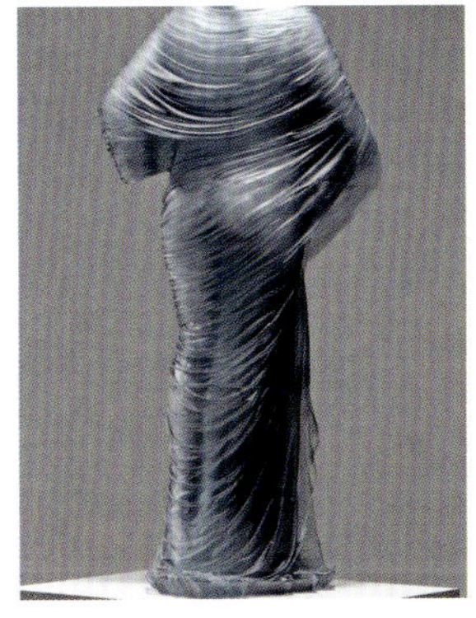

IOWA STATE UNIVERSITY MUSEUMS
Ames, Iowa

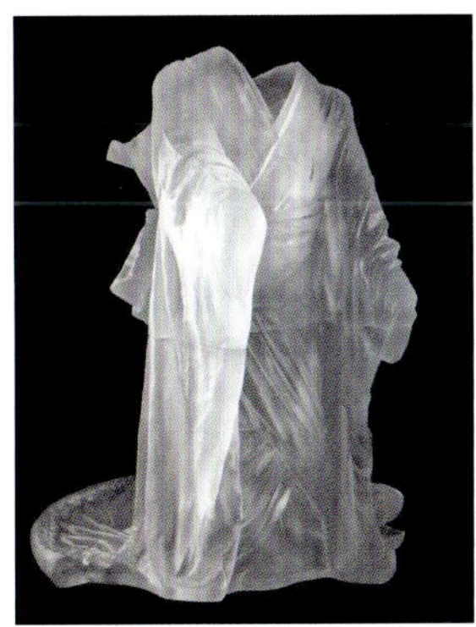

KNOXVILLE MUSEUM OF ART
Knoxville, Tennessee

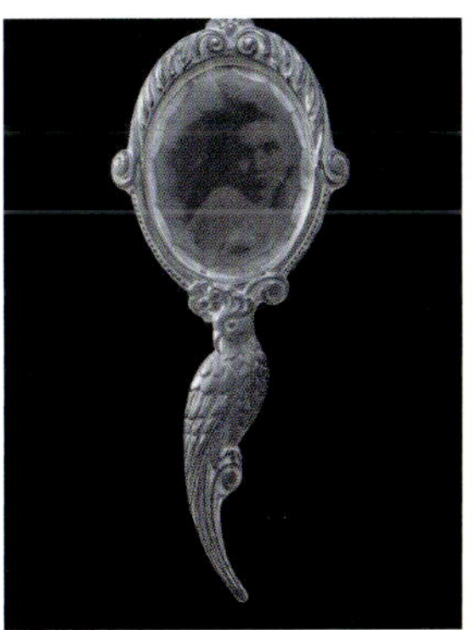

MUSÉE DES ARTS DÉCORATIFS
Paris, France

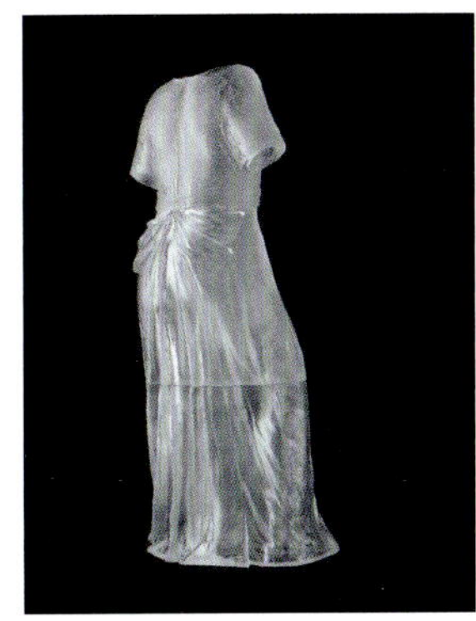

JOHN AND MABLE RINGLING MUSEUM OF ART
Sarasota, Florida

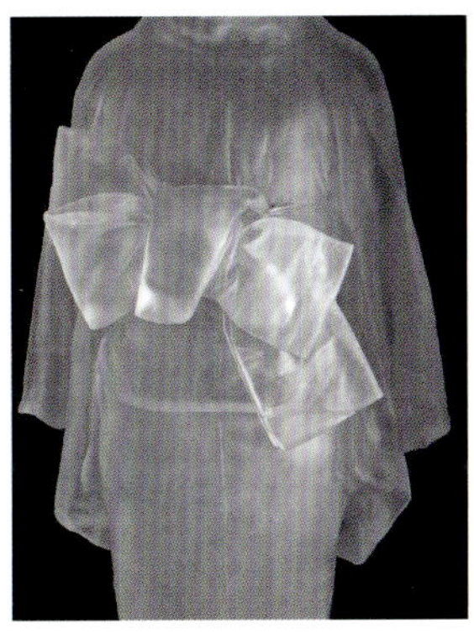

MONTGOMERY MUSEUM OF FINE ARTS
Montgomery, Alabama

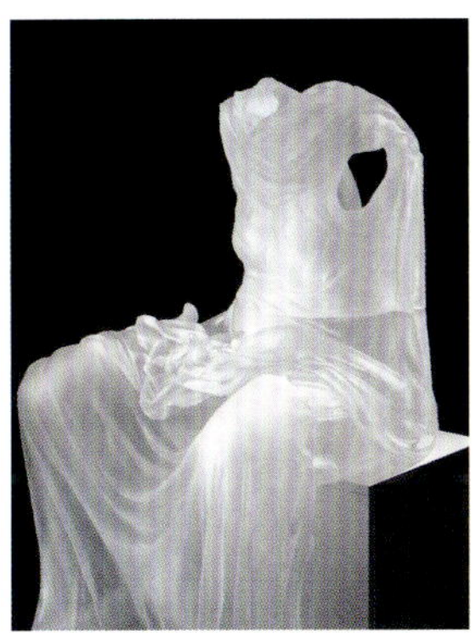

MUSÉE DU VERRE
Sars-Poteries, France

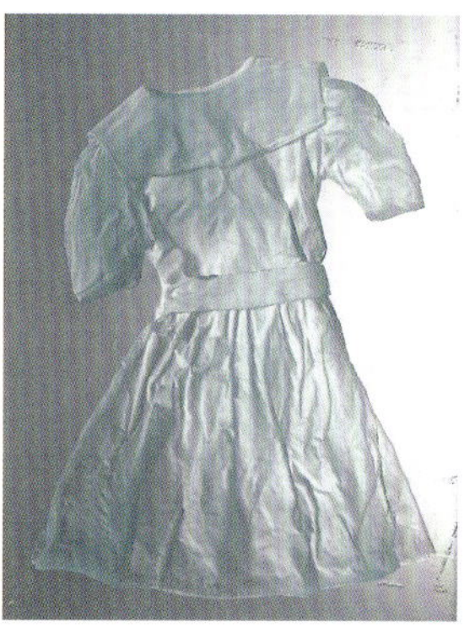

MUSEUM OF ART AND ARCHAEOLOGY, UNIVERSITY OF MISSOURI
Columbia, Missouri

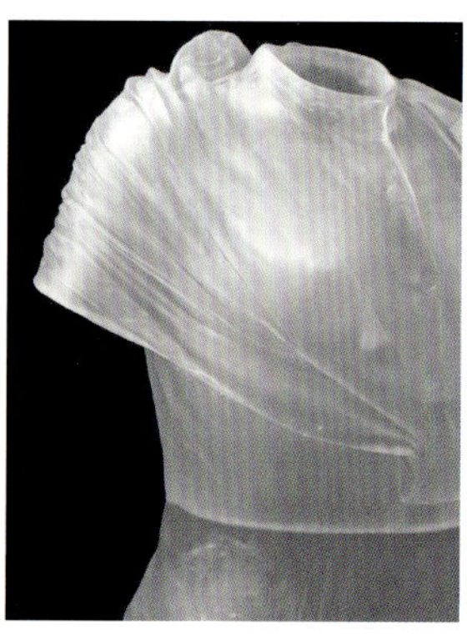

PALM SPRINGS ART MUSEUM
Palm Springs, California

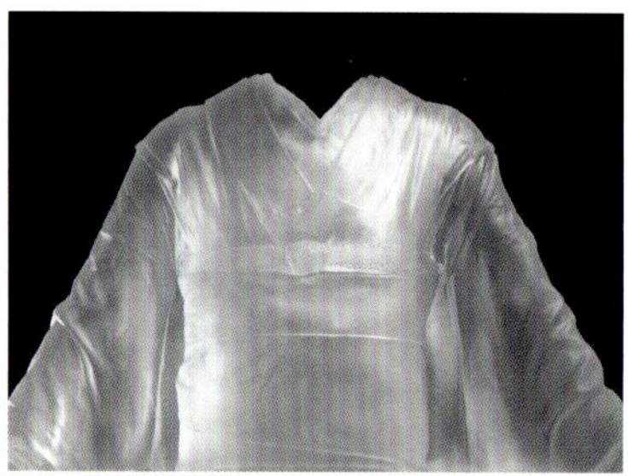

MUSEUM OF FINE ARTS, BOSTON
Boston, Massachusetts

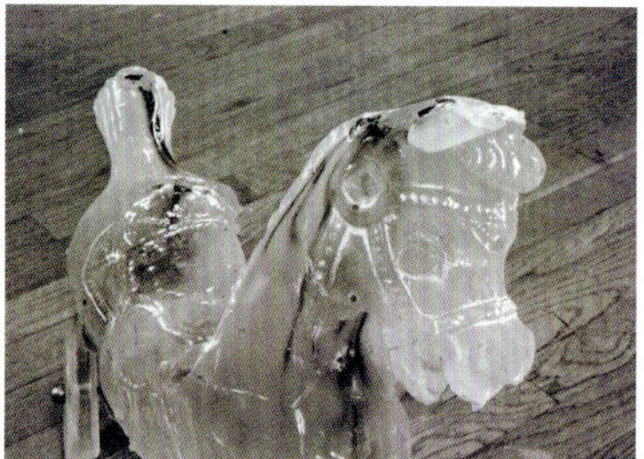

RACINE ART MUSEUM
Racine, Wisconsin

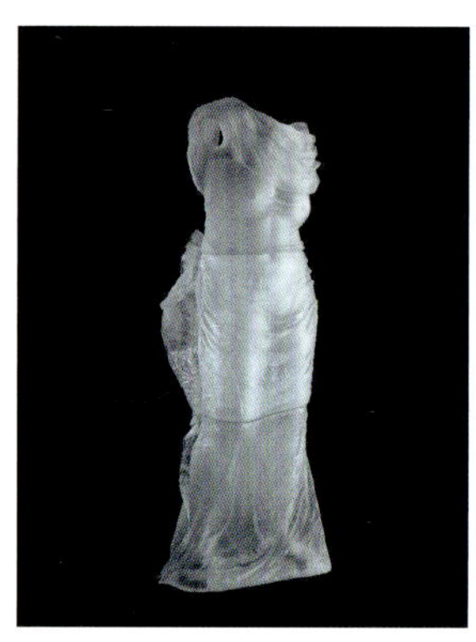

NATIONAL GALLERY OF AUSTRALIA
Parkes, Canberra, Australia

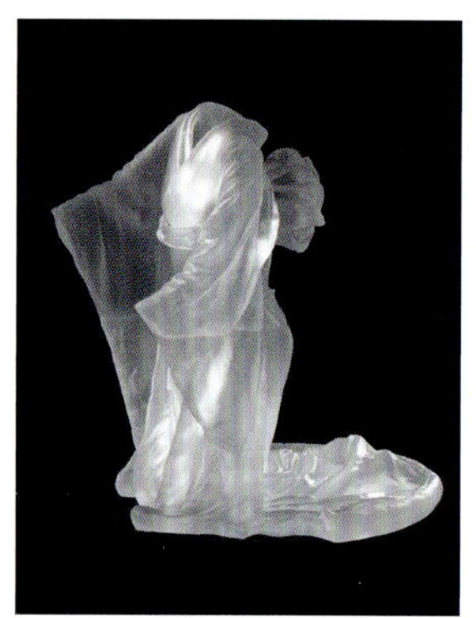

OKLAHOMA CITY MUSEUM OF ART
Oklahoma City, Oklahoma

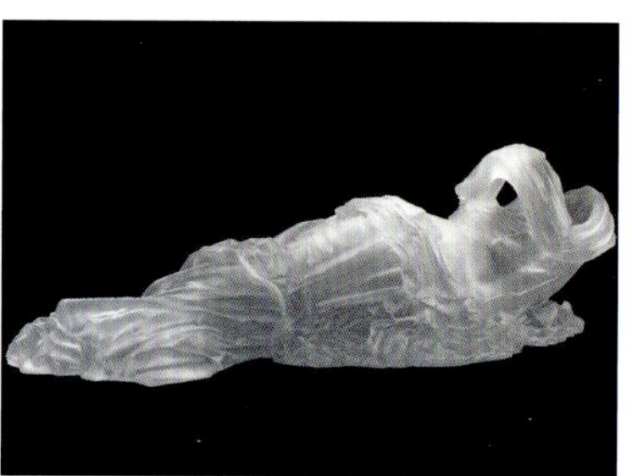

SMITHSONIAN AMERICAN ART MUSEUM RENWICK GALLERY
Washington, DC

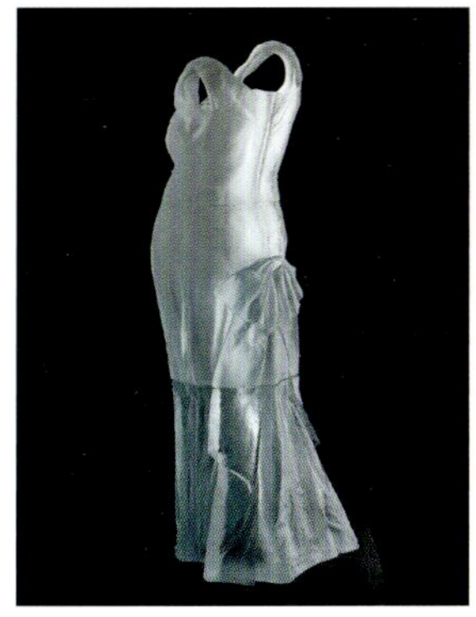

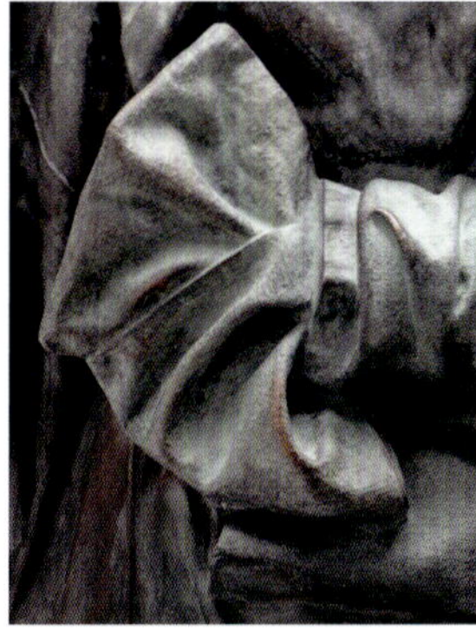

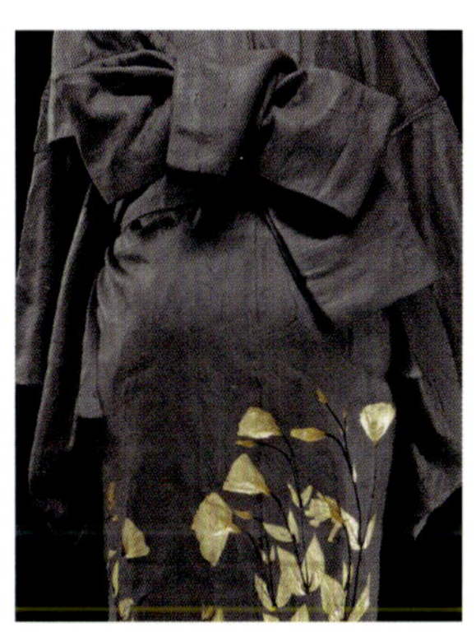

SEVEN BRIDGES FOUNDATION
Greenwich, Connecticut

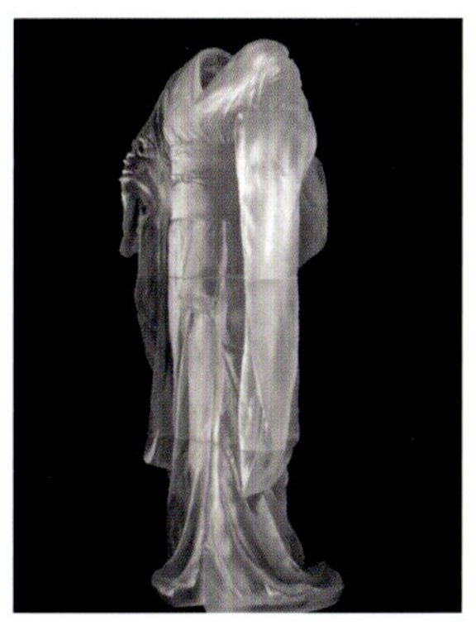

SPEED ART MUSEUM
Louisville, Kentucky

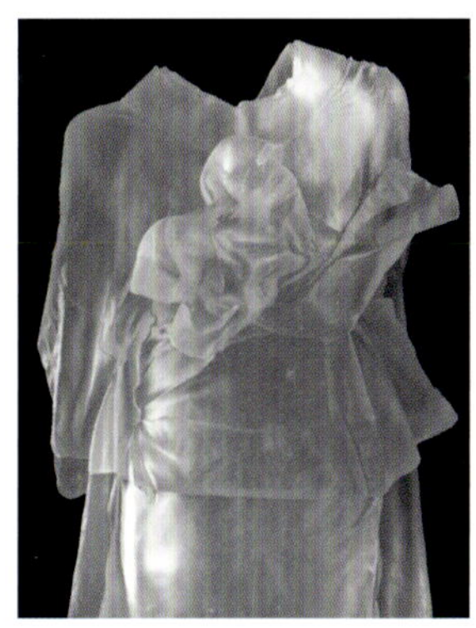

SPENCER MUSEUM OF ART
Lawrence, Kansas

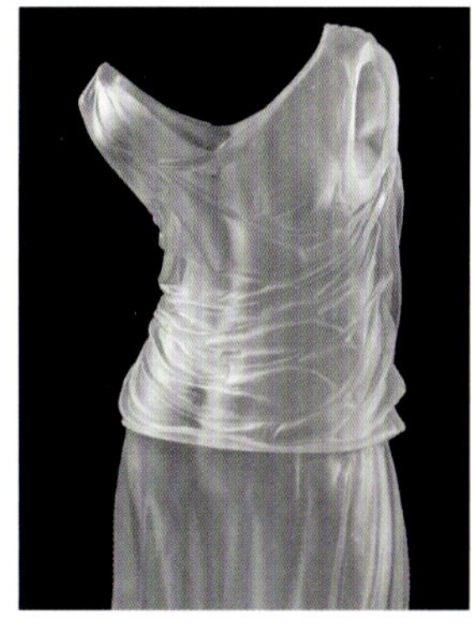

TOLEDO MUSEUM OF ART
Toledo, Ohio

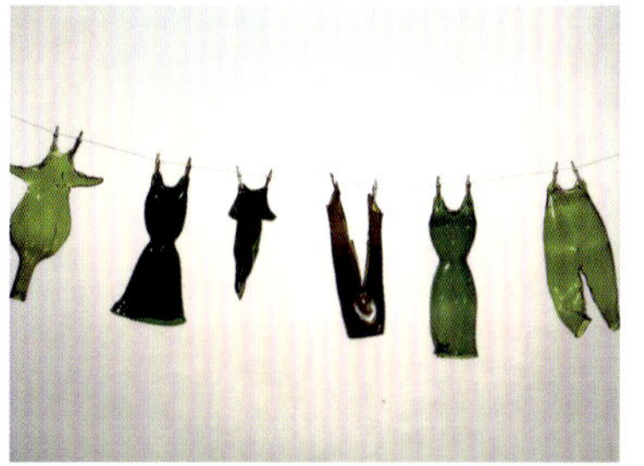

TUCSON MUSEUM OF ART
Tucson, Arizona

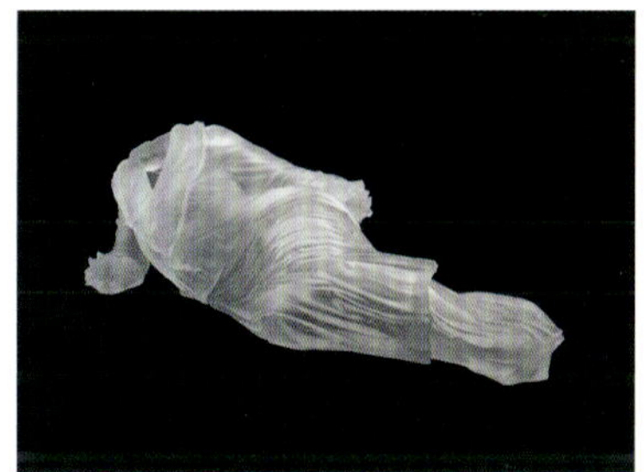

VERO BEACH MUSEUM OF ART
Vero Beach, Florida

Exhibitions
Selected

2020
Brunnier Art Museum, Ames, IA.
Contemplate Japan.

State Hermitage Museum, St. Petersburg, Russia. *Glasstress.*

2019
Fondazione Berengo at the 58th Biennale Arte, Venice, Italy. *Glasstress.* Exhibition catalogue.

Imagine Museum of Art, St. Petersburg, FL.
Karen LaMonte: Floating World.

Smithsonian American Art Museum, Renwick Gallery, Washington, DC. *Connections.*

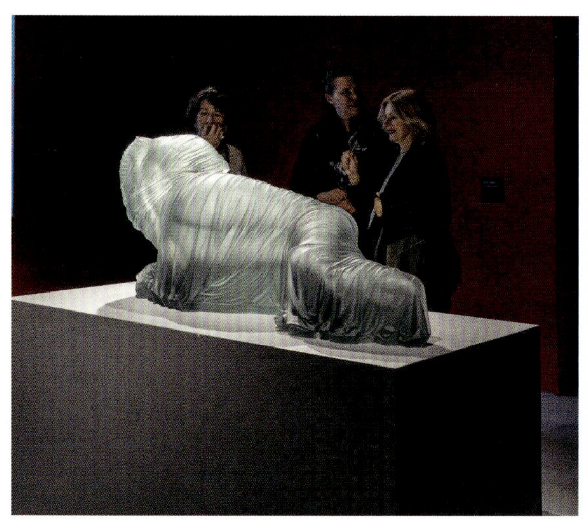

2018
GlazenHuis, Lommel, Belgium. *Tactile.*

Hunter Museum of American Art, Chattanooga, TN.
Embodied Beauty: Sculptures by Karen LaMonte.

Kampa Museum, Prague, Czech Republic.
Clothed in Light.

2017
Chazen Museum of Art, Madison, WI. *Karen LaMonte: Floating World.*

Fondazione Berengo at the 57th Biennale Arte, Venice, Italy. *Glasstress.* Exhibition catalogue.

Marshall M. Fredericks Sculpture Museum, Saginaw, MI. *Karen LaMonte: Floating World.*

Tucson Museum of Art, Tucson, AZ. *Dress Matters: Clothing as Metaphor*.

2016
Alexander Tutsek Foundation for Arts and Science, Munich, Germany. *Life is Not a Beach: Contemporary Art by International Artists.*

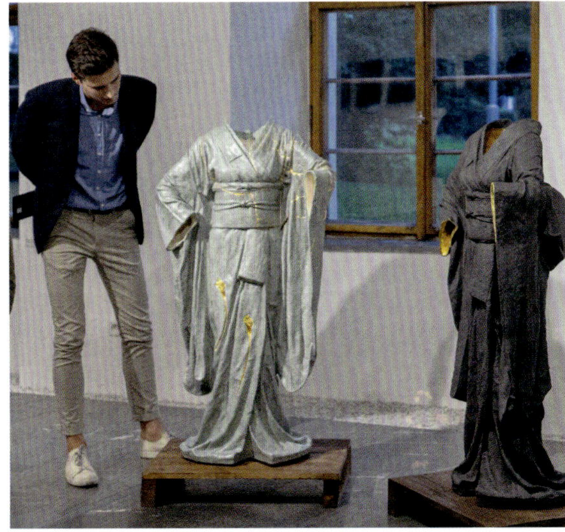

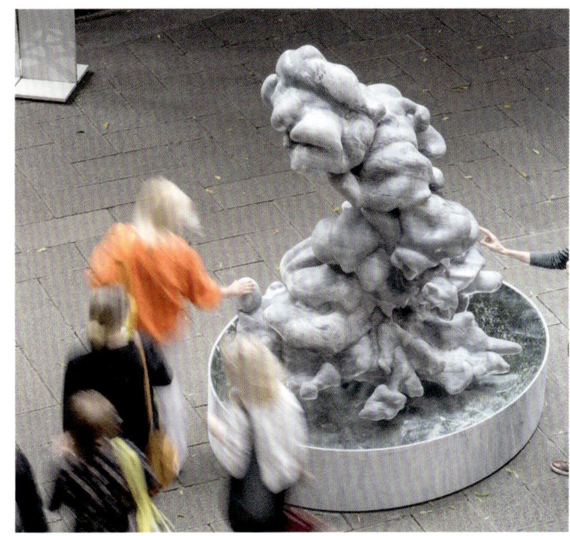

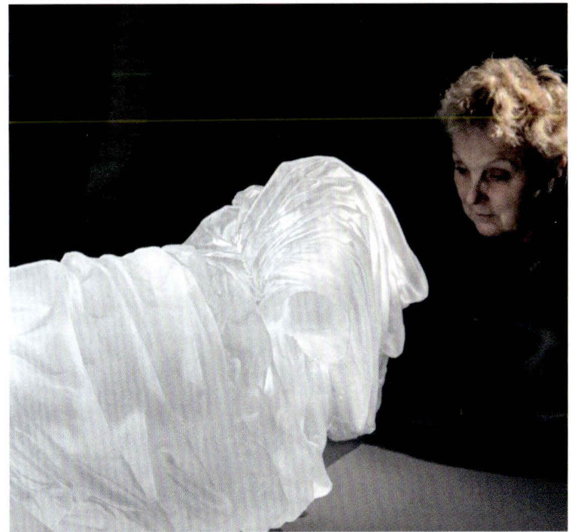

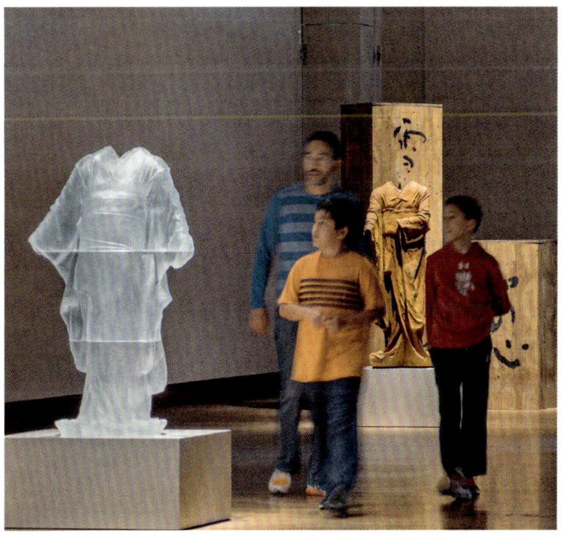

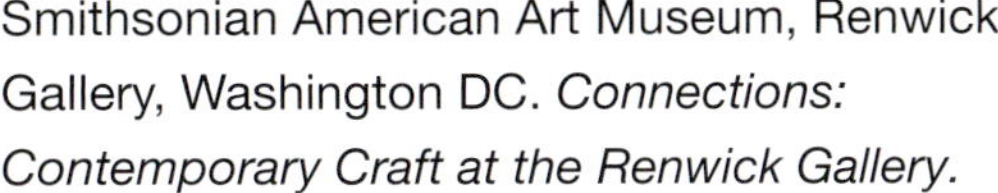

Smithsonian American Art Museum, Renwick Gallery, Washington DC. *Connections: Contemporary Craft at the Renwick Gallery.*

2015

West Bohemia Museum, Pilsen, Czech Republic. *Karen LaMonte: Floating World.* Exhibition catalogue.

Toyama Glass Art Museum, Toyama, Japan. *Inaugural Exhibition.* Exhibition catalogue.

2011

New Mexico Museum of Art, Santa Fe, NM. *Kimono: Karen LaMonte and Prints of the Floating World*.

2010

Musée du Verre, Sars-Poteries, France. *Karen LaMonte: Réflexions Féminines.*

2009

Chrysler Museum of Art, Norfolk, VA. *Contemporary Glass Among the Classics.*

2008

Glasmuseum Hentrich, Museum Kunst Palast, Düsseldorf, Germany. *Karen LaMonte Sculptures.*

New Mexico Museum of Art, Santa Fe, NM. *Flux: Reflections on Contemporary Glass.* Exhibition catalogue.

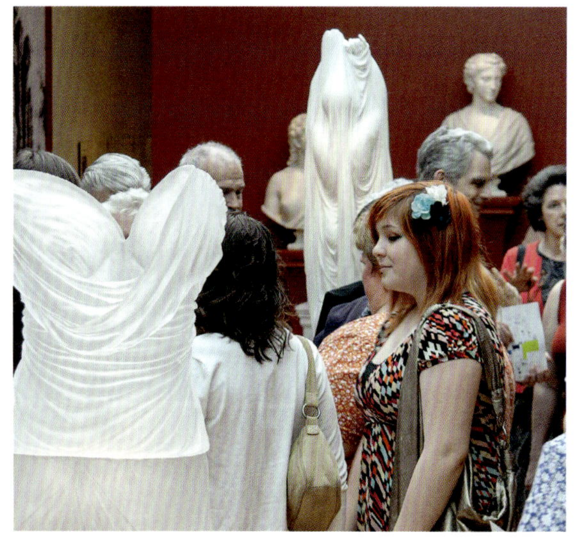

2006
Alexander Tutsek Foundation for Arts and Science, Munich, Germany. *The Face of Lost and Found Again.* Exhibition catalogue.

2005
Delaware Center for the Contemporary Arts, Wilmington, DE. *The Dress Makes the Woman.*

Museum of Glass International Center for Contemporary Art, Tacoma, WA. *Karen LaMonte: Absence Adorned.* Exhibition catalogue.

2004
Czech Museum of Fine Art, Prague, Czech Republic. *Karen LaMonte: Vanitas.* Exhibition catalogue.

2003
Camerino Municipal Salon, Camerino, Italy. *Stanze di Vetro.* Exhibition catalogue.

Klingspor-Museum Offenbach, Germany. *Corporal Identity-Body Language.* Exhibition catalogue.

Museum für Angewandte Kunst, Frankfurt, Germany. *Corporal Identity-Body Language.* Exhibition catalogue.

Museum of Art and Design, New York, NY. *Corporal Identity-Body Language.* Exhibition catalogue.

2002
Bevilacqua La Masa Foundation, Venice, Italy. *Stanze di Vetro.* Exhibition catalogue.

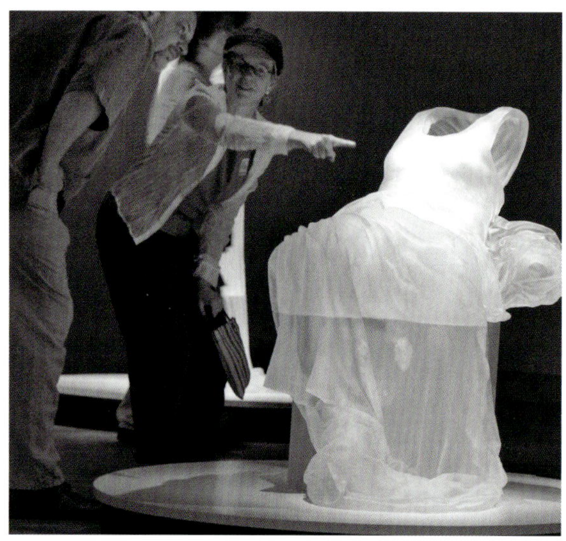

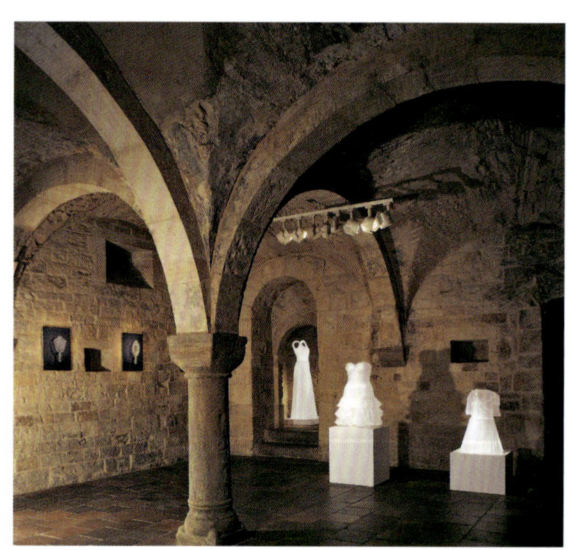

Awards

2018
Corning Museum of Glass, Corning, NY. Corning Incorporated Specialty Glass Residency

2015
James Renwick Alliance, Washington, DC. Master of the Medium Award

2012
Smithsonian Archives of American Art, Washington, DC. Oral history interview

2009
Corning Museum of Glass/Kohler Arts Center, Corning, NY. Joint Artist-in-Residence Program

2007
Kunst Palast, Düsseldorf, Germany. Jutta Cuny-Franz Memorial Award, Laureate

Museum of Glass, Tacoma, WA. Artist's Residency

2006
Japan-United States Friendship Commission, Washington, DC. NEA Creative Artists Exchange Fellowship Program

2005
The Virginia A. Groot Foundation, Minneapolis, MN. Recognition Award

2002
Wheaton Arts and Cultural Center, Millville, NJ. Creative Glass Center of America Fellowship

UrbanGlass, Brooklyn, NY. Award for New Talent in Glass

2001
The Louis Comfort Tiffany Foundation, New York, NY. Biennial Award

1999
Fulbright Scholar Program, Washington, DC. Fulbright Fellowship, Cast Glass Sculpture in the Czech Republic

1991
Wheaton Arts and Cultural Center, Millville, NJ. Creative Glass Center of America Fellowship

Bibliography
Selected

2019

Karen LaMonte: Nocturnes. Prague, Czech Republic: ArtWorks Publishing. Essays by Dr. Steven Nash and Karen LaMonte. Monograph.

LaMonte, Karen. Artist's lecture. Specialty Glass Artist-in-Residence. Corning Museum of Glass, NY.

——. Artist's lecture. Imagine Museum, St. Petersburg, FL.

——. Artist's lecture. Sophie Laumont '99 Lecturer. The Spence School, New York, NY.

2018

Dialogues: Studio Glass from the Florence and Robert Werner Collection. Lowe Art Museum, University of Miami. Exhibition catalogue, pp. 32–33. Essays by Jill Deupi, Davira S. Taragin, and Robert Werner.

LaMonte, Karen. Artist's lecture. *Embodied Beauty.* Hunter Museum of American Art, Chattanooga, TN.

——. Artist's lecture. Specialty Glass Artist-in-Residence. Corning Museum of Glass, Corning, NY.

2017

Glasstress 2017. Milan, Italy: Skira. Exhibition catalogue, pp. 122–33. Essays by Dimitri Ozerkov, et al.

Kovács, Ágnes Zsófia, and Sári B. László. *Space, Gender, and the Gaze in Literature and Art*. Newcastle upon Tyne, UK: Cambridge Scholars Publishing. Cover.

LaMonte, Karen. Artist's lecture. *Creative (R)evolution.* National Gallery of Australia, Canberra.

——. Artist's lecture. *Floating World*. Chazen Museum of Art, Madison, WI.

Townsend, Jen, and Reneé Zettle-Sterling. *Cast: Art and Objects Made Using Humanity's Most Transformational Process*. Atglen, PA: Schiffer Publishing.

Wright, Diane C., ed., *Glass: Masterworks from the Chrysler Museum of Art*. Norfolk, VA: Chrysler Museum of Art. Pp. 25, 192–93.

2016

Glass for the New Millennium: Masterworks from the Kaplan-Ostergaard Collection. Sacramento, CA: Crocker Art Museum, 2016. Exhibition catalogue, pp. 4, 11, 30–31, 84–85. Essays by Lial A. Jones, Tina Oldknow, Richard Whitely, Diana L. Daniels.

LaMonte, Karen. Artist's lecture. de Young Museum/Fine Arts Museums of San Francisco.

2015

Hampson, Ferdinand. *Studio Glass in America: A 50 Year Journey*. Atglen, PA: Schiffer Publishing.

Inaugural Exhibition. Toyoma, Japan: Toyama Glass Art Museum. Exhibition catalogue, pp. 115–17.

LaMonte, Karen. Artist's lecture. Master of the Medium. James Renwick Alliance, Washington, DC.

2013

Karen LaMonte: Floating World. Prague, Czech Republic: ArtWorks Publishing. Essays by Laura Addison and Karen LaMonte. Monograph.

Transparencies: Contemporary Art & a History of Glass. Des Moines, IA: Des Moines Art Center. Exhibition catalogue, pp. 46–51. Essay by Laura Burkhalter.

2012

LaMonte, Karen. Artist's lecture. *Beauty and Catastrophe*. Hunter Museum of American Art, Chattanooga, TN; Crystal Bridges Museum of American Art, Bentonville, AR; Palm Springs Art Museum, Palm Springs, CA; Spencer Museum of Art, Lawrence, KS.

2011

LaMonte, Karen. Artist's lecture. *Réflexions Féminines.* Musée du Verre, Sars-Poteries, France.

2010

Drapery Abstractions: Charting the Iconography of Desire. New York: Heller Gallery. Essay by Tina Oldknow.

LaMonte, Karen. Artist's lecture. Smithsonian American Art Museum, Washington, DC.

Studio Glass: Collection Anna Et Joe Mendel/ Anna and Joe Mendel Collection. Montreal, Quebec: Musée Des Beaux-Arts De Montréal/ Montreal Museum of Fine Arts. Pp. 87, 90, 130. Essay by Diane Charbonneau.

2009

Burgess, Anna, ed. *Seven Bridges Collection: The First Fifteen Years 1993–2008*. Seattle, WA: Marquand. Pp. 5, 76, 370.

2007

LaMonte, Karen. Artist's lecture. The Detroit Institute of Arts, Detroit, MI.

2005

Absence Adorned. Tacoma, WA: Museum of Glass International Center for Contemporary Art in association with University of Washington Press, Seattle and London. Essays by Arthur C. Danto, Karen LaMonte, Juli Cho Bailer, and Josi Irene Callan. Monograph.

Vanitas. Prague, Czech Republic: Czech Museum of Fine Arts. Essay by Petr Štěpán. Monograph.

2003

Corporal Identity—Körpersprache: 9. Triennale für Form und Inhalte, USA und Deutschland/Corporal Identity—Body Language: 9th Triennial for Form and Content, USA and Germany. Frankfurt am Main, Germany: Museum für Angewandte Kunst; Offenbach, Germany: Klingspor-Museum; New York: Museum of Arts & Design. Exhibition catalogue, pp. 307–9.

Kohler, Lucartha. *Women Working in Glass*. Atglen, PA: Schiffer Publishing.

Sculptures and Sartoriotypes. Prague, Czech Republic: Czech Museum of Fine Arts. Essay by Richard Drury.

Yelle, Richard. *International Glass Art*. Atglen, PA: Schiffer Publishing.

2002

Karen LaMonte: Absent Impressions. Prague, Czech Republic: National Gallery of Australia. Essay by Robert Bell.

2000

Yelle, Richard. *Contemporary Art from UrbanGlass*. Atglen, PA: Schiffer Publishing.

Acknowledgments

I thank my family and all those who have supported my work over the years.

For their contributions to this book, I am grateful to Lucy Lippard, Brett Littman, Arthur Danto, Laura Addison, Tina Oldknow, and Steven Nash, designer David Skolkin, photographer Martin Polák, and the terrific Rizzoli team of Charles Miers, James O. Muschett, and Elizabeth Smith. And of course my deepest gratitude to the amazing Steve, my husband, studio manager, and consigliere.

Contributors

Lucy R. Lippard is a writer, activist, sometime curator, and author of twenty-five books on contemporary art and cultural criticism, including *From the Center: Feminist Essays on Women's Art* (1976); *Eva Hesse* (1976); *Mixed Blessings: New Art in a Multicultural America* (1990); *The Lure of the Local: Senses of Place in a Multicentered* Society (1998); *Undermining: A Wild Ride through Land Use, Politics, and Art in the Changing West* (2014); and *Pueblo Chico: Land and Lives in Galisteo Since 1814* (2020). She was a cofounder of Ad Hoc Women Artists, Printed Matter, Political Art Documentation/ Distribution (PADD), and Heresies. Recipient of a number of awards, she lives off the grid in rural Galisteo, New Mexico, where for twenty-three years she has edited the monthly community newsletter *El Puente de Galisteo.*

Steven A. Nash served as the JoAnn McGrath Executive Director of the Palm Springs Art Museum from April 2007 until January 2015. Dr. Nash received his B.A. cum laude at Dartmouth College and his Ph.D. in art history at Stanford University. He was a museum professional for more than forty years, as research curator and chief curator at the Albright-Knox Art Gallery in Buffalo (1973–80), deputy director and chief curator at the Dallas Museum of Art (1980–88), associate director and chief curator at the Fine Arts Museums of San Francisco (1988–2001), and founding director of the Nasher Sculpture Center in Dallas (2001–07). Among the many exhibitions he has organized or co-organized are surveys on the modern artists Ben Nicholson, Naum Gabo, Pablo Picasso, Pierre Bonnard, Henry Moore, Wayne Thiebaud, Robert Arneson, Alberto Giacometti, Henri Matisse, and Richard Diebenkorn; several exhibitions on modern European sculpture, landscape art in California, masterworks from the Musée d'Orsay, the history of Crown Point Press in San Francisco, and numerous contemporary Californian artists. Each of these exhibitions featured catalogues that Dr. Nash authored solely or in part. His work on Pablo Picasso includes three exhibitions and catalogues: *Picasso the Printmaker* (Dallas Museum of Art, 1983), *Picasso the Sculptor* (Fine Arts Museums of San Francisco, 1996), and *Picasso and the War Years 1937–1945* (2003). During his career, Dr. Nash was responsible for the acquisition by his museums of literally thousands of works of art from many eras and cultures. He also carried out a wide variety of administrative and managerial duties, including participation in the design and installation of four new museums: the Dallas Museum of Art (1984), an expanded California Palace of the Legion of Honor (1995), the de Young Museum in San Francisco (2005), and the Nasher Sculpture Center (2003). As chief executive officer of the Sculpture Center, he was responsible for instituting and developing all operational and programmatic aspects of the new museum. Among other accomplishments at the Palm Springs Art Museum, he led the renovation of the museum's main building, oversaw the addition of two satellite facilities, helped develop the permanent collection significantly, and authored or contributed to several important publications. Now retired from museum life, he sits on various arts boards including those of the Nasher Sculpture Center, the Richard Diebenkorn Foundation (where he is president), and the Desert X Biennial. He also works as an art consultant and researcher. He is married and lives with his wife Carol in Palm Springs. The Nashes have two grown children, Colin and Jessica, and five grandchildren.

Brett Littman is the director of the Isamu Noguchi Foundation and Garden Museum in Long Island City, New York. He was the executive director of the Drawing Center from 2007 to 2018, the deputy director of MoMA PS1 from 2003 to 2007, the codirector of Dieu Donné Papermill from 2001 to 2003, and the associate director of UrbanGlass from 1996 to 2001. His interests are multidisciplinary; over the last decade, he has overseen more than seventy-five exhibitions and curated more than twenty dealing with visual art, craft, design, architecture, poetry, music, science, and literature. Littman is also an art critic, lecturer, and an active essayist for museum and gallery catalogues. He has written articles for a wide range of United States–based and international art, fashion, and design magazines.

Arthur C. Danto was an American art critic, philosopher, and Johnsonian Professor of Philosophy Emeritus at Columbia University. He was an art critic for *The Nation* from 1984 to 2009, an editor for *The Journal of Philosophy*, and a contributing editor of the *Naked Punch Review* and *Art Forum*. He published numerous books on philosophy and art, including an essay collection called *Encounters and Reflections: Art in the Historical Present* (1990), which won the National Book Critics Circle Prize for Criticism in 1990. He won the Frank Jewett Mather Award for art criticism from the College Art Association in 1996. His other titles include *Beyond the Brillo Box: The Visual Arts in Post-Historical Perspective* (1992); *Playing With the Edge: The Photographic Achievement of Robert Mapplethorpe* (1995); and *The Madonna of the Future: Essays in a Pluralistic Art World* (2001).

Laura Addison is curator of North American and European collections at the Museum of International Folk Art in Santa Fe, New Mexico. Previously, she was the curator of contemporary art at the New Mexico Museum of Art. Her projects focus on diverse genres and mediums, and the cross-pollination of art, craft, folk art, and design. Previous exhibitions include *No Idle Hands: The Myths & Meanings of Tramp Art* (Museum of International Folk Art, 2017–18), *Girard's Modern Folk* (Museum of International Folk Art, 2019–20), *James Drake: Salon of a Thousand Souls* (New Mexico Museum of Art, 2011–12), *Kimono: Karen LaMonte and Prints of the Floating World* (New Mexico Museum of Art, 2011), and *The Art & Artifice of Science* (Museum of Fine Arts/New Mexico, 2007). Addison has a B.A. from Cornell University and an M.A. from the University of New Mexico.

Tina Oldknow is an independent curator and art historian specializing in contemporary art, craft, and design in glass. In 2015, she retired as senior curator of modern and contemporary glass at The Corning Museum of Glass in Corning, New York—a position she held for fifteen years. She has served on the staff and as a consultant for several museums, including the J. Paul Getty Museum, the Los Angeles County Museum of Art, the Santa Barbara Museum of Art, and the Seattle Art Museum. Oldknow has curated more than thirty exhibitions, and has written more than one hundred books, articles, and other texts on glass. Her books include *Pilchuck: A Glass School* (1996), *Richard Marquis Objects* (1997), *Dante Marioni: Blown Glass* (2000), *Contemporary Glass Sculptures and Panels: Selections from The Corning Museum of Glass* (2008), *Voices of Contemporary Glass: The Heineman Collection* (2009), *Collecting Contemporary Glass: Art and Design after 1990 from The Corning Museum of Glass* (2014), and *Contemporary Glass Vessels: Selections from The Corning Museum of Glass* (2015). She was named an honorary fellow of the American Craft Council (2014) and an honorary fellow of The Corning Museum of Glass (2015). Oldknow, who has studied the history, culture, and artistic practice of glassmaking for over thirty years, holds a B.A. in art history from the University of California, Los Angeles, and an M.A. in art history from the University of Pennsylvania, Philadelphia.

First published in the United States of America in 2020 by

Rizzoli Electa, a division of
Rizzoli International Publications, Inc.
300 Park Avenue South
New York, NY 10010
www.rizzoliusa.com

An earlier version of "The Poetry of Meaning and Loss," by Arthur C. Danto (pp. 49–50), was published as "The Poetry of Meaning and Loss: The Glass Dresses of Karen LaMonte," in *Absence Adorned* (Tacoma, WA: Museum of Glass International Center for Contemporary Art in association with University of Washington Press, Seattle and London, 2005).

An earlier version of "Hauntings in the Floating World," by Laura Addison (pp. 85–87), was published as "Hauntings in the Floating World: The Kimono Sculptures of Karen LaMonte," in *Karen LaMonte: Floating World* (Prague, Czech Republic: ArtWorks Publishing, 2013).

An earlier version of "Charting the Iconography of Desire," by Tina Oldknow (pp. 131–33), was published as "Karen LaMonte: Charting the Iconography of Desire," in *Drapery Abstractions: Charting the Iconography of Desire* (New York: Heller Gallery, 2010).

An earlier version of "Night Becomes Her: Nocturnes, Etudes, and Tableaux," by Steven A. Nash (pp. 157–61), was published as "The Nocturnes: Music, Poetry, Art," in *Karen LaMonte: Nocturnes* (Prague, Czech Republic: ArtWorks Publishing, 2019).

Library of Congress Control Number: 2020933315
ISBN: 978-0-8478-6767-7

2020 2021 2022 2023 / 10 9 8 7 6 5 4 3 2 1

Printed in Italy

For Rizzoli Electa:
Charles Miers, Publisher
Margaret Rennolds Chace, Associate Publisher
James O. Muschett, Associate Publisher
Elizabeth Smith, Editor

Design by David Skolkin/David Skolkin Design, Santa Fe

Front cover: *Reclining Nocturne 3*, 2017
Cast glass, 20½ × 60 × 26 in. (51.5 × 153 × 65.5 cm)

Photography credits

Chazen Museum of Art: p. 87; **©CNAC/MNAM/Dist. RMN-Grand Palais / Art Resource, NY**: p. 50 (right); **Bruce Cole**: p. 174; **Corning Museum of Glass**: pp. 48, 266 (col. 1: 3); **Courtesy Estate of Pasquale De Antonis**: p. 20; **James Dee**: p. 28 (bottom); **Randy Dodson**: p. 14; **Nicola Gnesi**: pp. 192–93, 248–49, 254–55, 263 (from top, 3); **Tomas Hilger**: p. 268 (col. 2: 1); **Horst P. Horst, Vogue ©Conde Nast**: p. 50 (left); **Russell Johnson**: pp. 24–25, 51; **Karen LaMonte**: p. 28 (top); **Maryhill Museum of Art, Goldendale, Washington**: p. 160 (bottom); **©The Metropolitan Museum of Art. Image source: Art Resource, NY**: p. 158; **Martin Polák**: pp. 10, 12–13, 18 (all), 26, 30, 31 (all), 33, 34, 35, 36, 37, 41, 42, 43, 54, 55, 56–57, 58, 59, 60, 61, 62, 63, 64–65, 72, 73, 74, 75, 76–77, 84, 89, 94, 95, 96, 97, 98, 99, 102, 103, 104, 105, 106 (all), 107, 108–9, 110, 111, 112, 113, 116, 117, 118, 119, 120 (all), 121, 122, 123, 124, 125 (all), 126–27, 128–29, 137, 138, 139, 140, 141, 142, 143, 148, 154–55, 168–69, 172, 173 (all), 175, 176, 177, 178 (all), 179, 180, 181, 182, 183, 184–85, 186–87, 190, 191, 195, 196–97, 198 (all), 199, 200 (all), 202 (all), 203, 204, 205, 206, 207, 208 (all), 209, 210, 211, 212, 213, 214, 215, 216, 217, 218, 219, 220–21, 222, 223, 228, 232 (all), 233, 235, 236–37, 238, 239, 240 (all), 244–45, 246–47, 251, 252, 262 (from top: 2, 4), 264, 265 (row 1: 1, 3; row 2: all; row 3: 1), 266 (col. 1: 1, 2, 4, 5; col. 2: 2, 3; col. 3: all), 267 (col. 1: all; col. 2: 2, 3; col. 3: all; col. 4: all), 268 (col. 2: all; col. 3: 1, 3); 269 (col. 2: all; col. 3: 1), 271 (top left); **Steven Polaner**: pp. 2–3, 5, 22, 38–39, 44–45, 46–47, 52–53, 69, 82–83, 86, 88, 91, 92, 93, 100–101, 114 (all), 115, 130, 132, 133, 144–45, 146–47, 149 (all), 150, 151, 152–53, 156, 163, 164–65, 167, 188–89, 225, 226–27, 241, 242–43, 250, 253; **Ed Pollard**: pp. 6–7, 17, 66, 67; **Scala / Art Resource, NY**: p. 161; **Photographer M. Schreiner from the Archäologisches Landesmuseum Baden-Württemberg, Konstanz**: p. 230; **©Tate, London / Art Resource, NY**: p. 159; **Trinity Mirror / Mirrorpix / Alamy Stock Photo**: p. 19; **Gabriel Urbanek**: pp. 70, 71, 78–79, 81, 265 (row 3: 2), 266 (col. 2: 1), 267 (col. 2: 1), 268 (col. 1: 1), 269 (col. 1: 1; col. 3: 3); **Molly Wagoner**: pp. 170–71, 201.